# THE EARLY NATIONAL PERIOD

## AN EYEWITNESS HISTORY

# THE EARLY NATIONAL PERIOD

Sarah J. Purcell

☑®
Facts On File, Inc.

**The Early National Period**

Copyright © 2004 by Sarah J. Purcell
Maps copyright © 2004 by Facts On File, Inc.

Facts On File, Inc.
132 West 31st Street
New York NY 10001

**Library of Congress Cataloging-in-Publication Data**
Purcell, Sarah J.
   The early national period / Sarah J. Purcell.
      p.   cm. — (An eyewitness history)
   Includes bibliographical references and index.
   ISBN 0-8160-4769-3
   1. United States—History—1783–1865. 2. United States—History—1783–1865—Biography. 3. United States—History—1783–1865—Sources. I. Title. II. Series.
   E301.P87 2004
   973.4—dc22                                    2003014969

Facts On File books are available at special discounts when purchased in bulk quantities for businesses, associations, institutions, or sales promotions. Please call our Special Sales Department in New York at (212) 967-8800 or (800) 322-8755.

You can find Facts On File on the World Wide Web at
http://www.factsonfile.com

Text design by Joan M. Toro
Cover design by Cathy Rincon
Maps by Jeremy Eagle

Printed in the United States of America

VB JT 10 9 8 7 6 5 4 3 2 1

This book is printed on acid-free paper.

*For Ed and Mary Purcell*

# Note on Photos

Many of the illustrations and photographs used in this book are old, historical images. The quality of the prints is not always up to current standards, as in many cases the originals are from old or poor-quality negatives or are damaged. The content of the illustrations, however, made their inclusion important despite problems in reproduction.

# CONTENTS

# AUTHOR'S NOTE

This book provides an in-depth look at one of the most interesting and most misunderstood periods in all of American history—the early national period, sometimes called the early republic. Although many of the personalities and individuals who lived during this time are well known to the American public—John Adams, Thomas Jefferson, George Washington, Abigail Adams—many people do not really have a sense of what these people did or why they were important. Citizens of the United States often express a reverence for the "founding fathers," but they do not always know why or what for.

The early republican period was an era that helped to define the future of the United States, and it is far too easy to get caught up in the feeling that the Founding Fathers had everything figured out. They did not. Following the conclusion of the Revolutionary War in 1783, the country was fragile, and not everyone was sure that the new republic was an experiment that would succeed, although many people liked to think it was destined for greatness. By the end of the period covered in this book, 1828, the nation had survived a change in constitution; extensive changes in the electoral system; a major war with Great Britain; military conflicts with North African states, France, and many different American Indian nations; several economic booms and busts; and a whole host of significant social changes. None of those would have seemed fully evident to any observer in 1783.

In addition, the famous "founding fathers" (and perhaps a few founding mothers) were not solely responsible for the vibrant history of change during this period in the United States. During the early republic many more ordinary men and women, some well known and some obscure, left their marks on the fledgling country. Whether it was through marching with Daniel Shays and his rebels in western Massachusetts, participating in one of the nation's first labor strikes, or performing backbreaking labor growing cotton that would become the basis of huge national economic growth, many humble and obscure Americans contributed significantly to society. Other people just got on with the daily rhythm of life in an agricultural republic, but that life itself is of great interest and has shaped the character of the nation almost as much as its great political institutions have done.

This eyewitness history seeks to capture the points of view of both the famous and the more obscure players in early American history. Although the rich and articulate left many more records of their impressions of what life was like in the United States and Canada between 1783 and 1828, one can make the most of the humble voices to which one does have access, and one can often read between the lines of more elite perspectives to discern information about the rest of the population as well. When one reads a newspaper advertisement for a runaway slave, for example, one is seeing the world of the late 18th or early 19th century through the master's eyes, but one also sees what the slave took with him or her, one hears a bit about his or her personality, and one catches a glimpse of how he or she sought to break away to freedom.

When you read the eyewitness accounts of life and events during the early republic in this book, try to keep these multiple viewpoints in mind, and be critical of what you read. The narrative and chronology sections of each chapter are designed to help you put the eyewitness testimony in context. Not every observer was telling the truth about what he or she saw in the surrounding world. Take these eyewitness accounts with the appropriate grain of salt.

Many observations also tell us more about the mind-sets or prejudices of those who made them than they do about what or who was being observed. Just because a white observer saw "savages," for example, when he described Indians, his description did not make them so. You will find many examples of racism, sexism, classism, and downright ugliness in the eyewitness accounts told here. One should not try to erase the ugliness in the past but rather to understand it and figure out what it tells us about the society at large.

This is not to say that this book is all about conflict and ugly sentiments between people, however. Nor does it reveal the early republic to be a dry and boring place or time. On the contrary, one will find here a remarkable cast of characters: People who lived their lives to the fullest, often with a sense of goodwill and a sense of humor. Give up your preconceptions, and enjoy looking at the United States through their eyes.

# ACKNOWLEDGMENTS

My heartfelt thanks go out to the staff of Burling Library at Grinnell College, especially Sherry Shults and Christopher McKee. The staff of the Photographic Division of the Library of Congress was extremely helpful in gathering illustrations and information for this book. Thank you to Linda Price for computer and clerical support and Karen Groves and Margaret Hainline for clerical assistance in preparing the manuscript.

Thank you to Bert Holtje and Gene Brissie of James Peter Associates for guidance and management. Thanks to Nicole Bowen at Facts On File.

My greatest debt of gratitude for this project is owed to L. Edward Purcell for his unflagging support and soothing phone conversations, his editorial assistance, his untiring solace, and the loan of the Benson Lossing illustrations. No one could wish for a better role model of what a writer and historian should be.

# 1

# Post-Revolutionary Change
## 1783–1786

When the Revolutionary War came to a close in 1783, the United States was fully established as a free and independent nation after surviving nine years of war and disorder and the upheaval of breaking away from Great Britain. This change was certainly definitive, but at the same time, many crises brought on by the war and the Revolution remained unresolved. Americans spent much of the year 1783, and indeed many years thereafter, in a period of transition. The United States had become a country, but it remained to be seen whether it could function smoothly and how the everyday lives of its citizens would be affected by the political changes underway.

While most of the large-scale fighting of the Revolutionary War had concluded after the surrender by British major general Lord Cornwallis at Yorktown, Virginia, in 1781, sporadic skirmishes took place during the subsequent year even as peace commissioners were busy in Europe trying to hammer out terms for a treaty that would formally end the war. In the meantime, many American soldiers and sailors were still under arms, citizens were displaced from their homes, families continued to be divided by Revolutionary politics, and the British still occupied important American territories, including New York City.

The United States in the aftermath of the Revolutionary War was a society in the midst of political, social, and demographic changes that heightened a sense of contradiction in public life. The country was overwhelmingly rural, but after the war, it also began the process of becoming significantly more urban. Patriots valued freedom and independence, but the country as a whole still relied on Europe for financial support, and over 1 million American individuals lived in slavery. Although the Revolution helped to create the ideological framework that would lead increasing numbers of people to question slavery, the institution simultaneously became even more entrenched as a part of the southern economy. Americans had won the right to create governments for themselves, but stable political order sometimes seemed elusive as state governments disagreed with one another and as citizens remained wary of granting too much power to the central government.

British general Charles, earl (later, first marquis) of Cornwallis, had a long and successful career in the military following the Revolutionary War, but he never totally shook his reputation as the man who surrendered to the United States. *(Library of Congress, Prints and Photographs Division [LC-USZ62-45340])*

The Confederation government, which was weak but nevertheless represented the united voice of the 13 United States acting in concert, faced huge financial problems. Congress and the states had to find a way to pay for the war, and most especially to pay the soldiers and sailors who needed to be demobilized and who might represent a destabilizing force if left to reintegrate themselves into society while feeling disgruntled with their government. One of the main challenges in the immediate aftermath of the Revolution, and indeed in the entire era of the new nation, was for Americans to decide how to exercise the government authority they needed to run a country without trampling on the individual liberties they had come to prize so dearly during the Revolution. The first real test of this careful balance between power and liberty would come as Congress tried to raise enough money, through taxes of various kinds, to pay the American soldiers to return peacefully to their homes.

## The Legacy of Revolutionary Republicanism

At the beginning of the American Revolution, the Declaration of Independence had declared Americans' commitment to the proposition "that all Men are created equal, that they are endowed by their Creator with certain Unalienable rights, that among these are Life, Liberty, and the Pursuit of Happiness."[1] Once the war was over, the question of how Americans might best pursue their happiness, both individually and collectively, took on a new urgency. At the end of the 18th century, Americans faced large questions about what kind of government they wanted, what kind of society would best promote freedom, and whether social equality was a goal worth pursuing. The ramifications of building a society based on equality were certainly not settled in 1783, and indeed occupied Americans for most of the 19th and 20th centuries, but in 1783, many citizens of the United States claimed that their decision to form a republic gave them a special role in world history.

Before and during the Revolution, many Americans had come to believe that living in a republic, a country defined by representative government, carried with it special responsibilities. In keeping with the Roman and European traditions of republicanism with which many learned Americans were familiar, Revolutionary patriots called for Americans to be "virtuous." Republican virtue meant different things to different people, but in general it required putting the good of society ahead of selfish personal interests. The leaders of society would not be men born to hereditary privilege, but rather men who had proven their merit through intellectual or military accomplishments and public service. In this idealized vision of a new society, American citizens would choose to bond themselves together with a kind of political affection that would jealously guard against the misuse of power and "tyranny" that Great Britain had represented before the war. Under these circumstances, many aspects of daily life became politicized, as even the education of children, the style of clothing Americans wore, or the kinds of entertainments they found amusing could be read for signs of proper republican virtue.

These ideas of republicanism laid the way for many of the social and political developments that would happen over the next 50 years of American history, and they were remarkably flexible ideas. At the same time, the related issues of democracy and equality always lay in the background, ready to give the lie to the picture-perfect vision of American society. At the end of the Revolution there were almost 1 million slaves in the United States. Women were considered inferior and subordinate to men. Poverty was on the rise, especially in American cities. Though some state governments were more democratic than others, in many cases the rulers of the new nation came from the same ranks of rich and powerful white men who had ruled before the Revolution. But republicanism simultaneously opened up the opportunity for change. A good republic demanded an educated public, and some women, some African Americans, and some of the poor would soon get the idea that they might show merit and deserve a better place in American society as well.

The American republic was not perfect, but to understand the development of the new nation, and to understand how the United States survived all the crises it faced in the first few years of its secure existence, it is necessary to understand what ideals people hoped to live up to. Patriots were anxious for the war to end and to show the world that they could create a special kind of country.

## THE END OF THE REVOLUTION

At the beginning of 1783, it was clear that one of the greatest challenges facing the United States was a product of its greatest triumph, the victory in the Revolutionary War. The Continental army, and the loyalty of some particularly hard-pressed units, had already been severely tested by the lack of national financial resources since at least 1780. Congress and the secretary of finance, Robert Morris, a wealthy merchant and Pennsylvania patriot, had marshaled enough funds through foreign loans, taxes, and other financial maneuvering to keep the war going, but the question remained whether they would be able to come up with enough money to end it. The French, Spanish, and Dutch had lent or given the United States almost $10 million between 1777 and 1783, and the French had spent nearly $6 million on their own forces to provide military aid.[2] The United States owed a lot of money to foreign banks, foreign governments, foreign and domestic private individuals, and military officers and enlisted men. Each of these debts would present particular problems to the government as the peace was being concluded and the army began to demobilize.

Throughout 1782, American peace negotiators Benjamin Franklin, John Adams, and John Jay had carefully worked in Europe to gain a favorable political position for the United States as they tried to conclude a treaty that would end the war. Their efforts were hampered by the uncomfortable position the United States found itself in, not for the last time, between archrivals Britain and France (and to a lesser degree Spain). The French government had provided the staunchest support of the United States during the Revolutionary War, and by early 1783 the British were seeking to conclude a separate peace with France and Spain that would greatly influence the terms of the peace treaty between Britain and the United States. Some British negotiators were preoccupied with the settlement of disputes with France over the Caribbean sugar islands, and Franklin and his fellow diplomats managed to remain loyal to French interests, while always striving to gain the best possible position for the United States in the negotiations.

In January 1783, Great Britain concluded preliminary treaties with France and Spain that opened the way for the final phase of negotiations over the terms of peace with the United States and for a general armistice to go into effect in February. The biggest questions facing the negotiators concerned land and fishing rights, the status of Britain's Native American allies, and the treatment of the Loyalists who had fled the United States or been deprived of their property during the war. John Adams wrote in a letter that the negotiations that ended 1782 were "a constant Scuffle Morning, noon and night about Cod and Haddock on the Grand Bank, Deer skins on the Ohio and Pine Trees at Penobscat, and . . . all the Refugees."[3]

This print by London engraver Thomas Colley depicts the reconciliation between Britania and "her daughter" America, who is shown as an Indian woman. In the cartoon, Spain and France try to interfere with the reconciliation, while Holland looks on. *(Library of Congress, Prints and Photographs Division [LC-USZ62-1532])*

All these questions ended up being resolved in favor of the new United States, and the terms of the Treaty of Paris conferred generous territory and power upon the new nation. When the American and British diplomats finally signed the treaty on September 3, 1783, they created the basis for future American physical and economic expansion, though no one at the time could have conceived of quite how far that expansion would go. In the treaty, Great Britain retained control of Canada, whose southern boundary was fixed at the Great Lakes, but ceded to the United States all the territory south of the Lakes and east of the Mississippi River that it had won from the French just 20 years earlier. Britain promised to remove military forces from this territory "with all convenient speed," pledged not to maintain any permanent fortifications in U.S. territory, and did not insist on any particular protection for Indian territories within those boundaries. Although the British were generous to some of their former Indian allies, most notably Joseph Brant (Thayendanegea) and his band of Mohawk, whom they resettled on land in Ontario, Canada, the real losers in the treaty were the many other Native Americans who gained no protection from their wartime loyalty to the British and were left to contend for themselves against the United States.

The United States also secured generous fishing rights off the coast of Nova Scotia and Newfoundland, a particular issue of concern to New

Englanders who made considerable profits in those waters. The British guaranteed U.S. shipping rights on the Mississippi River, but this guarantee failed to take into account the power of Spain to dispute those rights—especially since Spain maintained control of New Orleans by the Treaty of Versailles, which commissioners simultaneously concluded with Great Britain. The United States promised in the Treaty of Paris to cover all prewar debts owed to British merchants, to reintegrate Loyalists as American citizens, and to return confiscated Loyalist property.

Western lands, shipping rights, and fishing rights all represented sources of financial capital for the fledgling United States, but most of that capital was not readily available and would have to await decades of economic development before Americans could take full advantage of it. At the same time, prewar debts to British merchants and wartime debts to people all over the world were of more immediate concern. Though the United States established the basis of its future growth in the Treaty of Paris, the treaty did not present many short-term solutions to the immediate problems of demobilization.

## DEMOBILIZATION

Those problems, both financial and political, were clear even while the treaty was still being negotiated. On January 6, 1783, three of the Continental army's most prominent officers, General Alexander McDouglass, Colonel John Brooks, and Colonel Matthias Ogden, petitioned Congress on behalf of their fellow officers to express their dissatisfaction with the financial settlement offered by Congress in the first stages of demobilization. Congress had made frequent promises of back pay and various pension schemes to keep both officers and enlisted men in the ranks during the war, and now that the end was approaching, soldiers were worried that they would never see their money. McDouglass, Brooks, and Ogden asked that Congress pay officers a lump-sum settlement after the war (instead of the half-pay for life Congress had previously settled upon) and that all back pay be disbursed before the army disbanded. Congress considered the officers' requests, though no easy solution was forthcoming.

The demands for back pay, half-pay pensions, and other postwar settlements posed serious threats not only to the economic but also to the political stability of the United States. Beyond the fact that a large body of armed men might be dangerous if they became truly disgruntled over pay issues, disaffected soldiers, particularly officers, threatened the new republican political order. If the United States was supposed to stand apart as a virtuous nation, in part *because* of the willingness of its soldiers to sacrifice themselves, then what did it mean if the nation was too "ungrateful" to pay them back? Or were the soldiers themselves being "unvirtuous" by caring for their pay? Many of the enlisted men who remained in the ranks at the end of the war were especially poor and had joined up because of the pay and promises of special bounties; their public protests risked exposing the Continental army as just another standing army for hire instead of the selfless band of patriots that Americans imagined it to be.[4]

For much of 1783, the crisis over pay threatened the political order that winning the war was supposed to ensure. In March, a group of army officers met in secret at the army encampment in Newburgh, New York, to discuss their displeasure with Congress's financial assurances. Unsigned letters, now known to have been written by Pennsylvania officer John Armstrong, circulated among them, denouncing Congress as ungrateful and threatening to turn military force against the government if officers' demands were not met. George Washington, the revered commander in chief of the army, learned of the letters, notified Congress of the unrest, and called together his officers to try and quell what became known as the "Newburgh Conspiracy." Washington addressed the officers at a meeting on March 15, and he managed to quiet the grumbling by stressing the honor of personal sacrifice for the cause. Members of Congress could not count on Washington's magnetic personality to get them out of all tight scrapes, however, and some national politicians like Alexander Hamilton hoped that the officers' actions might compel Americans to accept a stronger central government. Congress eventually voted to pay the officers a lump sum upon their discharge instead of half-pay for life.

Congress and the integrity of the new republic were not threatened only by Continental army officers. Enlisted men were also willing to push their grievances at the point of the bayonet before the year was out. At the end of May 1783, the army, except for a small force that stayed with Washington near New York City, was disbanded. Enlisted men were sent home with their muskets and a promise of a future settlement of three months' pay. It was unclear where the money to back up these promises would come from, however, and some men proved reluctant to go home. On June 14, a group of between 300 and 400 furloughed soldiers from the Third Pennsylvania Regiment surrounded the Pennsylvania State House where Congress was meeting in emergency session. Though the soldiers were armed, they allowed the Congressmen to leave the building unmolested. Congress retired to Princeton, New Jersey, and the disgruntled soldiers went home, but the threat of unrest cast a pall over national politics until well after the peace treaty went into effect.

## THE RETURN TO CIVILIAN ORDER

Despite the drama over the nation's financial obligations to retiring soldiers, the return to civilian order proceeded fairly smoothly after the Treaty of Paris was signed. George Washington departed Newburgh, New York, on October 18, 1783, and proceeded to New York City, which underwent a dramatic shift back to U.S. control. The final British troops evacuated the city on November 25 and took with them approximately 7,000 Americans who remained loyal to the Crown. At the beginning of December, Washington attended public celebrations honoring the peace treaty in New York, and he bid a tearful farewell to his closest officers at a dinner at Fraunces Tavern. Washington then rode to Annapolis, Maryland, where he tendered his resignation to Congress and returned to his plantation at Mount Vernon, Virginia, to resume life as a private citizen.

Washington's retirement earned him praise and admiration since it symbolized the willingness of military authority to subjugate itself to civilian order to create a peaceful republic. Thomas Jefferson wrote that Washington's personal restraint and willingness to return to his private life "probably prevented this Revolution from being closed, as most others have been, by a subversion of that liberty it was intended to establish."[5] The general was compared to

This 19th-century engraving depicts George Washington's Virginia estate, Mount Vernon, which overlooks the Potomac River. *(from Benson Lossing,* The Pictorial Field-Book of the Revolution, *1851–1852)*

Cincinnatus, a famed Roman farmer who became a powerful soldier but returned to his plow when the war was over. Washington's retirement held great symbolic power, especially in the aftermath of the Newburgh Conspiracy and the threats by armed men to impose a financial settlement on Congress. When the former officers of the Continental army founded a fraternal and honorary society among themselves in 1783, they named it the Society of the Cincinnati in a bid to associate themselves with the same Roman republican imagery (though the public was more dubious of what they saw as the aristocratic pretensions of the society).

Although Washington's personal magnetism and his peaceful retirement helped to ensure that peace really did take hold, many other Americans did not have plantations to which they could retire, nor did many find it easy to pick up the pieces of their lives following the war. Average soldiers returned home with no idea whether they would be paid for their service, and they had to find work during an economic slump. Most of the African-American men who had served as soldiers, sailors, or militiamen were granted their freedom in return, but free African Americans still faced racism and severe social restrictions, even in the most progressive urban areas like Philadelphia, which was home to the first antislavery society in the United States. Some women who had assumed control of businesses and farms during the war gladly gave up their wartime responsibilities to return to a subordinate position in their households, but others lost husbands and sons in the war and had to rebuild their own economic fortunes. African-American slaves who had fled their masters and been promised freedom by the British during the war faced uncertain futures as well. Some were allowed to move to Canada alongside other fleeing Loyalists, but others were resold into slavery in the Caribbean.

The Loyalist population, in general, faced the hardest task to find a new place for themselves in the postwar United States. Some did not even try. Between 70,000 and 100,000 Loyalists had fled the United States during the war, most to Great Britain or Canada, and now they faced the decision of whether or not to return. The stakes of such decisions were high, since many Loyalists were fighting after the war for the return of property that had been confiscated during the hostilities by private individuals or governments.

Many patriots did not want to see Loyalists return for political and economic reasons, and Loyalists who tried were often met with derision and even violence. In Charleston, South Carolina, Loyalists were openly mocked in the streets, and former patriots formed societies dedicated to retaining the social stigma of Loyalism. Some Loyalist families tried to move across the country and start over, but their political past might crop up to haunt them at unexpected moments.[6] Several states, including Massachusetts, had passed Banishment Acts that forbade Loyalists to return home, and these laws were repealed only slowly, if at all, over the course of the 1780s and 1790s. Pennsylvania had tried 500 Loyalists in absentia for treason, and it was unclear whether these men and women might ever be allowed to reclaim their homes. The 1783 Treaty of Paris guaranteed that Loyalists would be restored to full political rights, but that restoration came only after bitter political fights in many states, and some town meetings and state legislatures never agreed to abide fully by the terms of the treaty.

The Loyalists, many of whom had been among the most economically privileged Americans before the war, faced great obstacles in trying to reclaim their wealth and property. All 13 states had formally confiscated property from Loyalists during the war, in part as a way to help pay for militia and other war costs. Many Loyalists gave up trying to return home, resettled in Halifax, Nova Scotia, and began the task of building a new British colonial society there. Others tried to remain in England, where they petitioned the British government for financial compensation. While many did eventually receive money from the British government to cover lost property, nothing could restore their lost social status, especially since many of the former colonial elites could not maintain as high a standing in the more stratified English society.[7]

## ECONOMIC SLUMP

Probably the greatest challenge facing the United States in the aftermath of the Revolutionary War was economic. A combination of trade difficulties, debts, and a weak central government combined to send the country into a severe financial depression. The war itself had stimulated production and economic growth, as the American economy mobilized to feed and supply the army and to provide some of the goods cut off by the British, but that growth was accompanied by rampant inflation that made the lives of typical Americans much harder. Even though the vast majority of Americans lived on small farms that could produce food and basic necessities for an interdependent network of local farm families, the war had disrupted the agricultural economy and introduced more and more people to buying and selling goods. High wartime prices for most major staples began to fall steadily after 1783, but that was a mixed blessing since many farmers also made profits by marketing agricultural goods at home and abroad. At the same time, much of the hard currency in the United States was flowing overseas to pay off loans and to pay for imports, so many Americans lacked the means to pay for market goods, even if they were more affordable.[8]

The entire U.S. economy was weakened by the underlying structural problems of an oversupply of paper money and too much debt. During the war, Congress and the states had ordered almost $400 million worth of paper money to be printed, although they could rely on only about $30 million in hard currency reserves (the gold and silver that was supposed to back up paper money). During 1784 and 1785, Congress and the states engaged in a constant argument over who ought to assume responsibility to pay back some of the largest of these war debts. Although Congress convinced state governments to take over direct payment of some of the loans, it also promised to offer the states credit in the future for these payments, which threatened to further weaken the already low national tax revenue. Several states agreed to pay interest on the national war debt, but the issues of state versus federal power raised by these payments took much longer to settle. In addition to the debts owed by the Confederation and state governments to overseas powers and to former

This engraving depicts some of the Continental paper bills issued by Congress during and after the Revolutionary War that helped cause inflation and weaken the economy. *(from Benson Lossing,* The Pictorial Field-Book of the Revolution, *1851–1852)*

soldiers, many businesses and individuals also found themselves in severe debt. Trade imbalances and debts set off a chain reaction that led the country into deeper financial straits and threatened the political stability of the nation.[9]

After the war, trade patterns had to readjust, which caused considerable disruption to a U.S. economy still heavily dependent upon British imports, especially for luxury goods. Britain reopened its main trade with the United States, but the sudden flood of British goods overwhelmed American markets, especially because Americans lacked access to enough hard currency with which to pay foreign creditors. At the same time that British merchants continued to profit from American exports, Britain continued a wartime embargo on American products in the West Indies, and many American merchants and farmers who counted on selling their goods in the Caribbean suffered as a result. These trade restrictions encouraged Americans to seek new trade relations with China and other regions of Europe, but new avenues developed slowly and could not immediately replace the immense Caribbean trade that had grown up during the colonial period. The American South, which relied heavily on agricultural exports, particularly tobacco, suffered especially from declining trade, a situation worsened by the heavy indebtedness of many plantation owners to British tobacco merchants before the war and because the Treaty of Paris did nothing to relieve them of their obligations to pay. By 1784, there was a serious depression in American trade, and even internal markets, which carried on trade between American farms and cities, grew sluggish.[10]

The U.S. government could do very little to remedy the situation. It faced huge financial problems of its own. Under the Articles of Confederation, the constitution that established the terms of national government in the United States in 1781, the national government did not have the power to regulate trade or to levy direct taxes. A plan spearheaded by Robert Morris to raise national revenues by placing an impost tax on imports in 1782 failed because Congress could not impose any kind of national tax without the unanimous consent of every state, and Rhode Island, the smallest state, refused to agree to the impost. In almost every case, when the national government tried to raise money, one state or another stood in the way. Leaders who favored bolstering governmental power, such as Virginian James Madison, cited the unrest at the end of the Revolutionary War and the constant pressure on Congress to pay foreign debts as reasons to consider revising the Articles of Confederation. Immediately following the war, the republican suspicion of power overcame such ideas about the need for stronger central government, but the debts did not go away, and Congress could not command enough revenue from the states to cover its bills. The states, in turn, faced their own financial crises, especially related to their overissuance of bonds during the war.

As Congress, state governments, and merchants struggled with their war debts and commercial debts, the burden of the problem began to fall ever more on average American citizens. British merchants demanded payments in hard currency from American merchant debtors. Many of these merchants, in turn, sought government authorization to gain that currency by collecting on smaller loans, mortgages, and other kinds of promissory notes that had accumulated during the inflationary years. Americans who had contracted these debts often had access only to devalued paper currency and thus had no way to pay back their creditors. Many states, including Pennsylvania and Massachusetts, also issued new kinds of poll taxes and land taxes (both of which targeted small farmers) to pay back financial speculators who stood to make huge profits on the repayment of war bonds. Bankruptcies rose dramatically, especially since many creditors had the power to pursue their debtors in court and even to jail people who were unable to pay their debts in hard currency.

The central government lacked power to remedy the situation, and Congress was preoccupied with other concerns. Several state legislatures passed laws to protect debtors and farmers from legal action, and many courts, especially in the Middle Atlantic region, were hesitant to prosecute delinquent debtors. But in states where conservatives and financiers maintained political power, including Maryland and Massachusetts, legislation intended to shield individual debtors from prosecution failed. In Massachusetts, the problem was particularly acute, since residents were required to pay their taxes in hard currency, and sheriffs could bring legal action against anyone who did not pay.

## THE BEGINNING OF SHAYS'S REBELLION

In 1785 and 1786, with the economic depression continuing, matters came to a head in western Massachusetts, when indebted farmers began to protest loudly against their creditors, state tax officials, and the courts. Angry debtors held impromptu political conventions in Worcester and other towns and voted to publicize their grievances and petition the state government for relief. They denounced creditors and tax collectors in the newspapers as greedy beasts who sought to take away their hard-won rights, an especially sensitive point since many veterans were among the ranks of debtors pursued in court. Former soldiers who sold their pay certificates to financial speculators at less than face value felt twice wronged, once by the government and once by their creditors, whom they often still could not pay. Governor James Bowdoin, who drew his political support from eastern Massachusetts merchant interests, was unsympathetic to the demands of the debtors' meetings, and he signed a state Riot Act that outlawed unauthorized assemblies.

The disgruntled debtors saw this only as further proof of government "tyranny," and they began to take up arms. Late in 1786, bands of armed men, sometimes called Regulators in the manner of pre-Revolutionary resisters against the British, shut down county and local courts by preventing judges and other officials from meeting. While they continued to petition the state government seeking pro-debtor legislation, they used threats of force and intimidation to keep lawsuits against debtors from proceeding. The Regulators became more and more organized as the fall wore on; they met in taverns and followed the leadership of Revolutionary veteran Daniel Shays.[11]

Shays and his men may have understood their protests as part of a traditional pattern of agrarian unrest, and surely many of them had been schooled in protest by their participation in the Revolutionary War. But officials of the state government of Massachusetts, and many of the state's more privileged citizens, did not view their actions in the same terms. Newly formed state governments were fragile, and Governor Bowdoin warned the Massachusetts legislature that if armed men were allowed to control law enforcement, "[t]he great end of government, the security of life, liberty, and property, must be frustrated, and the government so far laid prostrate."[12] Smaller groups of armed

Regulators also challenged courts in New Hampshire, Pennsylvania, Connecticut, and New York, but the state of Massachusetts chose to take a strong stand against such resistance. As tensions escalated into the winter months, the state legislature authorized the organization of militia troops under former Revolutionary general and financial speculator Benjamin Lincoln and passed a series of laws intended to sanction any further armed protest. By the end of 1786, the issue of debt seemed to be forcing an internal military crisis in what had seemed to be one of the most stable of the United States.

In 1786, politicians concerned with the lack of power in the national government to prevent social upheaval—such as was evident in the early months of Shays's Rebellion—began to press much more forcefully their opinion that the Articles of Confederation needed revision. Nationalists, who believed that the financial and social difficulties facing the United States might be solved if the states were willing to grant more power to the central government, began to organize to further their political aspirations. Worried about trade problems, debtor unrest, and a lack of U.S. financial credibility, nationalists called a convention in Annapolis, Maryland, in September 1786 to discuss how to enhance the power of the national government to deal with these problems. Although the meeting was not well attended, with only five of the states' delegations showing up, the Annapolis Convention was important beyond its numbers. Meeting during the period of heightening tension in Massachusetts, the delegates issued a call for a new convention to convene in Philadelphia the following July, in order that delegates from all the states might consider altering the Articles. That meeting was to become the Constitutional Convention.

## LOOKING WEST

Although the U.S. government was clearly unable to solve most of the serious financial problems facing the country in the immediate aftermath of the Revolutionary War, Congress was not entirely impotent. In the development of western lands, the national government began to exert considerable authority. As with most postwar issues, the results of these actions were mixed and not without controversy, but advancing plans for western settlement did further the national goals of the United States. In their dealings with Native American bands to the immediate west of what was then the United States, government officials also set some patterns (both benign and nefarious) that would endure for decades.

Immediately following the war, many in the United States viewed western lands as a sort of pressure valve that might prevent unrest and provide needed financial resources to the U.S. government. Individual states and the Confederation government began issuing land certificates to war veterans as a way to pay off a portion of the back pay many were owed. Government negotiators fanned out to try to convince Indian nations bordering the United States that the Treaty of Paris had sapped them of some of their power and rights to the land, but very few Native Americans took the same view, and it was not yet entirely clear whether the United States would be able to back up any threats of force, especially against some of the better-organized Indian nations such as the Miami Confederacy and the Iroquois. Government agents forced a group of Iroquois to sign the unfavorable Treaty of Fort Stanwix in 1784, but in 1786 the Confederation's leaders backed off from the treaty and wanted to retake the lands they had given up west of New York. In 1785, the Cherokee, Choctaw, and Chickasaw nations ceded land claims in the Cumberland valley to the United States and opened formal relations with the government in the Treaty of Hopewell, but they also protested consistently when the national and several state governments failed to remove white settlers from within their sovereign territory. Neither the grants of western lands to veterans nor the initial efforts to negotiate with Native Americans proved likely to solidify national control over the entire west.

The United States faced at least four sets of problems when trying to begin its initial push westward. Thousands of U.S. citizens already lived beyond the defined borders of the 13 states, and it was unclear whether the government could control these people at all, even when it wanted to. The states often disagreed with one another about which had the rightful claim to western lands, and western settlers often disliked the control of their state governments, which tended to represent the eastern population centers most directly. Some western settlers, for example in Kentucky, which was part of western Virginia, openly flirted with foreign countries and threatened to secede from the United States to become Spanish or French colonies. Many white westerners provoked open conflicts with Native Americans, notably in Kentucky, the Carolinas, and the Ohio valley. This undeclared war between U.S. citizens and members of many Indian nations threatened both the authority and the stability of the U.S. government, which had dramatically decreased the size of the national military after 1783. Even in the midst of this sometimes chaotic atmosphere, land speculators drove up the cost of western property, and veterans' land bounties became commodities traded on the open market.

Congress wanted to solve all these underlying tensions by gaining better control of the western territories. At the end of 1783, Virginia ceded much of its vast western land claim to the U.S. government, and even though the legislature retained control of Kentucky, the cession paved the way for other states to follow suit and opened the way for Congress to set the terms for settlement of the Northwest Territory. In 1784, Congress passed a land ordinance drafted by Thomas Jefferson that established 10 federal districts in the west and set the terms for future statehood for the territories. The following year, another ordinance established procedures for the surveying and sale of land in the Northwest Territory. Some problems persisted in the Northwest, where land speculators held power, where Indians resisted surveying operations, and where the British failed to evacuate their forts in the Great Lakes region, but these land ordinances were nonetheless among the most successful government actions taken during the Confederation period.

Congress exercised less control over western territories south of the Ohio River, and the eastern states were not always successful at peacefully handling their western territories. In 1784, former Revolutionary War officers John Sevier and Arthur Campbell led settlers in present-day Tennessee to break away from the state of North Carolina and to form the state of Franklin. Their bid for statehood failed after several years of threatening back and forth but still showed the power of disillusioned westerners to cause problems for state governments. Franklin, though unsuccessful, was not an isolated case, and similar statehood movements were active in Kentucky and Vermont, both of which would not become separate states until the 1790s.

European powers took the opportunity to turn the lack of repose in the western territories to their advantage. As the first U.S. ambassadors to European countries, John Adams and Thomas Jefferson, were busy negotiating abroad, conditions at home sometimes complicated their diplomatic efforts. The British continued to court powerful Indian allies in the Great Lakes region, and they did not restrict their military posts to Canadian territory, as they had promised in the Treaty of Paris. U.S. secretary of foreign affairs John Jay negotiated a treaty that would open Spain to U.S. trade in 1785, but in return Spain demanded that the United States give up rights to navigate the Mississippi for 25 years, a requirement that would have severely sanctioned western U.S. settlers who relied on the river to send their goods to market. Only seven states out of the required nine in Congress agreed to ratify the Jay-Gardoqui Treaty, but westerners were shocked that a majority of states would agree to such conditions. Though the treaty failed, Spain revoked American trading rights anyway on the Mississippi for a time in 1786, and ironically the treaty negotiations may have also encouraged western settlers in Franklin and Kentucky who were secretly communicating with Spanish minister Gardoqui about the possibility of leaving the United States. The land ordinances of 1784 and 1785 may have been among the most powerful acts passed by the Confederation Congress, but western diplomatic dealings also revealed that the United States was still considered by Europeans to be a lesser international power.

## LIVING IN THE NEW NATION

Despite what must have seemed like considerable upheaval and unrest, the majority of Americans went about living relatively quiet lives in the first years after the Revolutionary War. Although the economic depression, pressures of military demobilization, efforts to reintegrate Loyalists, and conflicts over western lands certainly touched the lives of many, daily life in the United States in the mid-1780s was more defined by agricultural work than anything else. Though they may have had more interest in goods from abroad or trade with big cities than they would have had a few decades earlier, most women and men concerned themselves with producing food, clothing, and housing for themselves and their children. Some classes of people—especially those in cities and among the rising ranks of free African Americans—sought out new kinds of experiences, but most people, whether free or slave, continued to consider rural family life as the basic pattern of existence in the United States.

Community institutions—from the New England town meeting to the southern militia muster to the ever-growing number of churches—provided the most important contact between people in the new United States. In many states, government continued to promote particular forms of established religion, but members of dissenting denominations who no longer wanted to pay taxes for official church support were beginning to be heard. In 1786, Virginia set a new precedent by passing the Act for Establishing Religious Freedom, which formally declared a separation between religion and the state and no longer compelled citizens to support churches with tax money. The bill, drafted by Thomas Jefferson, owed its passage to a coalition of dissenters, including

Baptists and Methodists, the two fastest-growing American religious sects.[13] Just two years earlier, the American Methodist Church had broken off from the English church (which was still tied to the Church of England), and its energetic bishop, Francis Asbury, sent out dozens of circuit riders to win new American converts. His efforts would grow even more successful after the Virginia act. Aside from churches, Americans were also just beginning to enter the first phase of founding schools, clubs, benevolent societies, and a whole host of other social institutions that would come to define the early republic.

Although Americans undoubtedly identified most closely with their families and their local communities, large-scale participation in the Revolutionary War had opened Americans' eyes to one another. In the mid-1780s, more and more Americans read newspapers and began to be aware of national and state events and politics. An event like Shays's Rebellion showed how easily issues of local concern could quickly shade over into statewide or even national, political crises. In many ways, Americans were only beginning to feel the full effects of the new kind of republican society they had chosen to create. Even bigger changes were to come.

## CHRONICLE OF EVENTS

### 1783

Noah Webster publishes his *Blue-Backed Speller,* which begins his campaign to standardize spelling in America. The book will sell millions of copies and serve as a basis for future dictionaries.

Jedidiah Morse, one of the first important U.S. scientists, publishes his book *The American Geography.*

Rabbi Gershon M. Seixas successfully sues the state of Pennsylvania, forcing it to lift a ban on Jews holding public office.

Transylvania Seminary, the first college west of the Allegheny Mountains, is chartered in Kentucky.

Joseph Brant (Thayendanegea) leads his Mohawk followers to a settlement on the Grand River in Ontario, Canada, where the British have granted them tracts of land in repayment for support during the Revolutionary War.

Benjamin Franklin invents bifocal eyeglasses.

*January 16:* Continental army officers petition Congress for lump-sum payments at the end of the Revolutionary War instead of the half-pay for life that Congress had offered the previous year.

*January 20:* Articles of peace between Great Britain and France and Great Britain and Spain go into effect, fulfilling the precondition for a treaty between Britain and the United States.

*February 4:* A general armistice between the United States and Great Britain takes effect.

*February 22:* The first public celebrations of George Washington's birthday as a holiday take place in Virginia, New York, Massachusetts, and Maryland.

*March 10:* Unrest arises among the officers of the Continental army stationed at Newburgh, New York, when anonymous documents denouncing the Congress's promise of half pay and its inability to pay war debts circulate through the ranks.

*March 11:* George Washington alerts Congress that the army may be on the brink of mutiny.

*March 15:* George Washington quells the unrest at Newburgh, later known as the "Newburgh Conspiracy," by addressing his officers and appealing to their honor and loyalty.

*April 3:* Author Washington Irving is born in New York City.

*April 15:* Congress receives and ratifies the provisional treaty of peace between the United States and Great Britain.

*May 13:* A group of Continental army officers found the Society of the Cincinnati, an honorary organization whose membership they intend to pass along to their male heirs. George Washington is the society's first president.

*May 23:* James Otis, once a fiery opponent of the British before the Revolution, who now has gone mad, is struck by lightning and dies in Massachusetts.

*May 26:* Most of the U.S. Army begins to disband, and many soldiers leave camps without waiting for official orders. Noncommissioned officers and enlisted men leave Newburgh, New York, with promises of back pay, but Congress fails to indicate how they will be reimbursed. George Washington retains his command over a small force, and the British still occupy New York City.

*May 30:* In Philadelphia, Benjamin Towne begins publication of the first U.S. daily newspaper, *The Pennsylvania Evening Post.*

*June 15:* Congress, meeting in Philadelphia, is threatened by a mutinous band of furloughed soldiers from the Third Pennsylvania Regiment. The soldiers allow the Congressmen to adjourn unmolested, and Congress decides to move the seat of government.

*June 24:* Congress meets in Princeton, New Jersey.

*July 8:* The Massachusetts Supreme Court rules that slavery must be abolished in that state. This sparks a process of gradual emancipation across New England.

*August 13:* Charleston, South Carolina, is incorporated and officially changes its name from "Charles Town" to "Charleston."

*September 3:* Representatives of the United States and Great Britain sign the Treaty of Paris, formally concluding the Revolutionary War, assuring the independence of the United States, and defining the country's boundaries. In the treaty, the British Province of Quebec loses all lands south of the Great Lakes.

*September 22:* Congress proclaims that no private citizen may receive a gift or cession of Indian land without congressional permission.

*November:* Annapolis, Maryland, becomes the capital of the United States, and Congress convenes there in December.

This London cartoon depicts King George III discussing the ratification of the Treaty of Paris with his advisers as, in the background, Benjamin Franklin places a crown on the head of "America," represented by an Indian woman. *(Library of Congress, Prints and Photographs Division [LC-USZC4-5276])*

*November 25:* The British evacuate New York City along with almost 7,000 Loyalists, among them some of the city's most prominent citizens. George Washington and George Clinton enter the city to great public acclaim.

*December 20:* The Virginia Assembly cedes its huge western land claims to the United States, prompting other states to follow suit.

*December 23:* George Washington appears dramatically before Congress in Annapolis, Maryland, to resign his post as commander in chief of the Continental army. He is praised for his willingness to return to civilian life.

### 1784

Richard Allen and Absalom Jones become the first African Americans licensed to preach in the United States by the Methodist Episcopal Church.

Judith Sargent Murray publishes "Desultory Thoughts upon the Utility of Encouraging a Degree of Self-Complacency, Especially in Female Bosoms," an essay claiming that women are equal to men and arguing for female education.

Mother Ann Lee, the founder of the American Shaker religious movement, who believed herself to be Jesus Christ, dies.

British officials expel the last Acadians from Nova Scotia.

Thirteen-year-old Edward Warren makes the first U.S. hot-air balloon flight in a balloon produced by Peter Carnes in Baltimore, Maryland.

Many of New York's most prominent politicians and writers, including Thomas Paine, George Clinton, and John Jay, form the New York Society for Promoting Useful Knowledge.

*January 14:* Congress ratifies the Treaty of Paris.

*February 22:* The *Empress of China* sails from New York City carrying a cargo of ginseng root and seeking to open trade relations with China to counteract some of the economic harm caused by British commercial restrictions.

*February 23:* The Rhode Island legislature establishes the gradual abolition of slavery by voting that all blacks and "mulattoes" born in the state after March will be free.

*March 1:* Congress accepts the Virginia Act of Cession, which cedes most of Virginia's western territory, especially north of the Ohio River, to the national domain.

*April 23:* Congress adopts Thomas Jefferson's Territorial Ordinance of 1784, which sets out the basic rules of governance in the Northwestern territories that will serve as a basis for the 1787 Northwest Ordinance. Congress rejects Jefferson's proposal that slavery be disallowed in new states after 1800.

*May:* The *Gentlemen and Ladies' Town and Country Magazine* begins publication in Boston. Though the magazine lasts only a short time, it is notable as the first periodical in the United States aimed particularly at female readers.

*June:* The North Carolina legislature cedes its western lands (present-day Tennessee) to the U.S. government, outraging settlers in the territory who are hoping to control their own land claims. The legislature shortly reverses the cession, but settlers are not satisfied.

*August:* Congress appoints commissioners to consider laying out a permanent capital in a federal district.

A convention of residents of Western North Carolina, led by former revolutionary officers Arthur Campbell and John Sevier, defiantly declares the formation of the new state of Franklin. The declaration begins several years of wrangling among the settlers, the government of North Carolina, land speculators, and the U.S. government.

*August 30:* The *Empress of China,* a trading vessel captained by John Greene, arrives in Canton, China, beginning American trade with that country.

*October 22:* The United States signs the Treaty of Fort Stanwix with members of the pro-British Iroquois Confederacy. After they cede to military threats, the treaty forces the Iroquois to give up large amounts of land in Pennsylvania and all their claims west of New York State.

*November 18:* Although the archbishop of Canterbury objects, Scottish bishops consecrate Samuel Seabury the first Anglican bishop in the United States.

*November 24:* Zachary Taylor, future successful general and president of the United States, is born in Orange Court House, Virginia.

*December 5:* African-American poet Phillis Wheatley dies.

*December 24:* The Methodist Church is formally established in the United States at a Baltimore convention, and Francis Asbury is elected as the denomination's first bishop.

## 1785

Construction begins on the Little River Turnpike in Virginia, the nation's first turnpike.

Americans over the age of 15 consume an average of 40.3 gallons per person per year of alcoholic beverages.

*January 27:* The state of Georgia charters the University of Georgia, the first state nondenominational university in the country.

*February 24:* John Adams is appointed as the first U.S. ambassador to Great Britain.

*March 4:* New York City becomes the capital of the United States.

*March 10:* Thomas Jefferson is appointed the first U.S. ambassador to France.

*March 19:* The South Carolina Assembly charters the College of Charleston, the first city college in the United States.

*April–May:* John Adams and Thomas Jefferson negotiate to borrow money from Dutch bankers to help pay overdue U.S. war debts.

*May 10:* Thomas Jefferson publishes his book *Notes on the State of Virginia.* In addition to examining political theory, Jefferson also speculates on the reasons for the inferiority of the African race, and proposes that whites and blacks will never be able to live peacefully together in the United States.

*May 20:* Congress passes the Land Ordinance of 1785, which further defines plans to survey western territories so that they may be split up and sold.

*August 5:* In London, John Adams signs a treaty of friendship and trade with Prussia.

*August 23:* Naval hero Oliver Hazard Perry is born.

*November 18:* The United States concludes the Treaty of Hopewell with representatives of the Cherokee, Choctaw, and Chickasaw Nations, who declare themselves to be "under the protection" of the United States. The Cherokee send a deputy to the U.S. Congress, and the Indian nations are recognized as having sovereign borders, which the United States promises to protect from white encroachment (a promise that was later broken).

## 1786

Nicholas Biddle, future financier and head of the Second Bank of the United States, is born.

Mennonites from central Europe settle in Canada.

In Philadelphia, Charles Willson Peale establishes his very popular American Museum, which displays art, taxidermy animals, and natural history artifacts.

Printers in Philadelphia, Pennsylvania, hold the first organized strike in U.S. history; they successfully obtain a $6-a-week wage.

Inventor Ezekiel Reed produces a nail-making machine.

The first commercially produced ice cream in the United States becomes available in New York City.

The first golf club in the United States is founded in Charleston, South Carolina.

Ezra Stiles, president of Yale University, founds the Connecticut Society of Arts and Sciences.

*January 16:* Virginia adopts its Statute for Religious Freedom, which will become a model for the First Amendment to the U.S. Constitution. Thomas Jefferson, author of the statute, considers it one of the greatest accomplishments of his life.

*January 25:* John Adams concludes a treaty of friendship and peace with Morocco. Though treaties with Algiers, Tripoli, and Tunis fail to be signed, Americans hope that the Moroccan treaty will lessen tensions with other North African Barbary States, which have captured American sailors over the previous few years.

*August 7:* Congress establishes the first two federal Indian reservations and appoints a superintendent of Indian Affairs who will report to the secretary of war, Henry Knox.

*August 8:* Congress passes the Mint Act and adopts a decimal coinage system based on the Spanish dollar, although the central government does not produce many coins and many states continue to issue their own currency.

*August 15:* A county convention in Worcester, Massachusetts, sends a message to the state assembly in Boston protesting "abuses in the practice of law and the exorbitance of the fee-table."[14] Their message echoes the financial and political frustrations of people all over western Massachusetts, some of whom, like Daniel Shays, form armed bands of men to take action against courts that are pursuing indebted people.

*August 17:* David "Davy" Crockett, future congressman, fighter for Texas independence, and frontier character, is born in Hawkins County, Tennessee.

*August 29:* Armed insurgents close the court of common pleas in Northampton, Massachusetts.

*September 4:* Adam Hubbard leads a band of armed men who take over the courthouse in Worcester, Massachusetts. The next morning, they keep judges out by threatening them with bayonets.

*September 11–14:* Delegates from five states who are concerned about the lack of power demonstrated by the Confederation government convene in Annapolis, Maryland, and issue a call for states to send delegates to a Philadelphia convention the following year to revise the Articles of Confederation.

*December 26:* Daniel Shays's men use military force to close the Courts of Common Pleas and General Sessions in Springfield, Massachusetts.

## EYEWITNESS TESTIMONY

The army are now disciplined, and their wants as to food and clothing are relieved, but they are not paid. Their back accounts are not settled. If settled, the balances are not secured by competent funds. No provision is made for the half-pay promised them. Some persons, and indeed some States, pretend to dispute their claim to it. The army have swords in their hands. You know enough of the history of mankind to know much more than I have said, and possibly much more than they themselves yet think of. . . . I think it probable, that much of convulsion will ensue, yet it must terminate in giving to the government that power, without which government is but a name.

> *National financier and politician Gouverneur Morris,*
> *letter to John Jay, January 1, 1783, in Sparks,*
> Life of Gouverneur Morris, *249.*

Your Petitioner is not only innocent of any crime, but if a sincere affection for the independence and freedom of her Country, avowed and testified in the worst of times, be any Merit, she flatters herself she has some to plead. With regard to her banished husband, She has but little to say. Being a laborious hard-working man in a Mechanic employment, and not versed in the knowledge of publick troubles, it is not likely he could do any political good or harm.

> *Florence Cooke, wife of a banished South Carolina*
> *Loyalist, petition to the General Assembly of South*
> *Carolina, January 21, 1783, in Kerber,*
> Women of the Republic, *128.*

It is a favorite toast in the army, "a hoop to the barrel," or, "cement to the union." America will have fought and bled to little purpose, if the powers of government shall be insufficient to preserve the peace, and this must be the case without general funds. As the present constitution is so defective, why do not you great men call the people together, and tell them so. That is, to have a convention of the States to form a better constitution? This appears to us, who have a superficial view only, to be the most efficacious remedy. Let something be done before the peace takes place, or we shall be in a worse situation than we were at the commencement of the war.

> *Henry Knox, future secretary of war, letter to*
> *Gouverneur Morris, February 21, 1783, in Sparks,*
> Life of Gouverneur Morris, *256.*

If this, then, be your treatment, while the swords you wear are necessary for the defence [sic] of America, what have you to expect from peace, when your voice shall sink, and your strength dissipate by division? When those very swords, the instruments and companions of your glory, shall be taken from your sides, and no remaining mark of military distinction left but your wants, infirmities and scars? Can you then consent to be the only sufferers by this revolution, and retiring from the field, grow old in poverty, wretchedness and contempt? . . . I would advise you therefore, to come to some final opinion, of what you can bear and what you will suffer . . . carry your appeal from the justice to the fears of government. Change the milk and water style of your last memorial . . . tell them . . . that the slightest mark of indignity from Congress now, must operate like a grave, and part you forever: that in any political event, the army has its alternative. . . .

> *Disgruntled officer John Armstrong, The Newburgh*
> *Address "To the Officers of the Army," March 1783, in*
> *Rhodehamel,* The American Revolution, *775, 776.*

Let me entreat you, Gentlemen, on your part, not to take any measures, which, viewed in the calm light of reason, will lessen the dignity, and sully the glory you have hitherto maintained . . . express your utmost horror and detestation of the Man who wishes, under any specious pretences, to overturn the liberties of our Country, and who wickedly attempts to open the flood Gates of Civil discord, and deluge our rising Empire in Blood.

> *George Washington, speech to the Continental army*
> *officers at Newburgh, New York, March 15, 1783,*
> *in Rhodehamel,* The American Revolution, *784.*

I have seen a printed hand bill containing the preliminary Articles between Great Britain and the United States, and so far as I am able to judge, they are, upon the whole, as favorable as America, in her present situation, has a right to expect. The grand points are ceded to her, and as for the payment of debts contracted before the war, it is no more than justice requires, nor do I think it would have been sound policy in us to have abrogated them, had it been in our power.

> *Virginia plantation owner and politician George Mason,*
> *letter to Arthur Lee, March 25, 1783, in Rowland,*
> Life of George Mason, *II: 40.*

When soldiers advance without authority, who can halt them? We have many Clodiuses and Catalines in America, who may give a different direction to this business than either you or I expect. It is a critical business, and pregnant with dangerous consequences. Congress are fast declining, and their power and authority must expire, without more effectual support. What this may produce, time will manifest. I have done my duty, and wait events.

*Major General Nathanael Greene, letter to Gouverneur Morris, April 3, 1783, in Sparks,* Life of Gouverneur Morris, *251–252.*

This is to certify to whomsoever it may concern, that the Bearer hereof Cato Rammsay, a Negro, resorted to the British Lines, in consequence of the Proclamations of Sir William Howe, and Sir Henry Clinton, late Commanders in Chief of America; and that the said Negro has hereby his Excellency Sir Guy Carleton's Permission to go to Nova-Scotia, or wherever else he may think proper.

*British brigadier general Birch, pass for escaped slave to settle in Nova Scotia, April 21, 1783, in Johnson and Smith,* Africans in America, *119.*

We are now to rank among the nations of the world, but whether our independence shall prove a blessing or a curse, must depend on our own wisdom or folly, virtue or wickedness; judging the future by the past, the prospect is not promising. Justice and virtue are the vital principles of republican government; but among us a depravity of manners and morals prevails to the destruction of all confidence between man and man.

*George Mason, letter to Patrick Henry, May 6, 1783, in Rowland,* Life of George Mason, *II: 44.*

The prospect of speedily returning to the walks of private life fills my heart with raptures . . . The definitive treaty is not signed or if signed is not come to hand. Carlton is in possession of New York and no prospects of his speedily leaving it. To quit the field before our coast is clear would argue of a total want of sense. Neither shall we, but we remain inactive without imployment, and under such restrictions that we can make no arrangements for Domestic life.

*Lieutenant Benjamin Gilbert, letter to Daniel Gould, May 6, 1783, in Shy,* Winding Down, *104–105.*

A little before this time [June 1783] the officers of the army beginning to realize that the dissolution of the army was drawing nigh, and wishing to perpetuate that friendship which numerous hardships, sufferings, and common dangers had inspired in their breasts,—resolved to form themselves into a Society, by the name of the Cincinnati.

*Major General William Heath, from his 1798* Memoirs, *in Hart,* American History, *II: 626.*

Those brave men who were for the war and who have been fighting from four to eight years in defense of their Country and for the preservation of its liberty, are now discharged the service, and are retiring from the field of Glory with Joy in their counte-

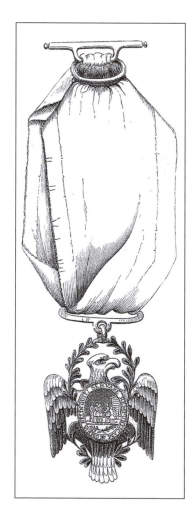

This emblem was worn by members of the Society of the Cincinnati, a controversial organization founded in 1783 by former officers in the Continental army. *(from Benson Lossing,* The Pictorial Field-Book of the Revolution, *1851–1852)*

nances, but poverty in their pockets. Not one man to twenty of them, has a single farthing to support him on his passage to his friends . . . an unprecedented piece of ingratitude.

*Lieutenant Benjamin Gilbert, letter to Charles Bruce, June 10, 1783, in Shy,* Winding Down, *107.*

The late prohibition to trade with the British Islands, unless in British bottoms, can do us no harm, and can do them no good. Our produce they must and will have. . . . I am persuaded the British Ministers cannot seriously intend the prohibition, although I am equally convinced, that a regard to the national prejudices renders it unavoidable at present.

*Gouverneur Morris, letter to John Jay, September 24, 1783, in Sparks,* Life of Gouverneur Morris, *259–260.*

. . . it only remains for the commander in chief to address himself once more, and that for the last time, to the armies of the United States . . . and to bid them an affectionate, a long farewell [sic]. . . . it is earnestly recommended to all the troops, that, with strong attachments to the union, they should carry with them into civil society the most conciliatory dispositions; and that they should prove themselves not less virtuous and useful as citizens, than they have been preserving and victorious as soldiers.

*Adjutant General Edward Hand delivers General Washington's farewell orders to his troops, November 2, 1783, in Warren,* History of the Rise, *II: 711, 712.*

Happy in the confirmation of our independence and sovereignty, and pleased with the opportunity afforded the United States, of becoming a respectable nation, I resign with satisfaction the appointment I accepted with diffidence—a diffidence in my abilities to accomplish so arduous a task; which however was superseded by a confidence in the rectitude of our cause, the support of the supreme power of the union, and the patronage of Heaven.

*George Washington, resignation speech to Congress, December 23, 1783, in Hart,* American History, *II: 628.*

The truth is, that though there are in that country [the United States] few people so miserable as the poor of Europe, there are also very few that in Europe would be called rich: It is rather a general happy

mediocrity that prevails. There are few great Proprietors of the soil, and few Tenants; most people cultivate their own lands, or follow some handicraft or merchandise; very few [are] rich enough to live idly upon their rents or incomes; or to pay the high prices given in Europe, for Painting, Statues, Architecture, and other works of Art that are more curious than useful.

*Benjamin Franklin,* Two Tracts: Information to Those Who Would Remove to America, *1784, in Hart,* American History, *III: 22.*

Princetown is a little country-town of only one considerable street in which few houses stand, but its elevated site makes the place especially agreeable . . . The College, a not uncomely building, stands in the middle of town, but is at this time in bad condition. . . . Recently Princetown had the honor of being for a while the place of assembly of the American Congress—after a handful of indelicate soldiers, demanding such a trifle as back pay for five or six years, had frightened the Congress from Philadelphia.

*German traveler Johann David Schoepf, travel narrative, 1784, in Morrison,* Travels in the Confederation, *41–42.*

These hunters or "backwoodsmen" live very like the Indians and acquire similar ways of thinking . . .

Nassau Hall, constructed in 1756, was the original building of Princeton University. *(from Benson Lossing,* The Pictorial Field-Book of the Revolution, *1851–1852)*

An insignificant cabin of unhewn logs; corn and a little wheat, a few cows and pigs, this is all their riches but they need no more. They get game from the woods; skins bring them in whiskey and clothes, which they do not care for of a costly sort. Their habitual costume is a "rifle-shirt," or shirt of fringed linen; instead of stockings they wear Indian leggings; their shoes they make themselves for the most part . . . They look upon the wilderness as their home and the wild as their possession; and so by this wandering, uncertain way of life, of which they are vastly fond, they become indifferent to all social ties, and do not like many neighbors around them, who by scaring off the game are a nuisance besides.

*German traveler Johann David Schoepf, travel narrative, 1784, in Morrison,* Travels in the Confederation, *238–239.*

True it is, that the general government wants energy, and equally true it is, that this want will eventually be supplied. A national spirit is the natural result of national existence, and although some of the present generation may feel colonial oppositions of opinion, yet this generation will die away and give place to a race of Americans.

*Gouverneur Morris, letter to John Jay, January 10, 1784, in Sparks,* Life of Gouverneur Morris, *266.*

In answer to Your request to be informed of the probable benefits on a Cargoe of Indentured Servants from hence [England] to Virginia, I can in a word say I know of nothing that can be sent from this Country to greater prospect of success. . . . You know the facility with which these Servants can be had from the numbers of poor now begging about.

*Author and diplomat Thomas Attwood Digges, letter to Thomas Trant, May 5, 1784, in Elias and Finch,* Letters of Thomas Attwood Digges, *399.*

I perfectly coincide with you in opinion that America is the country in the world, whose social state admits of the greatest portion of happiness. Such being my sentiment, I have commisserated [sic] the fate of those, who are exiled from among us. . . . With a very few exceptions, therefore, of old and powerful enemies, I would open wide the doors of that temple, which we have reared to liberty, and, in consecrating an asylum to the persecuted of mankind, I would not exclude those, who first drew the vital air, and first saw the light in America.

*Gouverneur Morris, letter to exiled Loyalist Peter Van Schaack, June 18, 1784, in Sparks,* Life of Gouverneur Morris, *270.*

Notwithstanding the languor of our direct trade with Europe, this country [Virginia] has indirectly tasted some of the fruits of Independence. The price of our last crop of Tobacco . . . has brought more specie into the country than it ever before contained at one time. The price of Hemp, however, has been reduced as much by the peace as that of Tobacco has been raised . . . Our crops of wheat have been rather scanty, owing partly to the rigors of the Winter, partly to an insect, which in many places has destroyed whole fields of that grain.

*Congressman James Madison, letter to Thomas Jefferson, August 20, 1784, in Madison,* Letters and Other Writings of James Madison, *I: 92.*

The payment of debts may indeed be expensive, but it is infinitely more expensive to withhold the payment. The former is an expense of money when money may be commanded to defray it; but the latter involves the destruction of the source from whence money can be derived when all other sources fail. That source, abundant, nay, almost inexhaustible, is public credit.

*Retiring national financier, Robert Morris, letter to Congress, November 1, 1784, in Oberholtzer,* Robert Morris, *210–211.*

I have not yet found leisure to scan the project of a Continental Convention with so close an eye as to have made up any observations worthy of being mentioned to you. In general, I hold it for a maxim, that the Union of the States is essential to their safety against foreign danger and internal contention; and that the perpetuity and efficacy of the present system cannot be confided in. The question therefore is, in what mode and at what moment the experiment for supplying the defects ought to be made. The answer to this question cannot be given without a knowledge greater than I possess of the temper and views of the different States. Virginia seems, I think, to have excellent dispositions towards the Confederacy. . . . Should a view of the other States present no objections against the experiment, individually, I would wish not to be presupposed here.

*James Madison, letter to Richard Henry Lee, December 25, 1784, in Madison,* Letters and Other Writings of James Madison, *I: 118–119.*

I have received letters from Brigadier-General Sevier, under the style and character of Governor . . . informing me that . . . the inhabitants of part of the territory lately ceded to Congress, had declared themselves independent of the State of North-Carolina, and no longer consider themselves under the sovereignty and jurisdiction of the same, stating their reason[s] for their separation and revolt—among which it is alleged, that the western country was ceded to Congress without their consent . . . I order, therefore, to reclaim such citizens, who, by specious pretences and the acts of designing men, have been seduced from their allegiance, to restrain others from following their example who are wavering, and to confirm the attachment and affection of those who adhere to the old government, and whose fidelity hath not yet been shaken, I have thought proper to issue this Manifesto, hereby warning all persons concerned in the said revolt . . .

*Governor Alexander Martin, Manifesto to the people of Franklin who had separated from North Carolina, 1785, in Hart,* American History, *III: 147–148, 149.*

I am authorized to say that no people can think more highly of your government than those who want the separation, and they only wish it to answer their better conveniency; but, though wanting to be separated in government, they wish to be united in friendship, and hope that mutual good offices may ever pass between the parent and infant State, which also is my wish and desire.

*John Sevier, leader of the state of Franklin, appeal to the North Carolina legislature, 1785, in Gilmore,* John Sevier, *88.*

The people of Massachusetts are for the most part of fine build . . . frank in their personal relationships, they reveal themselves as affable and courteous, and they do not abuse strong liquors as much as the inhabitants of the South. The women, too, are generally of fair and refined features, of ruddy and healthy complexions. . . . Before marrying they delight in pastimes, but without

slighting their housework, at which they keep themselves very busy. They also amuse themselves with music and reading, and they possess a natural vivacity and openness unspoiled by the refinements of gallantry.

*Italian traveler Luigi Castiglioni, observations in 1785, in Pace,* Luigi Castiglioni's Viaggio, *50–51.*

People think, act, and speak here [in Pennsylvania] precisely as it prompts them; the poorest day-laborer on the bank of the Delaware holds it his right to advance his opinion, in religious as well as political matters, with as much freedom as the gentleman or the scholar. And as yet there is to be found as little distinction of rank among the inhabitants of Philadelphia as in any city of the world.

*German traveler Johann David Schoepf, travel narrative, 1785, in Morrison,* Travels in the Confederation, *99.*

In 1785 I visited the rough and hilly country of Otsego [New York], where there existed not an inhabitant, nor any trace of a road; I was alone three hundred miles from home, without bread, meat, or food of any kind; fire and fishing tackle were my only means of subsistence. I caught trout in a brook, and roasted them on the ashes. My horse fed on the grass that grew by the edge of the waters. I laid me down to sleep in my watch-coat, nothing but the melancholy Wilderness around me. In this way I explored the country, formed my plans of future settlement, and meditated upon the spot where a place of trade or a village should afterward be established. In May 1786 I opened the sales of 40,000 acres, which, in sixteen days, were all taken up by the poorest order of men.

*Land speculator and judge William Cooper, discussing 1785–1786,* A Guide to the Wilderness, *1810, in Hart,* American History, *III: 97–98.*

I recollect, in 1785, when I visited Canada after the Peace, that there were no settlements except forts and Indian trading stations, and that I witnessed from 25 to 30,000 men, women and children driven from the United States to seek the protection of the British Government, who generously granted lands in Upper Canada and the River St. Lawrence above Montreal, and I saw the Military who had fought our battles convert their swords into tools of husbandry.

*English traveler Joseph Hadfield, remembering 1785 in a letter, March 26, 1818, in Robertson,* An Englishman in America, *107.*

So much has Canada been neglected that it remains to this day in language, principles, religions as attached to Old France as it was when subdued by British arms [in 1763]. . . . Had public schools been established in every parish, a college at Montreal, and another in Quebec where they might have learned both English and French, taking care that the masters who taught the latter were firmly attached to our laws and government, the people by degrees would have . . . become Englishmen. . . . The Loyalists in a few years will, from their superior knowledge of agriculture and the possession of better lands, gain such an ascendancy over the [French] Canadians that the latter will be obliged to follow their example . . .

> *English traveler Joseph Hadfield, diary entry, 1785, in Robertson,* An Englishman in America, *132–133.*

The Indians are generally hated here quite as much as they are pretty well throughout America. But this hate does not always spring from the same reasons, much less from those altogether just.—It is beginning to be extensively and learnedly posited that none of the Indian tribes, as many of them as are still scattered throughout the whole of broad America, have the remotest right to the land wherein they and their forefathers for unthinkable ages have lived.

> *German traveler Johann David Schoepf, travel narrative, 1785, in Morrison,* Travels in the Confederation, *277–278.*

Nature has given the use of the Mississippi to those who may settle on its waters, as she gave to the United States their independence. The impolicy of Spain may retard the former, as that of Great Britain did the latter. But as Great Britain could not defeat the latter, neither will Spain the former. . . . If the United States were to become parties to the occlusion of the Mississippi, they would be guilty of treason against the very laws under which they obtained and hold their national existence.

> *James Madison, letter to the Marquis de Lafayette, March 20, 1785, in Madison,* Letters and Other Writings of James Madison, *I: 137.*

The appointment of Mr. Adams to the Court of Great Britain is a circumstance which does not contradict my expectations; nor can I say it displeases me. Upon Geographical considerations New England will always have one of the principal appointments, and I know of no individual from that quarter who possesses more of their confidence, or would possess more of that of the other States; nor do I think him so well fitted for any Court of equal rank as that of London. I hope it has removed all obstacles to the establishment of Mr. Jefferson at the Court of France.

> *James Madison, letter to James Monroe, April 12, 1785, in Madison,* Letters and Other Writings of James Madison, *I: 143.*

I hear frequent complaints of the disorders of our coin, and the want of uniformity in the denominations of the States. Do not Congress think of a remedy for these evils? The regulation of weights and measures seem [sic] also to call for their attention. Every day will add to the difficulty of executing these works. If a mint be not established and a recoinage effected while the federal debts carry the money through the hands of Congress, I question much whether their limited powers will ever be able to render this branch of their prerogative effectual.

> *James Madison, letter to James Monroe, April 28, 1785, in Madison,* Letters and Other Writings of James Madison, *I: 152.*

You have often promised me, in talks that you sent me, that you would do me justice, and that all disorderly people should be moved off our lands; but the longer we want to see it done, the farther it seems off. Your people have built houses in sight of our towns. We don't want to quarrel with you, our elder brother. I therefore beg that you, our elder brother, will have your disorderly people taken off our lands immediately, as their being on our grounds causes great uneasiness . . . I also beg that you will send letters to the Great Council of America, and let them know how it is; that, if you have no power to move them off, they have, and I hope they will do it.

> *Cherokee leader Old Tassel, speech to North Carolina governor Richard Caswell, September 1785, in Gilmore,* John Sevier, *58.*

Although no man's sentiments are more opposed to any kind of restraint upon religious principles than mine are, yet I must confess, that I am not amongst the number of those, who are so much alarmed at the thoughts of making people pay towards the support of that which they profess, if of the denomination of Christians, or declare themselves Jews, Mahometans

[Muslims], or otherwise, and thereby obtain proper relief.

> *George Washington, letter to George Mason, October 3, 1785, in Rowland,* Life of George Mason, *II: 89.*

Relative to proper supplies of money, suffer me to say,—'twas not unwillingness to afford a sufficiency, but want of power to force collections any faster than by the laws enacted in May last, which prevented their doing anything on that subject.

> *Stephen Mix Mitchell, Connecticut legislator, letter to William Samuel Johnson, November 13, 1785, in Beardsley,* Life of William Samuel Johnson, *121.*

A decline or rather an extinction of public credit; a relaxation and corruption of manners, and a free use of foreign luxuries; a decay of trade and manufactures, with a prevailing scarcity of money; and, above all, individuals involved in debt to each other—these were the real, though more remote causes of the insurrection. It was the tax which people were required to pay, that caused them to feel the evils that have been enumerated—this called forth all their other grievances; and the first act of violence committed, was the burning or destroying of a tax bill. This sedition threw the state into a convulsion which lasted about a year; courts of justice were violently obstructed; the collection of debts was suspended; and a body of armed troops, under the command of General Lincoln, was employed, during the winter of 1786, to disperse the insurgents.

> *Jedidiah Morse, remembering the disorder during Shays's Rebellion in 1786 , in his* American Geography, *in Craven, Johnson, and Dunn,* Documentary History, *176.*

The business of education has acquired a new complexion by the independence of our country. The form of government we have assumed has created a new class of duties to every American. It becomes us, therefore, to examine our former habits upon this subject, and in laying the foundations for nurseries of wise and good men, to adapt our modes of teaching to the peculiar form of our government.

> *Benjamin Rush, Philadelphia doctor and educator,* A Plan for the Establishment of Public Schools and the Diffusion of Knowledge in Pennsylvania, *1786, in Johnson,* Reading the American Past, *I: 113.*

Philadelphia possesses in Mr. [Charles Willson] Peale an artist, native-born, who may be placed alongside of many in the old world. In an open saloon at his house, lovers and students of art may examine at any time a considerable number of his works. This collection consists for the most part of paintings of famous persons: Washington . . . Franklin, Paine, Morris,—most of the Major Generals of the American army—all the Presidents of the Congress; and others distinguished in the new states are to be found here.

> *German traveler Johann David Schoepf, travel narrative, 1786, in Morrison,* Travels in the Confederation, *89.*

The subscribers take this method to inform all officers and soldiers, who have served in the late war, and who are by a late ordinance of the honorable Congress to receive certain tracts of land in the Ohio country, and also all other good citizens who wish to become adventurers in that delightful region . . . that the lands in that quarter are of a much better quality than any other known to the New England people; that the climate, seasons, products, etc., are in fact equal to the most flattering accounts that have ever been published of them.

> *Land Speculators Rufus Putnam and Benjamin Tupper, promotional pamphlet, January 10, 1786, in Cutler and Cutler,* Life, Journals, and Correspondence of Rev. Manasseh Cutler, *179.*

No man shall be compelled to frequent or support any religious worship, place or ministry whatsoever, nor shall be enforced, restrained, molested, or burthened in his body or goods, nor shall otherwise suffer on account of his religious opinions or belief . . .

> Virginia Statute of Religious Liberty, *January 16, 1786, in Commager,* Documents, *I: 126.*

What is to become of this country? I am distressed on this subject. Unless some mode is adopted for a firmer union, and vesting Congress with the power of complying with her treaties, I tremble for the consequences. . . . I am frightened at our neglect of the necessary steps towards our political salvation. God help us!

> *Jonathan D. Sergeant, Pennsylvania attorney general, letter to William Samuel Johnson, February 18, 1786, in Beardsley,* Life of William Samuel Johnson, *124.*

I came here today to see you, to take you by the hand, and to be your brother. . . . I love you and all your people. The Choctaw and the Chickasaw form a single people, and I took you by the hand in the name of the two nations. . . . We want to take up the tomahawk for you [against the Creeks] and be always on your side. We have not come to receive gifts, but only to see you, who are the man we love.

*Choctaw representative Spkohummah, speech to South Carolina governor William Moultrie, March 16, 1786, in Pace, Luigi Castiglioni's Viaggio, 132.*

I am glad to hear that the opposition to the impost is likely to be overcome. It is an encouragement to persevere in good measures. I am afraid, at the same time, that, like other auxiliary resources, it will be overrated by the States, and slacken the regular efforts of taxation. It is also materially short of the power Congress ought to have with regard to trade.

*James Madison, letter to James Monroe, April 9, 1786, in Madison, Letters and Other Writings of James Madison, I: 230.*

To the Honourable Congress I Rachel do make this Complaint, Who am a Widow far advanced in years and Dearly have occasion of the Intrust for that Cash I Lent the States. . . . I was a [citizen] in [Jersey] when I Lent the States a considerable Sum of Moneys & had I justice done me it mite be [sufficient] to suporte me in the Contrey . . . I have Don as much to Carrey on the warr as maney that Sett Now at the healm of government.

*Elderly widow Rachel Wells, petition to Congress, May 18, 1786, in Kerber, Women of the Republic, 87.*

You talk, my good Sir, of employing influence to appease the present tumults in Massachusetts. I know not where that influence is to be found, or, if attainable, that it would be a proper remedy for the disorders. *Influence* is no *government*. Let us have one by which our lives, liberties, and properties will be secured, or let us know the worst at once. . . . Let the

reins of government then be braced and held with a steady hand, and every violation of the constitution be reprehended. If defective, let it be amended, but not suffered to be trampeled [sic] upon whilst it has an existence.

*George Washington, letter to Henry Lee, October 31, 1786, in Hart, American History, III: 188, 189.*

We learn that great commotions are prevailing in Massachusetts. An appeal to the Sword is exceedingly dreaded. The discontented, it is said, are as numerous as the friends of Government, and more decided in their measures. Should they get uppermost, it is uncertain what may be the effect. They profess to aim only at a reform of their Constitution, and of certain abuses in public administration; but an abolition of debts, public and private, and a new division of property, are strongly suspected to be in contemplation.

We also learn that a general combination of Indians threatens the frontier of the United States. Congress are planning measures for warding off the blow, one of which is an augmentation of federal troops to upwards of 2,000 men. In addition to these ills, it is pretty certain that a formidable party in Congress are bent on surrendering the Mississippi to Spain, for the sake of some commercial stipulations.

*James Madison II, letter to James Madison, November 1, 1786, in Madison, Letters and Other Writings of James Madison, I: 253–254.*

Be assured, that this body, now at arms, despise the idea of being instigated by British emissaries, which is so strenuously propagated by the enemies of our liberties: And also wish the most proper and speedy measures may be taken, to discharge both our foreign and domestick debt.

*Daniel Gray, "An Address to the People of the several towns in the country of Hampshire [Massachusetts] now at arms," December 1786 in Minot, History of the Insurrections in Massachusetts, 84.*

# 2

# Making a New Constitution
## 1787–1788

In the wake of post-revolutionary economic chaos, domestic upheaval, and insurrections such as Shays's Rebellion, a growing number of U.S. citizens were clamoring for some kind of change in American government. Many Americans, particularly nationalistic elites, worried that the new nation was facing an uncertain future because its government was simply too weak to be effective.

Although the American economy was growing, exports were not increasing quickly enough to equalize the balance of trade, and every state continued to face crushing debt incurred during the Revolutionary War. Unable to enact any sweeping taxes because the states could or would not agree, Congress could not raise enough revenue to pay back the national war debt, and the national government was close to being bankrupt. The actions of Daniel Shays and other Regulators, many of whom faced personal debt crises, frightened wealthy men like John Adams and Gouverneur Morris, who feared that economic crisis would lead to social revolution.

Most Americans would have agreed that the United States entered 1787 facing a crisis, and most were committed to finding solutions that fit with the republican ideals of the Revolution: a concern for the public well-being and a belief in representative government. Beyond these general principles, however, lay a large measure of disagreement over how national problems should be solved. Certainly not everyone was to have an equal say in the solutions.

## THE NEED FOR STRONGER GOVERNMENT

Advocates for stronger national government, who had not gotten far in their bid to increase the power of Congress since the end of the Revolutionary War, received a boost from Shays's Rebellion. The loosely coordinated rebellion of debtors in Western Massachusetts, which had led armed men to close down courts and to threaten government officials throughout late 1786, opened the year 1787 as a great topic of public concern. To prepare in case the military conflict escalated, James Bowdoin, the governor of Massachusetts, called up thousands of state militia forces late in 1786 and placed them under the command of former Revolutionary War general Benjamin Lincoln. Though Shays's

PENNSYLVANIA, ſſ.

# By the *Preſident* and the *Supreme Executive* Council of the Commonwealth of *Pennſylvania,*

## A PROCLAMATION.

WHEREAS the General Aſſembly of this Commonwealth, by a law entituled 'An act for co-operating with "the ſtate of Maſſachuſetts bay, agreeable to the articles of "confederation, in the apprehending of the proclaimed rebels "DANIEL SHAYS, LUKE DAY, ADAM WHEELER "and ELI PARSONS," have enacted, "that rewards ad-"ditional to thoſe offered and promiſed to be paid by the ſtate "of Maſſachuſetts Bay, for the apprehending the aforeſaid "rebels, be offered by this ſtate;" WE do hereby offer the following rewards to any perſon or perſons who ſhall, within the limits of this ſtate, apprehend the rebels aforeſaid, and ſecure them in the gaol of the city and county of Philadelphia, ——— viz. For the apprehending of the ſaid Daniel Shays, and ſecuring him as aforeſaid, the reward of *One hundred and Fifty Pounds* lawful money of the ſtate of Maſſachuſetts Bay, and *One Hundred Pounds* lawful money of this ſtate; and for the apprehending the ſaid Luke Day, Adam Wheeler and Eli Parſons, and ſecuring them as aforeſaid, the reward (reſpectively) of *One Hundred Pounds* lawful money of Maſſachuſetts Bay and *Fifty Pounds* lawful money of this ſtate: And all judges, juſtices, ſheriffs and conſtables are hereby ſtrictly enjoined and required to make diligent ſearch and enquiry after, and to uſe their utmoſt endeavours to apprehend and ſecure the ſaid Daniel Shays, Luke Day, Adam Wheeler and Eli Parſons, their aiders, abettors and comforters, and every of them, ſo that they may be dealt with according to law.

GIVEN in Council, under the hand of the Preſident, and the Seal of the State, at Philadelphia, this tenth day of March, in the year of our Lord one thouſand ſeven hundred and eighty-ſeven.

BENJAMIN FRANKLIN.

ATTEST

JOHN ARMSTRONG, jun. Secretary.

On May 19, 1787, the Pennsylvania Assembly issued this proclamation offering a reward for the capture of Daniel Shays and three other leaders of Shays's Rebellion. The proclamation shows how concern over the rebellion had spread outside Massachusetts. *(Library of Congress, Prints and Photographs Division [LC-USZ62-77992])*

men seemed to lose some of their enthusiasm during the coldest part of the New England winter, the stage was set for Massachusetts men, with many Revolutionary War veterans on both sides, to take up arms against one another.

The military phase of Shays's Rebellion came to a head in January 1787, when a group of Shaysite rebels planned to seize the weapons stored at the arsenal in Springfield, Massachusetts. On January 21, some 300 rebels surrounded the arsenal and trapped Gen. William Shepherd and his militia troops inside. After four days, mainly spent marching around the perimeter of the Springfield armory, the Shays rebels attacked the arsenal but were dispersed when the troops inside fired on them with cannon and grapeshot. Shays's forces were dismantled on February 4, when Lincoln invaded their camp at Petersham, Massachusetts, with 3,000 militia troops. By the end of the month, Shays himself had fled Massachusetts for New York, Vermont, and then Canada. From late February into April, small bands of Shaysite rebels, bolstered by new supplies and weapons given to them by British officials in Canada, tried to renew their attacks against lawyers and militia leaders, but they were never again able to mount a coordinated armed insurgency.[1]

Daniel Shays and his band of disgruntled debtors probably never posed a serious threat to the continuance of government in Massachusetts, but they had enough sympathizers in the state and elsewhere that nationalists were able to capitalize on the fright their military actions inspired. Thomas Jefferson, serving abroad as U.S. minister to France, was unconcerned by the rebellion, declaring in a letter: "Let them take arms. . . . the tree of liberty must be refreshed from time to time, with the blood of patriots and tyrants."[2] But his was the minority opinion among the elite class of politicians. Average Americans continued to push for a better government solution to the country's financial and trade crises, and many in power argued that the time had clearly come for the national government to be revised.

As had been the case since the end of the Revolution, people held various opinions of how the government should be changed, but most of them shared the opinion that something had to be done to preserve the new American republic intact. Some leaders, like Richard Henry Lee, thought that the states, as the closest representatives to each citizen, should chart their own courses and deal individually with economic depression and unrest like Shays's Rebellion. But others—including John Adams, George Washington, Benjamin Franklin, James Madison, and Alexander Hamilton—who thought of the United States less as a collection of autonomous states and more as *one* nation, believed the time had come to strengthen the national government.

Advocates of a stronger national government built upon conversations held at the failed Annapolis Convention of 1786 and asked Congress to authorize a new convention to revise the Articles of Confederation. In February 1787, Congress passed a resolution calling delegates to Philadelphia for the convention, but James Madison and Alexander Hamilton, among others, had far greater designs in mind. The Constitutional Convention would proceed, although many citizens remained skeptical, and Rhode Islanders refused to send any delegates at all.

## THE CONSTITUTIONAL CONVENTION

Americans in general may have continued to disagree over just what course government should take, but the Constitutional Convention called together delegates who seemed ready to take decisive action. Fifty-five delegates from the 12 other states came to Philadelphia in May. They were men from the top of American society—lawyers, merchants, plantation owners, and congressmen—but they thought of themselves as the direct representatives of "the people," on whose behalf they would revise the government. When the convention convened on May 25, its members immediately elected as presiding officer George Washington, the former Revolutionary War commander in chief, thought to be the most selfless leader in the country. The delegates also voted to conduct their deliberations in secret; they refused to speak to the press, and they had the windows nailed shut so "the people" could not overhear their deliberations.

Much of what is known about the Constitutional Convention comes from private notes taken by Virginian James Madison, who was probably the most important individual in the whole proceedings. Several of the highest-profile

This 1857 engraving is based on a Gilbert Stuart portrait of James Madison. *(Library of Congress, Prints and Photographs Division [LC-USZ62-106865])*

Revolutionary patriots were absent, including John Adams and Thomas Jefferson, who were serving as foreign ministers in Europe. Madison took the lead in shaping the convention's wide-ranging debates. He was a 36-year-old, Princeton-educated student of the European enlightenment, and he had bold plans to reshape entirely the American government.

Only four days after the start of the convention, Madison revealed his belief that the Articles of Confederation must be discarded altogether, and Edmund Randolph introduced Madison's template for a new national government, subsequently dubbed the Virginia Plan. By agreeing to discuss the plan, a majority of the delegates agreed to exceed their legal mandate and to consider creating a whole new form for the American republic.

The Virginia Plan would create a much stronger national government than had ever before existed in America: A two-house national legislature would have the power to veto any state law. A national judiciary and a president elected by the national legislature would provide checks and balances against the power of the two houses of Congress. Voters would directly elect the lower house, whose representatives would then choose the members of the upper house, and the size of each house would be determined by proportional representation, meaning that larger states with larger populations would have greater power than their smaller neighbors.

Madison's plan provided a valuable starting point for discussion, but several delegates, especially those from smaller states like Delaware, found this last point hard to swallow. By the middle of June, these men were supporting a different plan put forward by William Paterson of New Jersey, who was wary of completely discarding the Articles of Confederation and who favored greater state power. Paterson proposed keeping a single-house, or unicameral, legislature that would offer each state equal representation but provide Congress with greater powers of finance and taxation.

As the delegates struggled through an unusually hot summer, they used the contrasting plans to guide their debate. On July 16, they compromised on the question of representation in the national legislature and voted to adopt a house of representatives, directly elected by the people according to proportional representation, and a senate, elected by the state legislatures, in which each state would receive equal representation. In this, known as the Great Compromise, delegates effectively balanced the interests of large and small states and created a government about which they hoped advocates of both state and national power could agree.

Other issues remained to be solved, and compromises continued to form throughout the late summer. Disagreement over how to elect the president was settled by the creation of the electoral college, a body designed to act as a brake on an excess of popular democracy. More controversial was the issue of whether to include a bill of rights to guarantee in writing the personal liberties white Americans had come to expect. When a written bill of rights was rejected by the majority of delegates as unnecessary in a liberty-loving nation, several representatives became disenchanted and disavowed the work of the entire convention, an ominous sign that foreshadowed some of the divisions that developed during the subsequent fight for ratification.

The other major issue that required the constitutional delegates to compromise was slavery. The institution of slavery was increasingly on the defensive since the American Revolution had validated the idea that "all men are created equal," and the delegates, many of whom were slaveholders, had to decide the relationship both of the institution and of individual slaves to the government they proposed to create.

The main slavery issue considered by the delegates concerned not personal equality, but rather power and political representation. When representatives of large slave states argued that slaves ought to be counted as inhabitants for purposes of representation, delegates from less slave-populated states objected. The two sides eventually agreed that three-fifths of "other persons," as the Constitution referred to slaves, would be counted, thereby setting up an ambiguity in the definition of African-American citizenship that would vex the United States until after the Civil War. No delegate outright condemned slavery at the convention (only a few of them would ever do so), and the body also agreed to add a clause to prevent Congress from curtailing the slave trade until 1808.

When the convention closed on September 17, elderly delegate Benjamin Franklin urged unity, and only three delegates refused to sign the constitution they had helped to create. The Confederation Congress accepted the document, which would go into effect only when conventions of the voters in nine of the 13 states voted in favor of it. As the delegates returned to their states, it remained to be seen whether "the people" outside the closed hall in Philadelphia would be willing to ratify their work.

## LOOKING TO THE WEST

While the constitutional convention had been meeting in Philadelphia, the confederation government continued to meet as usual in New York, and Congress was not without important business of its own in the summer of 1787. A group of land speculators in the Ohio Company prevailed upon Congress to revise and expand land ordinances of 1784 and 1785 that had opened territory in the northwest to surveyors and settlers. Congress responded by passing the Northwest Ordinance, the most ambitious effort yet to organize and define new territory for the United States.

The ordinance mandated that lands north of the Ohio River and east of the Mississippi River would be organized into from three to five territories, and it established a clear process so that these territories might someday become states. At first, each territory would be ruled by a governor and officials appointed by Congress, but when 5,000 freemen settled there, they could elect a territorial legislature. When 60,000 free persons lived in a territory, it could apply for statehood.

This very orderly process masked much of the messy reality both of western settlement and of the government's role in integrating northwestern territories into the United States. Settlers had already moved into Ohio country and claimed land without observing the lines of the official surveyors and believing they would not have to pay anyone for their new land. Much of the territory that the ordinance projected would eventually become part of the United States was thickly populated by Miami, Chippewa, Shawnee, and Delaware native peoples who had other ideas.

The Northwest Ordinance did specify that Indian lands could not be indiscriminately confiscated; they had to be either purchased or ceded through negotiation. But American settlers who were beyond the reach of government control often paid little heed to this requirement, though they would come to expect government military forces to back them up when fighting broke out as a result.

On paper, the Northwest Ordinance also enforced remarkable civil liberties for territorial settlers. Four years before Americans had any national bill of rights, Congress guaranteed territorial civil rights, including religious freedom. The ordinance also forbade slavery in the Northwest Territory, though it ensured that fugitive slaves could be reclaimed from the free territory. Though this prohibition on slavery was by no means respected by everyone who settled in the Northwest Territory, it was significant because it marked the first time that the national government of the United States restricted slavery in any way.

In 1787, the U.S. government, which relied on the revenues generated from land sales in the absence of the national power to tax, was willing to overlook potential problems caused by the integration of new territories. Expansion would provide the land necessary to continue the development of the ideal republic populated by virtuous farmers, and many Americans were just beginning to envision a great national future for themselves. For the time being, Congress was able to ignore the ticking time bomb of Indian dissatisfaction and the threat of slavery's spread that westward movement accentuated.

## RATIFYING THE CONSTITUTION

Most political attention throughout fall 1787 into 1788 focused on whether and how the new Constitution would be ratified. Congress asked each state to hold a ratifying convention, in keeping with the tradition that special conventions could directly represent the will of the people in a republic. Delegates feared that the unanimous consent of all the state legislatures could never be gained. Since the states were being asked to give up a measure of their individual power to the new central government, it seemed only fitting that the new Constitution would have to be won or lost state by state. It was by no means a foregone conclusion that the new Constitution would succeed, and the refusal of two delegates from Virginia and one from Massachusetts to sign the document at the close of the Constitutional Convention provided merely a foretaste of the controversy and divided opinions about the Constitution that would develop in different states as the ratification contest progressed.

Advocates of the Constitution called themselves "Federalists" and launched a coordinated campaign to publicize and bolster the acceptance of the new Constitution. Federalist leaders included many of the leaders who had advocated stronger central government since the Revolution, notably James Madison, John Jay, and Alexander Hamilton, but the Federalist movement did not draw support only from those who had attended the Constitutional Convention or who held national political office. The Federalist cause won converts in American cities, seaports, and areas that drew income from commercial trade. Federalists favored a version of classical republicanism that would moderate democracy while at the same time allowing more government power to regulate trade, taxes, and relationships between the states.

The men and women who opposed the ratification of the Constitution, later termed "Anti-Federalists" by historians, were a much more loosely organized and diverse group. In general, people who were more dubious of power and more attached to their states were suspicious of the Federalists' motives, and many argued that the Constitutional Convention had seriously overstepped its authority. Backcountry settlers, urban politicians who had risen from humble origins, Revolutionary patriots with fresh memories of overarching British power, and people who were less afraid of an "excess" of democracy opposed the Federalists' vision of the Enlightenment. Many Anti-Federalists argued that the Constitution was too aristocratic, and some spoke in almost conspiratorial tones against the framers of the Constitution. One opponent of the Constitution claimed, for example, that at the Massachusetts ratifying convention "[t]hese lawyers and men of learning and monied men expect to be managers of this Constitution and get all the power and all the money into their own hands."[3] Many other Anti-Federalists were seriously concerned with the Constitution's lack of a bill of rights. Suspicion of the framers, and of the new government power they wished to create, was a force that drew opponents including New York governor George Clinton, small farmer Melancton Smith, well-bred Massachusetts writer Mercy Otis Warren, Revolutionary firebrand Patrick Henry, former president of Congress Richard Henry Lee, and Virginia plantation owner George Mason. These and others publicly and loudly opposed ratification.

The framers of the Constitution were, in general, suspicious of the power of lowly men to decide political matters for themselves. But when the state ratifying conventions began, these average men began to show serious influence. The ratifying process can best be understood as a complicated dance among competing economic interests, intellectual definitions of political institutions, and the demand of "the people" for recognition of their own rights. Though Madison, Hamilton, and Jay would assert during the New York ratification debate in one of their *Federalist* essays that the people had to be protected against "tyranny of their own passions," many of those same passions actually helped get the Constitution ratified.[4]

The first few state conventions to take up ratification passed the issue by wide margins, although the debates both within the conventions and in the states at large foreshadowed some of the severe divisions that would occur in states to come. Pennsylvanians ratified the Constitution by a vote of 46 to 23, but severe divisions between Federalists and Anti-Federalists and related tensions over how democratic the state's own constitution ought to be refused to die down, even after ratification. At the end of 1787, James Madison wrote to Thomas Jefferson: "The Constitution engrosses almost the whole political attention of America."[5]

As 1788 opened, New Jersey, Georgia, and Connecticut ratified the Constitution, but the Massachusetts ratifying convention, set to begin on January 9, was recognized as the biggest test yet of whether Federalists in large and powerful states could overcome their opposition to legitimize the new form of government. Sympathizers with Shays's Rebellion, many of whom had obtained political office in western counties of the state after the rebellion was put down, and Governor John Hancock, who himself rode into office on his perceived support for Shays, opposed the Constitution. But a coalition of conservative Federalists and Boston artisans who wanted more federal power to protect overseas trade won the day eventually, and Massachusetts narrowly ratified the Constitution in February.

Throughout the spring, Federalists and Anti-Federalists in the remaining states sharpened their attacks on one another. A referendum vote on the Constitution in Rhode Island failed in March, and tempers flared as the entire state of New York seemed to take up sides in the constitutional debate. The Federalists benefited from their coordinated campaign to promote their ideas, the most famous example of which remains the *Federalist* essays published in New York by Alexander Hamilton, John Jay, and James Madison. Madison, Hamilton, and Jay wrote under pseudonyms in an attempt to persuade the American public—and convention delegates in New York—that the federal Constitution represented good politics for a growing and powerful nation. The *Federalist* papers, which were published in book form in April, made a huge impact on the remaining ratification debates. They are still looked to as classic statements of American political theory.

As the Federalists and Anti-Federalists battled it out, Maryland, South Carolina, and New Hampshire ratified the document, by increasingly narrow margins. When New Hampshire ratified on June 21, 1788, the Constitution technically should have gone into effect, since nine of the 13 states had approved it. However, Congress knew that the new form of government would never survive without the support of New York and Virginia and so waited to declare confidence in the new Constitution until those states acquiesced. Two days later, Virginia delegates voted to approve the Constitution, although they strongly recommended the addition of a bill of rights and proposed 20 specific amendments. On June 26, New York followed suit, both ratifying the document and suggesting a slate of amendments. In August, North Carolina voted not to ratify the Constitution, but the remaining states paid little mind, since they had already accepted the document and considered it in effect.

Throughout the end of June and July, grand public parades and ceremonies in several American cities celebrated the ratification of the Constitution. On July 4, Philadelphians held the largest celebration in the country, dubbed the "Grand Federal Procession," as thousands of workingmen, organized according to trade and occupation, marched in a mile-and-a-half line through the streets. In New York, where a similar coalition of middle-class artisans and well-to-do political elites had finally achieved ratification, the parade was almost as large. The political and economic hopes of workingmen were displayed in the parade, for example, on a sign carried by the city's 120 blacksmiths that compared the Constitution to a merchant ship: "This federal ship will our commerce revive, And merchants and ship wrights and joiners shall thrive."[6] Not everyone was so sure of the prosperity of the national future, and many Anti-Federalists refused to participate in the public celebrations of the Constitution, but it was clear to everyone that a change in political fortunes was at hand.

## ENTERTAINMENT AND CULTURE

The parades that celebrated the ratification of the Constitution were typical large-scale public events of the late 1780s. As the postwar economic problems began to ease a bit in 1787 and as Americans emerged from the gloom of the Revolutionary War, public entertainments took on a new vitality in the United States. Americans were always interested in amusing themselves, but often with proper republican ideals and educational motives firmly in mind. American culture began to take on a new vitality in the late 1780s, even as citizens debated what forms of entertainment were most fitting in a proper republic. Though not always without controversy, theater, printed matter, social clubs, and other forms of entertainment were helping to define a new American cultural landscape, even as the political landscape seemed uncertain. Rough-and-tumble sports like cockfighting and wrestling were met with derision by the upper classes, but elites in several cities who formed themselves into polite tea societies or coed conversation clubs also met with public criticism for promoting dissipation and luxury. The most successful republican forms of culture were, in some ways, those that aimed at the vast middling ranks, which were developing into a powerful political and social force in the United States.

Print culture, especially cheap pamphlets and newspapers, had benefited from increased circulation during the war, and Americans in the late 1780s began to grow ever more attached to their news. The contributions of the *Federalist* essays to the ratification debate in New York shows how important publications were becoming to an American public, whose literacy outstripped that of almost every European nation. Local newspapers, which were becoming more numerous in the late 1780s, presented readers with a mixture of local, national, and international news, as well as fiction, poetry, gossip, and advertising. Papers were often passed around between acquaintances, and as had become the custom during the Revolutionary War, articles and sheets were often posted on the walls of public buildings or in taverns. Those who could not read might count on their friends to read the news to them.

Most Americans would have recognized that the quality of their books lagged behind any produced in European capitals, though some, who depended on American authors to create a native literature more in keeping with republican morality and simplicity, did not lament that fact. Philip Freneau, a diplomat and himself one of America's best-known poets, complained that there were "few writers of books in this new world, and amongst these very few that deal in works of imagination."[7] Some writers did try to apply their imaginations to the American domestic scene. A group of writers referred to as the "Rising Glory" poets published a series of satirical poems called *The Anarchiad* in late 1786 and 1787 in which they lampooned Shays's Rebellion, paper money crises, and the Anti-Federalists. In 1787, Joel Barlow published his epic poem *The Vision of Columbus,* which extolled the virtues of America. Several publishers, most notably Massachusetts printer Isaiah Thomas, printed editions of European novels, and Americans purchased European-printed books from itinerant booksellers who traveled a circuit up and down the eastern seaboard. By and large, however, Americans would have to wait for greater cultural and economic stability before a more extensive "native" literature became possible.

Americans could take part in any number of other forms of public culture and entertainment in 1787 and 1788, although some of these remained controversial as well. Although several cities, including Philadelphia, continued to flirt with statutes outlawing live theater productions, theater was becoming ever more popular. Theater companies thrived in New York City, Philadelphia, Boston, and outside Charleston, South Carolina (which would not allow productions within city limits). Sentimental plays, Shakespearean drama, and depictions of Revolutionary War heroism drew audiences, and in April 1787

American playwright Royall Tyler debuted his comedy *The Contrast,* which satirized American manners and morals. Attendance at Charles Willson Peale's American Museum in Philadelphia continued to rise, as city dwellers flocked to see the paintings, stuffed animals, and other artifacts displayed by the flamboyant artist (and to marvel at the live eagle that Peale kept tethered atop his building). Outside the bigger cities, almost every town and village in America held annual parades, complete with fireworks and festive public meals, to commemorate the Fourth of July, Washington's Birthday, or Revolutionary events of local importance. As with other public entertainments, these events fused politics and pleasure in a festive combination.

## SOCIAL EFFECTS OF REPUBLICANISM

In 1787 and 1788, as citizens of the United States were engaged in a discussion over what kind of republican government they wanted, the ideology of republicanism, which had been growing in importance since the Revolution, began to show some effects in American society outside the arena of formal politics. The notion that self-sacrificing individuals would set aside their selfish interests to serve the common good helped to define American patriotism in these years and also began to link that patriotism to a variety of nongovernmental matters. Average men and women shaped the meaning of republicanism when they sought to put it into effect in their daily lives, for example, in seeking an education. Republicanism began, in particular, to affect the definition of some social roles played by African Americans and white women.

In the late 1780s, the institution of slavery still overwhelmingly defined black life in the United States, but new opportunities for free African Americans opened up as well. At that time, almost 600,000 slaves lived in the United States; at the same time, the number of free African Americans grew dramatically.[8] African Americans, especially in the Middle Atlantic and New England states, sought new avenues to freedom, as private and public manumissions became possible, and the class of freemen created by the Revolutionary War began to swell. Racism and a strained economy ensured that most free African Americans remained in the lower ranks of society, working as farm laborers, wage laborers in urban workshops, or peddlers of goods on city streets.

However tenuous their economic status compared to the rest of the U.S. population, free African Americans formed strong community bonds, especially in Boston, New York, and Philadelphia. In April 1787, Richard Allen and Absalom Jones, both recently freed slaves who worked as laborers and who were licensed as Methodist preachers, helped to found the Free African Society in Philadelphia. The society provided crucial social ties among members of the city's black population and served as a means of benevolent financial support for those in need. The society was religious in outlook, though its membership was based on race rather than denomination, and it provided free blacks with the organizational support that would eventually help them found a black church in the city and seek greater political power.[9] In September 1787, Prince Hall, a former Revolutionary War soldier who owned a leather workshop in Boston, received a charter for the first African-American Masonic lodge in the nation. Throughout the late 18th and early 19th centuries, what would become known as the Prince Hall Lodge became a social center for Boston's growing circle of black professional men: hairdressers, merchants, and artisans. In 1788, Prince Hall also demonstrated his political leadership of the Boston free black community, which would take the lead in battling against slavery for decades to come, by leading a protest against the kidnapping of three black men by slave traders. Black community institutions like the Free African Society and the Prince Hall Lodge bonded African Americans together in mutual support, and their community service helped to provide the basis for future claims of republican citizenship by African Americans.

African Americans similarly made initial efforts to be included in the movement to increase educational opportunities in the United States, which also drew strength from republicanism. Educational advocates, most notably Philadelphia physician Benjamin Rush and the young essayist Judith Sargent Murray, had been arguing since shortly after the Revolutionary War that the United States would require an educational system that could produce good republican citizens and that freemen could not exist in ignorance. By 1787, these ideas were beginning to bear fruit, and not just for men. Very few public schools operated in the United States, though Massachusetts, Virginia, and other states were considering plans to make them a reality. African Americans in Boston petitioned to have their children included in that city's educational system, and a group of antislavery men in New York City founded a school for free African-American children.

Benjamin Rush argued in his 1787 treatise, *Thoughts on Female Education,* that women ought to be educated, not only to make good and amusing wives, but also so that they could help to educate the next generation of well-read republican citizens. Rush's ideas on education formed a part of what the historian Linda Kerber has dubbed the ideology of "republican motherhood," which defined a patriotic role for women as molders of the American future. In years to come, Rush's ideas and the influence of republicanism would lead both to the founding of many schools for American girls and to a heightened political importance for women's domestic roles.

Although the American republic seemed to be taking shape in different forms in government, African-American institutions, and educational advocacy, the debate over ratification of the U.S. Constitution had shown that the public was by no means unanimous in its view of the full meaning of republicanism. The political successes of the Shaysites in Massachusetts, the Anti-Federalist argument that the Constitution was too aristocratic, and even the large artisan participation in the state constitutional ratifying conventions and celebrations like the Grand Federal Procession all demonstrated how a more democratic vision of the United States was arising alongside the high-flown ideas of men like James Madison, Alexander Hamilton, and John Adams.

Benjamin Rush was the most respected physician in the early national period, and his theories about American education were also highly regarded. *(Library of Congress, Prints and Photographs Division [LC-USZ62-97104])*

# THE FIRST FEDERAL CONGRESS BEGINS

The full expression of the rise of new classes of citizens to political awareness would have to wait. As the Constitution went into effect, the elite group of men who had created it were chosen as the first political leaders under its terms. Though the Constitution had been approved, it remained to be seen whether and how the government it had created would function. Elections for the first federal Congress began in November 1788 but continued into the next year, because several states were slow to adopt electoral rules in keeping with the new Constitution.[10] By the end of the year it was clear that although the Anti-Federalists still held a lot of power in individual states, former proponents of the Federalist cause would hold a large majority in the new congress. Of the 91 men elected to the first federal Congress, 44 had taken part in the Constitutional Convention, and only eight men with Anti-Federalist sympathies were elected. The first Congress elected under the Constitution would seek to enforce its powers to the fullest extent imagined in 1787 by the framers of the document.

At the end of 1788, even as the congressional elections were being held in various states, political thoughts turned to the question of who would become the first president and vice president of the United States. Almost everyone acknowledged that the natural choice for president would be George Washington, although he initially protested that he was happily retired at his Mount Vernon plantation and had no desire to reenter the public eye or politics. It was thought to be unseemly and out of keeping with republican sacrifice to campaign for office or even to desire power too much, and probably at least part of Washington's reluctance stemmed from his adherence to republican values and traditions.

Because the office of U.S. president would create a new and powerful executive political force in American politics, the vast majority of politicians felt that Washington must be persuaded to take the office, since he had shown his reluctance to abuse power by retiring after the Revolutionary War in the first place. Less clear was who should be elected vice president, in some sense a question of who else politicians could view as president, since the vice president would be the candidate who received the second-highest number of votes in the electoral college. Political gossip favored John Adams or John Hancock because it seemed likely that northerners would want to balance George Washington's southern origins by electing one of their own to the vice presidency. No clear front-runner had emerged, even as Congress set January 7, 1789, as the day the first presidential electors should be chosen.

Americans ended 1788 having created a new form of government but still unsure of how power ought to be exercised in society. Tensions remained between Federalists and Anti-Federalists, debtors and merchants, and regions of the country. Although many more Americans had made some contribution to the political debate of the constitutional years, even if just by marching in or viewing a parade, the majority of "the people" were still excluded from voting or exercising any form of public power. But the republicanism that helped to create the new Constitution also helped to energize African-American community organizations and was beginning to shape a vision of the need for greater female education. Perhaps soon "the people" would begin to speak for themselves.

# CHRONICLE OF EVENTS

## 1787

Sacagawea (Sacajawea) is born into the Lemhi band of Shoshone (in present-day Idaho).

Philadelphia physician and educator Benjamin Rush publishes his *Thoughts on Female Education,* calling for increased schooling for girls. Rush is one of the foremost U.S. advocates of the educational ideas of British feminist Mary Wollstonecraft.

Dr. William Samuel Johnson is appointed as president of King's College (now Columbia University); he is the first nonordained person to head a U.S. college.

The first Methodist college in the United States, Cokesbury, opens in Abingdon, Maryland.

In New York City, the Manumission Society, a collection of the city's elite citizens who oppose slavery, founds the New York Free African School, which enrolls about 50 pupils.

John Cabot and Joshua Fisher establish the first U.S. cotton mill in Beverly, Massachusetts.

Oliver Evans, who had also developed the country's first mechanized flour mill, produces the first noncondensing, high-pressure steam engine in the United States.

South Carolina cedes its western lands, long in dispute, to the U.S. government, opening the way for increased U.S. settlement along the Ohio River.

The University of Pittsburgh is founded.

*January:* The Massachusetts legislature calls up 4,000 militia troops to put down the anticourt and antidebt violence, now referred to under the general name of Shays's Rebellion. Former Revolutionary general Benjamin Lincoln is called upon to command the troops.

*January 1:* Connecticut author Joel Barlow publishes his epic poem *The Vision of Columbus,* which envisions the United States as the ultimate expression of freedom in the New World.

*January 25:* Daniel Shays leads a band of armed men to attempt to seize the government arsenal at Springfield, Massachusetts, but his forces are routed in a skirmish with Massachusetts militia under General William Shepherd that kills four men.

*January 29:* Richard Allen, Absalom Jones, and other free African Americans in Philadelphia found the Free African Society, a religious and benevolent

association that also promotes the abolition of slavery, thought to be the first organization of its kind in the United States.

*February 4:* Daniel Shays's forces are completely dispersed after a skirmish with state militia forces at Petersham, Massachusetts.

*February 16:* The Massachusetts legislature passes the Disqualification Act, prohibiting men who took part in Shays's Rebellion from voting, holding public office, working as schoolmasters, or operating taverns. Several prominent Shaysite sympathizers, however, are nonetheless elected to the state legislature in following years.

*February 21:* Congress calls for a national convention in Philadelphia to revise the Articles of Confederation.

*February 27:* Shays's Rebellion comes to an end, and Daniel Shays flees the state of Massachusetts.

*April 16:* Royall Tyler's play, *The Contrast,* a comedy commenting on manners and morals and one of the first significant American plays, debuts in New York City.

*May–June:* John Adams negotiates with Dutch bankers for a third large loan to pay U.S. national debts.

*May 14:* The Constitutional Convention is set to begin in Philadelphia, but not enough delegates arrive, so the meeting is postponed.

*May 25:* With a quorum present, the Constitutional Convention begins.

*May 29:* At the Constitutional Convention, Virginia delegate Edmund Randolph proposes a plan essentially to throw out the Articles of Confederation and to draft a whole new constitution for the United States. He puts forth the Virginia Plan, authored primarily by James Madison, that calls for three branches of government with legislative representation based on population.

*June 15:* New Jersey delegate William Paterson proposes to the Constitutional Convention an alternative New Jersey Plan that is much closer to the Articles of Confederation and calls for equal representation for each state.

*July 16:* Connecticut delegate Roger Sherman proposes to the Constitutional Convention a compromise plan that incorporates a two-house legislature, a House of Representatives based on proportional representation, and a Senate on equal representation. His plan paves the way for the final compromise at the convention.

*July 16:* The Great Compromise (also known as the Connecticut Compromise), which settles the basic legislative form of the new federal government, is agreed upon at the Constitutional Convention.

*July 17:* Congress passes the Northwest Ordinance, building upon the land ordinances of 1784 and 1785. The Northwest Ordinance defines procedures for the Northwest Territory to be added as states, guarantees the civil rights of settlers, prohibits slavery in the territories, and calls for Indian land rights to be respected.

*August 16:* The Constitutional Convention approves a clause granting Congress the power to regulate foreign trade, interstate commerce, and trade with Indian nations. These powers represent a major change from the Articles of Confederation.

*August 21:* The delegates to the Constitutional Convention debate the place of slavery in the new Constitution. They eventually agree that slaves will be counted as three-fifths of a person for purposes of representation and that the slave trade will not be outlawed until 1808.

*August 22:* John Fitch calls on delegates to the Constitutional Convention to witness the first successful trial of his new invention, the 45-foot steamboat *Perseverance*. The boat achieves a speed of four miles per hour.

*August 31:* A local Act for the Prevention of Vice and Immorality that outlaws swearing, cockfighting, and professional theater takes effect in Philadelphia.

Constitutional Convention delegates approve the composition of the electoral college and decide on procedures in case the presidential election should ever result in a tie vote in the electoral college. They specify that in case of a tie, the House of Representatives will decide the election.

Virginia delegate George Mason, who has become disillusioned with the Constitutional Convention, announces that he "would sooner chop off his right hand than put it to the Constitution as it now stands."[11]

*September:* John Kendrick and Robert Gray sail from Boston aboard the *Columbia* and the *Lady Washington* to explore the Pacific Northwest. Their exploration will form the basis of the future U.S. claim to Oregon. Gray eventually sails around the tip of South America, to China, and around the world.

*September 8:* The Constitutional Convention chooses a committee of five members to draw up a final draft of the new document upon which they have agreed.

*September 12:* Black Revolutionary War veteran Prince Hall, a member of Boston's growing elite circle of free African Americans who had been inducted into Masonry by British soldiers during the war, receives a charter for an all-black Masonic lodge in Boston. In 1804, the lodge will be named the Prince Hall Grand Lodge.

Constitutional Convention delegates George Mason and Elbridge Gerry propose that a Bill of Rights be added to the Constitution to prevent the government from trampling on individual liberties. Their proposal is defeated, though James Madison promises that a Bill of Rights will be added in the future. The convention begins its final debate on the Constitution.

*September 15:* Disappointed Virginia delegates George Mason and Edmund Randolph propose beginning a second Constitutional Convention to discard the proposed constitution, but their suggestion is rejected unanimously by the rest of the delegates who vote to accept the document produced by the convention.

*September 17:* The Constitutional Convention concludes, all but three delegates sign the document, and the new federal Constitution is submitted to Congress.

*September 28:* Congress votes to submit the new Constitution to conventions in the states for ratification.

*October:* Congress recalls John Adams from his post as minister to Great Britain.

*October 5:* Congress appoints Arthur St. Clair as first governor of the Northwest Territory according to the rules set forth by the Northwest Ordinance.

*October 27:* The first *Federalist* essay appears in New York newspapers. John Jay, Alexander Hamilton, and James Madison write the series of papers to sway political opinion in favor of ratification of the federal Constitution.

*December 7:* A convention in Delaware unanimously ratifies the federal Constitution.

*December 12:* Pennsylvania ratifies the federal Constitution by a vote of 46 to 23 in its ratifying convention.

*December 18:* New Jersey's ratifying convention votes unanimously to ratify the federal Constitution.

Alexander Hamilton, one of the coauthors of the *Federalist* essays, became the first secretary of the treasury after the Constitution was ratified. He advocated greater use of federal power, and he was an important Federalist party leader before he was killed in a duel with Aaron Burr in 1804. *(Library of Congress, Prints and Photographs Division [LC-USZ62-96267])*

## 1788

New York becomes the capital of the United States under the terms of the new Constitution. The Constitution provides for the creation of a federal district for the U.S. capital, but Congress will take years to decide the exact location and layout of the district.

Daniel Shays is pardoned.

Phillip Freneau, the best-regarded U.S. poet of the early republic, publishes his collected works.

The state of Vermont outlaws slavery.

Susannah Rowson, America's first important professional woman author, publishes two novels and a book of poems.

The *Pennsylvania Gazette* newspaper calls for the founding of a national university, a botanical garden, and a scientific museum to be supported by public funds.

*January 2:* Georgia ratifies the federal Constitution by the unanimous vote of its ratifying convention.

*January 9:* Connecticut's convention votes 128 to 40 to ratify the federal Constitution.

*February 6:* The Massachusetts convention votes to ratify the federal Constitution by the narrow margin of 187 to 168.

*March 24:* A referendum on ratification of the Constitution in Rhode Island fails, and the state will not ratify the document until 1790.

*April 4:* The final *Federalist* paper is completed, and the collection of 85 essays is published in its entirety in book form, just in time to influence the bitter ratification debate in New York state.

*April 7:* Marietta, the first permanent settlement in the Northwest Territory under the terms of the Northwest Ordinance, is founded at the confluence of the Ohio and Muskingum Rivers.

*April 13–14:* After a young boy working for a New York City doctor recognizes his recently deceased mother on the dissection table, New Yorkers accuse doctors of stealing dead bodies to perform autopsies. Two days of riots against the doctors destroy several offices and damage hospital buildings in the city.

*April 28:* Delegates to Maryland's ratifying convention vote 63 to 11 to ratify the federal Constitution.

*May 23:* South Carolina ratifies the federal Constitution by a vote of 149 to 73.

*June 21:* New Hampshire becomes the ninth state to ratify the federal Constitution by a vote of 57 to 46. The New Hampshire ratifying convention also votes to recommend 12 amendments to the Constitution. The vote means that technically the Constitution has gone into effect. Because the largest states, Virginia and New York, have not yet ratified, Congress postpones declaring the Constitution in effect.

*June 25:* Virginia ratifies the federal Constitution, after recommending 20 amendments, by a close vote of 89 to 79 in its ratifying convention.

*June 26:* After a long and bitter public political battle between Federalists and Anti-Federalists, New York's convention ratifies the federal Constitution by a vote of 30 to 27.

*July 4:* To celebrate both Independence Day and the ratification of the Constitution, Philadelphians hold the Grand Federal Procession, the country's largest parade in honor of the Constitution.

*July 23:* New Yorkers hold a parade to celebrate the ratification of the Constitution in their state. The artisans of New York City have a particularly strong presence in the parade, as they begin to build the political coalition that will increase their power dramatically in the following years.

*August 2:* North Carolina's convention votes not to ratify the U.S. Constitution, though it has already gone into effect. The state, whose leaders claim that they will not agree until a Bill of Rights has been added, will not ratify the document until November 1789.

*September 13:* Congress designates New York as the U.S. capital and decides dates for the election and meeting of the first federal Congress, which will be chosen under the terms of the new Constitution.

*October 10:* Congress holds its last day of session in New York City under the Articles of Confederation.

*December 1:* Spain allows U.S. trade to be conducted from the port of New Orleans, but imposes a 15 percent tariff on American products.

*December 23:* In its last act before the new government defined by the U.S. Constitution takes effect, the Confederation government accepts 10 square miles of territory from the state of Maryland, which will become the future site of the District of Columbia.

## Eyewitness Testimony

No mention was made of negroes or slaves in this constitution, only because it was thought the very words would contaminate the glorious fabric of American liberty and government. Thus you see the cloud, which a few years ago was no larger than a man's hand, had descended in plentiful dews and at last covered every part of our land.

> *Philadelphia educator and doctor Benjamin Rush, 1787, in Johnson and Smith,* Africans in America, *201.*

I consent to this Constitution, because I expect no better, and because I am not sure it is not the best. The opinions I have had of its errors, I sacrifice to the public good.

> *Benjamin Franklin, speech near the closing of the Constitutional Convention, 1787, in Beardsley,* Life and Times of William Samuel Johnson, *128.*

The poor negro slaves work hard, and fare still harder. It is astonishing and unaccountable to conceive what an amazing degree of fatigue these poor but happy wretches undergo, and can support. The negro is called up about day-break, and is seldom allowed time enough to swallow three mouthfuls of homminy, or hoe-cake, but is driven out immediately to the field to hard labour . . . the poor slave generally fares the worse for his master's riches, which, consisting in land and negroes, their numbers increase their hardships, and diminish their value to their proprietor . . .

> *A northern magazine comments on a Virginia Plantation,* American Museum, *March 1787, in Pace, Luigi Castiglioni's* Viaggio, *194–195.*

. . . Absalom Jones and Richard Allen, two men of the African race, who, for their religious life and conversation have obtained a good report among men, these persons, from a love to the people of their complexion whom they beheld with sorrow, because of their irreligious and uncivilized state, often communed together upon this painful and important subject in order to form some kind of religious society . . .

> *Philadelphia Free African Society, charter preamble, April 12, 1787, in Aptheker,* Documentary History, *17.*

We understand that the discontents in Massachusetts, which lately produced an appeal to the sword, are now producing a trial of strength in the field of elec-

tioneering. The Governor will be displaced. The Senate is said to be already of a popular complexion, and it is expected that the other branch will be still more so. Paper money, it is surmised, will be the engine to be played off against creditors, both public and private.

> *James Madison, letter to George Washington, April 16, 1787, in Madison,* Letters and Other Writings of James Madison, *I: 292.*

There will not, nor cannot subsist harmony between the Northern and the Southern States. I would as soon undertake to cement the iron and clay of Nebuchadneezzar's image as to unite them cordially and sincerely.

> *Dr. Benjamin Gale, letter to William Samuel Johnson, April 19, 1787, in Beardsley,* Life and Times of William Samuel Johnson, *130.*

We are flattered with the prospect of a pretty full and very respectable meeting in next month. All the States have made appointments, except Connecticut, Maryland, and Rhode Island . . . The absence of one or two States, however, will not materially affect the deliberations of the Convention. Disagreement in opinion among the present is much more likely to embarrass us. The nearer the crisis approaches, the more I tremble for the issue.

> *James Madison, letter to Edmund Pendleton, April 22, 1787, in Madison,* Letters and Other Writings of James Madison, *I: 317.*

After every consideration my judgment was able to give the subject, I had determined to yield to the wishes of many of my friends who seemed anxious for my attending the Convention which is proposed to be holden in Philadelphia the 2d Monday of May, and though so much afflicted with a Rheumatick complaint . . . as to be under the necessity of carrying my arm in a sling for the last ten days, I had fixed on Monday next for my departure . . .

> *George Washington, letter to Henry Knox, April 27, 1787, in Ford,* Writings of George Washington, *XI: 138.*

We, the Free Africans and their descendants of the City of Philadelphia in the State of Pennsylvania or elsewhere do unanimously agree for the benefit of each other, to advance one shilling in silver, Pennsylvania currency, monthly and after one year's subscription from the date hereof then to hand forth to the needy of this society . . .

*Philadelphia Free African Society, financial rules, May 17, 1787, in Aptheker,* Documentary History, *18.*

There are among a variety some very eccentric opinions upon this great subject; and what is a very extraordinary phenomenon, we are likely to find the republicans, on this occasion, issue from the Southern and Middle States, and the anti-republicans from the Eastern; however extraordinary this may at first seem . . .

*George Mason, letter to George Mason, Jr., May 20, 1787, in Rowland,* Life of George Mason, *101–102.*

. . . The Articles of Confederation ought to be so corrected and enlarged as to accomplish the objects proposed by their institution; namely "common defense, security of liberty and general welfare." . . . the rights of suffrage in the National Legislature ought to be proportioned to the quotas of contribution, or to the number of free inhabitants, as the one or the other rule may seem best in different cases.

*The Virginia Plan, presented to the Constitutional Convention, May 29, 1787, in Commager,* Documents, *134.*

The business of this convention is as yet too much in embryo to form any opinion of the conclusion. Much is expected from it by some; not much by others; and nothing by a few. That something is necessary, none will deny; for the situation of the general government, if it can be called a government, is shaken to its foundation, and liable to be overturned by every blast. In a word, it is at an end; and, unless a remedy is soon applied, anarchy and confusion will inevitably ensue.

*George Washington, letter to Thomas Jefferson, May 30, 1787, in Ford,* Writings of George Washington, *XI: 159.*

Under the existing Confederacy, Congress represent the *States* and not the *people* of the *States;* their acts operate on the *States,* not on the *individuals.* The case will be changed in the new plan of government. The people will be represented; they ought therefore to choose the Representatives.

*George Mason, speech in the Constitutional Convention, June 6, 1787, in Rowland,* Life of George Mason, *116.*

The Convention continues to sit, and have been closely employed since the commencement of the session. I am still under the mortification of being restrained from disclosing any part of their proceedings. As soon as I am at liberty, I will endeavor to make amends for my silence . . . I have taken notes of everything that has yet passed, and mean to go on with the drudgery, if no indisposition obliges me to discontinue it. . . . The public mind is very impatient for the event, and various reports are circulating which tend to inflame curiosity. I do not learn, however, that any discontent is expressed at the concealment; and have little doubt that the people will be as ready to receive as we shall be able to propose a Government that will secure their liberties and happiness.

*James Madison, letter to Thomas Jefferson, July 18, 1787, in Madison,* Letters and Other Writings of James Madison, *I: 333–334.*

Upon what principle is it that the slaves shall be computed in the representation? Are they men? Then make them citizens, and let them vote. Are they property? Why, then, is no other property included? The houses in this city (Philadelphia) are worth more than all the wretched slaves who cover the rice swamps of South Carolina.

*Delegate Gouverneur Morris, speech before the Constitutional Convention, August 8, 1787, in Hart,* American History, *III: 215.*

A Government will probably be submitted to the people of the States, consisting of a President, cloathed with Executive power; a Senate chosen by the *Legislatures,* and another House chosen by the people of the States, jointly possessing the Legislative power; and a regular Judiciary establishment. The mode of constituting the Executive is among the few points not yet finally settled. The Senate will consist of two members from each State, and appointed sexennially. The other House, of members appointed biennially by the people of the States, in proportion to their number. . . . The extent of them may, perhaps, surprize [sic] you. I hazard an opinion, nevertheless, that the plan, should it be adopted, will neither effectually answer its national object, nor prevent the local mischiefs which everywhere excite disgusts against the State Governments.

*James Madison, letter to Thomas Jefferson, September 6, 1787, in Madison,* Letters and Other Writings of James Madison, *I: 338.*

This [proposed] government will set out a moderate aristocracy: it is at present impossible to foresee whether it will, in its operation, produce a monarchy, or a corrupt, tyrannical aristocracy; it will most probably vibrate some years between the two, and then terminate in the one or the other.

*George Mason, "Objections to This Constitution of Government," September 13, 1787. Available online. Gunston Hall Plantation website. URL: http://gunstonhall.org/documents/objections.html*

Met in Convention, when the Constitution received unanimous assent of 11 States and Colo. Hamilton's from New York (the only delegate from thence in Convention), and was subscribed to by every member present, except Govr. Randolph and Colo. Mason from Virginia, & Mr. Gerry from Massachusetts. The business being thus closed, the members adjourned to the City Tavern, dined together, and took a cordial leave of each other. After which I returned to my lodgings, did some business with, and received the papers from the Secretary of the Convention, and retired to meditate on the momentous wk. Which had been executed . . .

*George Washington, diary entry, September 17, 1787, in Ford,* Writings of George Washington, *XI: 154.*

We now have the honor to submit to the consideration of the United States in Congress assembled, that Constitution which has appeared to us the most advisable. The friends of our country have long seen and desired, that the power of making war, peace, and treaties, that of levying money and regulating commerce, and the correspondent executive and judicial authorities should be fully and effectively vested in the general government of the Union: But the impropriety of delegating such extensive trust to one body of men is evident.—Hence results the necessity of a different organization.

*George Washington, letter transmitting the Constitution to Congress, September 17, 1787, The University of Oklahoma Law Center website. Available online. URL: http://www.law.ou.edu/hist/tranmit.html*

It is the result of four months' deliberation. It is now a child of fortune, to be fostered by some and buffeted by others. What will be the general opinion, or the reception of it, is not for me to decide; nor shall I say any thing for or against it. If it be good, I suppose it will work its way; if bad, it will recoil on the framers.

*George Washington, letter to the marquis de Lafayette, September 18, 1787, in Ford,* Writings of George Washington, *XI: 155.*

No decisive indications of the public mind in the Northern and middle States can yet be collected. The reports continue to be rather favorable to the act of the Convention from every quarter; but its adversaries will naturally be latest in shewing themselves.

*James Madison, letter to George Washington, October 14, 1787, in Madison,* Letters and Other Writings of James Madison, *I: 342.*

. . . As we are willing to pay our equal part of these burdens, we are of the humble opinion that we have the right to enjoy the privileges of free men. But that we do not will appear in many instances, and we beg leave to mention one out of many, and that is the education of our children which now receive no benefit from the free schools in this town of Boston, which we think is a great grievance, as by wo[e]ful experience we now feel the want of a common education.

*Prince Hall leading a group of free African Americans, petition to the Massachusetts state legislature, October 17, 1787, in Aptheker,* Documentary History, *19.*

The States eastward of New York appear to be almost unanimous in favor of the new Constitution, (for I make no account of the dissension in Rhode Island). Their preachers are advocates for the adoption, and this circumstance, coinciding with the steady support of the property, and other abilities of the country, makes the current set strongly, and, I trust, irresistibly that way . . . What opinions prevail more southward I cannot guess. You are in better condition, than any other person, to judge of a great and important part of that country. I have observed, that your name to the new Constitution has been of infinite service.

*Gouverneur Morris, letter to George Washington, October 30, 1787, in Sparks,* Life of Gouverneur Morris, *288–289.*

All my informations from Richmond [Virginia] concur in representing the enthusiasm in favor of the new Constitution is subsiding, and giving place to a spirit of criticism. I was fearful of such an event from the influence and co-operation of some of the adversaries. . . . I enclose herewith the seven first numbers of the Federalist, a paper addressed to the people of this State [New York]. They relate entirely to the importance of the Union. If the whole plan should be executed, it will present to the public a full discussion of the merits of the proposed Constitution in all its relations.

> *James Madison, letter to George Washington, November 18, 1787, in Madison,* Letters and Other Writings of James Madison, *I: 360.*

I confess, as I enter the Building I stumble at the Threshold. I meet with a national Government, instead of a Federal Union of sovereign States. I am not able to conceive why the Wisdom of the Convention led them to give the Preference to the former before the latter. . . . You are sensible, Sir, that the Seeds of Aristocracy began to spring even before the Conclusion of our Struggle for the natural Rights of men, Seeds which like a Canker Worm lie at the Root of free Governments. So great is the Wickedness of some Men, & the stupid Servility of others, that one would be almost inclined to conclude that Communities cannot be free. The few haughty Families, think *They* must govern. The Body of the People tamely consent & submit to be their Slaves.

> *Opponent of the Constitution Samuel Adams, letter to Richard Henry Lee, December 3, 1787, in Lewis,* Anti-Federalists versus Federalists, *159, 160.*

When the constitution was first published, there appeared to prevail a misguided zeal to prevent a fair unbiased examination of the subject of infinite importance to this people and their posterity—to the cause of liberty and the rights of mankind . . .

> *Richard Henry Lee,* An Additional Number of Letters from the Federal Farmer . . . , *December 25, 1787 in* Lee, Additional, *1.*

But it is needless to enumerate other instances, in which the proposed constitution appears contradictory to the first principles which ought to govern mankind; and it is equally so to enquire into the motives that induced to so bold a step as the annihilation of the independence and sovereignty of the thirteen distinct states.—They are but too obvious through the whole progress of the business, from the first shutting up doors of the federal convention and resolving that no member should correspond with gentlemen in the different states on the subject under discussion; till the trivial proposition of *recommending* a few amendments was artfully ushered into the convention of the Massachusetts.

> *Mercy Otis Warren,* Observations on the New Constitution, and on the Federal and State Conventions by a Columbian Patriot, *1788, in* Lee, Additional, *1.*

The public here [New York] continues to be much agitated by the proposed federal Constitution, and to be attentive to little else. . . . [The Anti-Federalists are] made up, partly of deputies from the province of Maine, who apprehended difficulties from the new Government to their scheme of separation, partly of men who had espoused the disaffection of Shay's [sic], and partly of ignorant and jealous men, who had been taught, or had fancied, that the Convention at Philadelphia had entered into a conspiracy against the liberties of people at large, in order to erect an aristocracy for the rich, the *well born,* and the men of Education.

> *James Madison, letter to Thomas Jefferson, February 19, 1788, in Madison,* Letters and Other Writings of James Madison, *I: 376, 377.*

Petitioners are justly Allarmed at the [i]nhuman and cruel Treetment that Three of our Brethren free citizens of the Town of Boston lately Receved; The captain under a pretence that his vessel was in destres on a Island belo in this Hearber haven got them on bord put them in irons and carred them of, from their Wives & children to be sold for slaves . . .

> *Prince Hall leading a group of free African Americans, petition to the Massachusetts state legislature, February 27, 1788, in Aptheker,* Documentary History, *20.*

That the proposed constitution will admit of amendments is acknowledged by its warmest advocates; but to make such amendments as may be proposed by the several States the condition of its adoption would, in my opinion, amount to a complete rejection of it; for, upon examination of the objections, which are made by the opponents in different States, and the amendments, which have been proposed, it will be found, that what would be a favorite object with one State, is the very thing which is strenuously opposed by another.

*George Washington, letter to John Armstrong, April 25, 1788, in Ford,* Writings of George Washington, *XI: 251.*

Many in the opposition are friends to the Union, and mean well, but their principal leaders are very far from being solicitous about the fate of the Union. They wish and mean, if possible, to reject the constitution, with as little debate and as much speed as may be. . . . An idea has taken air, that the southern part of the State [New York] will at all events adhere to the Union, and, if necessary to that end, seek a separation from the northern.

*John Jay, letter to George Washington, May 29, 1788, in Ford,* Writings of George Washington, *XI: 270.*

One cannot avoid being pleased at the auspicious opening of the business of your [Virginia ratifying] convention. The decision of Maryland and South Carolina by so large majorities, and the almost certain adoption of the proposed constitution by New Hampshire, will make *all,* except desperate men, look before they leap into the dark consequences of rejection. The ratification by eight States without a negative, by three of them unanimously . . . is enough, one would think, to produce a cessation of opposition.

*George Washington, letter to James Madison, June 8, 1788, in Ford,* Writings of George Washington, *XI: 268–269.*

On the one hand I see my country on the point of embarking and launching into a troubled ocean, without chart or compass to direct her; one half of her crew hoisting sail for the land of *energy,* and the other looking with a longing aspect on the shore of *liberty.* . . . I really at this time think there is a decided majority for anterior amendments.

*Anti-Federalist Theodoric Bland, letter to Arthur Lee, June 13, 1788, in Rowland,* Life of George Mason, *241–242.*

The dangers to which we shall be exposed by a dissolution of the Union, have been represented; but, however much I may wish to preserve the Union, apprehensions of its dissolution ought not to induce us to submit to any measure which may involve in its consequences the loss of civil liberty. . . . I suppose a

government so organized, and possessing the powers mentioned in the proposed Constitution, will unavoidably terminate in the depriving us of that invaluable privilege.

*Anti-Federalist John Lansing, Speech at the New York ratifying convention, June 20–23, 1788, in Lewis,* Anti-Federalists versus Federalists, *233, 234.*

Henry Williams alarmed us a little this evening, when he returned from the Virginia shore: he brought information that our settlement was to be attacked this night by three strong parties of Chippewaw [sic] Indians . . . We have sent this information over to the garrison. It proved false, however; but it made some trouble for us. . . . At Boston we have frequent alarms of fire, and inundations of the tides; here the Indians answer the same purpose.

*Western settler Colonel John May, diary entry about the settlement at Marietta, July 23, 1788, in Hart,* American History, *III: 105.*

After a very tedious discussion, the Constitution has been ratified by the Convention of this State [New York]. It was carried by a majority of 5, the ayes being 30, the noes 25. Amendments, in general, sim-

Early American settlers in western territories such as Kentucky and Ohio often lived in fortifications and carried weapons to protect themselves against attack by Native Americans. *(from Benson Lossing,* The Pictorial Field-Book of the Revolution, *1851–1852)*

ilar to those of Virginia, are recommended, and a confidence expressed in the act of adoption that they will be incorporated in the Constitution. The Convention of North Carolina has not been heard from since it met. Congress are at present making the arrangements for putting the Government into operation.

*James Madison, letter to his son Colonel James Madison, July 27, 1788, in Madison, Letters and Other Writings of James Madison, I: 406.*

What a delight it was to wander along that long street whose simple wooden houses face Boston's magnificent harbor, and to stroll past the shops which displayed for sale all the products of the continent I had just left! How I enjoyed watching the shopkeepers, the workmen, and the seamen at their various tasks! This was not the noisy, distracting bustle of Paris; the people did not have the tense, harried look of the French, that intense preoccupation with pleasure, nor did they display the towering pride of the English. They had instead the simple and kindly but dignified look of men who are conscious of their liberty and to whom all other men are merely brothers and equals . . . Girls here enjoy the same freedom that they have in England and that they used to have in Geneva when that city was a republic and moral standards were respected. This freedom they do not abuse. Their sensitive and open hearts need not fear the deceits practiced by the roués of the Old World, and seductions are very rare.

*French traveler J. P. Brissot de Warville, travel narrative, July 30, 1788, in Brissot de Warville, New Travels, 84.*

The circulation of this paper has also resulted in a general lack of confidence. Silver is carefully hoarded and does not circulate. You can neither sell nor mortgage your land; in both cases, sellers and lenders are afraid of being paid in paper money which could continue to depreciate. Even friends do not dare trust one another, for examples of the most revolting perfidy have been known. The inevitable consequence is that patriotism dies out, clearing of land comes to a standstill everywhere, and trade falls into a decline.

*French traveler J. P. Brissot de Warville, travel narrative, August 25, 1788, in Brissot de Warville, New Travels, 156.*

The antifederalist party was strong in New York City, and three quarters of the members of the convention when they left from Poughkeepsie were opposed to the new Constitution. Mr. Hamilton, joining his efforts to those of the celebrated Mr. Jay, succeeded in convincing even the most obstinate among them that the refusal of New York would have disastrous consequences for the state and for the Confederation. Consequently they voted in favor of the Constitution. The celebration in New York following the ratification was magnificent.

*French traveler J. P. Brissot de Warville, travel narrative, August 1788, in Brissot de Warville, New Travels, 148.*

When you travel through Maryland and Virginia you think you are in a different world, and you think so again when you speak with the people of these states. Here there is no talk of freeing the Negroes, no praise of the antislavery societies in London and America . . . Virginians are convinced that it is impossible to grow tobacco without slaves, and they are afraid that if Negroes regain their freedom they will cause trouble. If the Negroes are freed they have no idea what place to assign them in society, whether to settle them in a separate country or to send them away . . . The strongest obstacle to abolition is in the character, inclinations, and habits of Virginians. They like to live off the sweat of their slaves, to hunt, and to display their wealth without having to do any work.

*French traveler J. P. Brissot de Warville, travel narrative, 1788, in Brissot de Warville, New Travels, 231.*

The merits and defects of the proposed constitution have been largely and ably discussed. For myself, I was ready to have embraced any tolerable compromise, that was competent to save us from impending ruin; and I can say there are scarcely any of the amendments, which have been suggested, to which I have much objection, except that which goes to the prevention of direct taxation. And that, I presume, will be more strenuously advocated and insisted upon hereafter, than any other.

*George Washington, letter to Thomas Jefferson, August 31, 1788, in Ford, Writings of George Washington, XI: 321.*

I . . . have come to a conclusion (in which I feel no hesitation), that every public and personal consideration will demand from you an acquiescence in what will *certainly* be the unanimous wish of your country [to become president]. The absolute retreat, which you meditated at the close of the late war, was natural and proper. Had the government produced by the revolution gone in a *tolerable* train, it would have been most advisable to have persisted in that retreat. But I am clearly of opinion, that the crisis, which brought you again into public view, left you no alternative but to comply; and I am equally clear in the opinion, that you are by that act *pledged* to take a part in the execution of the government.

*Alexander Hamilton, letter to George Washington,*
*September 1788, in Ford,* Writings of
George Washington, *XI: 329.*

I thought it best to maintain a guarded silence. . . . For, situated as I am, I could hardly bring the question [of being elected president] into the slightest discussion, or ask an opinion even in the most confidential manner, without betraying, in my judgment, some impropriety of conduct, or without feeling an apprehension, that a premature display of anxiety might be construed into a vainglorious desire of pushing myself into notice as a candidate. Now, if I am not grossly deceived of myself, I should unfeignedly rejoice in case the electors, by giving their votes in favor of some other person, would save me from the dreaded dilemma of being forced to accept or refuse.

*George Washington, letter to Alexander Hamilton,*
*October 3, 1788, in Ford,* Writings of
George Washington, *XI: 329,*
*330–331.*

The Presidency alone unites the conjectures of the public . . . As the President will be from a Southern State, it falls almost of course for the other part of the Continent to supply the next in rank. . . . The only candidates in the Northern States brought forward with their known consent are Hancock and Adams. Between these it seems probably the question will lie. Both of them are objectionable, and would, I think, be postponed by the general suffrage to several others, if they would accept the place. Hancock is weak, ambitious, a courtier of popularity, given to low intrigue, and lately reunited by a factious friendship with S. Adams. J. Adams has made himself obnoxious to many, particularly in the Southern States . . .

*James Madison, letter to Thomas Jefferson, October 17,*
*1788, in Madison,* Letters and Other Writings of
James Madison, *I: 422–423.*

At my time of life, and under my circumstances, nothing in this world can ever draw me from [retirement], unless it be a *conviction* that the partiality of my countrymen had made my services absolutely necessary, joined to a *fear* that my refusal might induce a belief that I preferred the conservation of my own reputation and private ease to the good of my country. . . . From this embarrassing situation I had naturally supposed that my declarations at the close of the war would have saved me; and that my sincere intentions, then publicly made known, would have effectually precluded me for every afterwards from being looked upon as a candidate for any office.

*George Washington, letter to Benjamin Lincoln, October*
*26, 1788, in Ford,* Writings of George Washington,
*XI: 336, 337.*

# 3

# A New Nation
## 1789–1792

In 1789, the new federal constitution took concrete form in the new federal government of the United States. Some of the uncertainty of the post–Revolutionary War period appeared to subside, as many Americans shifted their attention to what they hoped would be the stable new influence of the federal government. Those who had been proponents of creating more federal power saw the new government as an opportunity to solve the financial, diplomatic, and social problems created by the weak Articles of Confederation. Many hoped that the opening of the first federal congress and the inauguration of George Washington as president would mark a new era of growth for the United States.

The bitter political divisions created during the debate over the ratification of the Constitution and the polarized public debate between Federalists and Anti-Federalists subsided, but a new pattern of political opposition was just beginning to take shape. The disagreements over how much power ought to be wielded by government in American society had by no means disappeared, but the terms of the argument shifted once the federal government was firmly established. Political arguments, differences about economic policy, and, to some degree, disputes over the social origins of power in American society began to polarize national and local politicians as the dim outlines of partisan politics in the United States began to take shape.

The issue of how to form the United States into a nation that fulfilled the republican expectations created by the Revolution still hovered over social and political developments after 1789. The social impact of republicanism seemed even more relevant after the French Revolution began that same year. The American people, many of them energized by the radical democracy proposed in the initial phases of the French Revolution, did not count themselves out of the political battles that were beginning to develop among their elite leaders. Both political leaders and average Americans were engaged in deciding exactly how they wanted to live in a new nation.

## ESTABLISHING THE FEDERAL GOVERNMENT

When the first federal Congress fully began operation in 1789, it seemed likely that proponents of a strong national government would, at last, have their way in determining the public affairs of the nation. Former Federalists, supporters of the Constitution, held a solid majority in the Congress, and only nine representatives were former Anti-Federalists who had opposed ratification. The new Congress had much greater power to levy taxes than had the previous government under the Articles of Confederation, and though not everyone agreed on exactly what course the congressmen ought to take to solve the financial ills threatening the United States, most everyone agreed that some drastic action was needed. Congress quickly set about establishing a basic tax structure, including an assessment based upon the value of property. But raising sufficient basic revenues still seemed to present an overwhelming challenge to the new government.

To head the new federal government, the members of the electoral college met in February and elected George Washington, who had emerged as the clear and convincing choice to become the first president of the United States. Washington's heroic reputation as commander in chief during the Revolutionary War, his political restraint and acumen demonstrated both by his military retirement and his leadership of the Constitutional Convention, and his ability to represent the wealthy planter class of Virginia and the entire South made him by far the most attractive candidate. John Adams, the lawyer, Continental congressman, and former revolutionary from Massachusetts, was chosen to serve as the first vice president, an office left fairly undefined by the Constitution.

George Washington's election and inauguration, and in some sense the man himself, provided an important symbol of federal power to the American public that was still seeking to understand the workings of the new government created by the Constitution. Although Washington himself professed a healthy republican reluctance to accept political office—he said that traveling to his inauguration made him feel like "a culprit who is going to the place of his execution"—"the people" of America lauded Washington and seemed to fuse his personal strengths with the office of the presidency. During April 1789, men and women in towns and cities between Washington's estate at Mount Vernon, Virginia, and the capital of New York City turned out to celebrate the soon-to-be president with parades and triumphal arches as he journeyed to take the oath of office. As soon as Judge Robert R. Livingston swore in Washington on April 30, the huge crowd that had gathered outside New York's City Hall exclaimed: "Long live the President of the United States!"[1]

The monarchical flavor of this veneration for George Washington, the new president, was not lost on contemporary observers. Alexander Hamilton, who was perhaps the strongest proponent of centralized executive power, noted that although Americans would hold Washington in highest esteem, they would never think of him quite as a king because "[t]he notions of equality are as yet in my opinion too general and too strong."[2] Proposals in Congress to confer on the president the official title of "His Majesty, The President" or "His High Mightiness" were rejected in favor of the simpler form of address: "Mr. President." The President and the First Lady, Martha Washington, did encourage a formality in their relationships with the public and the Congress; they held weekly "levees" that resembled court receptions at their official residence and did not accept impromptu visitors. George Washington's birthday began to be celebrated more widely as a holiday in various cities around the country in 1790. The new president walked a thin line between high-style hero worship

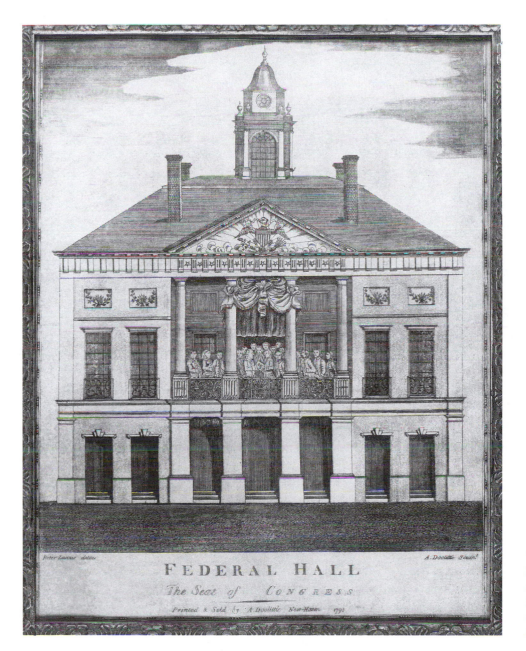

FEDERAL HALL

The Seat of CONGRESS

*Printed & Sold by A. Doolittle New-Haven.  1790*

This 1790 engraving by Amos Doolittle depicts the inauguration of George Washington at Federal Hall in New York City. *(Library of Congress, Prints and Photographs Division [LC-USZ62-126500])*

and the simplicity demanded by the citizens of a democratic republic. As political divisions worsened during his first term, the sometimes seemingly monarchical excesses of his office drew criticism from opponents.

The great public reverence for George Washington was not merely a personal or symbolic matter, however. The role of the executive became very important as a matter of substance as the federal government was taking shape. The Constitution was less specific about the powers of the president versus those of the Congress, and Washington's personal charisma went a long way toward enhancing the power of the office in its formative years. One of the most important ways in which Washington enhanced the power of the executive branch of government was by forming a very influential and activist cabinet in autumn 1789. George Washington's first cabinet contained men of high

This engraving depicts one of the weekly social receptions held by Martha Washington, which became important occasions for political discussion and contributed to the Washingtons' reputation for encouraging courtly splendor. *(Library of Congress, Prints and Photographs Division [LC-USZ62-103186])*

ability and strong opinion. They did not always agree with one another, but they would leave an indelible mark on American government.

The two most important and influential members of Washington's cabinet were Secretary of the Treasury Alexander Hamilton and Secretary of State Thomas Jefferson. Each man was a respected member of the elite class; each possessed a fierce intellect and a strong record of political experience. But the content and tone of their political opinions differed greatly. Hamilton, a New Yorker, favored strong federal power and constantly pushed the government to take action to solve financial and social problems. Jefferson, a Virginian, believed in a more decentralized form of government action that would continue to recognize the states as the primary locus of power in the United States. As Washington's first term progressed, the two men would disagree increasingly loudly in public over the ideological course of the U.S. government and over the implementation of specific policies.

Other governmental officials exercised public influence, but none would become quite the focus of political opposition as Jefferson and Hamilton did. Former Revolutionary War general Henry Knox took responsibility for the new War Department and assumed as his primary tasks the creation of a very small peacetime army and the need to negotiate with hundreds of Indian nations that opposed American expansionism. After Congress structured the Supreme Court and the federal district and circuit courts in the Judiciary Act of 1789, President Washington appointed John Jay as the first chief justice of the Supreme Court. But it would take several years before the nation's highest court began to exercise its full power. Although Vice President Adams presided almost daily over the Senate, in general he was disappointed with the level of responsibility of the vice president, which he referred to as "nothing" in one Senate debate.[3] The personalities of all these men would help to shape the course of the American nation.

## CONGRESS AND THE CABINET

One of the most important pieces of business facing the new Congress in 1789 was fulfilling the promise by leading Federalists that they would introduce a bill of rights to amend the Constitution. The promise had been instrumental in gaining ratification of the Constitution, especially in the final few states where voting had been close, and Congress began work almost immediately on drafting a bill of rights as an important sign of the victorious Federalists' fidelity to their promise. James Madison, a strong Constitutional proponent who represented Virginia in the House of Representatives, offered 19 specific amendments to be considered by Congress early in its first session. In September, Congress voted to approve 12 amendments and to submit them to the states for ratification. By November, the states had begun to ratify amendments, and the United States seemed well along the way to possessing a written guarantee of civil rights.

By 1791, the states had ratified the 10 constitutional amendments that have, together, come to be known as the Bill of Rights. In addition to protecting basic freedoms such as speech, religion, and a free press, the amendments served to knit together the nation, which might have been threatened by divisions between Federalists and Anti-Federalists. With the acceptance of the Bill of Rights, many former Anti-Federalists put aside their previous opposition to the federal government and established themselves as participants in the new processes of politics (although many of them kept up their opposition to individual Federalists whom they saw as their nemeses). While the Bill of Rights was in process of being adopted, the final two states that had refused to ratify the Constitution finally did so—North Carolina in November 1789 and Rhode Island in May 1790.

Aside from adopting the promised Bill of Rights, members of Congress and Washington's administration faced a variety of political challenges during their first few years in office. Many of the financial problems caused by economic speculation and a lack of coordination in the national economy since the Revolutionary War persisted, and as treasury secretary, Alexander Hamilton set the terms in which the solutions would be debated. Over the course of the first few years of the Washington administration, Hamilton laid out a financial program that proposed to enhance dramatically the role of centralized government in the national economy. It caused a firestorm of political opposition.

Hamilton, who had risen from humble origins, married well, and had served as Washington's aide-de-camp in the war, took the initiative to define a bold economic program in three reports he delivered to Congress in 1790 and 1791. From the beginning, Congress had ceded quite extensive decision-making authority to the executive branch, and Hamilton seized the initiative to define a proposed course of action to stabilize the economy and to encourage economic growth.

The first part of Hamilton's plan, proposed in his January 1790 "Report on the Public Credit," called for the federal government to buy back, or "redeem," at face value all financial notes issued by the national government under the Articles of Confederation. This proposal would have meant that speculators who had purchased government loan papers, soldiers' pay certificates, and other public notes at greatly depreciated prices over the years would redeem huge profits. Hamilton also urged Congress to fund a permanent public debt and to issue public interest-bearing securities, which would also likely benefit large financial institutions. The third proposal in Hamilton's "Report on Credit" called for the federal government to assume responsibility for the estimated $25 million of remaining state debts from the Revolutionary War.

Hamilton's report generated hot disagreement among representatives like Virginian James Madison (Hamilton's former fellow author of the *Federalist* papers), who argued that speculators ought not to benefit from notes that were initially issued to humbler individuals who wished to loan the government money. Hamilton hoped that providing repayment to large investors would cause them to stimulate the economy by reinvesting their capital. Several states, including Virginia, New York, Massachusetts, and Maryland, objected to the assumption of state war debts since they had already paid back all or most of their war loans. In April 1790, Congress voted to reject the assumption of state debts, but debate on the financial program was not over.

To gather support for his plan, and particularly for the most controversial part—the assumption of state debts—Hamilton engaged in some expert political maneuvering. He used the location of the proposed new federal capital city to bargain for congressional votes. After a deal to gain Pennsylvania's support from Robert Morris failed, Hamilton struck an agreement with Thomas Jefferson and James Madison. The two Virginians would gather southern support for Hamilton's assumption plan if he backed a plan to locate the new national capital on the Potomac River. Although Madison himself did not vote for the assumption plan, his deal with Hamilton—along with assurances that the federal government would reimburse states for any war loans already repaid—sealed the necessary votes. Legislation based on Hamilton's "Report on Public Credit" passed in July.

In December 1790, Hamilton revealed his second major financial proposal to the public and the Congress. He advocated the creation of a national bank. Hamilton envisioned that the Bank of the United States would be owned and operated jointly by the federal government and by private stockholders. Hamilton argued that the bank would solve a host of financial woes by stabilizing American currency, coordinating merchant loans, and handling government business, but his opponents worried that the bank would assume too much overweening power and enrich a few people without creating any actual financial stability. While it was true that almost every member of Congress was, in fact, a member of the very top economic elite of the country, those who opposed Hamilton's plan worried that the bank would do nothing to enhance small-scale farming, which was the economic base of the nation. The lure of financial stability overcame these objections, and Congress chartered the Bank of the United States. Thomas Jefferson urged George Washington to veto the charter, which, he argued, surpassed any governmental authority spelled out in the Constitution, but Washington signed the 21-year charter into law in February 1791.

Hamilton's third group of financial proposals, which he put forward in his December 1791 "Report on Manufactures," was the least successful of his plans. Hamilton's idea to stimulate domestic manufacturing with a related series of trade tariffs and domestic subsidies met with especially stiff resistance from southern plantation owners who opposed the notion of controlling trade through taxes and who did not want to question the agricultural base of the economy. American manufacturing, even in New England, where it was most advanced, was still very rudimentary and limited by comparison to Europe's. In December 1790, English immigrant Samuel Slater established the first water-powered cloth mill in the United States on the Blackstone River in Rhode Island, but even Slater's mill, which would become the basis of a huge and profitable American cloth manufacturing industry, started out small. Hamilton was unable to convince a majority in Congress that they should support his program to stimulate growth in industries just like this. Congress failed to pass Hamilton's suggested legislation to stimulate manufacturing, but his ideas about encouraging commerce would slowly continue to grow in influence.

During 1791, Hamilton did convince Congress to pass one final piece of financial legislation, whose full controversial importance would not become clear for several years. To pay for the national debt, which quickly reached the high level of $77 million, Congress levied a 25 percent excise tax on distilled liquor. The tax would prove particularly burdensome to western farmers, who could make much higher profits by refining corn into whiskey, which was easier to ship and more profitable than raw corn. The tax, which had to be paid when crops were brought to the distillery instead of when the whiskey was sold, aroused loud opposition almost from the beginning, and it instilled economic and regional resentments that would fester and grow well into Washington's second presidential term.

All in all, Hamilton's economic proposals helped to mark the new lines of political opposition in the national government. His plans, in addition to calling for specific financial measures, greatly enhanced the power of the central government. This seemed to confirm the fear of former Anti-Federalists who had hoped to avoid strong intervention by the central government. But even some politicians who had strongly favored the Constitution—like James Madison, himself the author of much of the document—found themselves coalescing in strong opposition to Hamilton and his ideas. Thomas Jefferson feared that President Washington was too easily swayed by Hamilton's ideas and too easily persuaded to exercise extreme federal power. Although not yet delineated into political parties, opposition camps were developing.

## THE PEOPLE IN THE NEW NATION

One event that would eventually make the political divisions even worse among elite politicians also energized the political sensibilities of the American people. The French Revolution, which began in late spring 1789, seemed to many Americans to confirm the worldwide relevance of their own commitment to republican principles. Most Americans assumed, however erroneously, that the French Revolution was the direct product of the fire of American liberty spreading across the Atlantic, and many felt that the French Revolution was just the first sign that American-style republicanism had started on its inevitable march across the globe. Although they would later disagree vehemently about the course it ran, political leaders from across the spectrum of American politics, including Hamilton, Jefferson, and Madison, initially praised revolutionary France's goals and supported its antimonarchical direction. At the same time, average Americans were filled with enthusiasm for French-style liberty. They toasted their "Gallic allies" at Fourth of July celebrations, celebrated French victories in the revolutionary war against Prussia that broke out in 1792, and began to incorporate liberty caps, tricolored flags and ribbons, and other French symbols into their own civic festivals.[4]

Public celebrations of the French Revolution, the Fourth of July, Washington's inauguration, and Washington's Birthday all showed the political vigor of an American public still trying to establish its role in the new nation. While some individuals who rose from humble origins came to prominence in the states, such as the former workingman William Findley, who became an influential Pennsylvania politician, the average man or woman did not have much influence either directly or indirectly on the workings of government. Most states maintained property limitations on voting, even for white men, and many federal officeholders, including U.S. senators, were not directly elected by the people. Some states experimented with widening the franchise; for example, starting in 1790, New Jersey allowed free blacks and even single women to vote in some state elections, as long as they owned considerable property.

The right to vote, while growing in importance, was not the only means of political expression. Even though they lacked much direct political influence, the American people showed political interest. They read political newspapers and debated current events in taverns and city streets. Public celebrations and festivals provided opportunities not only for individuals to feel connected to the American nation, but also to express their assent to public policies and politicians. In New York City, the Society of St. Tammany, a new fraternal organization that brought together workingmen, merchants, and traders to organize public celebrations and other benevolent activities, quickly took on an openly political tone. This group provided interaction between voters and nonvoters on such occasions as Evacuation Day, a New York City Revolutionary War anniversary celebration. Public awareness of and support for political causes would become an important part of the power base of the political parties that began to form late in Washington's first term.

Of course, some Americans were excluded altogether from the political sphere. The first federal census, completed in August 1790, counted 3,939,625 people in the United States, but 697,624 of them were slaves, who had no personal or political rights even under the new Constitution. Slave life in the early 1790s continued much as it had since the Revolution: Most slaves lived on small farms, where they engaged in agricultural labor and tried to build social and family networks in the face of daily control of their lives by the white master class. Urban slaves played important economic roles in cities ranging from Richmond, Virginia, to New York City, where they worked as artisans, servants, and day laborers. Some urban slaves lived more autonomous lives, in part because of the close proximity to free black communities that thrived in cities like Philadelphia. However, their wages were always returned to their owners, and even they did not have ultimate control over their own destinies. Any slave could be sold or returned to field work at any time, subject only to the discretion of her or his owner.

Poor white men and women exercised more control over their daily lives, but they also lived on the margins of society and outside the realm of high politics. By the beginning of the 1790s, the gap between rich and poor was growing in the United States, especially in cities, where an increasing proportion of the poor could be found. A boom in economic speculation brought on by Alexander Hamilton's financial program ended abruptly in mid-1791, ushering in mild financial panic and renewed inflation that reemphasized the uncertainty of the economy. The majority of Americans met their economic needs through subsistence farming or by exchanging local produce, but even those small farmers who had started to branch out into commerce felt threatened by some government actions, especially the excise tax on liquor.

At the same time, government actions opened up increasing amounts of land in the west to settlement, and white settlers poured into western territories hoping to find independence and economic opportunity. The subsiding of diplomatic tensions with Spain and Britain meant that the government ceased trying to discourage average citizens (who in many cases brought their slaves with them) from settling in territories west of the Appalachians or the Alleghenies. Westerners continued to seek greater political representation as they had since the Revolution, and they made inroads when they gained seats in several state legislatures. After decades of agitation, some western settlers achieved strong political recognition when their territories were carved away from eastern control and admitted to the Union as autonomous states—Vermont in 1791 and Kentucky in 1792. Even as political stability was being achieved, moving to territory such as Kentucky, however, was far from a secure proposition for the average white settler. One contemporary observer noted that Indians killed more Kentuckians in 1789 than in any prior year.[5]

In part, the new U.S. government approached the violence between Indians and white Americans as a problem to be solved through foreign policy. President Washington and Secretary of War Knox sent commissioners Benjamin Lincoln, David Humphreys, and Cyrus Griffin to negotiate with the belligerent Creek leader Alexander McGillivray and other southern tribal leaders in an attempt to calm conflicts between southern Indians and several southern states. In 1790 Congress passed the Trade and Intercourse Act to impose regulations on Americans who traded with Indians. Its intent was to exert some control over those interactions, especially in far western territories. In reality, however, unscrupulous traders paid little mind to American law, and a flood of U.S. citizens often took possession of Indian lands with little or no real legal claim or title.

The widespread nature of American contacts with Indians belonging to many different cultural groups, and the prejudices and shortsightedness of American politicians and military leaders, led the U.S. government to act much more aggressively in Indian policy than it would have in any other realm of foreign relations. In 1790 North Carolina ceded its final land claims to the U.S. government, and Congress formally created the Southwest Territory in a bid to keep organized control over western settlement. The U.S. commissioners sent to negotiate with the Creek met with such little success that their report argued for the creation of an American army capable of combating hostile Indian forces. Congress voted to authorize a small force, and though George Washington assured legislators in his first annual message to Congress in 1790 that "[t]o be prepared for war is one of the most effectual means of preserving peace," peace seemed to be less attainable than ever. [6] Americans continued to provoke the ire of strong tribal groups, especially in and around the states of Georgia and Kentucky and in the Ohio Territory.

Indians in the Ohio Territory had great success banding together to oppose American incursions. By 1790 they had created a strong confederacy including Chippewa, Lenni Lenape (Delaware), Ottawa, Shawnee, Potawatomi, and Miami peoples, many of whom repudiated land cessions that had been forced on them following the Revolutionary War. These united people faced the threat of military action, since once the United States had created an army, Americans deployed it into Indian territory to "assess" the belligerent situation. Secretary of War Knox sent military officers Josiah Harmar and Arthur St. Clair to head a combined force of army and militia troops in the Northwest Territory. Harmar and St. Clair were overmatched by their Indian military counterparts. The Miami war chief Little Turtle gathered an effective fighting force of warriors from the confederated Indian nations, and tensions continued to rise.

American military men had little success against Indian warriors. Harmar's forces were driven back by Little Turtle's combined military forces in September 1790 in the Ohio Territory. During a second engagement the following month, Harmar's group was entirely routed, and he set about destroying and burning Miami towns in retaliation. When Indian troops continued to attack settlements in the Ohio Territory, Congress authorized St. Clair to pursue another campaign into Miami territory in 1791. St. Clair was badly prepared for battle when he met Little Turtle's troops in November 1791, and he suffered one of the most decisive military defeats in American history. By 1792 it had become clear that peace with Northwest Indian nations would demand greater military force, more skillful diplomacy, or better control of American settlers.

## CULTURE BY DESIGN IN THE NEW NATION

After Congress had approved the idea of placing the new U.S. capital city on the Potomac River as part of the deal brokered to approve the assumption of state war debts, plans moved forward to create a blueprint for developing it. The planning of Washington, D.C., embodied some of the most important economic and ideological contradictions that were growing in American public life. Congress designated Philadelphia as the temporary capital to give planners of the new federal district time to create a new kind of city that would express true republican political ideals. Architectural designs for government buildings and for the city itself stressed classical ideals and symmetry in an attempt to create for the United States its own Greek and Roman–style temples to political democracy.

At the same time, economic considerations loomed large. Politicians did not necessarily view profits as contradictory to democracy, even though personal impartiality was one of the most highly prized political principles of the day. Drawing upon his long experience as a surveyor and land speculator, President Washington selected an exact site for the city near Alexandria, Virginia, which afforded excellent access to trade routes and the Chesapeake Bay. The site also benefited land speculators who had formed the Potomac Company, hoping to develop land along the river. Chief among them was George Washington himself. President Washington hired French designer Pierre L'Enfant, who designed a city centered around an open mall and impressive federal buildings. L'Enfant and a board of directors that took over responsibility for planning the capital city also blocked out miles of carefully organized territory around the mall. They hoped to sell this land to private investors for the development of businesses and housing. Although land speculators including Robert Morris, William Greenleaf, and James Nicholson all contributed much toward the growth of the capital city, each faced bankruptcy after becoming overzealous in his profit-making efforts. In creating tension between pure idealistic design as an expression of American politics and the rigors of economic speculation, the early planning of the U.S. capital city accurately represented the strong contradictory forces guiding public life in the new nation.

The city planning and architecture of the capital was not the only area of public culture in the early 1790s that developed deep contradictions. American literature was still dwarfed by European literary culture, although Americans' appetite for books was growing year by year, and the passage of a national copyright law in 1790 helped to encourage domestic publications. In 1789 William Wells Brown published what has often been termed "the first American novel," *The Power of Sympathy,* but the tale of seduction based on a famous true-life Massachusetts scandal was not much of a hit with readers until several years later.[7] The following year Royall Tyler met more success with his drama *The Contrast,* which lampooned various American social types, but the play still could not be performed in some cities around the country because of laws against live theater performances, and the broad satire was considered a bit coarse for the most refined reading audiences. Many educated readers bought editions of William Bartram's nature and travel writings, but by far the most popular books in the United States were European novels.

These novels appealed especially to female readers, who used their increasingly prevalent literacy skills to entertain themselves with tales of rakes, fallen women, and other dramatic characters. Opponents of female reading argued that women wasted their education, endangered their morals, and succumbed to frivolous fashion when they engaged in reading novels. But novels did open up an intellectual world, however limited, to American women who had sufficient time away from farmwork or child care to read them. Ironically, essayist Judith Sargent Murray's publications, especially her 1790 piece "On the Equality of the Sexes," called directly for female intellectual and social equality, but her writings found far fewer readers than light fiction containing stereotypical female characters. American female readers often found themselves caught between the desire to exercise their minds and the requirement that they not become too manly and "intellectual" or between the desire for refined entertainment and the accusation of womanly frivolity.

Even newspapers, which were still growing in popularity and number after 1789, were caught up in some of the important contradictions of American public culture, whose consequences would help to stoke the political conflict of the day. Eighteenth-century newspapers were by no means impartial or objective, but two important newspapers became such strong political advocates that they became an integral part of the development of the system of party opposition in American politics. In April 1789, almost as soon as the new federal government had begun operation, John Fenno began publication of his *Gazette of the United States,* which he envisioned as a newspaper to communicate government news of national interest. Fenno was a strong supporter of Alexander Hamilton, and the *Gazette of the United States* quickly became a strong advocate of Hamilton's policies and his use of strong federal power. Fenno also openly criticized Hamilton's opponents in the newspaper, and soon Jefferson, Madison, and their allies were considering how to publicize their own political points of view. In 1791, Madison and Jefferson aided poet Philip Freneau to found a rival newspaper, the *National Gazette,* to help them strike back against Fenno and other Hamiltonians.

In 1791 and 1792, when proponents of the two political camps attacked one another in the pages of each newspaper, the disagreements over financial and government policy that had taken place in Congress and the cabinet broke into open public battle. James Madison and Philip Freneau accused Alexander Hamilton of aristocratic tendencies and of having too great a love for Great Britain and monarchical-style government. Fenno even went so far as to begin criticizing President Washington, whose heroic reputation had previously protected him from personal attack. Hamilton and Fenno struck back and accused their opponents of threatening to undermine the stability of American government.

## A NEW POLITICAL ORDER ON THE HORIZON

The newspaper war between the *National Gazette* and the *Gazette of the United States* helped to cement a turn in American politics, as the opposition that had been developing between politicians started to become identifiable as political party conflict by the end of 1792. Because political parties were not accepted as benign parts of the American political system in the 1790s, no one involved in the conflict had a complete sense that loyal opposition to the other side was possible. Eighteenth-century political theory held that the nation should have *one* interest and that competing parties would weaken the strength of government by causing factional strife. But even though both sides did not view party conflict as wholly legitimate and healthy for American government, their activities nonetheless came increasingly to resemble those of true political parties. Jefferson and Madison, along with their supporters, disagreed with Hamilton, Adams, and their partisans, and each side was willing to organize opposition to the other. President Washington still tried to navigate between camps, but impartiality would grow increasingly difficult in years to come.

At the end of 1792, just as the partisan cast of American politics was hardening, the second presidential election was held. Despite thoughts earlier in the year that he might retire, Washington was unanimously reelected president with 132 electoral votes. However, the political division did find expression in the votes for vice president—an office that was, at the time, conferred on the candidate who received the second-highest total of electoral votes. John Adams was reelected with 70 electoral votes, but Adams's and Hamilton's opponents gathered 55 votes for rival candidate New Yorker George Clinton. Thomas

Jefferson and Aaron Burr each also received a few votes. Especially notable was that no southern electors cast votes for Adams.

The federal government had survived its first four years on solid footing and had begun to administer a variety of important economic and social programs. The new nation had some obvious diplomatic and military weaknesses, but they had not yet been severely tested. The ideological and partisan conflicts that emerged would harden in years to come when the two rival political camps came openly to do battle as the Federalist and Democratic-Republican Parties.

# CHRONICLE OF EVENTS

## 1789

William H. Brown publishes what is regarded as the first American novel, *The Power of Sympathy.*

Susannah Rowson publishes *Mary, or The Test of Honor.*

*January 7:* Members of the electoral college from 11 states convene to hold the first presidential election. New York fails to appoint any electors. Rhode Island and North Carolina have not ratified the Constitution, so they send no representatives.

*January 9:* The United States concludes the Treaty of Fort Harmar with the Wyandot and other Northwest Indian nations. The treaty fails to settle disputed land claims in the Ohio territory.

*January 23:* John Carroll, a Catholic clergyman and son of the prominent Maryland political family, establishes Georgetown College (later Georgetown University), the first Catholic college in the United States.

*February 4:* The members of the electoral college cast their ballots, which are kept secret.

*March 2:* The Pennsylvania legislature repeals its law against live theater performances.

*March 4:* The first federal Congress meets in New York, but no business can be conducted, because a quorum is lacking.

*April 1:* Pennsylvania politician Frederick Augustus Muhlenberg is elected first speaker of the House of Representatives.

*April 6:* The U.S. Senate elects New Hampshire senator John Langdon as temporary presiding officer. The electoral votes are counted, and George Washington is elected as the first president of the United States. John Adams is elected vice president.

*April 8:* The U.S. House of Representatives holds its first official session.

*April 11:* Editor John Fenno founds the newspaper the *Gazette of the United States,* which will become a powerful public advocate of the cause of the Federalist Party and will oppose the Democratic Republicans.

*April 23:* Congress creates a committee to determine the proper style of address for the U.S. president. Committee members reject high-sounding royal titles and settle on "Mr. President."

*April 30:* In New York City, Robert R. Livingston administers the oath of office, and George Washington is inaugurated as the first U.S. president.

*May 12:* The Society of St. Tammany, founded in New York City by a group of politically interested tradesmen, workingmen, and shopkeepers, receives its charter. The society, originally a fraternal order and civic organization, will become increasingly involved in politics and form the future basis of Tammany Hall, New York City's Democratic Party stronghold.

*July 4:* Congress passes the first Tariff Act, which is intended to encourage and enrich domestic manufacturers by taxing imported goods by as much as 15 percent.

*July 14:* The French Revolution begins when a mob of Paris citizens storms the Bastille. The marquis de Lafayette, a former Revolutionary War officer who ordered the storming of the prison, later attributes his love for liberty to the American Revolution when he sends the key to the Bastille to George Washington. Lafayette writes that the key is "a tribute which I owe as a son to my adoptive father."[8]

*July 27:* The Department of Foreign Affairs is established under the leadership of John Jay.

*August 7:* Congress establishes the U.S. Department of War. Control over Indian affairs is included in the duties of the War Department.

*September 1:* Former Continental army general Henry Knox is appointed first U.S. secretary of war.

*September 11:* The Department of Foreign Affairs is renamed the State Department. Alexander Hamilton, a New Yorsk politician and promoter of strong federal government power, is appointed secretary of the Treasury.

*September 22:* Congress creates the U.S. Postal Service. Samuel Osgood will become the first postmaster general.

*September 24:* Congress passes the Judiciary Act, which organizes the federal court system, including the Supreme Court (with a chief justice and five associate justices), 13 district courts, and three circuit courts.

*September 25:* Congress submits 12 amendments to the U.S. Constitution to the states for ratification. These amendments are proposed to form a bill of rights, which was promised to many opponents of the Constitution as a way to help get the document ratified in 1788.

*September 26:* Thomas Jefferson is named secretary of state and Edmund Randolph is named attorney general. John Jay is also appointed as the first chief justice of the Supreme Court, but since Jefferson is still in France, Jay continues also to run the State Department until Jefferson arrives home in 1790.

*September 30:* Congress creates a 1,000-member U.S. army.

*November 20:* New Jersey ratifies the Bill of Rights.

*November 21:* North Carolina ratifies the U.S. Constitution.

## 1790

Duncan Phyfe, a maker of fine furniture who has immigrated from Scotland, opens his shop in New York City.

Judith Sargent Murray publishes her essay "On the Equality of the Sexes."

Royall Tyler's play *The Contrast,* the first comedy to be performed in the United States, is published.

Universalist Christians, who dispute the divinity of Jesus Christ, hold a convention in Philadelphia.

John Fitch begins steamboat service between Trenton, New Jersey, and Philadelphia, Pennsylvania.

New York City prohibits residents from turning their pigs loose in the streets.

*January 4:* Alexander Hamilton issues his first report on the public credit, which suggests that Congress should fully fund federal debt and assume responsibility for most state debt incurred during the Revolutionary War.

*February 1:* The Supreme Court meets for the first time.

*February 11:* A group of antislavery Quakers send the first antislavery petition to Congress.

*March 26:* Congress establishes procedures for foreigners to become U.S. citizens in the first Naturalization Act.

*April 4:* Congress establishes the Revenue Marine Service, which later becomes the U.S. Coast Guard.

*April 10:* President Washington signs the Patent Act, establishing the Patent Office. When inventors register with the Patent Office and disclose how their inventions are made and how they work, they receive government protection for a period of years during which they have exclusive rights to develop the commercial use of the product.

*April 12:* Congress votes to reject Alexander Hamilton's idea of assuming state war debt. Southern states, some of which have already come up with schemes to repay their debts, oppose the idea, as do some investors who have sold their debt certificates for less than face value.

*April 17:* Benjamin Franklin, perhaps the most respected American citizen of his era in the world, dies in Philadelphia.

*May 29:* Rhode Island becomes the last of the 13 original states to ratify the U.S. Constitution.

*May 31:* The first national U.S. copyright law goes into effect, allowing writers, musicians, and artists the exclusive legal right to reproduce and sell their works.

*July 10:* The House of Representatives votes to locate the 10-mile federal district that will serve as the U.S. capital along the Potomac River. Some claim that the location is offered in exchange for southern support for federal assumption of state debts.

*July 22:* Congress passes the Trade and Intercourse Act, which defines terms of legal and trade relations with Indian nations.

*July 26:* The House of Representatives votes to assume state debts.

*August 1:* The first U.S. census is completed. The U.S. population is reported as 3,939,625, including 697,624 slaves and 59,544 free blacks.

*August 9:* Captain Robert Gray's merchant ship *Columbia* arrives in Boston after completing its trip around the world.

*August 15:* John Carroll is consecrated as the first Roman Catholic bishop for the United States. He is installed as bishop of Baltimore.

*September:* Little Turtle and his band of Miami Indian warriors defeat a force of Kentucky militia and U.S. army troops near the Maumee River after General Josiah Harmar attacks five Miami villages.

*October 3:* John Ross, future leader of the Cherokee nation, is born.

*December 6:* Philadelphia becomes the nation's capital for the next 10 years, while the permanent capital is planned and built in Washington, D.C.

*December 21:* On the Blackstone River in Pawtucket, Rhode Island, Samuel Slater begins operation of the first commercially successful water-powered cotton mill in the United States.

*December 22:* The state of North Carolina cedes the last of its western lands, which will later become part of the state of Tennessee, to the United States.

## 1791

French architect Pierre Charles L'Enfant is hired to design the capital city in the new District of Columbia.

Naturalist William Bartram publishes *Travels through North and South Carolina, Georgia, East and West Florida.*

Jeremy Belknap and other prominent citizens of Boston found the Massachusetts Historical Society, the country's first historical society.

Samuel Holyoke publishes his songbook *Harmonia Americana.*

*January:* Free African Americans in Charleston, South Carolina, petition the state legislature to ask for repeal of 1740 laws that placed them under severe social restrictions.

*January 1:* President Washington and Martha Washington hold a public reception, known as a presidential levee, beginning a tradition that will continue into the 20th century.

*February 15:* In a report to President Washington, Secretary of State Thomas Jefferson opposes Treasury Secretary Alexander Hamilton's plans to establish a national bank and to use federal powers to develop the economy by supporting domestic manufacturers.

*February 25:* Congress charters the First Bank of the United States for 21 years, and Washington reluctantly signs the bill.

*March 3:* Congress passes a tax on distilled liquor, the first internal revenue law passed in the United States. The law particularly targets rural interests and western farmers, who can make great profits from distilling their corn into whiskey. Opposition to the tax is almost immediate.

Congress approves the exact location of the District of Columbia.

This photograph depicts the building of the controversial First Bank of the United States, located on Third Street in Philadelphia. *(Library of Congress, Prints and Photographs Division [HABS, PA, 51-PHILA, 235-7])*

*March 4:* After almost 20 years of trying to break away from the state of New York, Vermont is admitted to the United States as the 14th state.

*April 27:* American inventor Samuel F. B. Morse is born.

*August 22:* Southern slave owners become alarmed when Haitian slaves rebel against their masters. The leader of the rebellion, Toussaint Louverture, manages to overthrow French control of the island for several years. Many wealthy French refugees flee to the southern United States.

*October 31:* Author and poet Philip Freneau founds the *National Gazette* newspaper, which is critical of Washington and Hamilton. Thomas Jefferson supports Freneau, and the paper becomes a main proponent of the Democratic-Republican Party.

*September:* George Washington offers money and weapons to the French government to help put down the slave rebellion in Haiti.

*November 4:* Miami, Delaware, Shawnee, Chippewa, Potawatomi, and Ottawa warriors, under the leadership of Little Turtle, inflict a severe defeat on General Arthur St. Clair's U.S. troops at the location now known as Fort Recovery, Ohio. The battle is the largest Indian victory ever against U.S. troops.

*December 5:* Alexander Hamilton delivers a report on domestic manufactures to Congress.

*December 15:* The Bill of Rights is ratified and goes into effect. Only 10 of the original 12 amendments proposed by Congress are approved.

## 1792

Commissioners of the District of Columbia fire Pierre Charles L'Enfant, who has been ignoring their wishes for construction of the district because they interfere with his design ideas. The African-American surveyor Benjamin Banneker completes L'Enfant's plan for the city from memory.

James Woodhouse founds the Chemical Society of Philadelphia, the first chemical society in the world and one of the first scientific societies in the United States.

The first edition of the *Farmer's Almanac* is published in Boston.

The first communal society and the second Shaker settlement in the United States, Mount Lebanon, is founded in New Lebanon, New York.

*January 12:* Gouverneur Morris becomes U.S. minister to France, and Thomas Pinckney becomes U.S. minister to Great Britain.

*February 21:* Congress passes the Presidential Succession Act, which establishes the order of succession in case the president or vice president is unable to fulfill his duties.

*April 2:* Congress establishes the U.S. Mint and reaffirms the decimal system of coinage.

*May 8:* Congress authorizes the Militia Act, which gives states the rights to mobilize men between the ages of 18 and 45. The act will prove especially significant in fighting against Indian nations in the Northwest Territory.

*May 11:* Robert Gray claims the Columbia River for the United States on his second trip around the world.

*May 17:* A group of New York merchants meet in a public coffeehouse to found a stock market, which later becomes the New York Stock Exchange.

*June 1:* After struggling throughout the 1780s to break away from the state of Virginia, Kentucky is admitted to the United States as the 15th state.

*July 18:* Revolutionary War naval hero John Paul Jones dies.

*August 21:* A convention of men who oppose the excise task on whiskey meets in Pittsburgh and adopts resolutions against the enforcement of the tax.

*September 29:* George Washington proclaims that he will enforce the excise tax on liquor and makes clear that the federal government will not countenance resistance.

*October 12:* A monument to Christopher Columbus is erected in Baltimore, Maryland.

*October 13:* In a ceremony complete with Masonic ritual, the cornerstone of the White House is laid.

*November 1:* The first regular general presidential election is held in the states to choose the members of the electoral college.

*December 5:* The electoral college votes are revealed, and Washington and Adams are reelected president and vice president.

## EYEWITNESS TESTIMONY

Besides this, a *national language* is a band of *national union*. Every engine should be employed to render the people of this country *national;* to call their attachments home to their own country; and to inspire them with the pride of national character. However they may boast of Independence, and the freedom of their government, yet their *opinions* are not sufficiently independent; an astonishing respect for the arts and literature of their parent country, and a blind imitation of its manners, are still prevalent among the Americans.

> *Noah Webster,* Dissertations on the English Language, *1789, in Kornfeld,* Creating an American Culture, *106.*

RAN AWAY . . . From the subscriber yesterday, A NEGRO FELLOW, named ISAAC, about six feet high, has lost one of his upper jaw fore teeth, and nearly all his under jaw teeth on the left side, and has a small scar over his left eye near his hair; he came from the Delaware state about a year ago, is an artful cunning fellow, very talkative, and endeavours to pass with strangers for a free man; he is well known in Savannah, as he has butchered and attended the market for Mr. Dickson some time; it is supposed he is harboured by some white person, as he has been encouraged in making his escape by one Clark, a waggoner or barber. Any person who will deliver the said fellow to me, or the Warden of the Workhouse, shall receive TWO GUINEAS REWARD, and, upon conviction of any white person harbouring him, THREE GUINEAS.

> *Samuel Iverson advertises for a runaway slave in the* Savannah Georgia Gazette, *January 1, 1789, in* Windley, Runaway Slave Advertisements, *IV: 162.*

I own myself the friend to a very free system of commerce, and hold it as a truth, that commercial shackles are generally unjust, oppressive, and impolitic; it is also a truth, that if industry and labor are left to take their own course, they will generally be directed to those objects which are the most productive, and this in a more certain and direct manner than the wisdom of the most enlightened Legislature could point out.

> *James Madison speaking in the House of Representatives against Congress's first tariff bill, April 9, 1789, in Hart,* American History, *III: 263.*

We shall do well upon the present Federal Constitution. Perhaps some things might be amended . . . But I wish to have no amendments made these twenty years; or not until by experience and good judgment we should be able to discern what amendments are necessary. The Constitution is so good and excellent, that I do not wish to have it shaken by any speedy alterations . . . I presume the public administration by the Federal Congress will be, in its initial operations, mild, gentle, clear in its reasons; but firm and steady, and of a growing weight. And I further presume without a doubt that the more the new federal system or police is contemplated, the more diffused will be the public conviction and satisfaction that LIBERTY is secure under it . . .

> *Yale president Ezra Stiles expresses hopes for the American republic in a letter to Columbia president William Samuel Johnson, April 13, 1789, in Beardsley,* Life and Times of William Samuel Johnson, *135–136.*

Attended the House. Ceremonies, endless ceremonies, the whole business of the day. I did not embark warmly this day. Otis, our Secretary, makes a most miserable hand at it. The grossest mistakes made on our minutes, and it cost us an hour or two to rectify them . . . The Vice-President, as usual, made us two or three speeches from the Chair. . . . God forgive me, for it was involuntary, but the profane muscles of my face were in tune for laughter in spite of my indisposition.

> *Pennsylvanian William Maclay records the early proceedings of the U.S. Senate in his journal, April 25, 1789, in Hart,* American History, *III: 257–258.*

When I was first honored with a call into the service of my country, then on the eve of an arduous struggle for its liberties, the light in which I contemplated my duty required that I should renounce every pecuniary compensation. From this resolution I have in no instance departed; and being still under the impressions which produced it, I must decline as inapplicable to myself any share in the personal emoluments which may be indispensably included in a permanent provision of the executive department, and must accordingly pray that the pecuniary estimates for the station in which I am placed during my continuance in it be limited to such actual expenditures as the public good may be thought to require.

> *George Washington announces in his first inaugural address that he will refuse to accept any pay, April 30, 1789, in Commager,* Documents, *151–152.*

As George Washington traveled from Virginia to New York for his inauguration, he was greeted and lauded by the public along the way. This mid-19th-century engraving by Currier & Ives depicts a famous incident at Trenton, New Jersey, where women erected a floral triumphal arch to welcome Washington. *(Library of Congress, Prints and Photographs Division [LC-USZ62-100505])*

We are informed that the President had assigned every Tuesday and Friday, between the hours of 2 and 3 for receiving visits; and that visits of compliment on other days, and particularly on Sunday, will not be agreeable to him. It seems to be a prevailing opinion that so much of the President's time will be engaged by the various and important business imposed upon him by the Constitution that he will find himself constrained to omit returning visits, or accepting invitations to entertainments.

Gazette of the United States, *May 2, 1789, in Seale,* The President's House, *I: 5.*

Mr. Madison according to notice, this day moved the house to go into a committee of the whole, in order to take into consideration the subject of amendments, In pursuance of the 5th article of the constitution. This motion was opposed by Mr. Jackson, Mr. Burke, &c. on the ground of its being improper to enter on such a subject till the government was perfectly organized and in operation. . . . Mr. Madison replied in a long and able speech, in which he enforced the propriety of entering, at an early period, into the subject of amendments . . . He then stated a number of amendments which he thought should be incorporated in the constitution, and enforced the propriety of each by various explanations and arguments.

The Daily Advertiser, *June 9, 1789, in Veit, Bowling, and Bickford,* Creating the Bill of Rights, *63.*

The Papers will Inform what has been doing this Week in Congress we are giving Every thing into the Hands of the President which we are not fit to manage ourselves[.] Perhaps we shall find this will lead us to a Greater length than we at first Conceited[.] I hope but don't believe we are acting wisely in Giving Power to the President to turn out the Great officers of the United States at Pleasure without giving any Reason for it. . . .

Connecticut congressman Benjamin Huntington in a letter to his wife, Anne, *June 20, 1789, in McCrackan,* Huntington Letters, *72–73.*

I hope Congress, before they adjourn, will take into very serious Consideration the necessary Amendments of the Constitution. . . . all are anxiously expecting them. They wish to see a Line drawn as clearly as may be, between the federal Powers vested in Congress and the distinct Sovereignty of the several States upon which the private & personal Rights of the Citizens depend. Without such Distinction there will be Danger of the Constitution issuing imperceptibly and gradually into a consolidated Government over all the States . . . I am fully persuaded that the population of the U.S. living in different Climates, of different Habits & feelings under one consolidated Government can not long remain free, or indeed remain under any kind of Government but despotism.

Samuel Adams in a letter to Elbridge Gerry, *August 22, 1789, in Cushing,* The Writings of Samuel Adams, *IV: 332.*

It is the opinion of all the Eastern States, that the climate of the Potomac is not only unhealthy, but destructive to northern constitutions. It is of importance to attend to this, for whether it be true or false, such is the public prepossession. Vast numbers of Eastern adventurers have gone to the Southern States, and all have found their graves there; they have met destruction as soon as they arrived.

*Congressman Theodore Sedgwick opposes locating the District of Columbia on the Potomac River, September 3, 1789, in Hart,* American History, *III: 272.*

By this and yesterday's papers, France seems travailing in the birth of freedom. Her throes and pangs of labor are violent. God give her a happy delivery! Royalty, nobility and vile pageantry, by which a few of the human race lord it over and tread on the necks of their fellow-mortals, seem likely to be demolished with their kindred Bastille, which is said to be laid in ashes. Ye gods! with what indignation do I review the late attempt of some creatures among us to revive this vile machinery! O Adams! Adams! what a wretch art thou!

*Pennsylvania senator William Maclay in his journal, September 18, 1789, in Hazen,* Contemporary American Opinion, *143–144.*

The People of this State [Rhode Island] . . . have apprehended danger by way of precedent—can it be thought strange then that with these impressions they should wait to see the proposed system organized and in operation? to see what further checks and securities would be agreed to, and established by way of amendments before they could adopt it as a constitution of government for themselves and posterity?

*Rhode Island governor John Collins in a letter to Congress and the president, September 26, 1789, in Veit, Bowling, and Bickford,* Creating the Bill of Rights, *298.*

A deputation from all the Creeks of the Tuccassee, the Hallowing & the Tellasee Kings waited upon us, to congratulate us upon our arrival, to express in general terms their desire for peace to smoke the pipe of friendship as a token of it . . . The next day McGillivray dined with us and although he got very much intoxicated, he seemed to retain his recollection, & reason, beyond what I had ever seen in a person, when in the same condition . . . He declared he

was really desirous of a peace, that the local situation of the Creeks required that they should be connected with us rather than with any other People, that, however, they had certain advantages in their Treaty with Spain, in respect to a guarantee & Trade, which they ought not in justice to themselves to give up without an equivalent.

*David Humphreys reports on the beginnings of his efforts to negotiate with the Creek in a letter to George Washington, September 26, 1789, in Humphreys,* Life and Times of David Humphreys, 6.

With respect to amendments matters have turned out exactly as I apprehended from the extra[ordinary] doctrine of playing the after game: the lower house sent up amendments which held out a safeguard to personal liberty in a great many instances, but this disgusted the Senate, and though we made every exertion to save them, they are so mutilated & gutted that in fact they are good for nothing, & I believe as many others do, that they will do more harm than benefit.

*William Grayson in a letter to Patrick Henry, September 29, 1789, in Veit, Bowling, and Bickford,* Creating the Bill of Rights, 300.

Slavery is such an atrocious debasement of human nature, that its very extirpation, if not performed with solicitous care, may sometimes open a source of serious evils. The unhappy man, who has long been treated as a brute animal, too frequently sinks beneath the common standard of the human species. . . . To instruct, to advise, to qualify those who have been restored to freedom, for the exercise and enjoyment of civil liberty; to promote in them habits of industry; to furnish them with employments suited to their age, sex, talents, and other circumstances; and to procure their children an education calculated for their future situation in life,—these are the great outlines of the annexed plan.

*Benjamin Franklin addresses the public on behalf of the Pennsylvania Society for Promoting the Abolition of Slavery, November 9, 1789, in Mellon,* Early American Views, 19–20.

I little thought that when the war was finished, that any circumstances could possibly have happened which would call the General into public life again. I had anticipated, that from this moment we should have been left to grow old in solitude and tranquility together . . . I will not, however, contemplate with too much regret disappointments that were enevitable [sic], though the generals [sic] feelings and my own were perfectly in unison with respect to our predilections for privet life, yet I cannot blame him for having acted according to his ideas of duty in obeying the voice of his country . . . I am persuaded that he has experienced nothing to make him repent his having acted from what he conceived to be alone a sense of indispensable duty: on the contrary, all his sensibility has been awakened in receiving such repeated and unequivocal [sic] proofs of sincear [sic] regards from all his country men. With respect to myself, I sometimes think the arrangement is not quite as it ought to have been, that I, who had much rather be at home should occupy a place with which a great many younger and gayer women would be prodigiously pleased.

*Martha Washington in a letter to Mercy Otis Warren, December, 26, 1789, in Fields,* Worthy Partner, *223–224.*

. . . To promote the encreasing [sic] respectability of the American name; to answer the calls of justice; to restore landed property to its due value; to furnish new resources both to agriculture and commerce; to cement more closely the union of the states; to add to their security against foreign attack; to establish public order on the basis of an upright and liberal policy. These are the great and invaluable ends to be secured, by a proper and adequate provision, at the present period, for the support of public credit.

*Secretary of the Treasury Alexander Hamilton, "Report on Public Credit," January 9, 1790, in Freeman,* Alexander Hamilton, *534.*

Since I wrote to you last, the current price of securities has rather dwindled . . . This may have arisen from other causes than meerly [sic] the want of confidence in the public faith. It will be a considerable time before Congress can decide on this perplexing and important business . . . It appears to me that matters have gone so far wrong that it is not an easy thing to find the right way out, and that men of the most upright intentions, who would wish to unite justice with policy, may judge & act very differently . . . Very little business has yet been completed in Congress. We go *slow* fast enough.

*Paine Wingate in a letter to Jeremy Belknap, January 18, 1790, in Hart,* American History, *III: 256–257.*

This colossal statue of George Washington dressed partially in a toga, which was erected in Massachusetts, shows evidence of his public reputation as a man of dignity and classical republican principles. *(from Benson Lossing,* The Pictorial Field-Book of the Revolution, *1851–1852)*

Bourne on the wings of time, another year
Sprung from the past, assumes its proud career;
From that bright spark which first illum'd these
    lands,
See Europe kindling, as the blaze expands,
Each gloomy tyrant, sworn to chain the mind,
Presumes no more to trample on mankind:
Even potent LOUIS trembles on his throne
The generous Prince that made our cause his own,
More *equal rights* his injur'd subjects claim
No more a country's strength—that
    country's shame;

Fame starts, astonish'd at such prizes won,
And rashness wonders how the work was done.
          *Philip Freneau, "On the American and French*
          *Revolutions," Daily Advertiser, March 6, 1790,*
          *in Hiltner,* The Newspaper Verse, *367.*

I am aware that there are many passages in the sacred oracles which seem to give the advantage to the other sex; but I consider all these as wholly metaphorical. . . . the exquisite delicacy of the female mind proclaimeth the exactness of its texture, while its nice sense of honour announceth its innate, its native grandeur. And indeed, in one respect, the pre-eminence seems to be tacitly allowed us, for after an education which limits and confines, and employments and recreations which naturally tend to enervate the body, and debilitate the mind; after we have from early youth been adorned with ribbons, and other gewgaws . . . being taught . . . that the ornamenting of our exterior ought to be the principal object of our attention . . . It is expected that with the other sex we should commence immediate war, and that we should triumph over the machinations of the most artful. We must be constantly upon our guard . . .
          *Judith Sargent Murray, "On the Equality of the Sexes,"*
          *March-April 1790, in Harris,* Selected Writings of
          Judith Sargent Murray, *9.*

Francis Asbury was the first bishop of the American Methodist Church, and he established a highly successful system of circuit-riding Methodist ministers. *(Library of Congress, Prints and Photographs Division [LC-USZC4-6153])*

We were compelled to ride through the rain, and crossed the Stone Mountain: those who wish to know how rough it is may tread in our path. What made it worse to me was, that while I was looking to see what was become of our guide, I was carried off with full force against a tree that hung across the road some distance from the ground, and my head received a very great jar. . . . We are now in a house in which a man was killed by the savages; and O, poor creatures! They are but one remove from savages themselves. I consider myself in danger; but my God will keep me whilst thousands pray for me . . . My soul is humbled before God, waiting to see the solution of this dark providence. The man of the house is gone after some horses supposed to be stolen by Indians. I have been near fainting; but my soul is revived again, and my bodily strength is somewhat renewed.
          *Circuit rider and Methodist bishop Francis Asbury*
          *records his travels through Tennessee in his diary, April*
          *6–11, 1790, in Thorp,* Southern Reader, *488–489.*

. . . A vast monied interest is to be created, that will forever be warring against the landed interest, to the destruction of the latter; and this evil, great as it would be, by funding the debts of the United States only, is to be increased ten fold, by the assumption of the state debts. By this plan the monied and the political speculator, will both be gratified; the former, by the way I have already stated, and the latter, by possessing the general government, with the sole cause, and consequently, with the whole power of taxation, and so converting the state legislatures into mere corporations.
          *Richard Henry Lee opposes Hamilton's debt plan in a*
          *letter to Patrick Henry, June 10, 1790, in Ballagh,*
          Letters, *II: 524.*

. . . The bill for adjourning Congress to Philadelphia after this Session, there to remain for ten years, and then to go to the Potomac; was this day passed in the Senate by a majority of two votes . . . It rests now with the H of Representatives, where we are assured by many Members, that a Majority will pass it into a Law—Thus, well has ended this very troublesome business—Truth is great & will prevail—

*Richard Henry Lee in a letter to Thomas Lee Shippen, July 6, 1790, in Ballagh, Letters, II: 531.*

I have the honor to inform you, that, on the 20th September, I marched with 320 federal troops, and 1,133 militia, total, 1,453. After encountering a few difficulties, we gained the Miami village. It was abandoned before we entered it, which I was very sorry for. The villanous [sic] traders would have been a principal object of attention. . . . The substance of the work is this, our loss was heavy, but the head quarters of iniquity were broken up. At a moderate computation, not less than 100 or 120 warriors were slain, and 300 log-houses and wigwams burned. Our loss about 180. The remainder of the Indians will be ill off for sustenance; 20,000 bushels of corn, in the ears, were consumed, burned, and destroyed, by the army, with vegetables in abundance.

*Brigadier General Josiah Harmar reports in a letter to Secretary of War Henry Knox, November 6, 1790 in, Thornbrough, Outpost on the Wabash, 268.*

The aspect of Philadelphia is cold and monotonous. In general the cities of the United States are lacking in monuments, especially old monuments . . . Almost nothing at Philadelphia, New York, Boston, rises above the mass of walls and roofs. The eye is saddened by this level appearance. The United States gives rather the idea of a colony than of a nation; there one finds customs, not mores. One has the feeling that the inhabitants do not have their roots in the ground. This society, so fine in the present, has no past; the cities are new, the tombs date from yesterday.

*French traveler François-René de Chateaubriand records his impressions of American cities in 1791, in Switzer, Chateaubriand's Travels, 14–15.*

As we find that education gives a strong turn or bias of mind in favor of the particular class of people one belongs to, and as the great bulk of the people in this district are laborious hard-working farmers; then a person from that class would more properly represent them. . . . If a man has been used to labor and industry himself . . . this will teach him to be saving and frugal

of the public money, and not to lavish enormous sums on useless officers and pensions.

*Controversial Vermont political candidate and publisher Matthew Lyon in a letter, 1791, in Austin, Matthew Lyon, 64.*

Annihilation of State government is undoubtedly the object of these people. The late conduct of our State Legislature has provoked them beyond all bounds. They have created an Indian war, that an army may spring out of it; and the trifling affair of our having eleven captives at Algiers (who ought long ago to have been ransomed) is made the pretext for going to war with them and fitting out a fleet. With these two engines, and the collateral aid derived from a host of revenue officers, farewell to freedom in America.

*Pennsylvanian William Maclay, speaking on the floor of the U.S. Senate, decries the overstepping of federal power in the proposed excise bill that will tax whiskey, January 28, 1791, in Baldwin, Whiskey Rebels, 67.*

Perhaps bank bills may be a more *convenient* vehicle than treasury orders. But a little *difference* in the degree of convenience cannot constitute the necessity which the Constitution makes the ground for assuming any non-enumerated power . . . Can it be thought that the Constitution intended that, for a shade or two of *convenience,* more or less, congress should be authorized to break down the most ancient and fundamental laws of several states . . . Nothing but a necessity invincible by other means, can justify such a prostration of laws, which constitute the pillars of our whole system of jurisprudence. Will Congress be too straight-laced to carry the Constitution into honest effect, unless they may pass over the foundation laws of state governments, for the slightest convenience to theirs?

*Secretary of State Thomas Jefferson argues that the creation of a national bank would be unconstitutional, February 15, 1791, in Commager, Documents, 160.*

In the present state of things, nothing has happened between us and France, to give a tolerable pretence, for breaking of our treaty of Alliance with that Power, and immediately forming one with you, a regard for National decorum, puts such a decisive step as this, out of our Reach, but I tell you candidly as an individual, that I think the formation of a treaty of commerce, would by degrees have led to this measure, which undoubtedly that Party with us, whose remaining animosities and French partialities influence their whole political conduct, regard with dissatisfaction.

*Secretary of the Treasury Alexander Hamilton tries to build ties in a letter to British Minister George Beckwith, February 16, 1791, in Combs,* The Jay Treaty, *59.*

A hope is entertained that it has, by this time, been made to appear, to the satisfaction of the President, that a bank has a natural relation to the power of collecting taxes—to that of regulating trade—to that of providing for the common defence [sic]—and that, as the bill under consideration contemplates the government in the light of a joint proprietor of the stock of the bank, it brings the case within the provision of the clause of the Constitution which immediately respects the property of the United States. . . . the Secretary of the Treasury, with all deference, conceives, that it will result as necessary consequence from the position that all the specified powers of the government are sovereign, as to the proper objects; that the incorporation of a bank is a constitutional measure . . .

*Secretary of the Treasury Alexander Hamilton explains his position that a national bank is constitutional, February 23, 1791, in Commager,* Documents, *158.*

Sir, suffer me to recall to your mind that time, in which the arms and tyranny of the British crown were exerted, with every powerful effort in order to reduce you to a state of servitude . . . you were then impressed with proper ideas of the great violation of liberty, and the free possession of those blessings, to which you were entitled by nature; but, Sir, how pitiable is it to reflect, that although you were so fully convinced of the benevolence of the Father of Mankind, and of his equal and impartial distribution of these rights and privileges, which he hath conferred upon them, that you should at the same time counteract his mercies, in detaining by fraud and violence so numerous a part of my brethren, under groaning captivity and cruel oppression that you should at the same time be found guilty of that most criminal act, which you professedly detested in others, with respect to yourselves.

*African-American intellectual, surveyor, and almanac author Benjamin Banneker appeals for black freedom in a letter to Thomas Jefferson, August 19, 1791, in Ducas,* Great Documents in Black American History, *24–25.*

FIVE POUNDS REWARD. Ran away from the subscriber on the 17th of August last, a likely young negro man named JAMES, about 21 years of age, five feet 7, or 8 inches high, of a yellowish complexion, by trade a blacksmith; most used to making axes, he stoops forward in his knees and body as if he had a burthen on his back—his back is marked with the whip, he has a scar on one of his elbows occasioned by a burn; has small legs and very large feet—has a bold look, speaks good English and can tell a smooth tale—born on Trent river . . .

*Aaron Lambert advertises for a runaway slave in the* North-Carolina Gazette, *September 24, 1791, in Parker,* Stealing a Little Freedom, *3.*

It may be worth your own consideration whether it might not produce successful attempts to withdraw the privilege now allowed to individuals, of giving freedom to slaves. It would at least be likely to clog it with a condition that the persons freed should be removed from this country . . .

*James Madison in a letter to Robert Pleasants, October 30, 1791, in* Letters and Other Writings of James Madison, *I: 542–543.*

The expediency of encouraging manufactures in the United States, which was not long since deemed very questionable, appears at this time to be pretty generally admitted. The embarrassments, which have obstructed the progress of our external trade, have led to serious reflections on the necessity of enlarging the sphere of our domestic commerce . . .

*Secretary of the Treasury Alexander Hamilton,* Report on the Subject of Manufactures, *December 5, 1791, in Freeman,* Alexander Hamilton, *647.*

Mr. Livermore of New Hampshire ridiculed with an uncommon degree of humor the idea that it could be of any consequence to the United States whether the head of Liberty were on their coins or not; the President was a very good emblem of Liberty, but what an emblematical figure might be he could not tell. A ghost had been said to be in the shape of the sound of a drum, and so might Liberty for aught he knew.

*Debate in Congress over whether George Washington's head should appear on American coins,* Annals of Congress, *March 1792, in Hazen,* Contemporary American Opinion, *151.*

[The] ground about the president's house [is] much too extensive. It may suit the genius of a despotic government to cultivate an immense and gloomy wilderness in the midst of a thriving city . . . I cannot think it suitable in our situation.

*District of Columbia Commissioner David Stuart objects to White House landscaping plans to George Washington, April 13, 1792, in* Seale, The President's House, *I: 24.*

. . . It was not till the last session that I became unequivocally convinced of the following truth: 'that Mr. Madison, cooperating with Mr. Jefferson, is at the head of a faction decidedly hostile to me and my administration; and actuated by views, in my judgement, subversive of the principles of good government and dangerous to the Union, peace, and happiness of the country.' . . . This conviction, in my mind, is the result of a long train of circumstances, many of them minute. To attempt to detail them all would fill a volume.

*Secretary of the Treasury Alexander Hamilton in a letter to Colonel Edward Carrington, May 26, 1792, in* Craven, Johnson, and Dunn, A Documentary History of the American People, *210.*

. . . A tax upon liquors which are the common drink of a nation operates in proportion to the number and not to the wealth of the people, and of course is unjust in itself, and oppressive upon the poor. . . . internal taxes upon consumption, from their very nature, never can effectually be carried into operation without vesting the officers appointed to collect them with powers most dangerous to the civil right of freemen, and must in the end destroy the liberties of every country in which they are introduced . . . The late excise law of Congress, from the present circumstances of our agriculture, our want of markets, and the scarcity of a circulating medium, will bring immediate distress and ruin.

*Declaration of a meeting in Pittsburgh to oppose the excise tax on whiskey, August 21–22, 1792, in* Slaughter, The Whiskey Rebellion, *116.*

Though little known to the people of America, I believe that, as far as I am known, it is not as an enemy to the republic, nor an intriguer against it, nor a waster of its revenue, nor prostitutor of it to the purposes of corruption, as the American [Alexander Hamilton] represents me; and I confide that yourself are satisfied that, as to the dissensions in the newspapers, not a syllable of them has ever proceeded from me; & that no cabals or intrigues of mine have produced those in the legislature . . .

*Thomas Jefferson in a letter to George Washington, September 9, 1792, in* Craven, Johnson, and Dunn, Documentary History of the American People, *216.*

That I wished to recommend Mr. Freneau to be appointed to his present Clerkship is certain. . . . But that the establishment of Mr. Freneau's press was wished in order to sap the Constitution, and that I forwarded the measure, or that my agency negociated it, by an illicit or improper connection between the functions of a translating clerk in a public Office and those of an Editor of a Gazette, these are charges which ought to be as impotent as they are malicious.

*James Madison defends himself against charges of partisanship in a letter to Edmund Randolph, September 13, 1792, in* Letters and Other Writings of James Madison, *I: 569, 570.*

[George Mason] said he considered Hamilton as having done us more injury than Great Britain and all her fleets and armies. That his [Mason's] plan of settling our debt would have been something in this way. He would have laid as much tax as could be paid without oppressing the people.

*Thomas Jefferson's notes of his last conversation with George Mason, September 30, 1792, in* Rowland, Life of George Mason, *II: 364.*

# 4

# Federalist Order
## 1793–1796

During George Washington's second presidential term between 1793 and 1796, the conflicts that had begun to polarize politicians into opposition parties during his first term grew deeper, and the Federalist and Democratic-Republican Parties took much more concrete form. Although party politics was still considered to be illegitimate, divisive, and potentially destructive to the American nation, domestic and foreign developments caused it to become more of a reality on the national scene. Inside the United States, social upheaval and reactions to the continuing course of the French Revolution made common ground between supporters of the two parties increasingly difficult to find. Members of the American public also continued to make it clear that politics was not a solely elite concern.

In the mid–1790s the United States was still a relatively minor presence on the world stage, but relationships with foreign governments and foreign wars still possessed great power to shape the character of U.S. domestic concerns. The United States was just beginning to try to assert its power in international relations, but American citizens who inserted themselves into international conflicts mostly managed to get themselves into trouble. The United States had not yet really come into its own, but it did begin to become clear what might be necessary in order to make that possible.

On the domestic front, conflicts also seemed to have the power to threaten national stability. The ideologies of the developing political parties represented deep divisions among politicians and in popular opinion about what course the country should take, and both sides thought the other would threaten the new republic with certain ruin. The Federalists and Democratic-Republicans differed on foreign relations, economic policy, the use of federal government authority, and the popular sources of government power. As foreign and domestic conflicts tested the strength of the new American republic, the parties would vie to see who would define and control the political and social order.

## THE FRENCH REVOLUTION AND AMERICAN POLITICS

By far the international event of the greatest importance and most continuing influence on both the foreign and the domestic fortunes of the United States was the continuing course of the French Revolution. The French Revolution took a violent turn at the end of 1792, and late in January 1793 Louis XVI and Marie Antoinette, along with hundreds of French aristocrats, lost their heads to the guillotine. When the French Revolution had begun in 1789, almost everyone in the United States viewed it as a good thing, and many viewed it as an extension of the liberty that the American Revolution had brought forth into the world. However, the execution of the monarch in France, the outbreak of war between France and Great Britain, and the increasing violence and social turmoil in the later phases of the French Revolution frightened some Americans. Support for the French Revolution became a divisive rather than a unifying or nationalistic force within the United States.

Disagreements over the course of the French Revolution became an increasingly clear dividing line between Federalists and Democratic-Republicans. Democratic-Republican leaders such as Thomas Jefferson and James Madison had for years used their party newspapers to accuse rival Federalist Alexander Hamilton and many of his supporters of harboring secret monarchical and pro-British beliefs, and now the course of world affairs seemed to offer a test of their accusations. The denunciation of aristocracy in the French republic also provided additional vocabulary for American party conflict, as the Democratic-Republicans accused the Federalists of being too aristocratic, and the Federalists accused the Democratic-Republicans of supporting dangerously radical and violent democracy. Events in France became a lens through which Americans could view their own political disagreements. If the French Revolution had copied the American Revolution, then the fate of the two nations might be linked. As pro-French editor Benjamin Franklin Bache wrote in his *General Advertiser* newspaper: "Upon the establishment or overthrow of liberty in France probably will depend the permanency of the Republic in the new world."[1]

Along with the more esoteric political considerations came a real diplomatic crisis brought on by the outbreak of a world-scale war between France and Great Britain. France had been at war with Prussia for several years, but in 1793 the war widened and republican France declared war on monarchist Great Britain. Partly because U.S. merchants had been building a steady overseas trade with both countries since the end of the American Revolution, the United States had to decide how to face the war between the two world powers. The question was further complicated by the treaty of alliance between the United States and France that had been in effect since the Revolutionary War, which seemed to make it possible that France could call upon American aid in the war against Great Britain.

In spring 1793, President Washington consulted his cabinet—which continued to contain both Democratic-Republican and Federalist leaders—about how to proceed in the foreign crisis. The cabinet members, though split along party lines, all advised that the United States recognize the new French government by receiving the French foreign minister who was en route to Philadelphia, but that the United States ought to proclaim itself strictly neutral in the war. On April 22, 1793, President Washington issued a proclamation of neutrality, drafted largely by Alexander Hamilton. Even though Jefferson, as secretary of state, had supported the proclamation, the public at large (and especially many of Jefferson's supporters) were divided over its propriety and its meaning. Radical Democratic-Republican newspaper editors complained loudly that the United States was abandoning its responsibilities to repay French help in the American Revolutionary War, and members of the public and politicians like James Madison alike complained that the proclamation exceeded the legitimate constitutional authority of the presidency. Alexander Hamilton countered in the press that it was up to the president to apply laws and treaties and "he had a right, and if in his opinion the interests of the Nation required it, it was his duty, as Executor of the laws, to proclaim the neutrality of the Nation, to exhort all persons to observe it, and to warn them of the penalties which would attend its non observance."[2] Even when the legality of the neutrality proclamation seemed settled, it still remained to be seen how effectively the United States would be able to maintain a neutral position in the war.

The issue became even more complicated because of the presence of the flamboyant French minister Edmond Charles Genet, who had arrived in Charleston, South Carolina, early in April 1793 just as the president was deciding to declare neutrality. Genet had been sent to the United States by the Girondist French government to whip up support for the French Revolution in the United States, Canada, and Louisiana, and to try to negotiate a new treaty that would strengthen the French-American alliance of 1778. Genet engaged in all the tactics he could summon to promote the French cause, and he outraged U.S. federal officials when he used his authority as a French diplomat to commission four American merchant ships as French privateers, thus positioning American sailors to fight battles for the French. When Genet met with President Washington, Secretary of State Jefferson, and other American diplomats in Philadelphia in May, he demanded money for the French cause, and he published thinly veiled anonymous newspaper articles that criticized the neutrality proclamation and the president. Genet generally behaved in a manner considered outrageous and undiplomatic by American politicians, especially the Federalists, who were less disposed toward France to begin with. Within four months of Genet's arrival, President Washington had decided to ask the French government to recall him, although the Girondist government was thrown out of power by Maximilien Robespierre before it could comply.

## DEMOCRATIC POPULAR POLITICS

To many Federalists like John Jay and Rufus King, what seemed even more outrageous than Genet's obvious efforts to draw the United States into the Anglo-French War was the great public acclaim and praise that met the French minister wherever he went. Throughout the spring, as Genet made his way between Charleston, South Carolina, and the temporary capital at Philadelphia, he was met by large and boisterous crowds of men and women who took the opportunity of his appearance to celebrate publicly the French Revolution and its democratic ideals. Once in Philadelphia, Genet was further honored by public dinners and receptions, to the great embarrassment of government officials stymied by his popularity. Even though Genet's diplomatic efforts met with little success, he had no trouble recruiting Americans to subscribe to his privateering efforts, even after he was out of favor with the government.

Genet's popularity gave him more power than most political elites, even the Democratic-Republican secretary of state Thomas Jefferson, might have wished for.

The public support for Edmond Charles Genet was not an isolated political phenomenon in the mid-1790s. In the streets of Philadelphia, congressmen could observe men and women wearing French tricolored ribbon rosettes, called cockades, to express their support for the French cause. Popular celebrations such as the Fourth of July also continued to have strong French symbolism in many cities and towns, especially those with Democratic-Republican sympathies. Philadelphia shoemakers took the egalitarian message of the French Revolution to heart by forming the first organized American labor union in May 1794. The union initially met with little success in raising pay or ameliorating working conditions for shoemakers, most of whom still worked in family-owned shops, but the organization of the union indicated a will for collective action by workingmen that would become a hallmark of democratic politics in the 19th century.

The most important manifestation of a newly energized form of popular politics was the spontaneous formation of what were called Democratic-Republican Societies in towns stretching across the country. The societies, which began to form in almost every state in the spring of 1793, dedicated themselves to fighting the power of the so-called aristocracy in the United States and to evaluating the equity of U.S. government policies. The societies were not directly linked to the Democratic-Republican Party, and elite party leaders like James Monroe and Thomas Jefferson were careful to keep their distance, yet their affinities with the Democratic-Republican view of politics were clear in most cases. Many of the societies openly criticized the federal government and President Washington himself, and George Washington viewed the societies not as a positive sign of democratization in America, but rather as a potentially dangerous "self-created" democratic faction.[3] The Democratic-Republican societies did use very radical egalitarian language in a variety of public proclamations to denounce the "wellborn" and their disproportionate influence on American public life. Members of the Democratic-Republican societies feared a "natural tendency in all [governments] arising from the imperfection of human nature itself, to slide gradually into the lap of slavery," and they saw their role as associating to fight this tendency.[4]

The contentious politics of Democratic-Republican societies became an issue during the events of 1794 that came to be known as the Whiskey Rebellion. As part of Alexander Hamilton's financial program in 1791, he had convinced Congress to pass an excise tax on distilled liquor, and the tax had drawn steady protest and opposition in western territories ever since. Westerners could make far greater profits by transporting their corn crops already distilled as whiskey, and many farmers in western Pennsylvania, Virginia, Kentucky, Maryland, North Carolina, and South Carolina simply refused to pay the tax. They explained their resistance in language reminiscent of the American Revolution, but the federal government was seriously vexed by the tax avoidance—especially since the excise had been approved by congressional representatives.

In 1794, resistance to the liquor tax broke into open rebellion in western Pennsylvania when a tax collector, John Neville, pressed charges against local farmers who refused to pay their duties. In July 1794, Neville and two federal marshals were attacked, and a crowd of 500 burned Neville's house to the ground. The resistance soon spread beyond the local level when thousands of farmers marched on Pittsburgh, Pennsylvania, to continue their protest against Neville and the tax. To Alexander Hamilton, the actions of the whiskey rebels seemed to confirm that an excess of democratic rhetoric could easily get out of hand. He also maintained that several Democratic-Republican societies had helped to plot the rebellion. Hamilton prevailed upon President Washington to send troops to put down the whiskey rebels, and he personally led a force of 15,000 militia and army soldiers into Pennsylvania in September 1794.

Although the rebellion had mostly subsided by the time Hamilton and his troops arrived, the soldiers captured 20 rebels, who were put on trial for their role in violently resisting the excise tax on liquor. Smaller local rebellions had occurred in other locations, such as western Kentucky, but Hamilton hoped to make an example of the Pennsylvania whiskey rebels to put a stop to all the tax rebellion. Two Pennsylvania men were convicted. After most of the ire had died down, however, they were pardoned by George Washington in the first-ever presidential pardons.

Democratic-Republican societies, some of which had openly encouraged the whiskey rebels if not conspired with them, were largely discredited by their association with the open rebellion. In a proclamation accompanying the call-up of troops to suppress the rebellion, George Washington dubbed the rebellion "treasonous."[5] The Whiskey Rebellion exceeded the perceived limits of legitimate popular opposition to government actions, but it also had larger effects. Although Thomas Jefferson, who had left his post as secretary of state at the end of 1793, and other Democratic-Republicans had never associated themselves with the radical societies, they were quite critical of Hamilton and Washington for sending troops against American citizens. While radical newspapers publicly criticized the Federalists for abusing federal power, Hamilton's influence over George Washington became even stronger following the rebellion. For the time being, the balance between federal power and the power of the people—and between the Federalists and the Democratic-Republicans—was far from settled.

## ECONOMIC CHANGE

Although the Whiskey Rebellion signaled that the controversy over Alexander Hamilton's post-Revolutionary economic plans had not entirely subsided, some postwar economic reforms did begin to bear fruit between 1793 and 1796 as the U.S. economy expanded and changed. Government stability helped to fuel growth in exports and imports, but the Anglo-French war also threatened to put this increasing American trade in harm's way. Economic prosperity in the mid-1790s engendered both optimism and fear that the United States might fall prey to European-style luxury and corruption. Preacher Samuel Deane worried in 1795 that "prosperity is apt to bring political evils in its train; such as luxury and idleness, dissipation and extravagant expenses; which tend to, and end in, wretchedness and ruin."[6] Despite such warnings, Americans pursued ever-greater economic activity, even as many avenues of economic growth threatened to bring harsh foreign or domestic problems along with them.

Western settlers, still angry about the tax on distilled liquor, demanded full access to the Mississippi River in order to send trade goods to the Atlantic Ocean. But Spain remained firmly in control of trading rights on the Mississippi and seemed less than open to American diplomatic overtures. Northern merchants exported ship masts, fish, rum, wood, and other raw materials to Europe in exchange for increasing amounts of British and French luxury goods like cloth, books, and dishware, but at the same time this healthy trade encouraged American ship captains to take risks in the midst of naval conflict between the French and the British. In November 1793, the British government issued the Orders in Council authorizing British naval vessels to seize trading ships as part of the war effort against France, and soon they began seizing U.S. ships trading in the West Indies, although Americans claimed the right to continue full trade as a neutral power. In the midst of naval conflict, the American South continued to trade large quantities of agricultural goods (many produced with slave labor) overseas.

Labor and productivity were of utmost concern to all enterprising or entrepreneurial American citizens, but they seemed especially important in the South, where slaves represented not only a major labor force but also a form of capital investment in and of themselves. White southerners in the planter class sought new ways to wring more profits from their labor force, which led some slaveholders to relax restrictions on their bondsmen to hire out their slaves as urban skilled laborers or to seek other flexible labor arrangements. The vast majority of slaves continued to live on small farms, where wheat had surpassed tobacco as the most frequently grown agricultural product.

The cotton gin, here depicted in an 1869 *Harper's Weekly* illustration, allowed cotton to become a staple crop and allowed the slave system to expand in the American South. *(Library of Congress, Prints and Photographs Division [LC-USZ62-103801])*

By far the most important labor-maximizing development in this period was the invention of the cotton gin in 1793. Eli Whitney, who had been hired to tutor the children of wealthy South Carolinian Catherine Greene, worked with her to perfect this invention, which quickly and efficiently separated the seeds and fiber of the cotton plant and drastically reduced the amount of time it took to process raw cotton. Whitney received a patent for the gin, and although it would take several years for the mechanical separation process to revolutionize southern agriculture, eventually cotton would become a southern staple crop because of his invention. The cotton gin also led to the further entrenchment of the slave labor system in the South and the development of widespread cloth manufacturing in the North.

Both state and federal governments continued to occupy themselves with ways to exploit western lands as further sources of economic growth and future development. In 1793 Congress passed the first federal fugitive slave law, making it a crime to harbor or help fugitive slaves. This law was intended to minimize the economic effects of outlawing slavery in the Northwest Territory. Slaveholders increasingly ignored the prohibition and often brought slaves with them in the North and Southwest when looking for new agricultural land to develop. In 1796 Congress passed a land act that divided public lands into townships and sections that could be auctioned in an orderly fashion to raise public money.

Land companies and speculators continued to make huge profits by speculating on western land and settlement deals. Some deals even stretched ethical boundaries enough to threaten the public vision of republican harmony in the U.S. economy. In the most striking example of fraudulent economic development, the Yazoo land company bribed all but one member of the Georgia legislature into granting it exclusive rights to 35,000,000 acres of western land for far less than market price. Fallout from the corrupt deal mired Georgia politics in controversy until well after the War of 1812, even though Georgia ceded its remaining western lands to the federal government in 1802.

The U.S. economy prospered between 1793 and 1796, but internal and external uncertainties caused many to question the stability of U.S. economic growth. Would the republic be able to avoid corrupt excesses on the one hand and the harsh consequences of European warfare on the other?

## DIPLOMACY AND POLITICS

After Britain began seizing American ships at the end of 1793, European warfare immediately threatened to drag the United States into an economic and diplomatic crisis. Thomas Jefferson resigned as secretary of state at the end of 1793, and President Washington replaced him with another pro-French Virginian, Edmund Randolph. The crisis with Great Britain, brought on by American neutral trading and the British violations of the 1783 Treaty of Paris that had ended the Revolutionary War, demanded vigorous diplomatic attention. Randolph was not left to deal with the crisis alone. Early in 1794, President Washington sent Chief Justice of the Supreme Court John Jay to London to negotiate with the British government.

Jay negotiated a wide-reaching treaty that avoided drawing the United States into war with Great Britain, but Jay's treaty also stirred up domestic political divisions to a dangerous degree. Even though Alexander Hamilton worked secretly behind the scenes to undercut John Jay's negotiating position, Jay persuaded the British to agree to several important concessions. The British government agreed to surrender trading posts in the northwest, to recognize American rights on the Mississippi River, and to open British trade in the East Indies to U.S. merchants. The treaty did not address the bigger issues of neutral trading rights or impressment of U.S. sailors into the Royal Navy, and Jay agreed to restrict American trade in the West Indies and Caribbean.

President Washington and his cabinet kept the exact provisions of the Jay Treaty a secret from the public, but as soon as the pro-British bent of the treaty became clear in the United States, James Madison and other prominent Democratic-Republicans denounced it. James Monroe, the U.S. minister to France, and Secretary of State Randolph both worked vigorously in the Senate to defeat ratification of Jay's treaty, and their efforts were bolstered by widespread public outcry against the agreement. Angry urban crowds up and down the eastern seaboard (concentrated heavily in Democratic-Republican cities) burned Chief Justice Jay in effigy. In the capital city of Philadelphia, the British minister's office was stoned and a mob threatened Vice President Adams's house. The French foreign minister, Pierre Adet, worked openly in Congress to help defeat the treaty. On the other side, President Washington and representatives of Federalist trading interests in states like New Jersey argued strongly for ratification, and eventually they won the day when the Senate ratified the Jay Treaty by a vote of 20 to 10.

During this battle over ratification, the United States was experiencing a much more clear-cut diplomatic and military success on the western frontier in a campaign against the Miami Indian Confederacy. After the blistering defeats inflicted by Little Turtle's warriors on U.S. military forces under Josiah Harmar and Arthur St. Clair in the early 1790s, President Washington appointed former Revolutionary general "Mad" Anthony Wayne as U.S. army commander in the West with a new mandate to subdue the Indian threat. In 1793 and 1794, Wayne led a force of over 3,000 militia and army troops into the Northwest Territory against the Miami and Shawnee Confederacy forces. Where Harmar and St. Clair had failed, he succeeded with great brutality. Wayne inflicted a crushing defeat on the confederacy forces at the Battle of Fallen Timbers in August 1794. After destroying Indian villages and building a series of forts in Indiana and Ohio, Wayne signed the Treaty of Greenville the following August with representatives of 12 Northwest Indian nations. The Treaty of Greenville guaranteed to U.S. settlers access to large tracts of land in the Northwest Territory. The treaty and military defeats left many Indians embittered, a fact not lost on British commanders in Canada, who promised to help clear out U.S. settlement in the Northwest Territory if a large-scale war should ever ensue.

With U.S.-Indian relations in the Northwest temporarily pacified and stronger U.S.-British ties in place, Spain also agreed to negotiate a new treaty with the United States in 1795. Buffeted between the British and French in the Anglo-French wars, Spain was afraid that Britain and the United States might join forces to clear Spain out of Florida and other territories in the Southwest after the Jay Treaty was ratified. Increasing numbers of U.S. citizens had begun settling in Florida, and westerners constantly assailed harsh taxes and restrictions on the Mississippi trade to New Orleans. U.S. Minister Thomas

Pinckney signed a treaty with Spain in 1795 (known as Pinckney's Treaty, or the Treaty of San Lorenzo). This treaty opened the Mississippi River fully to U.S. trade, guaranteed three years of tax-free trading in New Orleans, settled the boundaries of Florida in accordance with U.S. demands, and called for Spanish cooperation in stopping southern Indian attacks on U.S. settlers. The treaty was highly beneficial to U.S. interests.

The Jay Treaty, the Treaty of Greenville, and Pinckney's Treaty all improved the international diplomatic strength of the United States, but serious threats to peace and stability still existed. Both the French and the British encouraged North African Barbary states to attack U.S. shipping in the Mediterranean, and the United States had to sign treaties with Algeria and Tripoli between 1793 and 1796 that agreed to pay large sums of tribute to keep these states from seizing American ships and sailors. When President Washington publicly revealed all the terms of the Jay Treaty in February 1796, France retaliated by invalidating all previous treaties with the United States. Tensions with France threatened to worsen. The Federalists oversaw the construction of 11 frigates to form the first peacetime navy in the United States, and it seemed increasingly likely, despite extensive diplomatic activity, that the ships might see action.

## CITIES AND POLITICS

The vast majority of Americans in the 1790s continued to spend their lives in rural areas supporting themselves as part of an interdependent network of farm families. But at the same time, American cities, fueled by the boom in international trade, began to take on added importance. Cities provided the setting for much of the national political discourse carried on in newspapers, crowd protests, and celebrations for the likes of French minister Genet. Newspapers grew as a political force in new but quickly expanding western cities such as Lexington, Kentucky, and Cincinnati, Ohio. As Americans worked through their early party conflicts, they also helped to define the political space of the early republican city.

As plans for the new capital city in Washington, D.C., proceeded haltingly, the federal government continued to be housed in Philadelphia between 1793 and 1796. The commissioners charged with managing the capital's construction faced financial difficulties, and they continued battling over the best ways to implement the plans drawn up by the temperamental Frenchman Pierre L'Enfant. The commissioners did settle on a design for the new U.S. Capitol building, when Dr. William Thornton's Roman temple design was chosen in a competition in 1793. Thomas Jefferson praised Thornton's "simple, noble, beautiful" plan, which would house the legislative branch of the U.S. government in a building suited to its republican purpose.[7] The cornerstone of the building was laid in September 1793, even though complete architectural plans had yet to be finalized and it would take decades for the building to be finished. Work also proceeded slowly on the president's home, the White House, designed by Irish architect James Hoban.

Meanwhile, federal officials in Philadelphia, and everyone else there, were drastically affected by a yellow fever epidemic that struck in September 1793. Of the approximately 48,000 people who lived in Philadelphia in 1793, more than 20,000 fled the city, and almost 4,000 died of yellow fever by the end of October.[8] Congress adjourned, and the federal government removed from the city. City officials worried that hundreds of sick people remained, as Matthew Carey put it, "without a human being to hand them a drink of water, to administer medicines, or to perform any charitable office for them."[9]

In fact, members of the city's growing free African-American population did step forward to "administer medicines" and to offer their aid to help the city survive the epidemic. Philadelphia physician Benjamin Rush, who erroneously argued that African Americans were immune to yellow fever, prevailed upon black community leaders Absalom Jones and Richard Allen to organize people to provide medical and civic aid. Jones and Allen and their organization, the Free African Society, agreed. Philadelphia African Americans provided nursing care, food, and other comforts throughout the city. Although more than 400 African Americans themselves died in the epidemic, Rush claimed that the black Philadelphians had helped to save the city.

Once the epidemic was over, Jones and Absalom capitalized on some of the goodwill of local civic and religious leaders to support them when in 1794 they founded the Bethel African Methodist Episcopal Church, the first separate black Methodist church in the nation. Other Philadelphians, however, adhered to the racist idea that the yellow fever epidemic had somehow been spread by the African-American population, either on purpose or by accident.

The racist interpretation of the help offered by black Philadelphians during the yellow fever epidemic was far from an isolated sentiment in the mid-1790s. The free black population in American cities was rising, but this did not necessarily augur a new climate of tolerance and equality. After the former slave Toussaint Louverture led a successful black rebellion against French rule in the Caribbean colony of Saint-Domingue (now known as Haiti), many former French plantation owners sought refuge in southern U.S. cities. U.S. slaveholders feared, in many cases correctly, that their own slaves would find out about the successful political slave rebellion and get ideas about overthrowing slavery in the United States. Urban slaves and free blacks did have a better chance than rural blacks to gain literacy and to communicate with black sailors who could bring news of slave rebellions from afar. American cities, especially in the South, took on a quickly changing and highly unstable racialized atmosphere, the consequences of which were not yet fully clear.

## THE ELECTION OF 1796

Despite the efforts of some close advisers to persuade him otherwise, George Washington decided to retire from national politics, and he declined to be a candidate for a third term of office as president in 1796. In September 1796, Washington published a "Farewell Address" that urged the United States to avoid the dangers of faction and to chart an independent course in international affairs. The hot debates over the Whiskey Rebellion, financial policy, and especially the Jay Treaty in the previous years, however, made it clear that party divisions had become a serious force in American politics. Alexander Hamilton had resigned as secretary of the Treasury in 1795 to practice law and to devote himself more fully to political organizing. The presidential and congressional elections of 1796 would make it clear that, despite Washington's wishes, political parties had become much better defined and more important parts of the American political system.

Although the 1796 election did not bring with it the full-scale style of electioneering that would become popular in the early 19th century, the parties did face off over a well-defined ideological gulf. The pro-English Federalists fielded Vice President John Adams as their presidential candidate, and Thomas Jefferson stood as the candidate for the pro-French Democratic-Republicans. Although the Constitution did not provide the opportunity for presidential and vice-presidential candidates to run together on one ticket, each party also chose vice-presidential candidates—South Carolinian Thomas Pinckney for the Federalists and New Yorker Aaron Burr for the Democratic-Republicans.

Even though electioneering was not very widespread, political maneuvering behind the scenes certainly affected the election results. Alexander Hamilton was confident that the Federalists would be able to control most of the presidential electors once they had been chosen by the states, even though the Democratic-Republicans seemed likely to gain seats in Congress. After the states had already begun to select their presidential electors, Hamilton decided that he preferred Thomas Pinckney to John Adams, whose stiff personality he disliked and whose commitment to strong federalism he questioned. Hamilton lobbied Federalist electors to cast their votes for Pinckney instead of Adams, and the lack of strong party organization meant that his personal appeals held considerable sway in the process.

When the electors met to cast their votes at the end of 1796, Hamilton had convinced many Federalist electors to vote for Pinckney, but not enough to change the outcome of the presidential vote. His politicking did, however, result in an unexpected outcome in the vice-presidential vote. John Adams received 71 electoral votes; Thomas Jefferson received 68. Pinckney got 59 votes, and Aaron Burr received 30. Since the Constitution specified that the candidate with the second-highest number of total electoral votes would become vice president, Jefferson was elected to that office. John Adams would become the president, and his partisan rival would be vice president.

The results of the presidential election demonstrated that party politics had arrived as a force to be reckoned with, but they also demonstrated how the full effect and organization of modern political parties eluded even Alexander Hamilton. Hamilton's political maneuvering for a rival Federalist presidential candidate had managed to get his political nemesis, Thomas Jefferson, elected vice president. The electoral vote also showed that region played a large role in the political process: Adams received no votes from electors representing southern states, and Jefferson got little support from the North.

At the end of 1796, the United States would face a future without George Washington to lead the nation. International conflicts, most especially the Anglo-French wars, continued to threaten the political, economic, and military stability of the nation, and both parties would have access to power as the international and domestic situation continued to develop.

## CHRONICLE OF EVENTS

### 1793

William Thornton is awarded first prize in the competition to design the U.S. Capitol building.

Geographer Jedidiah Morse publishes his *American Universal Geography*.

Jacob Kimball publishes his collection of songs *The Rural Harmony*.

John Bill Ricketts founds his popular circus.

Slaves in Albany, New York, revolt.

France declares war on Great Britain. The war will cause trouble for the United States, both because politicians disagree about the diplomatic response and because Americans who try to continue trading with both sides will find themselves caught in naval conflict.

Explorer Sir Alexander Mackenzie completes his coast-to-coast journey across Canada.

*January 3:* Future women's rights activist Lucretia Mott is born.

*January 9:* Frenchman Jean-Pierre Blanchard completes the first successful travel by hot air balloon in the United States. He flies 15 miles between Philadelphia and Gloucester County, New Jersey.

*January 21:* In France, Louis XVI is executed. This signals the more violent turn of the French Revolution and causes further polarization between the Federalist and Democratic-Republican Parties in the United States.

*February 1:* Eleven days after the execution of the deposed Louis XVI, France declares war on Holland and Great Britain. The United States will face foreign policy challenges for decades during a protracted series of Anglo-French wars.

*February 12:* Congress passes the first U.S. Fugitive Slave Act, which makes it a crime to help slaves escape or to harbor escapees.

*March 4:* In Philadelphia, George Washington takes the oath of office for his second term as president. John Adams continues as vice president.

*April 8:* Edmond Charles Genet (popularly known as Citizen Genet), the flamboyant French minister to the United States, arrives in Charleston, South Carolina, and begins a trip north to Philadelphia, stopping to accept public accolades and to recruit public support for the French war effort along the way. Genet eventually helps to commission 12 American ships to act as French privateers.

*April 22:* President Washington issues a Proclamation of Neutrality in the war between Great Britain and France. Democratic-Republicans, who perceive the proclamation as de facto support for the British, are outraged.

*May 18:* President Washington receives Edmond Charles Genet in Philadelphia.

*May 25:* The first Catholic ordination in the United States takes place as French émigré Father Stephen Badin becomes a priest in Baltimore, Maryland.

*June 5:* Secretary of State Thomas Jefferson informs Genet that, in keeping with the U.S. Proclamation of Neutrality, he should stop recruiting the help of U.S. citizens in the French war. Genet does not stop trying to recruit or send out American privateers.

*June 8:* Great Britain issues an Order in Council that neutral ships carrying supplies to French ports will be seized and begins harassing commercial ships sailing under the flag of the United States.

*July 31:* Thomas Jefferson submits his resignation as secretary of state.

*August 19:* Samuel Goodrich, the author of the popular 19th-century children's book series *Peter Parley*, is born.

*August 23:* Thomas Jefferson sends a letter to France requesting the recall of Edmond Charles Genet. Washington and his cabinet, especially Alexander Hamilton, have grown increasingly wary of Genet's continued efforts to thwart U.S. neutrality. By the time Washington's request reaches France, the Girondist government that had originally dispatched Genet is out of power. Genet ends up staying in the United States, marrying, and settling on a farm in New York.

*September 18:* President Washington takes part in a Masonic ceremony to lay the cornerstone of the U.S. Capitol building.

*August–October:* A yellow fever epidemic strikes Philadelphia. Almost 4,000 people die, and 20,000 flee the city. Congress adjourns until December, and most government business stops as officials depart the city.

*October 7:* General "Mad" Anthony Wayne invades Ohio Indian territory with 2,600 U.S. Army troops.

*October 28:* Eli Whitney creates the definitive version of his pioneering invention, the cotton gin.

*November 6:* The British Privy Council issues secret orders to its navy, authorizing the capture of neutral ships trading with French ports, declaring open season on U.S. traders.

*December 31:* Thomas Jefferson's resignation as secretary of state takes effect, freeing him to engage in political activities opposing the Washington administration, which he perceives as increasingly anti-French.

## 1794

The nation's first major toll road, the Philadelphia-Lancaster Turnpike, opens.

One of the first canals in the United States is constructed on the Connecticut River in Massachusetts.

Susannah Rowson's hugely popular novel *Charlotte Temple* is published. It becomes the best-selling American novel until *Uncle Tom's Cabin* surpasses it in the 1850s.

Warfare between the Arikara and Sioux Indians drives the Arikara from their land (in present-day Nebraska). They move into the area currently occupied by South Dakota.

John Trumbull finishes his painting *The Declaration of Independence,* a version of which will later hang in the rotunda of the U.S. Capitol.

*January 2:* Edmund Randolph replaces Thomas Jefferson as secretary of state.

*February:* As tensions increase between the United States and Great Britain, Sir Guy Carleton, the British governor of Lower Canada, begins negotiations with Indian enemies of the United States to gain their favor in case of a future war. He promises to return land in the Northwest Territory to Indian nations if war should come.

*February 14:* Samuel Arnold's *The Castle of Andalusia,* perhaps the first opera performed in the United States, opens at the New Theater in Philadelphia.

*February 28:* After holding its first open, public debate, the U.S. Senate refuses to seat Albert Gallatin, the Swiss-born senator-elect from Pennsylvania, ostensibly because he had resided in the United States for fewer than nine years. The refusal was also affected by Gallatin's open support of the Whiskey rebels and his opposition to Alexander Hamilton.

*March 5:* Congress submits to the states for ratification a constitutional amendment to limit the ability of foreign and U.S. citizens' power to sue states in federal courts.

*March 14:* Eli Whitney receives a patent for the cotton gin, his device that makes it possible to separate cotton seeds mechanically from cotton fiber. Whitney's employer, Catherine Greene, who helped him perfect the invention, receives no credit.

*March 27:* In the face of rising naval tensions with both Britain and France, Congress authorizes the creation of a peacetime navy. Six frigates will be constructed to protect American shipping from attacks by the British and French and by Barbary pirates.

*April 19:* Chief Justice of the United States John Jay is sent to negotiate a treaty with Great Britain, which the Washington administration hopes will avert U.S. involvement in the French-British war.

*May 1:* Journeymen cordwainers (shoemakers) in Philadelphia establish the first trade union in the United States.

*May 27:* James Monroe is appointed U.S. ambassador to France.

*May 30:* John Quincy Adams is appointed U.S. minister to the Netherlands.

*June 5:* Congress passes the Neutrality Act, which prohibits U.S. citizens from serving in foreign military service or from operating privateers for foreign governments.

*June 10:* In Philadelphia, religious and community leader Richard Allen and the members of the Free African Society found the Bethel African Methodist Episcopal Church, the denomination's first church in the United States.

*June 19:* Richard Henry Lee, Revolutionary Virginian, dies.

*July 15:* Armed resistance to the federal excise tax on whiskey coalesces into open rebellion in western Pennsylvania.

*August 7:* President Washington calls up 12,000 militia forces to put down the Whiskey Rebellion and issues a proclamation ordering the rebels to cease their resistance to the liquor tax and their armed threats against government officials. Washington also forms the first presidential commission to investigate the effectiveness of and opposition to the tax.

*August 20:* Little Turtle's band of Indian warriors from the Miami, Lenni Lenape (Delaware), Shawnee, Chippewa, Potawatomi, and Ottawa nations are defeated at the Battle of Fallen Timbers by U.S. troops commanded by General "Mad" Anthony Wayne. The battle brings closure to Little Turtle's previously suc-

This engraving, based on a portrait painted by Alonzo Chappel, depicts American general "Mad" Anthony Wayne in a heroic light. Wayne's defeat of Indian forces at the Battle of Fallen Timbers in 1794 cleared the way for major Indian concessions in the Treaty of Greenville, but it also led to future military conflict. *(Library of Congress, Prints and Photographs Division [LC-USZ62-99093])*

cessful efforts to check the settlement of U.S. citizens in much of the Northwest Territory.

*September 24:* Confident of public support for his actions, President Washington orders U.S. militia troops into action against the Whiskey Rebellion. The rebels disband before any blood is spilled.

*November 11:* The United States signs a treaty with the Six Nations creating a reservation for the Iroquois people, who give up all their claims to lands in the United States in return for yearly payments of goods and money.

*November 19:* British and U.S. diplomats sign Jay's Treaty in London, but for the time being, the treaty remains secret within the United States. The controversial treaty does not prohibit Great Britain from stopping U.S. ships or impressing American sailors,

but it does seek to settle other important commercial and navigation conflicts.

*December 14:* The town meeting of Boston asks the state legislature to repeal a 40-year-old ban on live theater performances in Massachusetts.

## 1795

The Massachusetts State House, designed by one of America's greatest architects, Charles Bulfinch, is erected.

The Georgia legislature fraudulently grants 35 million acres of land (in present-day Mississippi and Alabama) to the Yazoo Land Company, a company largely designed to make money for members of the legislature themselves.

Ezra Stiles, the president of Yale University, dies.

Gilbert Stuart completes his first portrait of George Washington, which will become one of the most copied images in American art history.

Men stop wearing powdered wigs, and women's fashions change from bulky, heavy dresses to light, clingy shifts in the French style. Fashions are influenced, in part, by the popularity of the French Revolution in American cities.

*January 31:* Controversial treasury secretary Alexander Hamilton resigns to have more time to conduct Federalist party organizing.

*February 7:* The Eleventh Amendment to the Constitution is ratified.

*May:* In Philadelphia, trials begin for those indicted for their actions during the Whiskey Rebellion.

*June 24:* After an acrimonious debate that further polarizes the political parties in Congress and in the public at large, the Senate ratifies Jay's Treaty.

*July 10:* George Washington signs the first presidential pardon for participants in the Whiskey Rebellion, including two who had been sentenced to death for treasonous acts.

*August 3:* The United States concludes the Treaty of Greenville with representatives of 12 Northwest Indian nations. The treaty, which opens large tracts of land in Ohio and the Northwest Territory to white settlement, is the outcome of the Indian defeat at the Battle of Fallen Timbers the previous year.

*September 5:* In order to attempt to avoid having U.S. ships harassed and captured by pirates, the United States signs a treaty with Algiers that authorizes the payment of an expensive annual tribute.

*October 27:* Spain fully opens the Mississippi River to American commerce for a period of three years after U.S. diplomat Thomas Pinckney signs the Treaty of San Lorenzo (known in the United States as Pinckney's treaty) with Spanish officials.

*November 2:* James K. Polk, a future president of the United States, is born in Pineville, North Carolina.

*December 10:* Timothy Pickering replaces Edmund Randolph as secretary of state.

*December 15:* Reflecting its displeasure with his opposition to Jay's Treaty, the Federalist-controlled Senate refuses to confirm John Rutledge as chief justice of the Supreme Court despite the fact that Rutledge presided over the court in August. John Jay had resigned as chief justice when he was elected governor of New York.

## 1796

The first complete American edition of the plays of William Shakespeare is published.

Amelia Simmons publishes *American Cookery,* the first American cookbook.

James Finely constructs the first major U.S. suspension bridge over Jacob's Creek in Pennsylvania.

Oliver Ellsworth is confirmed as chief justice of the Supreme Court.

The federal government establishes an arsenal at the strategic location of Harpers Ferry, Virginia (later West Virginia).

*February 25:* The first U.S. Episcopal bishop, Samuel Seabury, dies.

*February 29:* As tensions between the United States and France grow, President Washington publicly declares the terms of Jay's Treaty with Great Britain (widely interpreted as a veiled threat against Revolutionary France).

*February:* Because the United States has signed Jay's Treaty with Great Britain, France issues a proclamation abrogating all previous U.S. treaties. This move represents a break from the traditional alliance between France and the United States forged during the American Revolution.

*March 8:* The U.S. Supreme Court delivers its ruling in the case of *Hylton v. United States,* the first case in which the court directly upholds the constitutionality of a congressional act.

*March 15:* The Senate ratifies the Treaty of San Lorenzo (Pinckney's Treaty).

*May 18:* Congress passes the Land Act, which divides public land into townships and sections that can be offered for auction.

*May 19:* Congress passes a game protection law to keep Americans from hunting in Indian territory.

*June 1:* Tennessee, formerly part of western North Carolina, becomes the 16th state in the union. John Sevier, who led the attempt to break away from North Carolina and found the state of Franklin in 1783, becomes Tennessee's first governor.

*July 2:* In an open threat against U.S. trade, France declares that it will stop, search, or capture all neutral ships headed for British ports.

*July 11:* U.S. troops take possession of the British fort at Detroit as British military forces begin their

George Washington was revered as a classical hero long after he left office as president. This 19th-century sketch shows the Horoatio Greenough statue of Washington in a toga that resides in the U.S. Capitol. *(from Benson Lossing,* The Pictorial Field-Book of the Revolution, *1851–1852)*

evacuation of the Northwest Territory under the terms of Jay's Treaty.

*August 22:* James Monroe is recalled as U.S. minister to France.

*September 17:* George Washington publishes his farewell address, in which he urges American politicians to avoid political party conflict and urges them not to bow to "foreign influence."

*October 29:* The trading vessel *Otter* becomes the first U.S. ship to sail into Monterey Bay in California (then Spanish territory).

*November 4:* U.S. representatives conclude a treaty of peace with the North African state of Tripoli, which supposedly insures that Tripolitan ships will cease their harassment of American shipping and capture of American sailors. The treaty is not effective, even though the United States pays Tripoli both tribute and ransom money.

*November 8:* The electoral college elects John Adams president of the United States. Thomas Jefferson receives the second-highest number of votes and so becomes vice president, even though he and Adams belong to different political parties.

## EYEWITNESS TESTIMONY

There is no land tax among the national revenues, nor is there any interior tax, or excise upon food, drink, fuel, lights, or any native or foreign manufacture, or native or foreign production, except a duty of about four pence sterling upon domestic distilled spirits. . . . The manufactures of the United States consist generally of articles of comfort, utility, and necessity. Articles of luxury, elegance, and shew are not manufactured in America, excepting a few kinds. The manufactures of the United States have increased very rapidly since the commencement of the revolutionary war, and particularly in the last five years.

*Assistant Secretary of the Treasury Tenche Coxe, 1793, in Hart,* American History, *III: 62, 63.*

The western Indians having proposed to us a conference in Auglaise, not far distant from Detroit, in the ensuing spring, I am now about to proceed to nominate three commissioners to meet and treat with them on the subject of peace. What may be the issue of the conference it is difficult to foresee; but it is extremely essential, that, whatever it be, it should carry with it the perfect confidence of our citizens, that every endeavour has been used to obtain peace, which their interests would permit.

*George Washington in a letter to Charles Carroll of Carrollton, January 23, 1793, in Sparks,* Writings of George Washington, *X: 313.*

You may recollect that I left a memorandum of what Theo. [Burr's daughter] was to learn. I hope it has been strictly attended to . . . I am more and more struck with the . . . cursed effects of fashionable education! of which both sexes are the advocates, and yours eminently the victims. If I could foresee that Theo would become a *mere* fashionable woman, with all the attendant frivolity and vacuity of mind, adorned with whatever grace and allurement, I would earnestly pray God to take her forthwith hence. But I yet hope, by her, to convince the world what neither sex appear to believe—that women have souls!

*Aaron Burr in a letter to his wife about their daughter's education, February 8, 1793, in Davis,* Memoirs of Aaron Burr, *I: 361–362.*

All our late accounts from Europe hold up the expectation of a general war in that quarter. For the sake of humanity I hope such an event will not take place; but, if it should, I trust that we shall have too just a sense of our own interest to originate any cause, that may involve us in it. And I ardently wish we may not be forced into it by the conduct of other nations. If we are permitted to improve without interruption the great advantages, which nature and circumstances have placed within our reach, many years will not revolve before we may be ranked, not only among the most respectable, but among the happiest people on this globe.

*George Washington in a letter to David Humphreys, March 23, 1793, in Sparks,* Writings of George Washington, *X: 331.*

Whereas it appears that a state of war exists between Austria, Prussia, Sardinia, Great Britain, and the United Netherlands on the one part and France on the other, and the duty and interest of the United States require that they should with sincerity and good faith adopt and pursue a conduct friendly and impartial toward the belligerent powers: I have therefore thought fit by these presents to declare the disposition of the United States to observe the conduct aforesaid toward those powers respectively, and to exhort and warn the citizens of the United States carefully to avoid all acts and proceeding whatsoever which may in any manner tend to contravene such disposition.

*George Washington's Proclamation of Neutrality, April 22, 1793, in Commager,* Documents, *163.*

Had you, Sir, before you ventured to issue a proclamation which appears to have given much uneasiness, consulted the *general* sentiments of your fellow-citizens, you would have found them, from one extremity of the Union to the other, firmly attached to the cause of France. You would not have found them disposed to consider it as a "duty" to forget their debt of gratitude to the French nation; or to view with unconcern, the magnanimous efforts of a faithful ally, to baffle the infernal projects of those despots who have confederated for the purpose of crushing her infant liberty. . . . to such a people it would have been a pleasing circumstance, to have been able to discover in the proclamation a recognition of the treaties with France.

*"Veritas" writes to President George Washington to protest the Proclamation of Neutrality in April 1793, in Hart,* American History, *III: 305, 306.*

You will perhaps think strange to Receive a Letter from [a] poor old woman who never had the Least [acquaintance] with you; But sir when you hear my Story I am very sure you will pity me at Least; if you Can Do no more for me—my Requ[e]st is in behalf of my grand Child who was taken Prisoner by the Indians in the wilderness Last fall 2 years her name is Salley . . . I am now old and very frail and Cannot rest Contented without trying Every method in my power for her Redemption from Captivity.

*Mary Mitchell in a letter to Kentucky governor Isaac Shelby, May 1, 1793. Available online. Library of Congress American Memory Project. URL: http://memory.loc.gov/cgi-bin/query/r?ammem/ faw:@field(DOCID+icufawcmc0023).*

The genuine display of affection for the cause of France, by the citizens, on the arrival of the minister [Genet], has once more banished aristocracy, and hailed equality triumphant. The bosoms of many hundred freemen beat high with affectionate transport, their souls caught the celestial fire of struggling liberty, and in the enthusiasm of emotion, they communicated their feelings to the worthy and amicable representative of the French nation.

*An "Old Soldier" writes in the* National Gazette, *May 22, 1793, in Waldstreicher,* In the Midst, *135.*

You must not make your final exit from public life till it will be marked with justifying circumstances which all good citizens will respect, and to which your friends can appeal. At the present crisis, what would the former think? What could the latter say? . . . I am anxious to see what reception Genet will find in Philadelphia. . . . I think it certain that he will be misled if he takes either the fashionable cant of the cities, or the cold caution of the Government, for the sense of the public.

*James Madison in a letter to Thomas Jefferson, May 27, 1793, in* Letters and Other Writings of James Madison, *I: 579–580.*

Every Gazette I see . . . exhibits a spirit of criticism on the Anglified complexion charged on the Executive politics. I regret extremely the position into which the President has been thrown. The unpopular cause of Anglomany is openly laying claim to him. . . . The proclamation was, in truth, a most unfortunate error. . . . It is mortifying to the real friends of the President that his fame and his influence should have

been unnecessarily made to depend in any degree on political events in a foreign quarter of the Globe.

*James Madison in a letter to Thomas Jefferson, June 19, 1793, in* Letters and Other Writings of James Madison, *I: 584.*

I had scarcely become settled in Philadelphia when in July, 1793, the yellow fever broke out, and, spreading rapidly in August, obliged all the citizens who could remove to seek safety in the country. . . . The horrors of this memorable affliction were extensive and heart-rending. Nor were they softened by professional skill. The disorder was in a great measure a stranger to our climate, and was awkwardly treated. Its rapid march, being from ten victims a day in August to one hundred a day in October, terrified the physicians, and led them into contradictory modes of treatment. . . . No hospitals or hospital stores were in readiness to alleviate the sufferings of the poor. For a long time nothing could be done other than to furnish coffins for the dead and men to bury them.

*Philadelphia merchant Samuel Breck, July 1793, in Hart,* American History, *III: 39, 40.*

What is to be done in the case of the *Little Sarah* now at Chester? Is the minister of the French Republic [Genet] to set the acts of this government at defiance *with impunity?* And then threaten the executive with an appeal to the people? What must the world think of such conduct, and of the government of the United States in submitting to it? These are serious questions.

*President George Washington to Secretary of State Thomas Jefferson in a letter, July 11, 1793, in Sparks, Writings of George Washington, X: 355–356.*

Money, to us, is of no value, & to most of us unknown, and as no consideration whatever can induce us to sell the lands on which we get sustenance for our women and children; we hope we may be allowed to point out a mode by which your settlers may be easily removed, and peace thereby obtained . . . We know that these settlers are poor, or they would never have ventured to live in a country which have been in continual trouble ever since they crossed the Ohio; divide therefore this large sum of money which you have offered to us, among these people . . . You have talked to us about concessions. It appears strange that you should expect any from us, who have only been defending our just Rights against your invasion; we want Peace; Restore to us our Country and we shall be Enemies no longer.

*Response of the Iroquois Council to American commissioners seeking to buy land west of the Ohio, August 16, 1793, in Van Evry,* Ark of Empire, *281.*

The President's House is ¾ of a mile East of the Creek dividing the City from Georgetown and one Mile from the River on a Hill yielding a sharp declivity to the River & commanding a fine view for several miles. . . . The Basement Story was laid & built of grayish white free Stone handsomely polished . . . the Front is a circular Room projecting from the House.

*Traveler James Kent describes the almost complete White House in his diary, September 1793, in Seale,* The President's House, *I: 59.*

The conduct of Genet . . . and his proceedings as exhibited in the newspapers, is as unaccountable as it is distressing. The effect is beginning to be strongly felt here, in the surprise and disgust of those who are attached to the French cause, and viewed this Minister as the instrument for cementing, instead of alienating the two Republics. These sensations are powerfully reinforced by the general and habitual veneration for the President.

*James Madison in a letter to Thomas Jefferson, September 2, 1793, in* Letters and Other Writings of James Madison, *I: 596.*

I have been extremely wounded, sir . . . that the President of the United States . . . did not speak to me at my first audience, but of the friendship of the United States towards France, without saying a word to me, without enouncing a single sentiment on our revolution; while all the towns, from Charleston to Philadelphia, had made the air resound with their most ardent wishes for the French republic . . . That, by instructions from the President of the United States, the American citizens who ranged themselves under the banners of France have been prosecuted and arrested; a crime against liberty unheard of. . . . I have done strictly my duty; I have defended my ground; and I will suffer no precedent against any of the rights of the French People while there remains to me a breath of life . . .

*Edmond Charles Genet in a letter to Thomas Jefferson protesting his treatment by George Washington's government and the fact that he has been recalled as French minister to the United States, September 18, 1793, in Hart,* American History, *III: 308, 309.*

This powerful nation [France] continues its friendship for the United States. It is a friendship of the utmost importance to our security, and should be carefully cultivated. Britain has not yet well digested the loss of its dominion over us; and has at times some flattering hopes of recovering it. Accidents may increase those hopes, and encourage dangerous attempts. A breach between us and France would infallibly bring the English again on our backs; and yet we have some wild beasts among our countrymen, who are endeavoring to weaken that connexion.

*An anonymous Democratic Republican in the* Pittsburgh Gazette, *December 14, 1793, in Link,* Democratic-Republican Societies, *54.*

Early in September [1793], a solicitation appeared in the public papers, to the people of colour to come forward and assist the distressed, perishing, and neglected sick; with a kind assurance, that people of our colour were not liable to take the infection . . . The black people were looked to. We then offered our services in the public papers, by advertising that we would remove the dead and procure nurses. Our services were the production of real sensibility;—we sought not fee nor reward, until the increase of the disorder rendered our labour so arduous that we were not adequate to the service we had assumed . . . Thus were our services extorted *at the peril of our lives,* yet you accuse us of exorting [sic] a *little money from you.*

*Absalom Jones and Richard Allen protest the treatment of African Americans during the Philadelphia yellow fever epidemic, 1794, in Aptheker,* Documentary History of the Negro People, *32–33, 36.*

Small riverboats like this one were used to ply tons of trade goods up and down the Mississippi River in the late 18th and early 19th centuries. *(from Benson Lossing,* The Pictorial Field-Book of the Revolution, *1851–1852)*

. . . about 1794, whiskey found a market at New Orleans. The first New Orleans boat from our section of the state was built at General Scott's landing, which was on the Kentucky river . . . The first cargo was made up of flour, whiskey and Irish potatoes.

*Kentuckian Allen Trimble reports on the opening of trade with New Orleans in his autobiography, 1794, in Appleby,* Recollections, *196.*

I yesterday received, with sincere regret, your resignation of the office of Secretary of State. It has been impossible to prevail upon you to forego any longer the indulgence of your desire for private life, the event, however anxious I am to avert it, must be submitted to. But I cannot suffer you to leave your station without assuring you, that the opinion, which I had formed of your integrity and talents, and which dictated your original nomination, has been confirmed by the fullest experience; and that both have been eminently displayed in the discharge of your duty.

*President George Washington accepting the resignation of Secretary of State Thomas Jefferson, January 1, 1794, in Sparks,* Writings of George Washington, *X: 390–391.*

[The West is] the grand nursery of the growing strength and future athletic power of America. Here will be her riches, here her population and here her weight in the great scale of political influence.

*South Carolinian Alexander Moultrie in a letter to Edmond Genet, January 9, 1794, in Link,* Democratic-Republican Societies, *66.*

Thear [sic] is a new French minister [Fauchet] arrived about ten days agoe—he seems to be a plain grave and good looking man.—but can't speak a word of English—he will soon learn if he stays hear, as far as we can judge from his looks, and manners he is a very agreeable a man.

*Martha Washington in a letter to Fanny Bassett Washington, March 2, 1794, in Fields,* Worthy Partner, *260.*

The Democratic and Republican Societies of the United States—May they preserve and disseminate their principles, undaunted by the frowns of power, uncontaminated by the luxury of aristocracy, until the Rights of Man shall become the supreme law of every land, and their separate fraternities be absorbed in one great democratic society comprehending the human race.

*A Philadelphia Democratic-Republican Society toast published in the* American Daily Advertiser, *May 5, 1794, in Link,* Democratic-Republican Societies, *109.*

We have observed with great pain that our councils want the integrity of spirit of republicans. This we attribute to the pernicious influence of stockholders or their subordinates; and our minds feel this with so much indignity, that we are almost ready to wish for a state of revolution and the guillotine of France for a short space in order to inflict punishment on the miscreants that enervate and disgrace our governments.

*The declaration of a meeting of Democratic Society delegates in Allegheny County, Pennsylvania, published in the* Gazette of the United States, *May 5, 1794, in Baldwin,* Whiskey Rebels, *98.*

This engraving, based upon a Gilbert Stuart portrait, portrays Martha Washington as the mild, supportive, motherly figure that characterized her public reputation, especially after her husband left office. *(Library of Congress, Prints and Photographs Division [LC-USZ62-3833])*

The baneful influence of war in Europe, has already too far extended itself into this remote region. A war of Kings and Nobles against the Equal Rights of Men. Their first object was to controul the common right of all civil societies, by frustrating the attempt of a magnanimous nation, to establish a Constitution of government for themselves, according to their own mind: More lately the nefarious design has been to crush the new formed Republic in its infancy . . . Great Britain takes an active part . . . But, whilst we have preserved the most strict neutrality towards the belligerent powers of Europe, in observance of the treaties made under the authority of the United States . . . [Britain] has employed her naval force in committing depredations on our lawful and unprotected commerce. Thus in fact, she has commenced hostilities. The Federal Government, although very solicitous if possible, to prevent the calamities of war, have mediated measures preparatory for the event.

*Samuel Adams to the legislature of Massachusetts, May 31, 1794, in Cushing,* The Writings of Samuel Adams, *IV: 364, 365.*

I felt myself mad with passion. I thought 250 dollars would ruin me; and to have to go [to] the federal court, at Philadelphia, would keep me from going to Kentucky this fall, after I had sold my plantation, and was getting ready. I felt my blood boil, at seeing general Neville along, to pilot the sheriff to my very door.

*Whiskey Rebellion leader William Miller on how he felt just before he refused a writ to make him pay his excise tax, July 15, 1794, in Baldwin,* Whiskey Rebels, *113–114.*

The four most Western Counties of Pennsylvania since the Commencement of those laws a period of more than three Years, have been in steady and Violent Opposition to them. . . . The Opposition has continued and matured, till it has at length broke out in Acts which are presumed to amount to Treason. Armed Collections of men, with the avowed design of Opposing the execution of the laws, have attacked the house of the Inspector of the Revenue, burnt and destroyed his Property and Shed the blood of Persons engaged in its defense. . . . a competent force of Militia should be called forth and employed to suppress the insurrection and support the Civil Authority in effectuating Obedience to the laws and the punish-

ment of Offenders . . . The force ought if attainable to be an imposing one, such if practicable, as will deter from opposition, save the effusion of the blood of Citizens and secure the object to be accomplished.

*Alexander Hamilton urges action against the Whiskey Rebellion in a letter to George Washington, August 2, 1794, in Freeman,* Alexander Hamilton, *823, 824, 825.*

Whereas combinations to defeat the execution of the laws laying duties upon spirits distilled within the United States and upon stills have from the time of the commencement of those laws existed in some of the western parts of Pennsylvania . . . it is in my judgment necessary under the circumstances of the case to take measures for calling forth the militia in order to suppress the combinations aforesaid, and to cause the laws to be duly executed . . .

*George Washington's proclamation calling out the militia to suppress the Whiskey Rebellion, August 7, 1794, in Commager,* Documents, *163–164.*

Your late orders for a detachment of militia, and your proclamation, give birth to a variety of sensations and opinions. All good citizens deplore the events, which have produced this conduct on your part . . . the great body of this State will exert themselves in whatever way you may direct, to the utmost of their power.

*Virginia Governor Henry Lee in a letter to President George Washington, August 17, 1794, in Sparks,* Writings of George Washington, *X: 560.*

It is with equal pride and satisfaction I add, that, as far as my information extends, this insurrection [the Whiskey Rebellion] is viewed with universal indignation and abhorrence, except by those, who have never missed an opportunity by side blows or otherwise to attack the general government. . . . I consider this insurrection as the first formidable fruit of the Democratic Societies, brought forth, I believe, too prematurely for their own views, which may contribute to the annihilation of them.

*President George Washington in a letter to Virginia Governor Henry Lee, August 26, 1794, in Sparks,* Writings of George Washington, *X: 429.*

Were it not then that I am principled against selling negroes, as you would do cattle at market, I would not in twelve months hence, be possessed of a single one as a slave. I shall be happily mistaken if they are not found to be a very troublesome species of property ere many years have passed over our heads.

*George Washington in a letter to Alexander Spotswood, November 23, 1794, in Phillips,* Plantation and Frontier, *II: 56.*

Many persons have been indicted in the Courts here for offenses in the late troubles [the Whiskey Rebellion]. I shall only mention, particularly, the persons who insulted the Commissioners at Greensburgh. I will further observe that the Grand Juries in the several counties have given such specimens of their sense of duty, as will justify at any future occasion, a confidence in the juries of this country in the most popular cases . . .

*A report in the Philadelphia* Aurora, *January 28, 1795, in Boyd,* The Whiskey Rebellion, *176.*

I have been so unhappy at Mrs. Woodbridges that I was obliged to leeve thare . . . But my Little son Jupiter who is now with Mrs. Woodbridge is my greatest care and from what she says and from the useage he meets with there is so trying to me that I am all most distracted. [T]herefore if you will be so kind as to write me how Long Jupiter is to remain with them as she tell me he is to live with her untill he is twenty five years of age. [T]his is something that I had no idea of. I all ways thought that he was to rcturn with me to new england or at Longest only ten years . . . I had much rather he wold return and Live with you as she allows all her sons to thump and beat him the same as if he was a Dog . . .

*Slave and mother Judith Cocks in a letter to Connecticut congressman James Hillhouse, March 8, 1795, in Blassingame,* Slave Testimony, *7.*

I mentioned in my last [letter] that the [Jay] Treaty was come, but kept a profound secret. In that state it remains. Its contents have produced conjectural comments without number. . . . I should hope it to be impossible that any stipulation, if any should be attempted, inconsistent with the Treaties with France, can ever be pursued into effect. I cannot even believe that such stipulation would be hazarded. The President, to say nothing of the people, would so certainly revolt at it, that more than wickedness would be requisite in the authors. At the same time, it is possible that articles may be included that will be ominous to

the confidence and cordiality of France towards the United States.

*James Madison in a letter to James Monroe, March 26, 1795, in* Letters and Other Writings of James Madison, *II: 41.*

I will now show you our colors, that you may know them to-morrow; formerly, they were displayed as ensigns of war and battle; now, they will be exhibited as emblems of peace and happiness. This Eagle, which you now see, holds close his bunch of arrows, whilst he seems to stretch forth, as a more valuable offering, the estimable branch of peace; the Great Spirit seems disposed to incline us all, to repose, for the future, under its grateful shade, and wisely enjoy the blessings which attend it.

*General Anthony Wayne displaying his flag to Little Turtle at the negotiations for the Treaty of Greenville, July 3, 1795, in Cayton,* Frontier Indiana, *165.*

Our tomahawk yet remains in your head; the English gave it to me to place there. Elder Brother: I now take the tomahawk out of your head; but with so much care, that you shall not feel pain or injury. I will now tear a big tree up by the roots, and throw the hatchet into the cavity which they occupied, where the waters will wash it away where it can never be found. Now I have buried the hatchet and I expect that none of my color will ever again find it out . . .

*Wyandot leader Tarke calling for peace and assenting to the land cessions in the Treaty of Greenville, July 1795, in Quaife,* Chicago, *124.*

. . . Washington ratified the Treaty with Britain & Hammond the British minister here immediately sail'd for England. Washington now defies the whole Sovreign [sic] that made him what he is—and can unmake him again. Better his hand had been cut off when his glory was at its height before he blasted all his Laurels!

*Massachusetts physician Nathaniel Ames in his diary, August 14, 1795, in Hart,* American History, *III: 336–337.*

The present period very forcibly evinces the justice of your remark "that science is the truest security of liberty," for if so great a body of ignorance as has been produced against the Treaty should be *in constant requisition* against every other act of government, we should soon have no government or Liberty left. It is lamentable to see the precipitancy, folly, and indecency with which so many rush into the condemnation of a measure . . . I wish the dignity of the President's answer may calm the motions of those who run after the cry of "liberty" and "constitution," without knowing what either means, and when they are at the same instant in the direct train to the most effectual measures to destroy both.

*Judge James Iredell in a letter to William Samuel Johnson, August 17, 1795, in Beardsley,* Life and Times of William Samuel Johnson, *139–140.*

According to the previous notification to the Senators, that branch assembled on the 28th of June . . . [and] after a few weeks consultation, ratified the Treaty, as you have seen. The injunction of secrecy was then dissolved by a full House, and quickly after restored, sub modo, in a thin one. Mr. Mason, disregarding the latter vote, sent the Treaty to the press, from whence it flew with an electric velocity to every part of the Union. The first impression was universally and simultaneously against it. Even the mercantile body, with the exception of Foreigners and demi-Americans, joined in the general condemnation. . . . As soon as it was known that the President had yielded his ratification, the British party were reinforced by those who bowed to the name of constituted authority, and those who are implicitly devoted to the President.

*James Madison in a letter to James Monroe, December 20, 1795, in* Letters and Other Writings of James Madison, *II: 64–65.*

Every day of age, is a day of strength to the [Jay] Treaty: not on account of the daily discovery of intrinsic merit but on account of the astonishing exertions and artifices employed to give it efficacy.

*Congressman William Branch Giles in a letter to Thomas Jefferson, December 20, 1795, in Combs,* The Jay Treaty, *172–173.*

The Treaty with Spain arrived on Tuesday last. It adjust[s] both the boundary and navigation in a very satisfactory manner. I have not yet been able to decide whether, on the latter point, it clashes or not with the British Treaty . . . The Algerine Treaty has some curious features. Among others, the sum of one million paid for the ransom and the peace does not appear before the Senate as any part of the Treaty, but has been paid as a

verbal part of the Contract. . . . The President's birthday has been celebrated with unexampled splendor. . . . It is remarkable, however, that the annual motion to adjourn for half an hour to pay the compliment of the day was rejected this year by 50 vs. 38.

*James Madison in a letter to Thomas Jefferson, February 29, 1796, in* Letters and Other Writings of James Madison, *II: 85.*

All Vessels belonging to the Citizens of the United States of North America Shall be permitted to enter the Different ports of the Regency to trade with our Subjects or any other Persons residing within our Jurisdiction . . . No Commander of any Cruiser belonging to this Regency shall be allowed to take any person of whatever Nation or denomination out of any Vessel belonging to the United States of North America in order to Examine them or under pretence of making them confess any thing desired neither shall they inflict any corporal punishment or any way else molest them.

Treaty of Peace and Amity between the United States *and Algiers, Proclaimed March 7, 1796. Available online. Avalon Project. URL:http://www.yale.edu/lawweb/avalon/diplomacy/barbary/bar1795t.htm.*

The Bill establishing Offices for the Sale of Land on the North West side of the River Ohio, has undergone the Discussion of 8 days, and a variety of Amendments . . . This Bill I have ever considered of the highest magnitude and importance, and I have strictly adhered to three principles in its Progress—1st. To exclude Monopoly as unfavorable to Liberty—2dly. So to lay off the Tracts as to accommodate the Grand Yeomanry of this Country by fixing the quantum so small as to place Purchases within the reach of their Pecuniary Resources— and 3dly. To adopt the mode the best calculated to render the Sales productive to our Treasury and at the same time correspondent with the above Principles.

*Virginia congressman Samuel J. Cabell in a circular letter to his constituents, March 7, 1796, in Cunningham,* Circular Letters, *I: 41.*

The People are alarmed and Petitions are coming from all Quarters, mostly in favor of the Treaty. . . . Mr. Madison looks worried to death. Pale, withered, haggard.

*John Adams in a letter to Abigail Adams, April 28, 1796, in Combs,* The Jay Treaty, *185.*

I have already intimated to you the danger of parties in the State, with particular reference to the founding of them on geographical discriminations. Let me now take a more comprehensive view, and warn you in the most solemn manner against the baneful effects of the spirit of party generally. . . . It serves always to distract the public councils and enfeeble the public administration. It agitates the community with ill-founded jealousies and false alarms; kindles the animosity of one part against another; foments occasional riot and insurrection. It opens the door to foreign influence and corruption, which find a facilitated access to the government itself through the channels of party passion. Thus the policy and the will of one country are subjected to the policy and will of another. . . .

> *George Washington's Farewell Address, September 17, 1796, in Commager, Documents, 170–171.*

Thair seems to Be no fear of God or but very little, in this place Religion is much oute [sic] of fashion. Sabbath Days are visiting or working Days with the biggest part of the people.

> *Vermonter Anna H. Weeks in a letter to Holland Weeks, October 20, 1796, in Link, Democratic-Republican Societies, 120.*

Exitus in dubio is still the motto to the election. You *must* reconcile yourself to the secondary, as well as the primary station, if that should be your lot. The prevailing idea is that Pinckney will have the greatest number of votes, and I think that Adams will be most likely to stand next. There are other calculations, however, less favorable to both.

> *James Madison in a letter to Thomas Jefferson, December 10, 1796, in Letters and Other Writings of James Madison, II: 107.*

This 19th-century engraving depicts a group of tourists visiting the ruins of the Revolutionary Fort Ticonderoga in New York State. Although the United States was changing rapidly, George Washington hoped in his farewell address that Americans would continue to pursue the unblemished ideals of the Revolution. *(from Benson Lossing,* The Pictorial Field-Book of the Revolution, *1851–1852)*

At end of year after violent conflict between partizans for French & Britons thro' United States to get President & Vice President it is confidently affirmed that Adams an aristocratic Lawyer in favor of British Dignities manners & Government will be President—And Jefferson late Gov. of Virginia a firm supporter of the Rights of Man & admirer of the French Revolution will be Vice President, which I hope will introduce him to be finally President & prevent a threatened war with France . . .

> *Massachusetts physician Nathaniel Ames in his diary, December 1796, in Hart, American History, III: 337.*

# 5

# Federalist Disorder
## 1797–1800

The hard-won diplomacy of the previous few years brought on a relatively stable relationship between the United States and Great Britain by 1797. Negotiations, military advances, and treaties also ushered in a period of rapproachment with western Indians and with Spain. But all was not calm, on either the foreign or the domestic front. While the Jay's Treaty stabilized relations with Great Britain, it served to worsen the U.S. relationship with France, which was still engaged in a series of revolutionary wars against Great Britain. And while John Adams (who became president in 1797) remained committed to George Washington's vision of a partyless system of American politics, the tensions with France constantly threatened to break into open war and stirred up the party contest between Federalists and Democratic-Republicans to new heights. The United States had achieved some stability as a nation, but international challenges precluded domestic tranquility.

## FRENCH DIPLOMACY AND THE XYZ AFFAIR

Although Alexander Hamilton held no official post in the first Adams cabinet, he continued to exercise a strong influence over the policies pursued by the executive branch of government. Hamilton did not always agree with President Adams about the course the nation should take. Nor did Hamilton think highly of President Adams, whom he had opposed in the 1796 presidential election. Hamilton agreed even less with his traditional partisan nemesis, Vice President Thomas Jefferson, and although President Adams initially sought to bring Jefferson into government decision making, he was soon alienated by other cabinet officials under Hamilton's influence, especially the strong Federalist secretary of state Timothy Pickering.

The pro-British stance of the Adams cabinet became immediately significant, given a dramatic increase in tensions between the United States and France. President Adams was hoping to avoid increased U.S. involvement in the Anglo-French wars, but the terms of the pro-British Jay Treaty that he inherited from George Washington and the second U.S. Congress made entanglement in foreign warfare impossible to avoid. Even from the beginning of 1797,

This 19th-century lithograph copies Gilbert Stuart's presidential portrait of John Adams. *(Library of Congress, Prints and Photographs Division [LC-USZ62-3992])*

before Adams was inaugurated in March, the French began seizing American ships and goods. France declared open season on American traders, who claimed to have rights to trade as neutrals in the Anglo-French wars with both Great Britain and France. The French, rather, viewed American trade as helping the cause of Great Britain, and they took the U.S. Congress's rejection of the 1778 alliance between France and the United States as an open invitation to hostilities.

By the time Adams became president, the French had already seized hundreds of U.S. ships, and at the beginning of March 1797 they threatened even greater intervention to halt the growing U.S. international trade, particularly with Great Britain. Adams, unlike some of his more staunch Federalist advisers, was determined to avoid open war with France. He wrote to his son: "My entrance into office is marked by a misunderstanding with France, which I shall endeavour to reconcile, provided that no violation of faith, no stain upon honor is exacted."[1] Adams called Congress into a special session in May 1797 with hopes that bipartisan legislation might empower him to calm the French situation.

But Federalists and Democratic-Republicans in Congress were not willing to work together in harmony, in part because they did possess very different views of France and its commercial grievances. President Adams wished to negotiate with the French, but he also called for U.S. military forces to be strengthened as a backup measure. Congress authorized construction of three modern and effective naval frigates, but Democratic-Republicans opposed Federalist efforts to build up the U.S. Army as well. With bipartisan cooperation seemingly nonexistent in Congress, Adams appointed a special diplomatic mission to France and sent a negotiating team, as the historian Reginald Horsman put it, to "convince the French that Jay's Treaty did not mean that the United States was now siding with Great Britain in the European war."[2] France had refused to receive Charles Cotesworth Pinckney as U.S. minister, but now Adams sent Virginia Federalist John Marshall and Massachusetts Democratic-Republican Elbridge Gerry to join him with the hope that the three-man team could reason with French foreign minister Charles-Maurice de Talleyrand.

The American diplomats met with great resistance from the very first, and as they became embroiled in what became known as the XYZ affair, their mission did nothing but enflame the anti-French sentiments within the United States. When the American negotiators arrived in Paris in October 1797, Talleyrand sent three agents named Bellamy, Hauteval, and Hottinguer (subsequently identified in American dispatches only as X, Y, and Z) to negotiate on the terms under which he would agree to meet them. The French agents demanded a loan of $12 million and a personal payment of $200,000 to Talleyrand before any negotiations could commence. The Americans, outraged, refused to pay what they viewed as blatant bribes.

President Adams reported to Congress in May 1798 that the French negotiations had failed. One month later, when the dispatches sent by Pinckney, Marshall, and Gerry describing the behavior of the French government were published in the United States, the public—and most especially Federalist politicians—were outraged. Federalists in Congress, with some considerable support from Democratic-Republicans, called for war against France. Congress established a Navy Department and appropriated money to increase dramatically the number of ships in the navy. Federalist legislators pushed ever harder to bolster army forces, though the Democratic-Republicans still resisted the idea of building a huge standing army (which seemed out of keeping with U.S. principles of republicanism). Congress also repealed all remaining treaties with France and prepared to defend American shipping against new French attacks.

## THE QUASI-WAR WITH FRANCE AND DOMESTIC DIVISIONS

After the public exposure of the XYZ affair, the United States entered two years of undeclared naval war with France. Although technically still neutral in the Anglo-French wars, the United States fought several pitched naval battles in the Caribbean against the French and commissioned privateers (private merchant ships sailing under the protection of the U.S. flag) to capture ships trading French goods. The French seized far more American merchant ships than the Americans did French, but the French government devoted few official resources to the naval conflict with the United States, and U.S. ships triumphed in each of the three major battles they fought with French ships of the line. The military battles in the Quasi-War with France caused turmoil in American shipping, and enhanced the power of the U.S. Navy and the newly created U.S. merchant marine, but the most dramatic effects of the Quasi-War were felt on the domestic front.

Congress was unwilling to create a huge army to fight any potential land war against France, but it did authorize 10,000 men to form a reserve army and augment the militia to 80,000 men in June 1798. Enthusiastic volunteers turned out for militia service around the country, particularly in northern areas loyal to the Federalists, and anti-French military displays became a regular feature at public celebrations, dinners, and parades.[3] But public support for military actions against France was far from universal, and the Quasi-War caused unrest in several cities. Rival pro-British and pro-French crowds clashed in the streets of Philadelphia until the militia had to be called out to restore public order. New York and Philadelphia theater audiences at largely segregated Federalist and Democratic-Republican theaters vied to outdo one another in patriotic outbursts and enthusiastic revelry. Belligerent crowds gathered to sing the patriotic song "Hail, Columbia," written by Charles Hopkinson as an anti-French anthem. Southern cities, such as Charleston, South Carolina, which had a sizable French population, were strongly Democratic-Republican, so the war against France found much less public support there as political divisions continued to exacerbate regional differences between North and South. The nation's newspapers, which had been growing in number, political vigor, and influence since the early 1790s, added to the sense of crisis by publishing daily denunciations of their local political enemies as well as of both France and Great Britain.

As the war frenzy against France and the competing pro-French sentiment continued to stir up the American public, Federalists in Congress sought to impose order on the domestic situation by passing a series of laws known collectively as the Alien and Sedition Acts. The Alien and Sedition Acts curtailed certain civil liberties and provided the Federalists means to control the domestic political scene, all with the rationale that the state of war with France demanded such actions. The provisions and enforcement of the Alien and Sedition Acts were so severe, however, that they caused controversy over whether the acts were constitutional or not. Reactions to the Alien and Sedition Acts further polarized U.S. domestic politics.

William Dunlap was one of the most successful playwrights, theater managers, and artistic entrepreneurs of the early national period. In 1798 and 1799, his play *André* was part of the public culture that allowed people to express their feelings about the Quasi-War with France. *(Library of Congress, Prints and Photographs Division [LC-USZ62-77612])*

Certainly the Alien and Sedition Acts were restrictive. The Naturalization Act of 1798 lengthened the amount of time an "alien" immigrant had to live in the United States before he could apply for citizenship from five to 14 years. Subsequent Alien acts not only made the naturalization process more complex but denied immigrants from "enemy" states the right to apply for citizenship altogether. Congress also granted the president wide powers to detain or deport any aliens whom he regarded as "dangerous to the peace and safety of the United States," which designation was left entirely up to his discretion. The Sedition Act, passed in July 1798, authorized prosecution and imprisonment of anyone, either alien or citizen, who sought to interfere with the operations of the U.S. government or who spoke or published false or malicious statements about U.S. government officials or their actions. The Sedition Act also prohibited public assemblies "with intent to oppose any measure . . . of the government."

Partisan tensions had already built to a fever pitch by the time the Alien and Sedition Acts were passed—in January 1798 Federalist Roger Griswold and Democratic-Republican Matthew Lyon had come to blows on the floor of the House of Representatives—but the fallout of restrictive legislation tore the two parties further apart than ever. Vermont congressman Lyon, who published a radical Anti-Federalist magazine called *The Scourge of Aristocracy,* and who had long characterized Alexander Hamilton and his political allies as "a set of aristocrats," was convicted of seditious libel under the Sedition Act in October 1798; when Lyon was imprisoned for four months, he became an even bigger martyr to the Democratic-Republican cause.[4] Several newspaper publishers, including Thomas Cooper and Anthony Haswell, were also prosecuted, imprisoned, and fined for publishing pieces critical of the government and its anti-French activities. Democratic-Republicans were outraged at these developments, many of which were aimed directly at sapping their political support, and even party leaders Thomas Jefferson and James Madison, who had remained apart from other public party actions such as Democratic-Republican societies earlier in the 1790s, sought new avenues of political action against the Federalist-controlled Congress.

Madison and Jefferson turned to the states to oppose the Alien and Sedition Acts. Jefferson, even though he was vice president of the United States, secretly authored a set of resolutions introduced into the Kentucky legislature by John C. Breckinridge on November 16, 1798, that denounced the Alien and Sedition Acts as unconstitutional. James Madison authored a similar set of resolutions passed in Virginia in December that announced the state's right and intention to resist enforcing federal acts it determined to be unconstitutional. A second set of Kentucky resolutions in November 1799 clearly declared that a state could nullify an unconstitutional federal law. New Hampshire and other northern states passed competing resolutions denying the right of states to nullify federal laws and calling on the courts to decide issues of legislative constitutionality. The principle of judicial review was not yet fully established, however, and the federal courts were so fully controlled by Federalist judges that southern Democratic-Republicans held little hope of successfully challenging the Alien and Sedition Acts in court.

Although later movements by states to nullify federal law, especially movements designed to protect the institution of slavery, would cite the Virginia and Kentucky resolutions as precedent, Madison and Jefferson never claimed that the resolutions sought to weaken the union. The states' actions seemed very bound to the political climate during the Quasi-War with France. The Alien and Sedition Acts remained in effect until they were repealed by the Democratic-Republican Congress that took power after Jefferson's inauguration in 1801.

## RESOLUTION OF THE FRENCH CRISIS

Even as domestic tensions over the politics of the French conflict accelerated, President Adams continued to seek new avenues to end the military clash with France. Relying on a message from his minister to The Hague in October 1798, Adams believed that the French were open to negotiation despite the tensions caused by the XYZ affair and the continuing naval clashes. In February 1799, Adams nominated William Vans Murray to be the new minister to France and announced his intentions to send Vans Murray to reopen peace talks with France. Facing overwhelming pressure from members of his own party, led by Alexander Hamilton, who opposed the French mission, Adams retired to his private home in Quincy, Massachusetts, for seven months. There he relied on his wife, Abigail, for political and domestic comfort against their attacks. In September 1799, Adams rejoined the cabinet and ordered new diplomats to France to reopen negotiations immediately.[5]

Adams's new peace mission to France succeeded in quelling military conflict with France. William Vans Murray and the other Americans sent to France in 1799 were received by the French government, and they negotiated an end to the naval war in early 1800. In September 1800, the two nations signed the Treaty of Mortefontaine, which formally ended the hostilities and drew to a close the two-year undeclared war.

The strongest effect of the Quasi-War with France was the complicated legacy of political division that carried the United States into the presidential election of 1800. The Federalist president, John Adams, was severely alienated from the more conservative elements in his own party, led by Alexander Hamilton and Timothy Pickering. The Democratic-Republicans had relied on the states to oppose Federalist actions and the Alien and Sedition Acts, and Vice President Jefferson seemed totally cut off from the executive branch, of which he was a member. Men and women in American cities had participated in the ideological battles between the two parties precipitated by the Quasi-War, and although most of them would have less of a direct role in the next presidential election, the divisive and politicized atmosphere that their actions helped to create would concretely affect one of the most contentious elections in American political history.

## ARMED INSURRECTION: SOCIAL ORDER AND DISORDER

During the final two years of the Adams administration, as the French crisis came to a head and reached a resolution, many Americans feared even worse damage from domestic armed insurrection. Armed insurrections—some real, some imagined, and some planned but never executed—threatened to cause great upheaval in American society, while at the same time dramatizing political and racial problems of long standing. One example of each kind of insurrection—the real violence of Fries's Rebellion, the largely imagined fear of violent secession by Democratic-Republican southern states, and the thwarted plot by slaves to free themselves in Gabriel's Rebellion—will show how the United States still faced considerable instability.

Fries's Rebellion, which took place in a heavily German area of Pennsylvania, called up memories of the Whiskey Rebellion and the political divisions caused by its suppression in 1794. At the beginning of 1799, Revolutionary War veteran John Fries led a group of angry Pennsylvanians to protest and disrupt the collection of a 1798 federal tax on land, houses, and other property. When an armed mob broke out of prison several of the rebels who had been arrested, President Adams called up militia troops to suppress the violence. The militia restored order fairly easily, and John Fries and several other men were imprisoned and sentenced to death after being convicted of treason. After the rebels lost a court appeal to overturn their convictions, President Adams, concerned that their executions would create martyrs for the antigovernment cause, pardoned them in spring 1800. Adams's pardon caused increased friction between himself and his fellow Federalists, who saw him as too conciliatory toward both France and the Democratic-Republicans.

The suspicions of these "High" Federalists were further heightened by rumors throughout 1798 and 1799 that southern states, which provided the Democratic-Republicans with much of their support, were arming and preparing to secede from the Union. The strident tone of the Virginia and Kentucky resolutions, which protested the Alien and Sedition Acts and openly challenged the states to nullify federal laws with which they disagreed, fueled fears of armed insurrection and secession. The newspaper wars between the parties, which the Sedition Acts never managed to quiet entirely, further fueled public paranoia with often violent party rhetoric. The historian James Roger Sharp has found some evidence that the Virginia legislature was indeed stockpiling weapons after the passage of the Virginia and Kentucky resolutions, but a real secession movement never took shape.[6]

Far more disturbing to Federalists and Democratic-Republicans alike was another armed plot that emerged in Virginia in 1800—a plan for a large-scale slave rebellion in the state capital, Richmond, led by an urban slave named Gabriel. Gabriel, a literate man rented out by his owner, Thomas Prosser, was exposed to radical French and democratic ideas during his time working as an independent blacksmith in Richmond. Gabriel organized a group of perhaps hundreds of slave men in an intricate plan to build weapons, take over Richmond, imprison Governor James Monroe, and end the institution of slavery in Virginia. Two rural slaves revealed the plot to their masters before Gabriel's rebels could act. Gabriel eluded capture for several months, but finally was caught. After the conspirators were tried, Gabriel and several other leaders were executed; many of their followers were sold to slave traders and removed from the state of Virginia. Following the scare of Gabriel's Rebellion, the Virginia legislature tightened the state's slave codes and restricted slave movement, literacy, and many other de facto freedoms that had grown up for urban slaves prior to 1800.

Whether these violent plots were executed by disgruntled Democratic-Republican farmers against federal tax collectors, the Democratic-Republican–controlled Virginia legislature against the Federalist Alien and

Sedition Acts, or the slaves of Virginia against their own Democratic-Republican and Federalist masters, they all showed continuing areas of instability in U.S. society and government. Some political arguments represented conflicts among members of the elite class, while others shaded over into ethnic and class conflict, such as was evident in Fries's Rebellion. Politics and class also played roles in Gabriel's Rebellion, but more than anything, the planned slave revolt dramatized how race and slavery could still cut across all other political categories both to threaten and to define American society.

## THE ELECTION OF 1800

One historian has written that Gabriel's Rebellion happened in 1800 for a reason: Gabriel was exposed to the fiery political rhetoric of the presidential election of 1800, and he thought the political divisions created the right circumstances for his own quest for freedom to succeed.[7] Even though Gabriel overestimated the degree to which even radical Democratic-Republicans would hold sympathy for armed black slaves, his conclusion was not out of line: The presidential election of 1800 dramatized the hardening of the divisions between the two parties and became one of the most controversial elections in American history. The election of 1800, dubbed by Thomas Jefferson "the Revolution of 1800," signaled the first time power passed peacefully from one political party to the other in the United States. However, the transition came only after a very hard-fought campaign that tested the American electoral system and ended up being settled in the House of Representatives. The results were so confusing that the final outcome of the election was not decided until early 1801.

Despite the Alien and Sedition Acts—or perhaps because of them—the Federalists and Democratic-Republicans traded extraordinarily strong criticisms and epithets during the election, even though the practice of widespread, formal campaigning for the office of president was still years away. Many arch-Federalists, led by Alexander Hamilton, were unhappy with President Adams, and Hamilton hatched a plan to replace Adams in the newly completed White House with southerner Charles Coatsworth Pinckney, whom he openly put forward as the Federalists' choice for vice president. Despite the electoral disaster that had ended with Thomas Jefferson being elected vice president in 1796, Hamilton tried to recruit equal support for Pinckney and Adams, hoping that a few southern electoral college votes might propel Pinckney over the top to victory. Adams caught on to most of Hamilton's plan and was furious.

Vice President Thomas Jefferson was the unambiguous Democratic-Republican candidate for president, and New Yorker Aaron Burr ran in the election hoping to become Jefferson's vice president. The Federalist campaign decried Jefferson as a godless radical who would betray the country to an excess of popular democracy, but at the same time, Hamilton and other Federalists continued to criticize Adams in public. Massachusetts politician Fisher Ames argued that "surely we have enough to fear from Jefferson" without creating opposition to the Federalists' own candidates, but vigorous opposition continued on all sides in speeches, pamphlets, and newspapers around the country.[8]

The voting to choose presidential electors commenced in some states as early as May 1800 and stretched out until November. It became clear that the election would be very close, but because of differences in the ways that states chose their electors, no one was sure exactly how close the electoral vote would be. The winner of the majority of electoral votes would become president, and the candidate who received the second-highest total would become vice president. Neither party managed its vice-presidential votes very well, the Federalists in part because of the disagreement over whether Pinckney was running for vice president or president. In December, the electors met to cast their ballots. The results were not revealed until the following month, but the vote totals set up an electoral gridlock that would be hard to resolve. Jefferson and Burr each received 73 electoral votes; Adams received 65, and Pinckney got 64 votes. Chief Justice John Jay received one vote. The lack of an electoral majority would mean that the House of Representatives (in which the Democratic-Republicans also won a majority) would have to decide what was already a contentious and controversial election.

## NATIONAL CULTURE

At the same time that public divisions over political, social, and economic issues seemed to threaten the stability of the new republic, many Americans also proceeded to form a stronger national identity in the late 1790s. Nationalism in this period did not necessarily mean unquestioning faith in the federal state, but Americans were generating a more concrete vision of themselves *as* Americans. Men and women maintained allegiances to their states, towns, ethnic groups, religious denominations, and families, but they found new ways to define themselves as citizens of the United States. In civic rituals, celebrations, and their devotion to American newspapers and literature, people bonded themselves more firmly to the United States.

Style, especially style befitting a free republic, seemed a matter of great concern. Although the vast majority of Americans still lived in relatively self-sufficient rural communities, markets were beginning to bring a greater variety of goods into the average American home, dramatically boosting demand for both domestic and imported goods. Although influenced by European designs in furniture, housing, and dishware, a distinctively American federal taste took shape. Clothing and hairstyles were modernizing as well, with changes starting in cities by the turn of the century. Women's dresses, fashioned after French designs, began to lighten and loosen up by the end of the decade, and full-length pants were challenging knee breeches as the dominant style for men. Very few men still wore powdered wigs by 1800, although most did wear their hair long and tied into a queue at the back. Clergymen held on to their wigs, but other public men gave them up; for example, in 1798, all but five members of the New York state legislature had given up their wigs.[9]

Books, although still expensive, began to play a larger role in many Americans' lives in the late 1790s. In April 1800 Congress chartered the Library of Congress and authorized $5,000 worth of book purchases to begin a national book collection. Bookshops flourished in cities, especially Philadelphia, Charleston, New York, and Boston, and itinerant book peddlers distributed both European and American volumes to rural areas. Wealthier book buyers subscribed to series offered by publishers who brought out works of both fiction and nonfiction. Novels appealed both to men and the growing ranks of women who were educated at the all-female academies designed to develop well-rounded women capable of raising good republican children. Despite a widespread concern that American morals might be threatened by the tales of dissipation and romance, novels increased in popularity and held wide influence in American society.

Increasingly, the novels popular with American readers were written by American authors, a fact that helped to encourage the development of a distinctly national culture. Many novels dealt with themes of threatened female purity; the most notable and popular of this genre was Susannah Rowson's *Charlotte Temple,* a seduction tale first published in 1791. Hannah Webster Foster published a similar and also highly successful novel, *The Coquette,* in 1797. By the turn of the century, Americans were also beginning to indulge in a Gothic sensibility that would mark the romanticism imported from Europe in the early 19th century. The best early example of American Gothic came in Charles Brockdon Brown's ghostly 1798 novel, *Wieland,* the first to be published by an author born in the United States who made his living entirely through fiction writing. Among the more political books that found success was Royall Tyler's *The Algerine Captive,* a tale that stressed the peril experienced by American sailors captured and held in "slavery" in Africa's Barbary States. In 1800, the Reverend Mason Locke Weems published the first edition of his highly laudatory and novelistic biography of George Washington, in which he hoped to offer Washington as a model of good behavior and American heroism to a growing reading public.

Weems's biography of Washington was successful, in part, because the death of George Washington in 1799 occasioned a great outpouring of public sentiment and grief that further solidified Washington's status as a national symbol. Washington died at his plantation at Mount Vernon on December 14, 1799, and as news of his demise spread across the country, he was eulogized in newspapers, sermons, public funerals, pamphlets, and speeches in every state of the union. Hundreds of funeral sermons and orations for George Washington were published following his death, and many women and men created visual tributes to the deceased national hero in paintings, needlework, and other textiles. The tributes to George Washington upon his death muted the political

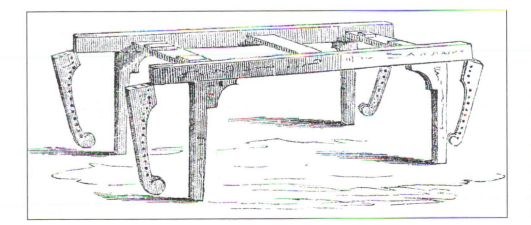

This bier was used to bear George Washington's coffin when he died in 1799. A tomb for Washington was constructed below the Rotunda of the U.S. Capitol, but Martha Washington had her husband buried at his Virginia estate, Mount Vernon, instead. *(from Benson Lossing,* The Pictorial Field-Book of the Revolution, *1851–1852)*

controversies that had engulfed him during his second term as president, as Americans sought to remember him as a nonpartisan war hero and true "father" of the nation. By celebrating George Washington, Americans were also celebrating their own commitment to the United States.

Not all public culture could avoid the partisan battles of the late 1790s so easily. It was not always clear where patriotism ended and partisanship began. Some groups, like the newly formed fraternal Society of St. Tammany, especially powerful in New York City, sponsored public holiday celebrations and also fostered strong ties to one political party or the other (in this case the Democratic-Republicans). When mixed groups of both respectable and less-respectable citizens (such as sailors and African Americans) celebrated French victories in the Anglo-French wars, they announced their commitment to the cause of the Democratic-Republican Party and to the cause of democracy in general. During the Quasi-War with France, urban theater audiences demonstrated their taste and their political beliefs by calling for patriotic songs, displaying partisan symbols on their clothing, and sometimes forcing authors to rewrite plays that did not seem sufficiently patriotic.

## A New Century

Americans entered the 19th century in an uncertain state. The presidency was undecided, and no one knew for sure whether the transition from rule by one party to another would go smoothly. Political parties themselves, which most Americans still viewed as illegitimate and divisive elements in society, had solidified their influence and differences during the Adams administration. The fights over the Quasi-War with France and the Alien and Sedition Acts had also caused considerable public upheaval. While the economic and international status of the United States seemed more stable than ever in some ways, much of that stability still relied on the ability of the country to remain on good terms with European nations—a feat not always easy to achieve in the midst of a world-scale war between Great Britain and France. Americans would embark on the new century wondering whether they would be able to chart their own course in the world.

## CHRONICLE OF EVENTS

**1797**

Isabella Graham and Elizabeth Ann Seton (who later will found a Catholic religious order and become a Catholic saint, but has not yet converted to Catholicism) found the Society for the Relief of Poor Widows with Small Children in New York City. Their society is the first benevolent association in the United States run by women.

Hannah Webster Foster publishes her novel *The Coquette,* which becomes one of the best-selling works of the late 18th and early 19th centuries.

Royall Tyler publishes his work of fiction, *The Algerine Captive,* which helps to arouse public sentiment against Africa's Barbary States, which continue to capture and ransom American sailors.

Charles Newbold of Burlington, New Jersey, invents a plow with a cast-iron blade, which makes tilling much easier and more efficient.

Dr. Samuel Latham Mitchell publishes the first U.S. medical journal, *The Medical Repository.*

Eli Terry patents his method for making wooden clockworks, the first U.S. patent granted for clock making, which would become a major U.S. industry.

*January 30:* Slaves in North Carolina, who had been freed by their Quaker masters, petition Congress for relief from a state law requiring them to be returned to slavery. Congress will reject their plea, the first antislavery petition to Congress by a group of African Americans.

*February 17:* John Burk's play *Bunker Hill,* which includes an onstage reenactment of the battle complete with cannon fire, inspires patriotic fervor when it is premiered. The play will enjoy popularity in several cities and in theaters supported by both Federalists and Democratic-Republicans.

*February 27:* The secretary of state, Timothy Pickering, delivers a report to Congress on the rising tensions between the United States and France.

*March 4:* On presidential inauguration day, John Adams, a Federalist, becomes president and Thomas Jefferson, a Democratic-Republican, becomes vice president.

*March 10:* The U.S. Navy launches its first frigate, *The United States.*

*May 15:* The diplomatic crisis with France heats up, as John Adams calls Congress into special session to discuss the French expulsion of Charles C. Pinckney, the U.S. minister to France, and issues related to naval conflict between the two nations.

*May 31:* Charles C. Pinckney, Elbridge Gerry, and John Marshall join together to negotiate a treaty with France.

*June 1:* John Adams appoints his son, John Quincy Adams, to be minister to Prussia.

*June 24:* Congress passes an act authorizing the call-up of 80,000 militia men, further indicating the fear of a possible war with France.

*July 8:* Tennessean William Blount is expelled from the U.S. Senate after he is accused of plotting to help the British wrest control of Florida and Louisiana from Spain.

*August 28:* The United States signs a naval treaty with Tunis and agrees to pay annual tribute to protect American shipping from Tunisian pirates.

*October 8:* U.S. negotiators Pinckney, Gerry, and Marshall are received in France by Foreign Minister Charles-Maurice de Talleyrand, but formal negotiations are postponed until Talleyrand can deliver his demands.

*October 18:* In France, government ministers identified only as X, Y, and Z demand a $240,000 bribe from U.S. negotiators. The incident eventually surfaces as the XYZ affair.

*October 21:* The U.S. Navy launches its newly constructed ship USS *Constitution,* which will become one of the most significant ships in U.S. naval history and is still an actively commissioned vessel.

**1798**

Charles Hopkinson publishes his patriotic poem "Hail, Columbia," which soon becomes the lyrics to a popular song.

Venture Smith publishes *A Narrative of the Life and Adventures of Venture,* which described his enslavement in Africa and his life as a Connecticut slave.

Eli Whitney, who has opened a musket factory in New Haven, Connecticut, designs the first manufacturing process for creating interchangeable parts in the United States.

Andrew Jackson becomes a justice of the Tennessee Supreme Court.

Yellow fever hits New York City and causes almost 3,000 deaths.

*January 30:* On the floor of Congress, Connecticut representative Roger Griswold and Vermonter

Mathew Lyon come to blows over a heated party issue, and Griswold tries to beat Lyon with a pair of iron fire tongs.

*March 18:* The French deliver a disappointing response to U.S. demands to protect shipping rights, and negotiations between the two nations break off.

*April:* Charles Brockdon Brown publishes *Alcuin, A Dialogue,* which argues for the equality of women and men.

*April 3:* President Adams makes public the dispatches from Gerry, Pinckney, and Marshall outlining the XYZ affair by sending them to the Senate. As tensions with France rise, so does talk of a possible war.

*April 7:* Congress defines the boundaries of the Mississippi Territory.

*April 30:* The Department of the Navy is formally separated from the Department of War, and a separate office of secretary of the navy is created.

*May 21:* Benjamin Stoddard is appointed first secretary of the navy.

*June 18:* The first Alien Act is adopted by Congress. The act amends the 1795 Naturalization Act to require aliens to reside in the United States for 14 years before they can apply for citizenship.

At a dinner in Philadelphia, South Carolina congressman and Federalist Robert Goodloe Harper offers a toast: "Millions for defense, but not one cent for tribute," in defiance of the French and their efforts to bribe American officials in the XYZ affair. The phrase becomes a popular Federalist rallying cry during the Quasi-War with France.

*June 25:* Congress passes the Alien Act, under which the president has authority to deport any alien whom he believes to be a threat to national security.

*July 6:* Congress passes the Alien Enemies Act, which authorizes the deportation of any citizen of a country hostile to the United States.

*July 7:* Congress expressly repeals the treaty of alliance with France signed in 1778 during the Revolutionary War. This is the first time Congress abrogates a specific treaty.

*July 11:* Congress reauthorizes the U.S. Marine Corps, which had been demobilized at the end of the Revolutionary War in 1783.

*July 14:* Congress passes the Sedition Act, which authorizes the imprisonment of anyone who interferes with the operations of government or who speaks or publishes false or malicious statements about members of the government or their actions.

*July 22:* The USS *Constitution* is first put to sea under Captain Samuel Nicholson.

*August 8:* Secretary of the Navy Benjamin Stoddard forbids black sailors on some U.S. sailing ships. In keeping with a long tradition of racially mixed sailing crews, African Americans had been accepted as sailors prior to this ruling.

*September:* Charles Brockton Brown publishes the novel *Wieland.*

*November 16:* The Kentucky legislature passes the "Kentucky Resolutions," which have been drafted by Thomas Jefferson, to protest the unconstitutionality of the Alien and Sedition Acts.

*November 20:* French naval forces capture the USS *Retaliation* off the coast of Guadeloupe, opening two years of undeclared naval warfare.

*December 14:* David Wilkinson patents a machine that cuts screw heads.

*December 24:* The Virginia legislature passes the "Virginia Resolutions," drafted by James Madison, which are very similar in form and content to the "Kentucky Resolutions" adopted the previous month.

## 1799

Handsome Lake's religious revitalization movement begins among the Seneca tribe of the Iroquois Confederation. Handsome Lake recovers from a severe illness and announces to his people in a series of Gaiwiio (Good Word) prophesies that they must give up alcohol, return to traditional Iroquois spiritual practices, and live in harmony with the United States. Handsome Lake's teachings become the basis for the Code of Handsome Lake, or the Longhouse Religion, later.

*January 30:* Congress prohibits private citizens from conducting negotiations with foreign governments.

*February 9:* In the Caribbean, the USS *Constellation* captures the French naval vessel *L'Insurgente.* The rising diplomatic tension and undeclared naval warfare between the United States and France threaten to worsen.

*February 25:* William Dawes, fellow Revolutionary rider with Paul Revere, dies.

*March 3:* Congress passes the Trade and Intercourse Act, which, among other things, establishes rules for trade and political negotiation with Indian nations.

*March 6:* John Fries leads a crowd to free 18 men jailed for interfering with tax collection in Bethlehem, Pennsylvania. The incident is part of a move-

This engraving depicts the fight between the USS *Constellation* and the French frigate *L'Insurgente* in February 1799. The engagement was part of the Quasi-War between the United States and France. *(National Archives/DOD, War & Conflict, # 71)*

ment known as Fries's Rebellion, which encompasses protests against federal property taxes.

*March 12:* President Adams orders John Fries and several of his supporters to be arrested.

*March 29:* The New York legislature passes a gradual emancipation law that grants eventual freedom to the children of slaves. Girls will be freed at the age of 25 and boys at 28.

*April 1:* Charles Brockdon Brown begins publication of the first quarterly literary review in the United States, *The American Review and Literary Journal.*

*June 6:* Patrick Henry dies.

*June 15:* The New Hampshire legislature issues resolutions that oppose the Kentucky and Virginia resolutions passed in protest against the Alien and Sedition Acts.

*October 16:* President Adams reopens diplomatic negotiations with France and hopes to avoid war by sending Oliver Ellsworth, William R. Davie, and William Vans Murray to France. Alexander Hamilton and other conservative Federalists disapprove of the president's new overture toward France.

*October 20:* James Iredell, one of the first justices of the U.S. Supreme Court, dies.

*November 22:* Kentucky once again backs the "Kentucky Resolutions" and reconfirms its commitment to state power. The resolutions claim for the first time that states should have the right to nullify federal law.

*December 14:* George Washington dies at his Mount Vernon plantation. Immediately, funeral ceremonies, sermons, and public commemorations are held across the United States. Washington's will provides for his slaves to be freed, and 122 of them go free.

*December 21:* Charleston, South Carolina, establishes that city's first public waterworks to bring water from Goose Creek to city residents.

## 1800

The second federal census reports that the U.S. population has grown extensively since 1790. The census records 5,308,483 Americans, 896,849 of whom are slaves.

Mason Locke Weems publishes the first edition of his popular yet highly fictionalized biography of George Washington.

John Chapman, known as "Johnny Appleseed," plants apple trees along a trail between Pennsylvania and Ohio.

Sailors based in New York City go on strike, and city officials, worried about spreading working-class agitation, forbid sailors to hold open meetings or to visit certain taverns.

Outside Boston, silversmith Paul Revere opens a mill to produce rolled sheet copper.

The first major navigable canal in the United States opens, connecting the Santee and Cooper Rivers in South Carolina.

Dr. Benjamin Waterhouse performs the first successful smallpox vaccination on a member of his family using a strain of vaccine made from cowpox.

Reverend Mason Locke Weems's biography of George Washington became one of the best-selling early American books. Weems created many of the most famous stories about George Washington, including the moral parable about him chopping down a cherry tree. *(from Benson Lossing,* The Pictorial Field-Book of the Revolution, *1851–1852)*

An offshoot of the Mennonite movement, the Church of the United Brethren in Christ, is officially organized. Martin Boehm and Philip W. Otterbein become the church's first bishops.

*January 6:* Congress reforms bankruptcy laws and outlaws imprisonment for debt.

*January 7:* Future president of the United States Millard Fillmore is born in Locke, New York.

*January 10:* The U.S. Senate ratifies a treaty of amity with Tunis aimed at preventing further piracy and capture of American sailors.

*January 18:* Congress passes the Peace Preservation Act, which establishes hefty fines for any western settlers convicted of inciting Indians to attack them to provoke U.S. military intervention.

*February 1:* The USS *Constellation* and the French frigate *La Vengeance* do battle, but no clear winner emerges.

*March 8:* Napoleon Bonaparte receives U.S. peace negotiators, but the Quasi-War with France continues.

*April 4:* Congress passes the first comprehensive federal bankruptcy law.

*April 24:* Congress charters the Library of Congress and authorizes an initial purchase of $5,000 worth of books.

*May:* President Adams dismisses Secretary of State Timothy Pickering and Secretary of War James McHenry, who oppose his policy of peace with France.

*May 7:* Congress divides the Northwest Territory and creates the new Indiana Territory to the west of the Ohio Territory.

*May 10:* Congress passes the Harrison Land Act, which creates district land offices, further opens public lands for private purchase, and helps encourage land speculators.

*May 21:* President Adams pardons John Fries, who was sentenced to death for his leading role in Fries's Rebellion.

*June:* The federal government settles in Washington, D.C.

*June 30:* A Baltimore newspaper publishes a mistaken report of the death of Thomas Jefferson, and the rumor spreads around the country.

*July:* Methodists in Logan County, Kentucky, hold the first recorded camp meeting revival.

*August 21:* The United States Marine band performs its first public concert.

This early engraving shows the U.S. Capitol in Washington, D.C., as it was when Congress moved in. Workmen in the foreground are still cutting stone for the building. *(Library of Congress, Prints and Photographs Division [LC-USZ62-1804])*

*August 30:* A slave rebellion in Richmond, Virginia, planned by Gabriel Prosser, which involved as many as 1,000 conspirators, is thwarted when disgruntled slaves warn authorities. Slave owners crack down on the freedom of urban slaves in the aftermath of fear created by the rebellion.

*September 30:* French and American officials sign a convention (later ratified in the Treaty of Mortefontaine) that ends the Quasi-War between the two nations. The U.S. Senate ratifies the convention, but the two countries continue to disagree over the status of their previous 1778 treaty of alliance.

*October 1:* Spain and France sign the secret Treaty of San Ildefonso, which transfers control over the Louisiana Territory and the Mississippi River to France.

*November:* John and Abigail Adams become the first presidential couple to inhabit the White House, which remains unfinished.

*November 17:* Congress holds its first session in the new capital of Washington, D.C.

*December 3:* Presidential electors meet to cast their votes. The tie vote between Thomas Jefferson and Aaron Burr that will force the election to be decided in the House of Representatives is not revealed until later.

## EYEWITNESS TESTIMONY

Nothing occurs to alleviate the crisis in our external affairs. The French continue to prey on our trade. The British, too, have not desisted. There are accounts that both of them are taking our East Indiamen. This is an alarming symptom . . .

*James Madison in a letter to Thomas Jefferson, January 29, 1797, in* Letters and Other Writings of James Madison, *II: 114.*

I have many acknowledgments to make for the friendly anxiety you are pleased to express in your letter of January 12 for my undertaking the office to which I have been elected. The idea that I would accept the office of president, but not that of vice president of the United States, had not its origin with me. I never thought of questioning the free exercise of the right of my fellow citizens to marshal those whom they call into their service according to their fitness, nor ever presumed that they were not the best judges of that.

*Thomas Jefferson in a letter to James Sullivan, February 9, 1797, in Hunt,* Essential Thomas Jefferson, *167.*

Last evening arrived in this city, on his way to Mount Vernon, the illustrious object of veneration and gratitude, GEORGE WASHINGTON. . . . At a distance from the city, he was met by a crowd of citizens, on horse and foot, who thronged the road to greet him, and by a detachment from Captain Hollingsworth's troop, who escorted him in through as great a concourse of people as Baltimore ever witnessed. On alighting at the Fountain Inn, the General was saluted with reiterated and thundering huzzas from the spectators.

*A Baltimore newspaper describes George Washington's reception in that city on his way to retire from office at home in Mount Vernon, March 13, 1797, in Sparks,* Writings of George Washington, *XI: 197.*

But the state of affairs externally and internally suggests the strongest imaginable auxiliary motives to avoid, if possible, at this time a rupture with France. Externally we behold France most formidably successful—extending too her connections and influence, while the affairs of her remaining enemies decline. . . . Those who may think an Invasion improbable ought to remember that it is not long

since there was a general Opinion the U States was in no danger of War. They see how difficult it has been and is to avoid one. . . . If France can transport her troops here what is to hinder an invasion?

*Alexander Hamilton in a letter to William Loughton Smith, April 10, 1797, in Freeman,* Alexander Hamilton, *870, 878.*

Mrs. Radcliffe's "Castles of Athlin & Dunbaine" is advertised in the New York papers, & as there is only one volume the expence of it will not be much—I intend buying it, & I think you will be pleased with it if you like such things as well as you used to—The Mysteries of Udolpho, have been so much caressed (poor things), that they have not had sufficient leisure [*sic*] to keep their *cloaths* in repair, a continual round of dissipation & visiting has preyed upon their *feeble frames,* & they have grown old in the days of their youth . . .

*Rachel Huntington jokes about her reading habits in a letter to her sister Anne, April 12, 1797, in McCrackan,* The Huntington Letters, *144.*

Such attempts ought to be repelled with a decision which shall convince France and the world that we are not a degraded people, humiliated under a colonial spirit of fear and sense of inferiority, fitted to be the miserable instruments of foreign influence, and regardless of national honor, character, and interest. . . . It is my sincere desire, and in this I presume I concur with you and with our constituents, to preserve peace and friendship with all nations; and believing that neither the honor nor the interest of the United States absolutely forbid the repetition of advances for securing these desirable objects with France, I shall institute a fresh attempt at negotiation . . .

*John Adams in his annual message to Congress, May 16, 1797. Available online. Avalon Project URL: http://www.yale.edu/lawweb/avalon/presiden/messages/ja97-03.htm.*

The speech is dispassionate but firm. The President, as becomes the chief Magistrate of an independent republic, appears disposed to adjust amicably, if possible, the difficulties, which subsist between the two nations, but resolved, at the same time, to vindicate our rights with energy.

*The* Walpole (New Hampshire) Farmer's Weekly Museum *comments on Adams's annual message, May 29, 1797, in Brown,* John Adams, *91.*

Today will be the 5th great dinner I have had, about 36 Gentlemen to day, as many more next week, and I shall have got through the whole of Congress, with their appendages. Then comes the 4 July which is a still more tedious day, as we must have then not only all Congress, but all the Gentlemen of the city, the Governour and officers and companies, all of whom the late President used to treat with cake, punch and wine . . . As we are here we cannot avoid the trouble nor expence . . . You will not wonder that I dread it, or think President Washington to blame for introducing the custom, if he could have avoided it.

*Abigail Adams laments the social commitments of being first lady in a letter, June 23, 1797, in Sprigg,*
Domestick Beings, *97.*

This 19th-century engraving depicts Gilbert Stuart's portrait of First Lady Abigail Adams. *(Library of Congress, Prints and Photographs Division [LC-USZ62-2045])*

The public buildings in the Federal city go on well. One wing of the Capitol (with which Congress might make a very good shift) and the President's House will be covered in this autumn; or to speak more correctly, perhaps the latter is *now* receiving its cover, and the former will be ready for it by that epoch. An elegant bridge is thrown over the Potomack at the little falls, and the navigation of the river above will be completed, nearly this season; through which an immensity of Produce must flow to the shipping Ports thereon.

*George Washington in a letter to David Humphreys, June 26, 1797, in Humphreys,* Life and Times of David Humphreys, *II: 261.*

The address to Mr. Monroe is another party finesse— intended, like the premature publication of the British Treaty, to forestall public opinion, by expressing an unequivocal approbation of the conduct of the late minister, before it has been examined, and before facts are known. Such tricks as these have become so common, as to lose their effect.

*Editorial comment in the Federalist newspaper* The Herald: A Gazette for the Country, *July 8, 1797.*

A letter is received here from Talleyrand, which says our envoys have been heard, that their pretensions are high, that possibly no arrangement may take place, but that there will be no declaration of war by France. . . . On the whole, I am entirely suspended as to what is to be expected.

*Thomas Jefferson in a letter to James Madison, January 24, 1798, in* Letters and Other Writings of James Madison, *II: 123.*

About a quarter past eleven o'clock, after prayers, whilst the SPEAKER was in his chair . . . Mr. GRISWOLD entered the House and observing Mr. LYON in his place (who was writing), he went up to him with a pretty strong walking stick in his hand with which he immediately began to beat him with great violence. . . . At length, getting behind the SPEAKER'S chair, Mr. L snatched up the tongs from the fire; the combatants then closed and came down together upon the floor . . .

*The Annals of Congress report the altercation between Matthew Lyon and Roger Griswold on the floor of the House of Representatives on January 30, 1798, in Rosenfeld,* American Aurora, *11, 13.*

I have well considered my journal . . . It is well suited to common readers; the wise need it not. . . . I have frequently skimmed along the frontiers, for four and five hundred miles . . . These places, if not the haunts of savage men, yet abound with wild beasts. I am only known by name to many of our people, and some of our local preachers; and unless the people were all together, they could not tell what I have had to cope with. I make no doubt the Methodists are, and will be, a numerous and wealthy people, and their preachers who follow us will not know our struggles but by comparing the present improved state of the country with what it was in our days, as exhibited in my journal and other records of that day.

*Methodist bishop and western traveler Francis Asbury in his journal, February 6, 1798, in Thorp,* Southern Reader, *491.*

There never was, perhaps, a greater contrast between two characters than between those of present President and his predecessor; although it is the boast and prop of the present that he treads in the steps of his predecessor. The one, cool, considerate, and cautious; the other, headlong, and kindled into flame by every spark that lights his passions; the one, ever scrutinizing into the public opinion, and ready to follow, where he could not lead it; the other, insulting it by the most adverse sentiments and pursuits. . . . the former chief magistrate pursuing peace every where with sincerity, though mistaking the means: the latter taking as much pains to get into war as the former took to keep out of it.

*James Madison contrasts George Washington and John Adams in a letter to Thomas Jefferson, February 1798, in* Letters and Other Writings of James Madison, *II: 127.*

Business thickens upon him. Officering all the frigates, contemplating what can be done at this critical period, *knowing what he thinks ought to be done,* yet not certain whether the people are sufficiently determined to second the Government, is a situation very painfull, as well as responsible.

*Abigail Adams describes John Adams's agonizing over whether to declare war against France in a letter, March 1798, in Brown,* John Adams, *93.*

The dispatches from the Envoys-extraordinary of the United States to the French Republic, which were mentioned in my message to both houses of Congress, on the 5th instant, have been examined and maturely considered. . . . Under these circumstances I cannot forbear to reiterate the recommendations, which have been formerly made, and to exhort you to adopt with promptitude, decision, and unanimity, such measures as the ample resources of the country afford, for the protection of our seafaring and commercial citizens; for the defence of any exposed portions of our territory; for replenishing our arsenals, establishing foundries, and military manufactures . . . In all your proceedings it will be important to manifest a zeal, vigor, and concert in defence of the national rights, proportioned to the danger with which they are threatened.

*President John Adams in a message to the U.S. Congress, March 19, 1798, in Cunningham,* Circular Letters, *111, 112.*

This Message is a declaration of war as far as the President's *ipse dixit* can go—it will be considered as such by France:—from the Message it would appear, that we had nothing to do but to enregister the Decree, and go on to drain our fellow-citizens of the hard earnings of their labors to support his projects, and this we are called on to do upon his bare declarations and opinions . . .

*Virginia congressman Anthony New in a circular letter to his constituents, March 20, 1798, in Cunningham,* Circular Letters, *112.*

To exercise the right of speech, and freedom of debate, recognized by the Constitution; to perpetuate the equal rights of man, to propagate political knowledge, and to revive the republican spirit of '76, are the great objects of this institution.

*The Republican Society of Norwalk, Connecticut, advertises its commitment to free speech in the* New London Bee, *April 4, 1798, in Link,* Democratic-Republican Societies, *113.*

The success of the war party in turning the [XYZ] Dispatches to their inflammatory views is a mortifying item against the enlightened character of our citizens. . . . I am glad to find, in general, that everything that good sense and accurate information can supply is abundantly exhibited by the newspapers to the view of the public. It is to be regretted that these papers are so limited in their circulation, as well as that the mixture of indiscretions in some of them should contribute to that effect. It is to be hoped, however, that any arbitrary attacks on the freedom of the press will find virtue enough remaining in the public mind to make them recoil on the wicked authors.

*James Madison in a letter to Thomas Jefferson, May 5, 1798, in* Letters *and Other Writings of* James Madison, *II: 139.*

In forming an army . . . I am at an immense loss whether to call on all the old generals, or to appoint a young set. If the French come here, we must learn to march with a quick step, and to attack, for in that way only are they said to be vulnerable. I must tax you sometimes for advice. We must have your name, if you will in any case permit us to use it. There will be more efficacy in it, than in many an army.

*President John Adams in a letter to George Washington, May 26, 1798, in Sparks,* Writings of George Washington, *XI: 246.*

I will never send another minister to France without assurances that he will be received, respected, and honored as the representative of a great, free, powerful, and independent nation.

*John Adams in a message to the U.S. Congress, June 21, 1798, in Brown,* John Adams, *99.*

In all ages of the world, a political projector or system-monger of popular talents, has been a greater scourge to society than a pestilence. . . . Let us never forget that the cornerstone of all republican governments is, that the will of every citizen is controlled by the laws or supreme will of the state.

*Federalist Noah Webster in a Fourth of July oration in New Haven, Connecticut, July 4, 1798, in Rollins,* The Long Journey of Noah Webster, *87, 88.*

Yesterday morning was ushered in with the ringing of bells and other demonstrations of joy; great numbers of opulent mercantile interest of this flourishing city assembled at the Coffee house to reciprocate their congratulations on the occasion—the *taking of a French schooner* after a desperate action of *one gun* . . .

*The Philadelphia* Aurora, *July 10, 1798, in Rosenfeld,* American Aurora, *187.*

A man must sing "Hail Columbia" and wear a black cockade or he is called by [the government party] a disorganizer, a Jacobin, a pensioned tool of the French . . . It would seem really the view of some of the loudest vociferators for union to excite a civil war in our country; they cannot expect that, by their denunciations, their insults & their abuse, they can bully the republicans into silence or an acquiescence in their sentiments or measures.

*The Philadelphia* Aurora, *August 1, 1798, in Rosenfeld,* American Aurora, *203.*

. . . there is a most respectable part of our state who have been enveloped in the XYZ delusion, and who destroy our unanimity for the present moment. This disease of the imagination will pass over, because the patients are essentially republicans. Indeed, the doctor is now on his way to cure it, in the guise of a tax gatherer. But give time for the medicine to work, and for the repetition of stronger doses, which must be administered.

*Thomas Jefferson in a letter to John Taylor, November 26, 1798, in Hunt,* The Essential Thomas Jefferson, *184.*

One Taylor (I believe his name is John) has brought forward a Resolution, in the Legislature of Virginia, which, I think, is at once the most foolish and the most impudent that I ever read or heard of. . . . This step on the part of the Virginians admits of no excuse; but, when they pretend to be actuated by an anxiety to preserve *liberty*, who can help despising them? They actuated by *a love of liberty!* They who live on the sweat of *slaves;* and who buy and sell those slaves with as little ceremony as the Pennsylvanians do hogs or sheep!!

*William Cobbett protests the Virginia Resolutions in his newspaper the* Country Porcupine, *December 26, 1798 in Hart,* American History, *III: 329, 330.*

The free spirited Resolves of Kentucky & Virginia with truth flashing thro' clouds of Aristocrat delusion have begun to stagger the people at the Westward who have been made to foam with rage against the French their benefact[ors.] It is amazing to see the apathy of the People under worse usurpation than that which once excited them to war—Now they can patiently see the Omnipotence of the British Parliament transfer'd to Congress usurping all State Jurisdiction retain'd by the Sovreign [sic] People in State governments.

*Massachusetts physician Nathaniel Ames in his diary, December 27, 1798, in Hart,* American History, *III: 337.*

PROPERTY PROTECTED. a la Francoise.

This 1798 British engraving mocks the United States in the aftermath of the XYZ affair. As "America," a female dressed in a feather headdress, is flattered, a French official plunders her treasures. In the background, other European nations look on as John Bull (Great Britain) watches haughtily from a hilltop. *(Library of Congress, Prints and Photographs Division [LC-USZ62-64187])*

Our government has not armies, nor a hierarchy, nor an extensive patronage. Instead of these auxiliaries of other governments, let it have the sword of public opinion drawn in its defence . . . A frame of government less free and popular might perhaps have been left to take some care of itself; but the people choose to have it as is, and therefore they must not complain of the burden, but come forward and support it; it has not strength to stand alone without such help from the wise and honest citizens.

*Massachusetts Federalist Fisher Ames warns that public opinion must be won over in 1799, in Davis,* The Fear of Conspiracy, 54.

The first thing in all great operations of such a Government as ours is to secure the opinion of the people. To this end, the proceedings of Virginia and Kentucke with the two laws complained of should be referred to a special Committee. That Committee should make a report exhibiting with great luminousness and particularity the reasons which support the constitutionality and expediency of those laws—the tendency of the doctrines advanced by Virginia and Kentucke to destroy the Constitution of the U States—and, with calm dignity united with pathos, the full evidence which they afford of a regular conspiracy to overturn the government. . . . The Government must not merely defend itself but must attack and arraign its enemies.

*Alexander Hamilton in a letter to Theodore Sedgwick, February 2, 1799, in Freeman,* Alexander Hamilton, 913.

The late nominations of the President for the purpose of renewing negotiations with France has given almost universal disgust. . . . There certainly will be serious difficulties in supporting Mr. Adams at the next election if he should be a candidate.

*Federalist Robert Troup in a letter to fellow party member Rufus King, April 19, 1799, in Brown,* John Adams, *111.*

The truth is, that negociation for a treaty with a government so totally unprincipled so shamelessly perfidious as that of France, would give us no security for peace or of compensation for injuries. . . . There will not be any safe treaty with France until its government (not the tyrants who successively administer it) shall be changed.

*Secretary of State Timothy Pickering expressing surprise and outrage that President Adams has appointed new commissioners to negotiate with France in a letter to William Vans Murray, July 10, 1799, in Elkins and McKitrick,* Age of Federalism, *622.*

We are here all wondering at the new mission to France. . . . The language used by the President *and his lady,* is in direct opposition to such a measure, and she has expressed much surprise that the intimations given in the papers of preparations for the envoys should be believed. This singular opposition of sentiment perplexes people very much, and many will not believe that the President intends they shall go on.

*Stephen Higginson in a letter to Oliver Wolcott, September 16, 1799, in Elkins and McKitrick,* Age of Federalism, *639.*

By a Gentleman from Vermont, we learn that Col. Matthew Lyon, Anthony Haswell, Editor of the Vermont Gazette, and Judah P. Spooner, Printer at Fairhaven, have been indicted for Sedition before the Circuit Court for the District of Vermont.

*The Philadelphia* Aurora, *October 24, 1799, in Rosenfeld,* American Aurora, *708.*

[I]t is a painful duty to advert to the ungrateful return which has been made . . . by some of the people in certain counties of Pennsylvania, where, seduced by the arts and misrepresentations of designing men, they have openly resisted the law directing the valuation of houses and lands. Such defiance was given to the civil authority as rendered hopeless all further attempts by judicial process to enforce the execution of the law,

and it became necessary to direct a military force to be employed . . .

*John Adams laments Fries's Rebellion in his annual message to Congress, December 3, 1799. Available online. Avalon Project. URL:http://www.yale.edu/lawweb/avalon/presiden/sou/adamsme3.htm#france.*

In consequence of the afflicting intelligence of the death of GENERAL WASHINGTON, Mrs. Adams' drawing room is deferred to Friday the 27th, when the Ladies are respectfully requested to wear white, trimmed with black ribbon, black gloves and fans, as a token of respect to the memory of the late President. . . . The universal Depression of the public Mind, on the Receipt of the afflicting Intelligence announced in our last Paper, continues unabated; and is demonstrated by the Anxiety every where displayed, to make an affectionate Acknowledgement of 'the vast Debt of Gratitude, which is due to the Virtues, Talents, and ever memorable services, of the illustrious Diseased.'

*The* Newport (Rhode Island) Mercury *reports on mourning rituals for the death of George Washington, December 31, 1799.*

Although I differed in opinion with him [Washington], on many principles both abstract and practical, though I disapproved of many of his acts while an officer of the government, though I am convinced his opinions of our Constitution and government were improper, erroneous and subversive of our liberties, I have never impeached the purity or goodness of his heart.

*Virginian Garritt Minor in a letter to Joseph C. Cabell, January 17, 1800, in Link,* Democratic-Republican Societies, *194.*

I have received with deep sensibility your sympathizing letter . . . To those only who have experienced losses like ours can our distresses be known—words are inadequate to convey an idea of them . . . If the mingling of the tears of numerous friends—if the sympathy of a Nation and every testimony of respect of veneration paid to the memory of the partners of our hearts could afford consolation you and myself would experience it in highest degree . . .

*Martha Washington in a letter to Janet Livingston Montgomery, the widow of Revolutionary War hero Richard Montgomery, April 5, 1800, in Fields,* Worthy Partner, *371.*

Many mourning portraits, such as this one, were published after George Washington's death in 1799. In this engraving, the goddess of liberty and the American eagle are depicted kneeling at Washington's side, as they are surrounded by symbols of peace and military glory. Beneath Washington is a depiction of the signing of the Declaration of Independence. *(from Benson Lossing,* The Pictorial Field-Book of the Revolution, *1851–1852)*

[I]t becomes you to reflect that the time you chose to rise up in arms to oppose the laws of your country was when it stood in a very critical situation with regard to France and on the eve of a rupture with that country . . . What remains for me is a very painful but a very necessary part of my duty . . . The judgment of the law is, and this Court doth award "that you be hanged by the neck *until dead*."

*U.S. Circuit Court judge Samuel Chase sentences James Fries to death for leading a rebellion against the government, May 2, 1800, in Rosenfeld,* American Aurora, *781.*

There will be an Antifederal Majority in the Ensuing Legislature, and this very high probability is that this will bring *Jefferson* into the Chief Magistracy; unless it be prevented by the measure which I shall now submit to your consideration . . . I shall not be supposed to mean that any thing ought to be done which integrity will forbid—but merely that the scruples of delicacy and propriety, as relative to a common course of things, ought to yield to the extraordinary nature of the crisis. They ought not to hinder the taking of a *legal* and *constitutional* step, to prevent an *Atheist* in Religion and a *Fanatic* in politics from getting possession of the helm of the State.

*Alexander Hamilton, discussing Jefferson, in a letter to John Jay, May 7, 1800, in Freeman,* Alexander Hamilton, *923, 924.*

You may well know, sir, the general state of the Indians residing on the Grand River, as well as in other parts. A considerable number of some of these nations have long since embraced Christianity, and the conversion of others must depend, under the influence of the Great Spirit, on the faithful labours of a resident minister, who might visit and instruct both here and elsewhere, as ways and doors might, from time to time, be opened for him. The establishment and enlargement of civilization and Christianity among the natives must be most earnestly desired by all good men . . .

*Mohawk warrior Joseph Brant in a letter to Aaron Burr, May 7, 1800, in Davis,* Memoirs of Aaron Burr, *II: 164.*

We insinuate nothing against the opposite ticket. Let the contest be considered as it really is, between Thomas Jefferson and John Adams. The former you know to be a sincere and enlightened Republican; whose greatness has been promulgated through the unavailing calumnies of his enemies, though he stands unshielded by a sedition law.

*The Democratic-Republican* Virginia Argus *urges readers to vote for Thomas Jefferson, July 11, 1800, in Brown,* John Adams, *132.*

*Porcupine's Gazette,* and Fenno's *Gazette,* from the moment of the mission to France, aided, countenanced, and encouraged by . . . Federalists in Boston, New York, and Philadelphia have done more to shuffle the cards into the hands of the jacobin leaders, than all the acts of administration, and all the policy of opposition from the commencement of the government. . . . If the election of a Federal President is lost by it, those who performed the exploit will be the greatest losers.

*John Adams comments on Federalist disagreements during the presidential election in a letter to John Trumbull, September 10, 1800, in Brown,* John Adams, *135.*

I have nothing more to offer than what General Washington would have had to offer, had he been taken by the British and put to trial by them. I have adventured my life in endeavoring to obtain the liberty of my countrymen, and am a willing sacrifice in their cause: and I beg, as a favour, that I may be immediately led to execution. I know that you have pre-determined to shed my blood, why then all this mockery of a trial?

*Testimony of a slave indicted in Gabriel's Rebellion, October 1800, in Johnson and Smith,* Africans in America, *256.*

Gabriel was appointed Captain at first consultation respecting the Insurrection, and afterwards when he had enlisted a number of men was appointed General. That they were to kill Mr. Prosser, Mr. Mosby, and all the neighbors, and then proceed to Richmond, where they would kill everybody, take the treasury, and divide the money among the soldiers; after which he would fortify Richmond and proceed to discipline his men, as he apprehended a force would be raised elsewhere to repel him.

*Ben, a slave, testifying in the trial about Gabriel's Rebellion, October 6, 1800, in Aptheker,* A Documentary History, *45.*

The house is upon a grand and superb scale, requiring about thirty servants to attend and keep the apartments in proper order, and perform the ordinary business of the house and the stables; an establishment very well proportioned to the President's salary. The lighting the apartments, from the kitchen to parlours and chambers, is a tax indeed . . . The

ladies from Georgetown and in the city have many of them visited me. Yesterday I returned fifteen visits.

*Abigail Adams describes life in the White House in a letter, November 21, 1800, in Hart,* American History, *III: 331, 332.*

I congratulate the people of the United States on the assembling of Congress at the permanent seat of their Government, and I congratulate you, gentlemen, on the prospect of a residence not to be changed. Although there is cause to apprehend that accommodations are not now so complete as might be wished, yet there is great reason to believe that this inconvenience will cease with the present session. . . . May this territory be the residence of virtue and happiness! In this city may that piety and virtue, that wisdom and magnanimity, that constancy and self-government, which adorned the great character whose name it bears be forever held in veneration! Here and throughout our country may simple manners, pure morals, and true religion flourish forever!

*John Adams in his annual message to Congress, November 22, 1800. Available online. Avalon Project. URL:http://www.yale.edu/lawweb/avalon/president/sou/adamsme4.htm#france.*

In December, 1800, a few days after Congress had for the first time met in our new Metropolis, I was one morning sitting alone in the parlour, when the servant opened the door and showed in a gentleman who wished to see my husband. The usual frankness and care with which I met strangers, were somewhat checked by the dignified and reserved air of the present visitor. . . . Mr. Smith entered and introduced the stranger to me as *Mr. Jefferson.* . . . I had long participated in my husband's political sentiments and anxieties, and looked upon Mr. Jefferson as the cornerstone on which the edifice of republican liberty was to rest, looked upon him as the champion of human rights, the reformer of abuses, the head of the republican party, which must rise or fall with him, and on the triumph of the republican party I devoutly believed the security and welfare of my country depended.

*Washington socialite Margaret Bayard Smith recalling her first meeting with Thomas Jefferson during the presidential election, December 1800, in Hunt,* The First Forty Years, *6, 7.*

Although we have not official information of the votes for president and vice-president, and cannot have until the first week in February, yet the state of the votes is given on such evidence as satisfies both parties that the two republican candidates stand highest. . . . it was badly managed not to have arranged with certainty what seems to have been left to hazard. It was the more material, because I understand several high-flying federalists have expressed their hope that two republican tickets may be equal, and their determination in that case to prevent a choice by the House of Representatives (which they are strong enough to do), and let the government devolve on a president of the Senate. Decency required that I should be so entirely passive during the late contest, that I never once asked whether arrangements had been made to prevent so many from dropping votes intentionally as might frustrate half the republican wish . . .

*Thomas Jefferson in a letter to fellow presidential candidate Aaron Burr, December 15, 1800, in Davis, Memoirs of Aaron Burr, II: 67, 68.*

I transmit to the Senate, for their consideration and decision, a convention, both in English and French, between the United States of America and the French Republic, signed at Paris on the 30th day of September last by the respective plenipotentiaries of the two powers.

*John Adams in a message to Congress, December 15, 1800. Available online. Avalon Project. URL: http://www.yale.edu/lawweb/avalon/president/ messages/ja00-01.htm.*

It is highly improbable that I shall have an equal number of votes with Mr. Jefferson; but, if such should be the result, every man who knows me ought to know that I would utterly disclaim all competition. Be assured that *the federal party can entertain no wish for such an exchange.*

*Aaron Burr in a letter to the public, December 16, 1800, in Davis, Memoirs of Aaron Burr, II: 75.*

New England is New England *still* and unless an earthquake could remove them and give them about ten degrees of our southern sun in their constitutions they will always remain so. You may as well attempt to separate the Barnacle from the Oyster, or a body of Caledonians as to divide New England. Not so our southern Gentry.

*South Carolina senator Charles Pinckney in his diary, December 20, 1800, in Hart, American History, III: 335–336.*

# 6

# Jeffersonian America
## 1801–1803

Thomas Jefferson dubbed his victory in the presidential election of 1800 and the transfer of national power from the Federalist to the Democratic-Republican Party "the Revolution of 1800." This phrase, for Jefferson, signaled that the Republicans' vision of democracy was triumphant over the Federalists and that the country had been saved from certain ruin by the peaceful transfer of power from one party to another. The casual observer in 1800 might have expected Jefferson's victory to mean the restraint of federal government power, a continued growth of the democratic voice of common men, more power for the states, and a national emphasis on rural farming instead of urban trade and commerce. These were all hallmarks of Democratic-Republican ideology, and although Jefferson and his compatriots kept their political beliefs intact, the real exercise of national power caused them constantly to compromise. The first few years of Jeffersonian America proved that many of the contradictions that characterized Thomas Jefferson, personally, would also play themselves out on the national stage. Competing forces—republicanism and democracy, growth and stability, power and the restraint of power, slavery and freedom—would all exert powerful influences on American life. There were real limits on the revolutionary nature of the Revolution of 1800.

## THE ELECTION OF 1800 AND THE TRANSITION OF POWER

Before Jefferson could take office, however, he had to be clearly elected president, and the chaos of the presidential election of 1800 caused gridlock that was not resolved until February 1801. The election of 1800 was characterized by political party activities that showed how the ideological rifts of the 1790s had hardened into concrete opposition groups, but at the same time, neither party exercised modern political management techniques, and the presidential electoral system did not function smoothly on its own. President John Adams ran for reelection, but he faced opposition from Alexander Hamilton, who led conservatives in the Federalist Party to criticize Adams and to work for the election of the supposed vice-presidential candidate Charles Coatsworth

Pinckney. The Democratic-Republicans clearly fielded Thomas Jefferson for president and Aaron Burr for vice president, but they did not manage the selection of electors in the states very carefully, to disastrous results.

According to the U.S. Constitution, the person who received the most electoral votes would be elected president, and the runner-up would be elected vice president, but if no candidate received a majority of electoral votes, the election would have to be decided by the House of Representatives. By the end of 1800, when the presidential electors met to cast their ballots, many politicians had an ill feeling that the vote would be close enough to throw the election into the House. When the votes were officially unsealed in February 1801, their suspicions were borne out. Thomas Jefferson and Aaron Burr were tied, with 73 electoral votes each. President Adams received 65 votes, and Charles C. Pinckney followed closely with 64. Former chief justice John Jay received one vote. Although it seemed clear that the next president would be a Democratic-Republican, the election would have to be decided in the House of Representatives, where no clear rules governed how such an election must be carried out, except that each state delegation could cast only one collective vote. In reality, anything could have happened.

The political composition of the House of Representatives and the personalities of the candidates prevented anyone from feeling sure about the eventual outcome of the election. The Democratic-Republican Party had won a decisive majority in the 1801 elections for the House of Representatives, but the new session of Congress did not begin until later in 1801, so it fell to the old Federalist-majority House to decide the presidential race. Many of the Federalist congressmen had participated in strong partisan opposition and mudslinging against Thomas Jefferson throughout the race, and subsequently they would cast ballots to decide on his political fate. Aaron Burr might have prevented considerable political stress if he had withdrawn from the race. It remains unclear whether Burr thought, given the tie, that he might overtake Jefferson and become president, but he was a man who carefully guarded his personal prestige and privileges, and for whatever reasons, he refused to take himself out of the running for the presidency.

The House of Representatives officially unsealed the electoral votes on February 11, 1801, and voted to enter continuous session until a president was elected. A severe snowstorm and the pressure to stay in session until the election was concluded led representatives to take up residence in the drafty Capitol building, as cots were constructed in the cloakrooms and meals were delivered to the floor of the House. During the first night of balloting, 27 rounds of voting were conducted, but neither Jefferson nor Burr achieved the needed majority of nine state votes to win the presidency.

The deadlock continued partly because of party maneuvering and partly because of regional divides among the states. In the first rounds of voting, Jefferson received the majority of his votes from southern states and Burr from northern states, with Vermont and Maryland casting no ballots. Many Federalist legislators threw their support to Burr because they hoped that he could be counted on to support Federalist causes if he were elected, and some historians have speculated ever since that Burr may have promised the Federalists favors in return for votes. Some Democratic-Republicans argued that the Federalists were conspiring to slow down the vote so that the Federalist-dominated Senate would be able to exert an influence if inauguration day passed with no clear presidential choice. The governors of Virginia and Pennsylvania communicated to Thomas Jefferson that they were willing to mobilize state militias to reject any election results that they considered illegitimate, and there were signs that Federalist militias in Massachusetts were also prepared for a call to action. As the election dragged on, the atmosphere of unrest only grew more dangerous.

As the crisis continued day after day, with no resolution in sight, Burr and Jefferson remained tied in round after round of voting. By the weekend of February 14 and 15, Delaware congressman James Bayard finally told fellow Federalists that since "Mr. Burr would not co-operate with us, I [am] determined to end the contest by voting for Mr. Jefferson."[1] Despite Alexander Hamilton's frantic warnings that Burr could not be trusted, Federalists had thrown their support to Burr hoping that he would actively seek to defeat Jefferson. But now, the Federalists seemed to accept defeat, and on February 17, Jefferson was finally elected. On the 36th round of balloting, Jefferson received 10 votes, Burr received four and two states declined to cast votes at all. Almost in spite of the electoral chaos and widespread fear that the system would fail outright, Jefferson received enough votes to become president, and Burr was elected vice president.

Aaron Burr flirted with Federalist support before becoming the Republican vice president after the election of 1800 was settled. Burr became one of the most controversial politicians in U.S. history. He not only killed Alexander Hamilton in a duel; he was subsequently indicted for treason. *(Library of Congress, Prints and Photographs Division [LC-USZ62-102555])*

President John Adams was very disappointed that he had not been elected for a second term in office, and he was determined to leave a strong Federalist power structure in place when he turned over the presidency to Thomas Jefferson. Just because Jefferson was convinced that "the Revolution of 1800" signaled public consensus that the Democratic-Republicans should be swept into office did not mean that Adams was content to go quietly out of office. In their final months in office before Jefferson's inauguration, Adams and the Federalist Congress worked to leave a lasting mark on the national government that would be hard for the Democratic-Republicans quickly to erase.

On January 20, 1801, John Adams nominated Virginian John Marshall to be the chief justice of the Supreme Court, a move that would turn into probably the longest-lasting Federalist stamp on the republic. Marshall was quickly confirmed by the Senate, and he served as chief justice for 34 years until his death in 1835. Marshall, a cousin of Thomas Jefferson, was a strong Federalist, but he was not dogmatic, and he prized nationalism and union above all else. Marshall favored using the power of the federal government to shape the republic into a strong nation, and as chief justice, he pursued every course of action that promoted strong federal powers. Marshall had served as one of Adams's ministers to France during the XYZ affair and served as secretary of state until his position as chief justice was confirmed, and his moderate Federalist opinions closely fit with the views of President Adams. John Marshall's personal charisma and intelligence, his strong nationalism, and his moderate

Federalism (all of which irked Thomas Jefferson) would become among the strongest influences in the history of the U.S. Supreme Court. The first early sign of Marshall's tremendous influence came in his 1803 decision in the seminal case of *Marbury v. Madison,* which established for the first time the right of the Supreme Court to determine the constitutionality of federal legislation, a concept referred to as the right of judicial review. John Marshall would never hesitate to use Supreme Court decisions to push his Federalist political ideas, even when they clashed with those of the sitting president.

Adams and the Federalist Congress worked to leave Jefferson with other vestiges of their beliefs in the American legal system. In February 1801, Congress passed a new judiciary act, which amended terms of the Judiciary Act of 1798 that had established the federal court system. The 1801 act reduced the number of justices on the Supreme Court from six to five, which meant that two justices would have to die or retire before Thomas Jefferson would be able to appoint anyone to the court. Congress further expanded the circuit court system and confirmed Federalist judges to fill almost all positions on the federal bench. Even though the new Democratic-Republican Congress repealed the February 1801 Judiciary Act at the beginning of March, the combined influence of Chief Justice John Marshall and the other Federalist federal judges meant that the judiciary would remain as a Federalist enclave ready to challenge Democratic-Republican legislative or executive actions.

On March 3, the evening before Jefferson took office as president, John Adams was still at work appointing Federalist judges, clerks, and other civil servants, hoping to extend Federalist influence over the next administration. The Jeffersonian newspapers published frenzied accounts of these so-called midnight appointments in an effort to paint Adams's acts as desperate and nefarious, but Adams was well within his rights to act as president until the very last minute. On March 4, John and Abigail Adams left the White House, of which they had been the first occupants, and retired to their home in Quincy, Massachusetts, without attending Thomas Jefferson's inauguration or pausing to pay the new president their respects. Thomas Jefferson quietly proclaimed in his inaugural address that "We are all Republicans, we are all Federalists," in an attempt to heal the party rifts of the past 10 years, but Adams was not present to hear his words.[2] Whether Federalists and Republicans could make up their differences remained to be seen, but no matter what his or her political persuasion, everyone could agree that a dramatic shift in power had occurred.

This lithograph copies an 1830 portrait of Chief Justice John Marshall by the painter Chester Harding. *(Library of Congress, Prints and Photographs Division [LC-USZCN3-35])*

## JEFFERSONIAN ENTERPRISE

When Thomas Jefferson took power, people expected a shift in federal economic policy away from the style and tone that had been set by Federalist Alexander Hamilton ever since the U.S. Constitution had gone into effect.

Although the Democratic-Republican Party gathered much of its political strength from artisan workingmen in eastern seaboard cities, Jefferson envisioned that the safety of the republic resided in encouraging a largely rural, agricultural society. Jefferson felt that farmers were blessed by God, and he argued that corruption could be avoided in a society that guaranteed wide ownership of land for self-sufficient yeoman households. Jefferson himself had designed many of the systems that split western lands into plots that could be auctioned to small landholders by the federal government, and he planned to pursue his agricultural economic program now that he was in office. Jefferson did not agree with his predecessors that the future of the U.S. economy depended on the encouragement of new developments in manufacturing and commerce. Jefferson believed that the United States ought to give "just weight to the moral and physical preference of the agricultural, over the manufacturing, man."[3]

Alongside Jefferson's vision of the ideal agrarian republic, however, the first few years of the 19th century witnessed the continued growth of American manufacturing. Although over 90 percent of Americans still lived on farms at the turn of the century, the market economy continued to expand and cause changes in economic life.[4] The entrepreneurial energy that had been released in the late 1790s began to bear fruit as an increasing number of Americans sought to increase their trade with Europe and to make money from new technologies. Thomas Jefferson, as secretary of state, had been required to administer the first U.S. patent system in 1790, when the federal government initially sought to encourage invention by offering innovators protection of their technological developments. By the time Jefferson was in office as president, however, the job of administering the U.S. Patent Office had grown too large to continue to be managed by the secretary of state. The number of patent applications had grown so large by 1802 that Jefferson's secretary of state, James Madison, established the office as a subdepartment of the State Department and appointed Dr. William Thornton as the superintendent of patents.

A number of early manufacturers began to make business advances during the first years after 1800. Slater's Mill in Pawtucket, Rhode Island, which had become the first mechanized cloth mill in the United States when it opened in 1793, expanded in 1801 to make room for more of the female workers who left their homes to spin and weave at the plant on the Blackstone River. The same year Eleuthère I. DuPont, a Paris gunpowder maker who had been forced to flee his factory during the French Revolution, relocated his company to the United States and began manufacturing gunpowder in Delaware. Du Pont's company would become one of the most successful manufacturers in the United States and the precursor of the huge DuPont chemical conglomerate. In 1802, Simon Willard patented the "banjo" clock, which, along with Eli Terry's all-wood clocks, would become one of the most widespread classes of early manufactured goods in the country. Other small-scale manufactories began to open, particularly in northern states. Ezekiel Case opened what would become his very profitable glove factory in Gloversville, New York, in 1803. Manufacturing was by no means the backbone of the U.S. economy, but increasing numbers of enterprising individuals with capital to invest were managing to open successful businesses.

This stereographic photo from the early 20th century shows Slater's Mill in Pawtucket, Rhode Island, which still retained many of its original features from the late 18th and early 19th centuries. *(Library of Congress, Prints and Photographs Division [LC-USZ62-116492])*

Manufacturing businesses were not the only spurs to increased American commerce at the turn of the 19th century, however. Agricultural production, fueled by a growing market economy that connected U.S. cities to the productive hinterlands, also provided goods for domestic and foreign trade. In 1803 cotton production surpassed tobacco and wheat production for the first time in U.S. history, signaling a major shift, especially in the southern economy. When cotton, grown using slave labor, became a significant staple crop, its supply both encouraged trade with European cloth manufactories and greater growth in American mills. When David Humphreys, a U.S. minister to Spain, returned from his posting abroad in 1802, he brought with him 100 merino sheep and began his quest to spread wool manufacturing as a major U.S. industry. Humphreys's work with the sheep earned him prizes from several American agricultural societies, who began to seize the opportunity to make U.S. agricultural products into trade goods.

The American appetite for manufactured goods continued to outpace domestic production after 1800, a fact that encouraged even more overseas trade. Americans remained willing to risk entanglement in the European wars for the sake of trading agricultural staples and other American exports for European finished goods. The risk posed by the Anglo-French wars had not significantly diminished since the 1790s, especially since Napoleon Bonaparte had risen to power in France. As the European wars waxed and waned, American traders continued to ply their wares and to seek the enforcement of neutral trading rights that had been very tenuously established at the end of the 1790s. The same entrepreneurial energy that fueled domestic economic growth sometimes caused Americans to get themselves into strange and unexpected international trouble, posing foreign and economic policy challenges to the Jefferson administration.

## THE FIRST TRIPOLITAN WAR

In his inaugural address, Thomas Jefferson had framed his vision of U.S. foreign policy by claiming that the nation ought to seek "Peace, commerce, and honest friendship with all nations, entangling alliances with none," but it soon became clear that peace and commerce might be mutually exclusive.[5] Trade in the Mediterranean proved immediately vexing, when the United States entered a new phase of conflict with the Barbary States of Algeria, Tripoli, Tunis, and Morocco. These Islamic states had a history of capturing American ships and sailors, sometimes at the behest of Britain or France, stretching back to the late 1770s—although negotiations and guarantees that the United States would make tribute payments had momentarily put a stop to the worst aggressive actions of the Barbary States in the 1790s. But the United States, focusing more attention on the French and English, had fallen behind on tribute payments, and by 1801 tensions were increasing as Barbary leaders began to threaten anew American shipping.

Yusuf Qaramanli, the pasha of Tripoli, took the initiative to force a crisis with the United States when he threatened all-out war if higher tribute payments were not delivered by the new Jefferson administration in 1801. Thomas Jefferson was not in favor of increasing American military power, generally, and he consistently proposed cutting the size of the U.S. Navy, a traditional favorite project of the Federalist Party. However, Jefferson was also not kindly disposed to use federal power to pay tribute to North African states, and he found himself choosing between increased tribute payments and the use of military force. Even though presidents Washington and Adams had paid tribute to various Barbary States to protect American shipping over the years, Jefferson turned instead to military action.

Yusuf Qaramanli eventually grew frustrated with stalled tribute payments and declared war on the United States by having the U.S. flag cut down in Tripoli in May 1801. His threatening war dispatches reached the United States at the end of 1801, and Jefferson reported to Congress in December that the national insult and the pressure to fight called for a strong American response. Jefferson had sent the U.S. naval ship *Enterprise* to the Mediterranean, where it had won a battle against a Tripolitan ship without any American casualties, and Congress was persuaded to back greater military involvement. In February 1802, Congress authorized the president to use greater naval power against Tripoli, although skeptical Federalists managed to win some restrictions on where and how naval battles could be staged. The U.S. Navy, in an alliance with Sweden, blockaded Tripoli, and Jefferson sent negotiators who managed to keep Morocco, Algeria, and Tunis from breaking the blockade.

Jefferson's administration, while successfully pursuing the blockade against Tripoli, was caught between the desire to restrain military power and the drive to use such power in the Mediterranean. Even as Jefferson was urging lower budgets for the navy, the newly constructed USS *Constitution* sailed for the Mediterranean, and in May 1803, Commodore Edward Preble moved to take command of a whole new squadron bound for the Tripolitan War. The Tripolitan War helped to win authorization in Congress in 1802 for an official U.S. Military Academy established at West Point, New York. Jefferson and his secretary of state, James Madison, found it difficult to successfully argue for the contraction of military forces during a time of war.

It became clear that the United States would not easily emerge from the foreign policy conundrum posed by the Barbary States in October 1803 when news arrived that the USS *Philadelphia* had run aground off Tripoli. The Tripolitans captured the *Philadelphia* and her crew of 300 and demanded ransom for their return. Alexander Hamilton's New York newspaper called the capture of the *Philadelphia* "a practical lesson in Jefferson's economy," since it might have been prevented if the navy were large or strong enough to wage an all-out war on Tripoli.[6] When news of the *Philadelphia's* capture reached the United States early in 1804, the Tripolitan War seemed far from settled and safe shipping in the Mediterranean seemed elusive.

## FEDERAL POWER AND LOUISIANA

Commercial conflict and problems with belligerent foreign powers were not restricted to the Mediterranean. Jefferson faced an even greater challenge to his desire to restrict federal power as international conflicts hit close to home along the Mississippi River. Napoleon Bonaparte, the leader of France, used a lull in France's wars against Great Britain to gather strength, and some of his policies regarding Louisiana provided Jefferson with great opportunity and great challenge for his vision of government.

French control of Louisiana became a threat to American commerce and stability almost immediately after Jefferson took office. In 1801, Spain sold the whole of the Louisiana Territory to France, which hoped to use the territory to provide food for the slave-populated sugar plantations in the colony of Saint-Domingue (modern-day Haiti). The following year, Spain, which still maintained control of New Orleans under the thumb of Napoleon, abruptly announced that the Mississippi River would be closed to American trade. This violation of the Jay-Gardoqui Treaty greatly threatened the economic prosperity of the western United States. Westerners relied on the Mississippi River to send their products to market; as Secretary of State Madison put it: "The Mississippi is to them everything. It is the Hudson, the Delaware, the Potomac, and all the navigable rivers of the Atlantic States formed into one stream."[7] France also moved to deny U.S. trading ships the right of deposit at the port of New Orleans, which specifically violated the terms of other French agreements of the 1790s.

Jefferson and Madison responded to the French and Spanish threats against the Mississippi trade with strong actions that led to an expansion of U.S. territory and the powers of the federal government. Jefferson caused havoc with French colonial policies by sending aid to Toussaint Louverture, the leader of a black rebellion against French rule in Haiti, and by decreeing that American Indians would have to be removed west of the Mississippi River. Even though the president was simultaneously trying to reduce the overall size of the U.S. military and fighting a war against Tripoli, Jefferson also asked Congress to authorize 80,000 militia troops and the construction of 15 gunboats to attack the lower Mississippi territory if Napoleon's obstructionism continued. All these actions, especially the possibility that Jefferson would aid a slave rebellion when he himself worried about such a rebellion occurring on American soil, indicated the high priority of free trade on the Mississippi.

Jefferson stretched his powers to the utmost in 1803, however, when he sent James Monroe and Robert Livingston to France to try to buy New Orleans and the Floridas from Napoleon outright. Napoleon, about to reenter another round of war with Great Britain and weary of French troubles in North America, instead surprised the American negotiators and offered to sell the entire Louisiana Territory to the United States for $15 million. In April, Jefferson agreed to the purchase, although he had to rely on a very wide reading of the Constitution to justify such a large purchase of territory. The Louisiana Purchase promised to double the size of the United States, open up far more land for cultivation and trade, push the United States farther west into Indian territory, and add unprecedented powers to the federal government, all in one fell swoop. On July 4, 1803, the government announced the purchase of the Louisiana Territory to the people of the United States, who responded, for the most part, enthusiastically. Public celebrations abounded. The Senate formally ratified the purchase in October.

The Louisiana Purchase confirmed that the United States would continue to look westward to ensure economic expansion. At the same time, other actions of the federal government solidified control over western territories. Ohio, the first state to be carved out of the Northwest Territory, formally entered the Union in March 1803, and Ohio's white settlers paid little heed to the protected nearby Indian hunting grounds guaranteed by the 1795 Treaty of Greenville. Three months later, Indiana's territorial governor, William Henry Harrison, forced several belligerent Indian nations to cede large tracts of land in the Treaty of Vincennes. The Kaskaskia nation alone ceded half of present-day Illinois in the treaty, which was later disavowed by some members of the Kaskaskia. In August 1803, military officials began construction of Fort Dearborn at the present-day site of Chicago, Illinois. Fort Dearborn would become an important post in Great Lakes trade and a symbol of U.S. military domination of new areas of western territory.

## AN EMPIRE FOR LIBERTY AND COMMERCE

Thomas Jefferson had always preferred to look toward the West rather than back to Europe for the future of the United States. But even though the Louisiana Purchase successfully removed French influence from the continent, Jefferson still had to reckon with a variety of power challenges in the new and unfamiliar territory. When the British explorer Alexander MacKenzie published his *Voyages from Montreal* in 1801, Jefferson was afraid that the tale of the first European exploration across Canada would signal a new surge of British power in North America. Jefferson, who had long been interested in the commercial and farming potential of western lands, also thought it wise to seek water routes across the continent that could increase the Pacific trade. Especially during a time when American shipping was plagued with wartime difficulties on the Atlantic and in the Mediterranean, Jefferson's westward thinking was amplified even further.

Jefferson believed that the western lands would provide an even greater spur for the growth of American democracy, since wide space would offer not only chances for economic prosperity but also room for political disagreements and factions to be diffused. He believed that the Native American population would naturally have to become more educated and "civilized" to give up their old ways of life and blend in with the white population, or be moved out of the way onto land reserved for their purposes. Jefferson never really offered a clear blueprint for Native American relations or the removal of native populations from desirable western lands, but his vision of American democracy read the West largely as consisting of vast, empty space ready for development by freedom-loving U.S. citizens.

As part of Jefferson's plans to develop the West into a commercial and democratic boon for the United States, he planned a voyage of scientific discovery and Indian diplomacy during the same time that he was negotiating the Louisiana Purchase. In 1803 Jefferson commissioned his private secretary, Meriwether Lewis, and a former officer, William Clark, to command an expedition across the North American continent. Jefferson charged Lewis and Clark to record western geography along with their impressions of the natural landscape and to send back scientific specimens from the territory they covered. The Lewis and Clark expedition would be responsible for informing Indian nations that the United States had purchased the Louisiana Territory and for establishing good relations with the nations to protect, as Jefferson put it in his instructions to Meriwether Lewis, the "commerce which may be carried on with the people inhabiting" the territory.[8] Lewis and Clark were also ordered to scout the possibilities for increasing the U.S. fur trade and to record the water routes that Jefferson was sure would allow easier Pacific trade.

Even as the Louisiana Purchase was being made public and the Senate was debating whether to ratify the land deal, Lewis and Clark prepared for their expedition. During October 1803, Lewis and Clark gathered together in the Indiana Territory the men (and later one woman, Sacagawea) who would form their Corps of Discovery. By the end of the year, they had gathered personnel, supplies, weapons, specially struck diplomatic medallions to offer Indian chiefs, and other trade goods into their large flat-bottomed bateau and were preparing to set out down the Mississippi to their embarkation point at the mouth of the Missouri River. Over the following three years, their party would provide the information that would help to define the "new West" for the American government and the American public alike.

## THE PUBLIC AND AWAKENING PROTESTANTISM

Thomas Jefferson and his political allies did not have a monopoly on defining the American social and political order in the first years of the 19th century. Many average American men and women were much more likely to define themselves in terms of religion than in political or economic terms. The religious movement that would sweep the United States throughout the first third of the 19th century, referred to by historians as the Second Great Awakening, was just beginning, sweeping up a new generation of Americans in the fervor of evangelical Christianity. The Second Great Awakening built upon the religious conversions and traditions of the First Great Awakening, which had taken place in America prior to the Revolutionary War in the 1730s and 1740s. The First Great Awakening introduced new styles of preaching and new religious denominations, especially Methodists and Baptists, to the United States. Both Methodist and Baptist churches, as well as new factions of Presbyterianism and Congregationalism influenced by the Awakening preachers, had grown in popularity throughout the 1780s and 1790s. But after the turn of the century, a dramatic surge of energy would cause another boost to American evangelical religion.

Francis Asbury, who had become bishop of the American Methodist Episcopal Church in 1785, established a very successful and popular system of circuit-riding preachers, who traveled around frontier areas on a regular course of sermonizing and missionary work. As a result, some of the greatest evangelical fervor built up in rural areas, many of which did not even have permanent churches or clergy. Yale president Timothy Dwight also sent out students he converted in the 1790s to serve as preachers in rural areas of the West, hoping to bring newly awakened religious fervor to the masses.

This is not to suggest that the Second Great Awakening was an elitist-driven movement. In fact, grassroots Protestantism demanded more and more attention at the turn of the century. The most dramatic symbol that evangelical religion was ready to break open into a full new Great Awakening came with the rise of the camp meeting, an entirely homegrown religious affair. The camp meeting, usually an interdenominational religious meeting held in a rural area that might be attended by both whites and blacks, became the quintessential symbol of the power of the early Second Great Awakening, especially in the South and the West.

The most notable camp meeting revival of all, dubbed the Great Revival, took place at Cane Ridge, Kentucky, in 1801. Organized in part by evangelist and founder of the Disciples of Christ denomination Alexander Campbell, it drew as many as 25,000 people to a spot in rural Bourbon County, Kentucky—a number more than 10 times larger than the population of that state's largest city. The Cane Ridge revival, like most of the camp meetings of the early Second Awakening, emphasized a personal experience with God, as participants danced, sang, listened to sermons, and even fell into trances when enthralled with ecstatic religious experience. The early Second Great Awakening communicated the message to individuals that they could be saved by God, perhaps granting them a sense of agency in a society that did not offer a very large social role for average persons (especially average women). The sense of social empowerment offered by the Second Great Awakening would grow over the next 20 years, but at the turn of the century, the camp meeting symbolized a new growth of energy at the grass roots of American culture.

## JEFFERSONIAN AMERICA AND POWER

By the end of 1803, the Revolution of 1800 that brought Thomas Jefferson and his fellow Democratic-Republicans into office was complete, but the change of party power in 1801 turned out to be revolutionary for reasons that even Jefferson himself might not have predicted. At the beginning of December 1803, Congress passed the Twelfth Amendment to the Constitution and sent it to the states for ratification. The amendment modified the electoral college procedure to allow presidential and vice-presidential candidates to run together on a ticket, a structure that would allow the country to avoid the kind of electoral disaster that had resulted in the deadlock between Thomas Jefferson and Aaron Burr in the election of 1800. In some ways, the passage of the Twelfth Amendment recognized once and for all that political parties could be a stabilizing force in American politics, even though Thomas Jefferson still worried that party opposition might merely create factions. Although Jefferson had declared in his inaugural speech that "We are all Republicans, We are all Federalists," each party would continue to have separate and defined membership, ideas, and agendas for government action.

Jefferson and his party also favored a restraint of federal power, but the year 1803 also ended with the confirmation of one of the strongest federal measures ever, entirely orchestrated by President Jefferson himself. On December 20, 1803, a large ceremony in New Orleans symbolically completed the transfer of the entire Louisiana Territory from France to the United States. Jefferson had used federal power almost to double the size of the United States. The consequences of the Louisiana Purchase would not be entirely clear for years to come, but in the meantime President Jefferson awaited word from the Lewis and Clark expedition and anticipated a great new era of western development for the American republic.

# CHRONICLE OF EVENTS

## 1801

Printer Matthew Carey helps to organize the American Company of Booksellers, which holds an annual book fair in New York City at the Beaver Street Coffee House.

Joseph Dennie founds *Port Folio* magazine, which becomes the most important magazine in the United States until after the War of 1812.

The *New York Evening Post* begins publication.

Josiah Ben begins baking hard-water crackers and selling them from his home in Milton, Massachusetts. The crackers will soon become a New England regional delicacy.

E. I. Du Pont establishes his gunpowder factory outside Wilmington, Delaware.

American inventor Robert Fulton tests the first entirely successful submarine, the *Nautilus.*

*January 1:* Peter Jones (Kahkewaquonaby) is born in Upper Canada. He later becomes an important Mississauga chief and Methodist missionary.

*January 20:* John Adams appoints John Marshall as chief justice of the U.S. Supreme Court. He will become one of the most significant justices in U.S. history.

*February 11:* The votes of the presidential electors in the 1800 presidential election are officially unsealed. The tie vote of 73 votes each for Thomas Jefferson and Aaron Burr means that the House of Representatives will be called upon to determine the winner. The House votes to enter continuous session until the election is decided.

*February 17:* The House of Representatives elects Thomas Jefferson the third president of the United States. The deadlock vote between Burr and Jefferson is broken only after an all-night session of balloting. Some critics accuse Democratic-Republican Aaron Burr of offering to throw his support to Federalist causes if he is elected.

*February 27:* Congress passes the Judiciary Act, which reduces the number of Supreme Court justices from six to five (in a last-ditch effort by the Federalist Congress to keep a Supreme Court appointment out of Jefferson's hands). The act also establishes 16 circuit courts.

*March 3:* President Adams works until his last minute in office; among his so-called midnight

This lithographic portrait of Thomas Jefferson depicts the president as a dignified character, yet also conveys the image of Jefferson as a man of the people. *(Library of Congress, Prints and Photographs Division [LC-USZ62-386])*

appointments, he elevates prominent Federalists to federal judgeships.

*March 4:* Thomas Jefferson is inaugurated as president at the first presidential inauguration held in Washington, D.C. Aaron Burr becomes vice president.

*March 8:* Congress repeals the Judiciary Act, which allowed John Adams to make his "midnight appointments" to pack the federal courts with Federalist judges.

*May 14:* Yusuf Qaramanli, the pasha of Tripoli, declares war on the United States and orders the flagpole at the American consulate to be cut down.

*May–August:* A smallpox epidemic sweeps across southern Canada and kills thousands of native peoples.

*June 14:* In London, traitorous Revolutionary War general Benedict Arnold dies.

*August 7:* A two-week revival meeting at Cane Ridge, Kentucky, which draws an estimated 25,000 people, signals the strength of the popular revivalism that will become a prominent feature of the Second Great Awakening religious movement.

## 1802

A group of New York elite individuals establishes the American Academy of Arts and sells stock in the organization.

Nathaniel Bowditch publishes the *New American Practical Navigator,* which will set the standard for navigation at sea for many years to come.

The New York state legislature bans public horse racing.

Colonel David Humphreys returns from his diplomatic post in Spain and introduces 100 merino sheep into the United States to provide the beginnings of a new and important wool industry.

Noah Webster publishes "The Rights of Neutral Nations in Time of War."

Simon Willard patents the "banjo" clock, which will become a very popular American timepiece.

The state of Georgia cedes its western land claims to the federal government in return for a guarantee (directly conflicting with treaty terms) that the federal government will confiscate all Native American lands within the Georgia borders.

*January 5:* The U.S. Senate first admits stenographers and note takers to record debate.

*January 29:* John Beckley is appointed the first librarian of Congress.

*February 6:* Congress grants the president authority to use naval power against Tripoli but is wary of all-out war and thus restricts naval action to open waters. The grant is considered by most Americans to be a formal declaration of war on Tripoli, which is already at war with the United States.

*March 8:* Congress repeals the Judiciary Act of 1801, which President Jefferson accuses of creating factional division in government by promoting a Federalist judiciary.

*March 16:* Congress authorizes a U.S. military academy and establishes the U.S. Army Engineer Corps.

*March 30:* Congress passes the Trade and Intercourse Act, which regulates Indian trade and empowers the president to restrict alcohol sales to tribal groups.

*April 29:* Congress passes the Judiciary Act of 1802, which returns the Supreme Court to six justices

from five and assigns each justice supervisory powers over certain federal circuit courts.

*May 3:* Congress incorporates Washington, D.C., as an independent city, and President Jefferson appoints Robert Brent as the city's first mayor.

*May 22:* Former first lady Martha Washington dies.

*July 4:* The U.S. Military Academy at West Point begins operation.

*July 6:* Revolutionary War general and frontiersman Daniel Morgan dies.

*September:* Journalist and former Democratic-Republican scandalmonger James Callender alleges in print that Thomas Jefferson has fathered several children by his slave and "concubine," Sally Hemings.

*October 16:* Spain abolishes American shipping rights on the Mississippi River. Although France formally owns the Louisiana Territory and rights to the river, Napoleon lets Spain set policy. Confusion over decision making and interference with commerce prompt Thomas Jefferson to consider negotiating or buying rights to Mississippi River traffic.

## 1803

Cotton overtakes tobacco as the primary export crop of the United States. The new dominance of cotton reflects the rise in production made possible by the 1793 invention of the cotton gin. The rise in cotton production also helps to entrench slavery more firmly in the southern states.

In Salisbury, Connecticut, publisher Caleb Bingham founds the Library of Youth, the first public library to be supported by tax money.

Ezekiel Case begins operation of his glove manufacturing business in Gloversville, New York.

The Middlesex Canal, which connects Boston Harbor and the Merrimack River, opens.

Benjamin Crehorne builds the first U.S.-made piano in Milton, Massachusetts.

New York's city hall opens.

Virginian William Wirt anonymously publishes his *Letters of a British Spy,* which provides commentary on American society and politics, in a Richmond newspaper.

In the war against Tripoli, the USS *Philadelphia* is captured after running aground. It will be dramatically recaptured and burned by Stephen Decatur the following year.

This painting depicts a port broadside view of the USS *Constitution*. *(Library of Congress, Prints and Photographs Division [LC-D416-20340])*

The USS *Constitution*, commanded by Edward Preble, sails to the Mediterranean to protect U.S. shipping.

Congress allocates $3,000 for the civilization and education of "heathen" Indians.

*January 12:* Thomas Jefferson sends James Monroe to France as an official envoy to negotiate for rights to New Orleans and Florida.

*January 18:* Thomas Jefferson requests funding from Congress to send a voyage of exploration to find a water route to the Pacific River. Jefferson directs Meriwether Lewis to begin preparing for a journey to the Pacific.

*February 24:* The Supreme Court issues a decision in the case of *Marbury v. Madison*, which establishes the right of judicial review—the court's power to decide whether acts of Congress are constitutional or not.

*March:* John Sibley explores the Red River.

*March 1:* Ohio, formerly a part of the Northwest Territory, enters the union as the 17th state. It becomes the first state admitted to the union under the procedures outlined in the Northwest Ordinance.

*April:* John James Audubon begins his observation of birds and other wildlife. He becomes the first person in the United States to track birds using a system of banding.

*April 11:* French foreign minister Talleyrand informs U.S. envoys that France is willing to sell the entire Louisiana Territory to the United States.

*April 19:* Spanish officials open the port of New Orleans to American trade.

*May 2:* Robert Livingston and James Monroe sign a treaty with France concluding the Louisiana Purchase. The United States buys the whole territory for under $15 million.

*May 23:* Captain Edward Preble assumes command of a naval squadron bound for the Mediterranean to do battle against Tripolitan forces.

*June 7:* William Henry Harrison, the governor of Indiana Territory, signs the Treaty of Vincennes with nine Indian nations, which are forced to cede land to the United States. The Kaskaskia nation cedes half of present-day Illinois.

*July 4:* The Louisiana Purchase is announced to the American public.

*August 17:* Construction of Fort Dearborn begins in the present-day location of Chicago, Illinois.

*August 31:* Thomas Jefferson sends Meriwether Lewis and William Clark to explore the Louisiana Territory, establish diplomatic relations with Indian nations, and scout commercial and trade opportunities.

*September 29:* Congregants dedicate the first Roman Catholic church built in Boston.

*October 2:* Former Revolutionary patriot and Massachusetts governor Samuel Adams dies.

*October 15–26:* Meriwether Lewis and William Clark bring together their exploration crew, dubbed the "Corps of Discovery," in Indiana Territory.

*October 20:* The Senate ratifies the purchase of the Louisiana Territory.

*November:* Charles Brockdon Brown begins publication of the *Memoirs of Carwin the Biloquist* a Gothic tale of ventriloquism and secret societies.

*December 9:* Congress passes the Twelfth Amendment to the Constitution, which seeks to provide for the separate election of president and vice president. This would make a tie vote in the presidential election, such as the one in 1800, less likely.

*December 20:* A ceremony in New Orleans signifies the formal transfer of Louisiana from French to U.S. control.

## EYEWITNESS TESTIMONY

It will be the wisdom, and probably the future effort of the American government, forever to maintain with unshaken magnanimity, the present neutral position of the United States. The hand of nature has displayed its magnificence in this quarter of the globe, in the astonishing rivers, lakes, and mountains, replete with the richest minerals and the most useful materials for manufacture. At the same time, the indigenous produce of its fertile lands yields medicine, food, and clothing, and every thing needful for man in his present condition.

*Mercy Otis Warren describes the state of the United States in 1801 in Warren,* History of the Rise, *II: 697.*

I sincerely wish Mr. Adams had taken the advice of his best friends, who counseled against sending the last mission to France, and had not made incurable inroads on the federal party, by taking a course which has lost him the Presidency, and led to his utter debasement. Where is all this to end? If the House of Representatives should choose Mr. Jefferson We undoubtedly have to apprehend a change in some most essential points of our Government, and great national interests. If Mr. Burr succeeds, we may flatter ourselves that he will not suffer the Executive power to be frittered into insignificance; but can we promise ourselves, that he will not continue to seek and depend upon his own party, for support?

*Federalist J. McHenry in a letter to Rufus King, January 2, 1801, in King,* Life and Correspondence of Rufus King, *III: 362.*

My extreme anxiety about the ensuing election of President by the House of Representatives will excuse to you the liberty I take in addressing you concerning it without being consulted by you. Did you know Mr. *Burr* as well as I do . . . You would be clearly of opinion with me that Mr. Jefferson is to be preferred.

*Alexander Hamilton in a letter to John Rutledge, Jr., January 4, 1801, in Freeman,* Alexander Hamilton, *972.*

Jefferson & Burr have each 73 votes & it is, as you well know, for the house to decide which shall be first: the Federalists in general are for Burr & great efforts are making to secure his preference in the

house. I think however they will not succeed & I think they ought not *unless Burr will & Jefferson will not* previously engage to uphold essential the existing policy.

*Federalist George Cabot in a letter to Rufus King, January 28, 1801, in King,* Life and Correspondence of Rufus King, *III: 378–379.*

It is now universally understood that Mr. Burr and Mr. Jefferson have received from the electors an equal number of votes . . . It is by no means impossible that they may also have an equal number of votes in the house of representatives . . . It is certainly of very great importance to decide what will be the result should neither of them have a constitutional majority . . . Congress . . . have the power to declare what officer shall act as President.

The Philadelphia Aurora *reports the sentiments of its rival the* Washington Federalist, *February 12, 1801, in Rosenfeld,* American Aurora, *898.*

I called on Mr. Adams. We conversed on the state of things. I observed to him that a very dangerous experiment was then in contemplation to defeat the Presidential election by an act of Congress declaring the right to devolve on him the government during any interregnum . . . He seemed to think such an act justifiable and observed that it was in my power to fix the election by a word in an instant, by declaring I would not turn out the federal [Federalist] officers.

*Thomas Jefferson reports on a conversation with John Adams, February 12, 1801, in Rosenfeld* American Aurora, *899.*

The crisis was at hand. The two bodies of Congress met, the Senators as witnesses the Representatives as electors. The question on which hung peace or war, nay, the Union of the States was to be decided. What an awful responsibility was attached to every vote given on that occasion. The sitting was held with closed doors. It lasted the whole day, the whole night. . . . Beds, as well as food were sent, for the accommodation of those whom age or debility disabled from enduring such a long protracted sitting—the balloting took place every hour—in the interval men ate, drank, slept or pondered over the result of the last ballot, compared ideas and persuasions to change votes, or gloomily anticipated the consequences, let the result be what it would. . . . For more than thirty hours the struggle was maintained, but finding the republican phalanx impenetrable . . . Mr. Jefferson was declared duly elected.

*Washington socialite Margaret Bayard Smith describes the presidential voting procedure in the House of Representatives in her notebook, February 1801, in Hunt,* The First Forty Years, *23, 24, 25.*

The conduct of Mr. Adams is not such as was to have been wished, or, perhaps, expected. Instead of smoothing the path for his successor, he plays into the hands of those who are endeavoring to strew it with as many difficulties as possible; and with this view, does not manifest a very squeamish regard to the Constitution. Will not his appointments to offices . . . be null?

*James Madison in a letter to Thomas Jefferson, February 28, 1801, in* Letters and Other Writings of James Madison, *II: 171.*

We have called by different names brethren of the same principle. We are all Republicans, we are all Federalists. If there be any among us who would wish to dissolve this Union or to change its republican form, let them stand undisturbed as monuments of the safety with which error of opinion may be tolerated where reason is left free to combat it. I know, indeed, that some honest men fear that a republican government can not be strong, that this Government is not strong enough; but would the honest patriot, in the full tide of successful experiment, abandon a government which has so far kept us free and firm on the theoretic and visionary fear that this Government, the world's best hope, may by possibility want energy to preserve itself? I trust not. I believe this, on the contrary, the strongest Government on earth.

*Thomas Jefferson in his first inaugural address, March 4, 1801. Available online. Avalon Project. URL: http://www.yale.edu/lawweb/avalon/ presiden/inaug/jefinau1.htm.*

I cannot describe the agitation I felt, while I looked around on the various multitude and while I listened to an address, containing principles the most correct, sentiments the most liberal, and wishes the most benevolent, conveyed in the most appropriate and elegant language and in a manner mild as it was firm. If doubts of the integrity and talents of Mr. Jefferson ever existed in the minds of any one, methinks this address must forever eradicate them. . . . The speech was delivered in so low a tone that few heard it.

*Washington socialite Margaret Bayard Smith describes attending Jefferson's inaugural address in a letter to Susan G. Smith, March 4, 1801, in Hunt,* The First Forty Years, *25–26.*

The change took place yesterday at 12 o'clock; when Mr. Jefferson, the new President, took the oath of office . . . The whole ceremony was conducted with the utmost propriety. As on the part of those who had supported the new President in the election, there was no unbecoming exultation; so his opposers manifested by their behavior, a cheerful acquiescence in the decision of the majority.

*South Carolina congressman Robert Goodloe Harper in a public letter to his constituents, March 5, 1801, in Cunningham,* Circular Letters, *247–248.*

No party that ever existed knew itself so little or so vainly overrated its own influence and popularity, as ours. None ever understood so ill the causes of its own power or so wantonly destroyed them. If we had been blessed with common sense, we should not have been overthrown by . . . Duane, Callender, Cooper and Lyon, or their great protector [Thomas Jefferson]. A group of foreign liars, encouraged by a few ambitious native gentlemen, have discomfited the education, the talents, the virtues, and the property of the country.

*John Adams in a letter to his former naval secretary Benjamin Stoddert, March 31, 1801, in Rosenfeld,* American Aurora, *901.*

I am not unacquainted with Mr. Jefferson, & if I can form a correct judgment of his system, he will be desirous of promoting the internal improvement of his country, and preserving it as much as possible from being entangled with *any European* connections: nobody will contradict the propriety of the first, and few will doubt the propriety of the last; tho' there may be those on this side of the Atlantic who might wish it to be otherwise.

*William Strickland in a letter to Rufus King, April 15, 1801, in King,* Life and Correspondence of Rufus King, *III: 431–432.*

The scene was awful beyond description; the falling, crying out, praying, exhorting, singing, shouting,

This 1819 engraving of a Methodist camp meeting shows participants engaged in some of the same kinds of ecstatic religious behavior described by people who attended the Cane Ridge revival in 1801. *(Library of Congress, Prints and Photographs Division [LC-USZ62-2497])*

&c. . . . few, if any, could escape without being afflicted. [I had the bodies] collected together, and laid out in order, on two squares of the meetinghouse; which, like so many dead corpses, covered a considerable part of the floor.

*Presbyterian minister Richard McNemar describes the new kind of revival religion that is beginning to sweep Kentucky, May 1801, in Eslinger,* Citizens of Zion, *203.*

I am conscious that the Mint, has been the subject of great Complaints particularly with regard to its expense—This has certainly been without just cause, as every plan for reducing the expence [sic] to government, has been uniformly rejected by all parties in various Committees of both Houses of Congress, on the policy that all the charge should be borne by the Govt. and the Depositors have every thing done without the least expense to them.

*Elias Boudinot, director of the U.S. Mint, in a letter to President Thomas Jefferson, June 16, 1801, in Boudinot,* Life, Public Services, Addresses, *II: 159–160.*

We found 20 persons present in a room where sat Mr. J. surrounded by the five Cherokee chiefs. After a conversation of a few minutes, he invited his company into the usual dining room, whose four large sideboards were covered with refreshments, such as cakes of various kinds, wine, punch, &c. All appeared to be cheerful, all happy. Mr. Jefferson mingled promiscuously with the citizens, and far from designating any particular friends for consultation, conversed for a short time with every one that came in his way.

*Washington socialite Margaret Bayard Smith describes the Fourth of July celebrations at the White House in a letter to Mary Ann Smith, July 5, 1801, in Hunt,* The First Forty Years, *30–31.*

I am on my way to one of the greatest meetings of the kind perhaps ever known; it is on a sacramental occasion. Religion has got to such a height here, that people attend from great distances; on this occasion. I doubt not but there will be 10,000 people, and perhaps 500 wagons. . . . The people encamp on the ground, and continue praising God, day and night, for one whole week before they break up.

*A Kentucky Baptist anticipates the great revival meeting at Cane Ridge, August 7, 1801, in Eslinger,* Citizens of Zion, *207.*

From 1801 for years a blessed revival of religion spread through almost the entire inhabited parts of the West, Kentucky, Tennessee, the Carolinas, and many other parts . . . The Presbyterians and Methodists in a great measure united in this work, met together, prayed together, and preached together. In this revival originated our camp meetings . . . They would erect their camps with logs or frame them, and cover them with clapboards or shingles. They would also erect a shed, sufficiently large to protect five thousand people from wind and rain . . . Ten, twenty and sometimes thirty ministers, of different denominations, would come together and preach night and day, four or five days together; and, indeed, I have known these camp-meetings to last three or four weeks, and great good resulted from them.

*Peter Cartwright remembers the great revival of 1801, in his memoirs, in Craven, Johnson, and Dunne* Documentary History, *265.*

The day is within my time as well as yours when we may say by what laws other nations shall treat us on the sea. And we will say it. In the meantime, we wish to let every treaty we have drop off without renewal.

*Thomas Jefferson in a letter to Albert Gallatin, September 5, 1801, in DeConde, The Quasi-War, 321.*

From Tunis and Leghorn I learn Commodore Dale had published a notification, purporting that 'the Bashaw of Tripoli having declared war against the United States, the port of Tripoli was blockaded by an armed force of the said States' . . . The Consul of the United States at Gibraltar writes to me that the timely arrival of the squadron under the orders of Commodore Dale, has prevented at least twenty-five merchant ships, belonging to citizens of the United States, with rich cargoes, from falling into the possession of those pirates.

*American ambassador to Spain David Humphreys reports on the Tripolitan War in a letter, September 10, 1801, in Humphreys, Life and Times of David Humphreys, II: 302, 303.*

As for my new "friend tobacco," he is like most of that name; has made me twice sick and is now dismissed.

*Daniel Webster in a letter to a college friend, October 26, 1801, in Webster, Private Correspondence of Daniel Webster, I: 98.*

I mentioned to you, that I had conceived a plan for a spoon manufacturing machine . . . I had it tried here and at Philadelphia, by different silversmiths, in the presence of a number of gentlemen; and have by me certificates to shew, that the product is more than 60 to one faster than with the hammer, and same number of hands. . . . I have laid out, in improvements and patents, all the money I ever had, and there is little encouragement either publick or private, for the most useful inventions, and he that does the most to lessen the enormous price of labour, unless he has the means of providing a capital, is like to be the poorest man.

*Inventor Thomas Bruff in a letter to President Thomas Jefferson, December 16, 1801, in McLaughlin, To His Excellency, 232, 233.*

The low price to which tobacco has for some years fallen in Europe, has occasioned the culture of it to be abandoned in these countries. That of the *Green-seed Cotton* has replaced it, very advantageously for the inhabitants, a great number of whom are already enriched by it. The separation of the seeds from the husks which enclose them, a tedious operation, which requires much manual labour, has been lately simplified by a machine, for which the inventor has obtained a patent from the American government. . . . In all the lower country the labours of the field are performed by negroes; and most of the planters employ them even in those which might be done with the plough.

*French traveler François André Michaux describes agriculture in the Carolinas and Georgia, 1802, in Hart, American History, III: 71, 72.*

The newspapers will have shown the position of the bill now before the Senate for the repeal of the act of last session establishing a new judiciary system . . . The constitutional right and power of abolishing one judiciary system and establishing another cannot be doubted.

*Vice President Aaron Burr in a letter to Barnabas Bidwell, February 1, 1802, in Davis, Memoirs of Aaron Burr, I: 169.*

Mine is an odd destiny. Perhaps no man in the U. States has sacrificed or done more for the present Constitution than myself—and contrary to all my anticipations of its fate, as you know from the very begginning [sic] I am still labouring to prop the frail and worthless fabric. Yet I have the murmurs of its friends no less than the curses of its foes for my rewards. What can I do better than withdraw from the Scene? Every day proves to me more and more that this American world was not made for me.

*Alexander Hamilton laments his political fate in a letter to Gouverneur Morris, February 29, 1802, in Freeman, Alexander Hamilton, 986.*

The judiciary storm has passed away for the present. I perceive, however, that an effort is making to improve the old system without increasing the number of judges; and we are once more unanimous at the bar of Philadelphia in rejoicing that Paterson, and not Chase, presides in our circuit. . . . There are some rumours of jealousy and dissatisfaction prevailing among the republican leaders, in the executive as well as the legislative departments of the federal as well as of our state government. It will be disgraceful, indeed, if the rumours are true.

*A. J. Dallas in a letter to Vice President Aaron Burr, April 3, 1802, in Davis, Memoirs of Aaron Burr, II: 84–85.*

Appearances in the Barbary are yet hostile—Tripoli has for some time carried on a predatory war against the United States, in consequence of which a small fleet has been ordered to the Mediterranean for the protection of our commerce and seamen in that and the adjoining seas—should Algiers and Tunis pursue the measures adopted by Tripoli, which is not improbable, however disagreeable such a step would be for a short time, it would, I presume, in its consequences, be productive of good effects, as it would furnish the United States with a sufficient cause for divesting themselves of a tribute as disgraceful as it is unjust.

*Tennessee congressman William Dickinson in a circular letter to his constituents, April 5, 1802, in Cunningham,* Circular Letters, *280.*

The cession of Louisiana and the Floridas by Spain to France, works most sorely on the United States . . . There is on the globe one single spot, the possessor of which is our natural and habitual enemy. It is New Orleans, through which the produce of three-eighths of our territory must pass to market . . . France, placing herself in that door, assumes to us the attitude of defiance.

*President Thomas Jefferson in a letter to Robert R. Livingston, the American minister to France, April 18, 1802, in Commager,* Documents, *189.*

. . . yesterday, I received the Medal in gold, which the Trustees of the Massachusetts Society for promoting Agriculture did me the honour to present to me from that Society, in consequence of my having introduced into New-England a small flock of the Merino breed of sheep . . . Should our mutual hope and expectation of meliorating the breed of sheep in America, by the introduction of this race, be fulfilled, I shall consider myself peculiarly fortunate for having been instrumental in producing an event, from which I shall derive more pleasure and consolation than from any other transaction of my life.

*David Humphreys in a letter to the Rev. S. Parker, April 23, 1803, in Humphreys,* Life and Times of David Humphreys, *II: 347.*

Black men if you have now a mind to join with me now is your time for freedom. All clever men who will keep secret these words I give to you is life . . . I have joined with both black and white which is the common man or poor white people, mulattoes will Join with me to help free the country, although they are free already. . . . I mean to lose my life in this way if they will take it.

*Arthur, a rebellious slave, calls for others to join his slave revolt, spring 1802, in Aptheker,* Documentary History, *50.*

Woodcuts such as this one were popular in the 19th century for their depiction of the Jeffersonian ideal of agrarian rural life. *(from Benson Lossing,* The Pictorial Field-Book of the Revolution, *1851–1852)*

The talent with which Heaven has intrusted me is small, very small, yet I feel responsible for the use of it, and am not willing to pervert it to purposes reproachful or unjust, nor to hide it, like the slothful servant, in a napkin. Now, I will enumerate the inducements that draw me towards the law. First and principally, it is my father's wish. . . . Secondly, my friends generally wish it. They are urgent and pressing. . . . and Mr. Thompson offers my tuition gratis, and to relinquish his stand to me.

*Daniel Webster describes his future career plans in a letter to a friend, May 18, 1802, in Webster,* Private Correspondence of Daniel Webster, *111.*

I imagine you will find it more difficult to return from European to American habits than the first change from American to European. It happens too that the state to which you return [Connecticut] as the adjoining one of Massachusetts is still under the paroxysm of party feelings, which the other states have worked through more quickly. Indeed we are no where as yet entirely clear of the wave of agitation which reached us from Europe in the year 1798, but I trust that the follies & violences first of one nation and then of another, will shortly have cured us all of European attachments & antipathies, and leave us under a conviction that we have no business to take part in them.

*President Thomas Jefferson in a letter to David Humphreys, the recently recalled American ambassador to Spain, July 15, 1802, in Humphreys,* Life and Times of David Humphreys, *II: 308.*

It has been asserted in various publications that Mr. Burr, during the late election for president and vice-president, entered into negotiations and agreed to terms with the federal party, or with certain individuals of that party, with a view to advance himself to the office of president to the exclusion of Mr. Jefferson. Mr. Burr, in a letter to Governor Bloomfield, dated the 21st of September last, declared that all such allegations were false and groundless . . .

*P. Irving in a letter to newspaper editor Daniel A. Ogden, November 24, 1802, in Davis,* Memoirs of Aaron Burr, *II: 95.*

The Indian tribes residing within the limits of the United States have, for a considerable time, been growing more and more uneasy at the constant diminution of the territory they occupy. . . . to provide an extension of territory which the rapid increase of our numbers will call for, two measures are deemed expedient. First: to encourage them to abandon hunting, to apply to the raising stock, to agriculture and domestic manufactures . . . Secondly: to multiply trading-houses among them, and place within their reach those things which will contribute more to their domestic comfort than the possession of extensive but uncultivated wilds.

*Thomas Jefferson in a message to Congress, January 18, 1803, in Hunt,* The Essential Thomas Jefferson, *207, 208.*

The business of New Orleans is much talked of here[.] In my opinion . . . we should immediately take possession, and then treat about it. We have no business to make excuses for the conduct of the Spanish government, by saying that they gave no orders to treat us in this manner. For my own part I do not fear a war with France and Spain. We could do more injury to them than they could do us.

*Charles Biddle in a letter to Aaron Burr, February 3, 1803, in Davis,* Memoirs of Aaron Burr, *II: 235.*

It is emphatically the province and duty of the judicial department to say what the law is. Those who apply the rule to particular cases, must of necessity expound and interpret that rule. If two laws conflict with each other the courts must decide on the operation of each. So if a law be in opposition to the constitution; if both the law and the constitution apply to a particular case, so that the court must either decide that case conformably to the law, disregarding the constitution; or conformably to the constitution, disregarding the law; the court must determine which of these conflicting rules governs the case. This is of the very essence of judicial duty. . . . It is also not entirely unworthy of observation, that in declaring what shall be the supreme law of the land, the constitution itself is first mentioned; and not the laws of the United States generally, but those only which shall be made in pursuance of the constitution, have that rank. Thus, the particular phraseology of the constitution of the United States confirms and strengthens the principle, supposed to be essential to all written constitutions, that a law repugnant to the constitution is void; and that courts, as well as other departments, are bound by that instrument.

*Chief Justice John Marshall delivers an opinion in the case of* Marbury v. Madison *and defines the principle of judicial review, February 24, 1803. Available online. Touro Law Center Website. URL: http:// law.tourlaw.edu/patch/Marbury/.*

But as to Louisiana, this new, immense, unbounded world, if it should ever be incorporated into this Union, which I have no idea can be done but by altering the Constitution, I believe it will be the greatest curse that could at present befall us; it may be productive of innumerable evils . . . as to what has been suggested of removing the Creeks and other nations of Indians from the eastern to the western banks of the Mississippi, and of making the fertile regions of Louisiana a howling wilderness, never to be trodden by the foot of civilized man, it is impracticable . . .

*A senator opposes the annexation of Louisiana, 1803, in* Hart, American History, *III: 373.*

You will find, also, that the Spanish Government has pretty promptly corrected the wrong done by its officer at New Orleans. This event . . . will be very soothing to those immediately interested in the trade of the Mississippi. The temper manifested by our Western Citizens has been throughout the best that can be conceived. The real injury from the suspension of the deposit was, however, much lessened by the previous destruction of the entire crop of wheat in Kentucky . . . Certain it is that the hearts and hopes of the Western people are strongly fixed on the Mississippi for the future boundary.

*James Madison in a letter to James Monroe, April 20, 1803, in* Letters and Other Writings of James Madison, *II: 180–181.*

The First Consul of the French Republic desiring to give to the United States a strong proof of his friendship, doth hereby cede to the said United States, in the name of the French Republic, forever and in full sovereignty, the said territory with all its rights and appurtenances, as fully and in the same manner as they have been acquired by the French Republic . . .

*The French government cedes Louisiana to the United States, April 30, 1803, in* Commager, Documents, *190.*

With respect to the marines I am happy to say that a change for the better has taken place in their conduct. We no longer see them intoxicated as formerly—nor is the neighborhood disturbed with their nocturnal riots and outrages—Not a single complaint has been made by any of the citizens since the arrival of Lieut. Keene so that as long as the present system of discipline is maintained it will not be necessary to rent a House and remove them from the Yard.

*The secretary of the navy reports good news in a letter to William W. Burrows, commandant of the Marine Corps, May 6, 1803, in* United States Office of Naval Records and Library, Naval Documents Related to the United States Wars with the Barbary Powers, *II: 400.*

I am truly sensible of the honor the President has conferred on me by committing to my direction the command of the Squadron destined for the Mediterranean service. . . . although I may err in judgment from a want of talents and experience, for so important Station, yet he may rest assured that I never shall from a want of Zeal for the Public service. The honor of the American Flag is very dear to me, and I hope it will never be tarnished under my command . . . I am making progress in preparing the *Constitution* for heaving down.

*Captain Edward Preble in a letter to the secretary of the navy, May 27, 1803, in* United States Office of Naval Records and Library, Naval Documents Related to the United States Wars with the Barbary Powers, *II: 423.*

In the journey which you are about to undertake, for the discovery of the course and source of the Missouri, and of the most convenient water communication from thence to the Pacific Ocean, your party being small, it is to be expected that you will encounter considerable dangers from the Indian inhabitants. . . . I hereby authorize you to draw on the secretaries of state, of the treasury, of war, and of the navy of the United States . . . for the purpose of obtaining money or necessaries for yourself and men . . .

*Thomas Jefferson in a letter to Meriwether Lewis, July 4, 1803 in* Hunt, The Essential Thomas Jefferson, *211.*

Yesterday was a day of joy to our citizens and of pride to our President. It is a day which you know he always enjoys. How much more must he have enjoyed it on this occasion from the great event that occasioned

Meriwether Lewis served as Thomas Jefferson's trusted secretary before leading one of the most daring transcontinental expeditions in American history. *(Library of Congress, Prints and Photographs Division [LC-USZ62-105848])*

it. The news of the cession of the Louisiana only arrived about 8 o'clock of the night preceding, just in time to be officially announced on this auspicious day. Next to the liberty of his country, peace is certainly the dearest to his heart. . . . This mighty event forms an era in our history, and of itself must render the administration of Jefferson immortal.

*Samuel Harrison Smith describes Fourth of July celebrations in Washington, D.C., in a letter to Margaret Bayard Smith, July 5, 1803, in Hunt,* The First Forty Years, *38.*

Our jacobins have already indulged their French feelings—they allow that the success of England—at least in defending herself—is necessary to keep France from troubling us; yet such is their profligacy and their hatred that they would rather risk the liberty of our country, than see England beat the French.

*Federalist George Cabot comments on the government's pro-French views in a letter to Rufus King, July 9, 1803, in King,* Life and Correspondence of Rufus King, *IV: 284.*

The following day every farmer came from the neighbourhood to the house, who had any children to send to my Academy, for such they did me the honour to term the log-hut in which I was to teach. Each man brought his son, or his daughter, and rejoiced that the day was arrived when their little ones could light their tapers and the torch of knowledge! . . . Of the boys I cannot speak in very encomiastic terms; but they were perhaps like all other school-boys, that is, more disposed to play truant than enlighten their minds.

*Schoolmaster John Davis describes his first days at the school he founded in Virginia, 1803, in Thorp,* Southern Reader, *193–194, 195.*

Novel reading has, I find, not only the ill effect of rendering people romantic, which, thanks to my father on earth, I am long past, but they really furnish no occupation to the mind. . . . A collection of images, which amuse only from their variety and rapid succession, like the pictures of a magic lantern; not like a piece of Vanderlyn, where the painter makes fine touches, and leaves to your vanity at least the merit of discovering them.

*Theodosia Burr Alston in a letter to her father, Aaron Burr, October 21, 1803, in Davis,* Memoirs of Aaron Burr, *II: 243.*

. . . the United States of America are under a great Calamity as a nation, and more especially some of our Cities and Capitals, in many parts of the Union, by reason of the Epidemical disease generally called the yellow Fever. . . . But when I contemplate of the many Thousands of our fellow men within the limits of the United States captivated to perpetual slavery, from generation to generation; either by law, or without Law . . . I am not at a loss for the special cause of the aforesaid calamity. . . . It obviously appears that the righteous Judge of Heaven and Earth, has marked out our great capitals and maritime Towns, and Cities, as the greatest offenders . . .

*Park Woodward in a letter to President Thomas Jefferson, November 28, 1803, in McLaughlin,* To His Excellency, *264, 265.*

# 7

# Rising Conflict
## 1804–1807

Since the end of the Revolutionary War, the United States had struggled to establish itself as a respected and independent nation. Having replaced the Articles of Confederation with the federal system defined by the U.S. Constitution, the nation's leaders sought to obtain a place for the United States in the world that would recognize what they believed to be its unique mission as a modern republic. Domestic life in the United States had changed since 1783, and the growth of commerce and market economic activities had given American citizens greater connections to one another and to the world outside. Improvements in transportation and increasing numbers of newspapers that provided better communication made Americans feel more connected than ever before, even as the addition of new land was vastly increasing the size of U.S. territory.

But although some Americans were feeling more confident of their internal connections as well as their place in the world, that did not mean the United States was ready to assume the status of a world power. The conflicts that had threatened to engulf the United States since the late 1790s—the series of Anglo-French wars, attacks by the Barbary States of North Africa, conflicts with Native Americans, and connections between domestic political turmoil and international strife—all seemed to grow worse at once between 1804 and 1807. During Thomas Jefferson's second term in office, conflagrations seemed to spread out in every direction, and the nation struggled to gain international respect, even as American citizens increasingly came to expect it as a matter of course. Some conflicts were solved, and some were not, but all together the challenges faced during these years questioned the place of the United States in the wider world.

## POLITICS IN JEFFERSONIAN AMERICA

In 1804, Thomas Jefferson was almost unanimously reelected president over the Federalist candidate, Charles Coatsworth Pinckney. The Democratic-Republican Party enjoyed a period of dominance over the Federalists during Jefferson's second term, and the president found support even in some traditional areas of Federalist strength, such as Connecticut and Massachusetts. By 1807,

Massachusetts had more Republican than Federalist representatives in Congress, and the party even showed signs of mounting a serious challenge for the governorship of that traditionally most Federalist of states. Although the Democratic-Republicans still drew most of their strength from the South and West as well as from urban New York City and Philadelphia, it seemed that their political appeal might be broader than ever.

The Democratic-Republicans did not have unfettered control of the federal government, however, even though the Federalists were in retreat. Jefferson and his partisans were still attempting to deal with the Federalist legacy left, particularly in the courts, by President Adams and his overwhelming number of judicial appointments. Neither party was above using government procedures to fight partisan battles. In January 1804, Virginia representative John Randolph introduced a resolution of impeachment against Federalist Supreme Court Justice Samuel Chase. Chase, a conservative who used his circuit court rulings to oppose democratic rabble-rousers, found himself on the wrong side of several political disputes with the ruling Democratic-Republicans. Chase was the first justice to be impeached by the House of Representatives, but he was acquitted at his Senate trial in 1805, when his Federalist lawyers effectively convinced even some staunch Jeffersonians that the political nature of the charges rendered them outrageous.

Presiding over the January 1805 Senate trial of Samuel Chase in one of his last official acts was the extraordinary controversial Vice President Aaron Burr. Burr's activities in 1804 and 1805 demonstrate that the Democratic-Republicans were far from a united party, and they also demonstrate how powerful personalities and traditional norms of behavior still had tremendous power to influence American politics. Burr had fallen out of political favor with Thomas Jefferson during his first term in office, partly because Burr's political battles against fellow Democratic-Republican George Clinton in New York State frequently took him away from presiding over the Senate and caused him to publish incendiary attacks against Clinton in pamphlets and newspapers. Jefferson chose to drop Burr as vice-presidential candidate in 1804. As his running mate, instead, he selected Burr's traditional enemy, George Clinton.

Disappointed that he would not return as vice president, Burr decided to run for the governorship of New York, given that Clinton would be out of the running for that office. Burr lost the race badly to Judge Morgan Lewis, another Jeffersonian politician, and he blamed the Federalists for his defeat—even though they fielded no candidate against him and despite the fact that Burr himself had courted Federalist political favors during the race. Burr was particularly bitter toward Alexander Hamilton, who had, in fact, campaigned for several years to keep power out of Burr's hands and who did not trust Burr.

Hamilton was correct to be leery of Aaron Burr. Burr accused Hamilton of making disparaging personal remarks against him during the New York governor's race, and when Hamilton refused to respond to the accusations during the summer of 1804, Burr challenged him to a duel. Dueling was a traditional means for gentlemen to protect their honor, and although its popularity was waning in the northern United States, the duel would remain a test of political masculinity for decades longer in the South. On July 11, Hamilton and Burr faced off with pistols in Weehawken, New Jersey. Burr shot Hamilton, and although eyewitness accounts later differed, Hamilton either failed to return the shot or deliberately missed Burr in return. Hamilton died the following day, and Burr fled south to escape murder indictments in both New York and New Jersey. When Burr returned to Washington, D.C., at the beginning of 1805 to finish his term as vice president and to preside over the Senate, he was under a considerable cloud for having killed Hamilton. The full political consequences of his fall from grace were not yet clear.

The consolidation of Democratic-Republican power and the overwhelming reelection of Thomas Jefferson as president, notwithstanding the antics of Aaron Burr, seemed to signal a turn toward democracy in national political life. But while Jefferson was an advocate for tapping into the political support of common Americans as a power base, the idea of democratic participation extended only so far. Jefferson and Clinton found much of their political support from white artisans and workingmen, but even the Democratic-Republicans often consciously excluded women and African Americans. One good example came in New Jersey, where some women had been voting in state elections since at least the 1780s, and where the state's growing free African-American population was trying to exert some small political influence. In 1807, the Democratic-Republican legislature of New Jersey disenfranchised both women and African Americans, in part because politicians thought them to be too pliant as many of them regularly voted for Federalist candidates. Even poor white men might run afoul of political leaders if their insistence on political rights included concrete economic demands. When the Philadelphia Society of Cordwainers organized one of the nation's first labor strikes to demand higher wages for shoemakers throughout the city, they were convicted of conspiracy and branded as criminals. The openness of Jeffersonian democracy extended only so far.

## RESOLVING THE TRIPOLITAN WAR

Jefferson had established a fairly tight hold on national political power by the time of his second term as president, and he would need all the political control he could muster to meet the international challenges that awaited his administration. One of the most immediate challenges stemmed from the ongoing war with Tripoli, which threatened to engulf the United States in an all-out Mediterranean war with the Barbary States of North Africa: Algeria, Morocco, Tunis, and Tripoli. In March 1804, just as Jefferson was about to be sworn in for his second term, news reached the United States that the USS *Philadelphia* had run aground off the coast of Tripoli, and her crew of over 300 had been captured to hold for ransom. Federalist legislators criticized Jefferson for demanding to "increase the revenue" of federal taxes to fund the

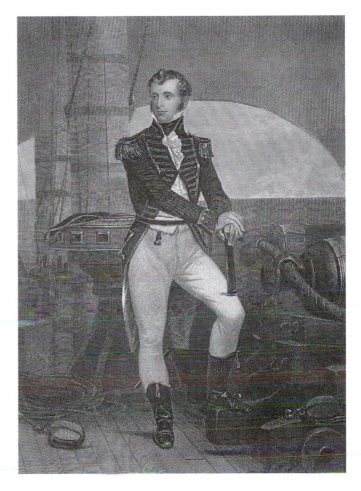

This engraving of an Alonzo Chappel portrait depicts Stephen Decatur, the American hero of the Tripolitan War, in a dignified naval pose. *(Library of Congress, Prints and Photographs Division [LC-USZ62-79109])*

In February 1804, Stephen Decatur led a naval expedition into the harbor of Tripoli to burn the captured U.S. ship *Philadelphia*. The action helped to bring the Tripolitan War to a climactic ending. *(National Archives/DOD, War & Conflict, # 75)*

Louisiana Purchase while simultaneously putting U.S. sailors at risk in a damaging war because he refused to pay an even cheaper tribute to Yusuf Qaramanli, the pasha of Tripoli.[1]

While Jefferson was battling his political opponents at home about how best to handle the Tripolitan conflict and continuing to argue for cutting the cost of U.S. naval forces, military events in the Mediterranean moved ahead to resolve the war. Naval officer Stephen Decatur, commander of the USS *Enterprise,* led a small sneak attack into the Tripolitan harbor and set the *Philadelphia* afire, assuring that the Tripolitans would not be able to turn the captured ship against the U.S. Navy. Meanwhile, the U.S. consul to Tunis, William Eaton, traveled to Egypt, where he convinced Yusuf Qaramanli's brother, Ahmed, whom Yusuf had deposed as pasha of Tripoli, to attempt a return to the throne. Eaton and Ahmed Qaramanli led a cross-country march from Egypt and daringly captured the Tripolitan port city of Derna in June 1805. But Eaton was unable to return Ahmed to the throne when the Tripolitan people did not cooperate, continuing to support Yusuf Qaramanli.

In the same month, American negotiators concluded a separate agreement with Yusuf Qaramanli that brought an end to the war. As part of the peace agreement, the United States paid $60,000 to Tripoli to ransom the crew of the *Philadelphia.* Tribute payments to the other North African states continued as well. Jefferson faced criticism from Federalists, and even some Democratic-Republicans, who insisted that the United States had submitted to poor terms to end the Tripolitan War. Federalists who represented the traders of New England argued that nothing in the agreement guaranteed the future safety of American shipping in the Mediterranean, especially as long as the French and the British both continued to encourage the Barbary States to interrupt American trade. Jefferson had concluded the war, but he had not guaranteed the safety of U.S. shipping or gained international respect.

## THE NAPOLEONIC WARS AND AMERICAN COMMERCE

Just after the Louisiana Purchase was concluded in 1803, France and Great Britain embarked on a whole new course of world-scale wars on both land and sea. The Napoleonic Wars would raise a whole new generation of commercial and military challenges for the United States and all of North America and would touch off almost a decade of foreign policy conflict that would culminate in the War of 1812. At first the Napoleonic Wars accelerated the rate of American overseas commercial trade. U.S. merchants used their status as neutral traders to infiltrate valuable European markets for food and other goods. But once France and Great Britain turned to naval blockade in their fight against each other, the United States was caught between them, and shipping was almost paralyzed. For a variety of reasons, not the least of which was the long-standing Democratic-Republican preference for France, the U.S. conflict with Great Britain turned particularly ugly.

For the first two years of the Napoleonic Wars, U.S. merchants benefited from the international strife, as they used the wartime opportunity to infiltrate Caribbean and European markets that had previously been closed to them by the belligerents. Between 1803 and 1805, both imports and exports climbed dramatically, each by almost $50 million, and total American trade was more

*This print depicts Robert Fulton discussing naval technology with Napoleon Bonaparte. Between 1800 and 1805, Fulton tried to sell both the French and the English on the idea of using torpedoes and submarines against each other. (Library of Congress, Prints and Photographs Division [LC-USZ62-117919])*

that three times larger than it had been in the entire decade of the 1790s. The United States quickly became the country with the largest neutral trade in the world by carefully negotiating between Great Britain and France and the other countries (Spain, Austria, Prussia, and Russia) that were quickly drawn into the wars on one side or the other.

In 1805, the smooth operation of neutral American shipping came to an abrupt halt, raising a new slew of problems as merchants sought to keep up their newfound and very lucrative trade. Great Britain gained the upper hand in the naval war in October 1805 when Admiral Horatio Nelson defeated the French and Spanish navies at the Battle of Trafalgar, but Napoleon's armies were much stronger than Britain's or those of Britain's allies, and the French soon won a decisive land victory at the Battle of Austerlitz. The French and British turned to naval blockade in their protracted conflict, much to the detriment of U.S. trade.

British interference with American shipping seemed particularly galling, since it began directly to contradict the terms of the 1794 Jay Treaty, and the British-American relationship turned quite sour. A British admiralty court ruled in the 1805 *Essex* decision that U.S. ships that tried to break the blockade to trade French goods from the Caribbean were liable to seizure. As early as 1803, British vessels had begun to stop American ships to search for British navy deserters who often reenlisted on American ships, and after 1805, the forcible removal, known as impressment, of these sailors increased dramatically. British naval officers did not distinguish carefully between British and U.S. citizens when they boarded American ships, and it is estimated that as many as 10,000 Americans were captured and impressed into the British navy between 1803 and 1812. The harsh conditions in the Royal Navy, and the combination of kidnapping and commercial threat posed by widespread naval impressment, caused great public outcry against the British practice. The British Orders-in-Council of 1806 declared that neutral ships must first visit British ports and obtain trading licenses before entering French ports, and the orders seemed particularly oppressive, given the constant threat to U.S. vessels of search and seizure by British ships.

Britain was not alone in viewing interference with American trade as a weapon in the European war. In 1806 and 1807, Napoleon imposed a "continental system" of decrees against English trading that placed severe restrictions on U.S. merchants and made many U.S. ships liable to French capture as well. The Berlin Decree of 1806 tightened the rules of the French blockade against Great Britain by closing all French-controlled ports to any ship that had stopped in a British port, and the Milan Decree the following year forbade neutral ships from carrying the trade licenses required by the English Orders-in-Council.

After having seen a huge rise in commercial profits, the United States seemed caught between Scylla and Charybdis after 1805. The total effect of the French and British actions was to declare all neutral trade illegal and to make U.S. ships liable to capture by both continental powers. The Jefferson administration focused first on how to respond to the British, in part because their abdication of the terms of Jay's treaty seemed to threaten to renew long-standing tensions between the two nations. Jefferson urged Congress to pass a non-importation act, which prohibited many kinds of British (and some French) goods from being imported into the United States after November 1806. Commercial sanctions appealed to Jeffersonian policymakers because they required no expensive military buildup that would enhance the power of the federal government and because they echoed the tactics of the nonimportation movement against Great Britain during the Imperial Crisis before the American Revolution.

Just after Congress took action by passing the Non-Importation Act, and in part because he may have realized that Americans relied heavily on British goods, Jefferson sent Marylander William Pinckney and Virginian James Monroe to London to try to negotiate a settlement with the British government. In December 1805, they negotiated a treaty that gained the United States little over the terms of Jay's treaty and failed to win any major concessions from Britain. Despite a clamor inside the United States for action to loosen the European trade restrictions, Jefferson refused to submit the treaty to the Senate for ratification, because he found its terms inadequate. Meanwhile, U.S. citizens continued to be impressed into the British navy, and both France and Britain went on threatening and capturing American ships.

In June 1807, the conflict with Great Britain escalated when the British navy vessel *Leopard* attacked the USS *Chesapeake,* engaged it in a battle that killed three Americans, hanged a British deserter, and kidnapped three American sailors from their ship. The attack took place only about 10 miles off the coast of Norfolk, Virginia, and this attack on a U.S. military ship in U.S. waters seemed to many an overt act of war that could not be justified by any of the draconian measures imposed against U.S. trade. American outrage reached a new fever pitch, with Thomas Jefferson noting: "Never since the battle of Lexington have I seen the country in such a state of exasperation as at present."[2] For years afterward, U.S. administrations demanded that the British pay restitution for the destruction caused in the *Chesapeake-Leopard* incident, but the British were very slow to admit wrongdoing.

Under tremendous public pressure, Congress moved to further tighten the commercial sanctions against Europe, since it was clear that nonimportation had not effected the desired change, especially in British behavior at sea. In December 1807, Thomas Jefferson signed into law a full embargo on all foreign trade. The embargo, which would be enforced with various degrees of stringency over the following few years, forbade American ships from sailing into European ports and severely restricted trade with European vessels, even along the coast of the United States. The purpose of the embargo was to cause severe economic damage (especially to Great Britain) by depriving the country of American trade goods, which would be felt "in her manufacturers, in the loss of naval stores, and above all in the supplies essential to her colonies."[3] What Congress and Jefferson did not anticipate, however, was that the embargo would cause even worse economic strife within the United States.

## EXPLORING THE WEST

At the same time that U.S. merchants saw their ships placed at great peril on the high seas because of the Napoleonic Wars, Thomas Jefferson's vision of looking westward for future sources of commerce and economic development was taking shape. Immediately following the Louisiana Purchase, which had almost doubled the size of the United States and which seemed to many to push the nation's destiny westward, Jefferson sent an official government party of exploration to find trade routes to the Pacific Ocean and to establish diplomatic relations with Indian nations in the vast Louisiana Territory and beyond. Meriwether Lewis and William Clark, the leaders of the expedition, gathered personnel and supplies through the end of 1803, and in May 1804, the Corps of Discovery, as they had dubbed their exploration party, set off from St. Louis on their journey.

In 1804, the Lewis and Clark expedition traveled up the Missouri River, and by the end of the year they chose to construct a fort and spend the winter at the present-day location of Bismarck, North Dakota. They dubbed their winter quarters Fort Mandan after the Mandan people with whom they had established friendly relations, and in honor of the fact that the Mandan provided them with great help along their journey. The following year, the Corps of Discovery continued along the Missouri River and then across the Rocky Mountains. The corps was surprised at how high the Rockies were and how difficult the overland passage was, obstacles that made the possibilities of transcontinental trade to the Pacific far less likely than hoped. After following western rivers to the Pacific, the party split in two in 1806 to try to find easier passes over the Rockies, but neither Lewis nor Clark found a significantly less difficult location to cross the mountains. In August 1806, the two parties rejoined at the Missouri River and continued homeward together, arriving back in St. Louis on September 23.

Although the Lewis and Clark expedition failed to find an easy overland or water trade route to the Pacific, the exploration was successful in several other ways. It created very accurate maps of western territory, and Lewis and Clark's journals recording scientific observations of the landscape, plants, and animals would serve as a valuable intellectual resource for centuries to come. The Corps of Discovery did establish trade networks with many Native American groups, especially using knowledge from French and mixed-race fur traders, several of whom were included in the expedition party. Lewis and Clark cemented good relations between the United States and several Indian nations, including the Mandan and some bands of the Shoshone. However, their diplomacy did not prevent fighting with other groups, including the Teton Sioux and the Piegan, although they avoided provoking all-out warfare.

Much of Lewis and Clark's success with some Native American nations, especially the Shoshone, came because they included as part of their party a Shoshone woman, Sacagawea, who acted as interpreter and facilitator for the exploration. Sacagawea joined the Corps of Discovery with her husband, a French Canadian trader named Toussaint Charbonneau. Charbonneau had purchased Sacagawea from the Minitari people, who had taken her as a war captive some years before. Sacagawea, who was only around 15 years old when she joined the Lewis and Clark expedition, gave birth to a son in February 1805, just after she had become part of the group. She took her newborn son along when she set out with the group from Fort Mandan in April. In August 1805, Sacagawea was reunited with her brother, Cameahwait, who by chance came upon the party of exploration. But even though she might have returned to her family, Sacagawea continued on to the Pacific Ocean and remained with the expedition.

Although Jefferson, Lewis, and Clark all viewed the expedition as a way for the United States to exercise its new legal authority and domination over the Louisiana Territory and beyond, the expedition might also be viewed as an indicator of the very complicated kinds of relationships between peoples that would develop in the American Far West. Lewis and Clark imposed military discipline on their Corps of Discovery, but their group functioned in reality as an assortment of many different kinds of individuals. American adventurers and men with military experience mixed with traders of different ethnicities who spoke different languages and followed different customs and habits. William Clark brought his slave, a man named York, as part of the exploration party, and York played an important role at several points along the journey. Clark refused to grant York his freedom when he requested to be let go in 1808. And although the Lewis and Clark exploration laid some of the groundwork for later American domination of western Indian nations, at the time the U.S. explorers were much weaker than their Indian allies and enemies, and they never would have survived the trip without Indian assistance. The day-to-day existence of the Lewis and Clark expedition relied on the power of many different individuals and groups to renegotiate constantly their relationships with one another and with the natural world.

In addition to the Lewis and Clark expedition, U.S. Army Lieutenant Zebulon Pike also explored parts of the West during 1805 and 1806, with an eye toward opening up commerce. Pike first set out in August 1805 to travel north to the source of the Mississippi River, a trip that led him to explore Pike's Peak (later named in his honor). In July 1806, Pike gathered a new exploration party and set out to explore territory in the Southwest, which brought him directly into conflict with Spanish officials, who did not look kindly on American explorers traversing their territory. Pike successfully charted the Santa Fe Trail, but then he was captured by Mexican officials, who slapped him in jail for several years. Despite his difficulties with Spanish Mexico, Pike's narrative of his journey was published before the long-delayed accounts of the Lewis and Clark exploration, and his vision of the West helped to promote the commercial appetite of U.S. merchants.

## WESTERN TENSIONS

Zebulon Pike was not the only U.S. citizen to become embroiled with Spanish officials in the Southwest. Former Vice President Aaron Burr and rogue military officer General James Wilkinson engaged in a plot, which is still not completely understood by historians, to plan an attack on Spanish Mexico that went horribly awry and resulted in Burr's being tried for treason. After Burr left office, he fled to the West, in part to escape the murder charges filed against him for killing Alexander Hamilton. In 1805 he began gathering troops and supplies for the attack on Spanish territory, which was probably calculated to open up new land for American settlers. After being acquitted of plotting against Spain in Kentucky at the beginning of 1806, Burr continued his activities. In the summer of 1806, Burr was on his way down the Ohio River when Wilkinson—who, unbeknown to any Americans, was actually a double agent also being paid by the Spanish—revealed the plans for the attack in a letter to President Thomas Jefferson.

Wilkinson most likely deliberately exaggerated Burr's role in the conspiracy, although Burr was certainly engaged with Wilkinson in planning illegal activities against Spanish territory. President Jefferson issued a proclamation aimed at Burr that expressly forbade American citizens to make war on Spain, and Wilkinson began to arrest some of Burr's coconspirators in New Orleans to help prove his own innocence. Burr was arrested and acquitted again in Mississippi state court early in January 1807 before finally being arrested by federal officials later the same month in Alabama and being indicted for treason for violating the terms of Jefferson's proclamation. Chief Justice John Marshall presided over Burr's treason trial in Virginia in the late summer. The government could not meet the stringent constitutional requirements to prove the charge of treason, and Burr was acquitted of all charges before fleeing to England in 1808.

The dubious exploits of Aaron Burr and James Wilkinson emphasized the tenuous control exerted by the American government over even some of the most prominent citizens of the United States who lived in the West. President Jefferson, who had long professed a desire to "civilize" Native Americans by

Tecumseh was the leader of the most powerful pan-Indian movement of the early 19th century. He sought to unite American Indian peoples against land incursions by the United States. *(Library of Congress, Prints and Photographs Division [LC-USZ62-8255])*

sending them to school to learn to adapt to American culture, did very little to keep American settlers from encroaching on Indian lands, even when they violated specific agreements such as the 1795 Treaty of Greenville. Jefferson's policies, in general, sought to win greater land cessions from Native American representatives, who many times did not even clearly represent their entire tribes. At the same time, ever greater numbers of white settlers spilled into previously Native-held areas west of Ohio, Alabama, and Georgia.

Starting in 1805, some Indians decided to strengthen their resistance to American encroachments, and a new movement coalesced under the leadership of the Shawnee military and political leader Tecumseh and his brother Tenskwatawa. Although some Native Americans had willingly entered negotiations to give up land rights to the United States over the previous decades, many continued to refuse to recognize treaties that they considered to be of dubious validity. In the years after 1800 Tecumseh, who had fought with Little Turtle's Miami warriors at the Battle of Fallen Timbers in 1794 and who had refused to sign the Treaty of Greenville, gathered a strong group of warriors together along the White River in Indiana. Tecumseh emphasized mutual aid among Native peoples and urged strong resistance to U.S. land claims.

In 1805, Tecumseh's political message received a boost from his brother's emergence as a religious seer. Tenskwatawa, referred to as "The Prophet" or "The Shawnee Prophet," experienced a series of visions that led him to preach a very particular native-centered religious message. Tenskwatawa urged Native peoples to return to older ways of living and to reject white culture in order that they might be saved from the encroaching power of the United States. Tenskwatawa's prophecies gained great popularity among many Native cultures after he correctly predicted the solar eclipse that took place on June 16, 1806. Tecumseh capitalized on the popularity of Tenskwatawa's religious message to begin building connections between native groups. Soon, Tecumseh would emerge as the leader of an extensive and well-organized Indian confederacy with great power to oppose the United States.

## OUTSIDERS AND AMERICAN SOCIETY

In the years of rising domestic and international conflict, American women continued to define for themselves a place in the United States that, while largely separate from the political sphere, remained influential to society as a whole. Most American women defined their positions in the world in familial terms. Married women were expected to be subordinate to their husbands, and although many women took an active part in family business, married women could not formally own property. Single women had a bit more freedom of action, although most were relegated to a marginal economic status; for support, they generally relied on their fathers or brothers or on hard labor doing laundry, taking in boarders, or sewing. Very poor women and most black women (especially slaves) did not have a choice but to work, and they occupied the lowest rungs of the economic ladder. A few professions, such as midwifery or teaching, made room for women, but even successful midwives and teachers faced increasing competition from male professionals in this period. Women's education continued to improve, especially in New England and the Middle Atlantic states, as the doctrine of republicanism stressed that women needed knowledge to raise their children to become good citizens. But very few women were allowed to pursue education solely for the purposes of fulfilling their own intellectual pursuits.

Even the few women who consistently tried to infiltrate the public or political sphere faced opposition during this period in American history. The 1807 bill that rescinded the right of New Jersey women to vote was submitted to the state legislature by John Condict, a Democratic-Republican politician who had been defeated in the 1790s in part by a heavy turnout of female Federalist voters. The legislature passed the bill in part because they believed disenfranchising women (and African Americans) would return "the safety, quiet, good order and dignity of the state."[4] When the former Revolutionary patriot and strident Anti-Federalist Mercy Otis Warren published her three-volume *History of the American Revolution* in 1805, she sparked scorn and opposition from her formerly friendly correspondent John Adams. Adams disliked Warren's Democratic-Republican politics, and he disagreed with much of her rendering of the history of the Revolution. In a series of critical letters, he questioned not only her historical interpretation but also whether women per se had the right and intellectual weight to write history. Adams's scorn for Mercy Otis Warren, whom he had previously respected as a talented writer, helped to dramatize that an intellectual woman still had a hard fight for acceptance in the United States.

African Americans made some measurable gains in American society between 1804 and 1807, even as they continued to face severe racism and restrictions on their social, personal, and political freedom. The overall status of African Americans tended to take one step forward and two steps back. The institution of slavery was becoming more entrenched across the South as cotton became more of a staple crop, but more northern states simultaneously moved ahead to outlaw slavery.

The conflicted legal status imposed, even on free African Americans, is well represented by developments in the state of New Jersey. In 1804, the New Jersey legislature passed a law for the gradual abolition of slavery in the state, but three years later the legislature also voted to deprive free African Americans of the long-held right to vote. Even though many northern states were phasing out the institution of slavery, that did not mean that African Americans were accepted or treated well. The newly created state of Ohio, which was experiencing a huge increase in population, passed legislation in 1804 to restrict severely the rights and movement of African Americans, even though slavery was not legal in the state. In 1806, Virginia officials, frightened in part by white refugees who had fled the successful black Haitian Revolution in which former slaves had wrested their country away from France two years earlier, restricted the rights of free African Americans to purchase and free slaves, and they insisted on the right to deport any freed people from the state.

The year 1807 ended on a note of great hope for African Americans, however, when the federal government took one of its boldest actions to date in regards to slavery. The U.S. Constitution had prohibited any interference with the international slave trade before the year 1808, but in the midst of the international commercial crisis in 1807, Congress started planning to outlaw the slave trading the following year. In March 1807, Congress passed legislation that would outlaw the foreign slave trade beginning on January 1, 1808. The law became the last federal action having to do with slavery that was not terribly controversial and that faced little opposition from southern representatives. In part because trade issues were so perilous because of the Napoleonic Wars, the slave trade was outlawed with little outcry.

## RISING CONFLICT

The full impact and importance of the end of the legal slave trade remained to be seen, and the institution of slavery was far from becoming extinct. Just as was true of many other aspects of American life in 1807, the country seemed on the cusp of change but also in the grips of great uncertainty as to the outcome of that change. Great new trade opportunities had pushed the United States increasingly into international markets. But the same trade that had increased economic prosperity drew the United States into diplomatic conflicts and military peril for which it was not necessarily prepared. The U.S. government had tried a host of approaches to respond to the threats posed by the Napoleonic Wars and had passed the embargo, hoping to demand respect from the world and to ensure safety for future American trade. Americans would wait cautiously to see whether this approach would work.

## CHRONICLE OF EVENTS

### 1804

Haitian slaves revolt, turn on their masters, and gain their country's independence from France. Many white refugees flee to the United States.

Andrew and Rachel Jackson construct the three-room cabin that will later become their plantation house, named The Hermitage.

Washington Allston publishes his Romantic pot-boiler *The Deluge.*

Chief Justice John Marshall publishes his five-volume *Life of Washington,* intended to record the history of America's greatest hero and to provide examples for American youth to emulate.

John Vanderlyn paints *The Death of Jane McCrea,* whose depiction of Indians capturing an innocent woman during the Revolutionary War reinforces the image of the noble savage in the public mind.

New York merchant John Pintard joins with other wealthy New Yorkers to found the New-York Historical Society.

Philadelphia inventor Oliver Evans invents a steam engine–powered amphibious vehicle, which he drives through the city's streets and into a river.

Levi Hollingworth builds his mining business, the Gunpowder Copper Works, in Maryland.

Residents of Marietta, Ohio, trade furs for books and establish the "Coonskin Library."

The New Jersey legislature passes a law providing for the gradual abolition of slavery in the state.

A group of Sauk and Fox Indians sign the Treaty of St. Louis, which cedes large sections of territory in the Midwest to the United States. The Sauk and Fox protest for years that the treaty signers did not represent the collective will of their tribes.

*January 5:* The legislature of Ohio passes laws prohibiting African Americans from moving about the state freely and severely restricting their rights.

*February 16:* Lieutenant Stephen Decatur leads a group of sailors into the harbor of Tripoli, where they destroy the USS *Philadelphia,* which had been captured when it ran aground on a reef.

*March 12:* The House of Representatives votes to impeach Supreme Court Justice Samuel Chase, in part because his Federalist rulings clash with Democratic-Republican ideas.

The Senate convicts Federal Judge John Pickering, who has already been impeached by the House, and he leaves office. The Pickering and Chase cases are the first impeachment proceedings to be held under the terms of the Constitution.

*March 26:* Congress creates two territories out of the land acquired in the Louisiana Purchase.

*April 25:* Vice President Aaron Burr is defeated in his race for governor of New York. He harbors bitterness against Alexander Hamilton, who helped insure his defeat.

*May 14:* The Lewis and Clark expedition embarks from St. Louis on a journey to explore the Louisiana Territory, negotiate with Indian nations, and find a water route to the Pacific Ocean.

*July 4:* Nathaniel Hawthorne future author of *The Scarlet Letter* and other important novels, is born.

*July 11:* In Weehawken, New Jersey, Aaron Burr shoots Alexander Hamilton in a duel, fought over personal insults exchanged after Burr felt slighted by his political defeat in the New York gubernatorial race.

*July 12:* Alexander Hamilton dies.

*August 18 and 27:* Territorial governor William Henry Harrison signs treaties with several Indian nations at Vincennes, Indiana, insuring cession of further land north of the Ohio River.

This mid-19th-century print depicts the duel between Alexander Hamilton and Aaron Burr on July 11, 1804. The print is sympathetic to Hamilton, who is depicted as firing into the air as Burr takes aim directly at him. *(Library of Congress, Prints and Photographs Division [LC-USZ62-75928])*

*September 7:* A large hurricane hits Charleston, South Carolina, severely damaging houses and wharves.

*September 24–28:* The Lewis and Clark expedition arrives at the mouth of the Teton River and meets with the Teton Sioux (Teton Lakota).

*September 25:* The Twelfth Amendment to the Constitution is adopted by the states. In the future, presidential and vice-presidential balloting will be conducted separately in the electoral college, instead of the vice presidency going to the candidate who receives the second-highest number of total votes.

*November 6:* Thomas Jefferson is reelected president, and New Yorker George Clinton is elected vice president.

*November 16:* Lewis and Clark take up their winter quarters with the Mandan Indians at "Fort Mandan."

*November 23:* Franklin Pierce, who will become the 14th president of the United States, is born.

## 1805

Congress fails to pass a proposed resolution calling for gradual emancipation of slaves in Washington, D.C.

The Pennsylvania Academy of Fine Art is founded. It will become the longest-lasting artistic institution in the United States.

Hugh Henry Brackenridge publishes the second part of his hugely popular satire *Modern Chivalry.*

Democratic-Republican Mercy Otis Warren publishes her *History of the Rise, Progress and Termination of the American Revolution,* which causes her longtime friend the Federalist John Adams, whom the book criticizes, to question the value of women writing history.

Hosea Ballou publishes his *Treatise on the Atonement,* which questions the notion of the Trinity and formally expresses the theological foundations of Universalism.

George Rapp and his fellow believers, who belong to a German pietist sect called the Harmonists, found a community at Harmony, Pennsylvania.

New Englander Frederick Tudor initiates the ice export trade to Martinique.

In the first antilabor organization court ruling in U.S. history, members of the Philadelphia Society of Cordwainers (shoemakers) are convicted of conspiracy after striking for higher wages.

Tenskwatawa (The Prophet), the brother of military and diplomatic leader Tecumseh, comes to prominence as a Shawnee spiritual leader who advocates Native separation from white culture.

*January 2:* The Senate trial of Justice Samuel Chase, who has been impeached by the House of Representatives, begins.

*January 11:* Congress forms the Territory of Michigan out of part of the Indiana Territory.

*March 2:* Vice President Aaron Burr delivers a farewell address to the Senate.

*March 3:* Congress formally reorganizes the Louisiana Territory and establishes St. Louis as its capital.

*April 7:* Lewis and Clark leave Fort Mandan to travel up the Missouri River with their exploration party.

*April 26:* The Lewis and Clark expedition reaches the mouth of the Yellowstone River.

The U.S. consul to Tunis, William Eaton, captures the city of Derna after leading a group of troops across Egypt. His victory, one of the most impressive of the Tripolitan War, becomes immortalized in the Marine Corps Hymn that praises actions on "the shores of Tripoli."

*June 4:* The United States negotiates a treaty ending the Tripolitan War, although the treaty includes a $60,000 ransom to free to the crew of the captured USS *Philadelphia.*

*June 11:* Detroit, Michigan, is nearly destroyed by fire.

*June 13:* The Lewis and Clark expedition observes the Great Falls of the Missouri River.

*June 21–July 2:* The Lewis and Clark party traverses the Great Falls of the Missouri River.

*July 1:* Congress establishes the Michigan Territory.

*August 9:* Zebulon Pike embarks from St. Louis to explore the source of the Mississippi River.

*September 20–October 7:* Lewis and Clark stay with the Nez Percé Indians.

*September 27:* William Moultrie dies.

*November 14:* The Lewis and Clark expedition reaches the Pacific Ocean, but only after admitting that their explorations found no easy route by water to the ocean.

## 1806

The first public school (for white children only) opens in Washington, D.C.

Virginia legislation restricts the rights of free African Americans to purchase slaves and grant them freedom. Former slaves may be deported from the state at the behest of county officials.

Journeyman shoemakers throughout the United States go on strike, but they are indicted for conspiracy for trying to gain higher wages.

Charles Willson Peale unveils his painting of the exhumation of a mastodon skeleton he had uncovered the year before in New York State.

Noah Webster publishes his *Compendious Dictionary*.

Bernard McMahon publishes *The American Gardener's Calendar*.

Jesse Hawley proposes plans for what will become the Erie Canal.

Future president Andrew Jackson duels with and kills a Kentucky man named Charles Dickinson, who had insulted Jackson's wife.

Stand Waite, who will become the leader of the Cherokee military forces that fight for the Confederacy in the Civil War, is born.

*January 17:* President Jefferson's grandson, James Madison Randolph, becomes the first child born in the White House.

*February 1:* A bridge spanning the Delaware River at Philadelphia is opened.

*February 12:* The Senate denounces Great Britain for seizing the cargo of ships protected by the U.S. flag. Britain ignores the resolution and continues to assert that many U.S. ships fail to meet the requirements of neutral traders in the war between Great Britain and France.

*March 23:* The members of the Lewis and Clark expedition begin their return trip to St. Louis.

*March 26:* Congress votes to endorse the construction of the Cumberland Road, which will run west to Ohio.

*April 10:* Revolutionary War commander Horatio Gates dies.

*April 18:* Congress passes the Non-Importation Act, intended to force Britain to observe American shipping rights by imposing a boycott on the importation of specific British goods.

*April 30:* Explorer Zebulon Pike returns to St. Louis after exploring the Mississippi River and charting Pike's Peak (in present-day Colorado).

*June 8:* George Wythe, noted Virginia jurist and law professor, dies.

*June 15:* The Lewis and Clark expedition begins to traverse the Rocky Mountains on the way back to St. Louis.

*July 3:* The Lewis and Clark expedition splits into two parties.

*July 15:* Zebulon Pike heads an exploration party that sets out from Fort Bellefontaine to explore the Southwest.

*July 15–August 3:* William Clark explores the Yellowstone River.

*August:* A group of Williams College students from "the Brethren," the first foreign missionary society in the United States.

*August 12:* The two parties of the Lewis and Clark expedition reunite at the Missouri River.

*September 23:* The Lewis and Clark expedition ends when the exploration party reenters St. Louis.

*October 25:* Revolutionary War general Henry Knox dies.

*November 15:* The Yale *Literary Cabinet* becomes the first college periodical published in the United States.

*November 27:* President Jefferson issues a proclamation intended to keep American citizens from joining military efforts against Spanish territory. Former Vice President Aaron Burr has been involved in a potentially treasonous plot to invade New Spain for several months.

*December 19:* President Jefferson suspends the Non-Importation Act.

*December 31:* James Monroe and William Pinckney negotiate a treaty (the Monroe-Pinckney Treaty) with Great Britain, designed to assure American neutral shipping rights.

## 1807

The first public school for free African-American children opens in Washington, D.C.

The Boston Athenaeum, a leading library, museum, and intellectual establishment, is founded.

Washington Irving and J. K. Paulding publish their *Salmagundi* essays, which provide a satirical look at contemporary New York society and spawn the Knickerbocker movement, a New York literary school.

Joel Barlow publishes his patriotic epic poem *The Columbiad*.

Jacob Albright founds the United States Evangelical Association.

*February 19:* Aaron Burr is arrested in Alabama for plotting to invade Spanish territory and to create an independent empire out of a combination of U.S. and Spanish land.

*February 27:* Poet Henry Wordsworth Longfellow is born in Portland, Maine.

*March 2:* Congress declares that the African slave trade will cease to be legal in the United States on January 1, 1808. The Constitution had prohibited such a law from taking effect before 1808.

*March 30:* Chief Justice John Marshall arraigns Aaron Burr on charges that he plotted to invade Spanish territory.

*June 22:* Off the coast of Norfolk, Virginia, the HMS *Leopard* attacks the USS *Chesapeake* and captures several American sailors on board (including three African Americans), whom the British claim to be deserted British sailors.

*June 24:* Aaron Burr is indicted for treason on the grounds that his plot to invade Spanish territory violated Jefferson's proclamation forbidding U.S. citizens to plot against foreign governments and that he encouraged the Louisiana Territory to secede from the United States.

*July 2:* In an effort to prevent all-out war, President Jefferson orders all British warships to leave U.S. waters.

*August 3:* Aaron Burr's treason trial begins.

*August 17:* The steamboat *Clermont,* run by Robert Fulton and Robert Livingston, begins its regular service between New York City and Albany, New York.

*September 1:* Aaron Burr is acquitted of treason.

Robert Fulton's steamboat *Clermont* was the first steam-powered commercial vessel in the United States. *(from Benson Lossing,* The Pictorial Field-Book of the Revolution, *1851–1852)*

*October 20:* Aaron Burr is tried for conspiracy in Richmond, Virginia, and acquitted again.

*November 4:* The Senate adopts Senator John Quincy Adam's proposal to form a committee to audit and control Senate expenses.

*December 22:* President Jefferson signs the Embargo Act, which places severe restrictions on both imports and exports in an effort to increase commercial pressures on Great Britain and France. Though Jefferson hopes the measure will force European powers to respect American shipping, the legislation has little effect except to cause economic damage inside the United States.

## EYEWITNESS TESTIMONY

New sources will be laid open for the employment of capital in the interior. . . . The coasting trade and internal commerce will receive a new impulse. . . . Domestic industry will put to shame idleness and dissipation. . . . Foreign nations will lose their influence over our councils. . . . The fertile lands of America will rise to their just value, by bringing a market to the door of the farmer. . . . The riches with which nature has so bountifully blessed this country will be explored and brought into use.

*Tenche Coxe in his* Essay on the Manufacturing Interest, *1804, in Watts,* Republic Reborn, *255.*

My family affairs go on pretty well; I have an old woman in the kitchen as a drudge, for she cannot cook; I have a miserably idle dirty girl as a waiter, whom I shall get rid of as soon as possible. Milly is my stand by, she cleans the house, makes beds, irons, clear starches, and attends Julia while I am in the kitchen, which is two or three hours every day, as I cook every dinner that is eat by the family and have even to assist in dishing up dinner. I have had a fine little girl of 5 yrs old bound to me by Dr. Willis. While I work, she plays with Julia and keeps her quiet. . . . I had to get over my pique to Mrs. Jones and she is not working for me. I giver her 12s. 6d. pr week and shall get her to do all my large work in the course of a week or two and shall then have leisure for my little things.

*Washington socialite Margaret Bayard Smith describes the domestic staff that keeps her house running in a letter to a friend, January 23, 1804, in Hunt,* The First Forty Years, *44–45.*

We, the subscribers, planters, merchants, and other inhabitants of Louisiana, respectfully approach the Legislature of the United States with a memorial of our rights, a remonstrance against certain laws which contravene them, and a petition for that redress to which the laws of nature, sanctioned by positive stipulation have entitled us. . . . Do political axioms on the Atlantic become problems when transferred to the shores of the Mississippi? . . . Where, we ask respectfully, where is the circumstance that is to exclude us from a participation in these rights?

*Petition by the citizens of Louisiana for a representative government, 1804, in Hart,* American History, *III: 377, 378.*

Reasons why it is desirable that Mr. Lansing rather than Col. Burr should succeed. . . . the ill opinion of Jefferson and jealousy of the ambition of Virginia is an inconsiderable prop of good principles in that Country. But these causes are leading to an opinion that a dismemberment of the Union is expedient. It would probably suit Mr. Burrs views to promote this result to be the chief of the Northern portion—And placed at the head of the state of New York no man would be more likely to succeed.

*Alexander Hamilton outlines the flaws of Aaron Burr in a speech advocating Burr's opponent in the New York governor's race, February 10, 1804, in Freeman,* Alexander Hamilton, *1004, 1005.*

The Bill in the Senate on the impressments of seamen, of which you have been apprized, was a few days ago postponed generally, with reasons assigned, which were meant to render such an issue conciliatory, without renouncing the right, or the eventual necessity of some such remedy. . . . This country wishes for justice, and thinks it has efficacious means in its own hands. It wishes, at the same time, not to resort, without absolute necessity, to any means that may interrupt harmony, or even wear an unfriendly aspect. This is certainly the sentiment of the Executive, in common with the other branches of the Government, and with the nation.

*James Madison in a letter to James Monroe, March 8, 1804, in* Letters and Other Writings of James Madison, *II: 200, 201.*

All the preparations being completed, we left our camp on Monday, May 14th, 1804. This spot is at the mouth of Wood [Du Bois] river, a small stream which empties into the Mississippi [on the east side], opposite the entrance of the Missouri . . . On both sides of the Mississippi the land for two or three miles is rich and level, but gradually swells into a high pleasant country . . . Not being able to set sail before 4 p.m., we did not make more than four miles, and camped on the first island, opposite a small creek called Coldwater.

*Meriwether Lewis describes the embarkation of the Lewis and Clark expedition, May 14, 1804, in Coues,* History of the Expedition, *I: 4, 5.*

Political opposition can never absolve Gentlemen from the necessity of a rigid adherence to the laws of honor and the rules of decorum: I neither claim such privilege nor indulge it in others.

*Aaron Burr declares that his honor is injured in a letter to Alexander Hamilton, June 21, 1804, in Freeman,* Alexander Hamilton, *1012.*

Col. Burr arrived first on the ground as had been previously agreed. When Genl. Hamilton arrived the parties exchanged salutations and the Seconds proceeded to make their arrangements. They measured the distance, ten full paces, and cast lots for the choice of positions as also to determine by whom the word should be given . . . The pistols were discharged within a few seconds of each other and the fire of Col. Burr took effect; Genl. Hamilton almost instantly fell. Col. Burr then advanced toward Genl. H—n with a manner and gesture of regret, but without Speaking turned about & withdrew.

*William P. Van Ness and Nathaniel Pendleton describe the Burr-Hamilton duel July 11, 1804, in an official statement, in Freeman,* Alexander Hamilton, *1027.*

General Hamilton died yesterday. The malignant federalists or tories, and the imbittered Clintonians, unite in endeavouring to excite public sympathy in his favour and indignation against his antagonist. Thousands of absurd falsehoods are circulated with industry. . . . I propose leaving town for a few days, and meditate also a journey for some weeks . . .

*Aaron Burr in a letter to Joseph Alston, July 13, 1804, in Davis,* Memoirs of Aaron Burr, *II: 327.*

On the subject of treaties, our system is to have none with any nation, as far as can be avoided. The treaty with England has therefore not been renewed, and all overtures for treaty with other nations have been declined. We believe that with nations, as with individuals, dealings may be carried on as advantageously, perhaps moreso, while their continuance depends on a voluntary good treatment. . . . Five fine frigates left the Chesapeake the 1st instant for Tripoli . . . I think they will make Tripoli sensible, that they mistake their interest in choosing war with us; and Tunis also,

This mid–19th-century Currier & Ives lithograph depicts the bombardment of Tripoli by U.S. forces during the Tripolitan War. The lithograph also demonstrates how the conflict lived on in American memory as a colorful and exotic military engagement. *(Library of Congress, Prints and Photographs Division [LC-USZ62-4])*

should she have declared war as we now expect, and almost wish.

*President Thomas Jefferson in a letter to Phillip Mazzei, July 18, 1804, in Hunt,* The Essential Thomas Jefferson, *231, 232.*

6. Our Navy. May its strength protect our Commerce and its glory confound its enemies at Washington and Tripoli. 7. Our little Army. May it never have to bear reproach from the brave, nor always to take it from the base. 8. HAMILTON. May our Country find indemnity for his loss, in the value of his Counsels.

*Toasts offered at a Federalist public dinner in Maine in honor of Rufus King, September 5, 1804, in King,* Life and Correspondence of Rufus King, *IV: 422.*

We invited the chiefs on board and showed them the boat, the air-gun, and such curiosities as we thought might amuse them. In this we succeeded too well; for after giving them a quarter of a glass of whisky, which they seemed to like very much, and sucked the bottle, it was with much difficulty that we could get rid of them. They at last accompanied Captain Clark on shore in a periogue with five men; but it seems they had formed a design to stop us; for no sooner had the party landed than three of the Indians seized the cable of the periogue, and one of the soldiers of the chief put his arms round the mast. The second chief, who affected intoxication, then said that we should not go on, that they had not received presents enough from us. Captain Clark told them that we would not be prevented from going on; that we were not squaws, but warriors; that we were sent by our great father, who could in a moment exterminate them.

*Meriwether Lewis describes his party's disagreement with the Teton Sioux, September 25, 1804, in Coues,* History of the Expedition, *I: 133.*

The object which appeared to astonish the Indians most was Captain Clark's servant York, a remarkably stout, strong negro. They had never seen a being of that color, and therefore flocked round him to examine the extraordinary monster. By way of amusement he told them that he had once been a wild animal, and caught and tamed by his master; and to convince them showed them feats of strength

which, added to his looks, made him more terrible than we wished him to be.

*Meriwether Lewis describes the effects of William Clark's slave, York, on the Native American population, October 9, 1804, in Coues,* History of the Expedition, *I: 159.*

West Florida is essential to the United States, both as their revenue on the Mississippi, and to the trade through the Mobile. Spain must also, sooner or later, swallow the claim for French injuries. All she can expect is, to have the pill wrapt up in the least nauseous disguise.

*James Madison in a letter to James Monroe, November 9, 1804, in* Letters and Other Writings of James Madison, *II: 208.*

Captain Clark with 14 men went out and found the Indians engaged in killing buffalo. The hunters, mounted on horseback and armed with bows and arrows, encircle the herd and gradually drive them into a plain or an open place fit for the movements of horses; they then ride in among them, and singling out a buffalo, a female being preferred, go as close as possible and wound her with arrows till they think they have given the mortal stroke. . . . Captain Clark killed ten buffalo . . .

*Meriwether Lewis describes a buffalo hunt, December 7, 1804, in Coues,* History of the Expedition, *I: 209.*

The effects of industry and enterprise appear in the numerous canals, turnpikes, elegant buildings, and well constructed bridges, over lengths and depths of water that open, and render the communication easy and agreeable, throughout a country almost without bounds. In short, arts and agriculture are pursued with avidity, civilization spreads, and science in full research is investigating all the sources of human knowledge. Indeed the whole country wears a face of improvement, from the extreme point of the northern and western woods, through all the southern states, and to the vast Atlantic ocean . . .

*Mercy Otis Warren,* History of the Rise, Progress, and Termination of the American Revolution, interspersed with Biographical, Political, and Moral Observations, *1805, II: 698.*

Brother, listen to what we say. There was a time when our forefathers owned this great island. . . . Brother, our seats were once large, and yours were small. You have now become a great people, and we have scarcely a place left to spread our blankets. You have got our country, but are not satisfied; you want to force your religion upon us. . . . Brother, you say there is but one way to worship and serve the Great Spirit. If there is but one religion, why do you white people differ so much about it? . . . Brother, we do not wish to destroy your religion or take it from you; we only want to enjoy our own.

*Sagoyewatha (Red Jacket), a Seneca religious leader, in a speech to a visiting American missionary, 1805, in Blaisdell,* Great Speeches, *41, 42.*

Early in the session a memorial was laid before Congress by deputies from a large portion of the citizens of the Territory of Orleans, praying an amelioration of the form of government that had been established in that territory by a law of last session. . . . at length a bill was introduced in the Senate and passed, authorizing the President of the United States to establish in that territory a government similar, in most respects, to that now exercised in the Mississippi Territory. By this bill the people of Orleans Territory will enjoy in some degree, the benefits of self-government.

*Tennessee congressman George W. Campbell in a circular letter to his constituents, February 26, 1805, in Cunningham,* Circular Letters, *388.*

Never, in all the time that we are here, have the Indians been in such a state of revolution as they are at present. . . . For the present they do not want to hear anything at all except what they learn through the extravagant visions.

*Moravian missionaries report on the revival of Indian spirituality among the Delaware, Miami, and Shawnee, March 1805, in Cayton,* Frontier Indiana, *205.*

I am honored and gratified by your Congratulations on my acquittal by the Senate of the Impeachment by the House of Representatives. It has ever been my wish to obtain and preserve the Esteem & Confidence of the virtuous and sensible part of my Fellow-Citizens. . . . It affords me great Pleasure to add, that a more fair and impartial trial, conducted with greater Dignity, never took place in any country.

*Impeached Supreme Court justice Samuel Chase in a letter to Rufus King, March 13, 1805, in King,* Life and Correspondence of Rufus King, *IV: 444, 445.*

Having made all our arrangements, we left the fort about five o'clock in the afternoon. The party now consisted of 32 persons. . . . The two interpreters were George Drewyer and Toussaint Chaboneau [sic]. The wife of Chaboneau [Sacagawea] also accompanied us with her young child, and we hope may be useful as an interpreter among the Snake Indians. She was herself one of that tribe, but having been taken in war by the Minnetarees, she was sold as a slave to Chaboneau, who brought her up and afterward married her.

*Meriwether Lewis describes Sacagawea (Sacajawea) as his expedition leaves its winter headquarters at Fort Mandan, April 7, 1805, in Coues,* History of the Expedition, *I: 253, 256–257.*

Arrived at Nashville on the 29th of May. One is astonished at the number of sensible, well-informed, and well behaved people which is found here. I have been received with much hospitality and kindness, and could stay a month with pleasure; but General Andrew Jackson having provided us a boat, we shall set off on Sunday, the 2d of June, to navigate down the Cumberland . . . Reached Massac on the Ohio, sixteen miles below, on the 6th. Here found General Wilkinson on his way to St. Louis. The general and his officers fitted me out with an elegant barge, sails, colours, and ten oars, with a sergeant, and ten able, faithful hands.

*Aaron Burr describes his western travels in a letter to his daughter, Theodosia, 1805, in Davis,* Memoirs of Aaron Burr, *II: 369, 370.*

The introduction of Slavery into this territory [Indiana] continues to be the Hobby horse of the influential men here. The members of the legislature have signed a petition to Congress praying for some reasonable modifications to the ordinance, but this favourite topic of Slavery, will I trust meet with a general disapprobation in Congress. Shallow politicians, who to obtain a transitory good are willing to entail on their Country a permanent evil.

*Indiana land official John Badollet laments one of the frequent attempts to introduce slavery into Indiana in a letter to Albert Gallatin, August 31, 1805, in Thornbrough,* Correspondence of John Badollet and Albert Gallatin, *49.*

England seems as ready to play the fool with respect to this country as her enemies. She is renewing her depredations on our Commerce in the most ruinous shapes, and has kindled a more general indignation among our Merchants than was ever before expressed. How little do those great Nations in Europe appear, in alternately smiling and frowning on the U. States, not according to any fixed sentiments or interests, but according to the winds and clouds of the moment!

*James Madison in a letter to G. W. Erving, November 1, 1805, in* Letters and Other Writings of James Madison, *II: 215.*

Personal Friendship for you and the love [of] my Country induce me to give you a warning about Cl. Burr's intrigues. You admit him at your table, and you held a long, and private conference with him a few days ago *after dinner* at the very moment he is meditating the overthrow of your Administration and what is more *conspiring against the State*. Yes Sir, his aberrations through the Western States *had no other object*.

*An anonymous letter to President Thomas Jefferson warns of the Burr Conspiracy, December 1, 1805, in* McLaughlin, To His Excellency, *5.*

I began with the disadvantage of a small capital, and the incumbrance of a large family, and yet I have already settled more acres than any man in America. There are forty thousand souls now holding directly or indirectly under me, and I trust, that no one amongst so many can justly impute to me any act resembling oppression. I . . . am proud of having been an instrument in reclaiming such large and fruitful tracts from the waste of creation.

*William Cooper, the founder of Cooperstown, New York,* A Guide in the Wilderness, *ca. 1806, in Hart,* American History, *II: 97.*

We were too poor to purchase other food from the Indians, so that we were sometimes reduced, notwithstanding all the exertions of our hunters, to a single day's provision in advance. The men, too, whom the constant rains and confinement had rendered unhealthy, might, we hoped, be benefited by leaving the coast and resuming the exercise of traveling. . . . the whole stock of goods on which we are to depend, for the purchase either of horses or of food, during the long tour of nearly 4,000 miles, is so much diminished that it might all be tied in two handker-

chiefs. We have in fact nothing but six blue robes, one of scarlet, a coat and hat of the United States Artillery uniform, five robes made of our large flag, and a few old clothes trimmed with ribbon. We therefore feel that our chief dependence must be on our guns . . .

*Meriwether Lewis paints a bleak picture as his exploration party prepares to set out to return to St. Louis from the West Coast, March 22, 1806, in Coues,* History of the Expedition, *III: 902.*

After much discussion of the various propositions which were submitted on this subject, a resolution was at length agreed to, for prohibiting the total importation of sundry important articles of the manufacture of that nation [Great Britain], which we can without a loss of much public revenue, and without much private inconvenience, either procure from other nations, or manufacture within the United States. This measure, it is believed, will not only greatly embarrass the commerce of Great Britain, by excluding from our markets so large and profitable a portion of her manufactures, but stimulate our own citizens to become the manufacturers of some of the articles so excluded.

*Kentucky congressman Matthew Walton in a letter to his constituents, March 27, 1806, in Cunningham,* Circular Letters, *I: 413.*

My butter which was as hard as in the middle of winter, was highly praised and when Mrs. Thornton observed my woman made excellent butter, I really felt a sensation of pride, which I do not often feel, in telling her it was my own making and that since the first of May, I had never missed churning but once. You can not think what a right down farmer's wife I am, but next winter will I hope convince you, that at least I am a good dairy maid, as you will eat of the fine butter I pack away. I have made about 60 lbs. This summer and have packed near 30 away.

*Washington socialite Margaret Bayard Smith brags about her domestic skills in a letter to Susan B. Smith, July 31, 1806, in Hunt,* The First Forty Years, *51–52.*

The party continued to slowly descend the river. . . . While there, they were overjoyed at seeing Captain Lewis' boats heave in sight about noon. But this feeling was changed into alarm on seeing the boats reach the shore without Captain Lewis, who they then learned had been wounded the day before, and was lying in the periogue.

*The Lewis and Clark expeditionary parties are reunited after splitting into two groups, August 12, 1806, in* Coues, History of the Expedition, *III: 1175.*

. . . descended to the Mississippi, and round to St. Louis, where we arrived at twelve o'clock; and having fired a salute, went on shore and received the heartiest and most hospitable welcome from the whole village.

*Meriwether Lewis reports on the conclusion of the Lewis and Clark expedition, September 23, 1806, in* Coues, History of the Expedition, *III: 1213.*

Negroes brought from the importers and carried home by the purchasers are ordinarily treated differently from the old ones. They are only gradually accustomed to work. They are made to bathe often, to take walks from time to time, and especially to dance; they are distributed in small numbers among old slaves in order to dispose them better to acquire their habits. . . . It happens too often that poor masters, who have no other slaves, or are too greedy, require hard labor of these fresh negroes, exhaust them quickly, lose them by sickness and more often by grief.

*French traveler C. C. Robin describes the breaking in of newly imported slaves in Louisiana, 1807, in* Phillips, Plantation and Frontier, *II: 31.*

. . . our great men are those who are most expert at crawling on all fours, and have the happiest facility in dragging and winding themselves along in the dirt like very reptiles. . . . It is not absolutely necessary to the formation of a great man that he should be either wise or valiant, upright or honorable. On the contrary, daily experience shows, that these qualities rather impede his preferment . . .

*Washington Irving denounces the morals of "great men" in his essay "On Greatness," 1807, in* Watts, Republic Reborn, *112.*

Some time in the latter part of September I received intimations that designs were in agitation in the Western country unlawful and unfriendly to the peace of the Union, and that the prime mover in these was Aaron Burr, heretofore distinguished by the favor of his country. . . . on the 25th of November, we learnt that a confidential agent of Aaron Burr had been deputed to him with communications, partly written

in cipher and partly oral, explaining his designs, exaggerating his resources, and making such offers of emolument and command to engage [General James Wilkinson] and the army in his unlawful enterprise as he had flattered himself would be successful.

*President Thomas Jefferson's message to Congress about the Burr conspiracy, January 22, 1807, in* Commager, Documents, *195, 196.*

With the Barbary powers in Africa, peace remains uninterrupted. The display of maritime force made by, and the inflexible perseverance of the United States, in the late war with Tripoli, have had a good effect, compelling the same powers to honor and respect the flag of the Union. With all the Indian tribes peace continues. The friendly measures adopted and pursued towards them, have a happy effect in conciliating their dispositions, in increasing their attachment to the United States, in divesting their savage habits, in promoting civilization among them, and in turning their attentions to agricultural pursuits . . .

*Tennessee congressman John Rhea in an open letter to his constituents, February 9, 1807, in* Cunningham, Circular Letters, *484–485.*

My Children, Chiefs of the Shawnee Nation . . . You express a wish to have your lands laid off separately to yourselves, that you may know what is your own, may have a fixed place to live on, of which you may not be deprived after you shall have built on it, and improved it. . . . With respect to reserves, you know they were made for the purpose of establishing convenient stations for trade and intercourse with the tribes within whose boundaries they are. . . . You wish me to name to you the person authorized to speak to you in our name, that you may know whom to believe, and not be deceived by imposters. My children, Governor Harrison is the person we authorize to talk to you in our name. You may depend on his advice, and that it comes from us.

*President Thomas Jefferson in a speech to the chiefs of the Shawnee nation, February 19, 1807, in* Hunt, The Essential Thomas Jefferson, *264, 265, 266–267.*

I think it my duty as a True American to give you my decided Oppinion [sic] considering all this noise about little Burr. . . . I don't like Burr nor never did but my dear Sir/ I have it from good authority directly—from the State of Ohio and the western country that our great general Wilkinson is as deep in the mud as little Burr is in the more which will Soon be proved and my friend also write me the people in general disiprove [sic] very much of Wilkinsons conduct and do realy [sic] Say that of the two Wilkinson is the greatest rouge and that he is in Spanish pay; therefore my dear Friend as a guardian of the people watch this impostor as well as the little divel [sic] . . .

*A concerned citizen writes to President Thomas Jefferson, February 24, 1807, in McLaughlin,* To His Excellency, *9–10.*

Captains Lewis and Clark, who with their associates, ascended the Missouri in the summer of 1804, as far up as Fort Mandan, about 1600 miles from its junction with the Mississippi, for the purpose of exploring the former river, and ascertaining the best communication from that to the Pacific Ocean, have at the hazard and expence of much danger, fatigue and personal privation, completed their expedition. . . . They ascertained with considerable accuracy the geography and commercial advantages of that country, as well as the character of its inhabitants, who on the Columbia are very numerous.

*Tennessee congressman George W. Campbell in a letter to his constituents, February 25, 1807, in Cunningham,* Circular Letters, *II: 497.*

It is indeed alarming, that private character weighs nothing in the scale of qualification for public office: as if a man had two hearts; a deceitful, depraved, wicked one towards his neighbor; an honest, pure, godly one toward his country! . . . I fear that our country is growing corrupt at a rate which distances the speed of every other. I do not say that the degree of positive corruption at present is so great, but the course towards total depravity is swift.

*Daniel Webster in a letter to a friend, March 8, 1807, in Webster,* Private Correspondence of Daniel Webster, *I: 225.*

The Treaty signed with the British Commissioners has not received the approbation of the President. . . . The case of impressments, particularly, having been brought to a formal issue, and having been the primary object of an Extraordinary Mission, a Treaty could not be closed which was silent on that subject—a subject which, whenever it shall no longer be seen through the mist with which practice enveloped

right, must excite wonder that the patience of the United States has remained so long unexhausted.

*James Madison in a letter to George Joy, May 22, 1807, in* Letters and Other Writings of James Madison, *II: 405.*

On Saturday morning General Wilkinson, with ten or eleven witnesses from New Orleans, arrived in Richmond[.] Four bills were immediately delivered to the grand jury against Blennerhassett and Burr; one for treason and one for misdemeanour against each. The examination of the witnesses was immediately commenced. They had gone through two-thirty last evening. There are about forty-six. General Eaton has been already examined. He came out of the jury-room in such rage and agitation that he shed tears, and complained bitterly that he had been questioned as if he were a villain. How else could he have been questioned with any propriety?

*Aaron Burr describes the early days of his trial in a letter to his daughter, Theodosia, June 18, 1807, in Davis,* Memoirs of Aaron Burr, *II: 406–407.*

[In] your History, you say that "after Mr. Adams's return from England he was implicated by a large portion of his countrymen as having relinquished the Republican system and forgotten the principles of the American Revolution, which he had advocated for near twenty years." I am somewhat at a loss for the meaning of the word "implicated" in this place. If it means suspected or accused or reproached, I know nothing of it. NO man ever accused or reproached me with any such relinquishment or oblivion . . . Now, Madam, I pray you to tell me who were the persons who composed that large portion of my countrymen who implicated me as having relinquished the Republican system? . . . Corruption is a charge that I cannot and will not bear. I challenge the whole human race, and angels and devils too, to produce an instance of it from my cradle to this hour.

*John Adams in a letter to Mercy Otis Warren about her* History, *July 20, 1807, in Adams,* Correspondence between John Adams and Mercy Warren, *332, 333, 335.*

I never had a wish to enter into a discussion of your motives of action while President of the United States, nor to give a particular detail of an Administration that rendered you unpopular indeed. This may be done by some one of that large majority of the people whose suffrages removed you from Presidential rank and placed another in the chair. I have frequently vindicated you as acting with honest intentions, however you might have been mistaken, or have varied from some gentlemen possessed of equal abilities, honor, and honesty, with yourself.

*Mercy Otis Warren responds to John Adams in a letter, July 28, 1807, in Adams,* Correspondence between John Adams and Mercy Warren, *360.*

We of the jury say that Aaron Burr is not proved to be guilty under this indictment by any evidence submitted to us. We therefore find him not guilty.

*The jury finds Aaron Burr not guilty of treason, September 1, 1807, in Davis,* Memoirs of Aaron Burr, *II: 384.*

To maintain the naval supremacy or perish as a Nation, is the prevalent doctrine of the day. The most candid Politicians admit that the manufacturing & commercial interests must suffer great detriment from a war; but they entertain a hope that their manufactures will find their way into Countries which have [not] been accustomed to receive them they judge, that we shall not be able by any means to dispense with the use of them, and they have a full conviction that a war will do us infinitely more harm than it will them, that it will be of short duration, and taking all circumstances into consideration, that it is preferable to an insidious neutrality—as they call the present system. . . . I perceive little chance of enjoying permanent safety, but by our becoming in a great degree an armed & united People, in effect, as well as in name.

*David Humphreys reports on British opinion about a potential war with the United States, September 25, 1807, in Humphreys,* Life and Times of David Humphreys, *363, 364.*

# 8

# Commercial Crisis and the Clamor for War
## 1808–1811

January 1, 1808, marked a big change for the United States of America. On that date, according to federal legislation passed at the end of the previous year, the foreign slave trade was outlawed. The change was hailed by antislavery activists, who hoped that this would be the first in a series of federal moves to curtail the institution of slavery in the United States. Even though more northern states were moving toward outlawing slavery, the end of the foreign slave trade did not signal a new era of national antislavery resolve. By contrast, the smuggling of slaves from Africa skyrocketed and the internal slave trade increased dramatically as cotton production spiked, making cotton the most important U.S. agricultural export. Even though the legal Atlantic trade in

This 1813 engraving by William Charles and Samuel Kennedy depicts three caricatures representing the United States, France, and Great Britain and lampoons the negotiations among them. Columbia lectures John Bull (Britain) to respect "free trade—Seamen's rights, etc." as Beau Napperty (France) looks on. John Bull's book reads, "Power constitutes Right." (*Library of Congress, Prints and Photographs Division [LC-USZ62-8869]*)

slaves had been curtailed, slave labor continued to fuel much of the rest of the U.S. trade economy.

That trade economy itself was far from peaceful in the following few years. Just prior to 1808 the United States had found itself increasingly embroiled in international conflicts ranging from the Tripolitan War to the latest in a long series of wars between Great Britain and France. U.S. trade had initially benefited from the Napoleonic Wars between Britain and France, as Americans grew increasingly dependent on both buying and selling goods abroad. U.S. shipping suffered severely when France and Britain imposed naval blockades on each other's coastlines and began seizing American ships that violated their respective blockades.

Even as the United States struggled to fight back against the aggressive actions of European nations, the government and citizenry questioned what the most effective countermeasures would be. The turmoil introduced into U.S. domestic life by international trade conflicts continued to increase between 1808 and 1811, as Great Britain seemed increasingly to become the chief enemy of the United States. The tensions wrought in Europe by the Napoleonic Wars seemed that they would spill over into North America, and loud voices began to call for war.

## COMMERCIAL SANCTIONS

U.S. ships, which were trying to carry wares as neutral traders in the Anglo-French wars, had become embroiled in the combustible situation caused by mutual British and French blockades. By the end of 1807, the tensions in foreign trade were beginning to hit home. After the HMS *Leopard* attacked the USS *Chesapeake* off the coast of Virginia, Congress retaliated by imposing a strict embargo on all foreign trade in December 1807. President Jefferson believed that commercial sanctions (which together were known as the restrictive system) would be the best way to combat European naval depredations without risking involvement in war, but the enforcement of the embargo and the subsequent series of commercial sanctions did not end up meeting either goal effectively.

Since the embargo forbade all U.S. exports, it thereby severely limited imports as well, since foreign ships were unlikely to enter U.S. ports. Thus it quickly began to cause economic hardships, especially in areas that were heavily export-dependent. The embargo caused acute and immediate damage in New England and parts of the Middle Atlantic states, which were beginning to rely ever more on exporting manufactured goods to support the local economies, and which protested loudly against trade restrictions. Southern planters were hit less hard, initially, since their agricultural exports were more seasonal, but as the embargo stretched into 1808, tobacco and cotton farmers began to feel a severe pinch. Smuggling was widespread, especially throughout the northern states, with their easy access to Canada. President Jefferson and New York governor Daniel D. Tompkins were even forced to call out troops to suppress rampant, violent smuggling on Lake Champlain.

The only place the embargo did not cause any perceptible economic harm was in Europe. Neither Britain nor France was much perturbed by it, and the domestic economic damage far outweighed any effectiveness of the embargo as a tool of foreign policy. Soon, the U.S. government was joining private citizens in the economic suffering, since most government revenues came from taxes on trade. U.S. tax revenues from imports declined by more than half to less than $8,000,000 in 1809.[1] Even some Democratic-Republicans grew critical of the embargo's terms; John Randolph remarked that it resembled an attempt "to cure corns by cutting off the toes."[2] The embargo was threatening to cripple the U.S. economy, and Britain and France, its intended victims, barely seemed to notice.

President Jefferson nonetheless stood by commercial sanctions as the best way to threaten European powers without risking a war that the United States might not be able effectively to prosecute. As his second term came to an end, his apparent Republican successor, James Madison, shared Jefferson's basic conviction in the power of economic coercion. As one Democratic-Republican newspaper contended, "peaceable coercion" ought to help the United States to avoid war while still boosting the country's international status and confirming its "national character."[3] Even though the economic hardships caused by the embargo caused a temporary surge in the popularity of the Federalists (especially in the North), Madison was easily elected president in 1808, with 122 of 179 electoral votes. The expected continuity between the Jefferson and Madison administrations was signaled by the fact that Jefferson's vice president, George Clinton, was reelected to office for Madison's first term.

Despite Madison's conviction that commercial sanctions provided a virtuous means for the American republic to avoid war, it was clear that the embargo was not working, and Congress repealed it just before Madison's inauguration in March 1809. The legislature did not abandon the idea of fighting British and French aggression using economic means, however. Congress replaced the embargo with the less stringent Non-Intercourse Act. The Non-Intercourse Act was at once both more complicated and even less effective than

This pen-and-ink drawing depicts the U.S. Capitol and Pennsylvania Avenue in Washington, D.C., prior to the War of 1812. *(Library of Congress, Prints and Photographs Division [LC-USZ62-4538])*

the embargo had been. Under its terms, all foreign trade with both Great Britain and France was forbidden to U.S. citizens (although they could now trade legally with other world powers). The Non-Intercourse Act tried to play Britain and France against each other by declaring that if either country were to recognize fully America's neutral trading rights, then the trade restrictions against that country would be relaxed.

The terms of the Non-Intercourse Act proved almost impossible to enforce. U.S. trading ships were allowed to leave port, and once they were out of American waters, many of them ended up trading with French and British agents, despite the legal restrictions. The historian Donald Hickey contends that the Non-Intercourse Act was so loose that it never was intended to be enforced; rather it was a way of saving U.S. diplomatic face after the failure of the embargo.[4] After some abortive efforts to work out trading terms by David M. Erskin, the British foreign minister in Washington, D.C., failed, the Non-Intercourse Act stayed in place. But it neither stopped Americans from trading overseas nor stopped the British and French from seizing American ships and impressing American sailors into their navies.

Still committed, in principle, to the policy behind the restrictive system, Congress again switched tactics. In May 1810, the legislature repealed the Non-Intercourse Act and passed, instead, Macon's Bill No. 2. This bill courted the favor of Britain and France by promising to retaliate against the enemy if either power could come to terms with the United States. Trade with Britain and France was legalized, but the bill promised that if either Britain or France lifted their sanctions against neutral trading rights and pledged to stop harassing U.S. ships, then Congress would reimpose nonimportation against the other nation. This formulation offered the advantage of allowing legal trade to continue, while still granting some diplomatic leverage with the European belligerents.

In August 1810, the French foreign minister, the duc de Cadore, pledged to meet the terms of Macon's Bill No. 2, and although his claims were probably fraudulent, the United States agreed to reimpose trade restrictions against Great Britain. Napoleon Bonaparte never intended to respect U.S. neutral trading rights, but the Democratic-Republicans, who controlled the national government, had always been more friendly to France than to Britain, and the French pledge served their political purposes. Madison proclaimed nonimportation terms against Great Britain in February 1811, and Congress backed his move in March. When Britain refused to repeal the Orders in Council, which detailed the restrictions on U.S. shipping, diplomatic relations between the United States and Great Britain came close to breaking. By the time it became clear that the United States had played right into Napoleon's hands, talk of war with Great Britain was beginning to be heard ever louder within the United States.

## NEW INTERNAL ENERGY

The clashes between the United States and Europe, and the restrictive system by which the U.S. government tried to manage them, did cause a great measure of domestic economic harm and upheaval, but they also had some rather unintended good effects. Because foreign trade was severely restricted by the series of laws enacted by Congress, internal trade and economic activity received an unexpected spur. The transition to a full-fledged market economy inside the United States that had been going on piecemeal for decades was energized by an increase in the flow of goods from country to city, especially since ports were often closed to outside trade with other parts of the world. Americans had grown used to buying a wider range of goods of all kinds, and if they could not receive them from overseas, they would have to begin manufacturing and trading more themselves. Even President Jefferson, never known as a friend of commerce and manufacturing, issued a call for increased domestic industry in his 1808 annual message to Congress.

Enterprising individuals made the most of these unusual economic opportunities. One of the most successful businessmen in all of American history, John Jacob Astor, began building his empire in the period, as he skillfully navigated the various trade restrictions to start his fur-trading business. Astor had already made a great deal of money in the early U.S. overseas trade with China around the turn of the century, and during the period when Congress placed restrictions on foreign trade, Astor concentrated on developing the interior trade networks that would form the basis of even bigger future profits. Astor, who possessed considerable business and personal connections in British Canada, sought to capitalize on the vast territory acquired by the United States in the 1803 Louisiana Purchase. Furs seemed to offer the most immediate and lucrative market (both domestically and overseas), and Astor founded his American Fur Company in 1808. Astor sought to expand his enterprise all the way to the Pacific by 1810, when he incorporated the Pacific Fur Company. The Pacific Fur Company established a trading post, dubbed Astoria, at the mouth of the Columbia River in present-day Oregon the following year. Astor's western holdings would become subject to British seizure during the War of 1812, but in the years leading up to the war, he successfully established a network of Indian, Canadian, and American traders, all of whom enriched him and his corporations to provide the basis of vast future wealth.

Other advances in trading made during the period leading up to the War of 1812 did not realize huge immediate profits, but they prepared the way for a great deal of future economic development. Several states, following the lead of New York, passed liberal incorporation laws that encouraged the development of factories and textile mills. Even in the midst of the controversy over the embargo in 1808, the United States established a trading post for maple sugar in the northern Michigan Territory to enhance further the profits generated by raw materials on the "frontier." The same year, Jesse Fell began experimenting with burning anthracite coal in Wilkes-Barre, Pennsylvania, and the later application of his coal-burning methods would literally lend fuel to U.S. industrialization and the home use of coal-burning stoves. Other industrial processes began to be perfected during these years. For example, the first aluminum works in the United States opened in Maryland in 1811.

Even as the British and French continued to capture large numbers of U.S. sailing ships that tried to trade their wares on the high seas, advancements in water transportation continued inside the United States that cleared the way for a future expansion in overseas trade. In May 1808, John Stevens launched his ship *Phoenix* on a trip between New York City and Philadelphia. The *Phoenix* was the first steam-powered ship to travel successfully on the Atlantic

Ocean, and within decades, steam travel would become vastly important for both foreign and domestic U.S. trade. In 1811, the steamboat *New Orleans* opened up western steamboat travel along the Ohio and Mississippi Rivers, making it possible to move internal trade more quickly and efficiently.

The pace of American scientific interest and discovery also quickened between 1808 and 1811, in part because of the increased interest in economic growth, but also as a function of new developments in medicine. American science certainly did not equal European or Asian accomplishments, and some intellectuals worried that after the demise of Benjamin Franklin, "there was nothing worthy of the name of national science" in the United States. But progress was made despite a lack of coordinated scientific efforts.[5] Fell's anthracite coal experiments were as much scientific as economic, and even though a group of professional scientists was beginning to develop, most discoveries continued to come from nonprofessionals like Fell. In 1809, William Maclure published the first scientific geological map of the United States, and that same year the noted medical pioneer Ephraim McDowell successfully removed a woman's ovarian tumor in the country's first successful abdominal operation. In 1810, Yale University founded its medical school, the country's sixth, signaling a new era of professionalization in American medical education and training. The chemist and natural scientist Benjamin Silliman also helped to build a solid reputation for pure scientific investigation at Yale during these years, although he was temporary blinded by a laboratory explosion in 1811.

Religious developments in the years before the War of 1812 caused much more popular enthusiasm than scientific ones, and they similarly laid the groundwork for greater future developments after the war. The evangelical fervor that had led since the 1780s to an increase in popularity of Protestant denominations, including Baptists and Methodists, continued, and a wide variety of Protestant individuals and sects experienced renewed fervor. The first U.S. temperance (anti-alcohol) society and Bible society sprang up during this period, both of which sought to apply the ideals of reform Protestantism to cure social ills. This trend would soon burst forth into a full-fledged reform movement fueled by the Protestant Second Great Awakening. In 1809, the Irish Presbyterian Alexander Campbell joined his father, Thomas, in western Pennsylvania, where they founded an interdenominational Christian association. The Campbells, who believed strongly in revival religion of the kind seen in 1801 at Cane Ridge, Kentucky, became dissatisfied with the Presbyterian Church and began the path of religious reform that would lead them to formally found the Church of Christ (Disciples of Christ) in the 1820s. Most Protestant women took part in religion as members of congregations, but a few—most notably Jarena Lee, who sought unsuccessfully during this period to be licensed as a preacher in Philadelphia's African Methodist Episcopal church—tried to become religious leaders.

Religious awakening was not confined to American Protestants in this period, however. Catholicism, also spreading in the United States, received its first designated archdiocese. One of the country's most important early Catholic advocates also began her important work in 1809. Elizabeth Bayley Seton, the daughter of a New York Anglican priest, had converted to Catholicism in 1805 after the death of her husband. Seton, who had a long history of involvement in charitable work, then turned her efforts toward education, founding a Catholic school in Baltimore, Maryland. In March 1809, Seton's religious devotion was confirmed when she accepted holy orders, and the following year she founded the Sisters of Charity of St. Joseph, the first religious order native to the United States. Mother Seton, as she was subsequently known, remained involved in parochial education and charity work for several decades, and in the 1970s she was canonized as the first American-born Catholic saint.

## THE PAN-INDIAN MOVEMENT

One of the most remarkable religious awakenings in the years before the War of 1812 took place outside the bounds of Christianity altogether, as a great Shawnee prophet led a spiritual movement that became the lifeblood of a whole new North American pan-Indian movement. The Shawnee "Prophet" Tenskwatawa and his brother, the warrior Tecumseh, expanded their religious and political movement after 1809 as their people seemed increasingly threatened by the United States. Tenskwatawa, a religious seer who advocated a withdrawal from European ways and a return to Indian spirituality and political sovereignty, continued the prophesizing that had brought him a wide variety of Indian followers since the early 1800s. The headquarters of Tecumseh and Tenskwatawa at Prophetstown on the Tippecanoe River (in present-day Indiana) became the base for a new phase in their pro-Indian activism. Indians from all over North America flocked to Prophetstown to hear Tenskwatawa's preaching, and Tecumseh began to emerge as a powerful military and political leader who called for a unified Indian resistance to the United States.

When Indiana's territorial governor, William Henry Harrison, extended an invitation for representatives from many of the most important Indian tribes across the region to enter a round of treaty negotiations in September 1809, Tecumseh and Tenskwatawa were alarmed, and they called for their allies to refuse to make any further land concessions to U.S. officials. Tecumseh was busy recruiting Indian military forces as Harrison opened negotiations with sympathetic representatives of the Lenni Lenape (Delaware), Potawatomi, Miami, Kickapoo, Wea, and Eel River peoples, who did not necessarily speak for the entire population of their tribes. Harrison concluded a treaty that gained an astounding 3 million acres of land in return for a small payment of $8,200. Known as the Treaty of Fort Wayne, it stood as one of the largest Indian land cessions to date.

The unfair terms of the Treaty of Fort Wayne, and the fact that many tribal lands (particularly Miami and Shawnee territories) had been included improperly in the treaty, fueled Tecumseh's efforts to recruit Indians to oppose the United States. Indeed, Tecumseh's biographer claims that the treaty "put Tecumseh on the road to war."[6] Tecumseh gradually emerged as the leader of the pan-Indian movement started by his brother, and by 1810 he claimed, "I am alone acknowledged head of all the Indians."[7] While that was certainly an exaggeration, Tecumseh had great success at recruiting disaffected Native peoples to his cause, and his military strength increased. Harrison encouraged American officials to believe that much of Tecumseh's power came from British encouragement in Canada. While it is true that Tecumseh did draw support from British officials, especially after he strengthened his Canadian alliance in 1810, his leadership had a broad and autonomous power base among Indians throughout the eastern half of North America.

After the Treaty of Fort Wayne was concluded, Tecumseh traveled up and down the eastern seaboard recruiting even more support for his movement of Indian unity. In September 1811, while Tecumseh was away, William Henry Harrison led a force of 1,000 militia troops toward Prophetstown, hoping to weaken the pan-Indian forces at a moment of vulnerability. Instead of catching Tenskwatawa unprotected, however, Harrison provoked an Indian offensive. The Prophet, emboldened by a belief that soldiers under his spiritual protection could not come to harm, led an attack on Harrison's camp near the modern-day location of Lafayette, Indiana, on November 7. Tenskwatawa's troops inflicted 180 casualties on the militiamen, but they did not win a decisive victory. On the following day, Harrison attacked and burned Prophetstown in retaliation.

The battle of Tippecanoe, as the attack came to be known, did much to boost Harrison's political reputation, and it diminished some of Tenskwatawa's and Tecumseh's power. But it did not disable the Shawnee brothers or the pan-Indian movement. In the winter of 1811, Tecumseh warned of more bloodshed when he told a group of Osage: "The red men . . . are determined on vengeance; they have taken up the tomahawk; they will make it fat with blood; they will drink the blood of the white people."[8]

## The Clamor for War

By 1811, Tecumseh was not the only person in North America calling for war. After the passage of Macon's Bill No. 2 and the imposition of nonimportation against Great Britain, Americans increasingly focused on Great Britain as the cause of their economic and foreign policy woes. Although the British and French both had seized hundreds of U.S. ships, French predations had slackened after 1810, and the British continued to impress American sailors into the Royal Navy. The United States and Britain had not been able to reach terms of compensation for the attack of the HMS *Leopard* on the USS *Chesapeake* in 1807, and rhetoric over the incident continued to run at fever pitch. In May 1811, tensions grew even worse when the USS *President,* sent by the U.S. Navy Department to police illegal British impressments, attacked the British ship *Little Belt* and killed three sailors in a short battle. The controversy that followed did not dispose British negotiators to pledge reparations for the earlier *Chesapeake* attack, and British public opinion against the United States grew more unfavorable.

Many American politicians also came, by 1811, to call for war against Great Britain. By the end of 1810, President Madison, who had been elected on the premise that he agreed with Thomas Jefferson's use of the restrictive system to prevent war, was beginning to believe that a war against Great Britain might not be prevented. Even more important, Madison faced considerable pressure in the Democratic-Republican Party from a new, young group of pro-war politicians who came to be known as the War Hawks. The War Hawks included western and southern Democratic-Republicans who were elected to Congress in 1810. Some of the most prominent politicians of the 19th century—including Henry Clay, John C. Calhoun, Felix Grundy, and Thomas Hart Benton—all got their start in national politics as members of the War Hawks, a term their opponent John Randolph coined because of their aggressive tendencies toward Great Britain.

The War Hawks pushed for the protection of their regional interests and stressed that a crisis point with Britain had been reached that required fighting a new "American Revolution" to restore American liberty and economic prosperity. John C. Calhoun argued that if the United States continued to "submit" to commercial and naval control by Great Britain, "the independence of this nation is lost."[9] The southern War Hawks were incensed by the harm caused to the cotton export economy by the restrictive system. Westerners loudly insisted that the British were to blame for stirring up Tecumseh and other Indians to violence along the western borders of the United States. Both southern and western War Hawks had expansionist aspirations, and they held out hopes of annexing Florida, Texas, and even Canada to the United States.

Before visions of war had entirely coalesced, the War Hawks did see some of their hopes realized. President Madison was already at work trying to seize the territory of West Florida from Spain around the time they were elected. The United States had unsuccessfully tried to negotiate the takeover of West Florida since shortly after the turn of the century, and early in 1810, President Madison sent secret agents to try a new path to annexation of the territory. The agents succeeded in spreading dissension, and in September 1810, a group of Americans seized the Spanish fort at Baton Rouge and declared their independence from Spain. The U.S. government quickly recognized their questionable independence, and the territory was annexed to the United States in October. Madison, aided the following spring by his new secretary of state, James Monroe, and secret authorization from Congress, then sent General George Matthews to East Florida to try to achieve a similar coup there. Matthews did not meet with much success, but Madison was intent on announcing to the world that the United States wished to end European control of parts of North America wherever possible and to eliminate East Florida as a refuge for runaway American slaves.

With the start of the Twelfth Congress in November 1811, the War Hawks gained powerful influence over national politics. Kentucky War Hawk Henry Clay was elected Speaker of the House of Representatives, and he used the position to promote the cause of war, even though some factions in his party were less belligerent than the War Hawks. The Federalist Party, still quite strong especially in New England, opposed the very idea of a new war with Great Britain, but they held only 25 percent of the House of Representative and 18 percent of the Senate.[10] The Federalists held out some vain hopes that President Madison would not support war, but increasingly all signs started to point in that direction. A report from the Senate Foreign Relations Committee at the end of November seemed to confirm that the executive branch was preparing to go to war, and Congress began to authorize the preparation of war materials and troops. Henry Clay wrote to a friend at the end of December: "The War preparations are advancing with the support of an immense majority."[11] Barring some daring move on the part of Great Britain or President Madison, war seemed imminent.

## A REPUBLIC IN CONFLICT

The end of 1811 was a frightening time in the United States. It looked as though the republic was on the brink of an all-out war for the first time since the conclusion of the Revolutionary War in 1783. Although the energy of territorial and cultural growth caused exciting changes inside the United States, some of the same energy led to instability and conflict with Native Americans. The U.S. economy had grown to the extent that international trade was ever more important, but that same fact had caused years of problems when the United States ran afoul of European powers engulfed in their own series of wars. Perhaps not surprisingly, given the origins and ideology of the American Republic, those tensions had grown highest with Great Britain by the end of 1811, and some Americans began to call for a "second American Revolution." Perhaps a new war would offer the United States a chance finally to gain full international respect and to expand its borders even more by conquering Indians and British possessions in Canada. The attempt might bring with it, however, a whole new set of problems for the still relatively young American republic.

## CHRONICLE OF EVENTS

**1808**

The New York Academy of Fine Arts is founded with U.S. Ambassador to France Robert R. Livingston as its first president.

The Theatre d'Orleans, a formal opera house, is constructed in New Orleans.

University of Maryland professor John Elihu Hall founds the *American Law Journal,* the first regularly published U.S. legal magazine.

Congressmen George W. Campbell of Tennessee and Barent Gardenier of New York engage in the first recorded duel between two members of Congress.

The first temperance society in the United States is organized in Moreau, New York.

The Catholic diocese in Baltimore becomes an archdiocese.

*The Missouri Gazette,* later known as the *St. Louis Republican,* begins publication as the first newspaper west of the Mississippi River.

The United States establishes a trading post for maple sugar in northern Michigan.

*January 1:* As of this date, the importation of slaves into the United States is illegal. Clandestine slave trading continues, and the slave population also continues to grow from natural population increase.

*January 9:* Congress expands the Embargo Act against international trade, which aims to bring diplomatic pressure to bear on Great Britain and, to a lesser degree, France.

*February 11:* Jesse Fell begins his experiments with burning anthracite coal in his home in Wilkes-Barre, Pennsylvania. The experiments will lead to a host of uses for the coal, which burned too hot to work effectively in previously available home stoves.

*March 12:* Congress again seeks to strengthen the terms of the embargo, which is starting to cause domestic economic harm while simultaneously failing to stop widespread international smuggling.

*April 6:* John Jacob Astor incorporates his American Fur Company, which will come to control the entire U.S. market in furs.

James N. Barker's play *The Indian Princess* or *La Belle Sauvage,* which dramatizes the life of Pocahontas, appears on the Philadelphia stage.

*April 17:* Napoleon Bonaparte issues the Bayonne Decree, which subjects all American ships in Euro-

Napoleon Bonaparte, emperor of the French, had forged some ties of friendship with the United States by selling the territory of Louisiana in 1803, but his double-dealing during the Anglo-French wars complicated U.S. diplomatic and military involvement in the wars and helped lead to the War of 1812. *(Library of Congress, Prints and Photographs Division [LC-USZ62-121171])*

pean ports to search and seizure. The decree will accelerate the pace of American commercial losses, and Napoleon's government will gain at least $10 million worth of seized goods.

*April 19:* President Jefferson and New York governor Daniel D. Tompkins move to put down insurrection in the Lake Champlain region, where smuggling in violation of the embargo runs rampant.

*May 6:* John Stevens's steamship *Phoenix* becomes the first steam-powered vessel to travel on the Atlantic. It uses a screw propeller to navigate between New York City and Philadelphia.

*November 8:* President Jefferson's annual message to Congress calls for an increase in domestic manufacturing and cites the trade embargo as a positive opportunity for internal economic development.

*November 10:* The United States signs a treaty at Ft. Clark, Kansas, with representatives of the Osage

Sioux. In the treaty, the Osage cede large tracts of land in present-day Missouri and Arkansas.

*December 7:* James Madison, a leader of the Democratic-Republican Party, is elected president with 122 of 179 electoral votes. George Clinton, who received 6 electoral votes for president, is reelected vice president.

*December 12:* In Philadelphia, William White founds the first Bible society in the United States.

*December 29:* Andrew Johnson, who will become the first U.S. president to be impeached in 1868, is born in Raleigh, North Carolina.

## 1809

Thomas Campbell publishes his popular story of an Indian "massacre" during the Revolutionary War, *Gertrude of Wyoming.*

William Maclure's *Observations on the Geology of the United States,* published this year, includes the first geological map of the United States.

The Seventy-Six Association is founded in Charleston, South Carolina. The group of elite Democratic-Republicans sponsors annual celebrations of Independence Day in the city that rival those sponsored by the Federalist Revolution Society.

Elizabeth Ann Seton founds the first Catholic school in the United States.

Washington Irving publishes his classic satirical *History of New York.*

Abel Stowel produces the first screw-cutting machine in the United States.

Dr. Ephraim McDowell performs the first abdominal operation in the United States when he removes a woman's ovarian tumor in Danville, Kentucky.

The state of Ohio begins to issue paper warrants to be used as currency because of a shortage of coins.

The state of Ohio allows African Americans who can prove their freedom with court papers to settle in the state.

*January 9:* Congress passes the Enforcement Act, which provides for the seizure of any goods suspected of being smuggled in or out of the United States in violation of the embargo.

*February 12:* Abraham Lincoln is born in Hodgenville, Kentucky.

*February 17:* Miami University, a state-sponsored college, is chartered in Oxford, Ohio.

*February 20:* In its ruling in the case of *United States v. Peters,* the Supreme Court reaffirms the doctrine of the supremacy of federal power over the states.

*February 23:* The governor of Connecticut, Jonathan Trumbull, protests that the embargo is unconstitutional. His sentiments echo widespread disaffection expressed throughout New England with the commercial sanctions.

*March 1:* The Embargo Act is repealed and replaced by the Non-Intercourse Act, which is less restrictive against international trade and makes it possible for the president to reestablish trade with Britain and France if they should begin to respect American shipping.

Congress creates the Illinois Territory.

*March 4:* On inauguration day, James Madison becomes the fourth president, and Thomas Jefferson retires to his Virginia estate, Monticello. Jefferson faces severe financial difficulties, and he will never again leave Virginia.

*April 19:* President Madison reopens trade relations with Great Britain on the condition that the British repeal their sanctions against neutral shipping rights.

*June 27:* President Madison appoints John Quincy Adams as U.S. ambassador to Russia.

This 19th-century engraving depicts Monticello, Thomas Jefferson's Palladian mansion at his Virginia estate. Jefferson designed the house himself and occupied many years of his life adding to it and pursuing his intellectual hobbies there. *(from Benson Lossing,* The Pictorial Field-Book of the Revolution, *1851–1852)*

*August 9:* Since Great Britain has failed to restore neutral shipping rights, President Madison again restricts American–British trade under the terms of the Non-Intercourse Act.

*September 30:* Indiana governor William Henry Harrison concludes the Treaty of Fort Wayne, in which Native Americans from the Delaware, Potawatomi, Miami, Kickapoo, Wea, and Eel River tribes cede 3 million acres of land to the United States for $8,200. Tecumseh, the Shawnee warrior who is organizing an Indian confederacy, protests the cession, claiming that Shawnee lands were illegally included in the treaty.

*October 11:* Meriwether Lewis commits suicide.

*November 1:* In New York City, visitors can view an exhibition of the Grand Panorama, an artistic view of the city and its surrounding countryside.

*December 7:* In Tennessee, Andrew Jackson and his wife, Rachel, legally adopt their first child, Andrew Jackson, Jr.

## 1810

The state of Maryland prohibits free African Americans from voting. The state also moves to allow all white men to vote by removing property-holding requirements.

Alexander and Thomas Campbell, Pennsylvania Presbyterians, found the Campbellite Church of Christ. They split off from the Presbyterian Church and unsuccessfully seek to become Baptists. Their church will form the basis of the Disciples of Christ denomination, which will be founded formally in 1827.

The Maryland legislature authorizes the Baltimore Washington Monument Society to conduct a lottery to raise funds for a monument to George Washington. Robert Mills will win the design competition for this, the first architectural monument to George Washington in the nation, in 1814, and its construction will be completed in 1829.

The Cumberland Presbytery in Kentucky is excluded from the Presbyterian Church.

Reverend Lyman Beecher becomes a charter member of the Connecticut Moral Society, which polices immoralities in society.

Congress forbids free African-American men from working as mail carriers.

The *Agricultural Museum,* America's first agricultural magazine, begins publication.

Architect Robert Mills won a competition begun in 1811 to design this monument in Baltimore, Maryland, to honor George Washington. Mills later designed the Washington Monument in Washington, D.C. *(from Benson Lossing,* The Pictorial Field-Book of the Revolution, *1851–1852)*

John Quincy Adams publishes a series of lectures he delivered at Harvard College between 1806 and 1809 as *Lectures on Rhetoric and Oratory.*

Charles Jared Ingersoll publishes *Inchiquin, The Jesuit's Letters,* which refutes the claims of European writers who have criticized America.

The Organization of the Society of Artists of the United States is founded.

In Boston, Johann Christian Gottlieb Graupner founds the first professional symphony orchestra in the United States, the Philharmonic Society.

Simeon Viets founds a cigar factory in West Suffield, Connecticut.

A. R. Hawley and Augustius Post fly a hot-air balloon from St. Louis to Canada.

Yale University founds a medical school.

Elizabeth Ann Seton founds America's first Catholic religious order, the Sisters of Charity of St.

This portrait depicts Elizabeth Ann Bayley Seton in her younger days at the time of her marriage. She went on to found a Catholic religious order and became the first American-born Roman Catholic saint. *(Library of Congress, Prints and Photographs Division [LC-USZ62-129040])*

Joseph, with four other women at St. Joseph's College in Emmitsburg, Maryland.

The American Museum opens in New York City.

Billy Bowlegs, the Seminole Tribal leader who will hold out against American troops in Florida during the 1835 Seminole War, is born.

*February 22:* American Gothic fiction author Charles Brockden Brown dies.

*March 16:* The Supreme Court issues its decision in the case of *Fletcher v. Peck,* ruling for the first time that a state law is unconstitutional.

*May 1:* Congress repeals the Non-Intercourse Act and passes Macon's Bill No. 2. Trade with both Great Britain and France is allowed, though the bill creates provisions for commercial retaliation against either power if it refuses to lift the ban on American neutral trading rights.

*June 23:* John Jacob Astor founds the Pacific Fur Company.

*July 12:* Members of the union of Journeymen Cordwainers go on trial for conspiracy for organizing a strike for higher wages. They are convicted and fined one dollar each.

*September 26:* Americans in West Florida declare independence from Spain and seize the fort of Baton Rouge.

*October 1:* The Berkshire Cattle Show in Pittsfield, Massachusetts, begins. The fair will spawn the first permanent agricultural association in the country.

*October 27:* President Madison annexes the West Florida Territory to the Louisiana Territory.

*November:* Democratic-Republican Elbridge Gerry is elected governor of Massachusetts.

*November 2:* Incorrectly informed that France has lifted commercial sanctions against the United States, President Madison declares his intent to close off commercial trade with Great Britain under the terms of Macon's Bill No. 2. Meanwhile, both the French and the British continue to search and seize American ships.

## 1811

The *Juvenile Magazine* begins publication.

The *Mobile Centinel,* Alabama's first newspaper, begins publication.

The country's first aluminum works opens in Cape Sable, Maryland.

The short-lived Columbian Chemical Society of Philadelphia is organized. The country's first chemical society, the Chemical Society of Philadelphia, had ceased to meet in 1803.

New York State issues its General Incorporation Statute for 1811 to try to encourage textile mills to manufacture thread for use by women in at-home weaving.

*January 8–11:* Federal troops help to put down two slave rebellions near New Orleans. Charles Deslondes, a freeman from Haiti, leads the band of 180 slaves who take part in the largest slave insurrection in U.S. history.

*January 14:* Harriet Beecher Stowe, future author of *Uncle Tom's Cabin,* is born.

*January 15:* Congress passes a secret act empowering President Madison to seek the annexation of East Florida to the United States. Technically, the United States was not supposed to seek actively the annexation of territory belonging to another country, in this case, Spain.

*February 11:* President Madison invokes Macon's Bill No. 2 once more and forbids American trade with Great Britain.

*February 20:* A vote in Congress to renew the charter of the Bank of the United States fails. Opponents of the bank, who dislike the bank's use of federal power and its British shareholders, rejoice.

*February 22:* At the urging of Abigail Adams, President Madison offers her son, John Quincy Adams, a position on the Supreme Court, but he turns down the position.

*March 2:* President Madison again suspends trade relations with Great Britain under the erroneous assumption that the French have finally agreed to respect American neutral trading rights.

*April 2:* President Madison names fellow Virginian James Monroe as secretary of state.

*April 12;* Americans working for John Jacob Astor's Pacific Fur Company found the first permanent American settlement in the Pacific Northwest at Fort Astoria in present-day Oregon.

*May 16:* After a misunderstanding over the impressment of American sailors, the USS *President* engages in a naval battle against the British ship *Little Belt.*

*September 11:* The steamboat *New Orleans* makes the first steamboat trip in the interior of the United States on the Ohio and Mississippi Rivers between Pittsburgh and New Orleans.

*September 26:* Territorial governor William Henry Harrison leaves Vincennes, Indiana, with 1,000 militia troops on an expedition to attack the Shawnee confederacy at Tippecanoe Creek.

*November:* A group of western and southern Democratic-Republicans dubbed the "War Hawks," which includes John C. Calhoun, Richard Mentor Johnson, Peter B. Porter, and Felix Grundy, gain new power in the House of Representatives. One of their number, Kentuckian Henry Clay, is elected Speaker of the House.

*November 7:* William Henry Harrison's troops are attacked by the Shawnee Confederacy near Tippecanoe Creek. The Shawnee, led by Tecumseh's brother Tenskwatawa "The Prophet," are defeated, and Harrison's men destroy their village. The defeat of Indian forces at Tippecanoe becomes the basis for Harrison's nickname "Old Tippecanoe" in the presidential election of 1840. Tecumseh himself was not present at the battle because he was traveling in the South recruiting support for a pan-Indian confederacy against western movement by the United States.

*December 12:* The entertainment establishment Vauxhall, owned by J. Delacroix, opens in New York City. Delacroix offers a saloon, tea room, cards, and private rooms for "genteel" entertainment.

*December 16:* A severe earthquake along the New Madrid fault, thought by some to be the worst in American history, changes the course of the Mississippi River.

## EYEWITNESS TESTIMONY

Let the first of January . . . be set apart in every year, as a day of publick thanksgiving. Let the history of the sufferings of our brethren, and of their deliverance, descend by this means to our children, to the remotest generations; and when they shall ask, in time to come, saying, What mean the lessons, the psalms, the prayers and the praises in the worship of this day? Let us answer them by saying, the Lord, on the day of which this is the anniversary, abolished the trade which dragged your fathers from their native country, and sold them as bond men in the United States of America.

*Philadelphia preacher Absalom Jones in a Thanksgiving sermon praising the outlawing of the slave trade, January 1, 1808, in Johnson and Smith,* Africans in America, *270.*

The Carolina slave dealers get frequent supplies from this state, particularly from the eastern shore; and never were my feelings more outraged or my notions of the freedom and liberty of my country more hurt, than by a scene which presented itself near Ellicott's—Two blanched and meagre looking wretches were lolling in their one-horse chair, protected from the excessive heat of the noon-day sun by a huge umbrella, and driving before them four beings of the African race, fastened to each other by iron chains fixed round the neck and arms . . .

*Observations in the anonymous pamphlet* A Tour in Virginia, *c. 1808, in Phillips,* Plantation and Frontier, *II: 55.*

I have always understood that there were two objects contemplated by the embargo laws . . . Precautionary, in saving our seamen, our ships and our merchandize from the plunder of our enemies, and avoiding the calamities of war. Coercive, by addressing strong appeals to the interests of both the belligerents. The first object has been answered beyond my most sanguine expectations. To make a fair and just estimate of this measure, reference should be had to our situation at the time of its adoption. At that time, the aggressions of both the belligerents were such, as to leave the United States but a painful alternative in the choice of one of three measures, to wit, the embargo, war, or submission. . . . It has pre-

served our peace—it has saved our honor—it has saved our national independence.

*Senator William Branch Giles argues that the embargo has worked in a speech, 1808, in Hart,* American History, *III: 403, 404.*

GENERAL EMBARGO. Upon whom is it to operate? On France? O, no—*On England* . . . For what? Because England had refused reparation for the attack on the *Chesapeake?* No. Because they had committed some new outrage? Not at all. Why then in the name of wonder! Because France had violated the laws of nations, and the obligation of treaties. *Therefore* was Great Britain to be injured, and we ourselves ruined!

*Editorial comment in the New York* Evening Post, *February 5, 1808, in King,* Life and Correspondence of Rufus King, *V: 78.*

With France we are in no *immediate* danger of war. Her future views it is impossible to estimate. The immediate danger we are in of a rupture with England is postponed for this year. This is effected by the embargo, as the question was simply between that and war. . . . A time would come, however, when war would be preferable to a continuance of the embargo. Of this Congress may have to decide at their next meeting.

*President Thomas Jefferson in a letter to Charles Coatsworth Pinckney, March 30, 1808, in Hunt,* The Essential Thomas Jefferson, *269.*

Many residents of Oswego, New York, who bitterly resented the Embargo, looked to their area's Revolutionary history for inspiration in their resistance against government trade restrictions. This engraving depicts a view of Fort Oswego, a constant reminder of the area's glorious past. *(from Benson Lossing,* The Pictorial Field-Book of the Revolution, *1851–1852)*

You will herewith receive a copy of the Embargo Laws. You will use the force under your direction to enforce these Laws within our Lines . . . You will so dispose the force under your command as to seize the Boats and vessels of American Citizens that may be found violating or attempting to violate the embargo Laws—to seize the boats and vessels belonging to Citizens or subjects of any other nation that may be found violating or attempting to violate, within the jurisdiction of the United States, the embargo Laws . . .

*Secretary of the Navy Robert Smith sends orders to Lieutenant Samuel Elbert, May 2, 1808, in Dudley,* Naval War of 1812, *I: 35.*

. . . it has become necessary to detach a Military force to the port and village, of Oswego, in the County of Onondaga, to compel obedience to the Laws, the execution of which has been forcibly resisted at that place . . . to suppress the existing insurrection and to aid the Collector of the said port to carry into effect the Laws of the United States against the armed and violent resistance made thereto at the said port and its vicinity . . .

*Daniel D. Tompkins, governor of New York, calls up the militia to enforce the embargo in upstate New York, August 19, 1808, in* Public Papers of Daniel D. Tompkins, *I: 194–195.*

The President and Madison have been greatly perplexed by the remonstrances from so many towns to remove the Embargo. You see they refer to Congress, and the evading it is a terrible thing. Madison is uneasy and feels bound to return to the seat of government, where I shall be sorry to go so soon.

*Dolley Madison in a letter to her sister-in-law Anna Payne, August 28, 1808, in* Madison, Memoirs and Letters, *66.*

It has been officially announced to the Commander in Chief of the State of New York, that on the shores and waters of Lake Champlain, within this State, there exists a combination of individuals who have repeatedly indulged themselves in armed and forcible resistance to the execution of the Laws by the constituted authorities. Those occurrences, in his opinion, occasion an emergency in which it is his duty to direct a

This popular portrait engraving of Dolley Madison captures some of the beauty, intelligence, and vivaciousness that made her into a popular figure and an able politician. *(Library of Congress, Prints and Photographs Division [LC-USZ62-68175])*

detachment of the Militia to depress such criminal combinations . . .

*New York governor Daniel D. Tompkins calls up the militia to suppress resistance to the embargo on Lake Champlain, September 7, 1808, in* Public Papers of Daniel D. Tompkins, *207–208.*

The conduct of the British Cabinet in rejecting the fair offer made to it, and even sneering at the course pursued by the United States, prove at once a very determined enmity to them, and a confidence that events were taking place here which would relieve it from the necessity of procuring a renewal of commercial intercourse, by any relaxations on its part. . . . I shall be much disappointed, however, if a spirit of independence and indignation [in the United States] does not strongly reinforce the past measures with others, which will give a severity to the contest, of privations, at least, for which the British Government would seem to be very little prepared, in any sense of the word.

*James Madison in a letter to William Pinkney, November 9, 1808, in* Letters and Other Writings of James Madison, *II: 425.*

I cannot believe that there is so much depravity or stupidity in the Eastern States as to countenance the reports that they will separate from their brethren, rather than submit longer to the suspension of their commerce. That such a project may lurk within a junto ready to sacrifice the rights, interests, and honor, of their Country, to their ambitious or vindic-

tive views, is not to be doubted; but that the body of an intelligent people, devoted to commerce and navigation, with few productions of their own, and objects of unceasing jealousy to G. Britain on account of their commerce and navigation, should be induced to abandon the Southern States, for which they are the Merchants seems to be impossible.

*James Madison in a letter to William Pinckney, December 5, 1808, in* Letters and Other Writings of James Madison, *II: 427–428.*

The prisoners in the gaol are kept to hard labour at smiths' work, within the walls; and their task, which ends at four o'clock in the afternoon, commences at four o'clock in the morning. . . . The prisoners were heavily ironed, and secured both by hand-cuffs and fetters; and, being therefore unable to walk, could only make their way by a sort of jump or hop. On entering the smithy, some went to the sides of the forges, where collars, dependent by iron chains from the roof, were fastened round their necks, and others were chained in pairs to wheelbarrows.

*English traveler Edward Augustus Kendall describes a prison in New York, 1808, in* Hart, American History, *III: 45.*

It was during the session of 1808–1809 that the embargo, unlimited in duration and extent, was passed, at the instance of Mr. Jefferson, as a retaliatory measure upon England. It prostrated the whole commerce of America, and produced a degree of distress in the new England States greater than that which followed upon the War. . . . A year passed away, and the evils, which it inflicted upon ourselves, were daily increasing in magnitude and extent; and in the mean time, our navigation being withdrawn from the ocean, Great Britain was enjoying a triumphant monopoly of the commerce of the world. . . . I became convinced of the necessity of abandoning it . . .

*Joseph Story, later a justice of the Supreme Court, reflects on his opposition to the embargo in his memoirs, 1809, in* Hart, American History, *III: 407.*

This caricature of Philadelphia merchant Stephen Girard shows him grasping for a Spanish dollar, because he has been ordered to pay his debts in hard currency. This cartoon mocks both monetary problems in the United States and those merchants who were thought to make them worse. *(Library of Congress, Prints and Photographs Division [LC-USZ61-908])*

Amidst the pressure of evils with which the belligerent edicts have afflicted us, some permanent good will arise, the spring given to manufactures will have durable effects. Knowing most of my own state I can affirm with confidence that were free intercourse opened again to-morrow she would never again import half of the coarse goods which she has done to the date of the edicts . . . My idea is that we should encourage home manufactures to the extent of our own consumption of every thing of which we raise the raw material.

*Thomas Jefferson in a letter to David Humphreys, January 20, 1809, in Humphreys,* Life and Times of David Humphreys, *378–379.*

The last vote taken . . . implies that a non intercourse with G. Britain and France, including an Embargo on exports to those two nations, [should?] be substituted for the general Embargo existing . . . If the non-intercourse, as proposed, should be adopted, it will leave open a trade to all the *Continent* of Europe, except France.

*James Madison in a letter to William Pinkney, February 11, 1809, in* Letters and Other Writings of James Madison, *II: 429.*

The present situation of the world is indeed without a parallel and that of our own country full of difficulties. The pressure of these, too, is the more severely felt because they have fallen upon us at a moment when the national prosperity being at a height not before attained, the contrast resulting from the change has been rendered the more striking.

*President James Madison in his first inaugural address, March 4, 1808. Available online. Avalon Project. URL: http://www.yale.edu/lawweb/avalon/presiden/inaug/madison1.htm.*

The Capitol presented a gay scene. Every inch of space was crowded and there being as many ladies as gentlemen, all in full dress, it gave it rather a gay than a solemn appearance . . . the high and low were promiscuously blended on the floor and in the galleries. . . . Mr. Madison was extremely pale and trembled excessively when he first began to speak, but soon gained confidence and spoke audibly.

*Washington socialite Margaret Bayard Smith describes James Madison's inauguration as president in a letter to her daughter, March 4, 1809, in Hunt,* The First Forty Years, *59.*

It was scarcely possible to elbow your way from one side to another, and poor Mrs. Madison was almost pressed to death, for every one crowded round her, those behind pressing on those before, and peeping over their shoulders to have a peep of her, and those

who were so fortunate as to get near enough to speak to her were happy indeed. . . . she was led to the part of the room where we happened to be, so that I accidentally was placed next her. She looked a queen. She had on a pale buff colored velvet, made plain, with a very long train, but not the least trimming, and beautiful pearl necklace, earrings and bracelets. . . . It would be *absolutely impossible* for any one to behave with more perfect propriety than she did. Unassuming dignity, sweetness, grace. It seems to me that such manners would disarm envy itself, and conciliate even enemies. The [ball] managers presented her with the first number,—"But what shall I do with it," said she, "I do not dance."

*Margaret Bayard Smith describes in her notebook Dolley Madison's comportment at the first-ever inaugural ball, March 5, 1809, in Hunt,* The First Forty Years, *61–62.*

He took us first to the garden he has commenced since his retirement. It is on the south side of the mountain and commands a most noble view. . . . We passed the outhouses for the slaves and workmen. They are all much better than I have seen on any other plantation, but to an eye unaccustomed to such sights, they appear poor and their cabins form a most unpleasant contrast with the palace that rises so near them. Mr. J. has carpenters, cabinet-makers, painters, and blacksmiths and several other trades all within himself, and finds these slaves excellent workmen.

*Margaret Bayard Smith describes the grounds of Thomas Jefferson's home, Monticello, in her journal, August 1, 1809, in Hunt,* The First Forty Years, *68, 69.*

It was very evident that the opinions of the people had undergone a great change in respect to the admission of negroes—three fourths were certainly against the admission—in this County only there was a small Majority in favor of admitting them the other three counties almost unanimously against it—There were two candidates in this County both friendly to the admission—The third from Clark opposed to them—The result of the Election was in favor of the latter . . .

*Governor William Henry Harrison writes about the controversy over whether Indianans will allow free African Americans into their territory in a letter to Albert Gallatin, August 29, 1809, in Thornbrough,* Correspondence of John Badollet and Albert Gallatin, *109–110.*

As to Mr. John Randolph, he certainly admires the British nation more than I do; and I think that some of his speeches respecting our foreign relations have been very wrong & have done some injury to America. But I never said what I am sure is false, that he was under British influence.

*Albert Gallatin in a letter to Indiana governor William Henry Harrison, September 27, 1809, in Thornbrough,* Correspondence of John Badollet and Albert Gallatin, *111–112.*

In the event of a War with any Nation having considerable maritime force, it is the opinion of revolutionary characters and of the inhabitants of this State generally that West Point ought to be so effectually fortified as to present a Barrier to a naval force from further ascending the Hudson. The objects to be accomplished by making that place impassable are that otherwise should a fleet enter the Harbour of New York sufficiently formidable to take possession of or pass the fortifications there, the vessels, Specie, Bank deposits, plate and other valuable moveable commodities in New York, might fall into their hands to one hundred times the expense of fortifying West Point.

*New York governor Daniel D. Tompkins in a letter to Secretary of War William Eustis, November 18, 1809, in* Public Papers of Daniel D. Tompkins, *II: 217–218.*

A most fatal mistake is made by parents of all classes in the present age. Many of them seem to think vice and irregularity the marks of sense and spirit, in a boy; and that innocence, modesty, submission to superiors, application to study, and to everything laudable, are the signs of stupidity.

*Caleb Bingham laments modern child rearing in the* American Preceptor, *1810, in Watts,* Republic Reborn, *112.*

Colonel Humphreys took great interest in the discipline and education of the apprentice boys attached to the factory. Seventy-three of these boys were indentured, I have been told, at the same time, from the New York alms-house, and others from the neigh–

The growth in both private and public education in the early 19th century led to the construction of countless schoolhouses around the country. Many of them, like this rural southern school, were quite small and crude, but they enabled students to gain an education during the times of year they were not occupied with agricultural labor. *(from Benson Lossing,* The Pictorial Field-Book of the Revolution, *1851–1852)*

boring villages. For these he established Sunday schools, with competent teachers; and indulged his military taste by uniforming them at no light expense as a militia company, drilling them himself. Of course so many lads, gathered from the lower classes of a great city, must have numbered some bad ones. Thefts and other small vices were sometimes discovered . . .

*Ann S. Stephens reports on the workers at David Humphreys's New York woolen mill, 1810, in Humphreys,* Life and Times of David Humphreys, *II: 386.*

Whilst the unyielding injustice of Foreign Powers continues to render our situation perplexing, and the preservation of peace more and more uncertain, the Councils of the General Government must find their confidence in the spirit and faculties of the nation greatly fortified by the co-operating patriotism of the States.

*James Madison in a letter to the General Assembly of North Carolina, January 1810, in* Letters and Other Writings of James Madison, *II: 463.*

*Macon's Bill*—Are we never to see the end of measures, equally repugnant to the recorded professions of our rulers, and subversive of the public welfare? After running through all the changes of commercial restrictions, which have humbled the spirit, impaired the morals, and utterly deranged the commerce of the country, is there no prospect of our administration being yet weaned from that folly, that spirit of *faction*, which is fast annihilating the sources of our wealth, as it has already emasculated and disgraced the nation?

*Editorial in the New York* Evening Post, *January 16, 1810, in King,* Life and Correspondence of Rufus King, *V: 194.*

I devoutly wish that the same disposition to cultivate peace by means of justice, which exists here, predominated elsewhere, particularly in G. Britain. . . . Let reparation be made for the acknowledged wrong committed in the case of the *Chesapeake*—a reparation so cheap to the wrong-doer, yet so material to the honor of the injured party; and let the orders in Council . . . be repealed also. as an expedient for substituting an illicit commerce in place of that to which neutrals have, as such, an incontestable right. The way will then be open for negotiation at large . . .

*James Madison in a letter to George Joy, January 17, 1810, in* Letters and Other Writings of James Madison, *II: 465, 466–467.*

From the moment that the affair of the Chesapeake rendered the prospect of war imminent, every faculty was exerted to be prepared for it, and I think I may venture to solace you with the assurance that we are, in a good degree, prepared. Military stores for many campaigns are on hand, all the necessary articles (sulphur excepted), and that art of preparing them among ourselves, abundantly; arms in our magazines for more men than will ever be required in the field, and forty thousand new stand yearly added . . .

*Thomas Jefferson in a letter to Polish Revolutionary War general Thaddeus Kościuszko, February 26, 1810, in Hunt,* The Essential Thomas Jefferson, *275.*

Dame Commerce will oppose domestic manufactures. She is a flirting, flippant, noisy jade, and if we are governed by her fantasies, we shall never put off the muslins of India and the cloths of Europe. But I trust that the yeomanry of this country, the true and genuine landlords of this tenement, called the United States, disregarding her freaks, will persevere in reform, until the whole national family is furnished by itself with the clothing necessary for its use. . . . There is a pleasure—a pride (if I may be allowed the expression, and I pity those who can not feel the sentiment)—in being clad in the productions of our own families. Others may prefer the cloths of Leeds and London, but give me Humphreysville.

*Kentucky congressman Henry Clay in a speech given before Congress, April 6, 1810, in Colton,* Life and Times, *II: 142–143.*

Some time ago the salt sent by the Governor to the Prophet was refused by him and sent back, and a young man named John Gamlin entrusted with the salt told me that the Prophet had declared to him, that, if any attempts were made to Survey the lands lately purchased, the Surveyors should survey no more. That Prophet, a Mahomet in miniature appears to have taken advantage of the indians' discontent to augment his influence by espousing their cause.

*John Badollet in a letter to Albert Gallatin, June 24, 1810, in Thornbrough,* Correspondence of John Badollet and Albert Gallatin, *151–152.*

The course adopted here towards West Florida will be made known by the Secretary of State. The occupancy of the Territory as far as the Perdido was called for by the crisis there, and is understood to be within the

This mill on the Walloomscoick River represents the kind of American business that grew rapidly in the years surrounding the War of 1812. *(from Benson Lossing,* The Pictorial Field-Book of the Revolution, *1851–1852)*

authority of the Executive. East Florida, also, is of great importance to the United States, and it is not probable that Congress will let it pass into any new hands. . . . The position of Cuba gives the United States so deep an interest in the destiny, even, of that Island, that although they might be an inactive, they could not be a satisfied spectator at its falling under any European Government.

*President James Madison in a letter to William Pinkney, October 30, 1810, in* Letters and Other Writings of James Madison, *II: 488.*

Sir, is the time never to arrive, when we may manage our own affairs, without the fear of insulting his Britannic majesty? Is the rod of British power to be for ever suspended over our heads? Does Congress put on an embargo to shelter our rightful commerce against the piratical depredations committed

upon it on the ocean? We are immediately warned of the indignation of offended England. Is a law of non-intercourse proposed? The whole navy of the haughty mistress of the seas is made to thunder in our ears. . . . Whether we assert our rights by sea, or attempt their maintenance by land—whithersoever we turn ourselves, this phantom incessantly pursues us.

*Kentucky senator Henry Clay in a speech to the Senate, December 25, 1810, in Colton,* Life and Times, *I: 161, 162.*

I am compelled to declare it as my deliberate opinion, that, if this bill passes, the bonds of this union are, virtually, dissolved; that the states, which compose it are free from their moral obligations, and that as it will be the right of all, so it will be the duty of some to prepare, definitely, for a separation; amicably, if they can, violently, if they must . . .

*New England Federalist congressman Josiah Quincy denounces legislation favoring the southern states in a speech, 1811, in Hart,* American History, *III: 410.*

Your son has not deceived you in the idea he has given of the banks of the Mississippi. There are I believe no lands in the U.S. that repay so richl[y] the toils of the husbandman. . . . If you contemplate a removal I dare [say] you cannot do better than coming over. . . . There are sugar lands I am told to be had very cheap. No sugar estate, at least very few are to be found there yet, owing to the expensiveness of this kind of establishment, but there are cotton plantations very superb indeed.

*Francois Xavier Martin in a letter to Colonel John Hamilton, March 22, 1811, in Phillips,* Plantation and Frontier, *II: 197.*

Brother!—You wish us to change our religion for yours. We like our religion, and do not want another. Our friends here . . . do us great good; they counsel us in trouble; they teach us how to be comfortable at all times. Our friends the Quakers do more. They give us ploughs, and teach us how to use them. They tell us we are accountable beings. But they do not tell us we must change our religion.—we are satisfied with what they do, and with what they say.

*Red Jacket (Sagoyewatha) in a speech to Indian agents at a Buffalo Creek Seneca Council, May 1811, in Blaisdell,* Great Speeches, *44–45.*

That you have become disgusted with the politics of our Country can excite no surprise. . . . The fate of the Election last year entirely destroyed the spirits of the Federalists, and the folly & wickedness of Congress the last winter appeared to strike them dumb and sink them in a state of desperate apathy. They awoke in Boston, but too late to make any excitement through the Commonwealth. They flatter themselves with the hope of a federal House of Representatives.

*Christopher Gore laments the decline of the Federalist Party in a letter to Rufus King, May 5, 1811, in King,* Life and Correspondence of Rufus King, *V: 245, 246.*

The whites are already nearly a match for us all united, and too strong for any one tribe alone to resist; so that unless we support one another with our collective and united forces; unless every tribe unanimously combines to give a check to the ambition and avarice of the whites, they will soon conquer us apart and disunited, as we will be driven away from our native country and scattered as autumnal leaves before the wind.

*Shawnee warrior Tecumseh pleads with the Chocktaw and Chickasaw to join his confederacy to resist the United States, September 1811, in Blaisdell,* Great Speeches, *50.*

I earnestly beseech you, before you act hastily in this great matter, and consider with yourselves how greatly you will err if you injudiciously approve of and inconsiderately act upon Tecumseh's advice. Remember the American people are now friendly disposed toward us. . . . You now have no just cause to declare war against the American people, or wreak your vengeance upon them as enemies . . . It is besides inconsistent with your national glory and with your honor, as a people, to violate your solemn treaty; and a disgrace to the memory of your forefathers, to wage war against the American people merely to gratify the malice of the English.

*Choctaw leader Pushmataha warns his people against joining in Tecumseh's anti-American pan-Indian movement, September 1811, in Blaisdell,* Great Speeches, *54, 55.*

The spirits of the mighty dead complain. The tears drop from the skies. Let the white race perish! They seize your land, they corrupt your women, they trample on your dead! Back! Whence they came, upon a trail of blood, they must be driven! Back! Back—ay, into the great water whose accursed waves brought them to our shores! Burn their dwellings! Destroy their stock! Slay their wives and children! The red man owns the country, and the pale-face must never enjoy it! War now! War forever!

*Shawnee warrior Tecumseh declares war against white society, October 1811, in Blaisdell,* Great Speeches, *58.*

The reparation made for the attack on the American frigate *Chesapeake* takes one splinter out of our wounds; but besides the provoking tardiness of the remedy, the moment finally chosen deprives it of much of its effect, by giving it the appearance of a mere anodyne to the excitements in Congress and the Nation produced by the contemporary disclosures.

*James Madison in a letter to John Quincy Adams, November 15, 1811, in* Letters and Other Writings of James Madison, *II: 517.*

Arrived in town last evening on his way to the Mississippi, Brigadier General Wade Hampton and suit, Commander in Chief of the western army, preceded by a division of fifty ragged, meagre looking negro infantry. Should his Excellency fail in obtaining laurels before Mobile, he will be able to make sugar at New Orleans.

*Racist commentary in the* Chronicle *of Augusta, Georgia, November 15, 1811, in Phillips,* Plantation and Frontier, *II: 196.*

The occasion is now presented, when the national character, misunderstood and traduced for a time by foreign and domestic enemies, should be vindicated. . . . That proud spirit of liberty and independence, which sustained our fathers in the successful assertions of their rights, against foreign oppression, is not yet sunk: The patriotic fire of the Revolution still burns in the American breast with a holy and unextinguishable flame, and will conduct this nation to those high destinies, which are not less the regard of dignified moderation, than of exalted valor.

*The House Foreign Relations Committee reports on rising tensions with Great Britain, November 29, 1811, in Watts,* Republic Reborn, *257–258.*

Supposing . . . that the United States should come into collision with either of the present great belligerent powers, a naval force of twelve sail of the line (74s) & twenty well constructed frigates, including those we now have rating generally not less than 38 guns, with the addition of our smaller vessels now in service judiciously directed, it is believed would be ample to the protection of our coasting trade generally-would, be competent to annoy extensively the commerce of an enemy-and uniting occasionally in operations with the gun boats already built, if equipped & brought into service and our fortifications also afford complete protection to our harbours.

*Secretary of the Navy Paul Hamilton assesses the nation's naval strength in a letter to Congressman Langdon Cheves, December 3, 1811, in Dudley,* Naval War of 1812, *I: 54.*

The Petition of Jemima Hunt (a free woman of color) of the County of Southampton, humbly sheweth—that sometime in the month of November in the Year 1805—Your petitioner entered into a contract with a certain Benjamin Barrett of said county for the purchase of Stephen a Negro man Slave, the property of said Barrett, & husband to your petitioner . . . Your petitioner farther states that she has paid the full amount of the purchase money and has obtained a bill of sale for the said Negro Stephen; who (being her husband) she intended to emancipate after she complyed with her contract,—but in some short time after as your petitioner has been informed an act of Assembly was passed, prohibiting slaves, being emancipated after the law went into operation, from residing in the state . . .

*Petition of Jemima Hunt to the Virginia legislature to allow her husband to remain in the state, December 9, 1811, in Aptheker,* Documentary History, *55.*

I understood the opinion of the Committee on Foreign Relations, differently . . . I certainly understood that the committee recommended the measures now before the House, as a preparation for war . . . why not declare war immediately? The answer is obvious: because we are not yet prepared. But, says the gentle-men, such language as is here held, will provoke Great Britain to commence hostilities. I have no such fears. She knows well that such a course would unite all parties here—a thing which, above all others, she most dreads. Besides, such has been our past conduct, that she will still calculate on our patience and submission, until war is actually commenced.

*South Carolina congressman John C. Calhoun speaking in Congress about the November report from the Committee on Foreign Relations and the prospects of war, December 12, 1811, in Crallé,* Speeches, *II: 1, 2, 13.*

The intrigues for President and Vice-President go on, but I think it may terminate as the last did. The Clintons, Smiths, Armstrongs, et cetera, are all in the field, and I believe there will be war. Mr. Madison sees no end to the perplexities without it, and they seem to be going on with the preparations. General Dearborn, you know, is nominated to command. Congress talks of adjourning for two months, but I believe it is merely a threatening, and they will sit until June.

*Dolley Madison in a letter to her sister-in-law Anna Payne, December 20, 1811, in Madison,* Memoirs and Letters, *73–74.*

The object of the force, he understood distinctly to be war, and war with Great Britain. It has been supposed, by some gentlemen, improper to discuss publicly so delicate a question. He did not feel the impropriety. It was a subject in its nature incapable of concealment . . . The assembling of armies, the strengthening of posts—all the movements preparatory to war, and which it is impossible to disguise, unfolded the intentions of the sovereign. . . . [Great Britain] may, indeed, anticipate us, and commence the war. But that is what she is in fact doing, and she can add but little to the injury which she is inflicting. If she choose to declare war in form, let her do so, the responsibility will be with her.

*Report of a speech by Speaker of the House Henry Clay, December 31, 1811, in Colton,* Life and Times, *I: 163, 164.*

# 9

# The War of 1812
## 1812–1815

The War of 1812, which pitted the United States against Great Britain and its Indian allies, was a confusing war. It left a mixed legacy for the United States and its political importance became only gradually apparent. Militarily, the war was not a success, yet it contained a few of the most famous and highly lauded victories in American military history. The United States gained very little in the peace settlement after the war, but the end of the Napoleonic Wars and the weakening of several important North American Indian powers brought about a new stability in American foreign affairs and politics. The War of 1812 was politically divisive, and it all but finished off the Federalist Party, but it also led into a notorious period of calm in U.S. politics. On an ideological level, the war did not materialize into the "Second War for Independence" hoped for by many at its beginning, but the war did provide a new spur to American patriotism. The War of 1812 confirmed the place of military force in supporting American nationalism, and many people would have agreed with President Madison's 1813 statement that "the war has proved . . . that our free Government, like other free governments, though slow in its early movements, acquires, in its progress, a force proportioned to its freedom."[1]

It cannot be said that the United States "won" the War of 1812. The country experienced both gains and losses in different areas of public and private life. The new nation did survive its first all-out war since the American Revolution, however, and many of the naval harassments occasioned by the Anglo-French wars stretching back to 1793 came to an end. Although the American military achieved a mixed record at best in the war, the public fastened on important battle victories as symbols of American strength and power. The war signaled the failure of the Democratic-Republican Party's foreign policy restraint and attempts to affect European behavior through commercial sanctions, but the party also emerged newly strengthened by the war. Part of the surge in patriotism created by the war would also carry a new generation of political leaders, particularly Andrew Jackson, into power in subsequent decades. The War of 1812 held great consequences for the American nation, although in some largely unexpected and subsequently forgotten ways.

## DECLARING WAR

Both Great Britain and France had harassed U.S. ships and sailors on the high seas for several decades preceding the War of 1812, but during the series of conflicts over commercial sanctions and blockades that had worsened since 1807, Great Britain increasingly became the focus of American political ire. U.S. politicians, particularly the belligerent group of Democratic-Republicans elected to Congress from the West and South in 1810, who became known as the War Hawks, expressed outrage at Britain's behavior. Although France actually seized slightly more American ships than Britain did between 1807 and 1812, the War Hawks focused their ire on British misdeeds, including the impressment of American sailors into the Royal Navy, British incitement of hostile American Indians across the West and South, and the continued enforcement of trade sanctions against the United States as spelled out in the British Orders in Council. The Democratic-Republicans were traditionally opposed to the British, and the War Hawks also contended that the time had come for Americans to reassert their independence from their former British colonial masters.

By the start of 1812 it seemed that President Madison was beginning to agree firmly with the War Hawks that war with Great Britain was inevitable. Some factions in the Democratic-Republican Party, and certainly most Federalist politicians, continued to deny that war was necessary, but they increasingly seemed to be struggling against the political grain. As Tennessee politician John Sevier put it: "Our Government have tried negociation until it is exhausted,

This 1812 engraving celebrates all the U.S. presidents to that date, reserving pride of place for George Washington, who is depicted in military uniform. *(Library of Congress, Prints and Photographs Division [LC-USZ62-90742])*

and there is no doubt in my mind the Executive have observed the most perfect uprightness, and impartial neutrality."[2] But now it looked as though war would be necessary to guarantee the honor and stature of the United States on the international stage. James Madison, the soft-spoken, unimposing chief executive, had firmly clung to the Jeffersonian ideal that war would not be good for the American republic, but he came to believe that the unnatural avoidance of war and overcompromising with the British might be even worse.

Regional tensions and interests helped complicate the move toward war, but they did not slow the momentum very much. Federalists, who continued to hold most of their political strength in New England, strongly opposed the idea of war with Great Britain, especially since they feared that the commercial trade economy, already weakened by years of commercial sanctions, would be further damaged by warfare. The War Hawks, who drew more support from the West and South, felt that the British were holding back further expansion of the United States, which retarded the growth of their regions' more agricultural economies. The War Hawks prepared to push for an invasion of Canada and strong moves against Native American groups, both of which initiatives might establish permanent U.S. control over vast new territories if successful. Southern politicians like Henry Clay and John C. Calhoun, who had written in a November 1811 congressional report, "The occasion is now presented, when the national character, misunderstood and traduced for a time by foreign and domestic enemies, should be vindicated," expressed hopes for future U.S. greatness based on the willingness to fight and win a war against Great Britain.[3]

Great Britain seemed undeterred by such rhetoric, and on June 1, 1812, President Madison delivered a message to Congress calling for a declaration of war. Madison maintained that Great Britain's aggression against the United States since the rekindling of the Napoleonic Wars in 1803 constituted "a series of acts hostile to the United States as an independent and neutral nation," and that since the "United States have in vain exhausted remonstrances and expostulations" against British depredations, no course was left except to react as though Great Britain were already in "a state of war against the United States."[4] The War Hawks had received the executive call to war for which they had been longing for many months.

After receiving Madison's war message, the Federalists in Congress pressed their opposition to war and party divisions hardened. Congress proceeded with a war resolution, nonetheless, and the prowar resolution received votes from every region of the nation. On June 18, the House of Representatives voted to go to war by a margin of 79 to 49, and the Senate followed with a vote of 19 to 13. The following month, Americans received word that the British government had actually repealed the Orders in Council trade restrictions just two days before the United States declared war, but by that time fighting had commenced, and President Madison was unwilling to back down and change course.

## THE UNITED STATES ON THE OFFENSIVE: 1812

The United States began its war against Great Britain with an elaborate plan to invade Canada, where both British and Indian power could be directly engaged. Although President Madison's war message had stressed British naval depredations as the cause of the war, U.S. military officials meant for the major campaigns to take place on land. Many U.S. citizens, particularly in the West, had harbored animosity toward British Canada for decades, and they viewed the war as an opportunity both to settle old scores and to seek territorial aggrandizement. Many of the most prominent British Canadians were descendants of Loyalists who fled the United States during and after the American Revolution, which lent some credence to the Democratic-Republicans' idea of the War of 1812 as a second Revolution, even if the reasons for the two wars were as different as the Federalists claimed. In addition, the War Hawks insisted that the British had incited Tecumseh and other Indians in the Northwest Territory to attack U.S. forces in the years before the war, and they preached dire warnings against any kind of British/Indian alliance. An overland attack was supposed to bring a chance for military glory and to provide a quick challenge to British authority on the North American continent.

The first phase of land attacks into Canada did neither. President Madison and his military strategists devised a three-pronged plan that would push American forces to attack Montreal, Niagara, and the frontier outside Detroit, and they put Major General William Hull in charge of the most important part of the plan, the western attack. In July 1812, Hull tried to attack Canada from his base in Detroit, but he was pushed back by a combined force led by the Shawnee warrior Tecumseh and British general Isaac Brock. Hull's overly cautious, even cowardly behavior led his men to lose confidence in his command. At the beginning of August, Hull ordered the evacuation of Fort Dearborn (at the present-day location of Chicago) and surrendered Detroit to the British. These were crushing blows to American progress, especially in addition to the British capture of the American fort on Mackinac Island at the end of July. American militia Major General Stephen Van Rensselaer did no better on the second front on the Niagara frontier in October, when his men openly rebelled against his command and he failed to take the heights of the city of Queenston. The British lost General Brock in the action, but combined American militia and army forces proved ineffective against the British army soldiers, Canadian volunteers, and Mohawk warriors. A young American captain, Winfield Scott, had to surrender his entire force. Major General Henry Dearborn's attack on Montreal in November turned out even worse. He wasted huge amounts of time preparing for the attack; many of his militia troops refused to cross the Canadian border; and his men grew confused and fired on one another before quickly retreating from the outskirts of the Canadian city.

The only major bright spot for the United States in the military campaign of 1812 came, surprisingly, at sea. The USS *Constitution,* the 54-gun American ship that had been commissioned during the Tripolitan War, fought a short battle in August off the coast of Halifax, Nova Scotia, against the 49-gun HMS *Guerrière.* The *Constitution* beat the *Guerrière* in an open engagement, a surprise since the British possessed unquestionably the most powerful navy in the world. The victory conferred an air of heroism and military mystique both on the American commander, Captain Isaac Hull, and on the *Constitution* itself, which was dubbed Old Ironsides in honor of its strength in battle (it remains the oldest commissioned ship in the U.S. Navy). Although the U.S. Navy did not face the full force of the Royal Navy in 1812 because it was occupied far

This cartoon by William Charles belittles the citizens of Alexandria, Virginia, for putting up little resistance when the British took their city in 1814. Johnny Bull, representing Great Britain, unfolds a list of "terms of capitulation" as two men kneel before him, and a soldier and sailor carry off trade goods behind his back. *(Library of Congress, Prints and Photographs Division [LC-USZ62-349])*

more with fighting the French in Europe, the victory of the *Constitution* (along with a few other, smaller naval victories) did prove that American naval power was far from trivial, and it provided a national morale booster.

That boost in morale was important, not only because the land battles in 1812 went badly, but also because the public remained severely divided over the war itself. The political controversies between the Democratic-Republicans and the Federalists over whether war ought to have been declared did not go away once the war had commenced, and neither were the disagreements in Congress totally detached from more general public opinion about the war. Although a surge in patriotic expression did occur at the outset of the war, so did a surge in antiwar feeling, and the two sides clashed openly.

The most famous example of fervent division came just after the war was declared in June 1812, when a series of prowar mobs in Baltimore, Maryland, attacked an antiwar Federalist newspaper publisher and dismantled his printing press. Between June 22 and early July, Baltimore was rocked by civil unrest as prowar mobs, undeterred by local militia troops trying to keep the peace, battled Federalist publisher Alexander Hanson, broke him out of protective custody, and severely injured Hanson and others. They also beat to death several men, including James Lignan, a Federalist former Revolutionary War general who was trying to protect Hanson.

The open violence in Baltimore, which went unpunished, stifled some expression of antiwar sentiments, but many in the more Federalist-dominated areas of New England continued openly to oppose the war. Many New England ministers, for example, used religious fast days to oppose the war as they asked "what christian, under the influence of christian principles, can dare pray for success" in such an unjust conflict.[5]

In the face of such divided public opinion and with, on balance, a poor record of performance in the first year of military campaigning, the year 1812 ended with one last U.S. effort to go on the offensive. Former Indiana governor William Henry Harrison was installed as the new commander of the

This cartoon by William Charles contrasts the stiff resistance offered to the British by the citizens of Baltimore to their easy reception at Alexandria. John Bull (who represents Great Britain) declares, "Mercy! Mercy on me—What fellows those Baltimoreans are— After the example of the Alexandrians I thought I had nothing to do but enter the Town and carry off the Booty—And here is nothing but Defeat and Disgrace!!" *(Library of Congress, Prints and Photographs Division [LC-USZ62-7431])*

northwestern U.S. land forces at the end of 1812, and he planned a new attack to try and regain Detroit from the British. Harrison's forces never made it to Detroit, however. They were cut apart on January 22, 1813, by British and Wyandot Indian troops in an engagement at Frenchtown (present-day Monroe, Michigan) along the river Raisin. The Wyandot killed around 40 wounded American prisoners after the battle, and after Harrison was forced to retreat south, "Remember the Raisin!" became a rallying cry for American military forces.

## GAINS AND LOSSES: THE CAMPAIGN OF 1813

The American military campaigns of 1813 began on a better note. On May 27, General Henry Dearborn and Commodore Isaac Chauncey renewed the attack on British Canada along the Niagara frontier, and their combined infantry and naval forces captured Fort George, located at the nexus of Lake Ontario and the Niagara River. The next day, the governor-general and British commander in chief of Canada, Sir George Prevost, attacked Commodore Chauncey's naval base at Sackets Harbor, New York. However, his blow was unsuccessful, and the American force gained an important advance look at newly built British ships meant to patrol the Great Lakes.

Despite holding on to Sackets Harbor, Henry Dearborn was unable to capitalize on the capture of Fort George or to make any further progress toward wresting Canada from British control. After an attempted assault further into Upper Canada failed when American forces retreated from a British attack on their camp at Stony Creek on June 6, Dearborn decided to hold the fort and withdraw his forces from the Canadian side of Lake Ontario. When another small American offensive on Beaver Dams north of Queenston failed on June 24, Dearborn was unceremoniously removed from command.

June events had also threatened to cast a pall over the bright spot in American morale, its record of success against the British Royal Navy. One of the U.S. Navy's most promising captains, James Lawrence, was killed on June 1, when his ship, the USS *Chesapeake,* engaged in a close, bloody fight with the expertly commanded HMS *Shannon* off the coast of Boston, Massachusetts. The *Chesapeake* became the first U.S. Navy ship to be captured during the war, although Lawrence's dying utterance—"Don't give up the ship!"—ironically survived to become an American rallying cry.

Lawrence's plea was heard, most famously and successfully, in September by Commodore Oliver Hazard Perry, who defeated the British on Lake Erie. The British had dominated Lake Erie, an important commercial and strategic waterway, since the beginning of the war. Perry gathered a fleet of nine ships to contend against the smaller British fleet, commanded by Captain Robert H. Barclay, a veteran of the British naval victory at Trafalgar. When the two fleets met in battle on September 10, Perry flew a flag stitched with the motto "Don't Give Up the Ship" in honor of Lawrence, and the winds favored the Americans' position from the start. Perry pulled off several brilliant maneuvers in the battle, not the least of which was abandoning his crippled ship *Lawrence,* rowing through the heat of the afternoon fire, and taking command of the fleet's second ship, *Niagara,* to complete the fight. By the end of the day, Perry's fleet had inflicted on the British one of their most humiliating defeats of the War of 1812; as he reported in a letter to an army colleague: "We have met the

This engraving depicts Oliver Hazard Perry's daring escape from his crippled ship *Lawrence* during the Battle of Lake Erie. He rowed out to take command of the *Niagara* and subsequently won the battle. *(National Archives/DOD, War & Conflict, # 83)*

enemy and they are ours." Perry almost instantly became a naval hero, capable of inspiring genuine American patriotism.

Perry's victory on Lake Erie, which secured American control of the lake for the remainder of the war, also helped to propel American ground troops to retake Detroit and push the British farther back into Canada. Major General William Henry Harrison, who had defeated Tecumseh's Shawnee troops at the Battle of Tippecanoe in 1811, met Tecumseh again in October at the Battle of the Thames. Harrison's large force of more than 4,000 pursued British, Canadian, and Indian troops commanded by Major General Henry Proctor, who were retreating from the Detroit area after the Battle of Lake Erie. Tecumseh urged Proctor to stay and fight, but he did not pause to engage the American forces until he had crossed into Canada and reached Moraviantown. The Americans, many of whom were directly commanded by U.S. congressman Richard Mentor Johnson, easily defeated the British troops, but the Indian fighters held out longer by defending a swamp near the river Thames. Eventually, even the Indians gave way, and Tecumseh himself was killed.

The death of Tecumseh, which ironically took place in an engagement commanded by his old nemesis William Henry Harrison, was an extraordinarily significant outcome of the battle. It also put Detroit firmly back into American control. Richard Mentor Johnson claimed personally to have killed the Shawnee leader, and although his claim was dubious, it helped solidify his political reputation for years afterward. Tecumseh had done much to convince the British to form Indian alliances in the Northwest, and he was the most prominent leader of the pan-Indian movement in all North America. Although Tecumseh himself was idolized in future American culture as the embodiment

This William Emmons engraving depicts a highly stylized vision of the death of Tecumseh at the Battle of the Thames. Richard Mentor Johnson aims and shoots Tecumseh. *(Library of Congress, Prints and Photographs Division [LC-USZ62-10173])*

of the noble Indian warrior, his loss did much to hurt the cause of real Indian peoples engaged in a fight against the United States for freedom and the preservation of their land.

## THE CREEK WAR

Tecumseh's death also came at a time when southern Indian peoples, inspired in part by his 1811 visit to stir up anti-American Indian support, were prosecuting their own cause against the military forces of the United States. The Creek Indians in Alabama and the Mississippi Territory lived very stable agricultural lives, and they were more highly assimilated into European-American culture than the tribes of the Northwest (they were one of the so-called Five Civilized Tribes). After Tecumseh's 1811 visit, however, some Creeks grew increasingly disenchanted with the tribe's pro-United States stance, and two factions grew up within the tribe. The Red Sticks advocated a return to Native American ways in keeping with the teachings of Tecumseh and his brother Tenskwatawa, "The Prophet," and some of their supporters fought alongside Tecumseh's troops early in the War of 1812. The White Sticks faction, on the other hand, wanted to continue strong ties with the United States and thought that accommodation to American culture would best guarantee the tribe's safety and land claims.

The pro-British Red Sticks and pro-American White Sticks came to blows and involved U.S. army and militia troops in the Creek War. After Red Sticks warrior William Weathersford (a mixed-race leader also known as Lamochattee, or Red Eagle) led an attack on the U.S. Fort Mims in lower Alabama and killed hundreds of soldiers, women, and children in August 1813, Tennessean Andrew Jackson organized a mixed force of U.S. militia, Cherokee, and White Sticks warriors to strike back. Jackson's force engaged Wethersford and the Red Sticks at Tallahatchee and Talladega, Alabama, in November and then again at Emuckfau Creek and Enitachopco Creek in January 1814, but he was unable to crush the Red Sticks until the climactic battle at Horseshoe Bend in March, 1814. Jackson's brutal tactics at Horseshoe Bend (in present-day Davison, Alabama) won the day and suppressed the Red Stick rebellion, but after the war ended, he showed no mercy for his White Stick Creek allies either. After the victory, Jackson forced the whole Creek nation to agree to give up 23 million acres of land to the United States. By early 1814, Tecumseh was dead, and the Creeks, one of the most powerful Indian nations in the Southeast, had lost much of their power. The War of 1812 was beginning to shape up as a disaster for Native Americans.

## THE CAMPAIGN OF 1814

U.S. military forces had failed yet again in a two-pronged attack on Montreal in November 1813, and the military campaigns of 1814 opened with a new set of commanders determined to press the advantages won in the West earlier in 1813. Unfortunately for the United States, the British finally defeated Napoleon Bonaparte in spring 1814, and they turned their full military attentions to the War of 1812. The end of the Napoleonic Wars brought a new level of British naval power to bear in North America, as ships were transferred from European waters to patrol the U.S. coastline. The British extended their naval blockade of the Atlantic coast, strengthened their naval presence in the Chesapeake Bay, and formed a plan to attack New Orleans from the Gulf of Mexico.

Despite severe financial difficulties, the American military hoped to meet the British on equal terms. Congress had been loath to impose the heavy taxes necessary to supply the army and to guarantee a strong program of shipbuilding, and the federal government had trouble borrowing money, in part because opponents of federal power had allowed the charter of the First Bank of the United States to expire before the war started. Some states, especially in strongly Federalist New England, were reluctant to fill their quotas of militia troops, forcing Congress to find creative incentives to fill the ranks. Congress passed a higher enlistment bounty, and the economic boost worked, pushing the size of the U.S. fighting forces to 40,000 in the spring of 1814—just in time to meet the increased British offensive.[6] Financial problems seemed to have been conquered for the time being, but conquering the British was another matter.

Jacob Brown, an American brigadier general who had taken over for disastrous commander Henry Dearborn on the Niagara frontier, launched a new American attack into Canada in July 1814. His goal was a decisive victory that could offset the arrival of new British naval power in the East. Brown's forces captured Fort Erie on July 3, and he pushed north all the way to the Chippewa River on July 4, 1814. The following day, the American troops, most of whom were regulars in the army, defeated a large group of well-trained British soldiers. Unfortunately, Jacob Brown was unable to follow up the victory at Chippewa because the reinforcements he expected Commodore Isaac Chauncey to provide never appeared. Brown's campaign into Canadian territo-

This 1812 William Charles cartoon fueled the War Hawks' demand for an attack on Canada by showing Great Britain paying Indians for American scalps. The caption reads "Arise Columbia's Sons and forward press/Your Country's wrongs call loudly for redress." *(Library of Congress, Prints and Photographs Division [LC-USZ62-89742])*

ry turned into a disaster on July 25 at the Battle of Lundy's Lane, the bloodiest engagement of the entire war. Although Brown's army troops once again showed admirable fighting skill against British regulars, an unusually high number of men suffered wounds, and the entire invasion into Upper Canada came to a halt. By the end of July, Brown's troops had to retreat to Fort Erie.

The most disastrous and morale-breaking American defeat of the war followed in August 1814, when the British invaded the U.S. capital at Washington, D.C., and set fire to many important federal government buildings. The British used their strong base along the Chesapeake and Pawtuxet Rivers to approach Washington, D.C., from Bladensburg, Maryland, which they attacked on August 24. As American military officials and political cronies of President Madison tried to arrange a hasty defense of the capital city, Secretary of State James Monroe rode out to try to help coordinate the American troops at Bladensburg. His meddling in battle plans only made matters worse, and the American response to British attacks was so disorganized as to be almost comical. (At one point President Madison, who was evacuating Washington, D.C., almost rode directly into the front lines of the battle.) The British force shattered American resistance and moved on to Washington, D.C., on August 25.

When the British troops marched into the nation's capital on the evening of August 25, many of the city's prominent citizens and government officials had evacuated only hours ahead of them. Although President Madison had left the previous day, his wife, Dolley, whose poise, beauty, and strong personality did much to bolster her husband's political status and credibility, stayed behind to gather up state papers, artifacts, and artworks from the White House. The British troops avoided damaging most private property, but they burned the White House, the Capitol, the Library of Congress, the Treasury, and many other buildings that housed official government departments. Canadian governor-general Prevost proclaimed the massive destruction "as a just retribution" for the destruction of York, the capital of Upper Canada, which American troops had burned in April 1813.[7]

Prevost himself was repelled in an attempt to attack the United States from Lake Champlain just when the country was reeling from the Chesapeake campaign. Prevost's combined naval and land attack on Plattsburgh, New York, failed miserably on September 11, 1814, which left open the possibility that the British might not be able to deliver a crushing blow on the East Coast. The following day, the British pressed the advantage gained at Washington, D.C., and began their attack on Baltimore, Maryland, whose capture they hoped would complete the success of the Chesapeake campaign. For three days, British land troops and ships made their way toward Fort McHenry, which protected the city. The troops inside Fort McHenry survived more than 24 hours of heavy and constant bombardment to fight off the British attackers. On September 15, the British retreated from Baltimore and admitted that the Chesapeake campaign had been only a partial success.

The dramatic events of August and September 1814 had a mixed effect on American morale and patriotism. Dashed by the destruction of federal government facilities in Washington, D.C., U.S. citizens again had their hopes raised by the victories at Plattsburgh and Fort McHenry. Francis Scott Key, an American diplomat who had observed the bombardment of Fort

McHenry, wrote the poem "The Star-Spangled Banner" to commemorate the American victory. It immediately caught on as the lyrics to a popular patriotic song. One American woman wrote that "the powerful effect produced by this soul-stirring song was not owing to any particular merit in the composition, but to the recollection of something noble in the character of a young heroic nation successfully struggling against the invasion of a mighty people for life, freedom, and domestic happiness."[8] The song had such a patriotic impact that it later became the official national anthem. Even the campaign that contained America's greatest domestic military disaster, the burning of its capital city, could contain the stuff of patriotic legend and national pride.

## WAR'S CONCLUSION

While the British were attacking the U.S. capital in August 1814, peace negotiations were already taking place in the Belgian city of Ghent. Diplomats on both sides had tried peaceful overtures almost since the beginning of the war, but now, though neither side was "winning," the talks took on real urgency. Partly, the British were willing to stop the war because they no longer needed to impress American sailors into their fight against France, and with the end of the Napoleonic Wars, the shipping difficulties that had plagued the United States since the 1790s were likely to cease.

At the same time that U.S. and British negotiators were trying to settle peace terms in Belgium, a separate diplomatic conference of sorts was taking place in New England. Twenty-six Federalist delegates from the states of Massachusetts, Connecticut, Rhode Island, New Hampshire, and Vermont met in Hartford, Connecticut, to discuss their continued opposition to the war and suggested remedies for the political and economic damage it inflicted upon their region. The delegates, who met between December 15, 1814, and January 5, 1815, discussed their dislike of federal embargoes, and they went so far as to propose amendments to the U.S. Constitution that would strengthen the hand of Federalist New England. They also discussed, but eventually discarded, the possibility of seceding from the Union if the war did not stop. Although the proposals at the Hartford Convention were soon rendered moot by the end of the war, the convention did lasting political damage to the Federalist Party because, having discussed secession, they were thought treasonous.

Opposition to the war would soon be irrelevant, since peace negotiations proceeded quickly and well. During November and December 1814, the American treaty negotiating team, composed of Henry Clay, John Quincy Adams, and Albert Gallatin, held off some aggressive British territorial demands, but they did not gain much for the United States, either. The United States did not directly gain territory in the treaty, but neither did the British recognize or protect their Indian allies, and the many Native Americans who had fought with the British became probably the biggest losers in the negotiations.

The Treaty of Ghent, which Britain and the United States signed on Christmas eve of 1814, effectively reinstated the status quo before the war. The United States did not expel Britain from Canada nor become the only dominant power in North America, as some of the War Hawks had hoped. The end of wars between Britain and France meant that things would be calmer after the War of 1812; nonetheless, the United States did not make many concrete gains in the treaty.

Although the Treaty of Ghent was concluded in Belgium at the end of 1814, the slow pace of transatlantic communication meant that the climactic battle of the War of 1812, the Battle of New Orleans, was fought *after* the war had technically ended. Despite the banality of the treaty settlement, the terrific battle triumph allowed Americans to feel as though they had won the war. The Battle of New Orleans also provided the American public with ongoing patriotic inspiration and greatly enhanced the heroic reputation of Andrew Jackson, who capitalized on his reputation to become one of the most significant military and political figures of the postwar decades. More than anything, the Battle of New Orleans showed how Americans turned the War of 1812 into a patriotic victory despite the fact that its real legacy was mixed at best.

British general Edward Pakenham and Admiral Alexander Cochrane planned to attack New Orleans from the Gulf of Mexico, and Jackson was sent to the city in December 1814 to prepare its defenses. Jackson put together a diverse force of army troops and militia composed of New Orleans Creoles, free Blacks, Tennessee and Kentucky riflemen, and the so-called Baratarian pirates, a group of Louisiana smugglers loyal to the flamboyant leader Jean Lafitte. Throughout December, Jackson tried to block the numerous water routes into the city by fortifying the bayous, swamps, and minor tributaries of the Mississippi that seemed to flow everywhere. After nearly a month of preliminary skirmishing, the full-scale battle took place on January 8, 1815. Jackson's men outmaneuvered the British, avoided inaccurate British cannon fire, used the weather to their advantage when fighting through a dense fog, and trained their accurate rifles on befuddled British regulars. When the battle ended, the British had suffered over 2,400 casualties and the Americans only 350.

Jackson's victory was instantly hailed as a glorious occurrence in U.S. history, and he found great personal admiration and praise as "the Hero of New Orleans." When the terms of the Treaty of Ghent became known in the United States early in February 1815, many Americans more easily swallowed its weaknesses because they could console themselves with thoughts of one of the worst-ever defeats of British troops by Americans. One congressman asked publicly in 1815: "Who is not proud to feel himself an American—our wrongs revenged—our rights recognized!"[9] Impressment had ceased, Tecumseh was dead, vast new Indian territories had been won in the Creek War, and America admired its new heroes like Winfield Scott, Oliver Hazard Perry, and, most of all, Andrew Jackson.

The real disharmony and destruction caused by the War of 1812 did not go entirely unnoticed. Congress voted to retain Washington, D.C., as the nation's capital, but it would take years of rebuilding before the city reached its former level of polish. On the national political scene, the Federalist Party found itself discredited by its opposition to the war and by talk of secession at the Hartford Convention, but individual politicians in New England held on to the old spirit of Federalism for years to come. The war had caused much economic damage, but it also spurred new industry like the Boston Manufacturing Company, incorporated in Lowell, Massachusetts, in 1814, which would soon become one of the world's largest textile manufacturing operations.

The victory at the Battle of New Orleans did confirm the War of 1812 as a builder of American patriotism, and perhaps for the first time Americans could convince themselves that they had won respect from Britain and other European powers. Andrew Jackson provided a symbol of masculine, militaristic American strength. In the years following the War of 1812, the United States would try to use that strength to emerge as a stronger nation.

## CHRONICLE OF EVENTS

### 1812

The White House hosts its first wedding, as First Lady Dolley Madison's sister, Lucy Payne Washington, marries Supreme Court Justice Thomas Todd.

The American Board of Commissioners for Foreign Missions sends the first American religious missionaries to Bombay, India.

The term *Uncle Sam* is used in public for the first time. It probably derives from the nickname of Samuel Wilson, a Troy, New York, butcher who supplied meat to American troops during the War of 1812. Later, the term will come to refer to the federal government.

Benjamin Rush publishes the first American book on mental health, *Medical Inquiries and Observations upon the Diseases of the Mind*.

James Kirke Paulding publishes his satirical novel *The Diverting History of John Bull and Brother Jonathan*, which lampoons the American Revolution.

Cochise, who will lead the Apache to war against the United States in 1863, is born.

*February 11:* Elbridge Gerry, governor of Massachusetts, signs a highly partisan redistricting law that creates oddly shaped districts that will favor his Democratic-Republican Party. A Federalist newspaper critiques the bill and dubs the practice of partisan redistricting *gerrymandering*.

*February 15:* William Hunt concludes his trek from St. Louis to Astoria, Oregon. He has blazed a trading route for John Jacob Astor's fur trading companies that closely parallels the later path of the Oregon Trail.

*March 3:* Congress votes to provide $50,000 in aid for victims of a Venezuelan earthquake. This is the first foreign aid provided by the United States.

*March 14:* Congress issues its first war bonds, created to pay for the War of 1812. All throughout the war, Congress is reluctant to raise taxes and has trouble funding the conflict.

*April 4:* Congress passes a 90-day trade embargo against Great Britain.

*April 10:* Great Britain informs the United States that the Orders in Council, which allow the search and seizure of American ships, remain in effect. France has failed to withdraw a similar order, so Britain wishes to keep its commercial sanctions against the United States in place.

Congress prepares for war by authorizing the call-up of 100,000 militia troops.

*April 20:* George Clinton, the vice president of the United States, dies in office.

*April 25:* Congress creates the General Land Office.

*April 30:* Louisiana is admitted to the union as the 18th state.

*May 16:* Martin Delaney, future African-American physician, army officer, and proponent of black nationalist African recolonization, is born in Virginia.

*May 18:* Southern Democratic-Republicans hold a congressional caucus and nominate James Madison for his second term as president. They nominate John

This mocking print depicts the wealthy Massachusetts Federalist congressman Josiah Quincy, who opposed the War of 1812, as the self-appointed king of New England, presiding over codfish. *(Library of Congress, Prints and Photographs Division [LC-USZ6-778])*

Langdon to replace George Clinton as vice president, but when Langdon declines the nomination, they choose Massachusetts governor Elbridge Gerry as their vice-presidential candidate.

*June 1:* President Madison delivers a message to Congress calling for a declaration of war against Great Britain.

*June 4:* The parts of the Louisiana Territory that have not been incorporated into the new state of Louisiana are reorganized as the Missouri Territory.

*June 18:* The War Hawk majority in Congress prevails, and Congress declares war on Great Britain. The War of 1812 begins.

*June 30:* The U.S. government issues its first interest-bearing treasury notes.

*July:* Violent riots take place in Baltimore, Maryland, as crowds protest against Alexander Hanson, a Federalist editor who openly opposes the War of 1812.

*July 1:* Congress doubles trade tariffs to raise money for the war.

*July 2:* Connecticut governor John Cotton refuses to authorize state militia to participate in the war. Many citizens throughout Federalist-dominated New England oppose the War of 1812. Federalists who oppose the war are dubbed "Coodies" by their opponents.

*July 17:* British troops capture the U.S. Fort Michilimacinac on Mackinac Island, off the coast of Michigan.

*August 15:* Potawatomie Indians destroy the largely abandoned Fort Dearborn (in the center of present-day Chicago) and kill the troops and families who are evacuating from Fort Dearborn to Fort Wayne.

*August 16:* General William Hull's invasion of Canada fails, and U.S. troops surrender the fort at Detroit to Great Britain. Later, Hull will be court-martialed for giving up the fort without a fight.

*August 19:* The USS *Constitution* defeats the British frigate *Guerrière* and is nicknamed "Old Ironsides" after cannon balls seem to bounce off its sides without causing harm. Among those aboard are Lucy Brewer, who served aboard the *Constitution* disguised as male sailor George Baker for three years.

*October 13:* General Stephen Van Rensselaer's invasion across the Niagara River and attempt to take the Queenston Heights fails. American casualties reach 1,000 after militia troops express an unwilling-

This 1813 cartoon by William Charles depicts a boxing match between caricatures of King George III and President James Madison. The king's bloody nose is the result of early U.S. naval victories in the War of 1812. *(Library of Congress, Prints and Photographs Division [LC-USZ62-5214])*

ness to respect his command to cross into Canada and engage a group of Mohawk warriors.

*October 24:* Printer Isaiah Thomas and other prominent citizens of Worcester, Massachusetts, found the American Antiquarian Society, which they dedicate to preserving historical books and documents.

*November:* Great Britain imposes a naval blockade on the Chesapeake and Delaware Bays. The blockade all but chokes off commercial traffic and causes a military threat to the U.S. capital.

*December 2:* James Madison is reelected president with a total of 129 of 217 electoral votes, and Elbridge Gerry is elected vice president. Although Madison and Gerry defeat their Federalist opponents, DeWitt Clinton and Jared Ingersoll, the Federalist Party gains seats in Congress.

*December 29:* The USS *Constitution* destroys the British frigate *Java*.

## 1813

The religious magazine *The Youth's Repository of Christian Knowledge* begins publication.

William Ellery Channing founds the liberal Unitarian magazine the *Christian Disciple*.

European traveler Bernard de Mandeville introduces the game of craps to New Orleans society.

Harriet Jacobs, who will become an abolitionist and author of the famous slave narrative *Incidents in the Life of a Slave Girl,* is born.

*January 22:* American forces lose the battle of Frenchtown, which stalls their attempt to retake Detroit.

*March 4:* James Madison is inaugurated to his second term as president.

*March 11:* Russia offers to try to bring peace between Great Britain and the United States.

*April 27:* American forces cross Lake Ontario, seize York (now Toronto), and burn all its public buildings.

*May 27:* The British naval blockade is extended north to New York and west along the Gulf Coast.

*June 1:* Naval Captain James Lawrence tells the crew of the USS *Chesapeake* "Don't give up the ship!" after he is mortally wounded as the British frigate HMS *Shannon* seizes his ship.

*August 30:* The Creek War opens in Alabama, when a band of Upper Creek warriors led by William Weathersford (Red Eagle) attacks Fort Mims near Mobile.

*September 5:* Secretary of War John Armstrong coordinates a plan to attack Montreal. He will send

This painting depicts the battle between the USS *Constitution* and the HMS *Java* off the coast of Brazil on December 29, 1812. The engagement was a decisive victory for the U.S. Navy. *(Library of Congress, Prints and Photographs Division [LC-D416-22694])*

General James Wilkinson's force from Sacketts Harbor, New York, and General Wade Hampton's force from Plattsburgh, New York, into Canada.

*September 10:* Captain Oliver Hazard Perry wins a daring victory over Captain Robert H. Barclay on Lake Erie. After his first ship is disabled, Perry rows through the fight and wins the battle aboard the *Niagara,* a second American vessel. He reports to William Henry Harrison: "We have met the enemy and they are ours." His actions solidify his heroic reputation.

*October 5:* William Henry Harrison's federal and militia troops defeat a combined force of British and Indian troops at the Battle of the Thames in Upper Canada. The famous Shawnee leader Tecumseh is killed in the battle. Kentuckian Richard Mentor Johnson will later take credit for killing Tecumseh, a claim that will help propel his political career.

*October 25:* Wade Hampton's attack on British troops at Chateaugay, Lower Canada (in present-day Quebec) fails, and he leads his troops back to Plattsburgh, New York.

*November 9:* Andrew Jackson's forces inflict a defeat on Creek Indian combatants led by William Wethersford (Red Eagle) at Talladega, Alabama. Jackson engages in brutal tactics against the Red Sticks, a band of Creeks that oppose the United States and the influence of white culture.

*November 11:* General James Wilkinson's attack on British and Canadian forces at Chrysler's Farm on the banks of the St. Lawrence River fails, and the second prong of John Armstrong's planned attack on Canada is destroyed.

*November 12:* Hector St. John de Crevecoeur, author of *Notes of an American Farmer,* a famous commentary on the American people and their surroundings, dies.

*December 18:* British forces capture Fort Niagara.

*December 29–30:* British troops burn Buffalo, New York.

## 1814

Ex-slave Catherine Ferguson opens a Sunday school to educate poor white and black children and unwed mothers in New York City.

Emma Willard opens the Middlebury, Vermont, Seminary, an academically challenging school for girls.

The Boston Manufacturing Company opens the world's first factory to manufacture cotton cloth under one roof. The factory becomes the basis of a huge cloth mill industry in Lowell, Massachusetts, which will fuel the Industrial Revolution in the United States.

*January 4:* Miles Macdonnel, governor of the Hudson's Bay Company's newly founded Red River Colony, composed of fur traders, their Indian wives, and Metis children, forbids the export of the dried-meat product pemmican from the colony (near present-day Winnipeg). Indian and Metis forces attack the colony over the following two years to attempt to reopen the food trade.

*January 18:* Congress appoints Henry Clay, Jonathan Russell, James A. Bayard, and John Quincy Adams as peace commissioners to begin negotiations to end the War of 1812 with Great Britain.

*February 8:* Congress adds Albert Gallatin to the list of peace commissioners empowered to negotiate with Great Britain.

*March 27:* Generals Andrew Jackson and John Coffee (along with allied Cherokee troops) defeat a combined force of Creek troops at Horseshoe Bend in present-day Alabama to end the Creek War. The Creek had supported the British in the War of 1812, but after losing almost 1,000 people at Horseshoe Bend, they conclude a separate peace with the United States.

*April 15:* In the face of continued commercial protests against the War of 1812 in New England, the embargo and the Non-Importation Acts are repealed by Congress.

*April 25:* Great Britain includes the coast of New England in its naval blockade.

*July 5:* Brigadier General Winfield Scott and Major General Jacob Brown defeat British troops in Upper Canada at the Battle of Chippewa.

*July 25:* Jacob Brown leads troops to engage the British at Lundy's Lane near Niagara Falls. His attack fails, but it provides further proof that U.S. troops can do well in open battle against British forces.

*August 8:* In Ghent, Belgium, the peace negotiations between Great Britain and the United States begin.

*August 9:* Creek representatives conclude the Treaty of Fort Jackson with American representatives and agree to cede 23 million acres of land in Georgia, Alabama, and the Mississippi Territory.

*August 19:* British forces put ashore at Benedict, Maryland, fight past the town of Bladensburg, and proceed toward Washington, D.C.

*August 24–25:* British forces enter Washington, D.C., and burn the White House, the Capitol, and many other government buildings. First Lady Dolley Madison rescues important executive papers and Gilbert Stuart's portrait of George Washington before evacuating the White House.

*August 27:* President Madison returns to the burned capital city.

*September 13–14:* The British bombard Fort McHenry but fail to take Baltimore. Francis Scott Key is inspired by the sight of the unsuccessful British bombardment to write the poem "The Star-Spangled Banner," which will later become the lyrics of the national anthem of the United States.

*October 14:* Congress authorizes the purchase of a large part of Thomas Jefferson's considerable personal library to replace books burned by the British at the Library of Congress. The $23,950 purchase also helps to alleviate some of Jefferson's financial troubles.

*October 29:* The *Demologos,* also known as *Fulton the First,* is launched as the world's first steam-powered warship.

*November 23:* Vice President Elbridge Gerry has a stroke while on the floor of the Senate and dies.

*December 24:* The United States and Britain sign a peace treaty at Ghent, Belgium. Neither side wins much in the treaty. Native American rights are not recognized in the treaty, and no Native Americans take part in the negotiations.

## 1815

By a slim margin, Congress votes to rebuild Washington, D.C., and to keep it as the nation's capital city. Congress takes up temporary residence in the Old Brick Capitol.

This 1814 cartoon by William Charles and Samuel Kennedy mocks the New England states that participated in the Hartford Convention and accuses them of plotting to abandon the United States. *(Library of Congress, Prints and Photographs Division [LC-USZ62-7831])*

Mason Locke Weems edits and publishes the first edition of Benjamin Franklin's *Autobiography*.

The Boston Society for the Moral and Religious Instruction of the Poor is founded.

In Boston, the Handel and Haydn Society, a vocal group that still exists, begins public performances.

*January 1:* General Andrew Jackson commands American artillery to keep British forces led by General Edward Pakenham from attacking New Orleans.

*January 5:* New England Federalists, who have vigorously opposed the War of 1812 throughout, conclude their convention at Hartford, Connecticut. They propose limiting the power of the federal government, although they fall short of calling for New England to secede from the Union, which they had considered.

*January 8:* Andrew Jackson leads a fierce defeat of British forces in the Battle of New Orleans. The battle, in which American forces inflicted 2,450 casualties on the British while losing only 350 soldiers themselves, provides the United States with a claim of victory to bolster public spirits at the end of the war and assures Jackson's heroic reputation.

*January 20:* President Madison vetoes a bill chartering a Second Bank of the United States.

*February 11:* News of the Treaty of Ghent, which ended the War of 1812, reaches the United States.

*February 16:* John Stevens obtains the first charter to build a railroad in the United States, though he never follows through on construction plans.

*March 3:* Congress declares war on Algiers, which is capturing American sailors and demanding tribute payments.

*May:* Jared Sparks publishes the first issue of the *North American Review,* which will become the literary journal of record for conservative cultural elites for decades to come.

*May 10:* Captain Stephen Decatur takes a fleet to Algiers to prevent the Algerians from taking captives and demanding tribute from American ships.

*June 17:* Decatur captures the Algerian flagship.

*June 30:* The Algerians, under considerable naval pressure from Decatur's fleet, agree to stop capturing American sailors and exacting tribute.

*July 3:* The United States and Great Britain agree to withdraw all trade restrictions against each other when diplomats sign a commercial convention. The East Indies are fully open to American trade for the first time since the Revolutionary War.

*July 4:* In Baltimore, the cornerstone of the monument designed by Robert Mills to honor George Washington is laid.

*July 26:* Stephen Decatur forces the government of Tunis to promise not to interfere with American ships or sailors without payment of tribute in return.

*August 5:* Stephen Decatur exacts a promise of commercial freedom from Tripoli.

*August 10:* Handsome Lake, a Turtle Clan Seneca Indian religious leader who preached a message of hard work that combined Iroquois and Anglo values, dies.

*September 24:* Former Revolutionary War officer and Tennessee governor John Sevier dies.

## Eyewitness Testimony

South of New Connecticut, few Bibles or religious tracts have been received for distribution among the inhabitants. The Sabbath is greatly profaned and but few good people can be found in any one place . . . within 30 miles of the falls of the Ohio. . . . We found the inhabitants in a very destitute state; very ignorant of the doctrines of the Gospel; and in many instances without Bibles, or any other religious books. The Methodist preachers pass through this country, in their circuits, occasionally. . . . At New Orleans . . . the greater part of the inhabitants are French Catholics, ignorant of almost every thing except what relates to the increase of their property; destitute of schools, Bibles and religious instruction.

*Protestant missionary to the West, Samuel J. Mills, reports to his sponsors on the state of western religion, 1812, in Carruth,* Encyclopedia of American Facts, *139.*

. . . all that we see from Great Britain indicates an adherence to her mad policy towards the United States. The newspapers give you a sufficient insight into the measures of Congress. With a view to enable the Executive to step at once into Canada, they have provided, after two months' delay, for a regular force requiring twelve to raise it, and after three months' for a volunteer force, on terms not likely to raise it at all for that object. The mixture of good and bad, avowed and disguised motives, accounting for these things, is curious enough . . .

*President James Madison in a letter to former president Thomas Jefferson, February 7, 1812, in* Letters and Other Writings of James Madison, *II: 525–526.*

The Indians have hitherto remained perfectly quiet, sending frequently messages for peace, but I am very much afraid that such a calm may eventually be followed by a storm, if by this time the Government has not taken some measures to avert it. . . . If the Indians have been excited to hostilities by the British, why does the President tell us that all the Tribes, the solitary instance of the Prophet excepted, are disposed for peace. . . . Plans of such a dangerous magnitude may well raise the indignation of the whole of the United S; it is not the first time that they have been gulled . . .

*John Badollet in a letter to Albert Gallatin, February 26, 1812, in Thornbrough,* The Correspondence of John Badollet and Albert Gallatin, *223.*

We behold . . . on the side of Great Britain, a state of war against the United States; on the side of the United States, a state of peace towards Great Britain. Whether the United States shall continue passive under these progressive usurpations, and these accumulating wrongs; or, opposing force to force in defence of their natural rights . . . is a solemn question, which the constitution wisely confides to the legislative department of the government.

*President James Madison in his war message to Congress, June 1, 1812, in Brannan,* Official Letters, *14.*

Be it enacted by the Senate and House of Representatives of the United States of America in Congress assembled, That war be and the same is hereby declared to exist between the United Kingdom of Great Britain and Ireland and the dependencies thereof, and the United States of America and their territories; and that the President of the United States is hereby authorized to use the whole land and naval force of the United States to carry the same into effect, and to issue to private armed vessels of the United States commissions or letters of marque and general reprisal, in such form as he shall think proper, and under the seal of the United States, against the vessels, goods, and effects of the government of the said United Kingdom of Great Britain and Ireland, and the subjects thereof.

*Congressional declaration of war, June 18, 1812. Avalon Project. Available online. URL: http://www. yale.edu/lawweb/avalon/statutes/1812-01.htm.*

. . . Each man who volunteers his services in such a cause [the War] or loans his money for its support, or by his conversation, his writings, or any other mode of influence, encourages its prosecution . . . loads his conscience with the blackest crimes.

*New England preacher David Osgood opposes the war in an 1812 sermon, in Hickey,* War of 1812, *257.*

I inclose a paper containing the Declaration of war . . . It is understood that the Federalists in Congress are to put all the strength of their talents into a protest against the war, and that the party at large are to be brought out in all their force.

*President James Madison in a letter to Thomas Jefferson, June 22, 1812, in* Letters and Other Writings of James Madison, *II: 536.*

War and [commercial] restriction may leave the country equally exhausted; but the latter not only leaves you poor,—but, even when successful, dispirited, divided, discontented, with diminished patriotism, and the manners of a considerable portion of your people corrupted. Not so in war. In that state the common danger unites all; strengthens the bonds of society, and feeds the flame of patriotism.

*John C. Calhoun in a speech before the House of Representatives, June 24, 1812, in* Speeches of John C. Calhoun, *II: 29.*

In addition to the strong French [Partia]lities & the desire to save the sincking [sic] party, the Southern people are determined on the acquisition of the Floridas . . . & the Western people covet the Indian possessions. Some few of the Northern & Eastern Men are flattered with the prospect of making their fortunes in Canada & poor Madison was threatened with abandonment in the Presidential election; unless he would aid their views. . . . We are now in a state of war unable to give satisfactory reasons, why or wherefore . . .

*Federalist Martin Chittenden in a letter to Jonathan Hubbard, June 27, 1812, in Brown,* Republic in Peril, *171–172.*

I duly received your favor of the 22d covering the declaration of war. It is entirely popular here, the only opinion being that it should have been issued the moment the season admitted the militia to enter Canada. . . . To continue the war popular, two things are necessary mainly: (1) to stop Indian barbarities; the conquest of Canada will do this; (2) to furnish markets for our produce, say indeed for our flour . . . For carrying our produce to foreign markets our own ships, neutral ships, and even enemy ships under neutral flag, which I would wink at, will probably suffice.

*Former president Thomas Jefferson in a letter to President James Madison, June 29, 1812, in Hunt,* Essential Thomas Jefferson, *293.*

The unprovoked declaration of war, by the United States of America, against the United Kingdom of Great Britain and Ireland and its dependencies, has been followed by the actual invasion of this province in a remote frontier of the western district, by a detachment of the armed forces of the United States. The officer commanding that detachment has thought proper to invite His Majesty's subjects not merely to a quiet and unresisting submission, but insults them with a call to seek voluntarily the protection of his government. . . . Where is to be found in any part of the world, a growth so rapid in wealth and prosperity, as this colony exhibits? Settled not thirty years by a band of veterans, exiled from their former possessions on account of their loyalty. . . . The unavoidable and immediate consequence of a separation from Great Britain must be the loss of this inestimable advantage . . .

*Major General Isaac Brock implores the people of Upper Canada to remain loyal to the Crown in a proclamation, July 22, 1812, in Hannay,* History of the War of 1812, *44–45.*

Our enemies have indeed said that they could subdue this country by proclamation; but it is our part to prove to them that they are sadly mistaken, that the population is determinedly hostile to them, and that the few who might be otherwise inclined will find it their safety to be faithful. . . . They will tell you that they are come to give you freedom. Yes, the base slaves of the most contemptible faction that ever distracted the affairs of any nation, the minions of the very sycophants who lick the dust from the feet of Bonaparte, will tell you that they are come to communicate the blessing of liberty to this province . . . Remember that, when you go forth to the combat, you fight not for yourselves alone, but for the whole world.

*Allan Maclean, speaker of the Commons House of Assembly of Upper Canada, exhorts his people to resist the U.S. invasion, August 5, 1812, in Hannay,* History of the War of 1812, *48.*

It was much to have been desired that simultaneous invasions of Canada, at several points, particularly in relation to Malden and Montreal, might have secured the great object of bringing all Upper Canada, and the channels communicating with the Indians, under our command; with ulterior prospects towards Quebec flattering to our arms. This systematic operation having been frustrated, it only remains to pursue the course that will diminish the disappointment as much as possible . . . the expedition against Montreal should be forwarded by all the means in your power.

*President James Madison in a letter to Major General Henry Dearborn, August 9, 1812, in* Letters and Other Writings of James Madison, *II: 538–539.*

At daylight [August 30] discovered a frigate lying in Nantucket Roads, cleared ship for action and stood for her. At 7 she proved the frigate *Constitution* from a cruise, having captured the British frigate *Guerrière*. This day moored ship in Boston harbor.

> *Naval midshipman Matthew C. Perry in his journal, August 31, 1812, in Allen,* Commodore Hull: Papers of Isaac Hull, *29.*

On Monday morning [August 31] the *Constitution* came up to town and was welcomed and honored by a federal salute from the Washington Artillery under Capt. Harris and by the hearty, unanimous, and repeated cheers of the citizens on the wharves, the shopping, and housetops.

> *The* Columbian Centinel *newspaper reports on the public acclaim in Boston for the* Constitution, *September 2, 1812, in Allen,* Commodore Hull: Papers of Isaac Hull, *29.*

Personally, we have arrived so near the close of the drama that we can experience but few of the evils which await the rising generation. We have passed through one revolution, and happily arrived at the goal; but the ambition, injustice, and plunder of foreign powers have again involved us in war, the termination of which is not given us to see. If we have not the 'gorgeous palaces or the cloud-capped towers' of Moscow to be levelled with the dust, nor a million of victims to be sacrificed upon the altar of ambition, we have our firesides, or comfortable habitations, our cities, our churches, and our country to defend, our rights, privileges, and independence to preserve. And for these are we not justly contending? Thus it appears to me. Yet I hear from our pulpits, and read from our presses, that it is an unjust, a wicked, a ruinous, and unnecessary war. . . . A house divided against itself,—and upon that foundation do our enemies build their hopes of subduing us. May it prove a sandy one to them!

> *Abigail Adams in a letter to Mercy Otis Warren, December 30, 1812, in Adams,* Correspondence between John Adams and Mercy Warren, *501–502.*

My brethren, the land in which we live gives us the opportunity rapidly to advance the prosperity of liberty.

On August 19, 1812, the USS *Constitution* achieved one of the most impressive naval victories of the War of 1812 against the HMS *Guerrière*. In the battle depicted here, the *Constitution* acquired its nickname, "Old Ironsides." *(Library of Congress, Prints and Photographs Division [LC-D43-T01-50208])*

This government founded on the principles of liberty and equality, and declaring them to be the free gift of God, if not ignorant of their declaration, must enforce it; I am confident she wills it, and strong forbodings of it is discernable. The northern sections of the union is fast conceding, and the southern must comply, although so biased by interest, that they have become callous to the voice of reason and justice . . . There could be many reasons given, to prove that the mind of an African is not inferior to that of an European; yet to do so would be superfluous. It would be like adding hardness to the diamond, or lustre to the sun.

*George Lawrence, a free black New Yorker, in a sermon to celebrate the anniversary of the ending of the external slave trade, January 1, 1813, in Aptheker,* Documentary History, *58.*

It is impossible that this country should ever abandon the gallant tars, who have won for us such splendid trophies. Let me suppose the genius of Columbia should visit one of them in his oppressor's prison, and attempt to reconcile him to his forlorn and wretched condition. . . . The poor tar would address her . . . and say: 'You owe me, my country, protection: I owe you, in return, obedience . . . I lost this eye in fighting under Truxton, with the Insurgente; I got this scar before Tripoli; I broke this leg on board the *Constitution* when the *Guerrière* struck' . . . I will not imagine the dreadful catastrophe to which he would be driven by an abandonment of him to his oppressor. It will not be, it can not be, that his country will refuse him protection. . . . if we fail, let us fail like men, lash ourselves to our gallant tars, and expire together in one common struggle, fighting for FREE TRADE AND SEAMEN'S RIGHTS.

*Speaker of the House Henry Clay in a speech before Congress, January 8, 1813, in Colton,* Life and Times of Henry Clay, *I: 178–179.*

I have the honour to acknowledge the receipt of your letter . . . accompanied by 332 Stockings and 200 mittens given by the ladies of the town of Montgomery to the soldiers in the service of the United States on the Canada Frontier. Such manifestations of liberality and patriotic feeling, cannot fail to inspire the brave defenders of their country with redoubled ardor in its service.

*New York governor Daniel D. Tompkins in a letter to a constituent, January 19, 1813, in* Public Papers of Daniel D. Tompkins, *III: 231.*

. . . The savages were suffered to commit every depredation upon our wounded which they pleased. An indiscriminate slaughter took place, of all who were unable to walk, many were tomahawked, and many were burned alive in houses.

*A group of officers describes the "massacre" at Frenchtown on January 21, 1813, in Brannan,* Official Letters, *135.*

A detachment from the left wing of the north-western army, under my command, at Frenchtown, on the river Raisin, was attacked on the 22d instant by a force greatly superior in number, aided by several pieces of artillery. . . . I was the more ready to make the surrender, from being assured, that unless done quickly, the buildings adjacent would be immediately set on fire, and that no responsibility would be taken for the conduct of the savages, who were then assembled in great numbers. . . . Our loss in killed is considerable.

*General James Winchester in a letter to the secretary of war, January 23, 1813, in Brannan,* Official Letters, *132, 133.*

The gentleman from Delaware sees in Canada no object worthy of conquest. . . . Other gentlemen consider the invasion of that country as wicked and unjustifiable. Its inhabitants are represented as unoffending, connected with those of the bordering States by a thousand tender ties, interchanging acts of kindness, and all the offices of good neighborhood. Canada innocent! Canada unoffending! Is it not in Canada that the tomahawk of the savage has been moulded into its deathlike form? From Canadian magazines, Malden, and others, that those supposes have been issued which nourish and sustain the Indian hostilities?

*Speaker of the House Henry Clay denounces the opinion that Canada should not be attacked in the war, 1813, in Hart,* American History, *III: 419.*

I have never allowed myself to believe that the Union was in danger, or that a dissolution of it could be desired, unless by a few individuals, if such there be, in desperate situations or of unbridled passions. In addition to the thousand affinities belonging to every part of the nation, every part has an interest, as deep as it is obvious, in maintaining the bond which keeps the whole together; and the Eastern part certainly not less than any other. . . . The great road of profitable intercourse for New England, even with old England, lies through the wheat, the cotton, and the tobacco fields, of her Southern and Western confederates.

*President James Madison expresses hopes that disagreement over the War of 1812 will not rip apart the Union in a letter to David Humphreys, March 23, 1813, in* Letters and Other Writings of James Madison, *II: 561–562.*

For the last week all the city and Georgetown (except the Cabinet) have expected a visit from the enemy, and were not lacking in their expressions of terror and reproach. . . . The fort is being repaired, and five hundred militia, with perhaps as many regulars, are to be stationed on the Green, near the Windmill, or rather Major Taylor's. The twenty tents already look well in my eyes, who have always been an advocate for fighting when assailed, though a Quaker. I therefore keep the old Tunisian sabre within reach.

*First Lady Dolley Madison in a letter to Edward Coles, May 12, 1813, in* Memoirs and Letters of Dolly Madison, *90–91.*

Don't give up the ship!

*Capt. James Lawrence as he was killed aboard the* USS Chesapeake, *June 1, 1813, in Hickey,* War of 1812, *155.*

. . . The British are such near neighbours and continue to menace us. Until the late alarm I have never been able to realize our being in a state of war; but now when such active preparations are made, when so many of our citizens and particular acquaintance have marched to meet the enemy, I not only believe but feel the unhappy state of our country. . . . There is so little apprehension of danger in the city, that not a single removal of person or goods has taken place.

*Washington, D.C., socialite Margaret Bayard Smith describes the atmosphere in the capital in a letter to her sister, July 20, 1813, in* Hunt, The First Forty Years, *89–90.*

We have met the enemy and they are ours: Two Ships, two Brigs {,} one Schooner & one Sloop.

*Oliver Hazard Perry describes his victory at the Battle of Lake Erie in a letter to William Henry Harrison, September 10, 1813, in Hickey,* War of 1812, *133.*

There is a report here, and generally believed, that captain Perry has captured the whole enemy's fleet on lake Erie. If this should prove true in all its details, (and God grant that it may) he has immortalized himself and not disappointed the high expectations formed of his talents and bravery.

*Secretary of the Navy Isaac Chauncey in a letter to General James Wilkinson, September 22, 1813, in Brannan,* Official Letters, *216.*

I have not been unaware of the disappointment and discontent gaining ground with respect to the war on Canada, or of the use to which they were turned against the Administration. I have not been less aware that success alone would put an end to them. This is the test by which public opinion decides more or less in all cases, and most of all, perhaps, in that of military events. . . . How far past failure is to be ascribed to the difficulties incident to the first stages of a war commenced as the present necessarily was; to the personal faults of those entrusted with command; to the course pursued by the National Legislature; or to mismanagements by the Executive Department, must be left to those who will decide impartially. . . . The utter inexperience of nearly all the new officers was an inconvenience of the most serious kind, but inseparable, as it always must be, from a country among whose blessings it is to have long intervals of peace, and to be without those large standing armies which even in peace are fitted for war.

*President James Madison in a letter to New Englander William Wirt, September 30, 1813, in* Letters and Other Writings of James Madison, *II: 573, 575.*

The Colonel [Johnson] most gallantly led the head of his column into the . . . enemy's fire, and was personally opposed to Tecumseh. . . . He rode a white horse, and was known to be an officer of rank; a shower of balls was discharged at him . . . his horse was shot under him—his clothes, his saddle, his person was pierced with bullets. At the moment his horse fell, Tecumseh rushed towards him with an uplifted tomahawk, to give the fatal stroke, but . . . he drew a pistol from his holster and laid his opponent dead at his feet.

*Samuel R. Brown recollects seeing Colonel Richard Mentor Johnson kill Tecumseh at the Battle of the Thames, October 5, 1813, in Sugden,* Tecumseh's Last Stand, *137.*

Suppose that our opponents [the Federalists], who object to everything, had been at the helm of government, and that an opposite line of policy had been pursued: —no embargoes—no non-intercourse—no non-importation acts—no war—and, in fact, no resistance to the injuries and aggressions of Great Britain; who can be ignorant of what would have been the consequence? They would have multiplied in number and degree, till our commerce would have been annihilated.

*John C. Calhoun in a speech before the House of Representatives, February 25, 1814, in* Speeches of John C. Calhoun, *II: 91.*

Your own observation and experience must prove to you the difficulty of recruiting men, and if you cannot get them in the very quarter of the union where they most abound, where are they to come from? The want of seamen has, as you have seen, compelled the Department to strip from ships that were ready for sea, to man those on the Lakes. Are we to strip the remainder in order to defend those that are building the Atlantic ports? If so, policy and economy would dictate the burning of the latter, in order to remove the temptation, rather than to defend them at an expence far transcending their value.

*Secretary of the Navy William Jones in a letter to Isaac Hull, June 17, 1814, in Allen,* Papers of Isaac Hull, *33–34.*

This morning on awakening we were greeted with the sad news, that our city was taken, the bridges and public buildings burnt, our troops flying in every direction. Our little army totally dispersed. Good God, what will be the event! . . . Oh how changed are my feelings, my confidence in our troops is gone, they may again be rallied, but it will require a long apprenticeship to make them good soldiers. Oh my sister how gloomy is the scene. I do not suppose Government will ever return to Washington. All those whose property was invested in that place, will be reduced to poverty.

*Margaret Bayard Smith describes her distress on hearing of the burning of Washington, D.C., in a letter to her sister, August 1814, in Hunt,* The First Forty Years, *100, 101.*

Mrs. M[adison] seem'd much depress'd, she could scarcely speak without tears. She told me she had

remained in the city till a few hours before the English enter'd. She was so confident of Victory that she was calmly listening to the roar of cannon, and watching the rockets in the air, when she perceived our troops rushing into the city, with the haste and dismay of a routed force. The friends with her then hurried her away, (her carriage being previously ready) and she with many other families . . . retreated with the flying army. In George town they perceived some men before them carrying off the picture of Genl. Washington (the large one by Stewart) which with the plate, was all that was saved out of the President's house. Mrs. M. lost all her own property.

*Margaret Bayard Smith describes First Lady Dolley Madison's conduct during the British attack on Washington, D.C., in a letter to her sister, August 1814, in Hunt,* The First Forty Years, *110.*

I have pressed as many Cabinet papers into trunks as to fill one carriage; our private property must be sacrificed, as it is impossible to procure wagons for its transportation. . . . French John (a faithful servant), with his usual activity and resolution, offers to spike the cannon at the gate, and lay a train of powder, which would blow up the British, should they enter the house.

*Dolley Madison describes evacuating the White House in a letter to her sister, Anna, August 23, 1814, in* Memoirs and Letters of Dolly Madison, *109.*

. . . The affairs of our country grow more and more gloomy . . . Every day we are hearing of new instances of the cruelty of the soldiery and individual suffering. It has been the poor who have been the principle sufferers. . . . In the army's march from Benedict they made tents and beds of all the green corn, for which purpose they cut down whole fields. I am told this country (from Benedict to Washington) is totally laid waste; you can scarcely get anything for man or horse to eat. They strip'd the people of their clothing, taking women's and even children's clothes.

*Margaret Bayard Smith describes the devastation outside Washington, D.C., in a letter to her sister, September 11, 1814, in Hunt,* The First Forty Years, *117.*

[Louisiana] is threatened on one side by the Spaniards of Mexico,—on the other side by Spaniards, English and Indians, and is filled with combustible materials within; the situation of the inhabitants is not the most secure: and they are less capable of self defence than any other part of the Union.

*Henry Marie Brackenridge describes the vulnerability of Louisiana in a letter, September 14, 1813, in Keller,* The Nation's Advocate, *151.*

I learn from the newspapers that the vandalism of our enemy has triumphed at Washington over science as well as the arts, by the destruction of the public library with the noble edifice in which it was deposited. . . . I presume it will be among the early objects of Congress to recommence their collection. This will be difficult while the war continues, and intercourse with Europe is attended with so much risk. You know my collection, its condition and extent. I have been fifty years making it, and have spared no pains, opportunity, or expense to make it what it is. . . . It is long since I have been sensible it ought not to continue private property, and had provided that at my death, Congress should have the refusal of it at their own price. But the loss they have now incurred, makes the present the proper moment for their accommodation. . . .

*Former president Thomas Jefferson offers his personal library for sale to Congress in a letter to Samuel H. Smith, September 21, 1814, in Hunt,* The Essential Thomas Jefferson, *300, 301.*

The whole compass of the diplomatic skill employed by the British Government in this negotiation has consisted in consuming time, without coming to any conclusion.

*Peace negotiator John Quincy Adams expresses frustration in a letter to his father, John Adams, October 27, 1814, in* Letters and Other Writings of James Madison, *II: 597.*

The principle Officers of the Ordinance department in this District [New York City], can employ twenty five boys from 10 to 15 years of age in preparing Cartridges. He will cloathe feed & school them if they remain a considerable time & will deal reasonably with them in other respects. It occurred to me that there might be boys of that Age in the Alms House who might be employed in that business advantageously for themselves & the public.

*New York governor Daniel D. Tompkins in a letter to De Witt Clinton, November 18, 1814, in* Public Papers of Daniel D. Tompkins, *III: 599.*

You are not mistaken in viewing the conduct of the Eastern States as the source of our greatest difficulties in carrying on the war; as it certainly is the greatest, if not the sole inducement with the enemy to persevere in it. The greater part of the people in that quarter have been brought by their leaders, aided by their priests, under a delusion scarcely exceeded by that recorded in the period of witchcraft; and the leaders themselves are becoming daily more desperate in the use they make of it. Their object is power.

*President James Madison in a letter to Wilson C. Nicholas, November 25, 1814, in* Letters and Other Writings of James Madison, *II: 593.*

Therefore resolved.—That it be and hereby is recommended to the Legislatures of the several States represented in this Convention to adopt all such measures as may be necessary effectually to protect the citizens of said States from the operation and effects of all acts which have been or may be passed by the Congress of the United States, which shall contain provisions, subjecting the militia or other citizens to forcible drafts, conscriptions, or impressments, not authorized by the Constitution of the United States.

*Declaration of the Hartfold Convention, December 1814. Avalon Project. Available online. URL: http://www.yale.edu/lawweb/avalon/amerdoc/hartconv.htm.*

Madam, the American army in Louisiana has gained immortal glory. It has made a defense against the most valiant and fortunate troops of Europe, excited to desperation by resistance, and staking its all of reputation on the die, unsurpassed in the annals of military warfare, its leader [Andrew Jackson] achieving in one hour the object of a whole campaign,—the preservation of the state from conquest, and the overthrow of its invaders. The 8th of January will form an epoch in the history of the Republic. . . . You may conceive, madam, what a spectacle of carnage must have met the eye, after the battle, when you learn that in killed,

The Battle of New Orleans turned Andrew Jackson into a national military hero, and images of Jackson at the battle, like this 19th-century lithograph, were popular throughout the century. *(Library of Congress, Prints and Photographs Division [LC-USZ62-21267])*

wounded, and missing, the loss of the enemy exceeded two thousand . . .

*Thomas B. Johnson reports on the Battle of New Orleans in a letter to First Lady Dolley Madison, January 19, 1815, in* Memoirs and Letters of Dolly Madison.

The brok'n clouds of the terrible fray
From our country have all rolled away,
In shameful defeat
Th' invaders retreat,
Even time shall hold sacred that day.
Latest star of the union rejoice,
'Mid the spheres ever bright be thy course;
Let Britons beware

Invasions who dare.
And let Jackson's bright fame with ages go down
In the land young in story, now in great renown.
*A poem by Henry Marie Brackenridge recited at the Pittsburgh Theater, February 13, 1815, in Keller,* The Nation's Advocate, *154.*

My father: What is this I see before me? A few knives and blankets? Is this all you promised us at the beginning of the war? Where is the fulfillment of those high speeches of promise you made us at Michilimackinac and sent to our villages on the Mississippi? You told us you would never let fall the hatchet till the Americans were driven beyond the Alleghenies! You said we should again be put in possession of our ancient hunting-grounds! You said that our British fathers would never make peace without consulting his Red children! . . . Will these paltry presents pay for the men we have lost in battle and on the road? Will they soothe the feelings of our friends? Will they make good your promises?
*Sioux Indian Wabashaw addresses a British military commander and denounces the British disregard for Indian peoples in the Treaty of Ghent, 1815, in Blaisdell,* Great Speeches, *69.*

The petition of Burke a free man of Colour humbly represents. That about the year of 1811 he purchased from his then master William P. Thoppson, Esqr. His freedom for the sum of four hundred dollars. That he was born in the State of Virginia where he has a wife and children in slavery, that although he is a person of colour, he has attachments and affections, perhaps as strong as if it had pleased heaven to give him a white skin. . . . The prayer therefore of your petitioner is that he have leave to remain in this Commonwealth free from any penalty whatever, that a law be passed for that purpose . . .
*A slave who has purchased his freedom petitions the Virginia legislature, December 9, 1815, in Aptheker,* Documentary History, *67.*

# 10

# The Era of
# Good Feelings?
## 1816–1819

In 1819, the New Yorker Washington Irving published a satirical book entitled *A Sketch-Book of Geoffrey Crayon, Gent,* which contained what would become two of his most famous and often-read stories, "Rip Van Winkle" and "The Legend of Sleepy Hollow." Irving had become known in the decade before 1819 for his stinging social and literary criticism and the way he used settings up the Hudson River in the Catskill Mountains of New York to provide commentary on American life. The story "Rip Van Winkle" continued in this tradition. In the story, which is set sometime in the 18th century, the character Rip Van Winkle goes into an enchanted sleep and awakens after 20 years to find the world around him dramatically changed. Rip notices that the King George III sign above the local tavern has been replaced by a mysterious General Washington; people talk of unfamiliar political parties; and a man presents an oration on the strange-sounding concepts of the "rights of citizens—elections—members of congress—liberty . . . and other words, which were a perfect Babylonish jargon" to Rip.[1]

Most of all, Rip notices a difference in the people around him: "The very character of the people seemed changed. There was a bustling, disputatious tone about it, instead of the accustomed phlegm and drowsy tranquility."[2] Although the character of Rip was probably seeing his formerly sleepy New York town sometime in the 1790s, his description of the changes in the American people fit even better, perhaps, the time of the story's publication in 1819. Washington Irving wanted his readers to note the dramatic shifts in American life since before the American Revolution, and in the befuddled character of Rip Van Winkle, he captured something of the speed of social change. Washington Irving was right: The United States was a vastly different place in 1819 than it had been in 1770, 1783, or even 1793. The "bustling, disputatious tone" noticed by Rip Van Winkle characterized very well the tone of American life in the years after the War of 1812. As the United States set itself on a new course and the market economy hastened political and social changes that had been brewing for decades, the pace of American life quickened.

# THE MARKET REVOLUTION

The U.S. economy had slowly been turning more and more toward a capitalist market system since the end of the 1780s, and following the War of 1812, the transition began to accelerate. The commercial difficulties and stresses of international warfare that had dogged the development of a swiftly increasing American trade since 1793 came to an end after both the War of 1812 and the Napoleonic Wars were settled. The vast majority of Americans still lived on farms, but buying and selling penetrated farther into even the most rural areas of the country. Both cotton and wheat grew more important as American trade goods, and after the War of 1812, the British opened their trade routes to the United States more fully than at any time since the Revolutionary War, spurring rapid growth in agricultural production. American cities grew larger, and ports like New York, Charleston, and Providence picked up additional speed from their capacity to act as points of connection among rural, internal, and international markets for goods of all kinds. Individual American citizens grew accustomed to engaging in more frequent cash transactions, more frequent borrowing, and the possession of a greater variety of manufactured goods.

Although European manufactured goods had been popular in the United States since the middle of the 18th century, by 1816, more and more of the products that American citizens desired were also being manufactured in the United States. Americans bought and sold a greater variety of goods than ever before: Great Britain flooded U.S. markets with trade goods after the war, and Americans also manufactured an ever increasing amount for themselves. Manufacturing, both in Europe and in the United States, also became an increasingly industrial process, as products began to be mass-produced using technologies and techniques developed over the previous decades, especially steam and water power. These fueled the growth in American manufacturing, and the factory system became increasingly common as a part of the economy, especially in New England and the Middle Atlantic states.

Cloth and shoe manufacturing quickly became the two leading industrial processes in the United States, in part because each industry had begun to convert to the factory system in the 1790s. During the late 1810s, Americans also manufactured chairs, clocks, machine parts, weapons, and other items, sometimes with interchangeable parts, but cloth and shoes led the way for all the other industries. The shoe industry was centered in Lynn, Massachusetts, where a group of Quaker merchants led by Micajah Pratt had incorporated a manufactory in 1814 to assemble under one roof and under central ownership the expertise of many of Lynn's long-standing families of shoemakers. At Pratt's shoe factory, most of the labor was done by hand: Men cut the shoe leather, women and children sewed the uppers, and young men joined the soles and uppers together. This system of labor caused a huge rise in productivity, and within a few years, Pratt's company was producing tens of thousands of pairs of shoes annually, which were sold throughout the United States and in Europe. The men and women of Lynn who could no longer sustain

Part of the effort to re-create stability following the War of 1812 involved looking to America's Revolutionary past for examples of heroism. In June 1818, the remains of Revolutionary War general Richard Montgomery were reinterred at this marble monument in his honor in New York City. *(from Benson Lossing,* The Pictorial Field-Book of the Revolution, *1851–1852)*

independently owned family shoe shops did not necessarily experience becoming wage laborers as a positive development, but the shift in the use and ownership of their labor facilitated the transition to capitalism. The older system of master craftsmen who ruled over journeymen and apprentices in a home-based shop began to be threatened in industry after industry, even though the changeover to large-scale factory production did not take place all at once.

The transition from home to factory was even more pronounced in cloth manufacturing, where centralization also became an important market force as the economy pulled out of the War of 1812 slump. In 1814, Francis Cabot Lowell and a group of other wealthy New England investors incorporated the Boston Manufacturing Company to produce cloth in the largest mechanized mill ever constructed under one roof, and in their first year of operation, the company made a 25 percent profit. Lowell intended from the beginning to capture as much of the market in manufactured cloth as possible, and he wanted to cause a significant decrease in the home manufacturing of textiles.

Spinning and weaving had been traditional female home occupations for hundreds of years, but Lowell's all-encompassing vision sought to change them into industrial processes. Lowell's mills, located originally in the town of Waltham, ran on steam and water power, much like Slater's Mill in Rhode Island, but the scale of production was even larger. Horace Bushnell commented, "This transition from mother-and-daughter power to water-and-steam power" would cause "a complete revolution in domestic life."[3] Bushnell was both right and wrong. The Waltham manufacturing system, as Lowell's process became known, still relied largely on female wage laborers to run the mechanized looms and bobbins, but the women had to leave home to sell their labor to the company. Lowell built large dormitories, and a whole town eventually grew up around the Waltham mills. But the girls who worked in the mills generally viewed their jobs as temporary ones that they would pursue for a few years before marrying and returning to a rural, farming life.

Nonetheless, Bushnell was correct that a "revolution in domestic life" was under way. As the market system penetrated the U.S. economy to a far greater extent, many industries followed shoes and cloth as production moved out of the home and into centralized factories. This meant that wage laborers, middle-class shop workers, and factory owners all experienced an increasing separation between home and work that had never been the case in a traditional farm economy. Although both men and women worked outside the home for wages, this separation helped to accelerate the development of a middle-class ideal of the "domestic woman" who did not work for wages, but rather was supposed to make the home into a leisured escape from the economic cares of the outside world. The separation between home and work helped to solidify both the class and the gender systems that would become even more polarized in the 1820s.

In economic terms, the stakes of this transition toward a more manufacturing-intensive, market-based system were very high. Along with a social transformation, the market changes had political consequences. A group of progress-minded Democratic-Republicans used their new political clout, enhanced by the fact that opposition to the War of 1812 had sapped the Federalist Party of much of its national power, to put together a program to strengthen national economic policy. The War of 1812 had necessitated higher federal taxes than ever before, and war policies combined with the development of manufacturing to stimulate renewed support for centralization of national finance and the exercise of economic power by the federal government.

Congress had allowed the charter of the Bank of the United States to expire in 1811, but wartime financial pressures led to an unprecedented growth in state-chartered banks and new private financial institutions of all kinds. The circulation of state and private banknotes in the absence of a stable central banking system had contributed to wartime inflation, and to combat this trend and stave off financial crisis, Congress moved to create a new Bank of the United States. President Madison vetoed the first attempt to charter the Second Bank of the United States in January 1815 because he believed the charter contained too much federal power, but when Congress again came into session at the beginning of 1816, both it and the president agreed that the financial situation demanded action. South Carolina Congressman John C. Calhoun argued that "the cause and states of the disorders of the national currency" required a new national bank, and he reintroduced charter legislation in January 1816.[4] Following its passage in March and April, President Madison set aside his lingering doubt over the constitutionality of national banking and signed the new charter on April 10, 1816, to create the Second Bank of the United States.

Madison's approval of the bank charter signaled a subtle shift in political party alignment and foreshadowed the activities of a new economic and political era. The Federalists, long the party that had supported the exercise of federal financial power, were fighting to hold on to any national influence at all, and a younger generation of Democratic-Republicans all but adopted the old ideas of Alexander Hamilton and advocated Federalist financial positions without the taint of Federalist politics. Henry Clay, John C. Calhoun, Albert Gallatin, and their Democratic-Republican supporters pushed for the use of federal power to improve trade, support manufacturing, stabilize the financial system, and encourage economic development. Through the course of 1816, it became clear that the Democratic-Republican Party would have the power to dominate totally the national political scene, but they did so, in part, on the coattails of traditional Federalist economic policies.

President Madison's acquiescence to the bank charter also signaled a shift in presidential politics. James Monroe, a Virginia protégé of Jefferson and Madison, was the clear choice to succeed Madison as president, but he entered office at a time when much of the old party system of Jefferson and Madison was passing away. The results of the 1816 presidential election dramatized how much power the Federalist Party had lost: Monroe was elected with 183 of 217 electoral votes, and he won every state except Massachusetts, Delaware, and Connecticut. One Federalist

Henry Clay, who rose to national prominence as a politician just before the War of 1812, was one of the most influential men in politics until the early 1850s, although he was never elected president. *(National Archives, Mathew Brady Photographs of Civil War Era Personalities and Scenes [NWDNS-111-B-4201])*

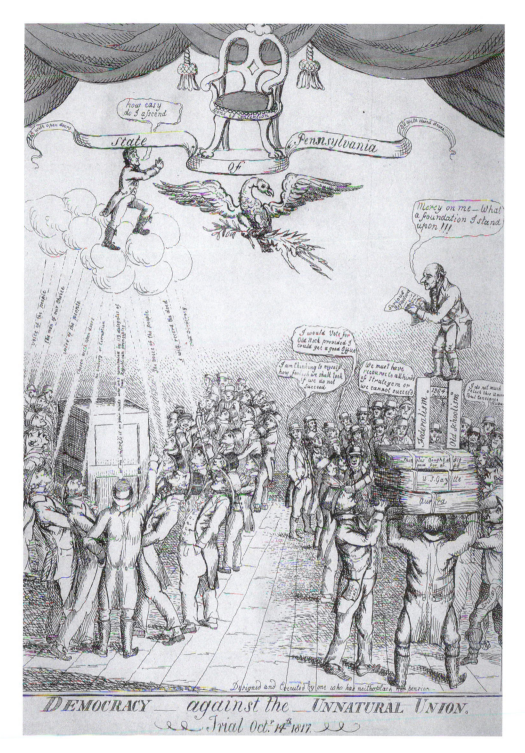

Even though national party tensions had subsided during the Era of Good Feelings, cartoons such as this one, which lampoons the Pennsylvania gubernatorial race of 1817, showed that politics remained contentious on a state and local level. *(Library of Congress, Prints and Photographs Division [LC-USZ62-89749])*

newspaper remarked that the diminished party contest meant that Monroe would preside over a new "era of good feelings" in American politics. Monroe's presidency did usher in a certain amount of political harmony with the dominance of the Democratic-Republican Party (or the Democratic Party, as it was increasingly becoming known). But factions and disagreements within the Democratic Party, caused by splits between the new nationalists and the remaining older-style Jeffersonian Democrats, did not go away. Some of the same political arguments about the nature of the American republic that had gone on since the end of the Revolution persisted, albeit in new political and economic circumstances.

Having won the new charter for the Second Bank of the United States, the nationalist Democrats continued to push their economic program in new directions that would encourage the new market and manufacturing developments in the U.S. economy. John C. Calhoun convinced Congress to continue many taxes that had been imposed on an emergency basis during the War of 1812, and he decided that there was sufficient support for a nationalist economic program to push for a new level of federal economic activism. Calhoun, along with Secretary of the Treasury Alexander Dallas and fellow South Carolina congressmen William Lowndes (with additional advice and support from mill owner Francis Cabot Lowell), called for the introduction of a trade tariff in 1816. The tariff would impose a 25-cent tax on every yard of imported cotton cloth and would impose additional trade taxes on imported iron, woolens, and a range of small manufactured goods.

Massachusetts congressman Daniel Webster, who represented older economic interests and shippers in New England, led the opposition to the tariff. The old-line New England merchants worried about a political alliance between northern industrialists and men like Calhoun, who wanted to increase southern manufacturing. The nationalists formed a strong coalition, however, and at the end of the 1816 congressional session, just before Monroe's election, the tariff passed. The unprecedented Tariff of 1816 kept most European cotton cloth out of the United States altogether and provided a further impetus for industrial growth.

Calhoun, Clay, and Gallatin—emboldened by their success with the tariff legislation, President Madison's reluctant approval of the bank charter, and the election of the more nationalist-minded—turned their attention at the end of 1816 to the subject of transportation. Gallatin proposed to use federal power and funding to build an interlocking system of roads and canals that would connect eastern and western markets to allow additional growth in American internal trade. Calhoun managed to win approval of a "Bonus Bill" that would have funded Gallatin's internal improvement projects, but as one of his last acts in office in March 1817, Madison again asserted an older, stricter interpretation of the Constitution and vetoed the bill. For the time being, federal sponsorship of transportation improvements came to a halt, but in some important cases particular states picked up the cause. As the historian Charles Sellers has written about the Madison veto: "Within two weeks De Witt Clinton persuaded the New York legislature to proceed with the Erie Canal on its own."[5]

The battle over the tariff and internal improvements demonstrated the new and complicated relationship among region, politics, and the dominance of the Democratic Party that had developed by the time of James Monroe's first year in office. After he was inaugurated in March 1817, Monroe went on an extensive tour of the United States. His tour was intended to dramatize the new power and unity with which the nation had emerged after the War of 1812. The New England leg of Monroe's tour was also meant to confirm the attachment of that region to the nation after the division of the War of 1812. Monroe appointed John Quincy Adams, a former Federalist and son of Federalist president and first lady John and Abigail Adams, to be secretary of state, a sign to some that his administration would bring together adherents of both the old parties in a new nationalist system. The economic coalition between southern nationalist politicians and northern industrialists like James Cabot Lowell also served as evidence that some new nationalist sentiment was taking effect. But in spite of any goodwill an executive tour might bring about, many Americans still greeted the "progress" of the market revolution with skepticism. Furthermore, plenty of southerners continued to invest in the system of slavery, an economic arrangement that was not necessarily part of a vision for an entirely capitalist future.

## SLAVERY AND TERRITORIAL EXPANSION

Although the institution of slavery continued to grow in importance, especially as domestically grown cotton became an important raw ingredient in the manufacturing economy of the northern United States, some American attitudes about slavery were changing after the War of 1812. For one thing, slavery continued its decades-long decrease in the North. In 1817, the legislature of New York State, one of the northern states that moved most slowly to end slavery, pushed forward the final portions of a gradual emancipation plan that would ensure freedom for all slaves in the state by 1827. Even in the South, where slave labor was firmly entrenched in both rural areas and cities, the free African-American population was growing. In the upper South, more than 10 percent of African Americans were free by 1810, and the disruptions of the War of 1812 caused the percentage to climb even higher.[6] The growing population of free people of color, by contrast, emphasized the oppressive nature of slavery both in the South and where it still existed in the North.

Some slave owners and antislavery activists alike were disturbed by the implications inherent in this coexistence between slavery and freedom. In 1816, prominent southern citizens, including Henry Clay and James Madison, joined together under the leadership of Presbyterian minister Robert Finley to found the American Colonization Society. The society advocated founding a colony in west Africa where freed slaves could be "repatriated" to start new lives as freed people (still under the paternal protection of the society itself). The society was founded on the racist principle, promoted heavily by Thomas Jefferson since the late 1780s, that slavery was an evil that must come to an end, but that blacks and whites could never peacefully live together. The American Colonization Society found much of its support in the upper South, where slave owners hoped to convert their livelihoods to a more modern, capitalistic style of production but were also wary of living close to scores of people whom they had recently held in bondage and believed to be inferior.

Although some African Americans, like the wealthy Massachusetts ship captain Paul Cuffe, took a positive black-nationalist perspective on the idea of emigrating to Africa and worked with the American Colonization Society, most free African Americans were appalled at the idea of being forcibly removed from their country. The abolitionist movement that would engage in a strenuous fight against American slavery and racism right up until the Civil War (1861–65) got an early start in 1817 when a group of "free men of color" in Philadelphia met to oppose the aims and proposals of the American Colonization Society. Many African Americans, like the prominent Philadelphia sail maker James Forten, were building successful free black families and communities, and they had no intention of letting colonizationists plan their futures.

Slaves who lived in the Deep South on rural plantations growing rice, cotton, and wheat had few chances to interact with urbanites and "free men of color" like James Forten. Their approach to freedom was much more personal, and their most direct means of opposing the system that held them in bondage was running away. It was difficult for runaways to escape, and it was not always clear where they could run to be safe (even in the North); nonetheless, the numbers of runaway slaves grew steadily after the War of 1812. Slaves who lived near frontier or foreign-controlled territories, like Florida, often sought protection across the borders. American officials and slaveholders worried, probably correctly, that fugitive slaves from Georgia, Alabama, and Mississippi sought refuge with the Seminole Indians or in Spanish Florida. The tension over slavery along the border helped to inflame an already fragile diplomatic situation in the Deep South.

Border tensions also increased because U.S. diplomacy in North America was readjusting after the War of 1812. The settlement of both the War of 1812 and the Napoleonic Wars changed the power structures on the continent, and Secretary of State John Quincy Adams was particularly keen to guarantee the primacy of the United States in North America. In 1817, the previous secretary of state, Richard Rush, had brokered an executive agreement with Great Britain (the Rush-Bagot pact) that lowered tensions with the British along the Canadian border and settled lingering military tensions around the Great Lakes. John Quincy Adams followed that up with the Convention of 1818, which set a stable border with Canada at the 49th parallel, guaranteed U.S. fishing rights off Newfoundland, and defined Oregon as open to settlement by both the United States and Great Britain.

Once the northern borders of the United States were secured and John Quincy Adams seemed to have brokered a new stability in the U.S. relationship with Great Britain, Monroe and his cabinet turned their attentions south. The Spanish held on to Florida under the settlement of the War of 1812, and their relative weakness in the region led both Indians and fugitive slaves to use Spanish lands as a base for actions against the United States. In 1816, Spanish officials had allowed American troops to destroy a fort occupied by runaway slaves near Pensacola, but Spanish territory was still seen as a haven for runaways, a reputation also encouraged by the Seminole Indians, harboring of fugitives there. The Seminole, a large and powerful coalition of southern Indian peoples, not only protected American slaves but also refused to recognize the terms that Andrew Jackson had dictated at the end of the Creek War, in which some of their lands near Georgia and Florida were promised away without their consent.

By November 1817, unrest along the Florida border broke into open warfare as Seminole and American fighters attacked and counterattacked along the Apalachicola River. At the start of this First Seminole War, Monroe and Adams ordered General Andrew Jackson to move south to take command of American operations, and they authorized American troops to cross into Spanish territory to pursue belligerent Seminole. John C. Calhoun, who had been appointed secretary of war in 1817, instructed Jackson to "adopt the necessary measure[s]" to pacify the Seminole, and Jackson responded in a letter to the president that he was ready to take "possession of the Floridas . . . in sixty days" if the President desired it.[7] Because of complications in the diplomatic communications between Florida and Washington, D.C., Jackson then thought that Monroe had communicated to him permission to seize Florida from Spain. Monroe later denied that he had directly authorized Jackson so explicitly, but the exact chain and content of their communications remains unclear to this day. On December 28, 1817, Jackson received a letter from Monroe that ordered him to take command of American troops fighting the Seminole and to prepare for "other services . . . depending on the conduct of the banditti at Amelia Island, and Galveston."[8] Whatever the meaning of this order, Jackson arrived on the Florida border with more than 1,000 troops by the beginning of March 1818, ready to fight both the Seminole and the Spanish.

At the beginning of 1818, Secretary of State Adams was negotiating with Spain's minister to the United States, Luis de Onís y González, to legitimize American claims to West Florida and to try to gain control of East Florida. But Jackson's military approach pushed the issue, and events began to overtake the negotiations. In early April, with his troops and a group of allied Creek troops, Jackson invaded Florida to pursue bands of Seminole and free blacks. Jackson seized the Spanish fort at St. Marks, burned several hundred houses, and executed two British citizens, Alexander Arbuthnot and Robert Armbrister, who, he claimed, were helping to incite the Seminole against the United States. On May 24, 1818, Jackson captured the Spanish town of Pensacola, drove out the Spanish governor, and issued a proclamation taking control of East Florida for the United States. Jackson himself was in bad health, so he returned home to Tennessee, but he had caused a powerful diplomatic shift that enhanced the power of the United States but created a mess for the executive branch.

Monroe and his cabinet faced a question over whether they would support Jackson's actions. Onís called for blood, London was outraged by the execution of Armbrister and Arbuthnot, and Henry Clay and other congressmen demanded that Jackson be censured for seizing Florida, but the executive also faced an immediate question of what to do with the territory. John Quincy Adams convinced a skeptical cabinet that they should support Jackson, and he managed to hold off British protests. Meanwhile, Adams continued negotiations with the Spanish, who soon decided to cut their losses and cede East Florida to the United States. Jackson was immensely popular, and the censure motion against him failed in Congress in February 1818.

Adams negotiated a wide-ranging treaty with Onís that further enhanced the position of the United States, not just in Florida but in the Far West as well. In the Adams-Onís, or Trans-Continental, Treaty, signed on February 22, 1819, Spain ceded all Florida to the United States and gave up any claims in Oregon and other parts of the Northwest. In return, the United States paid Spain $5 million and agreed to recognize Spanish control of Texas, although Adams refused to promise that the United States would not recognize Latin American countries that declared their independence from Spain in the future. The treaty was seen as a victory for Adams and the entire nation, one that enhanced its territory and legitimized Andrew Jackson's military aggression.

Other western territorial claims occupied American attention in 1818 and 1819 as well, and not all of them were settled as smoothly as the claim on Florida. In addition to subduing the Seminole (at least for the time being), Andrew Jackson continued his long-standing project of acquiring more Indian lands for the United States. While he was still in Florida, Jackson worked with Kentucky governor Isaac Shelby to conclude the terms of the "Jackson Purchase," an agreement in which dubious representatives of the Chickasaw Indians agreed to cede their lands between the Mississippi and Tennessee Rivers. The same year, the United States also purchased large tracts of land in central Indiana from a group of Delaware, Wea, Kickapoo, Miami, and Potawatomi peoples. The Treaty of Saginaw, concluded in December 1819 between the United States and several bands of Chippewa (Ojibway) Indians, also began the process of dislocating large numbers of Indian peoples around the Great Lakes. About that time as well, the United States moved quickly to bring territories in the Old Southwest and the former Louisiana Territory into the Union as states, a process that solidified American claims against Indian lands and further enhanced the country's continental spread. Indiana became a state in 1816, followed by Mississippi in 1817, Illinois in 1818, and Alabama in 1819. The country expanded at a rapid rate.

The territory of Missouri applied for admission to the Union at the end of 1819, but Missouri's application caused a political conflagration over the issue of slavery. Missouri was growing rapidly—it had been organized as a formal territory only at the beginning of 1819—and approximately 10,000 of its 60,000 inhabitants were slaves. The territory was settled heavily by southerners, who sought to expand their farming operations and to continue to use the slave labor they were used to relying upon. If Missouri were to enter the Union as a slave state, a careful balance that had been more or less consciously maintained over the years between slave and free states would be upset. The 22 states in 1819 were evenly divided—slave and free—and as the northern economic system was changing and slavery diminished there, a new slave state threatened to upset a political balance that seemed increasingly important. At a time when some moderate antislavery efforts (such as the American Colonization Society) were becoming more popular, even in the upper South, the Missouri statehood application set off a strenuous political fight over the power of the federal government to interfere with the institution of slavery and over the influence that slavery would have on national power itself.

The battle over Missouri statehood became even more polarized when New York Representative James Tallmadge, who had previously tried to disrupt slavery in the Missouri Territory, tried to amend the statehood bill to outlaw slavery in the future state of Missouri and gradually emancipate the slaves who already lived there. Even though a hope to restore the political balance between slave and free states arose at the very end of 1819 when Maine applied to split off from the state of Massachusetts and become an independent free state, a bitter political fight continued over whether the federal government could require the outlawing of slavery in Missouri. Tallmadge's amendments passed in the House of Representatives after a bitter debate, but as the debate moved to the Senate in 1820, the issue was not settled. While the United States rapidly expanded after the War of 1812 through military conquest, treaties, and the regularization of territories, in the case of Missouri that expansion threatened to bring about a crisis over slavery.

## NEW ECONOMIC WORLD/NEW ECONOMIC CRISIS

As all these territorial changes took place, the new market economy continued to surge forward, bringing with it political and social friction as well as economic growth. The nationalist Democratic-Republicans, who had put their transportation improvements on hold, continued to push for protectionist legislation to encourage internal American trade. In 1818, Congress augmented the trade tariffs established two years earlier and voted to extend the 25 percent tax on foreign cotton cloth until 1826. In 1818, Congress also voted for the first time to provide general pensions for Revolutionary War veterans, signaling a new level of willingness to use massive federal financial power.

The Supreme Court also evinced a new willingness to use federal power to protect private financial enterprise in the United States. In 1819, the Court announced two decisions that opened the floodgates for 19th-century corporate development. Chief Justice John Marshall, a Federalist who had exerted a powerful personal influence on the judiciary through decades of Democratic-Republican attempts to restrain federal power, now found a national climate more amenable to his progressive economic ideas. Marshall was a devotee of Alexander Hamilton's old-style Federalist belief in the power of the federal government to encourage a stable economy, and now his ideas went to work in a new capitalist age.

The court's first landmark economic decision came in the February 1819 case of *Dartmouth College v. Woodward*. Lawyer and congressman Daniel Webster had argued before the court on behalf of the trustees of Dartmouth College, his alma mater, that their rights as a private corporation had been violated when the state of New Hampshire altered their charter and sought to dictate administrative matters at the college. Marshall's decision in the case not only concurred with Webster's argument but took on ever broader importance. Chief Justice Marshall's bullying majority opinion in the case declared that a corporation was an "artificial being," whose contract rights could not be interfered with by state legislation.[9] The decision went far beyond simply protecting Dartmouth College from the state of New Hampshire. By broadly interpreting the contract clause of the Constitution, Marshall extended widespread protection to private corporations that would surely encourage new private business efforts.

One month later, the Court delivered a unanimous opinion in the case of *McCulloch v. Maryland* that went even further to define a strong interpretation of federal economic power. In 1818, Maryland imposed a tax on all banks not chartered in the state, a tax aimed directly at the Second Bank of the United States. Marshall's 1819 ruling in the case of *McCulloch v. Maryland* declared the tax to be unconstitutional. Marshall explained that even though the Constitution did not expressly allow the federal government in so many words to create chartered banks, Congress could, in fact, do so. The decision also reaffirmed Marshall's long-held idea that federal power superseded state power in many important ways. The court's decision in this case provided the basis for broad federal activism in the economy, and it set a precedent for interpreting the Constitution in a broad manner sympathetic to the exercise of federal power in general.

Although Marshall's decision in *McCulloch v. Maryland* confirmed the constitutionality of the Second Bank of the United States, the bank itself was not without problems in 1819. Land speculators and farmers had borrowed large amounts from it and other banks and financial institutions since the War of 1812, as their growing land prices and agricultural profits fueled their appetites for consumer goods and expansionism. The directors of the Second Bank of the United States decided to tighten credit in 1819 to avoid rampant inflation, and they began to call in banknotes and mortgages and to demand cash repayments from smaller banks around the country. The credit crunch resulted in a complete financial panic that caused prices to plunge and touched off an economic depression that would last for more than five years. Many Americans, especially in the credit-hungry West, blamed the Second Bank. As William Gouge proclaimed of 1819: "The Bank was saved, and the people were ruined."[10]

## GOOD FEELINGS?

By the end of 1819, the United States had clearly set itself on a new course of change following the War of 1812. The Federalist Party had all but disappeared from the national scene, and although the Democratic-Republican Party and President Monroe were said to preside over a new "era of good feelings," not everyone felt the same happy glow. A remarkable increase in manufacturing and market activity had spurred economic growth, but many individuals faced a tough transition to wage work and were in dire financial straits after the Panic of 1819. The Democratic-Republican Party took strong control of national politics, but the Federalists' demise did not entirely erase ideological differences between politicians who still disagreed over the extent and nature of national power in America. With the addition of new states and new territories and the success of Andrew Jackson's military adventures in Florida, the country expanded—which was not good news for the many Indian peoples who were dispossessed of their lands or the fugitive slaves who saw safe boundaries erased. The unsettled nature of the Missouri statehood question especially threatened to cause the breakdown of good feelings during Monroe's second term. Rip Van Winkle might have wished he could go back to sleep.

# CHRONICLE OF EVENTS

## 1816

Pittsburgh, Pennsylvania, is incorporated.

The U.S. Senate establishes a permanent system of standing committees.

Harvard Divinity School begins nondenominational theological education in the United States.

In Philadelphia, George Clymer builds the first hand printing press in the United States.

John Pickering publishes his *Vocabulary*, the first U.S. English grammar book.

Fort Dearborn, the site of present-day Chicago, is rebuilt after being destroyed during the War of 1812.

The country's first iron wire suspension bridge opens. The bridge, designed by Erskine Hazard and Josiah White, spans the Schuylkill River at Philadelphia.

New Yorkers form the American Bible Society, whose president, Elias Boudinot, wants to increase the number of people who own a copy of the Bible.

The first American prizefight takes place, and John Hyer beats Tom Beasley for the title of "American champion."

*March 14:* Congress passes authorization for a Second Bank of the United States, supported by both John C. Calhoun and Henry Clay. The bank is much needed owing to financial stresses caused by the commercial sanctions and war of the previous years.

*March 16:* A congressional caucus of Democratic-Republicans nominates Virginian James Monroe for president and New Yorker Daniel D. Tompkins for vice president.

*March 31:* Francis Asbury, Methodist missionary and bishop, dies.

*April:* Congress bans foreign citizens from participating in the U.S. fur trade. The move further strengthens John Jacob Astor's bid to create a monopoly in the lucrative fur trade.

*April 9:* In Philadelphia, the African Methodist Episcopal Church becomes a separate denomination. It is the first official autonomous black church in the United States. Former slave Richard Allen becomes the denomination's first bishop.

*April 27:* Congress passes the Tariff Act of 1816, which imposes levies on textiles, pig iron, leather, paper, and other goods that Congress hopes to encourage U.S. citizens to manufacture for themselves.

This 1819 engraving depicts a group of American Methodists on their way to a rural camp meeting. Camp meetings were among the most popular forms of religious participation among both whites and blacks in the early 19th century. *(Library of Congress, Prints and Photographs Division [LC-USZ62-2500])*

*June:* The Gas Light Company of Baltimore becomes the first city gas company in the United States.

A freak weather pattern causes 10 inches of snow to fall in parts of New England.

*June 10:* Delegates meet at Corydon, Indiana, to draw up a constitution and petition for statehood.

*June 19:* A group of traders and Metis outsiders kill 21 inhabitants of the Hudson's Bay Company Red River Colony (near present-day Winnipeg) at the Battle of Seven Oaks, waged over the right to trade food with the colony and in defiance of white rule.

*July 9:* The Cherokee nation agrees to cede land in present-day Alabama to the United States.

*July 27:* The United States invades Spanish Florida (which U.S. officials have been hoping to make part of the United States) to attack Fort Apalachicola, where army officers claim the Seminole Indians are harboring escaped slaves.

*December 4:* James Monroe is elected president by 183 electoral votes over Federalist opponent Rufus King, who receives just 34. Daniel Tompkins is elected vice president. The Federalist Party, hurt by its opposition to the War of 1812, loses seats in Congress.

*December 11:* Indiana is admitted to the Union as the 19th state.

*December 13:* The first savings bank in the United States, the Provident Institution for Savings, begins operation in Boston, Massachusetts.

*December 26:* Americans interested in gradually abolishing slavery and returning the freed slaves to Africa, including congressmen John C. Calhoun and Henry Clay, found the American Colonization Society in New York City.

## 1817

John C. Calhoun becomes secretary of war.

John Trumbull completes a new edition of his painting of the signing of the Declaration of Independence, which will become a popular print. A larger edition of the painting will grace the rotunda of the U.S. Capitol.

The first insane asylum in the United States begins operation in Frankford, Pennsylvania.

Thomas Gallaudet founds the Hartford School for the Deaf.

Harvard University begins the operation of a law school, signaling a change away from private study and apprenticeship toward more formal legal education.

The New York Stock Exchange receives an official charter.

The J. & J. Harper publishing house begins operation in New York City.

One of the country's first abolitionist newspapers, *The Philanthropist* of Mt. Pleasant, Ohio, begins publication.

This early photograph of the White House, taken in the 1840s, shows what it looked like shortly after it was reconstructed following the War of 1812. *(Library of Congress, Prints and Photographs Division [LC-USZ62-112293])*

President Monroe moves into the White House, which has been rebuilt following its burning by the British in the War of 1812.

It is likely that future abolitionist orator and newspaper publisher Frederick Douglass is born this year. Douglass never knew the exact date of his birth as a slave in North Carolina nor the identity of his father, whom he suspected to be his mother's master.

*January:* A meeting of free "colored" men in Philadelphia protests the American Colonization Society and declares that they will never consent to being sent to Africa or to leave behind their slave brothers and sisters.

*January 7:* The Second Bank of the United States opens in Philadelphia.

*January 11:* Timothy Dwight, the president of Yale University and the leader of a famous series of religious revivals on campus, dies.

*February 8:* John C. Calhoun sponsors a bill in Congress to fund $1.5 million worth of internal improvements for roads, canals, and other public infrastructure. President Madison vetoes the bill, which he claims exceeds the authority of the federal government.

*March 1:* Congress authorizes the Supreme Court to appoint a court reporter.

*March 4:* James Monroe and Daniel Tompkins are inaugurated as president and vice president, respectively.

*April 28–29:* Acting Secretary of State Richard Rush concludes an agreement with British ambassador Charles Bagot to limit the number of naval ships on the Great Lakes and to decrease the militarization along the Canadian border.

*May–June:* President Monroe tours New England and the Midwest to encourage nationalism and downplay the sectional division caused by the War of 1812. The Boston newspaper the *Columbian Centinel* declares that Monroe's presidency will usher in an "Era of Good Feelings."

*July 4:* Construction of the Erie Canal begins in Rome, New York.

*July 12:* Henry David Thoreau, the future transcendentalist author and political dissident, is born.

*August 18:* A committee is formed to investigate reports of a monster sea serpent spotted off the coast of Gloucester, Massachusetts.

This portrait engraving depicts President James Monroe seated in the White House with the U.S. Capitol in the background. Monroe was the last president who wore knee breeches and other 18th-century-style clothing while in office. *(Library of Congress, Prints and Photographs Division [LC-USX62-16956])*

*September:* William Cullen Bryant publishes his poem "Thanatopsis" in the *North American Review.* It becomes the first American poem to be highly regarded in Europe.

*September 7:* Paul Cuffe, the free African-American businessman who had settled some former slaves in Africa and championed the right of black suffrage in Massachusetts, dies.

*November:* The conflict between U.S. troops and Seminole warriors along the border between Florida and Georgia escalates into the beginning of the First Seminole War.

*December 10:* Mississippi enters the Union as the 20th state. The eastern part of the former Mississippi Territory is split off to form the new Alabama Territory.

*December 26:* War of 1812 hero General Andrew Jackson is placed in charge of American troops in the Seminole War.

## 1818

Romantic painter Washington Allston returns to the United States from England, where he had studied with Benjamin West.

The first American lithograph is produced.

Yale chemistry professor Benjamin Silliman begins publication of the *American Journal of Science.*

A group of Delaware, Wea, Kickapoo, Miami, and Potawatomi Indians give up their land rights to the "New Purchase" in central Indiana.

*January:* The ship *James Monroe* begins regular packet service between the United States and Great Britain.

*January 6:* General Andrew Jackson informs President Monroe that he will use the Seminole War as an occasion to capture Florida for the United States. President Monroe never responds, but Jackson continues with the military operation.

*March 18:* Congress passes the first federal legislation authorizing pensions for Revolutionary War veterans. Thousands of men pour into courts around the country to swear out affidavits describing their service in the Continental army in hopes of qualifying for pensions.

*April 4:* A law that formally sets the form of the U.S. flag takes effect. From this day forward, the flag will contain 13 red and white stripes and a number of stars equal to the number of states.

*April 7:* General Andrew Jackson's troops capture St. Marks, Florida, and the general arrests two British citizens who are suspected of assisting the Seminole Indians in their war against the United States.

*April 14:* Joseph Lovell becomes the first U.S. surgeon general of the Army Medical Corps.

*April 18:* General Jackson's troops defeat a combined force of Seminole Indian and African-American troops at the Battle of Suwannee, to end the First Seminole War.

*April 20:* Congress extends the Tariff Act to include more goods and raises rates on pig iron.

*April 29:* General Jackson orders Alexander Arbuthnot and Robert Ambrister, British citizens captured in the Seminole War, to be executed after they are court-martialed. Government officials are dismayed by Jackson's actions, which, they fear, will draw Great Britain into war.

*May 24:* General Jackson captures Pensacola, Florida.

*June 20:* The state of Connecticut opens voting to all white men, regardless of property holdings.

*October 19:* General Jackson and Kentucky governor Isaac Shelby negotiate the "Jackson Purchase," which causes the Chickasaw Indians to cede lands between the Mississippi and Tennessee Rivers.

*October 20:* An international convention establishes a clear northwestern border for the United States and opens Oregon formally to both U.S. and British settlement. The convention also settles American shipping rights off Newfoundland, which had been disputed since 1783.

*October 28:* Former first lady Abigail Adams dies.

*November 16:* At age 28, John H. Eaton becomes the youngest U.S. senator. He is sworn in despite the U.S. Constitutional requirement that senators must be 30 years old.

*November 28:* Secretary of State John Quincy Adams informs Spain that Seminole Indian violence in Florida may cause the United States to take control of the territory.

*December 3:* Illinois is admitted to the Union as the 21st state. Its northern border violates the terms of the Northwest Ordinance.

## 1819

Congress moves back into the U.S. Capitol, which has been restored since it was set on fire by the British during the War of 1812.

Norwich University in Vermont becomes the first American college to specialize in technical training.

Washington Irving publishes his collection of stories *The Sketch Book of Geoffrey Crayon Gent,* which contains "Rip Van Winkle," a rumination on how much America has changed since colonial times.

Mordecai Noah, a colorful figure in New York public life who will later proclaim himself to be a religious prophet, publishes the War of 1812 drama *She Would Be a Soldier.*

Academics at Yale University found the American Geological Society.

John J. Wood patents a plow manufactured with interchangeable parts.

Seth Boyden begins the manufacture of patent leather in the United States.

Congress offers a $50 reward for information about the illegal importation of slaves into the United States.

The Methodist Church establishes a mission to the Wyandot Indians.

*January:* A credit pinch and spiraling land speculation causes a severe financial panic that plunges the country into a four-year depression.

*January 25:* The state of Virginia grants a charter to Central College, which will become the University of Virginia.

*February 2:* The Supreme Court issues a landmark ruling in the case of *Dartmouth College v. Woodward* that strengthens the rights of private corporations and frees them from state interference.

*February 13:* Congress begins debate on an amendment proposed by New Yorker James Tallmadge that will outlaw slavery when the Missouri Territory becomes a state. The House passes the amendment, but the Senate does not. Debate over slavery in Missouri postpones its admission as a state.

*February 22:* Secretary of State John Quincy Adams concludes a treaty with Spanish minister Don Luis de Onís y González that grants the United States undisputed control over all of Florida and sets the boundaries between the United States and Mexico. The Senate quickly ratifies the treaty, but Spain is slower to do so.

*March 2:* The southern part of the Missouri Territory is split off to form the Arkansas Territory.

Congress establishes procedures to record the number of immigrants coming into the United States.

*March 6:* The Supreme Court rules in *McCulloch v. Maryland* that states cannot tax federal agencies, legitimizing the federal charter of the Second Bank of the United States and reaffirming the supremacy of federal over state power.

*April 2:* John Stuart Skinner founds the *American Farmer,* an extremely popular agricultural magazine, in Baltimore, Maryland.

*April 26:* The first U.S. chapter of the fraternal organization the Society of Odd Fellows begins operation at the Washington Lodge No. 1 in Baltimore, Maryland.

*May 24–June 20:* The steamship *Savannah* makes the first steam-powered transatlantic voyage.

*May 27:* Julia Ward Howe, who will compose the "Battle Hymn of the Republic" during the Civil War, is born.

*August 23:* Oliver Hazard Perry, the naval hero of the War of 1812, dies.

*September 24:* The Chippewa (Ojibway) Indians conclude the Treaty of Saginaw with the United States, the first in a series of treaties that give up land in the Saginaw Bay and cause the dislocation of many bands of Saginaw Chippewa.

*December 8:* The District of Maine, which has recently separated from the state of Massachusetts, petitions for statehood.

*December 14:* Alabama, a slave state, is admitted to the union as the 22nd state.

# EYEWITNESS TESTIMONY

During the six years I spent at Andover there were several revivals of religion. The master believed in their utility and did everything in his power to encourage them. We had prayer-meetings before school, after school, and in recess, and a strong influence was exerted to make us attend them.

*Josiah Quincy describes revivals at the Andover Academy (also known as Phillips Academy) in his memoir, 1816, in Hart,* American History, *III: 511.*

I have settled my purpose to remove from New Hampshire in the course of the summer. . . . On the whole I shall, probably, go to Boston; although I am not without some inducements to go into the Senate of New York. Our New England prosperity and importance are passing away. This is fact. The events of the times, the policy of England, the consequences of our war, and the Ghent Treaty, have bereft us of our commerce, the great source of our wealth. If any great scenes are to be acted in this country within the next twenty years, New York is the place in which those scenes are to be viewed.

*Daniel Webster in a letter to his brother Ezekiel Webster, March 26, 1816, in Webster,* Private Correspondence of Daniel Webster, *I: 256.*

What, then, are the effects of a war with a maritime power—with England? Our commerce annihilated, spreading individual misery and producing national poverty; our agriculture cut off from its accustomed markets, the surplus product of the farmer perishes on his hands, and he ceases to produce because he cannot sell. . . . The recent war fell with particular pressure on the growers of cotton and tobacco, and other great staples of the country . . . Neither agriculture, manufacturers, nor commerce, taken separately, is the cause of wealth; it flows from the three combined, and cannot exist without each.

*John C. Calhoun in a speech on the Tariff Bill before the House of Representatives, April 6, 1816, in Crallé,* Speeches of John C. Calhoun, *II: 165–166.*

Your indifference as to the result of the elections to the Presidency of the United States and to the office of governor of your own Commonwealth of Massachusetts . . . is the best of all possible political symptoms. It proves first, that you consider all the candidates as more likely to fill the respective stations, if suited to them, with credit to themselves and usefulness to the country. Secondly, that you consider no important principle of administration . . . to be involved in the issue. Thirdly, that the violence of party spirit continues to subside among us, and that there are no conflicting interests to immediate operation threatening our national union, or the unutterable horrors of civil war.

*John Quincy Adams comments on the political climate in a letter to his father, John Adams, April 8, 1816, in Ford,* Writings of John Quincy Adams, *VI: 2.*

So certain are the Effects of the requisite Arts of the Democracy, and so effectually prostrate is Federalism, that I have no kind of Expectation, that the latter can be again in Favor. The course remaining for Federalists, is to adhere to the integrity of their Principles; and they being out of the question as a rival Party, and the Republicans, so soon as this is understood, being sure to divide among themselves; the Federalists will be able to assist the true interest of Freedom & Justice, by giving their influence to the least wicked Section of the Republicans.

*Recently defeated Federalist candidate for governor of New York, Rufus King, in a letter to his son Edward, May 21, 1816, in King,* Life and Correspondence of Rufus King, *V: 537.*

During a long public life . . . the only great question, on which I have ever changed my opinion, is that of the bank of the United States.

*Congressman Henry Clay in an address to his Kentucky constituents, June 3, 1816, in Colton,* Life and Times of Henry Clay, *II: 10.*

. . . I have ever thought religion a concern purely between our God and our consciences for which we were accountable to him, and not to the priests. I never told my own religion nor scrutinized that of another. I never attempted to make a convert, nor wish to change another's creed. I have ever judged of the religion of others by their lives . . . for it is in our lives and not from our words, that our religion must be read. By the same test, the world must judge me.

*Thomas Jefferson in a letter to Washington socialite Margaret Bayard Smith, August 6, 1816, in Hunt,* The First Forty Years, *127.*

This engraving pictures Thomas Jefferson in his later years, which he spent in retirement at his estate, Monticello. *(Library of Congress, Prints and Photographs Division [LC-D429-29021])*

If the man may preach, because the Savior died for him, why not the woman? seeing he died for her also? Is he not a whole Savior, instead of a half one?

*African-American preacher Jarena Lee in her journal, 1817, in Johnson and Smith, Africans in America, 292.*

. . . To what can we direct our resources and attention more important than internal improvements? What can add more to the wealth, the strength, and the political prosperity of our country? . . . In fact, if we look into the nature of wealth, we will find that nothing can be more favorable to its growth than good roads and canals. . . . The more enlarged the sphere of commercial circulation, the more extended that of social intercourse; the more strongly we are bound together; the more inseparable our destinies.

*Representative John C. Calhoun advocates internal improvements in a congressional speech, 1817, in Hart, American History, III: 437, 438.*

Long and dismal are the complaints which the Indians make of European ingratitude and injustice. They love to repeat them, and always do it with the eloquence of nature, aided by an energetic and comprehensive language, which our polished idioms cannot imitate. Often I have listened to these descriptions of their hard sufferings, until I felt ashamed of being a *white man.*

*Moravian missionary John Heckewelder comments on the complaints of the Lenape Mohican people, 1817, in Hart, American History, III: 467.*

The establishment of a colony of free blacks in Africa, the land of their fathers, or some other distant quarter of the world, is beginning to be seriously agitated in different parts of the country, and will probably be brought before congress at the present session. . . . To the nation at large, the slave holding states in particular, this subject is full of interest. . . . Nor will the policy of such a measure be questioned by anyone who duly estimates the danger to which our tranquility is constantly exposed by having among us a race of people, possessing neither the rights of citizens nor the protection of slaves. With the example of Santo Domingo before our eyes, it is strange we would have permitted partial freedom to exist so long . . .

*The Milledgeville, Georgia, Journal comments on the movement to colonize free African Americans in Africa, January 1, 1817, in Phillips, Plantation and Frontier, II: 157–158.*

. . . they made up their minds to move to the far west, to Chatauqua County, N.Y. . . . we had a large covered wagon, a large yoke of oxen, and a large strong horse, just what we should want when we got there . . . We trudged on until we arrived in Albany, N.Y. This was the largest place I had ever seen. There we crossed the Hudson on a horse boat, which was a great curiosity to me. In those days there were no steamboats, canals, nor railroads, but a large public road, called the great western turnpike, with toll gates and taverns in plenty. . . . When we arrived in Buffalo . . . as we found the roads very bad, my brother-in-law took the heaviest of his goods from the wagon, and his family and shipped them on board a little sloop called the "Buffalo Packet."

*Lucky Fletcher Kellogg recalls travel conditions in 1817 in her diary, in Appleby, Recollections of the Early Republic, 149–150.*

Whereas our ancestors (not of choice) were the first successful cultivators of the wilds of America, we their descendants feel ourselves entitled to participate in the blessings of her luxuriant soil, which their blood and sweat manured; and that any measure . . . to banish us from her bosom, would not only be cruel, but in direct violation of those principles, which have been the boast of this republic. . . . We never will separate ourselves voluntarily from the slave population in this country; they are our brethren . . .

> *A meeting of free people of color in Philadelphia condemns plans to rid the United States of free blacks through the colonization of Africa, January 1817, in Aptheker,* Documentary History, 71.

Let it not be said that internal improvements may be wholly left to the enterprise of the States and of individuals. I know that much may justly be expected to be done by them; but, in a country so new and so extensive as ours, there is room enough for all the General and State Governments, and individuals, in which to exert their resources. But many of the improvements contemplated are on too great a scale for the resources of the States or individuals; and many of such a nature as the rival jealousies of the States, if left alone, would prevent.

> *John C. Calhoun advocates federal sponsorship of internal improvements in a speech before the House of Representatives, February 4, 1817, in Crallé,* Speeches of John C. Calhoun, II: 187–188.

I am not unaware of the great importance of roads and canals and the improved navigation of water courses, and that a power in the National Legislature to provide for them might be exercised with signal advantage to the general prosperity. But seeing that such a power is not expressly given by the Constitution . . . I have no option but to withhold my signature from it.

> *James Madison, in his last official act as president, vetoes the "Bonus Bill" that proposes to fund internal improvements, March 3, 1817, in Commager,* Documents, 212.

Our manufacturers will likewise require the systematic and fostering care of the Government. Possessing as we do all the raw materials, the fruit of our own soil and industry, we ought not to depend in the degree we have done on supplies from other countries. While we are thus dependent the sudden event of war, unsought and unexpected, can not fail to plunge us into the most serious difficulties It is important, too, that the capital which nourishes our manufacturers should be domestic, as its influence in that case instead of exhausting, as it may do in foreign hands, would be felt advantageously on agriculture and every other branch of industry Equally important is it to provide at home a market for our raw materials, as by extending the competition it will enhance the price and protect the cultivator against the casualties incident to foreign markets.

> *President James Monroe discusses the development of American commerce in his inaugural address, March 4, 1817. Available online. Yale University Avalon Project. URL: http://www.yale.edu/lawweb/avalon/ presiden/inaug/monroe1.htm.*

Among the first subjects which claimed the attention of Congress, was the act passed at the last session, altering the mode of compensation to the members of that body. It is unnecessary to remind you of the murmurs excited throughout the Union by this law. From every quarter it was severely anathematized, and all were forced to acknowledge that the great majority of the people required its repeal.

> *Congressman John Tyler in a letter to his Virginia constituents, March 7, 1817, in Tyler,* Letters and Times of the Tylers, I: 295.

These people are healthy, and the females and children better complexioned than their neighbours of the timbered country. It is evident, that they breathe better air. But they are in a low state of civilization, about half-Indian in their mode of life. . . . Their habits of life do not accord with those of a thickly settled neighbourhood. They are hunters by profession, and they would have the whole range of the forests for themselves and their cattle.—Thus strangers appear among them as invaders of their privileges; as *they* have intruded on the better founded, exclusive privileges of their Indian predecessors.

> *English land speculator Morris Birkbeck comments on white settlers in the Illinois Territory, July 1817, in Hart,* American History, III: 463, 464.

I assure you by this, that it is my wish to be good friends with the Americans, as well as all other people. I beg you to attend to no foolish talk or reports, that more any of my people wish to disturb the Americans who do not encroach on us. We are peaceable and wish to let others be so; but here are people with the Nation who make trouble. Listen not to them.

*Scottish trader Alexander Arbuthnot relays a message to U.S. officials on behalf of Creek Indian chiefs in Florida, July 1817, in Bassett,* Life of Andrew Jackson, *241.*

The man who has been introduced to the wonders and glories and pleasures of intellect feels himself elevated above the common sphere of mankind. He lives in an upper world and contemplates with calm indifference the labours of ordinary men, as of inferior beings, like the majestick eagle, who, heedless of the croakings of the ravens below, rises on his ample wing.

*George Bancroft in his commencement oration at Harvard University, August 27, 1817, in Howe,* Life and Letters of George Bancroft, *I: 30.*

. . . People seem to think we shall have great changes in social intercourse and customs. Mr. and Mrs. Monroe's manners will give a tone to all the rest. Few persons are admitted to the great house and not a single lady has as yet seen Mrs. Monroe, Mrs. Cutts excepted, and a committee from the Orphan Asylum . . . Altho' they have lived 7 years in W[ashington] both Mr. and Mrs. Monroe are perfect strangers not only to me but all the citizens. Everyone is highly pleased with the appointment of Mr. Wirt and Mr. Calhoun, they will be most agreeable additions to our society.

*Washington socialite Margaret Bayard Smith describes a change in Washington, D.C., at the start of the Monroe administration in a letter to a friend, November 23, 1817, in Hunt,* The First Forty Years, *141–142.*

The republican spirit of our country not only sympathizes with people struggling in a cause, so nearly if not precisely the same which was once our own, but it is working into indignation against the relapse of Europe into the opposite principle of monkery and despotism. And now, as at the early stage of the French Revolution, we have ardent spirits who are for rushing into the conflict, without looking to the consequences. Others are for proceeding more deliberately, and for waiting to ascertain what the nature and character of the governments in South America are to

Elizabeth Monroe, the wife of President James Monroe, was known as a quiet beauty whose reserve was a contrast to the previous first lady, Dolley Madison. *(Library of Congress, Prints and Photographs Division [LC-USZ62-113385])*

be, with whom we are to associate as members of the community of nations.

*Secretary of State John Quincy Adams in a letter to his father, John Adams, December 21, 1817, in Ford,* Writings of John Quincy Adams, *VI: 275–276.*

[Banks] hold the purse strings of society, and by monopolizing the whole of the circulating medium of the country, they form a precarious standard, by which all property in the country, houses, lands, debts and credits, personal and real estate of all descriptions, are valued, thus rendering the whole community dependent on them, and proscribing every man who dares oppose or expose their unlawful practices.

*A committee of the New York State legislature laments the lack of federal control over American banks, 1818, in Hart,* American History, *III: 442.*

Among the occupations to which my mother resorted, in order to support herself and her children, she established a circulating library . . . This collection of books comprehended the current literature of the day, and some of the standard English authors. It was kept in a room on the ground floor, appropriated to my mother as a "shop," in my grandmother's part of the old house. The circulation of the books, on the loan of which there was a small charge, brought in a little revenue; and as many of the books were the gifts of friends, who had purchased them for their own use, and after they had read them gave them to my mother, the expense for her of keeping of the collection with the new works of the time was inconsiderable. It was chiefly a collection of novels and poetry . . . The books were much sought for by the surrounding families.

*Benjamin Robbins Curtis remembers his mother establishing a lending library in 1818 in his memoirs, Curtis,* A Memoir of Benjamin Robbins Curtis, *I: 7–8.*

It was gratifying to be able once more to salute the President of the United States with the compliments of the season in his appropriate residence.

*The* National Intelligencer *newspaper rejoices at the reopening of the White House in time for the new year, January 3, 1818, in Seale,* The President's House, *I: 149.*

The Executive Government have ordered, and, as I conceive, very properly, Amelia Island to be taken possession of. This order ought to be carried into execution at all hazards, and simultaneously the whole of East Florida seized, and held as an indemnity for the outrages of Spain upon the property of our citizens. . . . This can be done without implicating the government. Let it be signified to me through any channel . . . that the possession of the Floridas would be desirable to the United States, and in sixty days it will be accomplished.

*General Andrew Jackson in a letter to president James Monroe, January 6, 1818, in Bassett,* Life of Andrew Jackson, *246.*

I am no propagandist. I would not seek to force upon other nations our principles and our liberty, if they do not want them. I would not disturb the repose even of a detestable despotism. But, if an abused and oppressed people will their freedom; if they seek to establish it; if, in truth, they have established it; we have a right, as a sovereign power, to notice the fact, and to act as circumstances and our interest require. . . . Whenever I think of Spanish America, the image irresistibly forces itself upon my mind, of an elder brother, whose education has been neglected, whose person has been abused and maltreated, and who has been disinherited by the unkindness of an unnatural parent. And, when I contemplate the glorious struggle which that country is now making, I think I behold that brother rising, by the power and energy of his fine native genius, to the manly rank which nature, and nature's God, intended for him.

*Henry Clay in a speech advocating liberty for Latin America and Mexico before the U.S. House of Representatives, March 24, 1818, in Colton,* Life and Times of Henry Clay, *I: 221.*

The late session of Congress has exhibited the parties of this country in a new and extraordinary point of view. The divisions heretofore so keen and bitter, between federalists and republicans, were scarce perceptible. Party spirit, inextinguishable in a country like ours, was in search of a leader, and the leader in search of party spirit, and both in search of pretexts. . . . the political atmosphere was calm and the attempts to blow up a gale were not successful. Neither South America, nor internal improvement, could be made to produce much agitation among the people. The foundations, however, were had for the future fabrication of opposition.

*Secretary of State John Quincy Adams in a letter to his mother, Abigail Adams, May 25, 1818, in Ford,* Writings of John Quincy Adams, *VI: 338–339.*

Last evening I received a note from the Spanish Minister informing me that he had just arrived here, and requesting an interview as soon as possible on affairs of the last importance to Spain and the United States. . . . As there was something tragical in the manner of both these gentlemen, I told them that they must take for nothing whatever I said to them, until I should have the honor of receiving your instructions; but that in my private opinion you would approve General Jackson's proceedings. That we could not suffer our women and children on the frontiers to be butchered by savages, out of complaisance to the jurisdiction which the King of Spain's officers avowed themselves unable to maintain against those same savages, and that when the governor of Pensacola threatened General Jackson, to drive him out of the province, *by force,* he left him no alternative but to take from him the means of executing his threat. Onis for the first time since I have held communication with him manifested symptoms of perturbation.

*Secretary of State John Quincy Adams in a letter to President James Monroe, July 8, 1818, in Ford,* Writings of John Quincy Adams, *VI: 384.*

Your attack of the Spanish posts, and occupancy of them, particularly Pensacola, [was] an occurrence of the most delicate and interesting nature . . . In calling you into active service against the Seminoles, and communicating to you the orders which had been given just before to General Gaines, the views and intentions of the government were fully disclosed in respect to the operations in Florida. In transcending the limit prescribed by those orders, you acted on your own responsibility.

*President James Monroe to General Andrew Jackson in a letter, July 19, 1818, in Colton,* Life and Times of Henry Clay, *I: 253.*

TEN DOLLARS REWARD. Ranaway From the Subscriber living in Jones County, on the 18th. Inst. A Negro Woman by the name of Amy, she is tall and stout built, Yellow Complexion, about 40 years of age, with several scars on her cheek and back of her neck, walks with her toes very much out, one of her fore-fingers is very crooked near the joint of the thumb, which prevents her from straightening it, and has a very sullen look.

*Joseph Hatch advertises for a runaway slave in the* Carolina Centinel *newspaper, July 25, 1818, in Phillips,* Plantation and Frontier, *II: 90.*

In attacking the posts of St. Marks and Pensacola, with the fort of Barrancas, General Jackson, it is under-stood, acted on facts which were, for the first time, brought to his knowledge, on the immediate theatre of war—facts, which, in his estimation, implicated the Spanish authorities in that quarter, as the instigators and auxiliaries of the war. . . . That his operations proceeded from motives of the purest patriotism, and from his conviction, that, in seizing and holding those posts, he was justified by the necessity of the case, and was advancing the best interests of the country, the character of General Jackson forbids a doubt.

The National Intelligencer *newspaper defends General Andrew Jackson's actions in the Seminole War, July 28, 1818, in Colton,* Life and Times of Henry Clay, *I: 258.*

In the fall of 1818, having been out on a frolic, when I came home Monday morning, my master threatened to flog me. I went into the field to ploughing without stopping to change my clothes. He came out in the forenoon and ordered me to take the horse to feed, evidently intending to whip me while the horse was eating. Thought I, if you flog me, old fellow, you will have to give me chase first. I loosed my horse from the plough, but instead of obeying his orders, I mounted and rode in haste to the opposite side of the field, dismounted and sculked [sic] into the woods.

*Slave David Barrett recalls running away from his master in fall 1818, in Blassingame,* Slave Testimony, *189.*

I have the honor to inform you that orders have already been forwarded to the commanding officers at Pensacola and St. Marks to deliver up those places . . . to the former governor of Pensacola and comman-dant of St. Marks respectively, or to any person duly authorized from you or from the governor general of the Havannah [Cuba] to receive them.

*Secretary of State John Quincy Adams in a letter to the Spanish foreign minister, Don Luis de Onís y González, August 24, 1818, in Ford,* Writings of John Quincy Adams, *VI: 445–446.*

I was sorry to find you understood your instructions relative to operations in Florida, different from what we intended. I was satisfied, however, that you had good reason for your conduct, and have acted in all things on that principle.

*President James Monroe in a letter to General Andrew Jackson, October 20, 1818, in Colton,* Life and Times of Henry Clay, *I: 253.*

You no doubt have learned long since of my being appointed on the Bank Investigating Committee. . . . Our wise men flattered us into the adoption of the banking system under the idea that boundless wealth would result from the adoption. Nature improved by art was to put on a more fascinating appearance. Mountains were to sink beneath the charm, and dis-tant climates, by means of canals, were to be locked in sweet embraces. Industry and enterprise were to be afforded new theatres of action, and the banks, like Midas, were to turn every thing into gold. The dream, however, is over,—instead of riches, penury walks the streets of our towns, and bankrupt-cy knocks at every man's door. They promised us blessings, and have given us sorrows; for the substance they have given the shadow; for gold and silver, rags and paper.

*Congressman John Tyler laments the collapse of the banking system in a letter, December 18, 1818, in Tyler* Letters and Times of the Tylers, *I: 303.*

Soon after landing I called at a hair-dresser's in Broadway, nearly opposite the city-hall: the man in the shop was a Negro. He had nearly finished with me, when a black man, very respectably dressed, came into the shop and sat down. The barber enquired if he wanted the proprietor or his *boss,* as he termed him, who was also black: the answer was negative; but that he wished to have his hair cut. My attendant turned upon his heel, and with the greatest contempt, muttered in a tone of proud importance. "We do not cut coloured men here, Sir." The poor fellow walked out without replying, exhibiting in his countenance confusion, humiliation, and mortification. . . . The most degraded white will not walk or eat with a negro; so that, although New York is a free state, it is such only on parchment . . .

*English visitor Henry B. Fearon comments on New York in his* Sketches of America, *1819, in Gilje and Rock,* Keepers of the Revolution, *236–237.*

*Resolved,* That the house of representatives of the United States, disapproves the proceedings in the trial and execution of Alexander Arbuthnot and Robert C. Ambrister.

*Resolution offered to the U.S. House of Representatives by Representative Nelson of Virginia, January 12, 1819, in Colton,* Life and Times of Henry Clay, *I: 252.*

We are engaged with Jackson and the President. I do not hesitate to say that the constitutional powers of the House of Representatives have been violated in the capture and detention of Pensacola and the Barancas; that Jackson overstepped his orders; that the President has improperly approved his proceedings, and that the whole are culpable. Yet I have greater confidence in Monroe than any other aspirant for the Presidency. He has justified a single violation of the Constitution; but they would establish all the roads asked for, all the National Banks which can be asked for, and do any-

thing which might, in their belief, promote the general welfare. Let us look well to our rights.

*Congressman John Tyler in a letter, January 19, 1819, in Tyler,* Letters and Times of the Tylers, *I: 304.*

Our triumph in the college cause has been complete. Five judges, only six attending, concur not only in a decision in our favor, but in placing it upon principles broad and deep, and which secure corporations of this description from legislative despotism and party violence for the future. The Court goes all lengths with us, and whatever trouble these gentlemen may give us in the future, in their great and pious zeal for the interest of learning, they cannot shake those principles which must and will restore Dartmouth College to its true and original owners.

*Joseph Hopkinson reports on the Supreme Court's decision in the Dartmouth College case, February 2, 1819, in Webster,* Private Correspondence of Daniel Webster, *I: 301.*

You observe that I have become a favorite target for the sharpshooters, but there appears to me to be something very whimsical in their choice of weapons . . . That the South American horse should be ridden as long as he had legs to stand on, and that he should if possible be spurred rough-shod over me, was to be expected. But that the champions of Puyrredon and Bolivar should, at the next breath, become the champions of Pizarro and Onis; that the sympathies of Buenos Ayrean patriotism should melt into tender mercies for Arbuthnot and Ambrister; that General Jackson should be insinuated a murderer for hanging murderers, and another officer extolled as a hero . . . all these, and numbers numberless more, are metamorphoses, logical and rhetorical, which put to shame all the metamorphoses poetical of Ovid. . . . The inveterate avowed enemies of the Administration have, however, been the most decided in their virulence against Jackson.

*Secretary of State John Quincy Adams laments congressional criticism of himself and General Andrew Jackson in a letter to his father, John Adams, February 14, 1819, in Ford,* Writings of John Quincy Adams, *VI: 528, 529.*

We have decided the great question as to the right of the States to tax the Bank of the United States, and have declared that they have no such power. This decision excites great interest, and in a political view is of the deepest consequence to the nation. It goes to establish the Constitution upon its great original principles.

*Supreme Court justice Joseph Story describes the court's decision in the case of* McCulloch v. Maryland *in a letter to his wife, Sarah Waldo Story, March 7, 1819, in Story,* Life and Letters of Joseph Story, *I: 325.*

You are pursuing, I observe, the true course with your Negroes in order to make their freedom a fair experiment for their happiness. With the habits of the slave and without the instruction, property, or employments of a freeman, the blacks, instead of deriving advantage from the partial benevolence of their masters, furnish arguments against the general efforts in their behalf. I wish your philanthropy could complete its object by changing their color as well as their legal condition.

*James Madison in a letter to Edward Coles, September 3, 1819, in* Memoirs and Letters of Dolly Madison, *164.*

A deep shadow has passed over our land: an commercial and individual gloom has created a universal stillness. In our remotest villages, the hammer is not heard, and in our larger cities the din and bustle of thrifty industry have ceased. . . . The . . . cause of distress is the sudden introduction of inordinate quantities of all species of foreign production, arising from false peace calculations, which have either deadened on the hands of our merchants, or paralyzed other operations . . . A remedy for this evil would be precious as rubies to him who values the institutions of his country, and glories in its indigenous greatness.

*An address on the national economy and the need for domestic manufacturing before the New York Tammany Society, October 4, 1819, in Colton,* Life and Times of Henry Clay, *II: 294.*

The Bank of the United States was chartered in 1816, and before 1820 had performed one of its cycles of delusive and bubble prosperity, followed by actual and wide-spread calamity. The whole paper system, of which it was the head and the citadel, after a vast expansion, had suddenly collapsed, spreading desolation over the land, and carrying ruin to debtors. The years 1819 and '20 were a period of gloom and agony. No money, either gold or silver: no paper convertible into specie: no measure, or standard of value, left remaining.

*Senator Thomas Hart Benton recalls the financial panic of 1819 in his memoirs, Benton,* Thirty Years' View, *I: 5.*

# 11

# Economic Crisis, Political Stability
## 1820–1823

The financial panic of 1819 left the United States in dire economic straits, and the country entered the 1820s on a shaky note. Average people suffered from the credit pinch caused by bank failures, and class divisions in U.S. society were ever more visible. In the midst of economic uncertainty, however, the new and different world of the 19th century began to take full form in the United States. The United States achieved, perhaps for the first time, some semblance of political stability, and the government extended its international influence.

During President Monroe's second term, the Democratic-Republican Party was firmly in control of national politics. But at the same time, new fault lines were developing in American politics, and in some ways the seeming consensus of the early 1820s hid the growth of new and very different political interests. Divisions within the Democratic Party began to develop that would shape the course of American politics right up until the Civil War. In the first years of the 1820s, the old, genteel world of republican politics had its swan song, as the new forces of institutionalized democracy that would coalesce around Andrew Jackson were gathering strength. Americans were about to begin living in a whole new political world, although none of them, including the politicians, were entirely aware of it.

## THE MISSOURI COMPROMISE

Even though the Democratic-Republicans had achieved party stability, issues remained that had the potential to cause political and social turmoil. Congress had spent much of the last part of 1819 not dealing with the economic crisis caused by the bank collapse, but rather debating the future of Missouri statehood. The initial petitions by territorial settlers asking that Missouri be admitted as a slave state were complicated when James Tallmadge and other congressmen tried to use Missouri statehood as a test case for the federal power to restrict the spread of slavery. Since Missouri would be the first state in the Union entirely west of the Mississippi River, its relationship to slavery seemed to point the way for future U.S. expansionism, but pro- and antislavery political interests were so sharply divided that forward movement on the issue was all but stalled at the beginning of 1820. Southern interests argued that the federal government did not have the power to restrict slavery in new states, just what several amendments to statehood legislation proposed by Tall-madge in 1819 intended to do. The philosophical and political dimensions of the question were still open at the end of 1819 when Maine sought to break off from Massachusetts to be admitted to the Union as a separate state. The balance provided by Maine, as a potential free state, offered the possibility of compromise on the Missouri question in 1820. However, the full relationship between federal and state power, as well as northern and southern interests, remained to be negotiated.

Throughout the early months of 1820, both the House of Representatives and the Senate, sometimes working at cross-purposes, took up the issue of how to bring both Missouri and Maine into the Union while smoothing over the slavery issue. All official Washington, D.C., seemed fixated on the question of Missouri statehood as proposals and counterproposals flew fast and thick (and while very little got done on any other legislative matter). Between January 13 and February 16, the Senate debated a Maine statehood bill sent up by the House of Representatives on January 3, and at the suggestion of the Senate Judiciary Committee, the body formally tied the issues of Maine and Missouri statehood together.

During the Senate debates, Illinois senator Jesse B. Thomas introduced an amendment that provided the basis for the eventual Missouri Compromise when he suggested admitting Missouri as a slave state, but establishing a line on the map at 36°30' latitude, north of which future slave states would not be allowed. One historian of the compromise, Glover Moore, writes: "Thomas was proposing in substance to make Maine a free state, admit Missouri with slavery, leave Arkansas and Oklahoma open to future settlement by slaveholders, and prohibit slavery forever in the remainder of the Louisiana Purchase north of 36°30', the southern boundary of the contemplated state of Missouri."[1] It immediately became clear that the idea was more popular with southerners than northerners, and although the Senate passed the measure on February 18, the bill still had a tough fight ahead in the House of Representatives.

The House of Representatives took a different approach, initially rejecting both the link between Missouri and Maine statehood and the 36°30' compromise line. The House twice rejected the Senate amendment that would have drawn a compromise on slavery, and instead passed its own amendment, put forth by New York's John W. Taylor, that would have outlawed slavery in Missouri outright. By the end of February 1820, Congress had committed the Missouri and Maine bills to a conference committee made up of members from both southern and northern states, in an attempt to reach some middle ground.

Even while the conference committee worked to put together a compromise bill for Maine and Missouri statehood, both senators and representatives continued to give rousing speeches in Congress that commanded great public attention and articulated as never before the country's divided opinion on the issue of slavery. So many people—black and white, men and women—crowded into the Capitol galleries to hear the speeches that Vice President Daniel D. Tompkins invited some of the more genteel female observers to take seats on the floor of the Senate (an act that irritated many senators who were deprived of their own seats). The attention of the nation's politicians and press seemed to be totally absorbed by the question of Missouri statehood and the broader issue of slavery.

Some observers worried that the open discussion of the slavery issue had only exposed unfortunate rifts in American public opinion, and some politicians worried that the Missouri question represented only the leading edge of a much larger conflict over slavery yet to come. Andrew Jackson worried that "The Missouri question so called, has agitated the public mind, and that I sincerely regret and never expected, but that now I see, will be the entering wedge to separate the union. . . . It is a question of political ascendancy and power . . .".[2]

Jackson's pronouncement that the division over Missouri involved a great deal of wrangling over power was correct, but his concern about regional division was temporarily set aside when the House and Senate finally reached a compromise at the beginning of March. Kentuckian Henry Clay had helped to broker a deal between pro- and antislavery legislators and between the House and Senate that brought both Maine and Missouri into the Union and, temporarily at least, preserved the balance between slave and free states in Congress. On March 15, 1820, Maine was admitted to the Union, and three days later Congress granted Missouri settlers the right to draw up a constitution with no restriction on slavery. Congress also approved the establishment of the 36°30' line to guide future admissions of slave or free territories, although that proviso remained the most controversial part of the overall Missouri compromise.

The compromise in Congress had not completely quashed public disagreement in the states over whether Missouri ought to be allowed to enter the Union as a slave state, and the fragile compromise threatened to fall apart when the citizens of Missouri drafted a controversial proposed state constitution. Missourians proposed in their new state constitution both to bar all African Americans from the state and to prohibit the state legislature from emancipating slaves in the future. The restriction on African Americans entering the state was especially controversial, since it applied to black citizens of other states and thereby seemed to conflict with the requirement in the U.S. Constitution that states not interfere with the rights of one another's citizens. Public and legislative debate dragged on throughout 1820. On December 12, the Senate passed a resolution admitting Missouri as a state but stating that they granted approval to nothing that "contravened" the U.S. Constitution.

The House of Representatives was slow to agree, and the legislative deadlock stretched into the next year. Henry Clay managed to broker a side deal that finessed the related matter of whether Missouri's electoral votes would count in the presidential election that reelected James Monroe at the beginning of 1821. But the final question of Missouri statehood remained unresolved. On February 22, 1821, Henry Clay convened a compromise committee of representatives and senators that worked out a deal to allow the president to proclaim Missouri to be a full state in the Union as soon as the Missouri legislature affirmed the supremacy of the U.S. Constitution. The House passed the compromise resolutions on February 26, and the Senate followed two days later. In June 1821, the Missouri legislature reluctantly promised to obey the federal constitution, and on August 10 President Monroe finally declared Missouri to be a state.

The Missouri Compromise never fully settled the issue of African-American citizenship, but its ingenious balancing of pro- and antislavery interests postponed deeper regional conflict for several decades. The compromise also began to reveal some new realities of political alignment in the United States. Monroe and the older generation of politicians seemed less effectual than ever, while Henry Clay and other younger men seemed fully to take on the role of statesmen. One senator called Clay the "Pacificator of ten millions of Brothers" for his role in brokering the two phases of the Missouri Compromise.[3] Clay had revealed himself to be a great compromiser, a skill that he would need in decades to come. The Missouri Compromise might have managed to moderate regional tensions, but it also made it clear that region would play a great role in the new era of American politics that was just beginning.

## DEMOCRATIC RUMBLINGS

The debate over slavery and the statehood of Missouri at times seemed to have very little to do with the lives of actual slaves, and white politicians mostly interested themselves in the larger political and regional issues that grew out of the compromise. But at bottom, the compromise revealed an increasingly difficult tension over race and slavery in the United States, especially now that the republic had begun to show real signs of democratization. The premise in the Declaration of Independence that "all men are created equal" had never been applied directly in the United States, but by the early 1820s an ever increasing number of outsiders in American society, including African Americans and some women, became more insistent about their democratic rights. After a conversation about slavery with Secretary of War John C. Calhoun of South Carolina during the Missouri debates, Secretary of State John Quincy Adams wrote in his diary: "What can be more false and heartless than this doctrine which makes the first and holiest rights of humanity to depend upon the color of the skin?"[4] Most politicians felt at a loss (or did not want) to find a solution to the political and moral problems posed by slavery, although more of them began to realize that the institution itself might pose increasingly difficult problems for the country. Former president Thomas Jefferson, who himself never freed his own large number of slaves, declared in 1820: "We have the wolf by the ears, and we can neither hold him, nor safely let him go. Justice is in one scale, and self-preservation in the other."[5]

Despite the ambivalence of the nation's leaders, some of the wolves, the slaves themselves, continued to try to break free. In the wake of the Missouri controversy, some African Americans took actions to reemphasize that slavery was both a personal and a political issue. One of the residents of Charleston, South Carolina, who had most closely followed the debates over Missouri statehood was Denmark Vesey, a former slave carpenter who had won the money in a lottery to purchase his own freedom. Vesey was a political man who had imbibed American democratic political rhetoric, and he professed an active faith in God and the kind of radical self-action pursued in the Haitian revolution. Although some historians now question how far Vesey's actual planning might have gotten, he worked together with slaves both in Charleston and on the surrounding rural plantations to plan a large-scale slave rebellion.

It is difficult to separate fact entirely from the exaggerated fear that gripped South Carolina after Vesey's plan for rebellion was uncovered, but he was accused of plotting to march on Charleston's arsenal to gather weapons for a huge revolt. The revolt was precipitated, in part, when local authorities closed a black Methodist church in Charleston, where Vesey was a regular worshiper. Vesey, who was given to using apocalyptic religious language, sanctioned the killing of white South Carolinians during the rebellion, and his message of violent resistance to the slave system found a number of strong supporters in and around Charleston. Before Vesey could take real action, however, his plot was betrayed, and the authorities intervened. In a wave of panic that swept the state, Vesey and 34 other African Americans were executed after short pro forma trials, and South Carolina courts banished 37 more people from the state.

Denmark Vesey's rebellion was a radical manifestation of what could happen when "lowly" Americans combined the power of democratic thinking with the hot-blooded reform Protestantism that was continuing to sweep the country in the late 1810s and early 1820s. Others took this combination in a less violent and radical direction, but they nonetheless used the twin ideas of democracy and reform religion to reflect on their social positions in a changing United States. One of the most popular movements that combined similar impulses, but in a completely different way than Denmark Vesey's, was a movement to reform and improve female education.

Following the American Revolution, a number of writers and schoolteachers, including Judith Sargent Murray and Benjamin Rush, had championed a rise in education for American girls and young women. To train women to raise children who could become successful citizens of a republic, new schools sprang up all over the country, and the educational level of girls, especially well-to-do girls, had risen steadily since the 1790s. Most of these girls' academies, as they were often called, provided a mix of academic and practical training, but in general female education remained less rigorous than male education. Girls, for example, seldom studied Greek and Latin, which were staples of formal male education and prerequisites for almost every college in the nation.

In the early 1820s, educators introduced a new and more rigorous kind of school for teenaged girls, the female seminary. Female seminaries—most of them founded, run, and staffed by women—offered a more rigorous curriculum than the girls academies. Moreover, they provided something closer to higher education for girls in an era when women were not accepted at any American college. Female seminaries trained a new generation of American women not just to be good republican mothers, but also to be active religious social reformers, public schoolteachers, and democratically minded housewives who supported their husbands' increasingly ambitious business ventures.

The most famous female seminary was founded by Emma Willard in Troy, New York. Willard, who had run a smaller girls' school in Vermont since 1814, tried in 1819 to convince the New York state legislature to endow a female seminary that would provide a rigorous education for girls and young women. When the legislature did not cooperate, Willard raised private funds and opened her school in Troy in 1821. Willard, who became a strong advocate for women's higher education and female intellectual capacity, taught a combination of classes that included classical languages, history, and science. Catharine

Beecher, the daughter of Second Great Awakening preacher Lyman Beecher, opened the Hartford Female Seminary in Connecticut in 1823. Beecher, who would become one of the most successful authors of the 19th century and an advocate of female domesticity, fostered her students' intellectual and spiritual development at the school, which combined academic with moral and religious education.

Although Beecher and Willard were not radical feminists, their schools trained a number of the most important political and women's rights activists of the next generation. Beecher's sister Harriet Beecher Stowe, the future author of *Uncle Tom's Cabin,* taught at the Hartford Seminary, and the future organizer of the Seneca Falls Women's Rights Convention, Elizabeth Cady Stanton, was a student of Willard's. On the surface, the education of white (mostly northern) women had very little to do with the kind of radical democratic action undertaken in Denmark Vesey's planned slave revolt, but both developments were outgrowths of the same kinds of social changes taking hold in the United States by the early 1820s. The rise of a more democratic and equalitarian strain in the American republic meant that very diverse groups of people, like slaves or middle-class white women, were able to define new courses of public action for themselves. Both slave rebellion and better female education signaled more extreme changes yet to come later in the century.

This photograph shows a statue erected in Troy, New York, in honor of women's educational advocate and teacher Emma Willard. *(Library of Congress, Prints and Photographs Division [LC-D4-18817])*

## DEMOCRATIC POLITICS AND DEMOCRATIC POLITICIANS

The impact of growing democratization upon formal politics was even more pronounced at the beginning of the 1820s. The Democratic-Republican Party remained in firm control of national (and most state) politics, and James Monroe was easily reelected for a second term as president in 1820. The seeming unanimity of the Democratic-Republican Party, however, hid the fact that a number of factions within the party were beginning to coalesce around different regional and ideologically divided leaders. A series of domestic political and international diplomatic events energized these leaders, some of whom—like Henry Clay, Andrew Jackson, and John Quincy Adams—had already started their rise to power in the years after the War of 1812. Each individual and each wing of the Democratic-Republican Party also took a slightly different approach to the new democratic developments that were promising to change both the tone and the content of American politics. Events caused a realignment of American politics that would take the population into a hot campaign far in advance of the 1824 presidential election, an election unlike any other that would redefine American political life for the rest of the 19th century.

The first signs that democratic and Democratic politics might be set for a realignment came in New York State, where Martin Van Buren consolidated his control over a new and more modern kind of political party organization. Whereas the Democratic-Republicans and the Federalists in the 1790s had considered party contests to be illegitimate and overly divisive (even though they engaged in quite a bit of campaigning against each other), Van Buren's political activities helped to legitimize the idea that political parties could represent the interests of democratic citizens and that an outright contest for power would not tear the nation apart. Van Buren led a democratic faction in New York politics, referred to as the Bucktails in honor of part of a ceremonial costume worn by their New York City allies the Tammany Society fraternal organization. Van Buren and the Bucktails built coalitions both with grassroots radical democratic organizations and with old-school Federalists to work against the elitist policies of New York governor De Witt Clinton at the beginning of the 1820s. During this period, Van Buren honed the skills that would enable him to build a whole new kind of Democratic Party.

Van Buren's commitment to democratic changes in the United States and his political organizational efforts were both tested in the New York constitutional convention of 1820–21. New York, like several other states, held a constitutional convention during these years that brought many of the ideas about more open and democratic politics under public examination. At the convention delegates from western New York advocated the removal of all property restrictions that kept poor white men from voting. Although conservative Democrats and De Witt Clinton were horrified at the idea of this "excessive" participatory democracy, Van Buren brokered a compromise. He claimed in the constitutional debate that "the character of the increased number of voters would be such as would render their elections rather a curse than a blessing," but he helped to push through the measure anyway, along with measures that destroyed most of the state institutions that propped up Clinton's excessive patronage power.[6]

Van Buren was ultimately more concerned that Clinton's executive power would stifle the general "democratical spirit" than he was worried about the effects of excessive democracy.[7] Even so, there were limits to the commitment of Van Buren and his Bucktail allies to pure democracy. At the same time that the New York constitutional convention removed all property requirements and enacted universal white male suffrage in 1821, they restricted black suffrage in the state more than ever before. After 1821, African-American men had to pay taxes on more than $250 in property, a large sum, to qualify as voters. New York was among several other states that simultaneously recognized greater political rights for white men while restricting black male suffrage.

Van Buren himself, who was seen as successfully moderating the interests of conservative and radical Democrats in New York, was elected to the Senate in 1821, where he hoped to take his party-organizing skills to new heights on the national scene. Van Buren especially hoped that he might rebuild a traditional alliance between New York and Virginia Democratic-Republicans that might allow him to wield power in the next presidential election.

Both John Quincy Adams and Henry Clay, who would emerge as presidential candidates in 1824, augmented their already highly respected reputations in the early 1820s. John Quincy Adams had gained particular notoriety for his successful negotiation of the Transcontinental (Adams-Onís) Treaty in 1818, and he was a powerful and influential secretary of state by the time the Senate ratified the treaty in 1821. Clay, who had built his reputation as speaker of the House, improved the political momentum he had gained from brokering the Missouri Compromise by also pushing his opinions on international diplomacy. A series of successful Latin American independence movements and European reactions to events in North and South America propelled Clay, and especially Adams, even more into the limelight by 1823.

John Quincy Adams was probably the most successful diplomat the United States had ever had. His considerable talents were put to the test by events that were quickly unfolding in Latin America and Europe. Chile, Peru, Mexico, Colombia, and Argentina were all agitating for independence from Spain. Henry Clay had been pushing hard since the late 1810s for the United States to support this movement and to aid these emerging nations in throwing off the colonial control of Spain. Adams was far more cautious, and he counseled President Monroe against prematurely interfering with Spain's colonies, especially since the ratification of the Transcontinental Treaty might be imperiled if he did so. In addition, Russia, Prussia, and Austria's so-called Holy Alliance was threatening to take the side of Spain, and the United States did not want to become embroiled in a larger European conflict.

In 1821, when Greece sought independence from the Ottoman Empire, Clay began to push even harder for the United States to aid and align itself with Latin American countries to provide a counterbalance to the Holy Alliance and other European powers, which might threaten republics in Latin America and Greece. Adams continued to hold out against such an alliance. He claimed in a widely read Fourth of July oration in 1821 that the United States "goes not abroad, in search of monsters to destroy. She is the well-wisher to the freedom and independence of all. She is the champion and vindicator only of her own."[8] Most American politicians held little regard for Latin Americans, and although they welcomed the end of Spain's colonial influence, they remained skeptical of the region's climate, Catholicism, and racial mixing. The U.S. consul in Brazil offered a typical assessment when he noted, "Hardly a worse state of society can be supposed to exist any where, than in this Country; where the climate also excites [them] to every sort of depravation and delinquency."[9] Despite this negative view, Adams, Monroe, and other American leaders recognized the benefits of strengthening Latin American trade and encouraging the spread of democracy and republicanism in South America. The question was how to do this.

By 1822, the Latin American independence movements had become so successful that Adams could no longer hold out against recognition of the newly formed republics. President Monroe, who had

This lithograph of an engraving by James Barton Longacre depicts John Quincy Adams, the brilliant diplomat and future president. *(Library of Congress, Prints and Photographs Division [LC-USZ62-126310])*

met with several visiting dignitaries and leaders of Latin American countries and had received letters from Thomas Jefferson encouraging recognition of the newly independent countries, instructed Adams to grant recognition and to open formal diplomatic relationships with Chile, Peru, Mexico, Colombia, and Argentina. Adams grudgingly announced recognition, but he was careful to specify that the United States would guarantee no intervention if the wars breaking out in Europe were to spread to South America. Henry Clay, who viewed supporting Latin American republics as part of his proposed "American System," which would enhance the economic power of the United States through internal improvements and strong alliances abroad, urged an even stronger intervention.

Ultimately, although Clay was pleased that Monroe and Adams recognized the Latin American republics, Adams's more restricted vision of U.S. foreign policy carried the day. The diplomatic wrangling over Europe and Latin America resulted in the creation of one of the most famous U.S. foreign policy statements, the Monroe Doctrine. Adams shaped the formal Monroe Doctrine as a response to British pressure to join a new alliance that would pledge to protect Latin America and to intervene if the Holy Alliance, which was meddling in Spanish affairs, found a way to help Spain regain its former colonies in the Western Hemisphere. Adams took advantage of Monroe's desire not to appear as the weaker relative of Great Britain, while still managing to keep the United States out of an alliance that would cause it to become overly involved in Latin America. Adams refused the British offer and carefully crafted the Monroe Doctrine, which would establish much of U.S. foreign policy for the rest of the century.

In his annual message to Congress on December 2, 1823, Monroe formally declared his new foreign policy to American politicians and to the rest of the world. Monroe expressed sympathy for Latin American and Greek independence, and he claimed that the United States had an interest in encouraging political liberty throughout the world. Nonetheless, Monroe outlined a policy of strict separation between European and North and South American affairs. The Monroe Doctrine proclaimed that the United States would not meddle in the problems of the "old world" as long as Europeans recognized that they could no longer interfere in the Western Hemisphere. Monroe spoke the words that Adams had written for him and made it clear that "The American continents . . . are henceforth not to be considered as subjects for future colonization by any European powers."[10] Monroe claimed that he did not wish the United States to become overly entangled in Latin American affairs by guaranteeing their independence, nor did he wish to overturn any currently existing European colonial governments. But he clearly established the view that the United States should be regarded as the preeminent power in the Western Hemisphere from that time on. Although John Quincy Adams would again have to deal with the consequences of Latin American independence for the United States during his own presidency, his formulation of the Monroe Doctrine established strong precedent for a whole era of U.S. foreign policy.

## THE EARLY CAMPAIGN FOR 1824

When politicking for the 1824 presidential election began early in 1821 and 1822, John Quincy Adams was the favored candidate of New England interests, although he described himself as a less than eager and charismatic campaigner. The other would-be candidates seemed fairly obvious choices to represent various regions and constituencies: Secretary of War John C. Calhoun, Secretary of the Treasury William Crawford (supported by Martin Van Buren), and Henry Clay. All these candidates enjoyed support from different wings of the Democratic-Republican Party, which began to hold caucuses to nominate them as presidential candidates.

The most magnetic force in the campaign, General Andrew Jackson, hardly seemed like a candidate in 1821 and 1822. In 1821, Monroe appointed Jackson as governor of the Florida Territory, which he had almost single-handedly won from Spain during and after the First Seminole War. Jackson proved to be an able governor, although his authoritarian style alienated many and aggravated political turmoil in the territory. In spring 1822, Jackson suffered an attack of ill health (exacerbated by bullet wounds received in several duels), and he retired to his Tennessee plantation, the Hermitage. Comfortably ensconced at home with his devoted wife, Rachel, Jackson seemed to be out of the public eye for the first time since the War of 1812. Nonetheless, he continued to receive letters and solicitations from political friends around the nation begging his opinion on political matters and the corruption scandals that made frequent headlines during the economic depression.

Rachel Jackson was beloved by her husband, Andrew Jackson. When she died before he took office as president in 1829, Jackson mourned her deeply for the rest of his life. *(Library of Congress, Prints and Photographs Division [LC-USZ62-25773])*

Jackson became so worried about the state of the republic that when a group of his friends and former political allies sought to have the Tennessee legislature nominate him as a presidential candidate, Jackson told them, "I have never been a candidate for office. I never will. But the people have a right to choose whom they will to perform their constitutional duties, and when the people call, the Citizen is bound to render the service required."[11] Jackson adopted the traditional republican tone of reluctant willingness to serve. Even though some prominent Tennesseans preferred Calhoun or Clay, the legislature unanimously voted to nominate Jackson for the presidency on July 20, 1822. In addition, to boost Jackson's chances in the presidential election, the Tennessee legislature also elected him to the U.S. Senate on October 1, 1823. Jackson had retired to the Hermitage in poor health and thinking that he would avoid public life, but instead, at the end of December 1823, he moved to Washington, D.C., to serve in the Senate and run as a presidential candidate. He wrote to a friend: "I am a senator against my wishes and feelings," but he took on the assignment with the vigorous approach that had always served him well as a military commander.[12]

The United States thus ended 1823 on the cusp of a momentous political change that not even the presidential candidates, who were beginning to campaign, fully grasped. The democratic ideals that had grown ever more influential in the American republic

The cover of this sheet music depicts Andrew Jackson as the "Heroe [sic] of New Orleans." Such heroic images of Jackson helped make him a successful political candidate. *(Library of Congress, Prints and Photographs Division [LC-USZ62-55789])*

since the 1790s now seemed poised to bear real fruit in the national electoral system, but vestiges of the old republican system remained. Democratic developments had affected life outside the halls of government, but Americans did not fully understand the long-term consequences of female education or thwarted slave rebellions. Soon, however, Americans would grasp that society and politics were changing, even if they were not completely prepared to deal with the consequences.

# CHRONICLE OF EVENTS

## 1820

An elementary school for free African-American children opens in Boston, Massachusetts.

Congress amends the charter of Washington, D.C., to provide for the direct election of the mayor.

Maria Hester Monroe, the president's daughter, is married in the White House to her cousin, Samuel Laurence Governeur.

The Pennsylvania Turnpike opens.

American missionaries travel to Hawaii.

Captain Nathaniel Brown Palmer of the Stonington, Connecticut, ship *Hero* discovers Antarctica.

Anton Philip Heinrich publishes *Dawning of Music in Kentucky,* which emphasizes the importance of American music.

In New York City, the Mercantile Library Association and the Apprentices' Library Association, public lending libraries, open.

The U.S. Lutheran Church founds its General Synod.

In Palmyra, New York, Joseph Smith experiences the first of his religious visions that will lead him to found the Church of Jesus Christ of Latter-day Saints.

Lambert Hitchcock opens his soon-to-be well-known chair factory in Hitchcockville (now Riverton), Connecticut. The factory produces chairs from interchangeable parts.

Rhode Islander Thomas R. Williams begins the mechanical production of felt cloth.

John C. Calhoun advocates that Indian tribal rights be destroyed and that the United States assume "guardianship" over Indian people.

*January 3:* The House of Representatives votes to admit Maine to the Union as a free state. The admission would tip the balance in Congress toward free states, so the slave states mobilize to oppose the bill.

*February 6:* The first recolonization of free African Americans begins as the American Colonization Society sends 86 people from New York to Sierra Leone, on the west coast of Africa, on the *Mayflower of Liberia.*

*February 15:* Susan B. Anthony, future reformer and women's suffrage activist, is born.

*February 16:* The U.S. Senate votes to admit Maine as a free state and Missouri as a slave state, which would preserve the balance between slave and free states.

*February 17:* The U.S. Senate adopts the key provision of the Missouri Compromise when it accepts an amendment accepting Missouri as a slave state, as long as slavery is outlawed in future states carved out of the Louisiana Territory north of a line drawn on the map at the 36°30' parallel of latitude.

*March 1:* The House of Representatives votes to admit Missouri to the Union as a free state.

*March 2:* In a compromise, the House of Representatives accepts the amendment that would admit Missouri as a slave state with the establishment of the 36°30' line.

*March 3:* The Missouri Compromise is formally adopted by both houses of Congress.

*March 6:* Congress passes the Missouri Enabling Act, which permits residents of Missouri to draw up a proposed state constitution.

*March 15:* Maine is admitted to the Union as the 23rd state.

*March 22:* Naval hero of the Tripolitan War Stephen Decatur is killed in a duel with James Barron.

*April 24:* Congress adopts a new Land Act that ends the policy of selling public lands on credit but lowers the sale price from $2.00 per acre to $1.25 per acre.

*May 15:* Congress proclaims that the illegal importation of slaves constitutes piracy, meaning that any citizens who import slaves may be punished with seizure of their ships and the death penalty.

*June 6:* Secretary of War John C. Calhoun sends Major Stephen H. Long on a journey from Pittsburgh to explore territory south of the Missouri River.

*June 19:* The new legislature of Maine charters Colby College.

*June 19:* A convention meeting in Missouri to draft a proposed state constitution votes to bar free blacks from the future state.

*September 26:* Daniel Boone, explorer and frontiersman, dies.

*October 18:* The United States forces the Choctaw nation to cede over 5 million acres of land and to establish definite boundaries for their territory in the Treaty of Doak's Stand.

*November 20:* The whaling ship *Essex* is sunk by a sperm whale in the Pacific Ocean. The incident will provide the inspiration for Herman Melville's novel *Moby-Dick*.

*November 27:* Edwin Forrest, who will become one of the most famous actors of the 19th century, debuts at Philadelphia's Walnut Street Theater.

*December 6:* James Monroe is reelected for a second term as president, with 231 out of 232 electoral votes, and Daniel D. Tompkins is reelected vice president.

## 1821

Mexico declares independence from Spain.

The first steamboat traffic on the Tennessee River begins.

James Fenimore Cooper publishes *The Spy,* his historical novel about Revolutionary War activity in upstate New York.

The first American book containing lithographs, *The Children's Friend,* is published.

William Cobett publishes *The American Gardener.*

Amherst College opens in Massachusetts.

This lithograph depicts Sequoyah holding a copy of the Cherokee alphabet, which he developed and which was adopted by the tribe in 1821. *(Library of Congress, Prints and Photographs Division [LC-USZ62-1292])*

Benjamin Lundy begins publication of his antislavery newspaper, *Genius of Universal Emancipation.*

The American Colonization Society founds the Republic of Liberia to provide a home for the freed slaves they hope to transport back to Africa. Very few people are ever settled in Liberia by the society.

The New York state legislature permits horse racing.

Junius B. Booth, the patriarch of the famous acting family that will produce President Lincoln's assassin, John Wilkes Booth, debuts as Richard III in Richmond, Virginia.

Massachusetts General Hospital opens in Boston.

The Cherokee officially approve Sequoyah's written alphabet for the Cherokee language.

Martin Van Buren begins serving in the U.S. Senate and building the Democratic partisan tactics and support in New York that will earn him the title "the father of modern American party politics."

The USS *Constitution,* under Captain Jacob Jones, is appointed as the flagship of the Mediterranean fleet.

*January 4:* Mother Elizabeth Ann Seton dies. She will later become the first American-born Roman Catholic saint.

*January 17:* The Mexican government makes a grant of land in Texas to Moses Austin, who begins to move American citizens into his colony there.

*February 7:* The crew of the U.S. ship *Cecilia* become the first documented people to set foot on Antarctica.

*February 22:* John Quincy Adams recommends to the U.S. Senate that the country adopt a uniform standard of weights and measures.

*March 5:* Having refused to be inaugurated on March 4, a Sunday, President Monroe is sworn in for his second term.

*April 15:* Andrew Jackson is appointed U.S. commissioner and governor of the East and West Florida Territories.

*May:* The English Classical School, the first American high school, opens in Boston, Massachusetts.

*May 31:* In Baltimore, Maryland, the Cathedral of the Assumption of the Blessed Virgin Mary, the first Roman Catholic cathedral in the United States, is dedicated.

*June 1:* Emma Willard founds the Waterford Academy for Young Ladies in Waterford, New York, where she provides female students with a rigorous

This 19th-century engraving depicts the official seal of the state of North Carolina. *(from Benson Lossing,* The Pictorial Field-Book of the Revolution, *1851–1852)*

academic educational program. Willard's school provides the first higher education for American girls and is the first female school to operate from an endowment fund.

*July 16:* Mary Baker Eddy, the future founder of the Church of Christ, Scientist (Christian Science), is born.

*August 10:* Missouri enters the Union as the 24th state.

*September:* The United States concludes a treaty with the Seminole Indians that requires them to move to central Florida, and, after 20 years, to move west to Indian territory.

*November 10:* Under the terms of a new state constitution, New York eliminates almost all property requirements that restrict poor white men from voting.

*November 16:* Missouri trader William Becknell arrives in Santa Fe after blazing what will become known as the Santa Fe Trail from Franklin, Missouri. The trail helps to open trade with northern Mexico.

*December 24:* Antonio Canova's *Statue of Washington,* which depicts George Washington as a Roman hero in a toga, is installed in the North Carolina state house in Raleigh.

## 1822

David Moncock, a Creek Indian, becomes the first Native American to graduate from the U.S. Military Academy at West Point.

The president of Yale University outlaws football on campus.

A 280-mile section of the Erie Canal between Rochester and Albany, New York, opens.

Bishop John England opens a Catholic seminary in Charleston, South Carolina, and begins publication of the first U.S. Catholic newspaper, the *U.S. Catholic Miscellany.*

Charles Willson Peale paints a self-portrait, *The Artist in His Museum,* that captures the fascination of his public museum in Philadelphia.

Washington Irving publishes *Bracebridge Hall.*

Mathew Carey's *Essays on Political Economy* advocate protective trade tariffs.

Nicholas Biddle assumes the presidency of the Bank of the United States. Biddle will do battle in the 1830s with President Andrew Jackson over the disestablishment of the bank.

Isaac McKim establishes the first steam-powered flour mill in the United States in Baltimore, Maryland.

Daniel Treadwell builds a steam printing press in Boston.

Vermonter William Church receives a patent for a machine to manufacture printing type.

Jedidiah Morse delivers a report to President Madison on the state of Indian tribes in the United States.

Red Cloud, who will become a war chief of the Oglala Lakota Sioux, is born.

*March 8:* President Monroe delivers a message to Congress calling for the recognition of the newly independent Latin American republics of Argentina, Brazil, Chile, Peru, Colombia, Mexico, and the Federation of Central American States.

*March 30:* Congress permits the formation of a territorial government in Florida.

*April 10:* Geneva College, now Hobart College, is chartered. The college will provide a "nonclassical" education to students who will become farmers and merchants.

*April 27:* Ulysses S. Grant is born.

*April 29:* Congress adopts a funding bill that will pay for repairs to the Cumberland Road with toll money. The road which will later become the nation's first federal highway runs between Cumberland, Maryland, and Vandalia, Illinois.

*May 4:* President Monroe vetoes the funding bill for the Cumberland Road because he believes the bill exceeds federal authority.

Congress agrees to diplomatic recognition of the Latin American republics.

*May 30:* A disgruntled slave betrays a plot by Denmark Vesey, a free black man from Charleston, South Carolina, to lead a slave rebellion.

*June 19:* The United States officially recognizes the Republic of Colombia.

*July 2:* After a short trial, the leader of a thwarted slave revolt in South Carolina, Denmark Vesey, and many of his coconspirators, are hanged. The fear caused by his planned revolt leads to the tightening of slave codes across the South.

*July 20:* The Tennessee legislature nominates Andrew Jackson for president.

*September 3:* The Sauk and Fox Indians conclude a treaty with the United States that will cede land to the United States but allow them to continue living and hunting on the land.

*October 4:* Rutherford B. Hayes, who will become the 19th president of the United States, is born in Delaware, Ohio.

*November 18:* The Kentucky legislature nominates Henry Clay for president.

*December 12:* The United States extends diplomatic recognition to the Republic of Mexico.

## 1823

Alexander Lucius Twilight receives a bachelor's degree from Middlebury College in Vermont and becomes the first-known black college graduate in the United States.

The St. Regis Seminary, the first missionary school in the United States for Native American boys, opens in Flourissant, Missouri.

Yale chemist Benjamin Silliman prepares the first hydrofluoric acid in the United States.

James Fenimore Cooper begins publication of his Leatherstocking tales with the publication of *The Pioneers.*

Clement Clarke Moore publishes "A Visit from St. Nicholas" anonymously in a newspaper.

The song "Home, Sweet Home" debuts in New York City as part of the opera *Clari.* It will become one of the most popular songs of the 19th and early 20th centuries.

The defensive post of Fort Clinton in New York City reopens as the Castle Garden auditorium, which will host popular entertainments and political events in the city throughout the 19th century.

John Dunn Hunter publishes his *Memoirs of a Captivity Among the Indians of North America.*

Charles J. Ingersoll defends American culture in his *Discourse Concerning the Influence of America on the Mind,* which he delivers at the American Philosophical Society.

Congress declares navigable waterways to be official post roads.

U.S. officials sign the Treaties of St. Louis with the Osage and Kansa Indians, who agree to cede large tracts of land in present-day Kansas, Missouri, and Oklahoma.

The first normal school, intended specifically to train teachers, opens in Concord, New Hampshire.

Andrew Jackson is elected to the U.S. Senate from Tennessee.

*January 27:* The United States formally recognizes Chile and Argentina as independent countries.

*July 17:* Secretary of State John Quincy Adams informs the Russian ambassador to the United States

This print depicting Andrew Jackson as the great hero of the War of 1812 is an example of the kind of widespread popular visual image that helped his political career, especially his campaigns for president. *(Library of Congress, Prints and Photographs Division [LC-USZCN4-188])*

that the United States will not recognize any Russian territorial claims or the formation of any new European colonies in North America. In 1821, Czar Alexander I had claimed all land north of the 51st parallel on the Pacific Coast.

*August 20:* George Canning, the British foreign secretary, asks American ambassador Richard Rush to have the United States join in a statement against European intervention in the Western Hemisphere. The British are dismayed at French actions in South America.

*September 4:* Gabriel Richard becomes the first Catholic priest to serve in Congress when he is elected as a nonvoting representative from the Michigan Territory.

*September 10:* The Champlain Canal, which connects the Hudson River and Lake Champlain, opens.

*November 7:* Secretary of State John Quincy Adams advocates a statement by the United States opposing European intervention in the Western Hemisphere, but he rejects the idea that the British should be included in the issuing of the statement.

*December 2:* President Monroe delivers his annual message to Congress. The message, mostly drafted by John Quincy Adams, proclaims the Monroe Doctrine.

## EYEWITNESS TESTIMONY

The students certainly considered the Faculty as their natural enemies. There existed between the two parties very little of kindly intercourse, and that was generally secret. If a student went unsummoned to a teacher's room it was almost always by night.

*Andrew Preston Peabody describes the student-teacher relationship at Harvard College in the early 1820s in his memoirs, quoted in Howe,* Life and Letters of George Bancroft, *I: 26.*

Our Vice President [Daniel D. Tompkins] was so gallant, that he admitted ladies in the senate chamber and appropriated to them those charming and commodious seats which belonged to foreign ministers and strangers of distinction, but their numbers were so great for some days, that they not only filled these and all other seats, that at last they got literally on the floor, to the no small inconvenience and displeasure of many gentlemen.

*Washington socialite Margaret Bayard Smith describes female attendance in the U.S. Senate, January 30, 1820, in Hunt,* The First Forty Years, *149.*

"Missouri" is the only word ever repeated here by the politician. The discussion is over in the Senate, and the decision is against the restriction by a respectable majority. I fear, however, that it is only a nominal majority, and one looking to a compromise. In our House the debate waxes warmer every day. When it will terminate cannot well be foreseen; and what may be the consequences is almost beyond the art of prophesy. We are abused and deeply aggrieved by the grossest ribaldry which newspaper editors and writers can bestow upon us, and to reach us, and affect us vitally, Missouri is the scape-goat. . . . Men talk of a dissolution of the Union with perfect non-chalance and indifference. I for one, however, will not be frightened at false fire.

*Virginia congressman John Tyler describes the mood in Congress as the Missouri Compromise is debated, in a letter, February 5, 1820, in Tyler,* Letters and Times of the Tylers, *I: 316.*

Slavery has been represented on all hands as a dark cloud, and the candor of the gentleman from Massachusetts (Mr. Whitman) drove him to the admission that it would be well to disperse this cloud. In this sentiment I entirely concur with him. How can you otherwise disarm it? Will you suffer it to increase in its darkness over one particular portion of this land, till its horrors shall burst upon it? . . . The man of the North is far removed from its influence; he may smile and experience no disquietude. But exclude this property from Missouri, by the exercise of an arbitrary power; shut it out from the Territories; and I maintain that you do not consult the interests of this Union.

*Congressman John Tyler comments on slavery and the debate over the Missouri Compromise in a letter, February 6, 1820, in Tyler,* Letters and Times of the Tylers, *I: 317.*

The Missouri question still depends in the House, but is approaching its termination, and several votes are trembling. . . . There is a great deal of heat and irritation, but most probably a compromise will take place, admitting Missouri into the Union without the restriction, and imposing it on all the other Territories. Virginia is most outrageous against the compromise; she insists that the Territories shall be free to have slaves, and uses all sorts of threats against all who dare propose a surrender of this privilege.

*Supreme Court Justice Joseph Story in a letter to his brother, February 27, 1820, in Story,* Life and Letters of Joseph Story, *I: 361–362.*

You will be no way surprised when I inform you that I am not at all pleased with my new profession—it requires more intense labour, more awful responsibility, and indeed it is in every respect less suited to my circumstances, and my disposition.—It is not in the scope of my powers of language to describe my feelings on the first occasion that a man was tried before me for his life—For I have just passed through two trials of that awful character.—The first was so critical that the weight of a hair would have saved or lost his life, & in that trying moment I was compelled to decide.

*North Carolina Superior Court judge Willie P. Magnum in a letter to his wife, Charity Magnum, in Shanks,* The Papers of Willie Person Magnum, *I: 21.*

. . . It is expedient to provide by law a suitable outfit and salary for such minister or ministers as the president, by and with the advice and consent of the senate, may send to any of the governments of South America, which have established, and are maintaining, their independence of Spain.

*Henry Clay supports opening diplomatic relations with
Latin American governments in a congressional
resolution, April 3, 1820, in Colton,* Life and Times
of Henry Clay, *I: 239.*

Since the first colonization of America, the principal direction of the labor and capital of the inhabitants, has been to produce raw materials for the consumption or fabrication of foreign nations. We have always had, in great abundance, the means of subsistence, but we have derived chiefly from other countries, our clothes, and the instruments of defense. . . . The limited amount of surplus produce, resulting from the smallness of our numbers, and the long and arduous convulsions of Europe, secured us good markets for that surplus in her ports, or those of her colonies. But those convulsions have not ceased, and our population has reached nearly ten millions. A new epoch has arisen . . .

*Congressman Henry Clay arguing in favor of the
proposed tariff of 1820 on the floor of the House of
Representatives, April 20, 1820, in Colton,* Life and
Times of Henry Clay, *II: 146–147.*

I am clearly of your opinion that, for the present, we ought to be content with the Floridas—fortify them, concentrate our population, confine our frontier to proper limits, until our country, to those limits, is filled with a dense population. It is the denseness of our population that gives strength and security to our frontier. With the Floridas in our possession, our fortifications completed, Orleans, the great emporium of the West, is secure.

*General Andrew Jackson in a letter to President James
Monroe, June 20, 1820, in Bassett,* Life of
Andrew Jackson, *272.*

. . . So much has been said, written and published on the "Missouri question" that the people, in general, are displeased with the mere sight of words in print, and few are willing to read much more on the subject. . . . It is *established* (so far as large majorities in both houses of congress can establish it), that the *power* to check the progress of a slave population within the *territories* of the United States, exists by the constitution; but admitted, that it was not expedient to exert that power in regard to Missouri and Arkansaw [sic].

*Newspaper editor Hezekiah Niles, fall 1820, in Hart,*
American History, *III: 455.*

On this day, the 25th of Nov. the APPRENTICES' LIBRARY of the city of New-York is to be opened . . . The free institutions of the United States rest on public opinion;—while this is correct and enlightened, we have a perpetual guarantee for their prosperity and duration. A people will never submit to the subversion of their rights, nor will usurpers dare to invade them, while the great mass of the community are possessed of intelligence, and think and act for themselves. Perhaps among no class of citizens is it more important to cultivate elementary education with assiduity, than among the different denominations of mechanics' apprentices. . . . Who can tell how many Franklins may be among you?

*Thomas Merecin in a public oration to honor the opening
of the Apprentices' Library in New York City,
November 25, 1820, in Gilje and Rock,*
Keepers of the Revolution, *52, 53.*

It shall be the duty of the general assembly, as soon as may be, to pass such laws as may be necessary, to prevent free Negroes and mulattoes from coming to or settling in this state, under any pretext whatsoever.

*A clause in the proposed Missouri constitution, 1820, in
Colton,* Life and Times of Henry Clay, *I: 280.*

The Missouri question is again up, and fills me with no small alarm . . . Missouri, I think, will not be admitted. The objection lies to the feature in her Constitution relative to free negroes, etc. This she can, if she be not carried away by passion, readily expunge, and next year she may come into the Union; but if she refuses to do so, I know not what may be the result.

*Virginia congressman John Tyler in a letter to a friend,
December 8, 1820, in Tyler,* Letters and Times of the
Tylers, *I: 336.*

The apprehended danger from the experiment of universal suffrage applied to the whole legislative department, is no dream of imagination. It is too mighty an excitement for the moral constitution of men to endure. The tendency of universal suffrage, is to jeopardize the rights of property, and the principles of liberty. . . . The growth of the city of New York is enough to startle and awaken those who are pursuing the *ignus fatuus* of universal suffrage. . . . It is rapidly swelling into the unwieldy and burdensome pauperism, of an European metropolis.

*Judge James Kent in a speech opposing constitutional changes in New York State, 1821, in Craven et al.,* Documentary History, *319.*

Our friend Webster has gained a noble reputation. He was before known as a lawyer; but he has now secured the title of an eminent and enlightened statesman. It was a glorious field for him, and he has had an ample harvest. The whole force of his great mind was brought out, and in several speeches he commanded universal admiration. . . . On the whole, I was never more proud of any display than his in my life.

*Supreme Court Justice Joseph Story comments in a letter on Daniel Webster's legislative success in the convention that split Maine from Massachusetts, January 21, 1821, in Story,* Life and Letters of Joseph Story, *I: 395–396.*

*Resolved,* That the state of Missouri be admitted into the Union on an equal footing with the original states, in all respects whatever, upon the fundamental condition, that the said state shall never pass any law preventing any description of persons from coming to and settling in the said state, who now are, or may hereafter become, citizens of any of the states of this Union . . . and provided, further, that nothing herein contained shall be construed to take from the state of Missouri, when admitted into the Union, the exercise of any right or power which can now be constitutionally exercised by any of the original states.

*A resolution of the U.S. House of Representatives, February 10, 1821, in Colton,* Life and Times of Henry Clay, *I: 282.*

On Sunday morning, about nine o'clock, we left Alexandria for Mount Vernon . . . Just below the slope of the hill on this side, and at no great distance from the river, is the tomb which contains the mortal remains of this truly great and wise man. It is a humble, family vault, built of brick, on the declivity of the hill, and covered over with soil; and an old wooden door above the ground, now kept locked, is all that hides his coffin from the vulgar gaze. A few scattered cedars surrounded the tomb; they are old and drooping, and seem long to have toiled with the wintry blast; all about the tomb has the air of neglect and decay. I felt awed as I gazed upon the scene; it was a melancholy mixed with profound feelings.

*Supreme Court Justice Joseph Story describes a visit to the tomb of George Washington in a letter to his wife, Sarah Waldo Story, February 27, 1821, in Story,* Life and Letters of Joseph Story, *I: 398–399.*

Twenty-five years ago the river Mississippi was shut up and our Western brethren had no outlet for their commerce. What has been the progress since that time? The river has not only become the property of the United States from its source to the ocean, with all its tributary streams (with the exception of the upper part of the Red River only), but Louisiana, with a fair and liberal boundary on the western side and the Floridas on the eastern, have been ceded to us. The United States now enjoy the complete and uninterrupted sovereignty over the whole territory from St. Croix to the Sabine. New States, settled from among ourselves in this and in other parts, have been admitted into our Union in equal participation in the national sovereignty with the original States. Our population has augmented in an astonishing degree and extended in every direction. We now, fellow-citizens, comprise within our limits the dimensions and faculties of a great power under a Government possessing all the energies of any government ever known to the Old World, with an utter incapacity to oppress the people.

*President James Monroe in his second inaugural address, March 5, 1821. Available online. Yale University Avalon Project. URL: http://www.yale.edu/lawweb/avalon/presiden/inaug/monroe2.htm.*

. . . Yesterday was the day appointed for the Inauguration of the President, upon his reappointment to office. A vast crowd was collected in the Capitol to witness the ceremony. It was, according to arrangement, to be performed in the Chamber of the House of Representatives. This is a most splendid and magnificent Hall . . . The hall was early thronged with ladies and gentlemen of the first distinction, who had come from the neighbouring cities to witness the scene. The whole area was crowded to excess, and the galleries appeared to be almost weighed down by their burden. About twelve o'clock the President came into the hall . . . His appearance was very impressive. . . . As soon as the speech was concluded, the marine corps of musicians who were in the gallery, played "Hail, Columbia," which was succeeded by "Yankee Doodle," and after some hurrahs from the crowd, the President received the congratulations of the assembly and retired. Altogether, the scene was truly striking and grand.

*Supreme Court Justice Joseph Story describes James Monroe's inauguration in a letter to his wife, Sarah Waldo Story, March 6, 1821, in Story,* Life and Letters of Joseph Story, *I: 399, 400, 401.*

. . .the statue of Washington, Executed at Rome by Canova, for the state of North Carolina . . . is intended to represent the immortal hero in the act of writing his farewell address. . . . He is clad in the roman costume . . . and the other emblems of Roman taste . . . The statue is of white marble of the finest kind. It rests upon a pedestal of the same kind of marble, upon the sides of which are represented in emblematical workmanship the four principal events of Washington's life. . . . It is said the artist has exercised his own taste entirely in the position and costume of the statue.

*The* Vermont Gazette *reprints a report from the* Norfolk Herald *about Canova's controversial statue of George Washington,* Vermont Gazette *(Bennington), July 17, 1821.*

[The] admission of the state of Missouri . . . was the exciting and agitating question of the session of 1820–'21. The question of restriction, that is, of prescribing the abolition of slavery within her limits, had been "compromised" the session before, by agreeing to admit the States without restriction, and abolishing it in all the remainder of the province of Louisiana, north and west of the State of Missouri, and north of the parallel of 36 degrees, 30 minutes. This "compromise" was the work of the South, sustained by the united voice of Mr. Monroe's cabinet, the united voices of the Southern senators, and a majority of the Southern representatives.

*Senator Thomas Hart Benton describes his 1821 view of the Missouri Compromise in his memoirs, Benton,* Thirty Years' View, *8.*

Mr. Scott arrived at the salt sulphur after we did, he came on here with us & staid [sic] a day & returned

to the Salt Sulphur with the intention of staying a week there, but was taken sick & went on to the warm springs. . . . I expect there is about twenty here at this time, or perhaps more. A gentleman died here about 4 weeks ago—with the consumption & there is a gentleman in the cabin next to us that the Dr's have despaired of, with the bilious fever, he has the most attentive & affectionate wife I ever saw.

*Martha A. Cain describes attendance at a Virginia sulfur spring, a popular health spa, in a letter to her sister, Charity Magnum, August 30, 1821, in Shanks,* The Papers of Willie Person Magnum, *I: 35–36.*

The first object of the popular leaders of the day is to win over to their own purposes those who are respectable and command influence; if they fail in this, their next object is to destroy that influence and respectability, by diminishing public confidence . . .

*Supreme Court Justice Joseph Story in a letter to a political associate, September 9, 1821, in* Life and Letters of Joseph Story, *I: 402–403.*

Nor need they expect any other than Mr. Adams to be supported in this state unless some Southern candidate should arise—and I am certain no man in the South could concentrate the votes of the South and West, but Mr. Calhoun—and you are at liberty to say in my name both to my friends and enemies—that I will as far as my influence extends support Mr. Adams unless Mr. Calhoun should be brought forward, and that I have no doubt but Mr. Adams will outpole [sic] Mr. Crawford in the South and West . . . As to Wm. H. Crawford you know my opinion. I would support the Devil first.

*Andrew Jackson assesses the early presidential candidates for 1824 (little realizing that he himself will eventually join the race) in a letter, December 6, 1821, in Bassett,* Life of Andrew Jackson, *326–327.*

. . . They are certainly an intelligent and noble part of our race, and capable of high moral and intellectual improvement. . . . They are a race, who on every correct principle ought to be saved from extinction . . . To remove these Indians far from their present homes . . . into a wilderness, among strangers, possibly hostile, to live as their new neighbors live, by hunting, a state to which they have not lately been accustomed, and which is incompatible with civilization, can hardly be reconciled with the professed views and objects of the Government in civilizing them.

*Jedidiah Morse reports on the state of American Indian society in the Great Lakes and along the Mississippi to President James Monroe, 1822, in* Chronology of the American Indian, *141.*

I know Denmark Vesey. On one occasion he asked me what news, I told him none; he replied we are free but the white people won't let us be so, and the only way is to rise up and fight the whites. . . . Vesey told me he was the leader in this plot. . . . Vesey induced me to join; when I went to Vesey's house there was a meeting there, the room was full of people, but none of them white. That night at Vesey's we determined to have arms made, and each man put in 12 ½ cents toward that purpose.

*One of Denmark Vesey's accused conspirators, Rolla, describes preparation for their armed slave rebellion at his trial in South Carolina, 1822, in Aptheker,* Documentary History, *76.*

There is much stir and buzz about Presidential candidates here. Mr. Clay's friends are certainly numerous; whether it be because his is the most recent nomination, or for what other reason, the fact is he is just now much talked about. I think it will be a busy winter, in talking and electioneering. My own opinion is, but I would not intimate it to others, that Mr. Clay considers himself a candidate, and means to run the race.

*Daniel Webster in a letter to Supreme Court Justice Joseph Story, January 14, 1822, in Webster,* Private Correspondence of Daniel Webster, *I: 319–320.*

We went to the President's on Monday to pay him our annual visit of ceremony. It so happened that, at the time, he was having an interview, and holding a talk with a considerable deputation of various tribes of Indians, from the most savage and distant parts. . . . It was to me as spectacle entirely new. The President first made a speech to them, which was interpreted by various interpreters in single sentences, and at the end of each they returned a sort of murmuring at sound in approbation. After this, the Chiefs stood up, and each in turn made a short speech to the President, which was in like manner interpreted. Their gestures and actions were very

strong and marked . . . Nothing could exceed the masculine cast of their forms, or the bold, decisive character of their movements.

*Supreme Court Justice Joseph Story reports on a visit to the White House in a letter to his wife, Sarah Waldo Story, February 10, 1822, in Story,* Life and Letters of Joseph Story, *I: 412–413.*

The members of the general assembly of the state of Tennessee, taking into view the great importance of the selection of a suitable person to fill the presidential chair at the approaching election for the chief magistracy of the United States, and seeing that those who achieved our independence, and laid the foundations of the American republic, have nearly passed away; and believing that moral worth, political requirements and decision of character, should unite in the individual who may be called to preside over the people of the United States, have turned their eyes to *Andrew Jackson,* late major-general in the armies of the United States. In him they behold the soldier, the statesman, and the honest man; he deliberates, he decides, and he acts; he is calm in deliberation, cautious in decision, efficient in action. Such a man we are willing to aid in electing to the highest office in the gift of a free people.

*The Tennessee legislature nominates Andrew Jackson as a presidential candidate, July 20, 1822, in Bassett,* Life of Andrew Jackson, *328.*

I have no desire, nor do I expect ever to be called to fill the Presidential chair, but should this be the case, contrary to my wishes or expectations, I am determined it shall be without any exertion on my part.

*Andrew Jackson in a letter to a friend, August 1, 1822, in Bassett,* Life of Andrew Jackson, *328–329.*

In entering the bay of New York I could do nothing but admire; I thought I had never seen such deep and beautiful green as I then saw all along the Jersey shore; it seemed to me, that no country has such neat and pretty villages, such cheerful townships, such a transparent atmosphere and glowing sky as our own. I was inclined to find everything agreeable and beautiful. Yet on traveling from New York to Worcester [Mass.] I could not but feel that, pleasant as the general surface of our country may be, it is not formed after the higher laws of beauty. I look in vain for the land of romance, for the bold scenery or the luxuriant landscapes, which charmed me in other countries . . . I remember, that our country is the land of our hearts for different and more serious reasons: I think of it as the place of refuge for pure religion, for civil liberties, for domestic happiness, and for all the kindly affections of social life . . . I love my country; I love it deeply.

*George Bancroft in a letter to his friend upon returning from his postgraduate education in Europe, September 24, 1822, in Howe,* Life and Letters of George Bancroft, *I: 159.*

. . . Disease and death, are making sad havoc in many parts of our country, and tho' some are more dreadfully affected, few are exempt. Our city is very sickly. . . . Meanwhile the awaken'd zeal of Mr. Post's congregation and other citizens is increasing; there are large assemblies every night, either at the churches or private houses. . . . They are introducing all the habits and hymns, of the Methodists into our Presbyterian churches, after the regular service is closed by the clergyman, the congregation rise, and strike up a methodist hymn, sung amidst the groans and sobs of the newly converted . . .

*Margaret Bayard Smith describes the cholera outbreak and religious awakening in Washington, D.C., in a letter, October 12, 1822, in Hunt,* The First Forty Years, *158, 159.*

. . . We beg leave to observe and to remind you that the Cherokee are not foreigners but original inhabitants of America, and that they now inhabit and stand on the soil of their own territory and that the limits of this territory are defined by the treaties which they have made with the government of the United States, and the states by which they are now surrounded have been created out of land which was once theirs, and they cannot recognize the sovereignty of any state within the limits of their territory.

*Cherokee Indian chiefs in a statement to President James Monroe, 1823, in* Chronology of the American Indian, *142.*

Games and healthful sports, promoting hilarity and securing a just degree of exercise, are to be encouraged. We are deeply impressed with the necessity of uniting physical with moral education . . . The whole subject of the union of moral and physical education is a great deal simpler, than it first may appear. And here, too, we may say, that we were the first in the new continent to connect gymnastics with a purely literary establishment.

*George Bancroft and Joseph Cogswell declare some of the principles of their new Round Hill boys' school in Northampton, Massachusetts, 1823, in Howe,* Life and Letters of George Bancroft, *I: 172–173.*

I hope we shall never present the example of coalition, intrigue or management advancing any citizens to the highest honor of the country. The influence of such an example would be pernicious in the extreme. If the people can be cheated, they will not be served. Virtuous servants would be discouraged and the unprincipled only would thrive.

*John C. Calhoun decries underhanded presidential campaigning in a letter to Andrew Jackson, July 31, 1823, in Bassett,* Life of Andrew Jackson, *335–336.*

It is unfortunate that, when called upon to form a constitution a territory is in the most unpropitious circumstances to success for the want of men of intellect and political knowledge, attending a country in the incipient state of population. This was woefully verified in our case, for although our convention contained several thinking men, the majority was composed of empty bablers [sic], democratic to madness, having incessantly the *people* in their mouths and their dear selves in their eyes . . .

*Land official John Badollet describes the political climate in Indiana in a letter to Albert Gallatin, September 10, 1823, in Thornbrough,* The Correspondence of John Badollet and Albert Gallatin, *260.*

I am particularly requested, by many friends of yours, to inquire if you are willing to serve in the Senate of the United States. The general wish here is that you may assent to what your friends earnestly desire, and enter upon a service which, though at war with your individual interest, is yet one which it is hoped you will not decline. . . . All we want is a belief that you will permit your name to be used.

*Abram Maury on behalf of the Tennessee legislature in a letter to Andrew Jackson, September 20, 1823, in Sargent,* Public Men and Events, *I: 39.*

There are many better qualified to meet the fatigues of the journey than myself . . . I have, therefore, earnestly to request my friends and beg of you, not to press me to an acceptance of the appointment. If appointed, I could not decline; and yet, in accepting, I should do great violence to my wishes and to my feelings. The length of time I have passed in public service authorizes me to make this request.

*Andrew Jackson tries to refuse a nomination for the U.S. Senate in a letter to Abram Maury, September 21, 1823, in Sargent,* Public Men and Events, *I: 40.*

The question presented by the letters you have sent me is the most momentous which has ever been offered to my contemplation since that of Independence. That made us a nation, this sets our compass and points the course which we are to steer through the ocean of time opening on us. . . . Our first and fundamental maxim should be never to entangle ourselves in the broils of Europe. Our second, never to suffer Europe to intermeddle with cisatlantic affairs. America, North and South, has a set of interests distinct from those of Europe, and peculiarly her own.

*Thomas Jefferson advises President James Monroe on the formation of the Monroe Doctrine in a letter, October 24, 1823, in Hunt,* Essential Thomas Jefferson, *327.*

There is a good deal of very fertile land between the Boat-Yard and Knoxville, but the want of a ready vent for its produce (it can be no other radical cause) has generated a system of miserable husbandry, more wasteful and injudicious even than that prevalent in Old Virginia. . . . The road abounds with houses of entertainment, that look neat and even genteel: most of them are said to be as comfortable as need be. The cheapness of their bills is wonderful.

*Lucian Minor comments on his travels in Tennessee in his diary, December 1, 1823, in Phillips,* Plantation and Frontier, *I: 256.*

In the wars of the European powers in matters relating to themselves we have never taken any part, nor does it comport with our policy to do so. It is only when our rights are invaded or seriously menaced that we resent injuries or make preparation for our defense. With the movements in this hemisphere we are of necessity more immediately connected, and by causes which must be obvious to all enlightened and impartial observers. The political system of the allied powers is essentially different in this respect from that of America. This difference proceeds from that which exists in their respective Governments; and to the defense of our own, which has been achieved by the loss of so much blood and treasure, and matured by the wisdom of their most enlightened citizens, and under which we have enjoyed unexampled felicity, this whole nation is devoted. We owe it, therefore, to candor and to the amicable relations existing between the United States and those powers to declare that we should consider any attempt on their part to extend their system to any portion of this hemisphere as dangerous to our peace and safety. . . . It is impossible that the allied powers should extend their political system to any portion of either continent without endangering our peace and happiness; nor can anyone believe that our southern brethren, if left to themselves, would adopt it of their own accord. It is equally impossible, therefore, that we should behold such interposition in any form with indifference.

*President James Monroe proclaims what will become known as the Monroe Doctrine in his annual message to Congress, December 2, 1823. Available online. Yale University Avalon Project. URL: http://www.yale.edu/lawweb/avalon/monroe.htm.*

In reviewing the proceedings of the Legislature it would seem that your body is more agitated on the subject of Presidential election than those nearer the grand political focus. . . . The thorough going '98 men complain of essential departures by the '23 republicans, from the good, old orthodox, democratic republican faith—Whereas the old Federal party take up a candidate some from one consideration & some from another without regard to any broad & obvious principle by which they are regulated in their selection. . . . Gen. Jackson has received very great attention since his arrival—more indeed than any person at Washington—but all concur in the belief that he has no chance of success. Mr. Clay is very popular in the House of Representatives, but that popularity is of a species not very enviable.

*North Carolina congressman Willie P. Magnum describes the mood in Congress in a letter to an associate, December 10, 1823, in Shanks,* The Papers of Willie Person Magnum, *I: 82, 83.*

The *old* Republicans, radicals if you please, disciples of the Jeffersonian school, are roused from their inactivity . . . Mr. C[alhoun] and A[dams] seem not such good friends as they were. I can not tell what is the matter, but our politicians think, they will no longer lend each other a helping hand. Whether they must fall without mutual aid, or whether they will get on better, separately, remains to be seen. There is no doubt of Mr. Jefferson's being decidedly for Mr. Crawford . . . If he were but well!

*Washington socialite Margaret Bayard Smith assesses the maneuvering of the presidential candidates in a letter to a friend, December 19, 1823, in Hunt,* The First Forty Years, *162–163.*

# 12

# Democracy
# 1824–1825

On July 4, 1826, vast numbers of people in the United States gathered to celebrate the 50th anniversary of the Declaration of Independence, the jubilee anniversary of the creation of the American nation. As they had for the past half century, people gathered in towns and cities to enjoy picnics, fireworks, and parades and to listen to patriotic and nationalistic orations, many of which tied U.S. history to predictions of a glorious future for the country. But while many of the themes of celebration on July 4, 1826, were familiar, much had changed in the United States over the previous 50 years—especially since the conclusion of the Revolutionary War in 1783. Although the republicanism and national identity that had motivated American politics since that time had remained quite consistent, new and more democratic ideas had now achieved a prominence that promised to send both national politics and the participation of average people in it in new directions.

July 4, 1826, also literally brought the passing of the older generation of politics in the United States. Both Thomas Jefferson and John Adams, former presidents whose political rivalry had shaped the national scene throughout the 1790s and into the early part of the 19th century, died on that day. Jefferson, the author of the Declaration of Independence, had lain mortally ill for days at his Virginia plantation home, Monticello. He seemed determined to die on the Fourth, however, and when he finally succumbed early that day, his last words were, "Is it the Fourth?"[1] Unbeknown to Jefferson, John Adams was also dying at his home in Braintree, Massachusetts. Adams, unaware that Jefferson had already passed away, declared with his dying breath: "Thomas Jefferson survives."[2] In their dying moments both Jefferson and Adams seemed to be holding on to the glory of the revolutionary past as embodied in the Fourth of July, and they both recognized that their passing signaled the end of an era. The death of Jefferson and Adams on the same day, the 50th anniversary of American independence, is not just a striking coincidence of history but a concrete symbol of the passing of an age.

The younger generation of politicians who had risen to power in 1826 still thought of themselves largely in terms defined by Adams and Jefferson. John Quincy Adams, Henry Clay, Andrew Jackson, and the other leaders of their era

Even as Americans looked forward to a new generation of politicians and a more modern world in the 19th century, they also looked back to their national history for inspiration. *(from Benson Lossing,* The Pictorial Field-Book of the Revolution, *1851–1852)*

defined themselves as public-spirited men chosen by the people to represent the best that the country had to offer. Yet, their recognition of a new level of direct democracy, and the rise of popular voting in many states, meant that this new generation had to deal directly with the American people and their opinions much more than Jefferson and Adams ever had. The new democracy also meant the triumph of a new style of politics in which campaigning and party division emerged as potent forces. The American people themselves also asserted their voices with greater confidence in the process. The transition to a more democratic style in the United States was not without severe growing pains, but even in the midst of those pains (contested elections, labor strikes, sectional disagreements), there was a sense of democratic possibility.

## THE ELECTION OF 1824

One of the most painful democratic exercises was the presidential election of 1824, among the most controversial elections in American history. The candidates in this election were technically, all members of the same Democratic-Republican Party, but they represented different sections and interests in the United States, and they opposed one another in ways that later generations might label as partisan. The democratization of the American electoral system had begun sufficiently so that attention had to be paid to what "the people," or at least white male voters, had to say. Yet despite that, the election was decided according to an older, more elite republican system established by the Constitution. The election was thrown into the House of Representatives, where representatives had full responsibility for the process and the selection of the president. The election of 1824 also exposed the new importance of personality in American politics. By losing the election in dramatic fashion, Andrew Jackson set himself up once and for all as a symbol of democracy for the new age—a democracy that would finally carry him to the presidency in 1828.

By 1823 five candidates had emerged for the presidential campaign, which had begun almost as soon as James Monroe was elected for his second term. The strongest early candidate was Secretary of the Treasury William H. Crawford, a Georgian who represented the Old Republican faction of the Democratic-Republican Party. The Old Republicans traced their intellectual heritage directly to Thomas Jefferson's wing of the party, and they disapproved of the gradual acceptance by the Democratic-Republicans over previous decades of policies of economic development and modernization. One of the strongest Democratic champions of those programs, Henry Clay, was also a candidate. Clay, a Kentuckian who was speaker of the House of Representatives, spoke mainly for westerners and interested parties who wished to see an expansion of the national economy. Clay advocated what he called an "American System," which would improve infrastructure, banking, foreign trade, and other sectors of the economy that would encourage economic growth.

Another candidate who hoped to capture southern and western votes in the election was Secretary of War, John C. Calhoun, a South Carolinian who hoped his Yale education and wide governmental experience might lend him broad appeal. Calhoun did not attract many northern supporters early on, however, because one of the other major candidates was Secretary of State John Quincy Adams, whose status as heir to his parents John and Abigail Adams gave him unassailable appeal in New England. While Adams had been a highly successful secretary of state and the architect of James Monroe's daring foreign policy, his less than dynamic persona, his status as a former Federalist, and his strong New England ties lessened his appeal in other parts of the country. The most dynamic candidate in the election, General Andrew Jackson, made a late entry into the race, but his candidacy quickly gained momentum. The fiery hero of the War of 1812, a renowned Indian fighter, and former governor of the Florida territory, Jackson had been elected to the U.S. Senate almost on a lark in 1823 after the Tennessee state legislature nominated him as a presidential candidate.

The usual practice of choosing presidential candidates by congressional caucuses fell out of favor in 1823 and 1824, and, like Jackson, the candidates gained nominations from state legislatures, conventions, and other special meetings around the country. As a result of this change and the large number of candidates, the election of 1824 saw some of the most open campaigning yet for the office of president. Even though the candidates themselves tried to maintain the appearance of republican impartiality by staying out of public campaigning, many of their representative waged strong efforts on their behalf. The most notable "agent" in the campaign was Representative Martin Van Buren, the fiery New York politician who had pioneered new party management and campaign techniques in the years just prior to 1824. Van Buren threw his support behind the early favorite, Crawford, in hopes that he could build up the cross-regional "nationalist" wing of the party and eventually enhance his own power.

Unfortunately for this plan, Crawford suffered a stroke in September 1823. Although he did not drop out of the race, he was totally incapacitated and bedridden until partway through 1824. It was a measure of how important electioneering had become that Van Buren and others continued campaigning on Crawford's behalf, but the stroke-weakened candidate was unable to pull any weight for his own election. At the same time, Andrew Jackson's candidacy quickly became popular, even outside the South and West, where many expected his support to be concentrated. Newspapers that supported Jackson found readers all over the country, and in spring 1824, a political convention in

This print depicts the presidential election of 1824 as a comical footrace. Henry Clay has fallen behind as Andrew Jackson, John Quincy Adams, and William Crawford race to the finish line. The cheering crowd in the cartoon (one man shouts "Hurra for our Jackson") demonstrates how the public was becoming increasingly important in electoral politics. *(Library of Congress, Prints and Photographs Division [LC-USZ62-89572])*

Harrisburg, Pennsylvania, nominated Jackson as their candidate for president. As Jackson began to draw support away from other candidates, John C. Calhoun dropped out of the race and concentrated his campaign on becoming vice president to whomever of his Democratic-Republican colleagues might win the presidential election.

Even after the election in November 1824, determining the winner was no easy matter. In the electoral college, Andrew Jackson received 99 electoral votes, John Quincy Adams got 84, William Crawford garnered 41, and Henry Clay received 37. According to the Constitution, the election would have to be decided by the House of Representatives, since no candidate had received a majority of electoral votes. Calhoun did receive a wide majority of electoral votes for vice president, so he was elected to that office even though it was unclear who would emerge as president. In 1824, a majority of states for the first time chose their presidential electors as determined by the results of the popular vote in the presidential election, although many states still chose electors in the state legislatures. The popular vote took on new importance, and there Andrew Jackson was the clear winner. Jackson received 42 percent of the popular vote, Adams got 33 percent, and Clay and Crawford each garnered only 13 percent.[3] Jackson, whose electoral votes came largely from the West and South, where electors tended to be chosen more directly by popular vote than in the northern states that supported Adams, put great stock in votes as representative of the voice of the common citizen and his choice for American politics.

Regardless of Jackson's reverence for the popular vote, it meant very little once the election passed into the House of Representatives. The Twelfth Amendment to the Constitution stipulated that the House would choose the president from among the top three candidates in the electoral vote, but beyond that there were few rules to guide the representatives in their choice. Each state delegation in the House would get one vote, just as they had when the 1800 election had been determined in the House. Ironically, Henry Clay, with the fourth-highest total of electoral votes, was out of the election, but he assumed new power in the process since he was Speaker of the House of Representatives. Most representatives recognized by now that William H. Crawford's bad health would prevent him from serving as president, so the election came down to a contest between John Quincy Adams and Andrew Jackson.

Congress convened on February 9, 1825, and the House had to determine a winner by March 4 for the inauguration to proceed according to the schedule set by the Constitution. All eyes were on Clay, who seemed to possess great power, not only by virtue of his office as Speaker, but also by his option to throw his supporters behind whichever candidate he might choose. Clay seemed to hold the power to decide the next president. Considerable political controversy, and subsequent historical disagreement, exists about just how Clay used his personal power to decide the election. Before the House ever convened, on January 9 Clay met with John Quincy Adams in private, a meeting in which Jackson's supporters later claimed the two struck a "corrupt bargain" to get Adams elected in return for political favors granted to Clay. Whether or not any such bargain existed (most historians think it did not), Clay threw his support behind Adams in the House, and Adams was elected. South Carolinian Robert Hayne wrote in a letter: "We are all in commotion about the monstrous union between Clay & Adams, for the purpose of depriving Jackson of the votes of the Western States where nine tenths of the people are decidedly in his favor."[4] Despite the objections of Hayne and others like him, John Quincy Adams would become president, even though Jackson had received both more popular votes and more electoral votes than Adams.

Martin Van Buren told one of the Kentucky representatives that by throwing his support to Jackson in the election, "You sign Mr. Clay's political death warrant." While that was far from true, Clay and the entire Democratic-Republican Party suffered severe aftereffects of the contested election.[5] As soon as he was elected, Adams appointed Henry Clay secretary of state, a move that prompted Jackson to dub Clay "The Judas of the West," a traitor who betrayed the people of his region for "thirty pieces of silver."[6] Clay spent much of the following years defending himself against charges that he had conspired to fix the election to gain office for himself. Jackson resigned his seat in the Senate, but his political allies remained in power, and they were more committed than ever to enacting electoral reform that would give direct voice to white male citizens and their votes. The disaffection caused by the election of 1824 set the stage of the dissolution of the unified Democratic-Republican Party and the virulent party contests of the next decades.

John Quincy Adams entered the presidency with extremely weak public and political support. Adams tried to mollify his opponents, and he claimed in his inaugural address, "that the will of the people is the source, and the happiness of the people the end of all legitimate government . . . [in a] representative democracy."[7] Adams had, in some respects, a successful presidency, although many of Andrew Jackson's supporters remained skeptical throughout Adams's tenure in office. Adams later became an advocate of the disenfranchised in American society, but at this point in his career, many doubted his full commitment to the idea of democracy.

## REPUBLICAN AND DEMOCRATIC IDEALISM

One of the unifying forces that kept the American nation together in the midst of electoral and political upheaval in 1824 and 1825 was the triumphal return visit to the United States of the marquis de Lafayette, the French aristocrat who had served as a general in the Revolutionary War. In February 1824, President Monroe invited Lafayette, who was revered as a great American warrior and a hero of the moderate phase of the French Revolution, to visit the United States to accept praise and gratitude from the American people as well as land and monetary grants from Congress. Lafayette had been imprisoned during the French Revolution and lost much of his family's fortune, so he happily accepted the invitation to return and tour the country for which he held so much affection and political fellow-feeling. U.S. citizens took the opportunity during Lafayette's visit to reconfirm their allegiances to the ideals of the American Revolution, now freshened with newer democratic ideas, and they used Lafayette's tour as an occasion to engage in an enormous nationalistic festival in celebration of both the general and of themselves.

On August 15, 1824, Lafayette landed in New York City and began his 13-month tour of all 24 of the United States, where he was

During the 13-month American tour of the marquis de Lafayette, many visual images and souvenirs bearing his image were sold to the American public. Such images often paired Lafayette with George Washington, as in this engraving that depicts them both as classical heroes wearing laurel wreaths. *(from Benson Lossing,* The Pictorial Field-Book of the Revolution, *1851–1852)*

received with great enthusiasm and pageantry. Newspapers all over the country followed the general's progress as he traveled from town to town, being received with pomp and ceremony at every stop. Every dignitary in U.S. politics, both local and national, vied to address Lafayette and to show off the great economic developments that had taken place since his last visit to the nation in the 1780s. Both social elites and average Americans greeted the general at a grand collection of ceremonies, balls, parties, and rallies. Wherever he went, Lafayette reviewed the local militia, spoke with politicians, shook hands with war veterans, and generally granted his approval to the developments in America since the end of the Revolution. Lafayette's traveling companion, Auguste Levasseur, recorded a typical scene that greeted Lafayette when he arrived in a city, where people of every race, class, and gender rushed to greet him:

> Mothers surrounded him, presenting their children and asking his blessing, which having obtained, they embraced their offspring with renewed tenderness; feeble old men appeared to become reanimated in talking to him of the numerous battles in which they had been engaged with him for the same of liberty. Men of colour reminded him with tenderness of his philanthropical efforts . . . young men with hard and blackened hands announced their laborious occupations, stopped before him and said with energy, "We also belong to the ten millions who are indebted to you for liberty and happiness!" Many others wished to speak to him.[8]

Lafayette, as a living symbol of the glory of the Revolution, allowed the newly democratic American public to swarm forward and express its reverence for the republican past that he also symbolized.

Lafayette's visit also provided an opportunity for political pageantry that created a scene of political unity, even as the nation was mired in electoral controversy. Lafayette visited the grave of George Washington, his close personal friend and commander in the war, and he spent time visiting with the surviving generation of Revolutionary politicians and former presidents: Thomas Jefferson, James Madison, John Adams, and James Monroe. But Lafayette also spent considerable time with the men who were so divided by the election of 1824: Andrew Jackson, Henry Clay, and John Quincy Adams. Lafayette himself was in Washington, D.C., while the election was being decided, and observers thought that his presence had a calming influence on political passions. Levasseur wrote, with perhaps only a pinch of exaggeration: "For nearly two months all discord and excitement produced by this election, which, it was said, would engender the most disastrous consequences, were forgotten, and nothing was thought of but Lafayette and the heroes of the revolution."[9] Lafayette also diverted attention to noble philanthropic and nationalistic projects as he traveled around the country. He laid the cornerstone for several important Revolutionary War monuments, most notably at an enormous ceremony on the Bunker Hill battlefield on the 50th anniversary of that battle, June 17, 1825. Lafayette also appeared at other commemorative exercises and presided over ceremonies inaugurating several public libraries and educational institutions. The Frenchman reminded Americans that "they had not quite forgotten to feel again as they felt in the Revolution," but that they also had new projects and new ideas to push forward into the future.[10]

To the marquis de Lafayette, one of the most important stops on his U.S. tour was his visit to George Washington's tomb. Lafayette gew very close to Washington during the Revolutionary War, and the association between them on Lafayette's visit further heightened American patriotism. *(from Benson Lossing,* The Pictorial Field-Book of the Revolution, *1851–1852)*

The response to Lafayette's visit was evidence of public enthusiasm for the memory of the old republican ideals of the United States; at the same time, it showed commitment to some of the new egalitarian ideals of American democracy. When women, African Americans, and working-class men participated in celebrations of the general's visit, they added their voices to the body of the people that made up the American nation. Others expressed their democratic enthusiasm in more radical and countercultural ways.

The 1820s saw the founding of several utopian communities dedicated to egalitarian, even socialist, ways of remaking American society. One of the most controversial communities was founded by Frances Wright, a Scottish writer and social activist who had returned to the United States for the second time in 1824 as a traveling companion to Lafayette. After Lafayette returned to France in 1825, Wright stayed behind and purchased land in Tennessee, where she set up an antislavery commune called Nashoba. It was designed to provide space where newly freed African Americans could gain education and a chance to live peaceably alongside whites. Nashoba became highly controversial not only for its racial mixing and the fact that it was led by a woman, but also for the free-love ideals expressed by some of its more outspoken residents. By 1828, Wright had left Nashoba to join fellow Scot Robert Dale Owen at his utopian society in New Harmony, Indiana.

Owen's society at New Harmony was based on the collective labor ideals of his father, the reform-minded industrialist Robert Owen. Wright and Robert Dale Owen together published a newspaper that gave them an outlet for their radical ideas about democracy, economic opportunity, education, and a number of other social issues. Although communities like Nashoba and New Harmony were far outside the mainstream in the mid-1820s, the alliance between Wright and Owen did eventually bear political fruit when both became involved with working-class politics in New York City later in the decade. They were far more radical than Lafayette, but both Owen and Wright, like the general, showed how Europeans visiting the United States could stir up enthusiasm for or against political ideas among the American populace.

## THE ECONOMY AND POLITICS

When John Quincy Adams took office as president in March 1825, he launched himself with full force into the new political alliance with Henry Clay that had emerged out of their bargaining over the contested election results. Adams decided to support Clay's long-standing goal of building up the national economy, a series of proposals that Clay had dubbed the American System, and adopted a version of it as his own presidential agenda. In his first annual message to Congress, Adams announced his intention to use the full power of the federal government to enhance the national infrastructure and provide the basis for economic growth. He proposed the creation of the Department of the Interior, a bankruptcy law, and a change to standardized weights and measures. Most important, he announced he would seek authorization for the widespread construction of roads and canals. Adams warned Congress that to keep up with Europe, American politicians must not be "palsied by the will of our constituents," but instead must push ahead with aggressive legislation to ensure economic prosperity.[11]

For a candidate who had been elected to the presidency by the House of Representatives despite losing both the popular and the electoral vote, Adams chose his words unwisely. President Adams was already vulnerable to criticism that he was undemocratic and aloof from the public. Detractors believed that as a member of one of the most aristocratic families in the United States, he had gained the presidency in part because he had inherited his father's fame. Some even accused the second president in the Adams dynasty of being openly monarchical, an exaggeration that Adams's own words did little to discourage. His style was ill-suited to an age when democratic ideas were becoming more important, and he played into the hands of his opponents by seeming to disregard the voice of the people in his message to Congress.

There was strong evidence, however, that many people did actually support the kind of economic activism that John Quincy Adams and Henry Clay advocated, even if that was not the basis for Adams's appeal for congressional support. All over the country, market activities, particularly those invigorated by new means of transportation, were expanding at a rapid rate. In March 1824, just before Adams was inaugurated, the U.S. Supreme Court ruled in the case of *Gibbons v. Ogden* that the federal government's constitutional power to regulate interstate commerce gave it ultimate authority over the states to define the rules of economic trade between states. The case had arisen when two steamboat ferry operators received conflicting authorizations from the federal government and the state of New York to ply their traffic on the Hudson River. By ruling in favor of the federal government's power to determine the legality of trade issues, the Supreme Court, particularly Chief Justice John Marshall, opened the way for the kind of exercise of federal power that would be necessary to make an expanded American system of roads and canals work.

Other transportation improvements of both national and local economic scale took on new importance in the mid-1820s. In 1825 the Erie Canal, which linked Buffalo and New York City, was completed, and crowds celebrated the canal as an economic and political success at well-attended opening ceremonies. New York governor De Witt Clinton poured a ceremonial cask of water into the canal to celebrate its opening and to celebrate his own political triumph in getting the canal constructed. The full opening of the Erie Canal, whose construction began during the first wave of enthusiasm for transportation improvements following the War of 1812, showed the economic benefits that could accrue from large-scale infrastructure projects. The canal improved the traffic in goods from the coastline to the interior of the entire northern United States and lowered the cost of shipping sufficiently to stimulate manufacturing and trade. The Erie Canal seemed to be a natural argument for the kind of big economic programs that Clay and Adams wanted. Smaller-scale efforts, like the railroad constructed to bring granite from a Quincy, Massachusetts, quarry to the construction site of the Bunker Hill Monument in 1827, also showed the benefits of ingenuity and investment in transportation improvements. The Adams administration appropriated money for national road-building projects, granted federal land to many state canal projects, and appropriated funds to invest in canal-building businesses.[12]

The large-scale economic program proposed by President Adams did little to address the immediate concerns of most working Americans, even though it promised to improve the overall economy and to offer great benefits in the long term by encouraging businesses to expand. American workers in the mid-1820s, especially those who worked in the very urban manufacturing industries that stood to gain from new improvements in transportation, seemed less interested in the economy as a whole than they were in their own plight as workers. This era saw a precipitous growth in labor activism, which warned politicians that economic development could sometimes take a toll on workers even as it encouraged a growth in aggregate trade and development. Many craft workers, who were losing status as they made the transition into the world of wage labor, experienced the market transition as personal and economic loss.

Despite the lack of a widespread or nationally organized labor movement in the mid-1820s, workers were increasingly willing to organize and strike to promote their local economic interests. In 1824, women and men employed at the Brown and Almay textile mills in Pawtucket, Rhode Island, went on strike, and the following year carpenters in Boston, Massachusetts, walked out of work demanding a 10-hour day from their employers. By 1827, such localized efforts were coalescing into networks of support for workers, and in that year workers in Philadelphia formed the first organized trade union in the United States, the Mechanics' Union of Trade Associations. Trade workers, and their discontents, served to remind politicians that their economic policies did not affect just aggregate trade and commerce but also influenced the lives of average people. It would take decades, however, before federal government power was brought to bear to protect the rights of workers.

Meanwhile, as Adams and Clay pursued a vigorous program of transportation improvements and pushed their political programs, Andrew Jackson and his political supporters began to gather strength in opposition to them. Jackson found perhaps an unlikely political ally in Vice President John C. Calhoun, who almost immediately upon taking office became isolated from President Adams and Secretary of State Clay. The president accused Calhoun of allowing Virginia senator John C. Randolph to denounce him on the floor of the Senate in violation of Senate rules, but Calhoun refused to contain Randolph, and the vice president vigorously defended his right to chair the Senate as he saw fit. By the summer of 1826, Calhoun had clearly decided that Jackson's advocacy of more limited use of federal power suited his South Carolina political sensibilities better than Adams's advocacy of the American system, and he wrote to Jackson in June that Adams seemed more interested in the "artful management of patronage" than in the proper "voice of the people.[13] Calhoun defined himself as a Jacksonian democrat, a group inside the Democratic-Republican Party that would soon begin seriously to vex President Adams. The split between the supporters of Jackson and the supporters of Adams also began to divide along lines that would eventually split the old Democratic-Republican Party into two new parties—the Democrats and the Whigs.

The biggest political fight that presaged what was to come in the 1828 presidential election arose, in fact, over an economic issue that very much involved ideological issues of federal government power and the ability to encourage economic growth. The Jacksonian Democrats and the Adams-Clay wing of the party came to blows over the issue of raising protectionist trade tariffs. Henry Clay had led the charge for higher trade tariffs that would stimulate particular agricultural industries since the end of the War of 1812, but now the fight took on a new urgency, as the national political battle got worse. In 1824 Clay had managed to get higher tariffs on hemp and wool passed through Congress, despite the opposition of New England manufacturing interests. But by 1827, even some New Englanders were convinced of Clay's arguments that the correct increase of trade taxes could stimulate industry. Massachusetts congressman Daniel Webster sponsored an increase in the Woolens Bill in 1827, which passed the House of Representatives but ran into deep trouble in the Senate. Vice President Calhoun, who had once been a proponent of Clay's American System, signaled the completion of his conversion to the support of weaker federal power by casting the tie-breaking vote in the Senate to defeat the Woolens Bill by tabling it.

Clay was outraged by Calhoun's actions, and he resolved to push forward other tariff increases to flush out his political enemies and expose them as a cabal working against the government and the Democratic-Republican Party. Clay got his wish of exposing a solid opposition party, although political activities surrounding higher tariffs went in sometimes confusing directions. After the midterm elections, when Congress returned to session in December 1827, both houses were dominated by Jacksonian Democrats, who then adopted the idea of passing tariffs that could appeal to Clay's own political allies in the West and New England in order to seal Andrew Jackson's chances for the presidency in 1828. Even if the Jacksonians' new push for higher trade taxes failed, they believed that they could not lose either way. If the tariffs were defeated, it could be construed as a political loss for Clay and Adams, who had supported higher tariffs all along. As a bonus, southern Jacksonians like John C. Calhoun would be happy. If the carefully targeted tariffs succeeded, newly elected congressman Martin Van Buren, who supported Jackson, would make sure that the Jacksonians could take credit and send Jackson to the White House.

In 1828, Congress indeed passed the new tariff bill. It was carefully constructed to raise the prices of almost all imported goods, but it also granted concessions to particular Jacksonian constituents in the Middle Atlantic and New England states. President Adams signed the tariff bill, since it was in keeping with the economic policies previously supported by his administration. Adams's support of the 1828 tariff backfired, however, forcing him into a no-win political situation. When southern Jacksonians, led by Vice President Calhoun, became outraged with the new bill and dubbed it "The Tariff of Abominations," they directed their ire at the president for promoting and signing the legislation. Henry Clay contended that the Jacksonian congressmen had purposely framed an objectionable bill so that it would be defeated and make the administration look bad; whether or not that was their true intention, the result was the same. Vice President John C. Calhoun, for one, was unalterably alienated from the policy of strong federal economic intervention, and he began to write a document, *The South Carolina Exposition and Protest,* that spelled out the right of a state to nullify any federal law that interfered with a state's rights to control its own economy.[14] Such nullification sentiments would separate Calhoun and other South Carolinians from the future Jackson administration in 1832, but for the time being Calhoun had nowhere else to go, and his political alliance with the Jacksonian Democrats remained strong in opposition to Clay and Adams and their National Republican wing of the Democratic-Republican Party.

# THE ELECTION OF 1828

Although Calhoun was the sitting vice president, he became Jackson's running mate in the 1828 presidential election. For Jackson, the 1828 election vindicated the results of 1824, confirmed the new voting power of average white men, cemented the rise of Van Buren's new style of political campaigning, and vaulted Andrew Jackson into the presidency.

New suffrage laws had taken hold in more states since the 1824 election, insuring both that the election would be witness to nearly universal white-male suffrage and that the popular vote would determine more of the electoral vote than ever before. Both developments were positive for Andrew Jackson, who appealed to the "common man" and saw direct voting as the best way for the "voice of the people" to be heard in government. Unlike the older generation of republican politicians, even more democratically minded politicians like Thomas Jefferson, Jackson wanted the government to be influenced by the direct voice and power of the people instead of filtered through layers of meritorious representatives. Although Jackson's vision of American democracy was still extremely restricted for some groups—in fact, it was predicated upon the exclusion of women, African Americans, and Indians—his politics did boost the power of the average white man to heights never before seen.

One measure of the success of the new democratic style of politics was the amount and style of campaigning that took place in 1828. New York politician Martin Van Buren, the father of modern campaign techniques, spearheaded Jackson's campaign against John Quincy Adams, and he tested to the fullest his ability to promote a candidate's appeal among the populace. Van Buren appealed both to the voters and to the larger public to support Jackson. The campaign played upon Jackson's reputation as a war hero and his renown for martial strength, which was summed up in his nickname "Old Hickory." In contrast to earlier presidential campaigns, which were largely genteel affairs in which gentlemen decided among supposedly equally disinterested candidates, this election was fought out in the streets. The Jacksonians held meetings and conventions in every state, and they bolstered public support for their candidate by throwing parades, barbecues, and parties that featured events such as the symbolic planting of hickory trees.

Adams partisans were not convinced that such campaign tactics had a place in national politics. One of their supporting newspapers, the *Washington National Journal,* wrote, for example, "Hickory trees! . . . What have hickory trees to do with republicanism and the great contest?"[15] John Quincy Adams held on to the older style of politics and largely stayed out of the campaigning fray, even as his cabinet seemed to lose confidence in his leadership and his ability to win the election. Some Adams supporters in the National Republican wing of the party, including John Quincy's wife, Louisa Catharine Adams, did campaign on his behalf, and some even adopted Van Buren–style tactics by attacking Jackson, his wife, and his mother in party newspapers. But for the most part, Adams wanted nothing to do with the new political world that Jackson's campaign heralded.

As a result, Adams lost the election. Twice as many men voted in 1828 as in the previous election, and they voted overwhelmingly for Andrew Jackson, who received 56 percent of the popular vote and 68 percent of the electoral vote.[16]

Jackson's support was strongest in the South, but he received healthy majorities in the Midwest and Middle Atlantic states; he lost only in Adams's native New England and in Delaware. Jackson had successfully vindicated his loss in 1824 and solidified his appeal among the masses. Of the huge crowds that showed up for Jackson's inauguration in 1829, Daniel Webster proclaimed, "They really seemed to think that the country is rescued from some dreadful danger."[17]

## DEMOCRACY

In some respects, the United States was much the same as it had been in 1783 at the conclusion of the Revolutionary War, but dramatic changes had also taken place. The country was still largely rural, although cities were coming to new prominence as manufacturing and the market economy experienced impressive growth. The republican political ideals that had defined American politics during and immediately after the Revolution still held a lot of appeal for Americans, as evidenced by public enthusiasm for the returned war hero the marquis de Lafayette. The compromises that had created the U.S. Constitution had been tested by 50 years of periodic domestic crisis, economic growth, and warfare, both threatened and real. The American republic had proved quite resilient, and representative government survived and flourished.

The United States had emerged from 50 years of existence with some important new political ideas and structures, as well. Andrew Jackson and his supporters represented not only a new generation of politicians, but also a willingness to embrace popular campaigning and a more grassroots style of rule. In 1828, average white men in the United States had more direct access to power than ever before. At the same time, slavery remained an extremely strong institution, and more than a million Americans lived lives of abject oppression under the slave system. Strong African-American voices were beginning to argue that the principles of republicanism and democracy demanded that all blacks be afforded equality. While slavery was declining in the northern United States, it would take decades of additional struggle and blood before the country eliminated slavery and undertook an even longer struggle against racism. White women fared better in the early republic, particularly as their educational opportunities improved, but they did not experience the same direct effects of Jacksonian democracy as their husbands, fathers, and sons.

Because the early republic was a time of constant and deep change in American life, many people living in the United States experienced a sense that they were part of a society in some kind of transition. The traditional world of the 18th century, in which it seemed unsure that the United States could even survive as an independent country, gave way to the early 19th century, when a sense of optimism accompanied improvements in communication and transportation. The United States had expanded over time but divisions between the regions of the nation were also hardening, and expansion was not always a smooth process as the implementation of state power often held unforeseen consequences. Many more trying times and changes lay ahead for the United States, but much had already been accomplished.

## CHRONICLE OF EVENTS

### 1824

Frances Wright arrives in the United States to meet the marquis de Lafayette. She will depart from Lafayette to travel as a lecturer and political activist for a variety of causes ranging from antislavery to women's rights.

Washington Irving publishes a collection of Gothic horror tales, *Tales of a Traveler.*

Lydia Maria Child publishes *Hobomok,* her novel about a "noble savage."

Members of the Kahal Kadosh Beth Elohim in Charleston, South Carolina, found the Reform Society of Israelites, inaugurating Reform Judaism in the United States.

Male and female weavers at the Brown and Almay mill in Pawtucket, Rhode Island, go on strike, the first U.S. strike to include both men and women.

The New York Common Council supports the idea of opening African Free Schools for black children.

Construction of the Capitol Rotunda is completed.

Explorer Jim Bridger scouts the Great Salt Lake.

Secretary of War John C. Calhoun creates the U.S. Bureau of Indian Affairs.

*January 24:* The Episcopal Church charters a theological seminary, Kenyon College, in Gambier, Ohio.

*February 14:* Democratic-Republicans in Congress nominate Treasury Secretary William H. Crawford for president.

*February 15:* Politicians in Boston nominate Secretary of State John Quincy Adams for president.

*March 2:* The Supreme Court issues its opinion in the case of *Gibbons v. Ogden,* which invalidates a state monopoly granted on steamboat travel between New York and New Jersey. The ruling broadly interprets the commerce clause of the Constitution to mean that federal power can take precedence over state control of commercial navigation, even within state boundaries.

*March 4:* A political convention in Harrisburg, Pennsylvania, nominates Andrew Jackson for president.

*March 30–31:* In a congressional debate over tariff policies, Kentuckian Henry Clay gives a speech advocating what he calls an "American System" that will promote American commerce through federal funding of internal improvements and will raise tariffs on imported goods.

*April 17:* Diplomats from the United States and Russia agree to establish a border between Russian and American claims on the U.S. West Coast at the 54°50' parallel of latitude.

*April 30:* Congress passes a general survey bill that expands the president's power to call for surveys for public improvements of the infrastructure.

Congress earmarks $10,000 for surveying the Great Sauk Trail, a road between Chicago and Detroit.

*May 22:* The Tariff Act of 1824 raises trade taxes on woolen and cotton cloth and imposes new rates on goods including glass, linen, and lead.

*May 25:* In Philadelphia, an ecumenical religious convention founds the American Sunday School Union.

*May 26:* The United States officially recognizes the Empire of Brazil.

*August 16:* Former Revolutionary War general the marquis de Lafayette arrives in New York City for a triumphal tour of the United States. Congress and President Monroe have invited Lafayette to honor him and to confer land and money on the general, who is facing financial problems.

*September 11:* A political convention in Philadelphia nominates Henry Clay for president.

*October 3:* The United States and Colombia conclude a treaty of amity and commerce.

*November:* A countrywide movement to liberalize voting regulations begins a series of suffrage reforms over the following years that will lead to almost universal suffrage for white males.

*December 1:* In the presidential election, no candidate receives a majority of the electoral vote. Andrew Jackson leads with 99 votes; John Quincy Adams receives 84 votes; William H. Crawford (who has become gravely ill) gets 44 votes; and Henry Clay receives 37 votes. The lack of a majority means that the House of Representatives will have to decide the presidential election. John C. Calhoun receives 182 electoral votes for vice president, and he will assume that office no matter who wins the presidential election.

*December 9:* The Senate receives the marquis de Lafayette as a visitor during its session and grants him a seat of honor.

## 1825

Henry Wadsworth Longfellow publishes his first poems in the *United States Literary Gazette*.

Fire destroys a large part of the collection of the Library of Congress.

Boston carpenters strike for a 10-hour day.

The Hudson River School of painters, which includes artists Asher B. Durand and Thomas Cole, thrives.

Frances Wright founds the utopian antislavery community of Nashoba in Tennessee. The community is widely condemned for promoting free love between whites and blacks.

The U.S. Postal Service opens its first dead-letter office.

*January 3:* Robert Dale Owen, the son of the English industrialist Robert Owen, acquires 20,000 acres of land in Indiana, where he founds the utopian community at New Harmony.

*February 12:* U.S. officials in Indian Springs, Georgia, conclude a treaty with representatives of the Creek Indians, who agree to cede their land in Georgia and move west of the Mississippi. Creeks protest that those who signed the treaty did not represent their whole community and that the treaty is invalid.

*February 25:* The House of Representatives elects John Quincy Adams president. Andrew Jackson, who received the most electoral votes, assumes no office.

*March 4:* John Quincy Adams is inaugurated as president. He is the first son of a president to become president himself.

*March 7:* John Quincy Adams names Henry Clay to be secretary of state. Andrew Jackson and his allies are outraged and allege that Henry Clay threw his presidential votes to John Quincy Adams in a "corrupt bargain" that guaranteed Clay the cabinet post.

President Adams names Joel R. Poinsett the first U.S. minister to Mexico.

*March 9:* The U.S. Senate defeats a proposed treaty with the nation of Colombia that proposed to help suppress the illegal African slave trade.

*June 17:* As many as 100,000 people turn out to see the marquis de Lafayette and other veterans of the Battle of Bunker Hill parade through the streets of Boston. Lafayette participates in a Masonic ritual to lay the cornerstone of the Bunker Hill Monument in Charlestown, Massachusetts. Daniel Webster's speech on the occasion boosts his national political reputation and his reputation as an orator.

*October 26:* Construction of the Erie Canal is completed. Public officials celebrate an elaborate ritual opening of the canal, which connects the Hudson River and Lake Erie.

*November 8:* Samuel F. B. Morse and other artists organize the New York Drawing Association, later to become the National Academy of Design.

*December 6:* President John Quincy Adams advocates the American System in his annual message to Congress.

*December 7:* The marquis de Lafayette, having visited all 24 states, completes his visit to the United States and returns to France.

*December 26:* President Adams urges Congress to approve U.S. delegates to attend an inter-American Congress organized by Simón de Bolívar.

## 1826

James Fenimore Cooper publishes *The Last of the Mohicans*.

Samuel F. B. Morse's portrait of the marquis de Lafayette becomes very popular.

John, Robert, and Edward Stevens operate the first railway steam locomotive in the United States.

New Hampshire resident Samuel Morey patents an internal combustion engine.

Faneuil Hall had served as an important market and commercial center since its construction in 1742. The adjacent Quincy Market project expanded both its size and its significance. *(from Benson Lossing,* The Pictorial Field-Book of the Revolution, *1851–1852)*

The Quincy Market, adjacent to Faneuil Hall in Boston, Massachusetts, begins to be constructed.

The Pennsylvania legislature outlaws kidnapping, which in effect nullifies the federal Fugitive Slave Act of 1793. The Pennsylvania law will later be invalidated by the Supreme Court case *Prigg v. Penn.*

*January 11:* The Senate Committee on Foreign Relations opposes President Adams's call to send delegates to the inter-American Congress.

*January 24:* Creek Indians sign the Treaty of Washington and agree to cede lands in western Georgia to the United States.

*February 13:* The American Temperance Society is founded in Boston, Massachusetts.

*February 17:* Georgia governor George M. Troop calls up state militia troops to prevent federal troops from surveying the land ceded by the Creek in the western part of the state.

*March 14:* The U.S. Senate approves the plan to send delegates to the inter-American Congress in Panama.

*March 25:* The U.S. House of Representatives also agrees to send U.S. delegates to Panama, but neither of the delegates participates in the inter-American Congress.

*April 8:* Secretary of State Henry Clay fights a duel with John Randolph, who keeps claiming publicly that Clay received his cabinet post as part of a "corrupt bargain" in the disputed presidential election.

*July 4:* Both Thomas Jefferson and John Adams die on this day, the 50th anniversary of the Declaration of Independence.

*August 2:* Daniel Webster delivers a stirring eulogy for John Adams.

*August 22:* Explorer Jedidiah Strong Smith leaves the Great Salt Lake to begin the first American overland journey to southern California.

*September:* Former Mason William Morgan is kidnapped after he publicly reveals the secrets of the fraternal order. The crime mobilizes anti-Masonic political activists, who form the Anti-Masonic political party.

*October 7:* The first railroad in the United States, the Quincy Tramway, opens. It hauls granite for the construction of the Bunker Hill Monument between Quincy and Charlestown, Massachusetts.

*November:* Jacksonian Democrats, who have all but split with Adams and Clay's wing of the Democratic Party, win a majority of seats in both houses of Congress.

## 1827

The U.S. Army builds Fort Leavenworth in the future Kansas Territory.

Edgar Allan Poe publishes his first book of poetry, *Tamerlane and Other Poems,* but the volume finds few readers.

James Fenimore Cooper publishes *The Prairie.*

One of the best-selling authors of the 19th century, Catherine Maria Sedgwick, publishes *Hope Leslie.*

John James Audubon publishes the first volume of *Birds of America.*

English author Francis Trollope begins her multi-year trip to the United States, which she will immortalize in her book *Domestic Manners of the Americans,* a European best-seller.

Sarah Josepha Hale uses her *Ladies' Magazine* to urge the United States to adopt Thanksgiving as an annual holiday.

*February 2:* The Supreme Court issues a ruling in the case of *Martin v. Mott* and affirms that in emergencies the president can take control of state militias over the objections of state governors.

*February 7:* Frenchwoman Francisquy Hutin introduces ballet to the United States when she stages *The Deserter* at New York's Bowery Theater.

*February 10:* The House of Representatives votes to raise trade tariffs on woolen cloth.

*February 28:* The Baltimore and Ohio railroad is chartered by the state of Maryland.

A close vote in the U.S. Senate, decided by the vote of Vice President John C. Calhoun, strikes down the rise in wool tariffs. The close debate exaggerates tensions between northern and southern states.

*March 16:* In New York City, John Russwurm and Samuel Cornish begin publication of the first U.S. newspaper run by African Americans, the *Freeman's Journal.*

*July 4:* Emancipation in New York State takes effect.

*July 26:* In a convention at New Echota, Georgia, the Cherokee nation adopts a constitution and a national government with three branches.

*July 30:* A trade convention in Harrisburg, Pennsylvania, calls for higher tariffs on woolens, iron, cotton cloth, and hemp.

*August 6:* The United States and Great Britain renew their commercial treaty of 1818 and agree to share jurisdiction over the Oregon Territory.

*November 15:* The Creek Indians cede all their remaining land in Georgia to the United States.

*December 17:* The U.S. Senate votes to create a special seating section for reporters in the Senate chamber, so that more accurate newspaper reports might be published.

*December 24:* The Harrisburg trade convention recommendations fail to gain approval in the Jacksonian Democratic-controlled Congress.

## 1828

Noah Webster publishes *The American Dictionary of the English Language.*

Nathaniel Hawthorne publishes his first novel, *Fanshawe.*

Minstrel show performer T. D. Rice popularizes the song "Jim Crow," a caricature of African-American behavior that will later lend its name to racist legislation in the United States.

Chester Harding completes his portrait of Chief Justice John Marshall.

Theodore Sedgwick Wright becomes the first African American to graduate from a theological seminary, Princeton Theological Seminary.

A factory in Jersey City, New Jersey, begins the first production of fine china in the United States.

Congress authorizes the construction of the first U.S. post office building.

The USS *Constitution* is found to be unseaworthy and is laid up at Boston, Massachusetts.

*January 31:* Jacksonian Democrats on the House Committee on Manufactures introduce legislation for extremely high trade tariffs, designed in part to embarrass President Adams if the bill is eventually defeated.

*February 21:* Cherokee editor Elias Boudinot begins publication of the *Cherokee Phoenix* newspaper in the Cherokee capital of New Echota.

*April 23:* The House of Representatives passes the Tariff Act, providing for a large increase in trade taxes.

*May 13:* The U.S. Senate passes the new trade tariffs.

*May 19:* President Adams signs the Tariff Act of 1828, which raises rates so high and damages trade in so many regions that some southerners name it the "Tariff of Abominations."

*July 4:* An elaborate ceremony inaugurates construction of the Baltimore and Ohio railroad.

President Adams breaks ground for the Chesapeake and Ohio Canal. The Baltimore and Ohio will race the Chesapeake and Ohio to reach across the Allegheny Mountains.

*July 24:* British Major General H. C. Darling issues an official report on conditions among Canadian Indians and recommends creating Indian reservations to educate and convert Indian peoples to Christianity.

*August 25:* U.S. negotiators conclude a treaty with Winnebago, Potawatomi, Ottawa, and Chippewa (Ojibway) Indians, who agree to cede lands in Michigan and Illinois.

*December 3:* Andrew Jackson is elected president with 178 electoral votes (over John Quincy Adams's 83 votes). John C. Calhoun is reelected vice president.

*December 19:* The South Carolina assembly condemns the new federal trade tariffs. Vice President Calhoun helps to draft the objections and anonymously publishes the "South Carolina Exposition and Protest," which decries the new tariff rates. South Carolina's objections to high tariffs will lead to a crisis over the nullification of federal law in 1832.

# EYEWITNESS TESTIMONY

The successful military or naval commander is almost the exclusive subject of story, of song, and of praise. Historians, orators, poets, sculptors, and painters, vie with each other, in their respective vocations, in recording, illustrating, proclaiming, and perpetuating his name, his person, and his deeds of renown. How different is the fate of the statesman!

*Henry Clay draws a comparison between public regard for military heroes and statesmen in a speech before the House of Representatives, 1824, in Colton,* Life and Times of Henry Clay, *I: 72.*

Resolved . . . that the President be requested to communicate to him [Lafayette] the assurances of grateful and affectionate attachment still cherished for him by the Government and people of the United States. And be it further resolved, That, whenever the President shall be informed of the time when the Marquis may be ready to embark, that a national ship (with suitable accommodations) be employed to bring him to the United States.

*Congressional resolution to invite the marquis de Lafayette to visit the United States, January 1824, in Brandon,* Lafayette, Guest of the Nation, *I: 28.*

What do you think of the probability of having the Marquis de Lafayette for a visit, for surely Montpelier will be the first place to fly to, when he comes to the United States. . . . We all attended Mrs. Adams's reception on the 8th, and it was really a very brilliant party, and very admirably well arranged. The ladies climbed the chairs and benches to see General Jackson, and Mrs. Adams very gracefully took his arm, and walked through the apartments with him, which gratified the general curiosity.

*Phoebe Morris in a letter to Dolley Madison, January 19, 1824, in* Memoirs and Letters of Dolly Madison, *169–170.*

You have observed the direction & progress of the present Administration and it seems to me that it cannot be doubted that the present fashionable ultra republicans have gone mad further than the sound Federalists of the old school—& that Mr. Calhoun is at the head of the new school cannot be questioned . . . The new school has taken the princi-

ples of the old Federalists but press their principles much further I mean on the subjects of internal improvements, etc., and especially in a latitudinous construction of the constitution generally—Mr. Macon informs me that even Rufus King told him that he was alarmed at the extent to which the new school were going.

*North Carolina congressman Willie P. Magnum in a letter to Thomas Ruffin, January 20, 1824, in Shanks,* The Papers of Willie Person Magnum: *I: 109.*

The Unitarians are universally steadfast, sincere, and earnest Christians. They all believe in the divine mission of Christ, the credibility and authenticity of the Bible, the miracles wrought by our Saviour and his apostles, and the efficacy of his precepts to lead men to salvation. They consider the Scriptures the true rule of faith, and the sure foundation of immortality. In short, their belief is as complete of the divine authority of the Scriptures, as that of any other class of Christians. It is a most gross calumny, therefore, to accuse them of treating the Bible and its doctrines as delusions and falsehoods . . .

*Supreme Court Justice Joseph Story in a letter to William Williams, March 6, 1824, in Story,* Life and Letters of Joseph Story, *I: 442.*

As to President, Jackson seems to be making head[way] yet . . . The truth is, he is the people's candidate in a great part of the southern and western country. I hope New England will support Mr. Calhoun for the Vice-Presidency. If so, he will probably be chosen, and that will be a great thing. He is a true man, and will do good to the country in that situation.

*Daniel Webster reports on the race for president and vice president in a letter to his brother Ezekiel, March 14, 1824, in Webster,* Private Correspondence of Daniel Webster, *I: 347.*

I think it perfectly certain that Gen. Jackson, tho strong, cannot in any event be elected President. I should be gratified to feel as sure that Mr. Adams is not to be the man, no material however that I know of—Crawford will get at least 90 votes in the electoral college—It is believed however that no election will be made, unless by the H. of Reps . . .

*North Carolina congressman Willie P. Magnum in a letter to Thomas Ruffin, March 24, 1824, in Shanks,* The Papers of Willie Person Magnum, *I: 131.*

And what is this tariff? It seems to have been regarded as a sort of monster, huge and deformed—a wild beast, endowed with tremendous powers of destruction, about to be let loose among our people, if not to devour them, at least to consume their substance. But let us calm our passions, and deliberately survey this alarming, this terrific being. The sole object of the tariff is to tax the produce of foreign industry, with the view of promoting American industry. The tax is exclusively levelled at foreign industry. . . . If it subjects any part of American industry to burdens, that is an effect not intended, but is altogether incidental, and preferably voluntary.

*Henry Clay defends the tariff against Southern objections in a speech before the House of Representatives, March 30–31, 1824, in Colton,* Life and Times of Henry Clay, *II: 163–164.*

It is well known that the General [Lafayette] is not rich . . . It is understood that he will be at no expense in the cities. He ought to be at no expense anywhere. It is hoped that he will not be permitted to expend one cent in the United States,—the people have proclaimed him to be their guest; let him be treated therefore, as such.

*The* National Journal *newspaper calls for the public to fund fully Lafayette's visit to the United States, August 5, 1824, in Brandon,* Lafayette, Guest of the Nation, *I: 29–30.*

I will pray my God to spare life until I see Andrew Jackson President of the United States, and then let me close my eyes in peace.

*Edward Patchell in a letter to Andrew Jackson, August 7, 1824, in Bassett,* Life of Andrew Jackson, *333.*

Agreeably to the arrangement previously made . . . the Marquis LA FAYETTE, the only surviving General of the seven year's war of our revolution was conducted from Staten-Island, and landed in this city, amidst every demonstration of joy and admiration that our citizens could bestow. The news of the General's arrival had spread through the surrounding country with the rapidity of lightening; and from the dawn of day until noon, the roads and ferryboats were thronged with people who were hastening to the city, to participate in the fete, and testify their gratitude for his services, and respect for the character of the illustrious 'National Guest.' Our citizens

also turned out in immense numbers, at an early hour, and, together with the military, presented the most lively and *moving* spectacle that we have witnessed on any former occasion.

*The New York* Commercial Advertiser *newspaper reports on the arrival of the marquis de Lafayette, August 17, 1824, in Brandon,* Lafayette: Guest of the Nation, *I: 36.*

I will ask, what is the real situation of the agriculturalist? Where has the American farmer a market for his surplus produce? Except for cotton, he has neither a foreign, nor a home market. . . . In short, sir, we have been too long subject to the policy of British merchants. It is time we should become a little more AMERICANIZED, and instead of feeding paupers and laborers of England, feed our own; or else, in a short time, by continuing our present policy, we shall be paupers ourselves. It is therefore my opinion, that a careful and judicious tariff is much wanted, to pay our national debt, and to afford us a means of that defence within ourselves, on which the safety of our country and liberties depends . . .

*Andrew Jackson in a letter to L. H. Coleman, August 26, 1824, in Colton,* Life and Times of Henry Clay, *II: 293.*

Mr. Jefferson is a man of whom one may form a very just account, as to person and manners, from description and pictures. We met him in the road, and I knew him at once, although he was on horseback, something straighter, and freer from the debility of age than I had expected. We found him uniformly pleasant, social, and interesting.

*Daniel Webster reports on a visit with the aged Thomas Jefferson in a letter, December 29, 1824, in Webster,* Private Correspondence of Daniel Webster, *I: 361.*

Soon after my arrival here, I thought the indications of public sentiment decisively favorable to Gen. Jackson. The members of Congress seemed not to have recovered from the astonishment created by his unexpected success . . . The election I think will depend upon the course that Mr. Clay may take. Of this I entertain scarcely any doubt. Mr. Clay & his friends have until very recently, maintained the utmost reserve, and the slight departure from that course, is still quite equivocal.—One thing I think sure, that he will not stand still, and that when he moves the first object will be success—Our notions of patriotism are quite low, when we see a gentleman occupying so much space in the public mind as Mr. Clay regulated by no higher considerations.—I learn from a source that I deem entitled to full faith, that sad measures have already been taken by Clay & his friends as to prevent Gen. Jackson from getting in any event the votes of Clay, that is, Clay's interest.

> *North Carolina congressman Willie P. Magnum in a letter to Duncan Cameron, January 10, 1825, in Shanks,* The Papers of Willie Person Magnum, *I: 173–174.*

As the 9th of February approaches, we begin to hear a little more about the election. I think some important indications will be made soon. A main inquiry is, in what direction Mr. Clay and his friends will move. There would seem at present to be some reason to think they will take a part finally for Mr. Adams. This will not necessarily be decisive, but it will be very important. After all, I cannot predict results. I believe Mr. Adams might be chosen if he or his friends would act somewhat differently. But if he has good counselors, I know not who they are.

> *Daniel Webster in a letter to his brother Ezekiel Webster, January 13, 1825, in Webster,* Private Correspondence of Daniel Webster, *I: 374.*

Would you believe, that men, professing democracy, could be found base enough, to lay the axe at the very root of the tree of liberty! . . . For some time past, the friends of Clay have hinted, that they, like the Swiss, would fight for those who pay best. Overtures were said to have been made, by the friends of Adams, to the friends of Clay offering him the appointment of secretary of state, for his aid to elect Adams. And the friends of Clay gave the information to the friends of Jackson, and hinted, that if the friends of Jackson would offer the same price, they would close with them. But none of the friends of Jackson would descend to such mean barter and sale. It was not believed by any of the friends of Jackson, that this contract would be ratified, by the members from the states which had voted for Clay. . . . The nation having delivered Jackson into the hands of Congress, backed by a large majority of their votes,

there was on my mind no doubt, that Congress would respond to the will of the nation, by electing the individual they had declared to be their choice. Contrary to his expectation, it is now ascertained to a certainty, that Henry Clay has transferred his interest to John Quincy Adams.

> *Letter to the editor in the Philadelphia* Columbian Observer *newspaper, January 25, 1825, in Colton,* Life and Times of Henry Clay, *I: 295–296.*

While the electoral votes were counting (which was done by the Senate and House conjointly) foreign ministers, strangers of distinction and General Lafayette were present. But when the Senate rose and the house formed itself into a *Body of States* to elect the President, the Senators withdrew from the floor, and all other persons from the House. "What even General Lafayette?" said I, "Yes," replied Mr. Lowry, "and had General Washington himself been there, he too must have withdrawn." . . . The whole proceeding was conducted with silence, order and dignity, and after the Ballots were collected Mr. Webster and Mr. Randolph were appointed the Tellers. It was Mr. Webster who with an audible and clear voice announced J. Adams elected.

> *Washington socialite Margaret Bayard Smith describes the presidential election in a letter, February 11, 1825, in Hunt,* The First Forty Years, *187.*

Peter Hook, a black boy, now in the possession of Mr. Perryman, of Holmesville, Pike County, Mississippi, says, that he is free. That he was born in Philadelphia. He seems from his statement, to have been kidnapped June, 1825. That he was induced one evening by a black man whom they called John, to go down to a schooner near Arch street wharf to get a dram. That a white man, whom they called Jo Johnson, took him down, tied his hands across and chained him to the pump.

> *Account of the kidnapping of Peter Hook in an interview with attorney Duncan S. Walker, June 1825, in Blassingame,* Slave Testimony, *181–182.*

Your arrival in the country, on this happy visit to your American brethren, was greeted by them with expressions of the liveliest satisfaction and joy. Your own observation since, will bear faithful witness how true are their hearts to the language of salutation, with which they first welcomed you. The population

This 1824 cartoon by James Akin Aquafortis criticizes attacks on presidential candidate Andrew Jackson by his opponents and by the press. Jackson stands tall above the pack of angry dogs who attack him. Aquafortis particularly criticized William Crawford and his supporter Martin Van Buren. *(Library of Congress, Prints and Photographs Division [LC-USZ62-5745])*

which has crowded your path-way, the prosperity which has smiled along your progress, in your tour through the Union, are but the fruits of events in which you largely and gloriously participated.

> *The governor of Massachusetts welcomes the marquis de Lafayette in a speech, June 16, 1825, in Butler, Memoirs of the Marquis de Lafayette, 402.*

At Canajoharie we took a canal boat for Utica. These packet boats are almost thirty-five feet long, with a single deck or story, in which there are two cabins, one for ladies, and the other for gentlemen. The one on board of which we were, was tolerably convenient, but some of them are said to be far more so. They are drawn by three horses attached to the boat by a long rope, and the largest horse is ridden by a driver who regulates the whole, and keeps them on a brisk walk, of about four miles an hour. Except when you pass a lock, not the slightest motion is felt in the boat, though the rapidity with which the surrounding objects pass by you, is very apt at first to make you a little dizzy.

*Supreme Court Justice Joseph Story describes travel on the Erie Canal in a letter, July 10, 1825, in Story,* The Life and Letters of Joseph Story, *I: 459.*

It is impossible to describe the Falls of Niagara in such a manner as to give an adequate idea of their stupendous magnificence. We have viewed them as yet only on the English side, meaning to cross over this morning to the American; but all travellers agree that the English Falls are far the most striking and awful . . . The form of the English Falls has been not unaptly compared to a horse-shoe, though from some positions it more nearly resembles a waving line in its form. The roar of the torrent is continual, and though often described as being as loud as thunder, it is wholly different, and is like the roar of Marblehead shore during a very heavy north-east storm. . . . Nothing can be more grand and imposing than the whole scene.

*Supreme Court Justice Joseph Story describes Niagara Falls in a letter, July 14, 1825, in Story,* The Life and Letters of Joseph Story, *I: 469.*

Since I have been on the Bench, I have carefully abstained from writing in the newspapers, and have endeavored to avoid mingling in political engagements, so far as I could without a surrender of my own independence. I have done this from the desire that my administration of justice should not be supposed by the public to be connected with political view or attachments; and from a fear that I might insensibly be drawn too much into the vortex of party excitements. I think the public opinion now points out this course to Judges . . .

*Supreme Court Justice Joseph Story in a letter to Edward Everett, August 4, 1825, in Story,* The Life and Letters of Joseph Story, *I: 363.*

It is conceived that any plan of emancipation, to be effectual, must consult at once the pecuniary interests and prevailing opinions of the southern planters, and bend itself to the existing laws of the southern states. In consequence, it appears indispensable, that emancipation be connected with colonization, and that it demand no pecuniary sacrifice from existing slaveholders, and entail no loss of property on their children.

*Radical reformer Francis Wright in the antislavery newspaper* Genius of Universal Emancipation, *October 1825, in Pease,* The Antislavery Argument, *39.*

In 1826, William Morgan, your free fellow citizen, was, by highly exalted members of the Masonic fraternity, with unlawful violence, seized,—secretly transported through the country more than one hundred miles, to a fortress of the United States [Niagara], then in charge of freemasons, who had prepared it for his reception,—there imprisoned, several days and nights, against his utmost efforts to escape,—and after suffering the most unmanly insults, and the most inhuman abuse, he was privately murdered. Previously to his seizure numerous meetings of freemasons, in lodges and otherwise, were held for the purpose of contriving and adopting the most certain means of carrying into effect, their unlawful objects upon him.

*An 1830 Anti-Masonic convention recalls the 1826 murder of William Morgan, whom the Anti-Masons depict as the victim of a conspiracy, in Davis,* The Fear of Conspiracy, *74.*

The Panama mission is yet undecided in the Senate. It is supposed to furnish some plausible grounds for opposition, and there will be a rallying of forces on the occasion . . . I have no doubt the mission will be approved, and the nominations confirmed by a large majority . . . when the correspondence is seen, it will probably be thought that the President decided right.

*Daniel Webster in a letter to his brother Ezekiel Webster, January 29, 1826, in Webster,* Private Correspondence of Daniel Webster, *I: 401–402.*

The infernal spirit of emancipation, generated by Colonizing & emancipating societies, is greatly felt in this State, and so is the free Negro suffrage in many Counties & almost all the towns—If the people of this State are not more awake to their rights and interest on this subject, a few years more will produce an influence here, greatly to be lamented & feared.

*Bartlett Yancey in a letter to Willie P. Magnum about the state of affairs in North Carolina, January 25, 1826, in Shanks,* The Papers of Willie Person Magnum, *I: 240.*

A Bill has passed the House of Representatives to increase our number [of Supreme Court justices] to ten, and it is very probable that it will receive the approbation of the Senate. It gave rise to one of the most vigorous and protracted debates which we have had this winter. . . . You may probably hear rumors that the Cabinet is divided by intestine discontents, but I can assure you that there is no foundation in fact for such rumors. . . . the opposition comes almost entirely from the slave-holding States, which were in favor of General Jackson, or Mr. Crawford, for President. The Western, Eastern, and Middle States, with the exception of Pennsylvania, are united in support of Mr. Adams. You may therefore easily judge how far he is likely to sustain himself in the Chair.

*Supreme Court Justice Joseph Story comments on politics in a letter to J. Evelyn Denison, March 15, 1826, in Story,* The Life and Letters of Joseph Story, *I: 494, 495.*

The King of England is the "fountain of honor": the President of the United States is the source of patronage. He presides over the entire system of Federal appointments, jobs, and contracts. He has "power" over the "support" of the individuals who administer the system. He makes and unmakes them. He chooses from the circles of his friends and supporters, and *may* dismiss them, and upon all the principles of human action, *will* dismiss them, as often as they disappoint his expectations.

*Senator Thomas Hart Benton in a congressional committee report, May 1826, in Bassett,* Life of Andrew Jackson, *388.*

Slaves are . . . placed on the footing of property, and he must be a wretched and misguided enthusiast who would now question the correctness of that decision. I always thought that the Northern politicians had gone a bow-shot too far when they attempted, as in the discussion of the Missouri question, to elevate to the condition of *citizens* the free blacks . . . This is, what you properly call it, a great question,—a question big with the fate of this Union; one that startles and is well calculated to alarm all the sensibilities of the patriot, and one the settlement of which I shall, along with yourself and our common constituents, watch with the deepest interest.

*Virginia governor John Tyler in a letter to Senator Littleton W. Tazewell, May 2, 1826, in Tyler,* Letters and Times of the Tylers, *I: 331.*

Thus has terminated, in the eighty-fourth year of his age, the life of one of the greatest and best of men. . . . Let his life be an instructive lesson to us, my countrymen. Let us teach our children to reverence his name, and even in infancy to lisp his principles. . . . Scarcely has the funeral knell of our Jefferson been sounded in our ears, when [we] were startled by the death-knell of another patriot, his zealous co-adjutor in the holy cause of the Revolution . . . Adams, the compeer of his early fame, the opposing orb of his meridian, the friend of his old age, and his companion to the realms of bliss. They have sunk together in death, and have fallen on the same glorious day into that sleep which knows no waking.

*Virginia governor John Tyler in a funeral oration in honor of Thomas Jefferson, July 11, 1826, in Tyler,* Letters and Times of the Tylers, *I: 353.*

. . . Each town or district within this Commonwealth, containing fifty families or householders, shall be provided with a teacher or teachers, of good morals, to instruct children in orthography, reading, writing, English grammar, geography, arithmetic, and good behavior, for such term of time as shall be equivalent six months for one school in each year.

*The Massachusetts legislature passes the nation's first law creating high schools, January, 1827, in Commager,* Documents, *247.*

Notwithstanding the vigilance of the powers now engaged to suppress the slave-trade, I have received information, that in a single year, in the single island of Cuba, slaves equal in amount to one half of the above-named number of fifty-two thousand, have been illicitly introduced. . . . If I could be instrumental in eradicating this deepest stain [slavery] from the character of our country, and removing all cause of reproach on account of it, by foreign nations . . . I would not exchange the proud satisfaction which I should enjoy, for the honor of all the triumphs ever decreed to the most successful conqueror.

*Henry Clay in a speech delivered to the American Colonization Society, January 20, 1827, in Colton,* Life and Times of Henry Clay, *I: 188, 189.*

The present administration is the most effective enemy of internal improvements that has ever appeared among us. They are ruining the cause by prostituting it to electioneering, and will be attacked upon that ground. I think it probable that Jackson will be catechized upon this subject, either by some overzealous friend or insidious enemy.

*Senator Thomas Hart Benton in a letter to Major W. B. Lewis about Andrew Jackson, February 22, 1827, in Bassett,* Life of Andrew Jackson, *397.*

A survey of the whole ground leads me to believe, confidently, in Mr. Adams's reelection. I set down New England, New Jersey, the greater part of Maryland, and perhaps all Delaware, Ohio, Kentucky, Indiana, Missouri, and Louisiana for him. We must then get votes enough in New York to choose him, and I think cannot fail of this.

*Daniel Webster incorrectly predicts that John Quincy Adams will be reelected in a letter, April 10, 1827, in Webster,* Private Correspondence of Daniel Webster, *I: 418.*

He [General Jackson] now stands before the nation as the direct public accuser of Mr. Clay and his friends, and by inference, of Mr. Adams also. The accusation has been *deliberately denied.* And if General Jackson should not sustain it by competent and credible proof, the American public will not be restrained by the grateful respect which they have hitherto cherished for him, from characterizing the charge, as in that event, it will deserve to be considered.

*The Washington* National Journal *newspaper, April 28, 1827, in Colton,* Life and Times of Henry Clay, *I: 323.*

. . .We of the Southern States feel, that we have been so long behind our Northern neighbors in the production of everything that substantially administers to the elegance or the comforts of life. It has been our own fault—not theirs. . . . From them we get not only our clothes, carriages, saddles, hats, shoes, flour, potatoes, but even our onions and horn buttons. . . . Let us change our policy, but without that spirit and those expressions which leave a festering sore in the hearts of those who should be brothers.

*Editorial in the Augusta, Georgia,* Courier, *June 21, 1827, in Phillips,* Plantation and Frontier, *I: 290.*

Here you may behold fathers and brothers leaving behind them the dearest objects of affection and moving slowly along in the mute agony of despair;

there a young mother stooping over an infant whose innocent smiles seem but to increase her misery. From some you will hear the burst of bitter lamentation, while from others a loud hysteric laugh breaks forth denoting still deeper agony.

*An* Alexandria Gazette *newspaper writer describes the slave market in Alexandria, Virginia, June 22, 1827, in Johnson and Smith,* Africans in America, *351.*

Let us then relieve ourselves from the odious stigma which some have long since cast upon us, that we are incapacitated by the God of nature, for the enjoyment of the rights of freemen, and convince them and the world that although our complexion may differ, yet we have hearts susceptible of feeling; judgment capable of discerning, and prudence sufficient to manage our affairs with discretion, and by example prove ourselves worthy of the blessings we enjoy.

*Nathaniel Paul in an oration to celebrate the abolition of slavery in New York, July 5, 1827, in Aptheker,* Documentary History, *88.*

When I took my last walk among the wharves in Charleston, and saw them piled up with mountains of Cotton, and all your stores, ships, steam and canal boats, crammed with and groaning under, the weight of Cotton, I returned to the Planters' Hotel, where I found the four daily papers, as well as the conversation of the boarders, teeming with Cotton! Cotton!! Cotton!!! . . . From this I continued on meeting with little else than cotton fields, cotton gins, cotton wagons . . . I arrived in Augusta; and when I saw cotton wagons in Broad-street, I whistled! . . . And you must know, that they have cotton warehouses there covering whole squares, all full of cotton; and some knowing ones told me, that there were then in the place from 40,000 to 50,000 bales. And Hamburg (as a Negro said) was worser, according to its size; for it puzzled me to tell which was the largest, the piles of cotton or the houses.

*A letter from a traveler along the Missouri River in the Augusta, Georgia,* Courier, *October 11, 1827, in Phillips,* Plantation and Frontier, *I: 284.*

Next week there is to be a Fair, for the benefit of the Orphan Asylum. Every female in the City, I believe, from the highest to the lowest has been at work for it. Mrs. Van Ness spares neither time [n]or expense and Mrs. Lovel for three weeks has been working night and day and enlisted her husband and sisters who have painted &c. &c, besides begging for scraps and pieces of all kinds to dress dolls and make pin cushions. From knit-stocking, clergyman's bands, to hats, caps, tables, and dresses the ingenuity of our ladies has been employed.

*Washington socialite Margaret Bayard Smith reports on female benevolent activities in Washington, D.C., in a letter, December 21, 1827, in Hunt,* The First Forty Years, *209–210.*

My traducers have attributed to me great facility in making a *bargain*. Whether I possess it, or not, there is *one* bargain, which, for their accommodation, I am willing to enter into with them. If they will prevail upon their chief, to acknowledge that he has been in error, and has done me injustice, and if they will cease to traduce and abuse me, I will no longer present myself before public assemblies, or in public prints, in my own defence. That is a bargain, however, which I have no expectation of being able to conclude; for men, who are in [a] long-established line of business, will not voluntarily quit their accustomed trade, and acknowledge themselves *bankrupts to honor, decency, and truth.*

*Henry Clay attacks Andrew Jackson and his political cronies, 1828, in Colton,* Life and Times of Henry Clay, *I: 108.*

There can be no doubt that, under a bald theory, a representation would be all the better if the most ignorant, profligate, and vagabond part of the community, were excluded from the right of voting. It is just as true, that if all the rogues and corrupt politicians, even including those who read Latin, and have well-lined pockets, could be refused the right of voting, honest men would fare all the better. . . . I do not mean to say that the suffrage may not, in most countries, be extended too far. I only wish to show you that it is not here.

*James Fenimore Cooper in,* Notions of the Americans . . ., *1828, in Craven and Johnson,* Documentary History, *321, 322.*

His scheme is to equalize property, or throw it into a common stock, so that no one will be very rich, and *none* poor. In order to accomplish this he would have society divided into communities,—no community to exceed 2000 individuals, nor be less than 800. This community, instead of living in towns or cities, should form a kind of village, extending over ten miles square,—each community should have within itself schools, manufactures, agricultural grounds, &c sufficient for the abundant supply of every comfort, nay every luxury of life. . . . Marriage is to be released from its present fetters and when a couple grew weary of each other, they would be allowed to separate and form new connections . . . I told him it would be nothing more than the Christian millennium.

*Margaret Bayard Smith reports on Robert Owen's plans for utopian communal living in a letter to her son, 1828, in Hunt,* The First Forty Years, *221, 222.*

The Tariff question not yet finally acted upon in the senate I fear we shall be beaten finally and that some further additions will be made on the imports. Our course however is clear, self defense, raise our Horses, mules & Pork, spin & weave at home buy nothing from these Tariff Gentlemen, that can be dispensed with, we can live as cheaply as they can, Let us take pride in what we can make & raise within ourselves and not in what we buy.

*Willis Alston comments on anti-tariff opinion in North Carolina in a letter to Willie P. Magnum, May 7, 1828, in Shanks,* The Papers of Willie Person Magnum, *I: 330.*

I am persuaded that I do not misinterpret the feelings of the people of the United States, as I certainly express my own, in saying, that the interest which was inspired in this country by the arduous struggles of South America, arose principally from the hope, that, along with its independence, would be established free institutions, insuring all the blessings of civil liberty. To the accomplishment of that object we still anxiously look.

*Henry Clay in a letter to Simón de Bolívar, October 27, 1828, in Colton,* Life and Times of Henry Clay, *I: 245.*

CASH FOR NEGROES. The Subscriber will give the highest price in Cash for Negroes of either sex

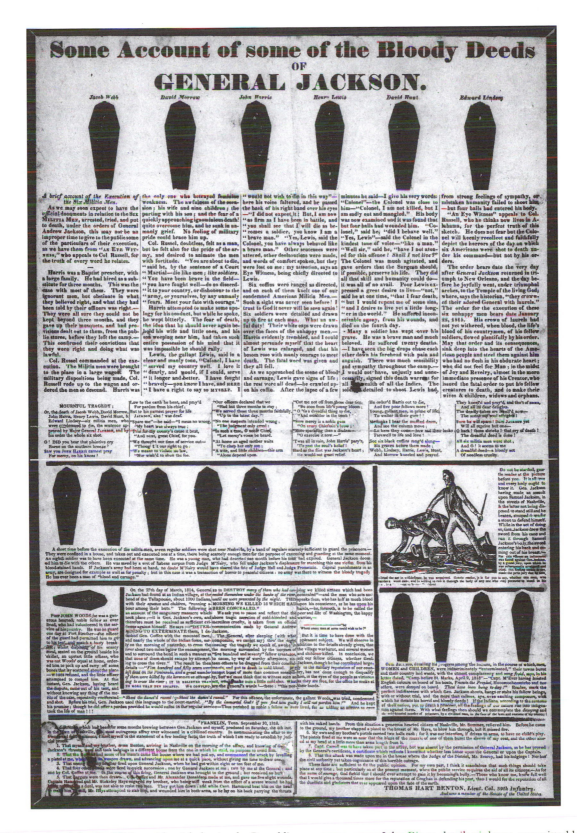

This handbill, produced for the 1828 presidential election by Republican newspaperman John Binns, details violence committed by Andrew Jackson and depicts him stabbing a man in Nashville, Tennessee. The 1828 campaign witnessed a dramatic growth in such negative campaign techniques. *(Library of Congress, Prints and Photographs Division [LC-USZ62-43901])*

delivered at Georgetown X Roads. Any person writing to the subscriber will be attended to.

*James Salisbury advertises his willingness to buy slaves in the Chestertown, Maryland,* Telegraph, *November 7, 1828, in Phillips,* Plantation and Frontier, *II: 55.*

The Senate and House of Representatives of South Carolina, now met, and sitting in General Assembly, through the Hon. William Smith and the Hon. Robert Y. Hayne, their representatives in the Senate of the United States, do, in the name and on behalf of the good people of the said commonwealth, solemnly PROTEST against the system of protecting duties, lately adopted by the federal government . . .

*The South Carolina legislature protests the "Tariff of Abominations," December 19, 1828, in Commager,* Documents, *249–250.*

# APPENDIX A
## Documents

1. Declaration for the Suspension of Hostilities in the Revolutionary War, signed January 20, 1783
2. The Treaty of Paris, signed September 3, 1783
3. The Northwest Ordinance, passed July 13, 1787
4. The Constitution of the United States of America, drafted 1787, ratified, 1788
5. The Bill of Rights, the first ten amendments to the Constitution of the United States, ratified, 1791
6. The Proclamation of Neutrality, April 22, 1793
7. The Treaty of Greenville, concluded August 3, 1795
8. An Act Respecting Alien Enemies, approved, July 6, 1798
9. The Sedition Act, approved, July 14, 1798
10. The Virginia Resolutions, agreed to by the Virginia Senate, December 24, 1798
11. The Louisiana Purchase, signed April 30, 1803
12. An Act to Prohibit the Importation of Slaves into any Port of Place within the Jurisdiction of the United States, From and After the First Day of January, in the Year of Our Lord One Thousand Eight Hundred and Eight, passed, March 2, 1807
13. An Act Declaring War between the United Kingdom of Great Britain and Ireland and the Dependencies Thereof and the United States of America and Their Territories, June 18, 1812
14. The Treaty of Ghent, signed December 24, 1814
15. The Monroe Doctrine, December 2, 1823

# 1. Declaration for the Suspension of Hostilities in the Revolutionary War, Signed January 20, 1783

We the underwritten Ministers Plenipotentiary of the United States of North America, having received from Mr Fitz-Herbert, Minister Plenipotentiary of his Britannic Majesty, a Declaration relative to a Suspension of Arms to be establish'd between his said Majesty and the said States, of which the following is a Copy. viz:

Whereas the Preliminary Articles agreed to and signed this Day between his Majesty the King of Great Britain, and his most Christian Majesty on the one Part, and also between his said Britannic Majesty and his Catholic Majesty on the other Part, stipulate a Cessation of Hostilities between those three Powers, which is to Commence upon the Exchange of the Ratifications of the said Preliminary Articles; And whereas by the Provisional Treaty signed the thirtieth of November last, between his Britannic Majesty and the United States of North America, it was stipulated that the said Treaty should have its Effect as soon as Peace between the said Crowns should be established; The underwritten Minister Plenipotentiary of his Britannic Majesty declares in the Name, and by the express, Order of the King his Master, that the said United States of North America, their Subjects and their Possessions, shall be comprised in the suspension of Arms above-mentioned, And that they shall consequently enjoy the Benifit [sic] of the Cessation of Hostilities, at the same Periods and in the same Manner as the three Crowns aforesaid and their Subjects and Possessions respectively On Condition however, that on the Part and in the Name of the Said United States of North America, there shall be deliver'd a similar Declaration expressing the Assent to the present Suspension of Arms, and containing an Assurance of the most perfect Reciprocity on their Part.

In faith whereof, we, the Minister Plenipotentiary of his Britannic Majesty, have signed this present Declaration, and have thereto caused the Seal of our Arms to be affixed, at Versailles this twentieth Day of January One Thousand seven hundred & Eighty three.

[Names.]

We have in the Name of the said United States of North America & in Virtue of the Powers we are vested with, received the above Declaration and do accept the same by these Presents, and we do reciprocally declare, that the said States shall cause to cease all Hostilities against his Britannic Majesty, his Subjects and Possessions at the Terms or Periods agreed to between his said Majesty the King of Great Britain, his Majesty the King of France, and his Majesty the King of Spain, in the same manner as is stipulated between these, three Crowns, and to have the same Effect.

In faith whereof, We Ministers Plenipotentiary from the United States of America, have signed the present Declaration and have hereunto affixed the Seals of our Arms. At Versailles the twentieth of January one thousand seven hundred and eighty three.

[Names.]

# 2. The Treaty of Paris, Signed September 3, 1783

In the name of the most holy and undivided Trinity.

It having pleased the Divine Providence to dispose the hearts of the most serene and most potent Prince George the Third, by the grace of God, king of Great Britain, France, and Ireland, defender of the faith, duke of Brunswick and Lunebourg, arch-treasurer and prince elector of the Holy Roman Empire etc., and of the United States of America, to forget all past misunderstandings and differences that have unhappily interrupted the good correspondence and friendship which they mutually wish to restore, and to establish such a beneficial and satisfactory intercourse, between the two countries upon the ground of reciprocal advantages and mutual convenience as may promote and secure to both perpetual peace and harmony; and having for this desirable end already laid the foundation of peace and reconciliation by the Provisional Articles signed at Paris on the 30th of November 1782, by the commissioners empowered on each part, which articles were agreed to be inserted in and constitute the Treaty of Peace proposed to be concluded between the Crown of Great Britain and the said United States, but which treaty was not to be concluded until terms of peace should be agreed upon between Great Britain and France and his Britannic Majesty should be ready to conclude such treaty accordingly; and the treaty between Great Britain and France having since been concluded, his Britannic Majesty and the United States of America, in order to carry into full effect the Provisional Articles above mentioned, according to the tenor thereof, have constituted and appointed, that is to say his Britannic Majesty on his part, David Hartley, Esqr., member of the Parliament of Great Britain, and the said United States on their part, John Adams, Esqr., late a commissioner of the United States of America at the court of Versailles, late delegate in Congress from the state of Massachusetts, and chief justice of the said state, and minister plenipotentiary of the said United States to their high mightinesses the States General of the United Netherlands; Benjamin Franklin, Esqr., late delegate in Congress from the state of Pennsylvania, president of the convention of the said state, and minister plenipotentiary from the United States of America at the court of Versailles; John Jay, Esqr., late president of Congress and chief justice of the state of New York, and minister plenipotentiary from the said United States at the court of Madrid; to be plenipotentiaries for the concluding and signing the present definitive treaty; who after having reciprocally communicated their respective full powers have agreed upon and confirmed the following articles.

## Article 1:

His Britannic Majesty acknowledges the said United States, viz., New Hampshire, Massachusetts Bay, Rhode Island and Providence Plantations, Connecticut, New York, New Jersey, Pennsylvania, Maryland, Virginia, North Carolina, South Carolina and Georgia, to be free sovereign and independent states, that he treats with them as such, and for himself, his heirs, and successors, relinquishes all claims to the government, propriety, and territorial rights of the same and every part thereof.

## Article 2:

And that all disputes which might arise in future on the subject of the boundaries of the said United States may be prevented, it is hereby agreed and declared, that the following are and shall be their boundaries, viz.; from the northwest angle of Nova Scotia, viz., that angle which is formed by a line drawn due north from the source of St. Croix River to the highlands; along the said highlands which divide those rivers that empty themselves into the river St. Lawrence, from those which fall into the Atlantic Ocean, to the northwesternmost head of Connecticut River; thence down along the middle of that river to the forty-fifth degree of north latitude; from thence by a line due

west on said latitude until it strikes the river Iroquois or Cataraquy; thence along the middle of said river into Lake Ontario; through the middle of said lake until it strikes the communication by water between that lake and Lake Erie; thence along the middle of said communication into Lake Erie, through the middle of said lake until it arrives at the water communication between that lake and Lake Huron; thence along the middle of said water communication into Lake Huron, thence through the middle of said lake to the water communication between that lake and Lake Superior; thence through Lake Superior northward of the Isles Royal and Phelipeaux to the Long Lake; thence through the middle of said Long Lake and the water communication between it and the Lake of the Woods, to the said Lake of the Woods; thence through the said lake to the most northwesternmost point thereof, and from thence on a due west course to the river Mississippi; thence by a line to be drawn along the middle of the said river Mississippi until it shall intersect the northernmost part of the thirty-first degree of north latitude, South, by a line to be drawn due east from the determination of the line last mentioned in the latitude of thirty-one degrees of the equator, to the middle of the river Apalachicola or Catahouche; thence along the middle thereof to its junction with the Flint River, thence straight to the head of Saint Mary's River; and thence down along the middle of Saint Mary's River to the Atlantic Ocean; east, by a line to be drawn along the middle of the river Saint Croix, from its mouth in the Bay of Fundy to its source, and from its source directly north to the aforesaid highlands which divide the rivers that fall into the Atlantic Ocean from those which fall into the river Saint Lawrence; comprehending all islands within twenty leagues of any part of the shores of the United States, and lying between lines to be drawn due east from the points where the aforesaid boundaries between Nova Scotia on the one part and East Florida on the other shall, respectively, touch the Bay of Fundy and the Atlantic Ocean, excepting such islands as now are or heretofore have been within the limits of the said province of Nova Scotia.

## Article 3:

It is agreed that the people of the United States shall continue to enjoy unmolested the right to take fish of every kind on the Grand Bank and on all the other banks of Newfoundland, also in the Gulf of Saint

Lawrence and at all other places in the sea, where the inhabitants of both countries used at any time heretofore to fish. And also that the inhabitants of the United States shall have liberty to take fish of every kind on such part of the coast of Newfoundland as British fishermen shall use, (but not to dry or cure the same on that island) and also on the coasts, bays and creeks of all other of his Britannic Majesty's dominions in America; and that the American fishermen shall have liberty to dry and cure fish in any of the unsettled bays, harbors, and creeks of Nova Scotia, Magdalen Islands, and Labrador, so long as the same shall remain unsettled, but so soon as the same or either of them shall be settled, it shall not be lawful for the said fishermen to dry or cure fish at such settlement without a previous agreement for that purpose with the inhabitants, proprietors, or possessors of the ground.

## Article 4:

It is agreed that creditors on either side shall meet with no lawful impediment to the recovery of the full value in sterling money of all bona fide debts heretofore contracted.

## Article 5:

It is agreed that Congress shall earnestly recommend it to the legislatures of the respective states to provide for the restitution of all estates, rights, and properties, which have been confiscated belonging to real British subjects; and also of the estates, rights, and properties of persons resident in districts in the possession on his Majesty's arms and who have not borne arms against the said United States. And that persons of any other description shall have free liberty to go to any part or parts of any of the thirteen United States and therein to remain twelve months unmolested in their endeavors to obtain the restitution of such of their estates, rights, and properties as may have been confiscated; and that Congress shall also earnestly recommend to the several states a reconsideration and revision of all acts or laws regarding the premises, so as to render the said laws or acts perfectly consistent not only with justice and equity but with that spirit of conciliation which on the return of the blessings of peace should universally prevail. And that Congress shall also earnestly recommend to the several states that the estates, rights, and properties, of such last mentioned persons shall be restored to them, they refunding to any persons who may be now in possession the bona

fide price (where any has been given) which such persons may have paid on purchasing any of the said lands, rights, or properties since the confiscation.

And it is agreed that all persons who have any interest in confiscated lands, either by debts, marriage settlements, or otherwise, shall meet with no lawful impediment in the prosecution of their just rights.

## Article 6:

That there shall be no future confiscations made nor any prosecutions commenced against any person or persons for, or by reason of, the part which he or they may have taken in the present war, and that no person shall on that account suffer any future loss or damage, either in his person, liberty, or property; and that those who may be in confinement on such charges at the time of the ratification of the treaty in America shall be immediately set at liberty, and the prosecutions so commenced be discontinued.

## Article 7:

There shall be a firm and perpetual peace between his Britannic Majesty and the said states, and between the subjects of the one and the citizens of the other, wherefore all hostilities both by sea and land shall from henceforth cease. All prisoners on both sides shall be set at liberty, and his Britannic Majesty shall with all convenient speed, and without causing any destruction, or carrying away any Negroes or other property of the American inhabitants, withdraw all his armies, garrisons, and fleets from the said United States, and from every post, place, and harbor within the same; leaving in all fortifications, the American artillery that may be therein; and shall also order and cause all archives, records, deeds, and papers belonging to any of the said states, or their citizens, which in the course of the war may have fallen into the hands of his officers, to be forthwith restored and delivered to the proper states and persons to whom they belong.

## Article 8:

The navigation of the river Mississippi, from its source to the ocean, shall forever remain free and open to the subjects of Great Britain and the citizens of the United States.

## Article 9:

In case it should so happen that any place or territory belonging to Great Britain or to the United States should have been conquered by the arms of either from the other before the arrival of the said Provisional Articles in America, it is agreed that the same shall be restored without difficulty and without requiring any compensation.

## *Article 10:*

The solemn ratifications of the present treaty expedited in good and due form shall be exchanged between the contracting parties in the space of six months or sooner, if possible, to be computed from the day of the signatures of the present treaty. In witness whereof we the undersigned, their ministers plenipotentiary, have in their name and in virtue of our full powers, signed with our hands the present definitive treaty and caused the seals of our arms to be affixed thereto.

Done at Paris, this third day of September in the year of our Lord, one thousand seven hundred and eighty-three.

[Names.]

## 3. THE NORTHWEST ORDINANCE, PASSED JULY 13, 1787

*An Ordinance for the government of the Territory of the United States northwest of the River Ohio.*

**Section 1.** *Be it ordained by the United States in Congress assembled,* That the said territory, for the purposes of temporary government, be one district, subject, however, to be divided into two districts, as future circumstances may, in the opinion of Congress, make it expedient.

**Sec. 2.** *Be it ordained by the authority aforesaid,* That the estates, both of resident and nonresident proprietors in the said territory, dying intestate, shall descent to, and be distributed among their children, and the descendants of a deceased child, in equal parts; the descendants of a deceased child or grandchild to take the share of their deceased parent in equal parts among them: And where there shall be no children or descendants, then in equal parts to the next of kin in equal degree; and among collaterals, the children of a deceased brother or sister of the intestate shall have, in equal parts among them, their deceased parents' share; and there shall in no case be a distinction between kindred of the whole and half blood; saving, in all cases, to the widow of the intestate her third part of the real estate for life, and one

third part of the personal estate; and this law relative to descents and dower, shall remain in full force until altered by the legislature of the district. And until the governor and judges shall adopt laws as hereinafter mentioned, estates in the said territory may be devised or bequeathed by wills in writing, signed and sealed by him or her in whom the estate may be (being of full age), and attested by three witnesses; and real estates may be conveyed by lease and release, or bargain and sale, signed, sealed and delivered by the person being of full age, in whom the estate may be, and attested by two witnesses, provided such wills be duly proved, and such conveyances be acknowledged, or the execution thereof duly proved, and be recorded within one year after proper magistrates, courts, and registers shall be appointed for that purpose; and personal property may be transferred by delivery; saving, however to the French and Canadian inhabitants, and other settlers of the Kaskaskies, St. Vincents and the neighboring villages who have heretofore professed themselves citizens of Virginia, their laws and customs now in force among them, relative to the descent and conveyance, of property.

**Sec. 3.** *Be it ordained by the authority aforesaid,* That there shall be appointed from time to time by Congress, a governor, whose commission shall continue in force for the term of three years, unless sooner revoked by Congress; he shall reside in the district, and have a freehold estate therein in 1,000 acres of land, while in the exercise of his office.

**Sec. 4.** There shall be appointed from time to time by Congress, a secretary, whose commission shall continue in force for four years unless sooner revoked; he shall reside in the district, and have a freehold estate therein in 500 acres of land, while in the exercise of his office. It shall be his duty to keep and preserve the acts and laws passed by the legislature, and the public records of the district, and the proceedings of the governor in his executive department, and transmit authentic copies of such acts and proceedings, every six months, to the Secretary of Congress: There shall also be appointed a court to consist of three judges, any two of whom to form a court, who shall have a common law jurisdiction, and reside in the district, and have each therein a freehold estate in 500 acres of land while in the exercise of their offices; and their commissions shall continue in force during good behavior.

**Sec. 5.** The governor and judges, or a majority of them, shall adopt and publish in the district such laws of the original States, criminal and civil, as may be necessary and best suited to the circumstances of the district, and report them to Congress from time to time: which laws shall be in force in the district until the organization of the General Assembly therein, unless disapproved of by Congress; but afterwards the Legislature shall have authority to alter them as they shall think fit.

**Sec. 6.** The governor, for the time being, shall be commander in chief of the militia, appoint and commission all officers in the same below the rank of general officers; all general officers shall be appointed and commissioned by Congress.

**Sec. 7.** Previous to the organization of the general assembly, the governor shall appoint such magistrates and other civil officers in each county or township, as he shall find necessary for the preservation of the peace and good order in the same: After the general assembly shall be organized, the powers and duties of the magistrates and other civil officers shall be regulated and defined by the said assembly; but all magistrates and other civil officers not herein otherwise directed, shall during the continuance of this temporary government, be appointed by the governor.

**Sec. 8.** For the prevention of crimes and injuries, the laws to be adopted or made shall have force in all parts of the district, and for the execution of process, criminal and civil, the governor shall make proper divisions thereof; and he shall proceed from time to time as circumstances may require, to lay out the parts of the district in which the Indian titles shall have been extinguished, into counties and townships, subject, however, to such alterations as may thereafter be made by the legislature.

**Sec. 9.** So soon as there shall be five thousand free male inhabitants of full age in the district, upon giving proof thereof to the governor, they shall receive authority, with time and place, to elect a representative from their counties or townships to represent them in the general assembly: Provided, That, for every five hundred free male inhabitants, there shall be one representative, and so on progressively with the number of free male inhabitants shall the right of representation increase, until the number of representatives shall amount to twenty five; after which, the number and proportion of representatives

shall be regulated by the legislature: Provided, That no person be eligible or qualified to act as a representative unless he shall have been a citizen of one of the United States three years, and be a resident in the district, or unless he shall have resided in the district three years; and, in either case, shall likewise hold in his own right, in fee simple, two hundred acres of land within the same; Provided, also, That a freehold in fifty acres of land in the district, having been a citizen of one of the states, and being resident in the district, or the like freehold and two years residence in the district, shall be necessary to qualify a man as an elector of a representative.

**Sec. 10.** The representatives thus elected, shall serve for the term of two years; and, in case of the death of a representative, or removal from office, the governor shall issue a writ to the county or township for which he was a member, to elect another in his stead, to serve for the residue of the term.

**Sec. 11.** The general assembly or legislature shall consist of the governor, legislative council, and a house of representatives. The Legislative Council shall consist of five members, to continue in office five years, unless sooner removed by Congress; any three of whom to be a quorum: and the members of the Council shall be nominated and appointed in the following manner, to wit: As soon as representatives shall be elected, the Governor shall appoint a time and place for them to meet together; and, when met, they shall nominate ten persons, residents in the district, and each possessed of a freehold in five hundred acres of land, and return their names to Congress; five of whom Congress shall appoint and commission to serve as aforesaid; and, whenever a vacancy shall happen in the council, by death or removal from office, the house of representatives shall nominate two persons, qualified as aforesaid, for each vacancy, and return their names to Congress; one of whom congress shall appoint and commission for the residue of the term. And every five years, four months at least before the expiration of the time of service of the members of council, the said house shall nominate ten persons, qualified as aforesaid, and return their names to Congress; five of whom Congress shall appoint and commission to serve as members of the council five years, unless sooner removed. And the governor, legislative council, and house of representatives, shall have authority to make laws in all cases, for the good government of the district, not repugnant to the principles and articles in this ordinance established and declared. And all bills, having passed by a majority in the house, and by a majority in the council, shall be referred to the governor for his assent; but no bill, or legislative act whatever, shall be of any force without his assent. The governor shall have power to convene, prorogue, and dissolve the general assembly, when, in his opinion, it shall be expedient.

**Sec. 12.** The governor, judges, legislative council, secretary, and such other officers as Congress shall appoint in the district, shall take an oath or affirmation of fidelity and of office; the governor before the president of congress, and all other officers before the Governor. As soon as a legislature shall be formed in the district, the council and house assembled in one room, shall have authority, by joint ballot, to elect a delegate to Congress, who shall have a seat in Congress, with a right of debating but not voting during this temporary government.

**Sec. 13.** And, for extending the fundamental principles of civil and religious liberty, which form the basis whereon these republics, their laws and constitutions are erected; to fix and establish those principles as the basis of all laws, constitutions, and governments, which forever hereafter shall be formed in the said territory: to provide also for the establishment of States, and permanent government therein, and for their admission to a share in the federal councils on an equal footing with the original States, at as early periods as may be consistent with the general interest.

**Sec. 14.** It is hereby ordained and declared by the authority aforesaid, That the following articles shall be considered as articles of compact between the original States and the people and States in the said territory and forever remain unalterable, unless by common consent, to wit:

**Art. 1.** No person, demeaning himself in a peaceable and orderly manner, shall ever be molested on account of his mode of worship or religious sentiments, in the said territory.

**Art. 2.** The inhabitants of the said territory shall always be entitled to the benefits of the writ of *habeas corpus,* and of the trial by jury; of a proportionate representation of the people in the legislature; and of judicial proceedings according to the course of the common law. All persons shall be bailable, unless for capital offenses, where the proof shall be evident or the presumption great. All fines shall be moderate; and

no cruel or unusual punishments shall be inflicted. No man shall be deprived of his liberty or property, but by the judgment of his peers or the law of the land; and, should the public exigencies make it necessary, for the common preservation, to take any person's property, or to demand his particular services, full compensation shall be made for the same. And, in the just preservation of rights and property, it is understood and declared, that no law ought ever to be made, or have force in the said territory, that shall, in any manner whatever, interfere with or affect private contracts or engagements, *bona fide,* and without fraud, previously formed.

**Art. 3.** Religion, morality, and knowledge, being necessary to good government and the happiness of mankind, schools and the means of education shall forever be encouraged. The utmost good faith shall always be observed towards the Indians; their lands and property shall never be taken from them without their consent; and, in their property, rights, and liberty, they shall never be invaded or disturbed, unless in just and lawful wars authorized by Congress; but laws founded in justice and humanity, shall from time to time be made for preventing wrongs being done to them, and for preserving peace and friendship with them.

**Art. 4.** The said territory, and the States which may be formed therein, shall forever remain a part of this Confederacy of the United States of America, subject to the Articles of Confederation, and to such alterations therein as shall be constitutionally made; and to all the acts and ordinances of the United States in Congress assembled, conformable thereto. The inhabitants and settlers in the said territory shall be subject to pay a part of the federal debts contracted or to be contracted, and a proportional part of the expenses of government, to be apportioned on them by Congress according to the same common rule and measure by which apportionments thereof shall be made on the other States; and the taxes for paying their proportion shall be laid and levied by the authority and direction of the legislatures of the district or districts, or new States, as in the original States, within the time agreed upon by the United States in Congress assembled. The legislatures of those districts or new States, shall never interfere with the primary disposal of the soil by the United States in Congress assembled, nor with any regulations Congress may find necessary for securing the title in such soil to the *bona fide* purchasers. No tax shall be imposed on lands the property of the United States; and, in no case, shall nonresident proprietors be taxed higher than residents. The navigable waters leading into the Mississippi and St. Lawrence, and the carrying places between the same, shall be common highways and forever free, as well to the inhabitants of the said territory as to the citizens of the United States, and those of any other States that may be admitted into the confederacy, without any tax, impost, or duty therefor.

**Art. 5.** There shall be formed in the said territory, not less than three nor more than five States; and the boundaries of the States, as soon as Virginia shall alter her act of cession, and consent to the same, shall become fixed and established as follows, to wit: The western State in the said territory, shall be bounded by the Mississippi, the Ohio, and Wabash Rivers; a direct line drawn from the Wabash and Post Vincents, due North, to the territorial line between the United States and Canada; and, by the said territorial line, to the Lake of the Woods and Mississippi. The middle State shall be bounded by the said direct line, the Wabash from Post Vincents to the Ohio, by the Ohio, by a direct line, drawn due north from the mouth of the Great Miami, to the said territorial line, and by the said territorial line. The eastern State shall be bounded by the last mentioned direct line, the Ohio, Pennsylvania, and the said territorial line: *Provided, however,* and it is further understood and declared, that the boundaries of these three States shall be subject so far to be altered, that, if Congress shall hereafter find it expedient, they shall have authority to form one or two States in that part of the said territory which lies north of an east and west line drawn through the southerly bend or extreme of Lake Michigan. And, whenever any of the said States shall have sixty thousand free inhabitants therein, such State shall be admitted, by its delegates, into the Congress of the United States, on an equal footing with the original States in all respects whatever, and shall be at liberty to form a permanent constitution and State government: *Provided,* the constitution and government so to be formed, shall be republican, and in conformity to the principles contained in these articles; and, so far as it can be consistent with the general interest of the confederacy, such admission shall be allowed at an earlier period, and when there may be a less number of free inhabitants in the State than sixty thousand.

**Art. 6.** There shall be neither slavery nor involuntary servitude in the said territory, otherwise than in the punishment of crimes whereof the party shall have been duly convicted: *Provided, always,* That any person escaping into the same, from whom labor or service is lawfully claimed in any one of the original States, such fugitive may be lawfully reclaimed and conveyed to the person claiming his or her labor or service as aforesaid.

*Be it ordained by the authority aforesaid,* That the resolutions of the 23rd of April, 1784, relative to the subject of this ordinance, be, and the same are hereby repealed and declared null and void. Done by the United States, in Congress assembled, the 13th day of July, in the year of our Lord 1787, and of their sovereignty and independence the twelfth.

# 4. The Constitution of the United States of America, Drafted 1787, Ratified 1788

We the People of the United States, in Order to form a more perfect Union, establish Justice, insure domestic Tranquility, provide for the common defence, promote the general Welfare, and secure the Blessings of Liberty to ourselves and our Posterity, do ordain and establish this CONSTITUTION for the United States of America.

## Article I.

**Section 1.** All legislative Powers herein granted shall be vested in a Congress of the United States, which shall consist of a Senate and House of Representatives.

**Section 2.** The House of Representatives shall be composed of Members chosen every second Year by the People of the several States, and the Electors in each State shall have the Qualifications requisite for Electors of the most numerous Branch of the State Legislature.

No Person shall be a Representative who shall not have attained to the Age of twenty five Years, and been seven Years a Citizen of the United States, and who shall not, when elected, be an Inhabitant of that State in which he shall be chosen.

Representatives and direct Taxes shall be apportioned among the several States which may be included within this Union, according to their respective Numbers, which shall be determined by adding to the whole Number of free Persons, including those bound to Service for a Term of Years, and excluding Indians not taxed, three fifths of all other Persons. The actual Enumeration shall be made within three Years after the first Meeting of the Congress of the United States, and within every subsequent Term of ten Years, in such Manner as they shall by Law direct. The Number of Representatives shall not exceed one for every thirty Thousand, but each State shall have at Least one Representative; and until such enumeration shall be made, the State of New Hampshire shall be entitled to chuse three, Massachusetts eight, Rhode-Island and Providence Plantations one, Connecticut five, New York six, New Jersey four, Pennsylvania eight, Delaware one, Maryland six, Virginia ten, North Carolina five, South Carolina five, and Georgia three. When vacancies happen in the Representation from any State, the Executive Authority thereof shall issue Writs of Election to fill such Vacancies.

The House of Representatives shall chuse their Speaker and other Officers; and shall have the sole Power of Impeachment.

**Section 3.** The Senate of the United States shall be composed of two Senators from each State, chosen by the Legislature thereof for six Years; and each Senator shall have one Vote.

Immediately after they shall be assembled in Consequence of the first Election, they shall be divided as equally as may be into three Classes. The Seats of the Senators of the first Class shall be vacated at the Expiration of the second Year, of the second Class at the Expiration of the fourth Year, and of the third Class at the Expiration of the sixth Year, so that one third may be chosen every second Year; and if Vacancies happen by Resignation, or otherwise, during the Recess of the Legislature of any State, the Executive thereof may make temporary Appointments until the next Meeting of the Legislature, which shall then fill such Vacancies.

No Person shall be a Senator who shall not have attained to the Age of thirty Years, and been nine Years a Citizen of the United States, and who shall not, when elected, be an Inhabitant of that State for which he shall be chosen.

The Vice President of the United States shall be President of the Senate, but shall have no Vote, unless they be equally divided.

The Senate shall chuse their other Officers, and also a President pro tempore, in the Absence of the Vice President, or when he shall exercise the Office of President of the United States. The Senate shall have the sole Power to try all Impeachments. When sitting for that Purpose, they shall be on Oath or Affirmation. When the President of the United States is tried, the Chief Justice shall preside: And no Person shall be convicted without the Concurrence of two thirds of the Members present.

Judgment in Cases of Impeachment shall not extend further than to removal from Office, and disqualification to hold and enjoy any Office of honor, Trust or Profit under the United States: but the Party convicted shall nevertheless be liable and subject to Indictment, Trial, Judgment and Punishment, according to Law.

**Section 4.** The Times, Places and Manner of holding Elections for Senators and Representatives, shall be prescribed in each State by the Legislature thereof; but the Congress may at any time by Law make or alter such Regulations, except as to the Places of Chusing Senators.

The Congress shall assemble at least once in every Year, and such Meeting shall be on the first Monday in December, unless they shall by Law appoint a different day.

**Section 5.** Each House shall be the Judge of the Elections, Returns and Qualifications of its own Members, and a Majority of each shall constitute a Quorum to do Business; but a smaller Number may adjourn from day to day, and may be authorized to compel the Attendance of absent Members, in such Manner, and under such Penalties as each House may provide.

Each House may determine the Rules of its Proceedings, punish its Members for disorderly Behaviour, and, with the Concurrence of two thirds, expel a Member.

Each House shall keep a Journal of its Proceedings, and from time to time publish the same, excepting such Parts as may in their Judgment require Secrecy; and the Yeas and Nays of the Members of either House on any question shall, at the Desire of one fifth of those Present, be entered on the Journal.

Neither House, during the Session of Congress, shall, without the Consent of the other, adjourn for more than three days, nor to any other Place than that in which the two Houses shall be sitting.

**Section 6.** The Senators and Representatives shall receive a Compensation for their Services, to be ascertained by Law, and paid out of the Treasury of the United States. They shall in all Cases, except Treason, Felony and Breach of the Peace, be privileged from Arrest during their Attendance at the Session of their respective Houses, and in going to and returning from the same; and for any Speech or Debate in either House, they shall not be questioned in any other Place.

No Senator or Representative shall, during the Time for which he was elected, be appointed to any civil Office under the Authority of the United States, which shall have been created, or the Emoluments whereof shall have been encreased during such time; and no Person holding any Office under the United States, shall be a Member of either House during his Continuance in Office.

**Section 7.** All Bills for raising Revenue shall originate in the House of Representatives; but the Senate may propose or concur with Amendments as on other Bills.

Every Bill which shall have passed the House of Representatives and the Senate, shall, before it become a Law, be presented to the President of the United States: If he approve he shall sign it, but if not he shall return it, with his objections to that House in which it shall have originated, who shall enter the Objections at large on their Journal, and proceed to reconsider it. If after such Reconsideration two thirds of that House shall agree to pass the Bill, it shall be sent, together with the Objections, to the other House, by which it shall likewise be reconsidered, and if approved by two thirds of that House, it shall become a Law. But in all such Cases the Votes of both Houses shall be determined by Yeas and Nays, and the Names of the Persons voting for and against the Bill shall be entered on the Journal of each House respectively. If any Bill shall not be returned by the President within ten Days (Sundays excepted) after it shall have been presented to him, the Same shall be a Law, in like Manner as if he had signed it, unless the Congress by their Adjournment prevent its Return, in which Case it shall not be a Law.

Every Order, Resolution, or Vote to which the Concurrence of the Senate and House of Representatives may be necessary (except on a question of Adjournment) shall be presented to the President of the United States; and before the Same shall take Effect, shall be approved by him, or being disapproved by him, shall be repassed by two thirds of the Senate and House of Representatives, according to the Rules and Limitations prescribed in the Case of a Bill.

**Section 8.** The Congress shall have Power To lay and collect Taxes, Duties, Imposts and Excises, to pay the Debts and provide for the common Defence and general Welfare of the United States; but all Duties, Imposts and Excises shall be uniform throughout the United States;

To borrow Money on the credit of the United States;

To regulate Commerce with foreign Nations, and among the several States, and with the Indian Tribes;

To establish an uniform rule of Naturalization, and uniform Laws on the subject of Bankruptcies throughout the United States;

To coin Money, regulate the Value thereof, and of foreign Coin, and fix the Standard of Weights and Measures;

To provide for the Punishment of counterfeiting the Securities and current Coin of the United States;

To establish Post Offices and post Roads;

To promote the Progress of Science and useful Arts, by securing for limited Times to Authors and Inventors the exclusive Right to their respective Writings and Discoveries;

To constitute Tribunals inferior to the Supreme Court;

To define and punish Piracies and Felonies committed on the high Seas, and Offences against the Law of Nations;

To declare War, grant Letters of Marque and Reprisal, and make Rules concerning Captures on Land and Water;

To raise and support Armies, but no Appropriation of Money to that Use shall be for a longer Term than two Years;

To provide and maintain a Navy;

To make Rules for the Government and Regulation of the land and naval forces;

To provide for calling forth the Militia to execute the Laws of the Union, suppress Insurrections and repel Invasions;

To provide for organizing, arming, and disciplining, the Militia, and for governing such Part of them as may be employed in the Service of the United States, reserving to the States respectively, the Appointment of the Officers, and the Authority of training the Militia according to the discipline prescribed by Congress;

To exercise exclusive Legislation in all Cases whatsoever, over such District (not exceeding ten Miles square) as may, by Cession of particular States, and the Acceptance of Congress, become the Seat of the Government of the United States, and to exercise like Authority over all Places purchased by the Consent of the Legislature of the State in which the Same shall be, for the Erection of Forts, Magazines, Arsenals, Dock-yards, and other needful Buildings;—And

To make all Laws which shall be necessary and proper for carrying into Execution the foregoing Powers, and all other Powers vested by this Constitution in the Government of the United States, or in any Department or Officer thereof.

**Section 9.** The Migration or Importation of such Persons as any of the States now existing shall think proper to admit, shall not be prohibited by the Congress prior to the Year one thousand eight hundred and eight, but a tax or duty may be imposed on such Importation, not exceeding ten dollars for each Person.

The Privilege of the Writ of Habeas Corpus shall not be suspended, unless when in Cases of Rebellion or Invasion the public Safety may require it.

No Bill of Attainder or ex post facto Law shall be passed.

No capitation, or other direct, Tax shall be laid, unless in Proportion to the Census or Enumeration herein before directed to be taken.

No Tax or Duty shall be laid on Articles exported from any State.

No Preference shall be given by any Regulation of Commerce or Revenue to the Ports of one State over those of another; nor shall Vessels bound to, or from, one State, be obliged to enter, clear, or pay Duties in another.

No Money shall be drawn from the Treasury, but in Consequence of Appropriations made by Law; and a regular Statement and Account of the Receipts and Expenditures of all public Money shall be published from time to time.

No Title of Nobility shall be granted by the United States: And no Person holding any Office of Profit or Trust under them, shall, without the Consent of the Congress, accept of any present, Emolument, Office, or Title, of any kind whatever, from any King, Prince, or foreign State.

**Section 10.** No State shall enter into any Treaty, Alliance, or Confederation; grant Letters of Marque and Reprisal; coin Money; emit Bills of Credit; make any Thing but gold and silver Coin a Tender in Payment of Debts; pass any Bill of Attainder, ex post facto Law, or Law impairing the Obligation of Contracts, or grant any Title of Nobility.

No State shall, without the Consent of the Congress, lay any Imposts or Duties on Imports or Exports, except what may be absolutely necessary for executing its inspection Laws: and the net Produce of all Duties and Imposts, laid by any State on Imports or Exports, shall be for the Use of the Treasury of the United States; and all such Laws shall be subject to the Revision and Controul of the Congress.

No State shall, without the Consent of Congress, lay any duty of Tonnage, keep Troops, or Ships of War in time of Peace, enter into any Agreement or Compact with another State, or with a foreign Power, or engage in War, unless actually invaded, or in such imminent Danger as will not admit of delay.

## Article II.

**Section 1.** The executive Power shall be vested in a President of the United States of America. He shall hold his Office during the Term of four years, and, together with the Vice President, chosen for the same Term, be elected, as follows:

Each State shall appoint, in such Manner as the Legislature thereof may direct, a Number of Electors, equal to the whole Number of Senators and Representatives to which the State may be entitled in the Congress: but no Senator or Representative, or Person holding an Office of Trust or Profit under the United States, shall be appointed an Elector.

The Electors shall meet in their respective States, and vote by Ballot for two persons, of whom one at least shall not be an Inhabitant of the same State with themselves. And they shall make a List of all the Persons voted for, and of the Number of Votes for each; which List they shall sign and certify, and transmit sealed to the Seat of the Government of the United States, directed to the President of the Senate. The President of the Senate shall, in the Presence of the Senate and House of Representatives, open all the Certificates, and the Votes shall then be counted. The Person having the greatest Number of Votes shall be the President, if such Number be a Majority of the whole Number of Electors appointed; and if there be more than one who have such Majority, and have an equal Number of Votes, then the House of Representatives shall immediately chuse by Ballot one of them for President; and if no Person have a Majority, then from the five highest on the List the said House shall in like Manner chuse the President. But in chusing the President, the Votes shall be taken by States, the Representation from each State having one Vote; A quorum for this purpose shall consist of a Member or Members from two-thirds of the States, and a Majority of all the States shall be necessary to a Choice. In every Case, after the Choice of the President, the Person having the greatest Number of Votes of the Electors shall be the Vice President. But if there should remain two or more who have equal votes, the Senate shall chuse from them by Ballot the Vice President.

The Congress may determine the Time of chusing the Electors, and the Day on which they shall give their Votes; which Day shall be the same throughout the United States.

No Person except a natural born Citizen, or a Citizen of the United States, at the time of the Adoption of this Constitution, shall be eligible to the Office of President; neither shall any Person be eligible to that Office who shall not have attained to the Age of thirty-five Years, and been fourteen Years a Resident within the United States.

In Case of the Removal of the President from Office, or of his Death, Resignation, or Inability to discharge the Powers and Duties of the said Office, the Same shall devolve on the Vice President, and the Congress may by Law provide for the Case of Removal, Death, Resignation or Inability, both of the President and Vice President, declaring what Officer shall then act as President, and such Officer shall act accordingly, until the Disability be removed, or a President shall be elected.

The President shall, at stated Times, receive for his Services, a Compensation, which shall neither be increased nor diminished during the Period for which he shall have been elected, and he shall not receive within that Period any other Emolument from the United States, or any of them.

Before he enter on the Execution of his Office, he shall take the following Oath or Affirmation:—"I do solemnly swear (or affirm) that I will faithfully execute the Office of President of the United States, and will to the best of my Ability, preserve, protect and defend the Constitution of the United States."

**Section 2.** The President shall be Commander in Chief of the Army and Navy of the United States, and of the Militia of the several States, when called into the actual Service of the United States; he may require the Opinion, in writing, of the principal Officer in each of the executive Departments, upon any Subject relating to the Duties of their respective Offices, and he shall have Power to grant Reprieves and Pardons for Offences against the United States, except in Cases of Impeachment.

He shall have Power, by and with the Advice and Consent of the Senate, to make Treaties, provided two thirds of the Senators present concur; and he shall nominate, and by and with the Advice and Consent of the Senate, shall appoint Ambassadors, other public Ministers and Consuls, Judges of the supreme Court, and all other Officers of the United States, whose Appointments are not herein otherwise provided for, and which shall be established by Law: but the Congress may by Law vest the Appointment of such inferior Officers, as they think proper, in the President alone, in the Courts of Law, or in the Heads of Departments.

The President shall have Power to fill up all Vacancies that may happen during the Recess of the Senate, by granting Commissions which shall expire at the End of their next Session.

**Section 3.** He shall from time to time give to the Congress Information of the State of the Union, and recommend to their Consideration such Measures as he shall judge necessary and expedient; he may, on extraordinary Occasions, convene both Houses, or either of them, and in Case of Disagreement between them, with respect to the Time of Adjournment, he may adjourn them to such Time as he shall think proper; he shall receive Ambassadors and other public Ministers; he shall take Care that the Laws be faithfully executed, and shall Commission all the Officers of the United States.

**Section 4.** The President, Vice President and all civil Officers of the United States, shall be removed from Office on Impeachment for, and Conviction of, Treason, Bribery, or other high Crimes and Misdemeanors.

### Article III.

**Section 1.** The judicial Power of the United States shall be vested in one supreme Court, and in such inferior Courts as the Congress may from time to time ordain and establish. The Judges, both of the supreme and inferior Courts, shall hold their Offices during good Behaviour, and shall, at stated Times, receive for their Services a Compensation, which shall not be diminished during their Continuance in Office.

**Section 2.** The judicial Power shall extend to all Cases, in Law and Equity, arising under this Constitution, the Laws of the United States, and Treaties made, or which shall be made, under their Authority;—to all Cases affecting Ambassadors, other public ministers and consuls;—to all Cases of admiralty and maritime Jurisdiction;—to Controversies to which the United States shall be a Party;—to Controversies between two or more States;—between a State and Citizens of another State;—between Citizens of different States;—between Citizens of the same State claiming Lands under Grants of different States, and between a State, or the Citizens thereof, and foreign States, Citizens or Subjects.

In all Cases affecting Ambassadors, other public Ministers and Consuls, and those in which a State shall be Party, the supreme Court shall have original Jurisdiction. In all the other Cases before mentioned, the supreme Court shall have appellate Jurisdiction, both as to Law and Fact, with such Exceptions, and under such Regulations as the Congress shall make.

The Trial of all Crimes, except in Cases of Impeachment, shall be by Jury; and such Trial shall be held in the State where the said Crimes shall have been committed; but when not committed within any State, the Trial shall be at such Place or Places as the Congress may by Law have directed.

**Section 3.** Treason against the United States, shall consist only in levying War against them, or in adhering to their Enemies, giving them Aid and Comfort. No Person shall be convicted of Treason unless on the Testimony of two Witnesses to the same overt Act, or on Confession in open Court.

The Congress shall have Power to declare the Punishment of Treason, but no Attainder of Treason shall work Corruption of Blood, or Forfeiture except during the Life of the Person attainted.

## Article IV.

**Section 1.** Full Faith and Credit shall be given in each State to the public Acts, Records, and judicial Proceedings of every other State. And the Congress may by general Laws prescribe the Manner in which such Acts, Records and Proceedings shall be proved, and the Effect thereof.

**Section 2.** The Citizens of each State shall be entitled to all Privileges and Immunities of Citizens in the several States.

A Person charged in any State with Treason, Felony, or other Crime, who shall flee from Justice, and be found in another State, shall on Demand of the executive Authority of the State from which he fled, be delivered up, to be removed to the State having Jurisdiction of the Crime.

No Person held to Service or Labour in one State, under the Laws thereof, escaping into another, shall, in Consequence of any Law or Regulation therein, be discharged from such Service or Labour, but shall be delivered up on Claim of the Party to whom such Service or Labour may be due.

**Section 3.** New States may be admitted by the Congress into this Union; but no new State shall be formed or erected within the Jurisdiction of any other State; nor any State be formed by the Junction of two or more States, or Parts of States, without the Consent of the Legislatures of the States concerned as well as of the Congress.

The Congress shall have Power to dispose of and make all needful Rules and Regulations respecting the Territory or other Property belonging to the United States; and nothing in this Constitution shall be so construed as to Prejudice any Claims of the United States, or of any particular State.

**Section 4.** The United States shall guarantee to every State in this Union a Republican Form of Government, and shall protect each of them against Invasion; and on Application of the Legislature, or of the Executive (when the Legislature cannot be convened), against domestic Violence.

## Article V.

The Congress, whenever two thirds of both Houses shall deem it necessary, shall propose Amendments to this Constitution, or, on the Application of the Legislatures of two thirds of the several States, shall call a Convention for proposing Amendments, which, in either Case, shall be valid to all Intents and Purposes, as Part of this Constitution, when ratified by the Legislatures of three fourths of the several States, or by Conventions in three fourths thereof, as the one or the other Mode of Ratification may be proposed by the Congress; Provided that no Amendment which may be made prior to the Year One thousand eight hundred and eight shall in any Manner affect the first and fourth Clauses in the Ninth Section of the first Article; and that no State, without its Consent, shall be deprived of its equal Suffrage in the Senate.

### Article VI.

All Debts contracted and Engagements entered into, before the Adoption of this Constitution, shall be as valid against the United States under this Constitution, as under the Confederation.

This Constitution, and the Laws of the United States which shall be made in Pursuance thereof; and all Treaties made, or which shall be made, under the Authority of the United States, shall be the supreme Law of the Land; and the Judges in every State shall be bound thereby, any Thing in the Constitution or Laws of any State to the Contrary notwithstanding.

The Senators and Representatives before mentioned, and the Members of the several State Legislatures, and all executive and judicial Officers, both of the United States and of the several States, shall be bound by Oath or Affirmation, to support this Constitution; but no religious Test shall ever be required as a Qualification to any Office or public Trust under the United States.

### Article VII.

The Ratification of the Conventions of nine States, shall be sufficient for the Establishments of this Constitution between the States so ratifying the Same.

Done in Convention by the Unanimous Consent of the States present the Seventeenth Day of September in the Year of our Lord one thousand seven hundred and Eighty seven and of the Independence of the United States of America the Twelfth. In witness whereof We have hereunto subscribed our Names,

[Names]

## 5. THE BILL OF RIGHTS, THE FIRST TEN AMENDMENTS TO THE CONSTITUTION OF THE UNITED STATES, RATIFIED, 1791

### Amendment I

Congress shall make no law respecting an establishment of religion, or prohibiting the free exercise thereof; or abridging the freedom of speech, or of the press; or the right of the people peaceably to assemble, and to petition the Government for a redress of grievances.

### Amendment II

A well regulated Militia, being necessary to the security of a free State, the right of the people to keep and bear Arms, shall not be infringed.

### Amendment III

No Soldier shall, in time of peace be quartered in any house, without the consent of the Owner, nor in time of war, but in a manner to be prescribed by law.

### Amendment IV

The right of the people to be secure in their persons, houses, papers, and effects, against unreasonable searches and seizures, shall not be violated, and no Warrants shall issue, but upon probable cause, supported by Oath or affirmation, and particularly describing the place to be searched, and the persons or things to be seized.

### Amendment V

No person shall be held to answer for a capital, or otherwise infamous crime, unless on a presentment or indictment of a Grand Jury, except in cases arising in the land or naval forces, or in the Militia, when in actual service in time of War or public danger; nor shall any person be subject for the same offence to be twice put in jeopardy of life or limb; nor shall be compelled in any criminal case to be a witness against himself, nor be deprived of life, liberty, or property, without due process of law; nor shall private property be taken for public use, without just compensation.

### Amendment VI

In all criminal prosecutions, the accused shall enjoy the right to a speedy and public trial, by an impartial jury of the State and district wherein the crime shall have been committed, which district shall have been previously ascertained by law, and to be informed of the nature and cause of the accusation; to be confronted with the witnesses against him; to have compulsory process for obtaining witnesses in his favor, and to have the Assistance of Counsel for his defence.

### Amendment VII

In suits at common law, where the value in controversy shall exceed twenty dollars, the right of trial by jury shall be preserved, and no fact tried by a jury, shall be otherwise reexamined in any Court of the United States, than according to the rules of the common law.

### Amendment VIII

Excessive bail shall not be required, nor excessive fines imposed, nor cruel and unusual punishments inflicted.

### Amendment IX

The enumeration in the Constitution, of certain rights, shall not be construed to deny or disparage others retained by the people.

### Amendment X

The powers not delegated to the United States by the Constitution, nor prohibited by it to the States, are reserved to the States respectively, or to the people.

## 6. THE PROCLAMATION OF NEUTRALITY, APRIL 22, 1793

### A Proclamation

Whereas it appears that a state of war exists between Austria, Prussia, Sardinia, Great Britain, and the United Netherlands, of the one part, and France on the other; and the duty and interest of the United States require, that they should with sincerity and good faith adopt and pursue a conduct friendly and impartial toward the belligerent Powers;

I have therefore thought fit by these presents to declare the disposition of the United States to observe the conduct aforesaid towards those Powers respectfully; and to exhort and warn the citizens of the United States carefully to avoid all acts and proceedings whatsoever, which may in any manner tend to contravene such disposition.

And I do hereby also make known, that whatsoever of the citizens of the United States shall render himself liable to punishment or forfeiture under the law of nations, by committing, aiding, or abetting hostilities against any of the said Powers, or by carrying to any of them those articles which are deemed contraband by the modern usage of nations, will not receive the protection of the United States, against such punishment or forfeiture; and further, that I have given instructions to those officers, to whom it belongs, to cause prosecutions to be instituted against all persons, who shall, within the cognizance of the courts of the United States, violate the law of nations, with respect to the Powers at war, or any of them.

In testimony whereof, I have caused the seal of the United States of America to be affixed to these presents, and signed the same with my hand. Done at the city of Philadelphia, the twenty-second day of April, one thousand seven hundred and ninety-three, and of the Independence of the United States of America the seventeenth.

—George Washington

## 7. THE TREATY OF GREENVILLE, CONCLUDED AUGUST 3, 1795

A treaty of peace between the United States of America, and the tribes of Indians called the Wyandots, Delawares, Shawanees, Ottawas, Chippewas, Pattawatimas, Miamis, Eel Rivers, Weas, Kickapoos, Piankeshaws, and Kaskaskias.

To put an end to a destructive war, to settle all controversies, and to restore harmony and friendly intercourse between the said United States and Indian tribes, Anthony Wayne, major general commanding the army of the United States, and sole commissioner for the good purposes above mentioned, and the said tribes of Indians, by their sachems, chiefs, and warriors, met together at Greenville, the head quarters of the said army, have agreed on the following articles, which, when ratified by the President, with the advice and consent of the Senate of the United States, shall be binding on them and the said Indian tribes.

### Art. 1:

Henceforth all hostilities shall cease; peace is hereby established, and shall be perpetual; and a friendly intercourse shall take place between the said United States and Indian tribes.

### Art. 2:

All prisoners shall, on both sides, be restored. The Indians, prisoners to the United States, shall be immediately set at liberty. The people of the United States, still remaining prisoners among the Indians, shall be delivered up in ninety days from the date hereof, to the general or commanding officer at Greenville, fort Wayne, or fort Defiance; and ten chiefs of the said tribes shall remain at Greenville as hostages, until the delivery of the prisoners shall be effected.

## Art. 3:

The general boundary line between the lands of the United States and the lands of the said Indian tribes, shall begin at the mouth of Cayahoga river, and run thence up the same to the portage, between that and the Tuscarawas branch of the Muskingum, thence down that branch to the crossing place above fort Lawrence, thence westerly to a fork of that branch of the Great Miami river, running into the Ohio, at or near which fork stood Loromie's store, and where commences the portage between the Miami of the Ohio, and St. Mary's river, which is a branch of the Miami which runs into lake Erie; thence a westerly course to fort Recovery, which stands on a branch of the Wabash; thence southwesterly in a direct line to the Ohio, so as to intersect that river opposite the mouth of Kentucke or Cuttawa river. And in consideration of the peace now established; of the goods formerly received from the United States; of those now to be delivered; and of the yearly delivery of goods now stipulated to be made hereafter; and to indemnify the United States for the injuries and expenses they have sustained during the war, the said Indian tribes do hereby cede and relinquish forever, all their claims to the lands lying eastwardly and southwardly of the general boundary line now described: and these lands, or any part of them, shall never hereafter be made a cause or pretence, on the part of the said tribes, or any of them, of war or injury to the United States, or any of the people thereof.

And for the same considerations, and as an evidence of the returning friendship of the said Indian tribes, of their confidence in the United States, and desire to provide for their accommodations, and for that convenient intercourse which will be beneficial to both parties, the said Indian tribes do also cede to the United States the following pieces of land, to wit:

1. One piece of land six miles square, at or near Loromie's store, before mentioned.
2. One piece two miles square, at the head of the navigable water or landing, on the St. Mary's river, near Girty's town.
3. One piece six miles square, at the head of the navigable water of the Auglaize river.
4. One piece six miles square, at the confluence of the Auglaize and Miami rivers, where fort Defiance now stands.
5. One piece six miles square, at or near the confluence of the rivers St. Mary's and St. Joseph's, where fort Wayne now stands, or near it.
6. One piece two miles square, on the Wabash river, at the end of the portage from the Miami of the lake, and about eight miles westward from fort Wayne.
7. One piece six miles square, at the Ouatanon, or Old Wea towns, on the Wabash river.
8. One piece twelve miles square, at the British fort on the Miami of the lake, at the foot of the rapids.
9. One piece six miles square, at the mouth of the said river, where it empties into the lake.
10. One piece six miles square, upon Sandusky lake, where a fort formerly stood.
11. One piece two miles square, at the lower rapids of Sandusky river.
12. The post of Detroit, and all the land to the north, the west and the south of it, of which the Indian title has been extinguished by gifts or grants to the French or English governments: and so much more land to be annexed to the district of Detroit, as shall be comprehended between the river Rosine, on the south, lake St. Clair on the north, and a line, the general course whereof shall be six miles distant from the west end of lake Erie and Detroit river.
13. The post of Michilimackinac, and all the land on the island on which that post stands, and the main land adjacent, of which the Indian title has been extinguished by gifts or grants to the French or English governments; and a piece of land on the main to the north of the island, to measure six miles, on lake Huron, or the strait between lakes Huron and Michigan, and to extend three miles back from the water of the lake or strait; and also, the Island De Bois Blane, being an extra and voluntary gift of the Chippewa nation.
14. One piece of land six miles square, at the mouth of Chikago river, emptying into the southwest end of lake Michigan, where a fort formerly stood.
15. One piece twelve miles square, at or near the mouth of the Illinois river, emptying into the Mississippi.
16. One piece six miles square, at the old Piorias fort and village near the south end of the Illinois lake, on said Illinois river. And whenever the United

States shall think proper to survey and mark the boundaries of the lands hereby ceded to them, they shall give timely notice thereof to the said tribes of Indians, that they may appoint some of their wise chiefs to attend and see that the lines are run according to the terms of this treaty.

And the said Indian tribes will allow to the people of the United States a free passage by land and by water, as one and the other shall be found convenient, through their country, along the chain of posts hereinbefore mentioned; that is to say, from the commencement of the portage aforesaid, at or near Loromie's store, thence along said portage to the St. Mary's, and down the same to fort Wayne, and then down the Miami, to lake Erie; again, from the commencement of the portage at or near Loromie's store along the portage from thence to the river Auglaize, and down the same to its junction with the Miami at fort Defiance; again, from the commencement of the portage aforesaid, to Sandusky river, and down the same to Sandusky bay and lake Erie, and from Sandusky to the post which shall be taken at or near the foot of the Rapids of the Miami of the lake; and from thence to Detroit. Again, from the mouth of Chikago, to the commencement of the portage, between that river and the Illinois, and down the Illinois river to the Mississippi; also, from fort Wayne, along the portage aforesaid, which leads to the Wabash, and then down the Wabash to the Ohio. And the said Indian tribes will also allow to the people of the United States, the free use of the harbors and mouths of rivers along the lakes adjoining the Indian lands, for sheltering vessels and boats, and liberty to land their cargoes where necessary for their safety.

## Art. 4:

In consideration of the peace now established, and of the cessions and relinquishments of lands made in the preceding article by the said tribes of Indians, and to manifest the liberality of the United States, as the great means of rendering this peace strong and perpetual, the United States relinquish their claims to all other Indian lands northward of the river Ohio, eastward of the Mississippi, and westward and southward of the Great Lakes and the waters, uniting them, according to the boundary line agreed on by the United States and the King of Great Britain, in the treaty of peace made between them in the year 1783.

But from this relinquishment by the United States, the following tracts of land are explicitly excepted:

**1st.** The tract on one hundred and fifty thousand acres near the rapids of the river Ohio, which has been assigned to General Clark, for the use of himself and his warriors.

**2nd.** The post of St. Vincennes, on the River Wabash, and the lands adjacent, of which the Indian title has been extinguished.

**3rd.** The lands at all other places in possession of the French people and other white settlers among them, of which the Indian title has been extinguished as mentioned in the 3d article; and

**4th.** The post of fort Massac towards the mouth of the Ohio. To which several parcels of land so excepted, the said tribes relinquish all the title and claim which they or any of them may have.

And for the same considerations and with the same views as above mentioned, the United States now deliver to the said Indian tribes a quantity of goods to the value of twenty thousand dollars, the receipt whereof they do hereby acknowledge; and henceforward every year, forever, the United States will deliver, at some convenient place northward of the river Ohio, like useful goods, suited to the circumstances of the Indians, of the value of nine thousand five hundred dollars; reckoning that value at the first cost of the goods in the city or place in the United States where they shall be procured. The tribes to which those goods are to be annually delivered, and the proportions in which they are to be delivered, are the following:

**1st.** To the Wyandots, the amount of one thousand dollars.

**2nd.** To the Delawares, the amount of one thousand dollars.

**3rd.** To the Shawanees, the amount of one thousand dollars.

**4th.** To the Miamis, the amount of one thousand dollars.

**5th.** To the Ottawas, the amount of one thousand dollars.

**6th.** To the Chippewas, the amount of one thousand dollars.

**7th.** To the Pattawatimas, the amount of one thousand dollars, and

**8th.** To the Kickapoo, Wea, Eel River, Piankeshaw, and Kaskaskia tribes, the amount of five hundred dollars each.

Provided, that if either of the said tribes shall hereafter, at an annual delivery of their share of the goods aforesaid, desire that a part of their annuity should be furnished in domestic animals, implements of husbandry, and other utensils convenient for them, and in compensation to useful antificers who may reside with or near them, and be employed for their benefit, the same shall, at the subsequent annual deliveries, be furnished accordingly.

## Art. 5:

To prevent any misunderstanding about the Indian lands relinquished by the United States in the fourth article, it is now explicitly declared, that the meaning of that relinquishment is this: the Indian tribes who have a right to those lands, are quietly to enjoy them, hunting, planting, and dwelling thereon, so long as they please, without any molestation from the United States; but when those tribes, or any of them, shall be disposed to sell their lands, or any part of them, they are to be sold only to the United States; and until such sale, the United States will protect all the said Indian tribes in the quiet enjoyment of their lands against all citizens of the United States, and against all other white persons who intrude upon the same. And the said Indian tribes again acknowledge themselves to be under the protection of the said United States, and no other power whatever.

## Art. 6:

If any citizen of he United States, or any other white person or persons, shall presume to settle upon the lands now relinquished by the United States, such citizen or other person shall be out of the protection of the United States; and the Indian tribe, on whose land the settlement shall be made, may drive off the settler, or punish him in such manner as they shall think fit; and because such settlements, made without the consent of the United States, will be injurious to them as well as to the Indians, the United States shall be at liberty to break them up, and remove and punish the settlers as they shall think proper, and so effect that protection of the Indian lands herein before stipulated.

## Art. 7:

The said tribes of Indians, parties to this treaty, shall be at liberty to hunt within the territory and lands which they have now ceded to the United States, without hindrance or molestation, so long as they demean themselves peaceably, and offer no injury to the people of the United States.

## Art. 8:

Trade shall be opened with the said Indian tribes; and they do hereby respectively engage to afford protection to such persons, with their property, as shall be duly licensed to reside among them for the purpose of trade; and to their agents and servants; but no person shall be permitted to reside among them for the purpose of trade; and to their agents and servants; but no person shall be permitted to reside at any of their towns or hunting camps, as a trader, who is not furnished with a license for that purpose, under the hand and seal of the superintendent of the department northwest of the Ohio, or such other person as the President of the United States shall authorize to grant such licenses; to the end, that the said Indians may not be imposed on in their trade. And if any licensed trader shall abuse his privilege by unfair dealing, upon complaint and proof thereof, his license shall be taken from him, and he shall be further punished according to the laws of the United States. And if any person shall intrude himself as a trader, without such license, the said Indians shall take and bring him before the superintendent, or his deputy, to be dealt with according to law. And to prevent impositions by forged licenses, the said Indians shall, at lease once a year, give information to the superintendent, or his deputies, on the names of the traders residing among them.

## Art. 9:

Lest the firm peace and friendship now established, should be interrupted by the misconduct of individuals, the United States, and the said Indian tribes agree, that for injuries done by individuals on either side, no private revenge or retaliation shall take place; but instead thereof, complaint shall be made by the party injured, to the other: by the said Indian tribes or any of them, to the President of the United States, or the superintendent by him appointed; and by the superintendent or other person appointed by the President, to the principal chiefs of the said Indian tribes, or of the tribe to which the offender belongs; and such prudent measures shall then be taken as shall be necessary to preserve the said peace and friendship unbroken, until the legislature (or great council) of the United States, shall make other equitable provision in the case, to the satisfaction of both parties. Should any Indian tribes meditate a war against the United States, or either of them, and the same shall come to the knowledge of the before mentioned tribes, or either of them, they do hereby engage to give immediate notice thereof to the general, or officer commanding the troops of the United States, at the nearest post. And should any tribe, with hostile intentions against the United States, or either of them, attempt to pass through their country, they will endeavor to prevent the same, and in like manner give information of such attempt, to the general, or officer commanding, as soon as possible, that all causes of mistrust and suspicion may be avoided between them and the United States. In like manner, the United States shall give notice to the said Indian tribes of any harm that may be meditated against them, or either of them, that shall come to their knowledge; and do all in their power to hinder and prevent the same, that the friendship between them may be uninterrupted.

## Art. 10:

All other treaties heretofore made between the United States, and the said Indian tribes, or any of them, since the treaty of 1783, between the United States and Great Britain, that come within the purview of this treaty, shall henceforth cease and become void.

In testimony whereof, the said Anthony Wayne, and the sachems and war chiefs of the before mentioned nations and tribes of Indians, have hereunto set their hands and affixed their seals. Done at Greenville, in the territory of the United States northwest of the river Ohio, on the third day of August, one thousand seven hundred and ninety five.

WYANDOTS.
[Names.]
DELAWARES.
[Names.]
SHAWANEES.
[Names.]
OTTAWAS.
[Names.]
CHIPPEWAS.
[Names.]
OTTAWA.
[Names.]

PATTAWATIMAS OF THE RIVER ST. JOSEPH.
[Names.]
PATTAWATIMAS OF HURON.
[Names.]
MIAMIS.
[Names.]
MIAMIS AND EEL RIVERS.
[Names.]
EEL RIVER TRIBE.
[Names.]
MIAMIS.
[Names.]
WEAS, FOR THEMSELVES AND THE PIANKE-
    SHAWS.
[Names.]
KICKAPOOS AND KASKASKIAS.
[Names.]
DELAWARES OF SANDUSKY.
[Names.]

H. De Butts, first A.D.C. and Sec'ry to Major Gen. Wayne, Wm. H. Harrison, Aid de Camp to Major Gen. Wayne . . . [Names.]

## 8. An Act Respecting Alien Enemies, Approved, July 6, 1798

*SECTION 1. Be it enacted by the Senate and House of Representatives of the United States of America in Congress assembled,* That whenever there shall be a declared war between the United States and any foreign nation or government, or any invasion or predatory incursion shall be perpetrated, attempted, or threatened against the territory of the United States, by any foreign nation or government, and the President of the United States shall make public proclamation of the event, all natives, citizens, denizens, or subjects of the hostile nation or government, being males of the age of fourteen years and upwards, who shall be within the United States, and not actually naturalized, shall be liable to be apprehended, restrained, secured and removed, as alien enemies. And the President of the United States shall be, and he is hereby authorized, in any event, as aforesaid, by his proclamation thereof, or other public act, to direct the conduct to be observed, on the part of the United States, towards the aliens who shall become liable, as aforesaid; the manner and degree of the restraint to which they shall be subject, and in what cases, and upon what security their residence shall be permitted, and to provide for the removal of those, who, not being permitted to reside within the United States, shall refuse or neglect to depart therefrom; and to establish any other regulations which shall be found necessary in the premises and for the public safety: Provided, that aliens resident within the United States, who shall become liable as enemies, in the manner aforesaid, and who shall not be chargeable with actual hostility, or other crime against the public safety, shall be allowed, for the recovery, disposal, and removal of their goods and effects, and for their departure, the full time which is, or shall be stipulated by any treaty, where any shall have been between the United States, and the hostile nation or government, of which they shall be natives, citizens, denizens or subjects: and where no such treaty shall have existed, the President of the United States may ascertain and declare such reasonable time as may be consistent with the public safety, and according to the dictates of humanity and national hospitality.

*SECTION 2. And be it further enacted,* That after any proclamation shall be made as aforesaid, it shall be the duty of the several courts of the United States, and of each state, having criminal jurisdiction, and of the several judges and justices of the courts of the United States, and they shall be, and are hereby respectively, authorized upon complaint, against any alien or alien enemies, as aforesaid, who shall be resident and at large within such jurisdiction or district, to the danger of the public peace or safety, and contrary to the tenor or intent of such proclamation, or other regulations which the President of the United States shall and may establish in the premises, to cause such alien or aliens to be duly apprehended and convened before such court, judge or justice; and after a full examination and hearing on such complaint. and sufficient cause therefor appearing, shall and may order such alien or aliens to be removed out of the territory of the United States, or to give sureties of their good behaviour, or to be otherwise restrained, conformably to the proclamation or regulations which shall and may be established as aforesaid, and may imprison, or otherwise secure such alien or aliens, until the order which shall and may be made, as aforesaid, shall be performed.

*SECTION 3. And be it further enacted,* That it shall be the duty of the marshal of the district in which any alien enemy shall be apprehended, who by the

President of the United States, or by order of any court, judge or justice, as aforesaid, shall be required to depart, and to be removed, as aforesaid, to provide therefore, and to execute such order, by himself or his deputy, or other discreet person or persons to be employed by him, by causing a removal of such alien out of the territory of the United States; and for such removal the marshal shall have the warrant of the President of the United States, or of the court, judge or justice ordering the same, as the case may be.

## 9. THE SEDITION ACT, APPROVED, JULY 14, 1798

*SECTION 1. Be it enacted by the Senate and House of Representatives of the United States of America, in Congress assembled,* That if any persons shall unlawfully combine or conspire together, with intent to oppose any measure or measures of the government of the United States, which are or shall be directed by proper authority, or to impede the operation of any law of the United States, or to intimidate or prevent any person holding a place or office in or under the government of the United States, from undertaking, performing or executing his trust or duty, and if any person or persons, with intent as aforesaid, shall counsel, advise or attempt to procure any insurrection, riot, unlawful assembly, or combination, whether such conspiracy, threatening, counsel, advice, or attempt shall have the proposed effect or not, he or they shall be deemed guilty of a high misdemeanor, and on conviction, before any court of the United States having jurisdiction thereof, shall be punished by a fine not exceeding five thousand dollars, and by imprisonment during a term not less than six months nor exceeding five years; and further, at the discretion of the court may be holden to find sureties for his good behaviour in such sum, and for such time, as the said court may direct.

*SECTION 2. And be it farther enacted,* That if any person shall write, print, utter or publish, or shall cause or procure to be written, printed, uttered or published, or shall knowingly and willingly assist or aid in writing, printing, uttering or publishing any false, scandalous and malicious writing or writings against the government of the United States, or either house of the Congress of the United States, or the President of the United States, with intent to defame the said government, or either house of the said Congress, or the said President, or to bring them, or either of them, into contempt or disrepute; or to excite against them, or either or any of them, the hatred of the good people of the United States, or to stir up sedition within the United States, or to excite any unlawful combinations therein, for opposing or resisting any law of the United States, or any act of the President of the United States, done in pursuance of any such law, or of the powers in him vested by the constitution of the United States, or to resist, oppose, or defeat any such law or act, or to aid, encourage or abet any hostile designs of any foreign nation against United States, their people or government, then such person, being thereof convicted before any court of the United States having jurisdiction thereof, shall be punished by a fine not exceeding two thousand dollars, and by imprisonment not exceeding two years.

*SECTION 3. And be it further enacted and declared,* That if any person shall be prosecuted under this act, for the writing or publishing any libel aforesaid, it shall be lawful for the defendant, upon the trial of the cause, to give in evidence in his defence, the truth of the matter contained in Republication charged as a libel. And the jury who shall try the cause, shall have a right to determine the law and the fact, under the direction of the court, as in other cases.

*SECTION 4. And be it further enacted,* That this act shall continue and be in force until the third day of March, one thousand eight hundred and one, and no longer: Provided, that the expiration of the act shall not prevent or defeat a prosecution and punishment of any offence against the law, during the time it shall be in force.

## 10. THE VIRGINIA RESOLUTIONS, AGREED TO BY THE VIRGINIA SENATE, DECEMBER 24, 1798

RESOLVED, That the General Assembly of Virginia, doth unequivocally express a firm resolution to maintain and defend the Constitution of the United States, and the Constitution of this State, against every aggression either foreign or domestic, and that they will support the government of the United States in all measures warranted by the former. That this assembly most solemnly declares a warm attachment to the Union of the States, to maintain which it pledges all its powers; and that for this end, it is their duty to watch over and oppose every infraction of those principles which constitute the only basis of that Union, because

a faithful observance of them, can alone secure its existence and the public happiness. That this Assembly doth explicitly and peremptorily declare, that it views the powers of the federal government, as resulting from the compact, to which the states are parties; as limited by the plain sense and intention of the instrument constituting the compact; as no further valid that they are authorized by the grants enumerated in that compact; and that in case of a deliberate, palpable, and dangerous exercise of other powers, not granted by the said compact, the states who are parties thereto, have the right, and are in duty bound, to interpose for arresting the progress of the evil, and for maintaining within their respective limits, the authorities, rights and liberties appertaining to them.

That the General Assembly doth also express its deep regret, that a spirit has in sundry instances, been manifested by the federal government, to enlarge its powers by forced constructions of the constitutional charter which defines them; and that implications have appeared of a design to expound certain general phrases (which having been copied from the very limited grant of power, in the former articles of confederation were the less liable to be misconstrued) so as to destroy the meaning and effect, of the particular enumeration which necessarily explains and limits the general phrases; and so as to consolidate the states by degrees, into one sovereignty, the obvious tendency and inevitable consequence of which would be, to transform the present republican system of the United States, into an absolute, or at best a mixed monarchy.

That the General Assembly doth particularly protest against the palpable and alarming infractions of the Constitution, in the two late cases of the "Alien and Sedition Acts" passed at the last session of Congress; the first of which exercises a power no where delegated to the federal government, and which by uniting legislative and judicial powers to those of executive, subverts the general principles of free government; as well as the particular organization, and positive provisions of the federal constitution; and the other of which acts, exercises in like manner, a power not delegated by the constitution, but on the contrary, expressly and positively forbidden by one of the amendments thereto; a power, which more than any other, ought to produce universal alarm, because it is levelled against that right of freely examining public characters and measures, and of free communication among the people thereon, which has ever been justly deemed, the only effectual guardian of every other right.

That this state having by its Convention, which ratified the federal Constitution, expressly declared, that among other essential rights, "the Liberty of Conscience and of the Press cannot be cancelled, abridged, restrained, or modified by any authority of the United States," and from its extreme anxiety to guard these rights from every possible attack of sophistry or ambition, having with other states, recommended an amendment of that purpose, which amendment was, in due time, annexed to the Constitution; it would mark a reproachable inconsistency, and criminal degeneracy, if an indifference were now shewn, to the most palpable violation of one of the Rights, thus declared and secured; and to the establishment of a precedent which may be fatal to the other.

That the good people of this commonwealth, having ever felt, and continuing to feel, the most sincere affection for their brethren of the other states; the truest anxiety for establishing and perpetuating the union of all; and the most scrupulous fidelity to that constitution, which is the pledge of mutual friendship, and the instrument of mutual happiness; the General Assembly doth solemnly appeal to the like dispositions of the other states, in confidence that they will concur with this commonwealth in declaring, as it does hereby declare, that the acts aforesaid, are unconstitutional; and that the necessary and proper measures will be taken by each, for co-operating with this state, in maintaining the Authorities, Rights, and Liberties, referred to the States respectively, or to the people.

That the Governor be desired, to transmit a copy of the foregoing Resolutions to the executive authority of each of the other states, with a request that the same may be communicated to the Legislature thereof; and that a copy be furnished to each of the Senators and Representatives representing this state in the Congress of the United States.

## 11. THE LOUISIANA PURCHASE, SIGNED APRIL 30, 1803

### Treaty between the United States of America and the French Republic

The President of the United States of America and the First Consul of the French Republic in the name of the French People desiring to remove all Source of misunderstanding relative to objects of discussion mentioned in the Second and fifth articles of the Convention of the 8th Vendémiaire on 9/30 September 1800 relative to the rights claimed by the United States in virtue of the Treaty concluded at Madrid the 27 of October 1795, between His Catholic Majesty & the Said United States, & willing to Strengthen the union and friendship which at the time of the Said Convention was happily reestablished between the two nations have respectively named their Plenipotentiaries to wit The President of the United States, by and with the advice and consent of the Senate of the Said States; Robert R. Livingston Minister Plenipotentiary of the United States and James Monroe Minister Plenipotentiary and Envoy extraordinary of the Said States near the Government of the French Republic; And the First Consul in the name of the French people, Citizen Francis Barbé Marbois Minister of the public treasury who after having respectively exchanged their full powers have agreed to the following Articles.

### Article I

Whereas by the Article the third of the Treaty concluded at St Ildefonso the 9th Vendémiaire on 1st October 1800 between the First Consul of the French Republic and his Catholic Majesty it was agreed as follows.

> "His Catholic Majesty promises and engages on his part to cede to the French Republic six months after the full and entire execution of the conditions and Stipulations herein relative to his Royal Highness the Duke of Parma, the Colony or Province of Louisiana with the Same extent that it now has in the hand of Spain, & that it had when France possessed it; and Such as it Should be after the Treaties subsequently entered into between Spain and other States."

And whereas in pursuance of the Treaty and particularly of the third article the French Republic has an incontestable title to the domain and to the possession of the said Territory—The First Consul of the French Republic desiring to give to the United States a strong proof of his friendship doth hereby cede to the United States in the name of the French Republic for ever and in full Sovereignty the said territory with all its rights and appurtenances as fully and in the Same manner as they have been acquired by the French

Republic in virtue of the above mentioned Treaty concluded with his Catholic Majesty.

## Article II

In the cession made by the preceeding article are included the adjacent Islands belonging to Louisiana all public lots and Squares, vacant lands and all public buildings, fortifications, barracks and other edifices which are not private property.—The Archives, papers & documents relative to the domain and Sovereignty of Louisiana and its dependances will be left in the possession of the Commissaries of the United States, and copies will be afterwards given in due form to the Magistrates and Municipal officers of such of the said papers and documents as may be necessary to them.

## Article III

The inhabitants of the ceded territory shall be incorporated in the Union of the United States and admitted as soon as possible according to the principles of the federal Constitution to the enjoyment of all these rights, advantages and immunities of citizens of the United States, and in the mean time they shall be maintained and protected in the free enjoyment of their liberty, property and the Religion which they profess.

## Article IV

There Shall be Sent by the Government of France a Commissary to Louisiana to the end that he do every act necessary as well to receive from the Officers of his Catholic Majesty the Said country and its dependances in the name of the French Republic if it has not been already done as to transmit it in the name of the French Republic to the Commissary or agent of the United States.

## Article V

Immediately after the ratification of the present Treaty by the President of the United States and in case that of the first Consul's shall have been previously obtained, the commissary of the French Republic shall remit all military posts of New Orleans and other parts of the ceded territory to the Commissary or Commissaries named by the President to take possession—the troops whether of France or Spain who may be there shall cease to occupy any military post from the time of taking possession and shall be embarked as soon as possible in the course of three months after the ratification of this treaty.

## Article VI

The United States promise to execute Such treaties and articles as may have been agreed between Spain and the tribes and nations of Indians until by mutual consent of the United States and the said tribes or nations other Suitable articles Shall have been agreed upon.

## Article VII

As it is reciprocally advantageous to the commerce of France and the United States to encourage the communication of both nations for a limited time in the country ceded by the present treaty until general arrangements relative to commerce of both nations may be agreed on; it has been agreed between the contracting parties that the French Ships coming directly from France or any of her colonies loaded only with the produce and manufactures of France or her Said Colonies; and the Ships of Spain coming directly from Spain or any of her colonies loaded only with the produce or manufactures of Spain or her Colonies shall be admitted during the Space of twelve years in the Port of New-Orleans and in all other legal ports-of-entry within the ceded territory in the Same manner as the Ships of the United States coming directly from France or Spain or any of their Colonies without being Subject to any other or greater duty on merchandize or other or greater tonnage than that paid by the citizens of the United States.

During that Space of time above mentioned no other nation Shall have a right to the Same privileges in the Ports of the ceded territory—the twelve years Shall commence three months after the exchange of ratifications if it Shall take place in France or three months after it Shall have been notified at Paris to the French Government if it Shall take place in the United States; It is however well understood that the object of the above article is to favour the manufactures, Commerce, freight and navigation of France and of Spain So far as relates to the importations that the French and Spanish Shall make into the Said Ports of the United States without in any Sort affecting the regulations that the United States may make concerning the exportation of the produce and merchandize of the United States, or any right they may have to make Such regulations.

## Article VIII

In future and for ever after the expiration of the twelve years, the Ships of France shall be treated upon the footing of the most favoured nations in the ports above mentioned.

## Article IX

The Particular Convention Signed this day by the respective Ministers, having for its object to provide for the payment of debts due to the Citizens of the United States by the French Republic prior to the 30th Sept. 1800 (8th Vendémiaire an 9) is approved and to have its execution in the Same manner as if it had been inserted in this present treaty, and it Shall be ratified in the same form and in the Same time So that the one Shall not be ratified distinct from the other.

Another particular Convention Signed at the Same date as the present treaty relative to a definitive rule between the contracting parties is in the like manner approved and will be ratified in the Same form, and in the Same time and jointly.

## Article X

The present treaty Shall be ratified in good and due form and the ratifications Shall be exchanged in the Space of Six months after the date of the Signature by the Ministers Plenipotentiary or Sooner if possible.

In faith whereof the respective Plenipotentiaries have Signed these articles in the French and English languages; declaring nevertheless that the present Treaty was originally agreed to in the French language; and have thereunto affixed their Seals.

Done at Paris the tenth day of Floreal in the eleventh year of the French Republic; and the 30th of April 1803.

**Robt R Livingston [seal]**
**Jas. Monroe [seal]**
**Barbé Marbois [seal]**

## 12. An Act to Prohibit the Importation of Slaves into any Port of Place within the Jurisdiction of the United States, From and After the First Day of January, in the Year of Our Lord One Thousand Eight Hundred and Eight, Passed, March 2, 1807

*Be it enacted by the Senate and House of Representatives of the United States of America in Congress assembled,* That from and after the first day of January, one thousand

eight hundred and eight, it shall not be lawful to import or bring into the United States or the territories thereof from any foreign kingdom, place, or country, any negro, mulatto, or person of colour, with intent to hold, sell, or dispose of such negro, mulatto, or person of colour, as a slave, or to be held to service or labour.

**SEC 2.** *And be it further enacted,* That no citizen or citizens of the United States, or any other person, shall, from arid after the first day of January, in the year of our Lord one thousand eight hundred and eight, for himself, or themselves, or any other person whatsoever, either as master, factor, or owner, build, fit, equip, load or otherwise prepare any ship or vessel, in any port or place within the jurisdiction of the United States, nor shall cause any ship or vessel to sail from any port or place within the same, for the purpose of procuring any negro, mulatto, or person of colour, from any foreign kingdom, place, or country, to be transported to any port or place whatsoever, within the jurisdiction of the United States, to be held, sold, or disposed of as slaves, or to be held to service or labour: and if any ship or vessel shall be so fitted out for the purpose aforesaid, or shall be caused to sail so as aforesaid, every such ship or vessel, her tackle, apparel, and furniture, shall be forfeited to the United States, and shall be liable to be seized, prosecuted, and condemned in any of the circuit courts or district courts, for the district where the said ship or vessel may be found or seized.

**SEC. 3.** *And be it further enacted,* That all and every person so building, fitting out, equipping, loading, or otherwise preparing or sending away, any ship or vessel, knowing or intending that the same shall be employed in such trade or business, from and after the first day of January, one thousand eight hundred and eight, contrary to the true intent and meaning of this act, or any ways aiding or abetting therein, shall severally forfeit and pay twenty thousand dollars, one moiety thereof to the use of the United States, and the other moiety to the use of any person or persons who shall sue for and prosecute the same to effect.

**SEC. 4.** *And be it further enacted,* If any citizen or citizens of the United States, or any person resident within the jurisdiction of the same, shall, from and after the first day of January, one thousand eight hundred and eight, take on board, receive or transport from any of the coasts or kingdoms of Africa, or from any other foreign kingdom, place, or country, any negro, mulatto, or person of colour, in any ship or vessel, for the purpose of selling them in any port or place within the jurisdiction of the United States as slaves, or to be held to service or labour, or shall be in any ways aiding or abetting therein, such citizen or citizens, or person, shall severally forfeit and pay five thousand dollars, one moiety thereof to the use of any person or persons who shall sue for and prosecute the same to effect; and every such ship or vessel in which such negro, mulatto, or person of colour, shall have been taken on board, received, or transported as aforesaid, her tackle, apparel, and furniture, and the goods and effects which shall be found on board the same, shall be forfeited to the United States, and shall be liable to be seized, prosecuted, and condemned in any of the circuit courts or district courts in the district where the said ship or vessel may be found or seized. And neither the importer, nor any person or persons claiming from or under him, shall hold any right or title whatsoever to any negro, mulatto, or person of colour, nor to the service or labour thereof, who may be imported or brought within the United States, or territories thereof, in violation of this law, but the same shall remain subject to any regulations not contravening the provisions of this act, which the legislatures of the several states or territories at any time hereafter may make, for disposing of any such negro, mulatto, or person of colour.

**SEC. 5.** *And be it further enacted,* That if any citizen or citizens of the United States, or any other person resident within the jurisdiction of the same, shall, from and after the first day of January, one thousand eight hundred and eight, contrary to the true intent and meaning of this act, take on board any ship or vessel from any of the coasts or kingdoms of Africa, or from any other foreign kingdom, place, or country, any negro, mulatto, or person of colour, with intent to sell him, her, or them, for a slave, or slaves, or to be held to service or labour, and shall transport the same to any port or place within the jurisdiction of the United States, and there sell such negro, mulatto, or person of colour, so transported as aforesaid, for a slave, or to be held to service or labour, every such offender shall be deemed guilty of a high misdemeanor, and being thereof convicted before any court having competent juris-

diction, shall suffer imprisonment for not more than ten years nor less than five years, and be fined not exceeding ten thousand dollars, nor less than one thousand dollars.

**SEC. 6.** *And be it further enacted,* That if any person or persons whatsoever, shall, from and after the first day of January, one thousand eight hundred and eight, purchase or sell any negro, mulatto, or person of colour, for a slave, or to be held to service or labour, who shall have been imported, or brought from any foreign kingdom, place, or country, or from the dominions of any foreign state, immediately adjoining to the United States, into any port or place within the jurisdiction of the United States, after the last day of December, one thousand eight hundred and seven, knowing at the time of such purchase or sale, such negro, mulatto or person of colour, was so brought within the jurisdiction of the Unified States, as aforesaid, such purchaser and seller shall severally forfeit and pay for every negro, mulatto, or person of colour, so purchased or sold as aforesaid, eight hundred dollars; one moiety thereof to the United States, and the other moiety to the use of any person or persons who shall sue for and prosecute the same to effect: Provided, that the aforesaid forfeiture shall not extend to the seller or purchaser of any negro, mulatto, or person of colour, who may be sold or disposed of in virtue of any regulation which may hereafter be made by any of the legislatures of the several states in that respect, in pursuance of this act, and the constitution of the United States.

**SEC. 7.** *And be it further enacted,* That if any ship or vessel shall be found, from and after the first day of January, one thousand eight hundred and eight, in any river, port, bay, or harbor, or on the high seas, within the jurisdictional limits of the United States, or hovering on the coast thereof, having on board any negro, mulatto, or person of colour, for the purpose of selling them as slaves, or with intent to land the same, in any port or place within the jurisdiction of the United States, contrary to the prohibition of this act, every such ship or vessel, together with her tackle, apparel, and furniture, and the goods or effects which shall be found on board the same, shall be forfeited to the use of the United States, and may be seized, prosecuted, and condemned, in any court of the United States, having jurisdiction thereof And it shall be lawful for the President of the United

States, and he is hereby authorized, should he deem it expedient, to cause any of the armed vessels of the United States to be manned and employed to cruise on any part of the coast of the United States, or territories thereof, where he may judge attempts will be made to violate the provisions of this act, and to instruct and direct the commanders of armed vessels of the United States, to seize, take, and bring into any port of the United States all such ships or vessels, and moreover to seize, take, and bring into any port of the United States all ships or vessels of the United States, wheresoever found on the high seas, contravening the provisions of this act, to be proceeded against according to law, and the captain, master, or commander of every such ship or vessel, so found and seized as aforesaid, shall be deemed guilty of a high misdemeanor, and shall be liable to be prosecuted before any court of the United States, having jurisdiction thereof; and being thereof convicted, shall be fined not exceeding ten thousand dollars, and be imprisoned not less than two years, and not exceeding four years. And the proceeds of all ships and vessels, their tackle, apparel, and furniture, and the goods and effects on board of them, which shall be so seized, prosecuted and condemned, shall be divided equally between the United States and the officers and men who shall make such seizure, take, or bring the same into port for condemnation, whether such seizure be made by an armed vessel of the United States, or revenue cutters hereof, and the same shall be distributed in like manner, as is provided by law, for the distribution of prizes taken from an enemy: Provided, that the officers and men, to be entitled to one half of the proceeds aforesaid, shall safe keep every negro, mulatto, or person of colour, found on board of any ship or vessel so by them seized, taken, or brought into port for condemnation, and shall deliver every such negro, mulatto, or person of colour, to such person or persons as shall be appointed by the respective states, to receive the same, and if no such person or persons shall be appointed by the respective states, they shall deliver every such negro, mulatto, or person of colour, to the overseers of the poor of the port or place where such ship or vessel may be brought or found, and shall immediately transmit to the governor or chief magistrate of the state, an account of their proceedings, together with the number of such Negroes, mulattoes, or persons of colour, and a descriptive list of the same, that he may give directions respecting such Negroes, mulattoes, or persons of colour.

**SEC. 8.** *And be it further enacted,* That no captain, master or commander of any ship or vessel, of less burthen than forty tons, shall, from and after the first day of January, one thousand eight hundred and eight, take on board and transport any negro, mulatto, or person of colour, to any port or place whatsoever, for the purpose of selling or disposing of the same as a slave, or with intent that the same may be sold or disposed of to be held to service or labour, on penalty of forfeiting for every such negro, mulatto, or person of colour, so taken on board and transported, as aforesaid, the sum of eight hundred dollars; one moiety thereof to the use of the United States, and the other moiety to any person or persons who shall sue for, and prosecute the same to effect: Provided however, That nothing in this section shall extend to prohibit the taking on board or transporting on any river, or inland bay of the sea, within the jurisdiction of the United States, any negro, mulatto, or person of colour, (not imported contrary to the provisions of this act) in any vessel or species of craft whatever.

**SEC. 9.** *And be it further enacted,* That the captain, master, or commander of any ship or vessel of the burthen of forty tons or more, from and after the first day of January, one thousand eight hundred and eight, sailing coastwise, from any port in the United States, to any port or place within the jurisdiction of the same, having on board any negro, mulatto, or person of colour, for the purpose of transporting them to be sold or disposed of as slaves, or to be held to service or labour, shall, previous to the departure of such ship or vessel, make out and subscribe duplicate manifests of every such negro, mulatto, or person of colour, on board such ship or vessel, therein specifying the name and sex of each person, their age and stature, as near as may be, and the class to which they respectively belong, whether negro, mulatto, or person of colour, with the name and place of residence of every owner or shipper of the same, and shall deliver such manifests to the collector of the port, if there be one, otherwise to the surveyor, before whom the captain, master, or commander, together with the owner or shipper, shall severally swear or affirm to the best of their knowledge and belief, that the persons therein specified were not imported or brought into the United

States, from and after the first day of January, one thousand eight hundred and eight, and that under the laws of the state, they are held to service or labour; whereupon the said collector or surveyor shall certify the same on the said manifests, one of which he shall return to the said captain, master, or commander, with a permit, specifying thereon the number, names, and general description of such persons, and authorizing him to proceed to the port of his destination. And if any ship or vessel, being laden and destined as aforesaid, shall depart from the port where she may then be, without the captain, master, or commander having first made out and subscribed duplicate manifests, of every negro, mulatto, and person of colour, on board such ship or vessel, as aforesaid, and without having previously delivered the same to the said collector or surveyor, and obtained a permit, in manner as herein required, or shall, previous to her arrival at the port of her destination, take on board any negro, mulatto, or person of colour, other than those specified in the manifests, as aforesaid, every such ship or vessel, together with her tackle, apparel and furniture, shall be forfeited to the use of the United States, and may be seized, prosecuted and condemned in any court of the United States having jurisdiction thereof; and the captain, master, or commander of every such ship or vessel, shall moreover forfeit, for every such negro, mulatto, or person of colour, so transported, or taken on board, contrary to the provisions of this act, the sum of one thousand dollars, one moiety thereof to the United States, and the other moiety to the use of any person or persons who shall sue for and prosecute the same to effect.

**SEC. 10.** *And be it further enacted,* That the captain, master, or commander of every ship or vessel, of the burthen of forty tons or more, from and after the first day of January, one thousand eight hundred and eight, sailing coastwise, and having on board any negro, mulatto, or person of colour, to sell or dispose of as slaves, or to be held to service or labour, and arriving in any port within the jurisdiction of the United States, from any other port within the same, shall, previous to the unlading or putting on shore any of the persons aforesaid, or suffering them to go on shore, deliver to the collector, if there be one, or if not, to the surveyor residing at the port of her arrival, the manifest certified by the collector or surveyor of the port from whence she sailed, as is herein before

directed, to the truth of which, before such officer, he shall swear or affirm, and if the collector or surveyor shall be satisfied therewith, he shall thereupon grant a permit for unlading or suffering such negro, mulatto, or person of colour, to be put on shore, and if the captain, master, or commander of any such ship or vessel being laden as aforesaid, shall neglect or refuse to deliver the manifest at the time and in the manner herein directed, or shall land or put on shore any negro, mulatto, or person of colour, for the purpose aforesaid, before he shall have delivered his manifest as aforesaid, and obtained a permit for that purpose, every such captain, master, or commander, shall forfeit and pay ten thousand dollars, one moiety thereof to the United States, the other moiety to the use of any person or persons who shall sue for and prosecute the same to effect.

## 13. An Act Declaring War between the United Kingdom of Great Britain and Ireland and the Dependencies Thereof and the United States of America and Their Territories, June 18, 1812

*Be it enacted by the Senate and House of Representatives of the United States of America in Congress assembled,* That war be and the same is hereby declared to exist between the United Kingdom of Great Britain and Ireland and the dependencies thereof, and the United States of America and their territories; and that the President of the United States is hereby authorized to use the whole land and naval force of the United States to carry the same into effect, and to issue to private armed vessels of the United States commissions or letters of marque and general reprisal, in such form as he shall think proper, and under the seal of the United States, against the vessels, goods, and effects of the government of the said United Kingdom of Great Britain and Ireland, and the subjects thereof.

## 14. The Treaty of Ghent, Signed December 24, 1814

Treaty of Peace and Amity between His Britannic Majesty and the United States of America. His Britannic Majesty and the United States of America desirous of terminating the war which has unhappily subsisted between the two Countries, and of restoring upon principles of perfect reciprocity, Peace, Friendship, and good Understanding between them, have for that purpose appointed their respective Plenipotentiaries, that is to say, His Britannic Majesty on His part has appointed the Right Honourable James Lord Gambier, late Admiral of the White now Admiral of the Red Squadron of His Majesty's Fleet; Henry Goulburn Esquire, a Member of the Imperial Parliament and Under Secretary of State; and William Adams Esquire, Doctor of Civil Laws: And the President of the United States, by and with the advice and consent of the Senate thereof, has appointed John Quincy Adams, James A. Bayard, Henry Clay, Jonathan Russell, and Albert Gallatin, Citizens of the United States; who, after a reciprocal communication of their respective Full Powers, have agreed upon the following Articles.

## Article the First.

There shall be a firm and universal Peace between His Britannic Majesty and the United States, and between their respective Countries, Territories, Cities, Towns, and People of every degree without exception of places or persons. All hostilities both by sea and land shall cease as soon as this Treaty shall have been ratified by both parties as hereinafter mentioned. All territory, places, and possessions whatsoever taken by either party from the other during the war, or which may be taken after the signing of this Treaty, excepting only the Islands hereinafter mentioned, shall be restored without delay and without causing any destruction or carrying away any of the Artillery or other public property originally captured in the said forts or places, and which shall remain therein upon the Exchange of the Ratifications of this Treaty, or any Slaves or other private property; And all Archives, Records, Deeds, and Papers, either of a public nature or belonging to private persons, which in the course of the war may have fallen into the hands of the Officers of either party, shall be, as far as may be practicable, forthwith restored and delivered to the proper authorities and persons to whom they respectively belong. Such of the Islands in the Bay of Passamaquoddy as are claimed by both parties shall remain in the possession of the party in whose occupation they may be at the time of the Exchange of the Ratifications of this Treaty until the decision respecting the title to the said Islands shall have been made in conformity with the fourth Article of this Treaty. No disposition made by this Treaty as to such possession of the Islands and territories claimed by both parties shall in any manner whatever be construed to affect the right of either.

## Article the Second.

Immediately after the ratifications of this Treaty by both parties as hereinafter mentioned, orders shall be sent to the Armies, Squadrons, Officers, Subjects, and Citizens of the two Powers to cease from all hostilities: and to prevent all causes of complaint which might arise on account of the prizes which may be taken at sea after the said Ratifications of this Treaty, it is reciprocally agreed that all vessels and effects which may be taken after the space of twelve days from the said Ratifications upon all parts of the Coast of North America from the Latitude of twenty three degrees North to the Latitude of fifty degrees North, and as far Eastward in the Atlantic Ocean as the thirty sixth degree of West Longitude from the Meridian of Greenwich, shall be restored on each side:-that the time shall be thirty days in all other parts of the Atlantic Ocean North of the Equinoctial Line or Equator:-and the same time for the British and Irish Channels, for the Gulf of Mexico, and all parts of the West Indies:-forty days for the North Seas for the Baltic, and for all parts of the Mediterranean-sixty days for the Atlantic Ocean South of the Equator as far as the Latitude of the Cape of Good Hope.-ninety days for every other part of the world South of the Equator, and one hundred and twenty days for all other parts of the world without exception.

## Article the Third.

All Prisoners of war taken on either side as well by land as by sea shall be restored as soon as practicable after the Ratifications of this Treaty as hereinafter mentioned on their paying the debts which they may have contracted during their captivity. The two Contracting Parties respectively engage to discharge in specie the advances which may have been made by the other for the sustenance and maintenance of such prisoners.

## Article the Fourth.

Whereas it was stipulated by the second Article in the Treaty of Peace of one thousand seven hundred and eighty three between His Britannic Majesty and the

United States of America that the boundary of the United States should comprehend all Islands within twenty leagues of any part of the shores of the United States and lying between lines to be drawn due East from the points where the aforesaid boundaries between Nova Scotia on the one part and East Florida on the other shall respectively touch the Bay of Fundy and the Atlantic Ocean, excepting such Islands as now are or heretofore have been within the limits of Nova Scotia, and whereas the several Islands in the Bay of Passamaquoddy, which is part of the Bay of Fundy, and the Island of Grand Menan in the said Bay of Fundy, are claimed by the United States as being comprehended within their aforesaid boundaries, which said Islands are claimed as belonging to His Britannic Majesty as having been at the time of and previous to the aforesaid Treaty of one thousand seven hundred and eighty three within the limits of the Province of Nova Scotia: In order therefore finally to decide upon these claims it is agreed that they shall be referred to two Commissioners to be appointed in the following manner: viz: One Commissioner shall be appointed by His Britannic Majesty and one by the President of the United States, by and with the advice and consent of the Senate thereof, and the said two Commissioners so appointed shall be sworn impartially to examine and decide upon the said claims according to such evidence as shall be laid before them on the part of His Britannic Majesty and of the United States respectively. The said Commissioners shall meet at St Andrews in the Province of New Brunswick, and shall have power to adjourn to such other place or places as they shall think fit. The said Commissioners shall by a declaration or report under their hands and seals decide to which of the two Contracting parties the several Islands aforesaid do respectedly belong in conformity with the true intent of the said Treaty of Peace of one thousand seven hundred and eighty three. And if the said Commissioners shall agree in their decision both parties shall consider such decision as final and conclusive. It is further agreed that in the event of the two Commissioners differing upon all or any of the matters so referred to them, or in the event of both or either of the said Commissioners refusing or declining or wilfully omitting to act as such, they shall make jointly or separately a report or reports as well to the Government of His Britannic Majesty as to that of the United States, stating in detail the points on which they differ, and the grounds upon which their respective opinions have been formed, or the grounds upon which they or either of them have so refused declined or omitted to act. And His Britannic Majesty and the Government of the United States hereby agree to refer the report or reports of the said Commissioners to some friendly Sovereign or State to be then named for that purpose, and who shall be requested to decide on the differences which may be stated in the said report or reports, or upon the report of one Commissioner together with the grounds upon which the other Commissioner shall have refused, declined or omitted to act as the case may be. And if the Commissioner so refusing, declining, or omitting to act, shall also wilfully omit to state the grounds upon which he has so done in such manner that the said statement may be referred to such friendly Sovereign or State together with the report of such other Commissioner, then such Sovereign or State shall decide ex parse upon the said report alone. And His Britannic Majesty and the Government of the United States engage to consider the decision of such friendly Sovereign or State to be final and conclusive on all the matters so referred.

### Article the Fifth.

Whereas neither that point of the Highlands lying due North from the source of the River St Croix, and designated in the former Treaty of Peace between the two Powers as the North West Angle of Nova Scotia, nor the North Westernmost head of Connecticut River has yet been ascertained; and whereas that part of the boundary line between the Dominions of the two Powers which extends from the source of the River St Croix directly North to the above mentioned North West Angle of Nova Scotia, thence along the said Highlands which divide those Rivers that empty themselves into the River St Lawrence from those which fall into the Atlantic Ocean to the North Westernmost head of Connecticut River, thence down along the middle of that River to the forty fifth degree of North Latitude, thence by a line due West on said latitude until it strikes the River Iroquois or Cataraquy, has not yet been surveyed: it is agreed that for these several purposes two Commissioners shall be appointed, sworn, and authorized to act exactly in the manner directed with respect to those mentioned in the next preceding Article unless otherwise specified in the present Article. The said

Commissioners shall meet at St Andrews in the Province of New Brunswick, and shall have power to adjourn to such other place or places as they shall think fit. The said Commissioners shall have power to ascertain and determine the points above mentioned in conformity with the provisions of the said Treaty of Peace of one thousand seven hundred and eighty three, and shall cause the boundary aforesaid from the source of the River St Croix to the River Iroquois or Cataraquy to be surveyed and marked according to the said provisions. The said Commissioners shall make a map of the said boundary, and annex to it a declaration under their hands and seals certifying it to be the true Map of the said boundary, and particularizing the latitude and longitude of the North West Angle of Nova Scotia, of the North Westernmost head of Connecticut River, and of such other points of the said boundary as they may deem proper. And both parties agree to consider such map and declaration as finally and conclusively fixing the said boundary. And in the event of the said two Commissioners differing, or both, or either of them refusing, declining, or wilfully omitting to act, such reports, declarations, or statements shall be made by them or either of them, and such reference to a friendly Sovereign or State shall be made in all respects as in the latter part of the fourth Article is contained, and in as full a manner as if the same was herein repeated.

## Article the Sixth.

Whereas by the former Treaty of Peace that portion of the boundary of the United States from the point where the forty-fifth degree of North Latitude strikes the River Iroquois or Cataraquy to the Lake Superior was declared to be "along the middle of said River into Lake Ontario, through the middle of said Lake until it strikes the communication by water between that Lake and Lake Erie, thence along the middle of said communication into Lake Erie, through the middle of said Lake until it arrives at the water communication into the Lake Huron; thence through the middle of said Lake to the water communication between that Lake and Lake Superior:" and whereas doubts have arisen what was the middle of the said River, Lakes, and water communications, and whether certain Islands lying in the same were within the Dominions of His Britannic Majesty or of the United States: In order therefore finally to decide these doubts, they shall be referred

to two Commissioners to be appointed, sworn, and authorized to act exactly in the manner directed with respect to those mentioned in the next preceding Article unless otherwise specified in this present Article. The said Commissioners shall meet in the first instance at Albany in the State of New York, and shall have power to adjourn to such other place or places as they shall think fit. The said Commissioners shall by a Report or Declaration under their hands and seals, designate the boundary through the said River, Lakes, and water communications, and decide to which of the two Contracting parties the several Islands lying within the said Rivers, Lakes, and water communications, do respectively belong in conformity with the true intent of the said Treaty of one thousand seven hundred and eighty three. And both parties agree to consider such designation and decision as final and conclusive. And in the event of the said two Commissioners differing or both or either of them refusing, declining, or wilfully omitting to act, such reports, declarations, or statements shall be made by them or either of them, and such reference to a friendly Sovereign or State shall be made in all respects as in the latter part of the fourth Article is contained, and in as full a manner as if the same was herein repeated.

## Article the Seventh.

It is further agreed that the said two last mentioned Commissioners after they shall have executed the duties assigned to them in the preceding Article, shall be, and they are hereby, authorized upon their oaths impartially to fix and determine according to the true intent of the said Treaty of Peace of one thousand seven hundred and eighty three, that part of the boundary between the dominions of the two Powers, which extends from the water communication between Lake Huron and Lake Superior to the most North Western point of the Lake of the Woods;-to decide to which of the two Parties the several Islands lying in the Lakes, water communications, and Rivers forming the said boundary do respectively belong in conformity with the true intent of the said Treaty of Peace of one thousand seven hundred and eighty three, and to cause such parts of the said boundary as require it to be surveyed and marked. The said Commissioners shall by a Report or declaration under their hands and seals, designate the boundary aforesaid, state their decision on the points thus referred to them, and particularize the Latitude and Longitude of the most North Western point of the Lake of the Woods, and of such other parts of the said boundary as they may deem proper. And both parties agree to consider such designation and decision as final and conclusive. And in the event of the said two Commissioners differing, or both or either of them refusing, declining, or wilfully omitting to act, such reports, declarations or statements shall be made by them or either of them, and such reference to a friendly Sovereign or State shall be made in all respects as in the latter part of the fourth Article is contained, and in as full a manner as if the same was herein revealed.

## Article the Eighth.

The several Boards of two Commissioners mentioned in the four preceding Articles shall respectively have power to appoint a Secretary, and to employ such Surveyors or other persons as they shall judge necessary. Duplicates of all their respective reports, declarations, statements, and decisions, and of their accounts, and of the Journal of their proceedings shall be delivered by them to the Agents of His Britannic Majesty and to the Agents of the United States, who may be respectively appointed and authorized to manage the business on behalf of their respective Governments. The said Commissioners shall be respectively paid in such manner as shall be agreed between the two contracting parties, such agreement being to be settled at the time of the Exchange of the Ratifications of this Treaty. And all other expenses attending the said Commissions shall be defrayed equally by the two parties. And in the case of death, sickness, resignation, or necessary absence, the place of every such Commissioner respectively shall be supplied in the same manner as such Commissioner was first appointed; and the new Commissioner shall take the same oath or affirmation and do the same duties. It is further agreed between the two contracting parties that in case any of the Islands mentioned in any of the preceding Articles, which were in the possession of one of the parties prior to the commencement of the present war between the two Countries, should by the decision of any of the Boards of Commissioners aforesaid, or of the Sovereign or State so referred to, as in the four next preceding Articles contained, fall within the dominions of the other party, all grants of land made previous to the commencement of the war by the party having had such possession, shall be as valid as if such Island or Islands had by such decision or decisions been adjudged to be within the dominions of the party having had such possession.

## Article the Ninth.

The United States of America engage to put an end immediately after the Ratification of the present Treaty to hostilities with all the Tribes or Nations of Indians with whom they may be at war at the time of such Ratification, and forthwith to restore to such Tribes or Nations respectively all the possessions, rights, and privileges which they may have enjoyed or been entitled to in one thousand eight hundred and eleven previous to such hostilities. Provided always that such Tribes or Nations shall agree to desist from all hostilities against the United States of America, their Citizens, and Subjects upon the Ratification of the present Treaty being notified to such Tribes or Nations, and shall so desist accordingly. And His Britannic Majesty engages on his part to put an end immediately after the Ratification of the present Treaty to hostilities with all the Tribes or Nations of Indians with whom He may be at war at the time of such Ratification, and forthwith to restore to such Tribes or Nations respectively all the possessions, rights, and privileges, which they may have enjoyed or been entitled to in one thousand eight hundred and eleven previous to such hostilities. Provided always that such Tribes or Nations shall agree to desist from all hostilities against His Britannic Majesty and His Subjects upon the Ratification of the present Treaty being notified to such Tribes or Nations, and shall so desist accordingly.

## Article the Tenth.

Whereas the Traffic in Slaves is irreconcilable with the principles of humanity and Justice, and whereas both His Majesty and the United States are desirous of continuing their efforts to promote its entire abolition, it is hereby agreed that both the contracting parties shall use their best endeavours to accomplish so desirable an object.

## Article the Eleventh.

This Treaty when the same shall have been ratified on both sides without alteration by either of the contracting parties, and the Ratifications mutually exchanged, shall be binding on both parties, and the Ratifications shall be exchanged at Washington in the space of four months from this day or sooner if practicable. In faith whereof, We the respective Plenipotentiaries have signed this Treaty, and have hereunto affixed our Seals.

Done in triplicate at Ghent the twenty fourth day of December one thousand eight hundred and fourteen.

[Names.]

## 15. THE MONROE DOCTRINE, DECEMBER 2, 1823

From President Monroe's seventh annual message to Congress, December 2, 1823:

. . . At the proposal of the Russian Imperial Government, made through the minister of the Emperor residing here, a full power and instructions have been transmitted to the minister of the United States at St. Petersburg to arrange by amicable negotiation the respective rights and interests of the two nations on the northwest coast of this continent. A similar proposal has been made by His Imperial Majesty to the Government of Great Britain, which has likewise been acceded to. The Government of the United States has been desirous by this friendly proceeding of manifesting the great value which they have invariably attached to the friendship of the Emperor and their solicitude to cultivate the best understanding with his Government. In the discussions to which this interest has given rise and in the arrangements by which they may terminate the occasion has been judged proper for asserting, as a principle in which the rights and interests of the United States are involved, that the American continents, by the free and independent condition which they have assumed and maintain, are henceforth not to be considered as subjects for future colonization by any European powers . . .

It was stated at the commencement of the last session that a great effort was then making in Spain and Portugal to improve the condition of the people of those countries, and that it appeared to be conducted with extraordinary moderation. It need scarcely be remarked that the results have been so far very different from what was then anticipated. Of events in that quarter of the globe, with which we have so much intercourse and from which we derive our origin, we

have always been anxious and interested spectators. The citizens of the United States cherish sentiments the most friendly in favor of the liberty and happiness of their fellow-men on that side of the Atlantic. In the wars of the European powers in matters relating to themselves we have never taken any part, nor does it comport with our policy to do so. It is only when our rights are invaded or seriously menaced that we resent injuries or make preparation for our defense. With the movements in this hemisphere we are of necessity more immediately connected, and by causes which must be obvious to all enlightened and impartial observers. The political system of the allied powers is essentially different in this respect from that of America. This difference proceeds from that which exists in their respective Governments; and to the defense of our own, which has been achieved by the loss of so much blood and treasure, and matured by the wisdom of their most enlightened citizens, and under which we have enjoyed unexampled felicity, this whole nation is devoted. We owe it, therefore, to candor and to the amicable relations existing between the United States and those powers to declare that we should consider any attempt on their part to extend their system to any portion of this hemisphere as dangerous to our peace and safety. With the existing colonies or dependencies of any European power we have not interfered and shall not interfere. But with the Governments who have declared their independence and maintain it, and whose independence we have, on great consideration and on just principles, acknowledged, we could not view any interposition for the purpose of oppressing them, or controlling in any other manner their destiny, by any European power in any other light than as the manifestation of an unfriendly disposition toward the United States. In the war between those new Governments and Spain we declared our neutrality at the time of their recognition, and to this we have adhered, and shall continue to adhere, provided no change shall occur which, in the judgement of the competent authorities of this Government, shall make a corresponding change on the part of the United States indispensable to their security.

The late events in Spain and Portugal shew that Europe is still unsettled. Of this important fact no stronger proof can be adduced than that the allied powers should have thought it proper, on any principle satisfactory to themselves, to have interposed by force in the internal concerns of Spain. To what extent such interposition may be carried, on the same principle, is a question in which all independent powers whose governments differ from theirs are interested, even those most remote, and surely none of them more so than the United States. Our policy in regard to Europe, which was adopted at an early stage of the wars which have so long agitated that quarter of the globe, nevertheless remains the same, which is, is not to interfere in the internal concerns of any of its powers; to consider the government de facto as the legitimate government for us; to cultivate friendly relations with it, and to preserve those relations by a frank, firm, and manly policy, meeting in all instances the just claims of every power, submitting to injuries from none. But in regard to those continents circumstances are eminently and conspicuously different. It is impossible that the allied powers should extend their political system to any portion of either continent without endangering our peace and happiness; nor can anyone believe that our southern brethren, if left to themselves, would adopt it of their own accord. It is equally impossible, therefore, that we should behold such interposition in any form with indifference. If we look to the comparative strength and resources of Spain and those new Governments, and their distance from each other, it must be obvious that she can never subdue them. It is still the true policy of the United States to leave the parties to themselves, in hope that other powers will pursue the same course. . . .

# APPENDIX B
# Biographies of Major Personalities

**Adams, Abigail Smith** (November 11, 1744–October 28, 1818) *first lady*

As the wife and mother of two early presidents of the United States, Abigail Adams showed how an intelligent woman with direct access to power could exercise influence even when she played a traditional and restricted role as an 18th-century woman.

Although she had only limited formal education, a fact she greatly lamented, Adams was one of the most dutiful and eloquent letter writers of the Revolutionary and early republican periods. She married John Adams in October 1764 and bore four children over the subsequent 10 years. While John was away from home off and on for almost 10 years during the Revolution, Abigail ran the family farm in Braintree (now Quincy), Massachusetts, and proved a capable businesswoman.

In 1784, Abigail joined John in Paris and then London, where he served as a diplomat for four years, and her letters to friends and political associates such as Thomas Jefferson and Mercy Otis Warren helped to spread diplomatic information and news. When her husband was elected as the first vice president in 1789, Abigail supported him, and by the time he was elected president in 1796, she conveyed an increasing sense of allegiance to the Federalist Party. She encouraged her husband's conservative politics, for example, as a strong supporter of the Alien and Sedition Acts. During John Adams's presidency, he and Abigail moved frequently between Massachusetts and the various national capitals, but at the end of his term in 1800, they became the first presidential couple to occupy the newly built White House in Washington, D.C.

The family retired to Braintree, Massachusetts, in 1801, and Abigail helped John to recover from his political wounds. She spent much of the rest of her life encouraging the political talents and ambitions of her son, John Quincy Adams, but she did not live to see him elected president in 1824. Late in life, Abigail played a large part in the reconciliation between her husband and Thomas Jefferson, whose political conflicts had broken up their friendship during the 1790s.

**Adams, John** (October 19, 1735–July 4, 1826) *diplomat, vice president, president*

John Adams's statesmanship helped to shape the political character of the United States in the immediate post-Revolutionary period, and he was a key figure in the country's first era of political party contest.

Adams graduated from Harvard College in 1755 and then became a lawyer in Massachusetts. He married Abigail Adams in October 1764 and fathered four children over the subsequent 10 years, the same period in which he became prominent in politics. Adams was a political activist against Great Britain during the Imperial Crisis, and he authored several important pamphlets, resolutions, and tracts that helped to define the Patriot cause. Adams served in the Continental Congress from 1774 to 1776 and again for a short period in 1777, and he was active in Massachusetts state politics. During most of the American Revolution, Adams served as a diplomat for the United States in the Netherlands and France, where he helped to arrange loans for the American government. Adams helped to negotiate the Treaty of Paris, which ended the Revolutionary War in 1783.

Following the war, John was joined in Europe by his wife, Abigail, and he served as the first U.S. minister to Great Britain during the Confederation period, while he continued to publish popular philosophical and political tracts in the United States. Adams was elected as the first vice president of the United States under the terms of the new federal Constitution in 1789.

During his term as vice president, Adams influenced President Washington, although he was criticized for being too pro-British and for seeming to value the trappings of aristocracy and even monarchy over republican simplicity. Adams was dubious of the French Revolution, and he found himself increasingly alienated in political matters from Secretary of State Thomas Jefferson.

Jefferson's supporters were beginning to form the Democratic-Republican Party in opposition to the Federalist policies of Adams and Secretary of the Treasury Alexander Hamilton, and when Adams was reelected vice president in 1792, he faced opposition from the Jeffersonian politician George Clinton. Even though many Americans, especially George Washington, were dubious of the legitimacy of political party contests, Adams and Hamilton outright opposed Jefferson and other Democratic-Republicans during Washington's second term.

In 1796, Adams was elected president over Jefferson, who received the second-highest number of electoral votes and became vice president. Adams's presidential term was rocky because of the domestic party conflict and rising troubles between the United States and France. Adams managed the XYZ affair (a scandal that ensued when France demanded a bribe) well, but differences of opinion over France increasingly divided the nation, as evidenced in Adams's enforcement of the Alien and Sedition Acts. Although they were both Federalists, Adams often ran afoul of Alexander Hamilton, who criticized Adams for being too soft on France, and who sometimes used his political influence to compromise the president's support. Adams avoided an open war with France, but he was defeated in the contentious 1800 presidential election by his ultimate political rival, Thomas Jefferson.

After making many last-minute political appointments that helped to insure a Federalist influence in national politics over the next decade, Adams retired with his family to Braintree (now Quincy), Massachusetts, in 1801. Adams spent the rest of his life writing, studying, and encouraging the political career of his son, John Quincy Adams, who became president in 1825. Adams was reconciled with Thomas Jefferson late in life, and the two men died on the same day, July 4, 1826, the 50th anniversary of American independence.

## Adams, John Quincy (July 11, 1767–February 23, 1848) *diplomat, secretary of state, president*

John Quincy Adams shaped the foreign policy of the United States more than any other single individual during the early republic, and his fairly unsuccessful term as president served merely as a prelude to his even more important political career during the 1830s and 1840s.

John Quincy Adams was the son of Abigail Adams and John Adams (the second president of the United States), and from an early age both of his famous parents encouraged his political development and ambition. He was educated in Europe while traveling on his father's diplomatic missions, with which he assisted at a young age, and he graduated from Harvard College in 1787. Soon thereafter, he became a lawyer in Boston, then began serving as U.S. minister to the Netherlands in 1794. He married the intelligent and vivacious Louisa Catherine Johnson while in England in 1797. Adams stayed in Europe and represented the United States in Berlin until his father was voted out of office in 1800.

Back in Boston, Adams became a Federalist politician, and he was elected to the U.S. Senate in 1803. When the Federalist Party became disillusioned by his support for many of President Jefferson's policies, he resigned from office, became a Democratic-Republican, and later served as U.S. minister to Russia during James Madison's first term as president, where he worked to secure help from Russia during the War of 1812. In 1813, Adams went to England and then Ghent, Belgium, as one of the commissioners who negotiated the treaty that ended the War of 1812 in 1815. Afterward he served as U.S. minister to Great Britain.

James Monroe appointed Adams secretary of state in 1817, and the office well suited Adams's talents and diplomatic experience. Adams refused to censure Andrew Jackson for his hasty takeover of Spanish Florida during the First Seminole War, and in the midst of a storm of controversy over Jackson's actions, Adams calmly negotiated a treaty with Spain legalizing the American takeover of the territory, the Adams-Onís Treaty of 1818. Adams also negotiated the Intercontinental Treaty with Great Britain in 1818, which settled various disputed trade and territorial rights and stabilized the relationship between the two countries. Adams's considerable influence over Monroe's foreign policy came to a head in 1823 when Adams drafted the Monroe Doctrine, a policy designed to keep European powers out of the affairs of the Western Hemisphere, which the president announced in his annual message to Congress.

By 1823, Adams was also fully embroiled in the hotly contested presidential campaign for the election of 1824. Although Adams adhered to an older style of politics and personally shunned campaigning, he was the presidential candidate in that election who represented the interests of New England. After none of the candidates received a majority of the electoral vote, the election was decided in the House of Representatives, where Adams was elected president, although he had won neither the most electoral votes nor the most popular votes. Rival candidate Andrew Jackson charged that Adams won the presidency only because of a supposed "corrupt bargain" in which he promised Henry Clay personal political power in exchange for supporting him in the House of Representatives.

Jackson never proved his case, but Adams did appoint Clay as secretary of state as soon as he took office in 1825. Adams's term as president was not terribly successful, in part because partisans who supported Jackson (including Vice President John C. Calhoun) did everything to oppose him and to set their candidate up for a more successful run for the office in 1828. During his term, Adams supported a strong program of internal improvements and financial developments. After the Jacksonians achieved a majority in Congress in 1827, however, Adams's support of a high trade tariff in 1828 backfired, when Jackson used the move to cost Adams support in the South, where the tariff was hugely unpopular. Adams was voted out of office after one term.

In 1831, Adams made a political comeback when he was elected to the U.S. House of Representatives from Massachusetts, and he was reelected for the subsequent 17 years. In Congress, he backed internal improvements, and he became active against the institution of slavery, most famously opposing the "Gag Rule," that prohibited discussion of slavery on the floor of Congress until 1844. Adams also successfully argued before the U.S. Supreme Court on behalf of the mutineer slaves of the *Amistad* in 1841, securing their release and passage back to Africa. At the end of his life, Adams opposed the annexation of Mexico and the Mexican-American War, and he was an active legislator until the day he died from a stroke while sitting at his desk on the floor of the House of Representatives.

### Adams, Louisa Catherine Johnson (February 12, 1775–May 15, 1852) *first lady*

Louisa Catherine Adams, the wife of John Quincy Adams, was a steadfast campaigner and supporter for her husband and a highly skilled diplomatic wife.

Louisa Catherine Johnson, born in London to an English mother and an American father, married John Quincy Adams when he was serving in Europe as an American diplomat in 1797. She spent much of her married life in poor reproductive health; pregnant 14 times, she had nine miscarriages, one stillborn child, and four live children. Louisa fit uncomfortably at first into American life when she and John Quincy returned to Boston in 1801, but her spirits soared when she accompanied her husband on his diplomatic posting to Russia in 1809. She traveled both alone and with small children around Europe in her husband's wake, sometimes suffering from severe depression that was probably linked to her failed pregnancies.

When the Adamses returned to the United States and John Quincy Adams took up his post as secretary of state in 1817, Louisa Catherine turned herself into one of Washington, D.C.'s most gracious hostesses. She organized parties, salons, and other public events, in part in an effort to get her husband elected president in 1824. He was elected, and Louisa Catherine lived a fairly quiet life as first lady.

The Adamses retired from Washington, D.C., after John Quincy's single term as president. Louisa Catherine was disappointed when her husband returned to enter the House of Representatives in 1830. When she died in 1852, Congress adjourned in her honor, a mark of the respect she still commanded among the nation's leaders.

### Burr, Aaron (February 6, 1756–September 14, 1836) *vice president, controversial politician and personality*

Burr was perhaps the most notorious political figure of the early republic. He served as vice president but was indicted for murder during his term and treason not long thereafter.

Born in New Jersey, Burr graduated from Princeton University, of which his father was president, and then served with distinction as a military officer in the Revolutionary War until 1779. Burr became a lawyer and moved to New York, where he began to pursue political ambitions. He was elected to the U.S. Senate in 1791 in a campaign that began his long political and personal feud with Alexander Hamilton. In the Senate, Burr adhered to the Democratic-Republican Party, and the party nominated him to be Thomas Jefferson's running mate for the election of 1800.

When bad party management resulted in a tied electoral vote in 1800, the election was thrown into the House of Representatives. Over the objections of party leader Alexander Hamilton, some Federalists cast their ballots for Burr in the House, thinking they could get Burr to support Federalist positions if they gave him the presidency over Jefferson. After 35 rounds of balloting, Jefferson was elected president and Burr vice president, but Burr's position in the Democratic-Republican Party was severely compromised by the electoral maneuvering.

Burr spent much of his vice-presidential term meddling in New York politics, and he ran for governor of New York in 1804. Burr blamed Hamilton for his defeat in that election, and the personal and political ill will between the two men came to a head when they fought a duel on July 11, 1804. Burr killed Hamilton in the duel, and he spent the next several months trying to evade prosecution for murder, even as he presided over the U.S. Senate at the end of his vice-presidential term.

In 1805 and 1806, Burr traveled Ohio, Kentucky, Tennessee, and Missouri, where he met with the shady U.S. military official James Wilkinson. The two engaged in a plot, which was perhaps intended to seize Spanish territory in the West to create a private empire, and although Burr was tried for treason for his role in the scheme, he was acquitted in Virginia Circuit Court in 1807.

Burr spent the following four years in Europe, and when he returned to the United States, he built up a new law practice in New York State. He had some influence over the younger generation of New York politicians, including Martin Van Buren, but for the most part he remained out of the public eye until his death in 1836.

**Calhoun, John C.** (March 18, 1782–March 31, 1850) *U.S. senator, cabinet member, vice president*
John C. Calhoun, the son of a prosperous South Carolina plantation family, graduated from Yale University in 1804 and completed his education by becoming a lawyer in South Carolina. Calhoun was elected as a Democratic-Republican member of Congress in 1811, where he immediately became influential as the chair of the House Foreign Relations Committee and one of the most outspoken of the "War Hawks," who demanded war against Great Britain. After the War of 1812, Calhoun became an advocate of nationalism and the strong use of federal power, and he authored the charter of the Second Bank of the United States and the "Bonus Bill," which would have paid for internal improvements had it not been vetoed by President Madison.

Calhoun served as secretary of war during the Monroe administration, an office he used to author important government reports and to shape expansionist policies against Native American tribes. In the cabinet, Calhoun strongly supported censuring General Andrew Jackson for his unauthorized takeover of Spanish Florida after the Seminole War in 1818, but President Monroe and Secretary of State John Quincy Adams refused to censure Jackson.

Calhoun stood as a candidate for president in 1824, but when Andrew Jackson also entered the race and sapped much of his support, Calhoun decided to run for vice president instead. He was elected vice president in 1824, even as the presidential race was thrown into the House of Representatives. While serving as vice president under John Quincy Adams, who emerged victorious in the 1824 election, Calhoun joined forces with New York senator Martin Van Buren to oppose the president's policies, and Calhoun came to support the Jacksonian wing of the increasingly divided Democratic-Republican Party. Calhoun promoted the power of the office of vice president by taking an active role in the Senate. Although he had previously supported tariffs as part of his nationalist political program, Calhoun was outraged by President Adams's support of the 1828 "Tariff of Abominations," and he led opposition against the tariff and authored the *South Carolina Exposition and Protest,* a scathing antitariff defense of states' rights.

Calhoun served as vice president during Andrew Jackson's first presidential term beginning in 1829, but he became ever more alienated from Jackson and his cabinet, and he was dropped from the ticket in 1832. Calhoun was an important figure during the Nullification Crisis that same year, when South Carolina opposed a new, higher series of tariffs. Calhoun spent most of the next 20 years in the U.S. Senate, where he was increasingly known as an advocate of states' rights and a virulent defender of the institution of slavery. He also ran unsuccessfully for president a second time in 1843. Calhoun opposed the Compromise of 1850, and when he died that same year, his earlier career as a nationalist politician during the early republic was all but forgotten. He was remembered primarily as a promoter of southern sectional interests.

## Clark, William (August 1, 1770–September 1, 1838)
*explorer, territorial governor, Indian superintendent*

William Clark was born in rural Virginia, the youngest brother of George Rogers Clark, a western hero of the French and Indian War and the Revolutionary War. When William Clark was a young man, his family moved to Kentucky, and he took up a career as a frontier military man. In the late 1780s and early 1790s, Clark participated in attacks on bands of Indians as part of the Kentucky militia, and in 1792 he became a lieutenant in the U.S. Army. He continued to serve in Indian campaigns, and he fought at the Battle of Fallen Timbers under General "Mad" Anthony Wayne.

Clark left the military for a time to become a merchant, but in 1803, Meriwether Lewis, a longtime military companion, asked Clark to serve as his fellow commander on an expedition to the Pacific Ocean organized by President Jefferson. Between 1804 and 1806, Lewis, Clark, and the other members of their "Corps of Discovery" traveled between St. Louis, Missouri, and the Pacific coast, keeping records of the natural world and establishing diplomatic relations with many Indian peoples along the way. Clark's maps of the West made during the journey were considered standard for decades to come.

In 1807, William Clark became the chief Indian agent for the Louisiana Territory, and he was appointed territorial governor of Missouri in 1813. In 1820 he was appointed superintendent of Indian affairs at St. Louis in 1822, a post that allowed him to supervise the process of Indian removal until just before his death in 1838.

## Clay, Henry (April 12, 1777–June 29, 1852)
*legislator, Speaker of the House, secretary of state*

Although he never became president, to his personal disappointment, Henry Clay was one of the most influential politicians of the early 19th century.

Henry Clay was born in Virginia, where he received little formal education. His intelligence and talent earned him respect, and by the age of 15, he was serving as a clerk in the state chancery office. There he came to the notice of George Wythe, who decided to give Clay a legal education. Clay became a lawyer in 1797, and at the age of 20, he moved to Lexington, Kentucky, where he set up an immediately prosperous law practice. Clay married the wealthy Lucretia Hart, rose through Kentucky politics, and became a leader in the state legislature. He also served a brief stint in the U.S. Senate in 1806, when he filled out the term of a Kentucky senator who had died.

Clay was elected to the U.S. House of Representatives in 1811, where he was immediately elected Speaker of the House and began to issue the strong calls for war against Great Britain that marked him as one of the "War Hawks." Clay wanted to promote western expansion and economic development, and he supported war as a way to clear Great Britain (and Indians) out of the way. Clay was a strong legislator throughout the war, and he served as one of the negotiators of the Treaty of Ghent that ended the war in 1815.

Clay continued in the House after the war, where he especially promoted his plans for internal improvements, higher tariffs, and the attempts to charter the Second Bank of the United States. Clay broke with the Monroe administration in 1817 when he sharply criticized General Andrew Jackson's invasion of Florida; Clay and Jackson were soon to become bitter and long-standing political enemies. Clay was the crucial negotiator of the Missouri Compromise of 1820–21, and he left Congress briefly before returning to office in 1823. In the early 1820s, Clay championed what he dubbed the "American System," which linked his economic plans and support of internal improvements to strong support for Latin American independence movements.

Clay ran in the 1824 presidential election as a representative of western interests, but Andrew Jackson stole much of his thunder, and Clay came in fourth in the electoral balloting. However, when the election was thrown into the House of Representatives, Clay, as House Speaker, wielded much power to influence the ultimate choice among the top three candidates. When Clay threw his support behind John Quincy Adams, Jackson accused Clay of being part of a "corrupt bargain" to grab power. Clay denied the charge for the rest of his life. Whatever the arrangement, when Adams took office in 1825, he immediately appointed Clay to be secretary of state.

Clay used the office of secretary of state to promote his interest in Latin American independence, although Jackson's supporters in Congress thwarted some of his more creative diplomatic efforts. When Jackson became president in 1829, Clay retired to Kentucky.

Clay did not stay out of politics, however. He was elected to the U.S. Senate in 1831, and he ran against Jackson for president in 1832. Clay was badly defeated, but he continued to organize opposition to Jackson, and he was one of the founders of the Whig Party in 1834. Clay resigned from the Senate in 1842, and he was the Whig candidate for president in 1844, but he lost to expansionist Democrat James K. Polk. Clay was returned to the Senate in 1849, where he played a crucial role in brokering the Compromise of 1850. He died two years later, after a career of almost 50 years in politics.

## Cuffe, Paul (January 17, 1759–September 7, 1817) businessman, black nationalist, advocate of African colonization

Paul Cuffe, the son of a West African father and a Wampanoag Indian mother, was a sailor who worked his way up to become a successful merchant and shipowner by 1806. Although Cuffe was one of the wealthiest African Americans in the country, his race kept him from being fully accepted by the Massachusetts merchant community, and he became increasingly interested throughout his life in enhancing African-American power and strengthening ties to Africa. Cuffe worked to gain political and educational rights for blacks in Massachusetts.

Cuffe became a Quaker in 1808, and he sailed on two trips to help establish the English colony for former slaves in Sierra Leone, West Africa. During the War of 1812, Cuffe worked to free slaves and to try to settle them in Sierra Leone, and after the war he transported 38 black settlers to West Africa. Always skeptical of American racism, Cuffe saw African colonization as a positive solution to the problem of American slavery, and just before his death he endorsed the formation of the American Colonization Society (ACS). Although other free African Americans would subsequently oppose the ACS as a racist and ineffectual organization, Cuffe was one of

the first Americans to suggest returning to Africa as a way to promote black nationalism, a strategy that would be taken up by other activists in decades to come.

## Dearborn, Henry (February 23, 1851–June 6, 1829) politician, soldier

Henry Dearborn served as an officer throughout the Revolutionary War, and after the war he moved to the Maine frontier. He was elected to Congress from Massachusetts in 1793, where he served as a loyal Democratic-Republican partisan. His party loyalty and military experience earned him an appointment as secretary of war under President Thomas Jefferson, an office Dearborn kept for the duration of Jefferson's presidency.

At the beginning of the War of 1812, President Madison appointed Dearborn as senior major general of the U.S. Army and put him in charge of the entire northeastern theater of the war, including the invasion of Canada at Lake Champlain. Dearborn took little action, and his poor performance hindered the U.S. war effort from the outset. He was relieved of command in July 1813, after basically failing in every campaign he planned, although he continued to serve in the army until his discharge in 1815. Dearborn served as U.S. minister to Portugal from 1822 to 1824.

## Hamilton, Alexander (January 11, 1757–July 12, 1804) Federalist party leader, secretary of the treasury

Alexander Hamilton rose from humble beginnings to become one of the most powerful politicians in the early years of the U.S. republic, before his life ended in a duel with Vice President Aaron Burr.

Born on the West Indian island of Nevis, Hamilton was orphaned at a young age. He became a trusted merchant's apprentice in St. Croix, and his intelligence led backers to send him at the age of 15 to be educated at Princeton University, in New Jersey. Disillusioned with Princeton, Hamilton moved to New York to attend King's College (now Columbia University). In New York, Hamilton was caught up in the Revolutionary movement, and he published political pamphlets and became an artillery captain in 1776.

In 1777, he became a lieutenant colonel and was appointed aide-de-camp to General George Washington, for whom he became a trusted adviser. In 1780, Hamilton married Elizabeth Schuyler, a daughter of one of America's richest families, and continued to serve in various posts in the Continental Army until 1782.

After serving a short stint in Congress, practicing law in New York, and becoming a New York state legislator, Hamilton became a delegate at the 1787 constitutional convention, where he advocated strengthening the powers of the federal government. During the fight to ratify the new U.S. Constitution, Hamilton became one of its strongest advocates. Along with James Madison and John Jay, he coauthored the *Federalist* essays that helped to seal ratification in New York State.

When he assumed the presidency in 1789, George Washington appointed Alexander Hamilton to serve as the first U.S. secretary of the Treasury. Hamilton used the office to argue for use of federal power in all things, especially in financial affairs, and he exerted a profound influence over President Washington. Controversies and divisions over Hamilton's proposed fiscal policies, which included the creation of the First Bank of the United States, helped to create the first political parties in the United States. Hamilton became a primary leader of the Federalist Party, although President Washington continued to assert that he himself was nonpartisan. Hamilton opposed the excesses of democracy he observed in the French Revolution, and he urged President Washington to take action to suppress symptoms of such excess in the United States, such as the 1794 Whiskey Rebellion. Hamilton became a symbol of strong federal power, which brought him in particular conflict with Secretary of State Thomas Jefferson, and eventually both men resigned from the cabinet to devote themselves to partisan politicking.

Although he returned to private law practice in 1795, Hamilton was never far from politics. He continued to advise George Washington. He also remained an active leader of the Federalist Party, even after John Adams was elected as President Washington's successor. Hamilton frequently criticized fellow Federalist John Adams, whom he saw as being too soft on France. In the 1800 election, Hamilton worked to defeat Adams by campaigning for Charles Coatsworth Pinckney, but his plan backfired when a very contested process led to the election of his greater nemesis, Thomas Jefferson, as president. Despite Jefferson's presidency, Hamilton retained much political influence, especially in New York, and

he continued to promote Federalist causes. He helped to ensure Aaron Burr's defeat in the 1804 gubernatorial campaign in New York. Burr took offense at Hamilton's behavior and some alleged rude remarks he had made, and challenged Hamilton to a duel. Burr shot and killed Hamilton in the duel at Weehawken, New Jersey, in July 1804.

**Harrison, William Henry** (February 9, 1773–April 4, 1841) *territorial governor, military leader, U.S. president*

William Henry Harrison made the political reputation that would later carry him to the presidency as a territorial official, Indian fighter, and military leader in the War of 1812. Harrison got an early taste of western Indian warfare in the early 1790s, when he served in the U.S. Army during "Mad" Anthony Wayne's campaigns against Little Turtle. By 1799 Harrison had risen quickly in the political world, and he was appointed territorial governor of Indiana at the age of 27.

As Indiana governor, Harrison worked to take over as much Indian land as possible. He concluded the coercive Treaty of Fort Wayne in 1809, which gained title to large tracts of Northwest Territory Indian land but also invigorated the anti-American pan-Indian movement led by the Shawnee warrior Tecumseh. After a confrontational meeting with Tecumseh at Vincennes, Indiana, in 1810, Harrison attacked the Shawnee headquarters at Tippecanoe (or Prophetstown) in November 1811, while Tecumseh was away recruiting support for his movement. Harrison defeated Tecumseh's brother, Tenskwatawa, and used the victory to bolster his calls to the Madison administration for more military support against Indians across the Northwest.

Such calls helped lead the United States into the War of 1812 the following year. Harrison fought in the war, first as a major general of the Kentucky militia and later as a major general in the U.S. Army. Harrison was put in command of the northwestern theater of the war in 1813 after the first year of the military campaign had gone badly, and he ordered the construction of forts and lent support to Oliver Hazard Perry's naval campaign on Lake Erie, both of which helped drive the British back into Canada and led to the death of Tecumseh at the Battle of the Thames in October 1813. After a series of conflicts with Secretary of War John Armstrong, Harrison resigned his military commission in 1814, but he continued as an Indian negotiator to gain large tracts of land for the United States.

After the War of 1812, Harrison took short turns in the House of Representatives, the Senate, and as U.S. minister to Colombia. He became a prominent farmer in Ohio and reentered politics in 1836 as a Whig candidate for the presidency. He was elected president in 1840 but died in April 1841, just weeks after his inauguration.

**Irving, Washington** (April 3, 1783–November 28, 1859)  *author, diplomat*
Washington Irving was one of the first American authors to become a highly respected literary figure, and his often-satirical fiction helped Americans accept with a sense of humor the great changes underway in their society during the early republic. In 1807–08, Irving published his first book, *Salmagundi,* written with William Irving and J. K. Paulding, and he followed in 1809 with *A History of New York,* which he published under the pseudonym Diedrich Knickerbocker. The Knickerbocker series inaugurated an American style of satire that remained popular throughout much of the 19th century.

Irving's *Sketch Book of Geoffrey Crayon, Gent.,* which appeared at the beginning of the 1820s, contained his most famous stories, "Rip Van Winkle" and "The Legend of Sleepy Hollow." They continued his tradition of slightly comical social commentary and cemented his worldwide literary reputation. Over the following years, Irving set himself up as a literary gentleman and published numerous popular works including *Astoria* (1836) and a biography of Christopher Columbus (1828). Irving served as U.S. minister to Spain from 1842 to 1846.

**Jackson, Andrew** (March 15, 1767–June 8, 1845)  *military hero, politician, U.S. president*
Andrew Jackson was one of the most important personalities of the late 18th and early 19th centuries. Jackson's pugnacious character was influenced by his youthful service in the Revolutionary War, during which he lost several close members of his family. He became a lawyer in 1787, and he was active in Tennessee politics before being elected to the U.S. Congress in 1796 and the U.S. Senate in 1797. Jackson then resigned from the Senate and became a Tennessee Supreme Court judge.

As a major general during the War of 1812, Jackson gained a reputation for heroism and for taking decisive action against Native Americans. He led engagements against the Creek Indians in 1813 and 1814 that subdued the Red Sticks rebellion against the United States and forced the Creek to cede 23 million acres of land. Jackson then moved to capture Pensacola (West Florida) and marched his troops to defend New Orleans against the final British attack of the War of 1812. Jackson won his most glorious military victory at the Battle of New Orleans on January 15, 1815. His effective strategy and tactics allowed Americans to claim victory in a war that was, at best, a stalemate. Moreover, his brilliant victory at New Orleans caused Jackson to be anointed as a national hero.

Jackson led military forces against the Seminole Indians in 1818, and he followed his victory with an invasion of Spanish-controlled West Florida, a move that may not have been authorized by President Monroe. Even though Jackson risked escalating the conflict when he executed two British citizens who, he said, were helping the Seminole, President Monroe and Secretary of State John Quincy Adams refused to censure his actions, and Spain was forced to cede control of Florida to the United States. After serving a brief term as territorial governor of Florida, Jackson retired from public life for a time and returned to enjoy the company of his beloved wife, Rachel, at their Tennessee plantation, the Hermitage.

In 1823, a political caucus in the state of Tennessee nominated Jackson as a presidential candidate, and he was subsequently elected again to the U.S. Senate. Jackson's presidential candidacy caught on, although he ran against several other important politicians. Jackson received the most popular votes and the greatest number of electoral votes in the 1824 presidential election, but since no candidate got a majority of electoral votes, the election was decided in the House of Representatives. House members at length chose John Quincy Adams over Jackson, in part because Speaker of the House and rival presidential candidate Henry Clay supported Adams.

Jackson resigned from the Senate, but he immediately became the front-runner for the 1828 election. Opposition to President Adams coalesced around Jackson and his political supporters, who maintained a more democratic outlook and reverence for popular politics than Adams. Jackson was decisively elected president in 1828 in a campaign orchestrated by Martin Van Buren using extensive electioneering techniques that played on Jackson's heroic reputation and democratic ideals.

Jackson served two terms as president and presided over many of the most important political issues of his era: Indian Removal, the Nullification Crisis, the demise of the Second Bank of the United States, and the rise of a new two-party system in American politics.

Jackson's strong personality—he fought numerous duels in which he killed other men and took bullets himself—and daring exploits combined with great political savvy to make him a symbol of his age.

## Jay, John (December 12, 1745–May 17, 1829)
*diplomat, chief justice of the U.S. Supreme Court*

John Jay started as a New York lawyer who served in the Revolutionary War, was active in state politics, and served as president of the Continental Congress in 1778. Jay, who also had served as a diplomat during the war, was one of the peace commissioners who negotiated the Treaty of Paris that ended the Revolutionary War.

Jay was frustrated by weak federal power when he served as U.S. foreign minister (the precursor to secretary of state) during the Confederation period, and he became a strong supporter of the proposed U.S. Constitution in 1787. He coauthored the *Federalist* papers with Alexander Hamilton and James Madison in an effort to persuade residents of New York to ratify the Constitution.

President Washington appointed Jay as the first chief justice of the U.S. Supreme Court in 1789, and Jay defined many court procedures in the first years of its existence. In 1794, while still chief justice, Jay was sent to negotiate with the British, who continued to encroach on American power, especially by interfering with trade and maintaining forts on the northwestern frontier. Jay concluded the so-called Jay Treaty, which Jeffersonians strongly opposed and used to accuse their opponents of rampant pro-British and anti-French sympathies. The controversial treaty was ratified in secret by the Senate in June 1795, and when its terms were revealed, a new controversy erupted as Democratic-Republican societies protested its terms and secret handling.

In 1795, Jay resigned as chief justice and became governor of New York, an office to which he had been elected while in England negotiating the treaty. He gave up the governorship in 1800, and at the end of the year he declined a second nomination as chief justice of the Supreme Court. This opened the way for President John Adams to appoint John Marshall, who became one of the court's most influential justices. Jay retired from public life and lived out his remaining days on his farm in Bedford, New York.

## Jefferson, Thomas (April 13, 1743–July 4, 1826)
*diplomat, vice president, president*

Thomas Jefferson was one of the most influential politicians and thinkers in the early United States, and he has come to stand as a symbol both of the democratic nature of the U.S. republic and of some of its most difficult contradictions.

The oldest son of a wealthy Virginia plantation family, Jefferson graduated from the College of William and Mary in 1762, then spent five years studying law with George Wythe, Virginia's most famous legal scholar and judge. Jefferson's political career soon overtook his legal career, and he practiced law only until 1775. Jefferson served in the Virginia House of Burgesses, where he was an outspoken opponent of the British during the Imperial Crisis; he especially attacked King George III in his 1774 pamphlet *A Summary View of the Rights of British America.*

By then, Jefferson had also established himself as one of the leading gentlemen of Virginia, whose intelligence and polish garnered him wide respect. Jefferson married Martha Wales Skelton in 1772, and although he never remarried after she died 10 years later, he did remain very close to his two daughters who survived into adulthood. Jefferson's home, Monticello, was the focal point of his 10,000-acre estate, which included over 150 slaves. It is now widely believed by historians that Jefferson also fathered several children with Sally Hemings, one of his slaves, who was his constant companion for many years.

Thomas Jefferson was elected to the Continental Congress in 1775, and in 1776, when the Congress moved the country toward independence, Congress members chose Jefferson to draft the Declaration of Independence. Jefferson's eloquent words, including the invocation that "all men are created equal," became the ideological basis for American democracy, even if Jefferson himself and many of his contemporaries defined the category of "all men" much more narrowly than later generations of Americans would.

Jefferson retired from national political office for a time during the American Revolution to return to Virginia politics. He served in the Virginia legislature and on a board that revised the state's legal code (including changes in primogeniture and the support of religious freedom), and Jefferson was elected governor of Virginia in 1779. Criticism of Jefferson's poor handling of the British invasion of Virginia in 1781 helped him decide to retire as governor that same year. Jefferson stayed at Monticello from 1781 to 1783 working on his *Notes on the State of Virginia* and grieving the death of his wife, but he was again called into national service when he was elected to Congress in 1783.

In 1784, Jefferson went on a diplomatic mission to France, and he was appointed U.S. minister to France in 1785. Upon his return to the United States in 1790, Jefferson accepted the post of secretary of state in George Washington's first cabinet, a position that allowed him to exercise considerable influence over the fledgling Democratic-Republican Party that grew in opposition to the Federalists throughout the 1790s. As secretary of state, Jefferson strongly opposed the policies proposed by Secretary of the Treasury Alexander Hamilton, especially his proposed use of strong federal power to boost the U.S. economy. Jefferson also admired the French Revolution, and he consistently accused Hamilton of being too pro-British.

Jefferson resigned as secretary of state in 1793, and this allowed him to devote even more time to party organizing and to his opposition to Hamilton and the Federalists. Jefferson ran for president in 1796, but he came in second in the electoral vote and was therefore elected to serve as the vice president under Federalist John Adams. Jefferson was a strong presence as vice president, even though he often opposed the policies of Adams and other Federalists. For example, he secretly authored the "Kentucky Resolutions" in opposition to the Alien and Sedition Acts in 1798.

In the 1800 presidential election, Thomas Jefferson and Aaron Burr tied in the electoral college, and after many rounds of balloting Jefferson was elected president by the House of Representatives. In what Jefferson himself termed "the Revolution of 1800," the smooth transition to Jefferson's administration proved for the first time that the U.S. government could survive a change in party control, something of which contemporaries had been far from certain.

Although Jefferson was consistently a proponent of limiting the power of the federal government since its creation in 1789, as president he did not hesitate to use federal power when it suited him or seemed to benefit the entire country. One of his greatest achievements as president was the Louisiana Purchase, which added millions of acres of territory to the United States. He did not always support such use of government power, however, particularly in financial matters. He dramatically reduced the federal debt and the size of the military during his two terms.

Jefferson's second term as president was marked by commercial and diplomatic difficulties when the United States got caught in the Anglo-French wars. Jefferson wanted to protect American neutrality and trading rights, but his strategy of pressuring Britain and France through commercial sanctions, including the 1807 embargo, was not very effective at containing European aggression. When Jefferson left office in 1809, the U.S. economy was suffering from the series of economic sanctions he had supported, and France and England had not stopped harassing U.S. ships.

After leaving the presidency, Jefferson retired to Monticello, and he rarely ventured far from home during the almost 20 more years that he lived. Jefferson was an active political correspondent who dispensed frequent advice to President Madison and others, but he did not personally take part in the political world again. He worked on improvements to Monticello, and he designed the buildings of the University of Virginia, which he helped to found in 1819.

Jefferson, who had always spent extravagantly to maintain his genteel habits, suffered greatly in the financial crisis of 1819, and his personal debt grew larger by the year. In 1815, Congress had purchased Jefferson's 10,000-volume personal library to form the basis of the Library of Congress after the British burned public buildings in Washington, D.C., but that cash infusion was not enough to restore Jefferson's solvency. Partly as a result of his large debts, Jefferson, the author of the Declaration of Independence and champion of American democracy, never emancipated his slaves, including the ones who likely were his own children. He recognized that slavery as an institution was damaging to the American people, but he was unable to form a solution to the problem.

Jefferson died on July 4, 1826, the 50th anniversary of the adoption of the Declaration of Independence. He was a giant political and intellectual influence on 18th- and early 19th-century America, but he wished only for a simple epitaph. In all his contradiction and ambiguity, Thomas Jefferson helped to define the first era of American "independence."

## marquis de Lafayette (Marie Joseph de Motier) (September 6, 1757–May 20, 1834)
*Revolutionary general*

The marquis de Lafayette first became important to the fledgling United States when he volunteered, as a 20-year-old French aristocrat, to serve as an officer in the Continental army during the Revolutionary War. Lafayette became a close confidant of George Washington during the war, and he pledged some of his personal fortune to help American troops. He played a key part in the defeat of the British at Yorktown in 1781 that all but ended the Revolutionary War.

Back in France, Lafayette fell on hard times during the French Revolution. Although he helped to lead the liberation of the Bastille and served in various Revolutionary governments until 1792, he was persecuted by Jacobin radicals and had to flee the country. He was imprisoned in Austria for several years before Napoleon Bonaparte freed him.

Americans, who venerated Lafayette as a hero of their own Revolution and an advocate of moderate French-style democracy, anxiously followed Lafayette's fate during the French Revolution, and in 1824 President Monroe invited the general to return to the United States to accept praise and money from the American people. Lafayette spent over a year touring the 24 United States, where he was greeted by enthusiastic public celebration. In the 1820s, Lafayette stood as a great symbol of Americans' reverence for their own revolution and for the ideals of democracy.

## Lewis, Meriwether (August 18, 1774–October 11, 1809) *explorer*

Meriwether Lewis was born and raised on a series of plantations in Virginia and Georgia. He joined the Virginia militia in 1794 and marched to help put down the Whiskey Rebellion in western Pennsylvania. He enlisted in the U.S. Army in 1795, was posted to the Western division commanded by "Mad"

Anthony Wayne, and was present at the signing of the Treaty of Greenville.

Lewis served in the army until 1801, when President Thomas Jefferson, a family friend, appointed Lewis as his private secretary. Jefferson then chose his trusted assistant in 1803 to lead the "Corps of Discovery," which he planned to send on an expedition to the Pacific Ocean. Lewis set out with his fellow commander, William Clark, to St. Louis, and their party explored to the Pacific and back between 1804 and 1806. Lewis's journals of their journey provided Jefferson, and subsequent readers, with extensive knowledge of the flora and fauna the explorers encountered. Although he was not always successful at it, Lewis also sought to establish diplomatic relations with many Indian nations on the journey.

Lewis was often unhappy after returning from the journey of exploration. He served as territorial governor of Upper Louisiana for one year but resigned after a series of squabbles with other government officials. While staying at Nashville, Tennessee, on his way back to Washington in October 1809, Lewis died from what was most likely a self-inflicted gunshot wound.

## Little Turtle (Michikinkwa) (ca. 1752–July 14, 1812) *Miami war chief*

Little Turtle led some of the most successful Indian engagements ever against U.S. military forces in the early 1790s. Little Turtle led a confederation of Indian forces, including predominantly Miami and Shawnee, to oppose U.S. citizens who settled west of the Appalachian Mountains after the Revolutionary War. He also defeated U.S. forces under General Josiah Harmar in Ohio in 1790 and inflicted an even greater loss on General Arthur St. Clair's forces at St. Mary's the following year. After losing 600 men in the engagement, St. Clair was forced to retreat from the Miami Territory.

In response to Little Turtle's victories, General "Mad" Anthony Wayne invaded the Northwest Territory with an even larger combined force of militia and U.S. Army troops, who finally defeated Little Turtle's troops (although he was not personally in command) at the Battle of Fallen Timbers in 1794. Following Indian capitulation in the 1795 Treaty of Greenville, Little Turtle lost much of his power among the Miami. He visited President Washington in 1797 and had his portrait painted by Gilbert Stuart. Little Turtle subsequently tried to keep his people out of the pan-Indian resistance movement led by Tecumseh after the turn of the century. Little Turtle died just at the beginning of the War of 1812, which inflicted further damage on his people.

**Macon, Nathaniel** (December 17, 1757–June 1837)
*Democratic-Republican congressman, vice-presidential candidate*

Nathaniel Macon was a strong advocate of small government and states' rights who maintained his political support of the Jeffersonian order throughout the late 18th and early 19th centuries. After serving in the Revolutionary War, Macon was elected first to the North Carolina legislature and then the House of Representatives in 1791. Macon was a strong Jeffersonian Republican; he supported the French Revolution and opposed the Jay Treaty, the Alien and Sedition Acts, and the Quasi-War with France.

After Thomas Jefferson was elected president in 1800, Macon served as Speaker of the House from 1801 to 1807, an office he used to bridge gaps between Democratic-Republicans and Federalists during that period. Although he was deposed as Speaker, Macon spearheaded several bills bearing his name that supported commercial sanctions against Great Britain in the years leading up to the War of 1812, which he ultimately championed as well. Following the war, Macon was elected to the U.S. Senate, where he became a strong critic of Henry Clay's plans to use federal government power to build banks, roads, canals, and other infrastructure projects. Macon was a strong defender of slavery, and in 1820 he strongly opposed the Missouri Compromise. He served as William H. Crawford's running mate in the presidential election of 1824, although he later endorsed Andrew Jackson. Macon retired from politics in 1828.

**Madison, Dolley Payne Todd** (May 20, 1768– July 12, 1849) *first lady*

Dolley Madison was one of the most renowned first ladies in U.S. history, and her political acumen, patriotism, and personality left a lasting mark on the position of first lady.

Dolley was born in North Carolina but raised and educated in Virginia, before her parents sold their slaves and moved to Pennsylvania in 1783. Dolley married John Todd in 1790, and before he died three years later, they had one son together. She married James Madison in 1794, just as he was coming to prominence as a Democratic-Republican congressman from Virginia. For the rest of their married life, Dolley's lively personality and vivacious presence balanced her husband's quiet intellect and personal reserve. This powerful political couple rarely spent more than a few days apart.

Between 1797 and 1801, the Madisons resided on their Virginia estate, Montpelier, but when James was called into service as secretary of state under President Thomas Jefferson, the couple moved to Washington, D.C. Dolley served as official hostess for state occasions at the White House, because both President Jefferson and Vice President Burr were widowers, and her skills at planning the perfect social occasion at which politics might be conducted won her great influence among the most powerful residents of the capital. The fact that Federalists sometimes criticized her showed how successful she was at promoting Democratic-Republican causes through the channels of polite society.

When her husband assumed office as president in 1809, Dolley Madison's political and social activities accelerated. At the White House, which she personally decorated and furnished, she held weekly receptions on Wednesday evenings that provided powerful men with opportunities to interact. The fashionable Dolley had a personality that could put others at ease, and she created a perfect social atmosphere for the transaction of political business.

Dolley remained calm in the face of crisis during the War of 1812. When the British invaded Washington, D.C., in August 1814 and marched on the White House, she removed important cabinet papers, Gilbert Stuart's portrait of George Washington, and other valuables in her own carriages when she fled, almost at the last minute—acts that would gain her wide renown.

The Madisons retired to Montpelier after John's second term as president ended in 1817, and Dolley continued to entertain visitors, though she seldom left the plantation. After James Madison died in 1836, Dolley moved back to Washington, where her house on Lafayette Square once again became a political salon. She was a social presence at the White House until her death in 1849.

## Madison, James (March 5, 1751–June 28, 1836)
*president*

James Madison shaped much of the course of the early U.S. government by personally drafting much of the U.S. Constitution, working for its ratification, then becoming an important politician once it went into effect.

James Madison was raised in Orange County, Virginia, and educated at Princeton University, from which he graduated in 1771. Poor health kept Madison out of the military during the Revolutionary War, so the student of history and law became a politician instead. He helped to draft the constitution of Virginia in 1776, a document that shared much in common with the later U.S. Constitution. During the Revolution, he served in the Virginia legislature and in the Continental Congress; when the Revolution ended, he returned to the Virginia legislature, where he became one of its most influential members.

As a Virginia legislator and later a member of Congress, Madison grew weary of the problems caused by the weakness of the central government, so he helped push for the Philadelphia Convention that drafted a new U.S. Constitution in 1787. At the Philadelphia Convention, Madison drafted many of the most important plans and planks that became part of the final document, and his personal notes on the proceedings remain the best record of what took place during the framing of the Constitution. After the convention, Madison became one of the strongest advocates for ratification of the new Constitution. He coauthored the *Federalist* papers, which helped push the Constitution through in the crucial state of New York.

When Congress convened under the new Constitution in 1789, Madison immediately became one of its most powerful and prominent legislators. He guided the Bill of Rights to ratification, and he battled against Secretary of the Treasury Alexander Hamilton's financial program. Even though he had wanted a stronger federal government, Madison now favored restraining its overwhelming power, and in the 1790s he became a leader, along with Thomas Jefferson, of the Democratic-Republican Party. When Madison married Dolley Payne Todd in 1794 he tried to retire from politics, but he was not successful.

When Thomas Jefferson became president in 1801, he appointed Madison secretary of state. Madison kept this office until he himself became president in 1809. In both roles, Madison presided over the rising commercial and military tensions among the United States, Great Britain, and France, as the United States was caught up in the Anglo-French wars. During Jefferson's administration, Madison supported commercial sanctions and tried to keep the country out of war, but after he became president, he faced increasing pressure from militant members of his own party. In June 1812, Madison yielded to these "War Hawks" and asked for a congressional declaration of war against Great Britain.

The War of 1812 was not a military success, and Madison proved to be a weak commander in chief. He did little to control the squabbling of his cabinet and military officers, and he was not an effective military strategist. His popularity suffered from the British invasion and burning of public buildings in Washington, D.C., in August 1814. Madison recovered politically, however, and capitalized on Andrew Jackson's success at the Battle of New Orleans, at the end of the war in January 1815, to frame the war as perhaps more successful than it had been. Madison presided over a postwar economic recovery, and he approved several improvements to the national economic and transportation systems, although he remained wary of too much federal power. In particular, he vetoed the "Bonus Bill" as going too far to promote an unconstitutional use of power on internal improvements.

After his term ended in 1817, Madison returned to his Virginia plantation, Montpelier, where he lived a quiet life, but he continued to write influential letters filled with political and philosophical advice and insight. He remained in retirement until his death in 1836.

## Marshall, John (September 24, 1755–July 6, 1835)
*chief justice of the U.S. Supreme Court*

Arguably the most influential chief justice to preside over the U.S. Supreme Court, John Marshall personally shaped the character of early American jurisprudence during his long term of service on the bench between 1801 and 1835.

Marshall, a cousin of Thomas Jefferson, was born in Virginia and served as a minor officer during the Revolutionary War. Immediately after the Revolution, Marshall began to practice law, and he was elected to the Virginia legislature, where he favored ratification of the U.S. Constitution.

Marshall was a Federalist who evinced a strong belief in national union and the use of federal power to enhance the economy and the quality of American life. During the diplomatic difficulties with France during John Adams's presidency, Marshall went to France as one of the diplomats who was to negotiate a settlement that would avoid war. Instead, when French officials sought to exact bribes from the American diplomats, Marshall found himself embroiled in what became known as the XYZ affair. His dispatches reporting on the situation to Adams helped to diffuse political tensions over the controversy inside the United States. Marshall was elected to Congress in 1799. Adams nominated Marshall to be chief justice at the very end of his term as president. The Senate confirmed the appointment just before Thomas Jefferson, a rival Democratic-Republican, took office.

For the next 34 years, Marshall used his political skills, intelligence, and force of personality to unify the Supreme Court and shape its decisions to enhance the power of the federal government. He authored more than 500 decisions during his tenure, including the important cases *Marbury v. Madison* (1803), *Fletcher v. Peck* (1810), *McCulloch v. Maryland* (1819), *Dartmouth College v. Woodward* (1819), and *Gibbons v. Ogden* (1824). Marshall not only shaped the public understanding and legal interpretation of the U.S. Constitution but almost single-handedly defined the role of chief justice.

Although Marshall was often ill after 1831, he did not step down from the court until almost the end of his life.

### Monroe, James (April 28, 1758–July 4, 1831)
*cabinet official, legislator, president*

James Monroe was born in Virginia, where he was a student at the College of William and Mary when the American Revolution broke out. He served with distinction as an officer and was wounded in the Revolutionary War. In 1780, he took up the study of law under Virginia governor Thomas Jefferson. After the war, Monroe practiced law and served in the Confederation Congress.

Monroe then served in the state legislature of Virginia and was a delegate to the 1788 convention in the state that deliberated the ratification of the new U.S. Constitution. Monroe opposed the Constitution, and he was defeated in a campaign for a seat in the first federal Congress by the strong supporter of the Constitution, James Madison. Monroe was appointed to fill a vacant chair in the U.S. Senate in 1790. Although he was a fairly undistinguished legislator, he served his time as a strong supporter of Jefferson and an opponent of Secretary of the Treasury Alexander Hamilton at every turn.

In 1794, Monroe was appointed U.S. minister to France, but he did not feel he was effective because of the simultaneous negotiations between John Jay and officials in Great Britain, the bitter enemy of France. Monroe returned to the United States in 1796, and he served as governor of Virginia from 1799 to 1802. The following year, President Jefferson sent Monroe back to France to negotiate the Louisiana Purchase. Afterward, Monroe went to London to negotiate trade agreements with Britain.

With the rising European tensions that would lead to the War of 1812, Monroe returned to the governorship of Virginia for a short time in January 1811, before James Madison appointed him secretary of state two months later. As secretary of state, Monroe was not successful at gaining diplomatic concessions from Great Britain, and he began to advocate war. During the War of 1812, Monroe feuded constantly with Secretary of War John Armstrong, whom Monroe eventually replaced to hold two cabinet posts simultaneously.

Although Democratic-Republican Party leaders had little enthusiasm for him, Monroe was nominated to succeed Madison as president, and he handily won the election of 1816. During his two terms as president, Monroe presided over the so-called Era of Good Feelings, which witnessed the demise of the Federalist Party as a national political force, the economic crisis that followed the panic of 1819, and the Missouri Compromise. Monroe's administration achieved much in the realm of foreign policy, owing mostly to the talents of his secretary of state, John Quincy Adams. Monroe was influenced by Adams to support Andrew Jackson's annexation of Florida, to pursue treaties strengthening the American relationship to European nations, and to declare that Europeans should not meddle in the affairs of the Western Hemisphere (a policy later known as the Monroe Doctrine).

When Monroe left office in 1825, he retired to rural Virginia and reentered politics only for the Virginia constitutional convention of 1829. Revered as one of the last surviving heroes of the American Revolution, Monroe died in 1831.

### Rush, Benjamin (January 4, 1746–April 19, 1813)
*physician, social activist*

Benjamin Rush was born outside Philadelphia, graduated from Princeton University at the age of 14, and received his early medical education at the College of Philadelphia. In 1766, he studied medicine at the University of Edinburgh (Scotland) and subsequently interned with the world-famous physician William Hunter in London. When Rush returned to the United States in 1769 and took up a post as professor of chemistry at the College of Philadelphia, he quickly became one of the most respected physicians in North America.

During the American Revolution, Rush served in the Continental Congress, where he signed the Declaration of Independence, then became a surgeon general in the Continental army. Upon returning to his private medical practice in 1778, he spent the rest of his life as a teacher and doctor who treated both physical and mental ailments.

Rush's medical expertise was particularly tested during the Yellow Fever epidemic that hit Philadelphia and killed thousands of people in 1793. Rush advocated the use of drastic bleeding and heavy purgatives, both of which provided some success in treating the fever's victims.

During the 1780s and 1790s, Rush also advocated a number of reforms. He opposed capital punishment and was a strong advocate of public education, education for women, and broader access to higher education. From 1797 until his death in 1813, Rush supplemented his medical earnings by serving as a treasurer of the U.S. Mint.

### Shays, Daniel (ca. 1747–September 29, 1825)
*Revolutionary soldier, leader of "Shays's Rebellion"*

Born to a humble family in Hopkinton, Massachusetts, Daniel Shays as a young man was a hired farm worker. The Revolutionary War brought opportunity to Shays, who began his service at the war's outbreak at the Battle of Lexington and steadily rose through the ranks from 1775 through 1780. After distinguished service at the battles of Bunker Hill, Fort Ticonderoga, Saratoga, and Stony Point, Shays was commissioned a captain in the Continental army in 1777.

Shays resigned his commission in 1780 and returned to life as a farmer in western Massachusetts. A town leader, he was fairly prosperous, but he also quickly built up a large debt during the postwar economic crisis. Shays was drawn into a popular movement in western Massachusetts that sought to prevent the prosecution of debtors by closing courts using armed force. Shays himself was not one of the more aggressive leaders of the movement, which became known as Shays's Rebellion, but in 1786 when Shaysites marched on the federal arsenal at Springfield, Shays helped to keep military discipline. The Shaysite movement was put down by Massachusetts militia forces under General Benjamin Lincoln in 1787. Shays fled to Vermont, but after he was pardoned, he moved to New York and lived out the rest of his life there.

Shays's Rebellion helped push nationalist-minded political elites into supporting the calls for a convention to consider strengthening the federal constitution in 1787.

### Smith, Margaret Bayard (February 20, 1778– June 7, 1844) *socialite, writer*

Margaret Bayard Smith's letters, diaries, and public writings provide some of the keenest chronicles of life in Washington, D.C., in the early 19th century.

Margaret Bayard was born to a prominent merchant family in Pennsylvania and was raised by her sister in New Jersey, where she received a strong education and developed a love for books. Margaret married her cousin, Samuel Harrison Smith, in 1800, and the couple moved to Washington, D.C., where Samuel started the Jeffersonian newspaper, the *National Intelligencer.* Margaret Bayard Smith took part in the social life of Washington, D.C., in which politics was often conducted in parlors and at parties as well as in the halls of Congress. As her husband rose through the ranks of official Washington, becoming an officer of the Bank of the United States in 1828, Margaret wrote letters, hosted gatherings, and bore four children.

Following the War of 1812, Margaret Bayard Smith increasingly exercised her talent for writing, as she filled reams of letters and notebooks with commentary on life in the national capital. She wrote two books in the 1820s and was a frequent and lively magazine contributor until her death in 1844.

**Tecumseh** (ca. 1768–October 5, 1813) *Shawnee chief, military leader, pan-Indian organizer*
Tecumseh was a fierce military leader who built political support for a pan-Indian movement and advocated resistance to the takeover of Indian lands by the United States. Tecumseh first took part in war against the United States in 1780, when he joined the fight to avenge the murdered Shawnee chief Cornstalk. He took part in Little Turtle's military maneuvers against the United States in the 1790s and was present at the defeat at the Battle of Fallen Timbers in 1794, but he refused to sign the Treaty of Greenville, which ceded large amounts of Indian land in the Northwest Territory.

Tecumseh advocated the idea that Indian land was not "owned" in the same sense that Europeans or Americans thought of ownership, and therefore, he argued, land could not be legally ceded or sold. He also maintained a great sense of racial and cultural solidarity among Indian peoples. With his brother Tenskwatawa, who began to preach a sympathetic cultural and religious message in 1805, Tecumseh set out to create a pan-Indian movement. After establishing the village of Tippecanoe (or Prophetstown) (in present-day Indiana) in 1808 as a rallying point for Indian activists, Tecumseh went south on the first of several trips to build support for Indian resistance to the United States.

In 1810, Tecumseh met with Indiana territorial governor William Henry Harrison to insist that Indians would not cede any more western lands to the United States, but the following year, while Tecumseh was away on another recruiting trip, Harrison attacked Tenskwatawa at Tippecanoe and defeated the main body of Tecumseh's forces.

Tecumseh allied himself with the British in the War of 1812, and he bravely led Shawnee and other Indian troops in several important engagements against the United States in Canada and the Northwest Territory. Tecumseh viewed the British pragmatically as a bulwark against U.S. expansion, but he was disappointed with the weak strategy of British commander General Henry Proctor. Thus he took a strong stand with his Indian forces at the Thames River in October 1813, even as Proctor was planning to retreat. Tecumseh was killed at the battle of the Thames.

Richard Mentor Johnson based much of his future political career on his claim to be the man who killed Tecumseh. Tecumseh became a figure of cultural fascination in the United States, as well as a symbol of strong Indian pride and resistance, even after his death extinguished many hopes for effective Indian military opposition to the United States.

**Tenskwatawa (Laulewasika, Lalawethika, The Prophet, The Shawnee Prophet)** (ca. 1775–November 1837) *Shawnee spiritual and political leader*
Tenskwatawa was the religious leader of a widespread pan-Indian movement in the early 19th century whose political leader was his brother Tecumseh. In 1805, Tenskwatawa experienced a spiritual conversion that led him to denounce Euro-American culture. He called for Indian peoples to reject American and European ideas, dress, intermarriage, and alcohol as a way to counter the power of the United States and to preserve Indian lands. As Tecumseh traveled throughout the Northwest and Southwest exhorting Indians to resist the encroachments of the United States, Tenskwatawa gained spiritual converts after correctly predicting a solar eclipse in 1806.

In 1808, Tecumseh and Tenskwatawa established a headquarters at Tippecanoe (or Prophetstown) on the Tippecanoe River in present-day Indiana, where they attracted followers from many Northern Indian groups. Indiana territorial governor William Henry Harrison pursued a military campaign against Tippecanoe in 1811, while Tecumseh was away, and Tenskwatawa led his people against Harrison before being forced to retreat in defeat. Although Tecumseh's movement continued when the Shawnee allied themselves with the British in the War of 1812, Tenskwatawa was fairly discredited by the battle at Tippecanoe. After Tecumseh was killed in 1813, the pan-Indian movement largely dissolved. Tenskwatawa lived in Canada until 1826, and later moved to Missouri and Kansas, where he died in 1837.

**Washington, George** (February 22, 1732–December 14, 1799) *Revolutionary commander, president*
George Washington was born the son of a privileged plantation family in Virginia. Although he received little formal schooling, his social position, talent, and political acumen helped him rise to become the most influential and powerful man in the early years of the United States.

As a young man in Virginia, George Washington schooled himself in the polite habits of the gentry class, acquiring the sociability, skills as a horseman, great physical presence, and force of personality that would serve him well his whole life. By the age of 17, Washington had trained as a surveyor and begun a lifelong interest in western land speculation. By the age of 19, Washington had inherited his brother's estate, Mount Vernon, and he was commissioned an officer in the Virginia colonial militia.

Washington's actions with the militia in 1753, when he was supposed to deliver an ultimatum demanding French withdrawal from Ohio territory, helped to precipitate the beginning of the French and Indian War. In that war, during which he rose to the rank of colonel and commander in chief of Virginia militia, Washington gained military experience as he participated in key battles, including Braddock's defeat in 1755 and the British capture of Fort Duquesne in 1758. In 1759, George Washington married Martha Custis, a wealthy widow who further enhanced his social standing as the leading gentleman in Virginia.

Washington began serving in the Virginia House of Burgesses in 1759, where he steadily supported the increasing measures of resistance against British imperial control over the colonies. As an opponent of the British, Washington was elected to the Continental Congress in 1774 and 1775. His military fame, along with Congress's desire to unite the southern colonies to the Revolutionary cause, led to the appointment of Washington as commander in chief of the Continental army after the Revolutionary War broke out in spring 1775.

Washington's main military strategy during the Revolution was to make the American army into a respected European-style fighting force while avoiding as many pitched battles as possible, since the British military was better supplied, better staffed, and more experienced. After driving the British out of Boston in 1775, Washington fell back from New York City in 1776, retreated into New Jersey, and fought to a standstill in 1777, despite notable victories at Trenton and Princeton. After indecisive fighting in Pennsylvania in late 1777, Washington wintered with his army at Valley Forge between 1777 and 1778. When fighting shifted to the south, Washington marched his forces to Virginia, coordinated an attack with southern commanders and with French army and navy forces, and forced British general Cornwallis to surrender at Yorktown in October 1781. Washington's fame and military reputation were secured by winning the war, even though fighting continued sporadically for two more years until a formal peace treaty was concluded.

After the Revolutionary War, Washington gained further admiration from the citizens of the new United States for voluntarily retiring from military office and returning to civilian life on his Virginia plantation. He worried that the Articles of Confederation had created a central government that was far too weak, however, and so he consented to join the Philadelphia convention in 1787 that drafted a new constitution for the United States. Washington presided over the convention, although he seldom spoke during the proceedings.

While he continued to express a reluctance to take on personal power, in keeping with his reverence for republican political ideology, George Washington realized that the public demanded his services in the new executive branch of government when he was unanimously chosen by the electoral college to be the first president of the United States in 1789. Washington's decisions did much to shape the character of the office of the presidency for some time to come. He refused to accept a salary, so as to stress the impartial nature of his service; eventually he accepted the $25,000 annual payment that Congress insisted upon.

One of the most important ways that Washington affected the early government of the United States was in his selection of cabinet officers. Along with his vice president, John Adams, Washington's most influential cabinet ministers were Secretary of the Treasury Alexander Hamilton and Secretary of State Thomas Jefferson, between whom personal enmity and party rancor grew steadily throughout the 1790s as Washington counseled a middle course.

Even though Washington always tried to avoid party conflict, he was rather conservative and tended to favor the advice of Hamilton over that of Jefferson. Washington supported most of Hamilton's financial and funding programs in the early years of his administration, despite the fact that Jefferson, Madison, and other soon-to-be Democratic-Republicans decried them as unconstitutional. In 1793, Washington issued a proclamation of neutrality in the war between Great Britain and France that led Jefferson's supporters to accuse Washington of being too pro-British, because he seemed to repudiate the French-American alliance left over from the American Revolution. During his second term, Washington came under increasing criticism, especially for sending troops to put down the Whiskey Rebellion in western Pennsylvania in 1794 and for supporting the controversial Jay Treaty the following year.

Washington set one of his most important precedents as president by refusing to accept a third term in office. He issued a Farewell Address in 1796 that warned politicians of the evils of party contest and cautioned the United States to avoid entangling alliances with foreign nations.

After leaving office, George Washington retired to a quiet life on his plantation. He died of an infection in December 1799. Upon his death, Washington freed all his slaves according to the terms of a will drawn up the year before. When news of his passing spread around the country, Americans everywhere mourned. George Washington, a symbol of the resolve and strength of the early United States, became heroic and enduring figure in American culture.

**Willard, Emma Hart** (February 23, 1787–April 15, 1870) *educator*
Emma Willard was born to a very large farm family in Connecticut at the end of the 18th century, a time when girls were just beginning to reap the educational opportunities offered in the post-revolutionary period. She would grow into the most important female educator of the 19th century.

Willard received her early education at home, but she entered the Berlin Academy, in Berlin, Connecticut, in 1802. She thus became one of many middle-class young women of her age who sought academic opportunities in the scores of new schools opening at the turn of the century. By the time she was 21 years old in 1807, she already had experience as a teacher, and she became preceptor of a female academy in Middlebury, Vermont. She married Dr. John Willard in 1809, but continued her rising career as an educator of girls. She opened her own school in Middlebury in 1814. It was hugely successful, in part because she put into practice the radical idea that girls should receive a rigorous aca-

demic education, including instruction in science and classical languages.

In the late 1810s, Willard began a campaign to persuade the state of New York to endow a public school for girls that would provide the approximate equivalent of a college education. Her official campaign failed, but she moved her own school to Waterford, New York, in 1819. When the Troy, New York, city government offered to support her scheme, she opened the Troy Female Academy in 1821. Willard spent the rest of her life teaching, writing, and turning the school into one of the premier educational institutions for girls in the United States. Her school still exists as a private institution; it was renamed the Emma Willard School in her honor in 1895.

**Wright, Frances** (September 6, 1795–December 13, 1852) *political activist, reformer*
Born in Scotland in 1795 and self-educated, Frances Wright first visited the United States as a young woman just after the War of 1812. She traveled around the country and, upon her return to Europe, published her highly laudatory *Views of Society and Manners in America.*

When Wright returned to the United States in 1824 with the French Revolutionary War general the marquis de Lafayette, she again traveled extensively. On this trip she formed plans to put into action her increasingly radical political and social ideas. She departed from Lafayette in 1825 and traveled to the South, where she was increasingly seized with the desire to do something about the evils of slavery. She published an antislavery tract, *A Plan for the Gradual Abolition of Slavery in the United States,* and purchased land in Tennessee on which she constructed a community to test her antislavery ideas. The colony, called Nashoba, housed a collection of white, black, and mixed-race people, all of whom supported Wright's plans for gradual abolition and education for free African Americans. Some in the colony were accused of practicing free love, a scandal that helped bring Nashoba to ruin by 1828.

Following the disbanding of Nashoba, Wright took her political activism in new directions. She stayed at New Harmony, the Indiana utopian community established by Scottish industrialist Robert Owen, where she published a newspaper with Owen's son, Robert Dale Owen. The two promoted a radical program of free education as a way to ameliorate class tensions in the United States. Their ideas gained wider support in the following years, when Wright traveled as a highly controversial lecturer and as they built a political following, particularly in New York City. Wright's ideas helped to build the Workingmen's political movement in New York City in the early 1830s.

After marrying a French physician, Guillaume D'Arusmont, Wright stepped in and out of public life for the next few decades. Ill health plagued her. She died in 1852 as one of the most famous, even notorious, women of her period, who had once been dubbed "The Red Harlot of Infidelities" for her radical ideas and public activism.

# APPENDIX C

## Maps and Charts

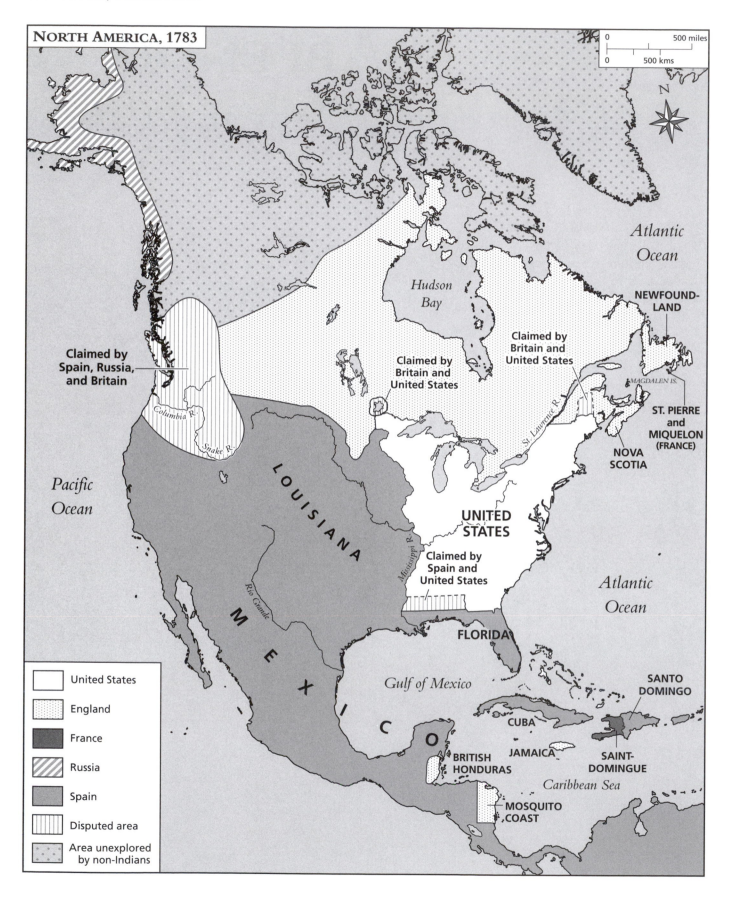

**NORTH AMERICA, 1783**

Atlantic Ocean

Hudson Bay

NEWFOUND-LAND

Claimed by Spain, Russia, and Britain

Claimed by Britain and United States

Claimed by Britain and United States

MAGDALEN IS.

Columbia R.

ST. PIERRE and MIQUELON (FRANCE)

Snake R.

NOVA SCOTIA

Pacific Ocean

L O U I S I A N A

UNITED STATES

St. Lawrence R.

Mississippi R.

Claimed by Spain and United States

Atlantic Ocean

M E X I C O

Rio Grande

FLORIDA

SANTO DOMINGO

Gulf of Mexico

CUBA

JAMAICA

SAINT-DOMINGUE

BRITISH HONDURAS

Caribbean Sea

MOSQUITO COAST

United States

England

France

Russia

Spain

Disputed area

Area unexplored by non-Indians

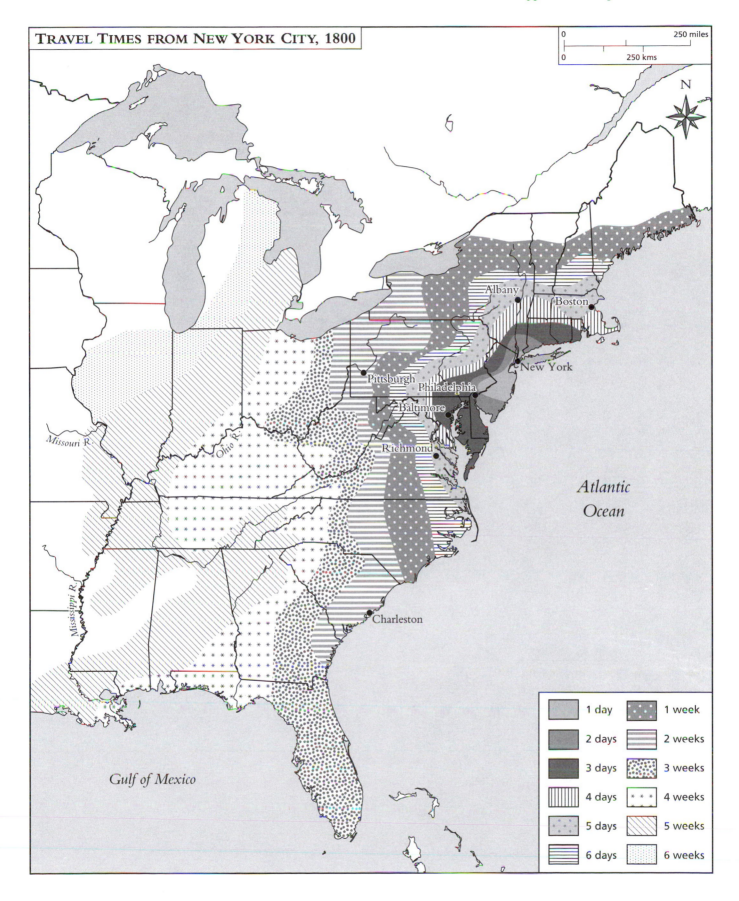

TRAVEL TIMES FROM NEW YORK CITY, 1800

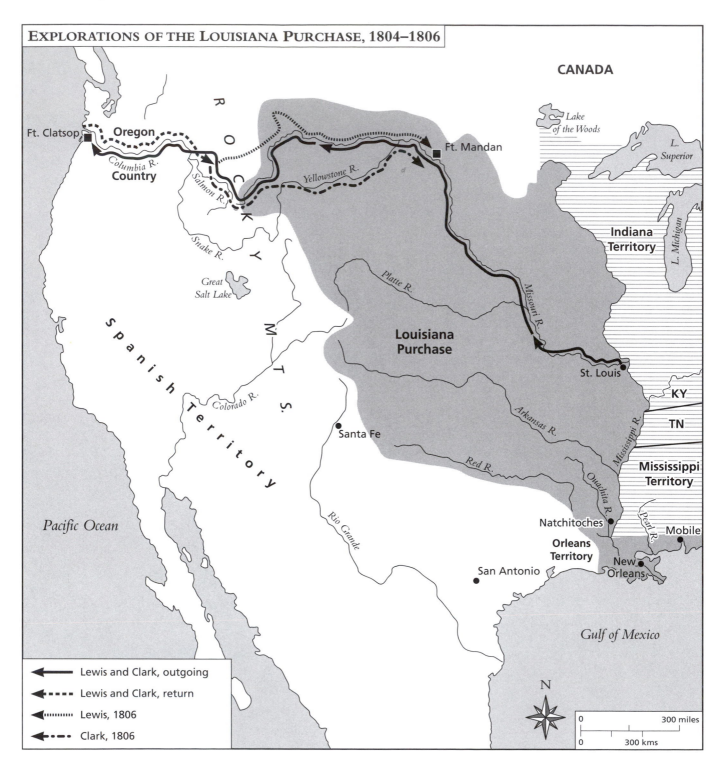

**EXPLORATIONS OF THE LOUISIANA PURCHASE, 1804–1806**

CANADA

Lake of the Woods

L. Superior

Ft. Clatsop

Oregon

Country

Columbia R.

Salmon R.

Ft. Mandan

Yellowstone R.

R O C K Y

Snake R.

Indiana Territory

L. Michigan

Great Salt Lake

Platte R.

Louisiana Purchase

Missouri R.

M T S.

St. Louis

KY

Colorado R.

Spanish Territory

Arkansas R.

TN

Santa Fe

Red R.

Mississippi R.

Mississippi Territory

Ouachita R.

Pearl R.

Pacific Ocean

Rio Grande

Natchitoches

Mobile

Orleans Territory

New Orleans

San Antonio

Gulf of Mexico

N

Lewis and Clark, outgoing

Lewis and Clark, return

Lewis, 1806

Clark, 1806

0          300 miles

0          300 kms

## WAR OF 1812

British Canada

*Lake Superior*

Ft. Mackimac

**Illinois Territory**

*Lake Michigan*

**Michigan Territory**

*Lake Huron*

Ft. Dearborn

Detroit
Aug. 16, 1812

Ft. Detroit

*Hull*

*The Thames*
*Oct. 5, 1813*

York (Toronto)
April 27, 1813

Chrysler's Farm
Nov. 11, 1813

Montreal

*St. Lawrence R.*

Quebec

**Maine**
**(part of Mass.)**

Lake Champlain
Sept. 11, 1814

*Dearborn*

*Lake Ontario*

**Vermont**

**New Hampshire**

Lundy's Lane
July 25, 1814

**New York**

Erie

*Lake Erie*

*Perry*

**Massachusetts**

Boston

**Connecticut**

Tippecanoe
Nov. 7, 1811

*Harrison*

Put-in-Bay
Sept. 10, 1813

**Ohio**

**Rhode Island**

**Pennsylvania**

Philadelphia

Godly Wood
Sept. 12, 1814

**New Jersey**

Cincinnati

**Unorganized**

*Missouri R.*

St. Louis

**Indiana Territory**

*Mississippi R.*

*Ohio R.*

**Territory**

Washington, D.C.
Aug. 24–28, 1814

Washington

Baltimore

**Delaware**

**Maryland**

*Chesapeake Bay*

**Kentucky**

**Virginia**

**Tennessee**

*Jackson*

**North Carolina**

**Mississippi Territory**

Horseshoe Bend
March 27, 1814

*Jackson*

**South Carolina**

**Georgia**

**Louisiana**

Pensacola
Nov. 7, 1814

*Jackson*

New Orleans
Jan. 8, 1815

*Jackson*

New Orleans

Pensacola

**Spanish Florida**

*Hudson R.*

*Atlantic Ocean*

*Gulf of Mexico*

N

**Legend:**

U.S. state in 1812

U.S. territory in 1812

U.S. movement

British movement

U.S. victory

British/Indian victory

Fort

0      200 miles

0      200 kms

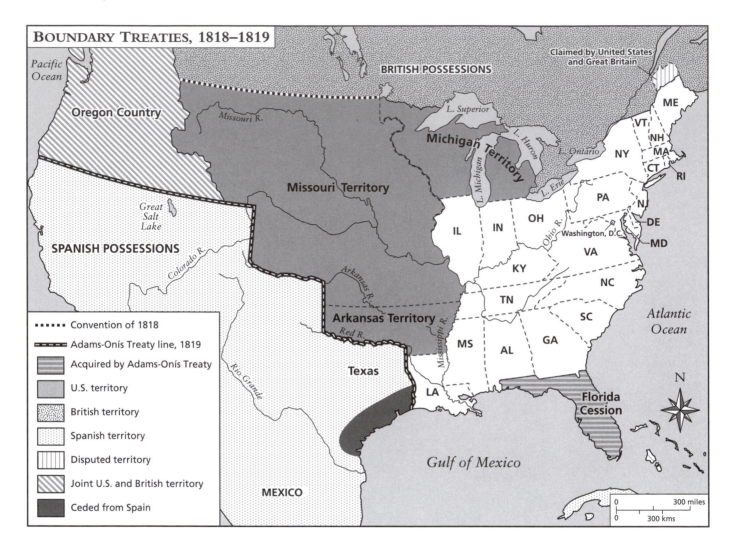

BOUNDARY TREATIES, 1818–1819

Pacific Ocean

BRITISH POSSESSIONS

Claimed by United States and Great Britain

Oregon Country

Missouri R.

L. Superior

ME

Michigan Territory

L. Huron

VT

NH

Missouri Territory

L. Michigan

L. Ontario

NY

MA

CT

RI

Great Salt Lake

L. Erie

PA

NJ

SPANISH POSSESSIONS

IL

IN

OH

Ohio R.

DE

Colorado R.

Washington, D.C.

MD

VA

KY

Arkansas R.

NC

TN

SC

Arkansas Territory

Red R.

MS

AL

GA

Atlantic Ocean

Texas

Mississippi R.

Rio Grande

LA

N

Florida Cession

MEXICO

Gulf of Mexico

• • • • •  Convention of 1818

━━━  Adams-Onís Treaty line, 1819

Acquired by Adams-Onís Treaty

U.S. territory

British territory

Spanish territory

Disputed territory

Joint U.S. and British territory

Ceded from Spain

0          300 miles
0          300 kms

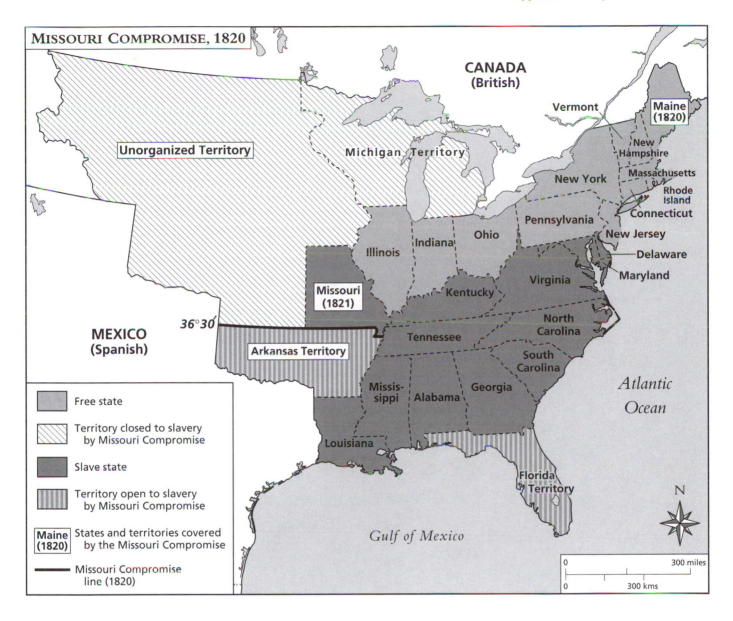

MISSOURI COMPROMISE, 1820

CANADA
(British)

Unorganized Territory

Michigan Territory

Vermont

Maine
(1820)

New
Hampshire

New York

Massachusetts

Rhode
Island

Connecticut

Pennsylvania

New Jersey

Delaware

Maryland

Illinois

Indiana

Ohio

Missouri
(1821)

Kentucky

Virginia

MEXICO
(Spanish)

36°30'

North
Carolina

Arkansas Territory

Tennessee

South
Carolina

Missis-
sippi

Alabama

Georgia

Atlantic
Ocean

Louisiana

Florida
Territory

Gulf of Mexico

N

Free state

Territory closed to slavery
by Missouri Compromise

Slave state

Territory open to slavery
by Missouri Compromise

Maine
(1820)   States and territories covered
by the Missouri Compromise

Missouri Compromise
line (1820)

0                    300 miles

0          300 kms

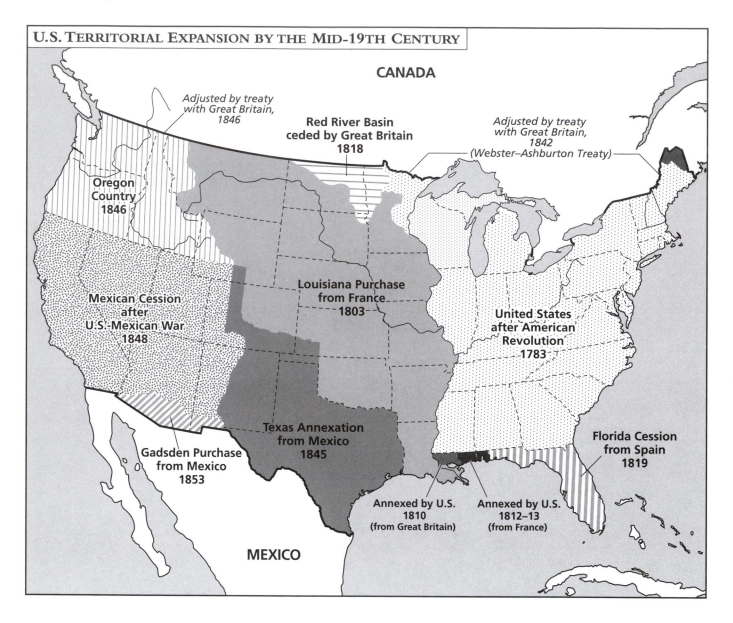

U.S. TERRITORIAL EXPANSION BY THE MID-19TH CENTURY

CANADA

*Adjusted by treaty with Great Britain, 1846*

**Red River Basin ceded by Great Britain 1818**

*Adjusted by treaty with Great Britain, 1842 (Webster–Ashburton Treaty)*

**Oregon Country 1846**

**Mexican Cession after U.S.-Mexican War 1848**

**Louisiana Purchase from France 1803**

**United States after American Revolution 1783**

**Texas Annexation from Mexico 1845**

**Gadsden Purchase from Mexico 1853**

**Florida Cession from Spain 1819**

**Annexed by U.S. 1810 (from Great Britain)**

**Annexed by U.S. 1812–13 (from France)**

**MEXICO**

## 8. ADMISSION OF STATES INTO THE UNION, 1787–1821

| State | Date of Admission | State | Date of Admission |
|---|---|---|---|
| Delaware | December 7, 1787 | Rhode Island | May 29, 1790 |
| Pennsylvania | December 12, 1787 | Vermont | March 4, 1791 |
| New Jersey | December 18, 1787 | Kentucky | June 1, 1792 |
| Georgia | January 2, 1788 | Tennessee | June 1, 1796 |
| Connecticut | January 9, 1788 | Ohio | March 1, 1803 |
| Massachusetts | February 6, 1788 | Louisiana | April 30, 1812 |
| Maryland | April 28, 1788 | Indiana | December 11, 1816 |
| South Carolina | May 23, 1788 | Mississippi | December 10, 1817 |
| New Hampshire | June 21, 1788 | Illinois | December 3, 1818 |
| Virginia | June 25, 1788 | Alabama | December 14, 1819 |
| New York | July 26, 1788 | Maine | March 15, 1820 |
| North Carolina | November 21, 1789 | Missouri | August 10, 1821 |

## 9. PRESIDENTIAL ELECTIONS, 1789–1828

| Year | Candidates | State of Residence at Time of Election | Parties | Popular Vote | Percentage of Popular Vote | Electoral Vote | Percentage of Voter Participation |
|---|---|---|---|---|---|---|---|
| 1789 | **George Washington** | Virginia | | | | 69 | |
| | John Adams | | | | | 34 | |
| | Others | | | | | 35 | |
| 1792 | **George Washington** | Virginia | | | | 132 | |
| | John Adams | | | | | 77 | |
| | George Clinton | | | | | 50 | |
| | Others | | | | | 5 | |
| 1796 | **John Adams** | Massachusetts | Federalist | | | 71 | |
| | Thomas Jefferson | | Democratic-Republican | | | 68 | |
| | Thomas Pinckney | | Federalist | | | 59 | |
| | Aaron Burr | | Federalist | | | 30 | |
| | Others | | | | | 48 | |
| 1800 | **Thomas Jefferson** | Virginia | Democratic-Republican | | | 73 | |
| | Aaron Burr | | Democratic-Republican | | | 73 | |
| | John Adams | | Federalist | | | 65 | |
| | C. C. Pinckney | | Federalist | | | 64 | |
| | John Jay | | Federalist | | | 1 | |
| 1804 | **Thomas Jefferson** | Virginia | Democratic-Republican | | | 162 | |
| | C. C. Pinckney | | Federalist | | | 14 | |
| 1808 | **James Madison** | Virginia | Democratic-Republican | | | 122 | |
| | C. C. Pinckney | | Federalist | | | 47 | |
| | George Clinton | | Democratic-Republican | | | 6 | |
| 1812 | **James Madison** | Virginia | Democratic-Republican | | | 128 | |
| | De Witt Clinton | | Democratic-Republican | | | 89 | |
| 1816 | **James Monroe** | Virginia | Democratic-Republican | | | 183 | |
| | Rufus King | | Federalist | | | 34 | |
| 1820 | **James Monroe** | Virginia | Democratic-Republican | | | 231 | |
| | John Quincy Adams | | Democratic-Republican | | | 1 | |
| 1824 | **John Q. Adams** | Massachusetts | Democratic-Republican | 108,740 | 30.5 | 84 | 26.9 |
| | Andew Jackson | | Democratic-Republican | 153,544 | 43.1 | 99 | |
| | William H. Crawford | | Democratic-Republican | 46,618 | 13.1 | 41 | |
| | Henry Clay | | Democratic-Republican | 47,136 | 13.2 | 37 | |
| 1828 | **Andew Jackson** | Tennessee | Democratic | 647,286 | 56.0 | 178 | 57.6 |
| | John Quincy Adams | | National Republican | 508,064 | 44.0 | 83 | |

## 10. VICE PRESIDENTS AND CABINET MEMBERS, 1789–1829

### The Washington Administration (1789–1797)

| | | |
|---|---|---|
| Vice president | John Adams | 1789–97 |
| Secretary of state | Thomas Jefferson | 1789–93 |
| | Edmund Randolph | 1794–95 |
| | Timothy Pickering | 1795–97 |
| Secretary of treasury | Alexander Hamilton | 1789–95 |
| | Oliver Wolcott | 1795–97 |
| Secretary of war | Henry Knox | 1789–94 |
| | Timothy Pickering | 1795–96 |
| | James McHenry | 1796–97 |
| Attorney general | Edmund Randolph | 1789–93 |
| | William Bradford | 1794–95 |
| | Charles Lee | 1795–97 |
| Postmaster general | Samuel Osgood | 1789–91 |
| | Timothy Pickering | 1791–94 |
| | Joseph Habersham | 1795–97 |

### Adams Administration (1797–1801)

| | | |
|---|---|---|
| Vice president | Thomas Jefferson | 1797–1801 |
| Secretary of state | Timothy Pickering | 1797–1800 |
| | John Marshall | 1800–1801 |
| Secretary of treasury | Oliver Wolcott | 1797–1800 |
| | Samuel Dexter | 1800–1801 |
| Secretary of war | James McHenry | 1797–1800 |
| | Samuel Dexter | 1800–1801 |
| Attorney general | Charles Lee | 1797–1801 |
| Postmaster general | Joseph Habersham | 1797–1801 |
| Secretary of navy | Benjamin Stoddert | 1798–1801 |

### Jefferson Administration (1801–1809)

| | | |
|---|---|---|
| Vice president | Aaron Burr | 1801–05 |
| | George Clinton | 1805–09 |
| Secretary of state | James Madison | 1801–09 |
| Secretary of treasury | Samuel Dexter | 1801 |
| | Albert Gallatin | 1801–09 |
| Secretary of war | Henry Dearborn | 1801–09 |
| Attorney general | Levi Lincoln | 1801–05 |
| | Robert Smith | 1805 |
| | John Breckinridge | 1805–06 |
| | Caesar Rodney | 1807–09 |
| Postmaster general | Joseph Habersham | 1801 |
| | Gideon Granger | 1801–09 |
| Secretary of navy | Robert Smith | 1801–09 |

### Madison Administration (1809–1817)

| | | |
|---|---|---|
| Vice president | George Clinton | 1809–13 |
| | Elbridge Gerry | 1813–17 |
| Secretary of state | Robert Smith | 1809–11 |
| | James Monroe | 1811–17 |
| Secretary of treasury | Albert Gallatin | 1809–13 |
| | George Campbell | 1814 |
| | Alexander Dallas | 1814–16 |
| | William Crawford | 1816–17 |
| Secretary of war | William Eustis | 1809–12 |
| | John Armstrong | 1813–14 |
| | James Monroe | 1814–15 |
| | William Crawford | 1815–17 |
| Attorney general | Caesar Rodney | 1809–11 |
| | William Pinkney | 1811–14 |
| | Richard Rush | 1814–17 |
| Postmaster general | Gideon Granger | 1809–14 |
| | Return Meigs | 1814–17 |
| Secretary of navy | Paul Hamilton | 1809–13 |
| | William Jones | 1813–14 |
| | Benjamin Crowninshield | 1814–17 |

### Monroe Administration (1817–1825)

| | | |
|---|---|---|
| Vice president | Daniel Tompkins | 1817–25 |
| Secretary of state | John Quincy Adams | 1817–25 |
| Secretary of treasury | William Crawford | 1817–25 |
| Secretary of war | George Graham | 1817 |
| | John C. Calhoun | 1817–25 |
| Attorney general | Richard Rush | 1817 |
| | William Wirt | 1817–25 |
| Postmaster general | Return Meigs | 1817–23 |
| | John McLean | 1823–25 |
| Secretary of navy | Benjamin Crowninshield | 1817–18 |
| | Smith Thompson | 1817–18 |
| | Samuel Southard | 1818–23 |

### Quincy Adams Administration (1825–1829)

| | | |
|---|---|---|
| Vice president | John C. Calhoun | 1825–29 |
| Secretary of state | Henry Clay | 1825–29 |
| Secretary of treasury | Richard Rush | 1825–29 |
| Secretary of war | James Barbour | 1825–28 |
| | Peter Porter | 1828–29 |
| Attorney general | William Wirt | 1825–29 |
| Postmaster general | John McLean | 1825–29 |
| Secretary of navy | Samuel Southard | 1825–29 |

# NOTES

## 1. POST-REVOLUTIONARY CHANGE: 1783–1786

1. *The Declaration of Independence,* Yale University, Avalon Project. URL:http://yale.edu/lawweb/avalon/declare.htm.
2. John J. McCusker and Russell R. Menard, *The Economy of British America, 1607–1789* (Chapel Hill: University of North Carolina Press, 1985), 363.
3. John Adams, quoted in *The Book of Abigail and John: Selected Letters of the Adams Family, 1762–1784,* ed. L. H. Butterfield, Marc Friedlaender, and Mary-Jo Klein (Cambridge, Mass.: Harvard University Press, 1975), 327.
4. Charles Patrick Neimeyer, *America Goes to War: A Social History of the Continental Army* (New York: New York University Press, 1996).
5. Thomas Jefferson, quoted in Barry Schwartz, *George Washington: The Making of an American Symbol* (New York: Free Press, 1987), 136.
6. See Laurel Thatcher Ulrich, *A Midwife's Tale: The Life of Martha Ballard, Based on Her Diary, 1785–1812* (New York: Alfred A. Knopf, 1990).
7. William H. Nelson, *The American Tory,* rev. ed. (Boston: Northeastern University Press, 1992), 166–69; Merrill Jensen, *The New Nation: A History of the United States during the Confederation, 1781–1789* (Boston: Northeastern University Press, 1981), 265.
8. Thomas L. Purvis, "Price Indexes," *Revolutionary America: 1763 to 1800* (New York: Facts On File, 1995), 116–17; Jensen, *New Nation,* 187.
9. Jensen, *New Nation,* 389, 392–93.
10. Christopher Clark, *The Roots of Rural Capitalism: Western Massachusetts, 1780–1860* (Ithaca, N.Y.: Cornell University Press, 1990), 44–45.
11. David P. Szatmary, *Shays' Rebellion: The Making of an Agrarian Insurrection* (Amherst: University of Massachusetts Press, 1980), 62–65.
12. James Bowdoin, quoted in Szatmary, *Shays' Rebellion,* 71.
13. Jon Butler, *Awash in a Sea of Faith: Christianizing the American People* (Cambridge, Mass.: Harvard University Press, 1990), 264.
14. Quoted in Charles Martyn, *The Life of Artemas Ward* (New York: Artemas Ward, 1921), 280.

## 2. MAKING A NEW CONSTITUTION: 1787–1788

1. David P. Szatmary, *Shays' Rebellion: The Making of an Agrarian Insurrection* (Amherst: University of Massachusetts Press, 1980), 110–13.
2. Thomas Jefferson, letter to William Stephens Smith, November 13, 1787, in Adrienne Koch and William Peden, eds., *The Life and Selected Writings of Thomas Jefferson* (New York: Random House, 1993), 403.
3. Amos Singletary, quoted in Alfred F. Young, "The Framers of the Constitution and the 'Genius' of the People," *Radical History Review* 42 (1998): 15–16.
4. "Publius," quoted in Liah Greenfeld, *Nationalism: Five Roads to Modernity* (Cambridge, Mass.: Harvard University Press, 1992), 429.
5. James Madison, quoted in Catharine Drinker Bowen, *Miracle at Philadelphia* (Boston: Little, Brown, 1966), 278.
6. *New York Packet,* August 5, 1788, quoted in American Social History Project, *Who Built America?,* vol. 1 (New York: Worth, 2000), 273.
7. Philip Freneau, quoted in Kenneth Silverman, *A Cultural History of the American Revolution* (New York: Columbia University Press, 1987), 565.
8. Young, "The Framers," 9–10.
9. Gary B. Nash, *Forging Freedom: The Formation of Philadelphia's Black Community, 1720–1840*

(Cambridge, Mass.: Harvard University Press, 1988), 94–99.

10. Stanley Elkins and Eric McKitrick, *The Age of Federalism* (New York: Oxford University Press, 1993), 33.

11. George Mason, quoted on Gunston Hall Plantation website. URL: http://gunstonhall.org/georgemason/timeline.html.

## 3. A New Nation: 1789–1792

1. James Roger Sharp, *American Politics in the Early Republic* (New Haven, Conn.: Yale University Press, 1993), 17–18.

2. Alexander Hamilton, quoted in Simon Newman, *Parades and the Politics of the Street: Festive Culture in the Early American Republic* (Philadelphia: University of Pennsylvania Press, 1997), 50.

3. John Adams, quoted in Jack D. Warren, "John Adams," in *The Vice Presidents: A Biographical Dictionary,* ed. L. Edward Purcell (New York: Facts On File, 1998), 5.

4. Boston militia Fourth of July toast, 1791, quoted in Len Travers, *Celebrating the Fourth: Independence Day and the Rites of Nationalism in the Early Republic* (Amherst: University of Massachusetts Press, 1997), 90.

5. Dale Van Every, *Ark of Empire: The American Frontier, 1784–1803* (New York: Arno Press, 1977), 208.

6. Ibid., 211.

7. Cathy N. Davidson, *The Revolution and the Word: The Rise of the Novel in America* (New York: Oxford University Press, 1986), 91–98.

8. Marquis de Lafayette, quoted in Lloyd Kramer, *Lafayette in Two Worlds* (Chapel Hill: University of North Carolina Press, 1996), 35.

## 4. Federalist Order: 1793–1796

1. Benjamin Franklin Bache, quoted in James Roger Sharp, *American Politics in the Early Republic: The New Nation in Crisis* (New Haven, Conn.: Yale University Press, 1993), 72.

2. Alexander Hamilton, "Pacificus No. 1," *Gazette of the United States,* June 29, 1793, in *Alexander Hamilton: Writings,* Joanne B. Freeman, ed. (New York: Library of America, 2001), 809.

3. See Stanley Elkins and Erik McKitrick, *The Age of Federalism: The Early American Republic,*

*1788–1800* (New York: Oxford University Press, 1993), 484–485.

4. Proclamation of the German Democratic Society, quoted in Richard Buel, Jr., *Securing the Revolution: Ideology in American Politics, 1789–1815* (Ithaca, N.Y.: Cornell University Press, 1972), 104.

5. Reginald Horsman, *The New Republic: The United States of America, 1789–1815* (New York: Longman, 2000), 58.

6. Samuel Deane, quoted in Drew R. McCoy, *The Elusive Republic: Political Economy in Jeffersonian America* (Chapel Hill: University of North Carolina Press, 1980), 172.

7. Thomas Jefferson, quoted in Elkins and McKitrick, *Age of Federalism,* 178.

8. Sam Bass Warner, Jr., *The Private City* (Philadelphia: University of Pennsylvania Press, 1968), 103; Gary B. Nash, *Forging Freedom: The Formation of Philadelphia's Black Community, 1720–1840* (Cambridge, Mass.: Harvard University Press, 1988), 124.

9. Matthew Carey, quoted in Nash, *Forging Freedom,* 122.

## 5. Federalist Disorder: 1797–1800

1. John Adams to John Quincy Adams, March 31, 1797, quoted in David McCullough, *John Adams* (New York: Simon and Schuster, 2001), 476.

2. Reginald Horsman, *The New Republic: The United States of America, 1789–1815* (New York: Longman, 2000), 70.

3. David Waldstreicher, *In the Midst of Perpetual Fetes: The Making of American Nationalism, 1776–1820* (Chapel Hill: University of North Carolina Press, 1997), 156–157.

4. Robert E. Shalhope, *Bennington and the Green Mountain Boys: The Emergence of Liberal Democracy in Vermont, 1760–1850* (Baltimore, Md.: Johns Hopkins University Press, 1996), 202, 207.

5. James Roger Sharp, *American Politics in the Early Republic* (New Haven, Conn.: Yale University Press, 1993), 212–213.

6. Ibid., 203–205.

7. Douglas Egerton, *Gabriel's Rebellion: The Virginia Slave Conspiracies of 1800 & 1802* (Chapel Hill: University of North Carolina Press, 1993).

8. Fisher Ames, quoted in Stanley Elkins and Erik McKitrick, *The Age of Federalism* (New York: Oxford University Press, 1993), 737.

9. Russel Blaine Nye, *The Cultural Life of the New Nation, 1776–1830* (New York: Harper and Row, 1960), 133.

## 6. Jeffersonian America: 1801–1803

1. James Bayard, quoted in James Roger Sharp, *American Politics in the Early Republic: The New Nation in Crisis* (New Haven, Conn.: Yale University Press, 1993), 271.

2. Thomas Jefferson, "First Inaugural Address," Yale University, Avalon Project, URL: http://www.yale.edu/lawweb/avalon/presiden/inaug/jefinau1.htm.

3. Thomas Jefferson, quoted in Drew R. McCoy, *The Elusive Republic: Political Economy in Jeffersonian America* (New York: W. W. Norton, 1982), 195.

4. Steven Mintz and Susan Kellogg, *Domestic Revolutions: A Social History of American Family Life* (New York: Free Press, 1988), 49.

5. Thomas Jefferson, "First Inaugural Address," Yale University, Avalon Project. URL: http://www.yale.edu/lawweb/avalon/presiden/inaug/jefinau1.htm.

6. New York *Evening Post,* quoted in Robert J. Allison, *The Crescent Obscured: The United States and the Muslim World, 1776–1815* (Chicago: University of Chicago Press, 1995), 29.

7. James Madison, quoted in Walter LaFeber, *The American Age: United States Foreign Policy at Home and Abroad since 1750* (New York: W. W. Norton, 1989), 53.

8. Thomas Jefferson's instructions to Meriwether Lewis, June 20, 1803, in Gunther Barth, ed., *The Lewis and Clark Expedition* (New York: Bedford/St. Martin's, 1998), 19.

## 7. Rising Conflict: 1804–1807

1. New York *Evening Post,* quoted in Robert J. Allison, *The Crescent Obscured: The United States and the Muslim World, 1776–1815* (Chicago: University of Chicago Press, 1995), 29.

2. Thomas Jefferson, quoted in Gordon S. Wood et al. *The Great Republic,* vol. 1, 4th ed. (Lexington, Mass: D.C. Heath, 1992), 362.

3. *National Intelligencer,* quoted in Drew R. McCoy, *The Elusive Republic: Political Economy in Jeffersonian America* (New York: W. W. Norton, 1982), 217.

4. New Jersey State Legislature, quoted in Mary Beth Norton, *Liberty's Daughters: The Revolutionary Experience of American Women, 1750–1800* (Boston: Scott, Foresman, 1980), 193.

## 8. Commercial Crisis and the Clamor for War: 1808–1811

1. Reginald Horsman, *The New Republic* (New York: Longman, 2000), 191.

2. John Randolph, quoted in Donald Hickey, *The War of 1812: A Forgotten Conflict* (Urbana: University of Illinois Press, 1989), 20.

3. *National Intelligencer and Washington Advertiser,* December 28, 1807, quoted in Drew R. McCoy, *The Elusive Republic* (New York: W. W. Norton, 1982), 218.

4. Hickey, *War of 1812,* 22.

5. Simon Newcomb, quoted in George H. Daniels, *American Science in the Age of Jackson* (New York: Columbia University Press, 1968), 6.

6. John Sugden, *Tecumseh: A Life* (New York: Henry Holt, 1997), 187.

7. Tecumseh, quoted in ibid., 187.

8. Tecumseh, quoted in *Great Speeches by Native Americans,* ed. by Bob Blaisdell (New York: Dover, 2000), 60.

9. John C. Calhoun, quoted in Hickey, *War of 1812,* 26.

10. Hickey, *War of 1812,* 29.

11. Henry Clay, quoted in Roger H. Brown, *The Republic in Peril: 1812* (New York: W. W. Norton, 1971), 56.

## 9. The War of 1812: 1812–1815

1. James Madison, *State of the Union,* 1812 quoted in "James Madison: His Legacy," James Madison Center, James Madison University. URL:http://www.jmu.edu/madison/madison.thm#Warof1812.

2. John Sevier, quoted in Roger H. Brown, *The Republic in Peril: 1812* (New York: W. W. Norton, 1971), 65.

3. House Foreign Relations Committee Report, November 29, 1811, quoted in Steven Watts, *The Republic Reborn* (Baltimore, Md.: Johns Hopkins University Press, 1987), 257.

4. James Madison, "War Message to Congress," June 1, 1812, "Casebook: The War of 1812." URL: http://warof1812.casebook.org/documents/text.html?id=603755124902f765f2d9249ccb354143.

5. David Osgood, quoted in Sarah J. Purcell, *Sealed with Blood: War Sacrifice and Memory in Revolutionary America* (Philadelphia: University of Pennsylvania Press, 2002), 161.

6. Donald Hickey, *The War of 1812: A Forgotten Conflict* (Urbana: University of Illinois Press, 1989), 183.

7. George Prevost, quoted in John R. Elting, *Amateurs to Arms! A Military History of the War of 1812* (New York: Da Capo Press, 1991), 220.

8. Julia Anne Hieronymus Tevis, quoted in *Recollections of the Early Republic,* ed. by Joyce Appleby (Boston: Northeastern University Press, 1997), 77.

9. Charles J. Ingersoll, quoted in Hickey, *War of 1812,* 309.

## 10. The Era of Good Feelings?: 1816–1819

1. Washington Irving, "Rip Van Winkle," The Rip Van Winkle Site. URL:http://www.cwrl.utexas.edu/~daniel/amlit/rvw.rvwtext.html.

2. Ibid.

3. Horace Bushnell, quoted in Charles Sellers, *The Market Revolution* (New York: Oxford University Press, 1991), 28.

4. John C. Calhoun, quoted in Bray Hammond, *Banks and Politics in America* (Princeton, N.J.: Princeton University Press, 1985), 234.

5. Sellers, *Market Revolution,* 79.

6. Peter Kolchin, *American Slavery, 1619–1877* (New York: Hill and Wang, 1993), 81.

7. John C. Calhoun and Andrew Jackson, quoted in Robert V. Remini, *The Life of Andrew Jackson* (New York: Harper and Row, 1988), 118.

8. Ibid., 119.

9. John Marshall, quoted in Sellers, *Market Revolution,* 87.

10. William Gouge, quoted in Hammond, *Banks,* 259.

## 11. Economic Crisis, Political Stability: 1820–1823

1. Glover Moore, *The Missouri Controversy, 1819–1821* (Gloucester, Mass.: Peter Smith, 1967), 89.

2. Andrew Jackson, quoted in Robert V. Remini, *The Life of Andrew Jackson* (New York: Harper and Row, 1988), 129.

3. Thomas Hart Benton, quoted in Moore, *Missouri,* 159.

4. John Quincy Adams, quoted in Lynn Hudson Parsons, *John Quincy Adams* (Madison, Wisc.: Madison House, 1998), 161.

5. Thomas Jefferson, quoted in Peter Kolchin, *American Slavery, 1619–1877* (New York: Hill and Wang, 1993), 89.

6. Martin Van Buren, quoted in Edward Pessen, *Jacksonian America: Society, Personality, and Politics* (Homewood, Ill.: Dorsey Press, 1969), 207.

7. Martin Van Buren, quoted in Charles Sellers, *The Market Revolution* (New York: Oxford University Press, 1991), 111.

8. John Quincy Adams, quoted in Parsons, *John Quincy Adams,* 149.

9. Robert Lowry, quoted in Lars Schoultz, *Beneath the United States: A History of U.S. Policy toward Latin America* (Cambridge, Mass.: Harvard University Press, 1998), 9.

10. James Monroe, quoted in Walter LaFeber, *The American Age* (New York: W. W. Norton, 1989), 84.

11. Andrew Jackson, quoted in Remini, *Life of Andrew Jackson,* 145.

12. Andrew Jackson, quoted in Remini, *Life of Andrew Jackson,* 146.

## 12. Democracy: 1824–1825

1. Thomas Jefferson, quoted in Andrew Burstein, *America's Jubilee* (New York: Alfred A. Knopf, 2001), 263; Burstein notes that there may be a healthy dose of historical mythmaking in the reports of both Jefferson's and Adams's final words.

2. John Adams, quoted in Burstein, *America's Jubilee,* 268.

3. Charles Sellers, *The Market Revolution* (New York: Oxford University Press, 1991), 197.

4. Robert Y. Hayne, quoted in Robert V. Remini, *The Life of Andrew Jackson* (New York: Harper and Row, 1988), 153.

5. Martin Van Buren, quoted in Remini, *Life of Andrew Jackson,* 153.

6. Andrew Jackson, quoted in Remini, *Life of Andrew Jackson,* 155.

7. John Quincy Adams, quoted in Lynn Parsons, *John Quincy Adams* (Madison, Wisc.: Madison House, 1998), 176.

8. Auguste Levasseur, quoted in Marian Klamkin, *The Return of Lafayette, 1824–1825* (New York: Charles Scribner's Sons, 1975), 13, 16.

9. Auguste Levasseur, quoted in Klamkin, *Return of Lafayette,* 117–118.

10. New York *Commercial Advertiser,* quoted in Sarah J. Purcell, *Sealed with Blood: War Sacrifice and Memory in Revolutionary America* (Philadelphia: University of Pennsylvania Press, 2002), 177.

11. John Quincy Adams, quoted in Parsons, *John Quincy Adams,* 181.

12. Sellers, *Market Revolution,* 290.

13. John C. Calhoun, quoted in Mark G. Malvasi, "John Caldwell Calhoun," in *The Vice Presidents of the United States, A Biographical Dictionary,* ed. by L. Edward Purcell (New York: Facts On File, 1998), 64.

14. Robert V. Remini, *The Election of Andrew Jackson* (New York: J. B. Lippincott, 1963), 178.

15. *Washington National Journal,* May 24, 1828, quoted in Robert V. Remini, *The Jacksonian Era,* 2d ed. (Wheeling, Ill.: Harlan Davidson, 1997), 19.

16. Sellers, *Market Revolution,* 297, 299.

17. Daniel Webster, quoted in Sellers, *Market Revolution,* 301.

# BIBLIOGRAPHY

Adams, Charles F., ed. *Correspondence between John Adams and Mercy Warren.* Reprint ed. New York: Arno Press, 1972.

Allen, Gardner Weld, ed. *Commodore Hull: Papers of Isaac Hull, Commodore, United States Navy.* Boston: Boston Athenaeum, 1929.

Allison, Robert J. *The Crescent Obscured: The United States and the Muslim World, 1776–1815.* Chicago: University of Chicago Press, 2000.

Altschuler, Glenn C., and Stuart M. Blumin. *Rude Republic: Americans and Their Politics in the Nineteenth Century.* Princeton, N.J.: Princeton University Press, 2000.

American Social History Project. *Who Built America?* Volume 1. New York: Worth, 2000.

Appleby, Joyce. *Capitalism and a New Social Order: The Republican Vision of the 1790s.* New York: New York University Press, 1984.

———. *Recollections of the Early Republic.* Boston: Northeastern University Press, 1997.

Aptheker, Herbert, ed. *A Documentary History of the Negro People in the United States.* New York: Citadel Press, 1969.

Austin, Aleine. *Matthew Lyon: "New Man" of the Democratic Revolution, 1749–1822.* University Park: Pennsylvania State University Press, 1981.

Baepler, Paul, ed. *White Slaves, African Masters: An Anthology of American Barbary Captivity Narratives.* Chicago: University of Chicago Press, 1999.

Baldwin, Leland D. *Whiskey Rebels: The Story of a Frontier Uprising.* Pittsburgh, Pa.: University of Pittsburgh Press, 1976.

Ballagh, James Curtis, ed. *The Letters of Richard Henry Lee.* Volume 2. New York: Da Capo Press, 1970.

Banner, James A. *To the Hartford Convention: The Federalists and the Origins of Party Politics in the Early Republic, 1789–1815.* New York: Alfred A. Knopf, 1970.

Banning, Lance. *The Jeffersonian Persuasion: Evolution of a Party Ideology.* Ithaca, N.Y.: Cornell University Press, 1978.

Barth, Gunther, ed. *The Lewis and Clark Expedition.* New York: Bedford/St. Martin's, 1998.

Bassett, John Spencer. *The Life of Andrew Jackson.* New York: Macmillan, 1925.

Baym, Nina. *American Women Writers and the Work of History, 1790–1860.* New Brunswick, N.J.: Rutgers University Press, 1995.

Bear, James A., Jr. *Jefferson at Monticello: Recollections of a Monticello Slave and of a Monticello Overseer.* Charlottesville: University Press of Virginia, 1967.

Beardsley, E. Edwards. *Life and Times of William Samuel Johnson, LL.D.* New York: Hurd and Houghton, 1876.

Beeman, Richard, Stephen Botein, and Edward C. Carter II, eds. *Beyond Confederation: Origins of the Constitution and American National Identity.* Chapel Hill: University of North Carolina Press, 1987.

Belohalavek, John M. *"Let the Eagle Soar!" The Foreign Policy of Andrew Jackson.* Lincoln: University of Nebraska Press, 1985.

Benton, Thomas Hart. *Thirty Years' View.* Volume 1. New York: D. Appleton, 1880.

Bergen, Frank, ed. *The Journals of Lewis & Clark.* New York: Penguin Books, 1989.

Berlin, Ira. *Many Thousands Gone: The First Two Centuries of Slavery in North America.* Cambridge, Mass.: Harvard University Press, 1998.

Blaidsdell, Bob, ed. *Great Speeches by Native Americans.* Mineola, N.Y.: Dover, 2000.

Blassingame, John W., ed. *Slave Testimony: Two Centuries of Letters, Speeches, Interviews and Autobiographies.* Baton Rouge: Louisiana State University Press, 1977.

Bloch, Ruth. *Visionary Republic: Millennial Themes in American Thought, 1756–1800.* Cambridge, Mass.: Harvard University Press, 1985.

Blumin, Stuart M. *The Emergence of the Middle Class: Social Experience in the American City, 1760–1900.* New York: Cambridge University Press, 1989.

Boudinot, J. J., ed. *The Life, Public Services, Addresses, and Letters of Elias Boudinot.* Volume 2. Reprint ed. New York: Da Capo Press, 1971.

Bowen, Catharine Drinker. *Miracle at Philadelphia.* Boston: Little, Brown, 1966.

Boyd, Steven R. *The Whiskey Rebellion: Past and Present Perspectives.* Westport, Conn.: Greenwood Press, 1985.

Brandon, Edgar Ewing. *Lafayette, Guest of the Nation: A Contemporary Account of the Triumphal Tour of General Lafayette through the United States in 1824–1825 as Reported by the Local Newspapers.* Volume 1. Oxford, Ohio: Oxford Historical Press, 1950.

Brannan, John, ed. *Official Letters of the Military and Naval Officers of the United States, During the War With Great Britain in the Years 1812, 13, 14, and 15.* Reprint ed. New York: Arno Press, 1971.

Brigham, David R. *Public Culture in the Early Republic: Peale's Museum and Its Audience.* Washington, D.C.: Smithsonian Institution Press, 1995.

Brissot de Warville, J. P. *New Travels in the United States of America, 1788.* Durand Echeverria, ed. Cambridge, Mass.: The Belknap Press of Harvard University Press, 1964.

Brown, Roger H. *The Republic in Peril: 1812.* New York: W. W. Norton, 1971.

Brown, Walt. *John Adams and the American Press: Politics and Journalism at the Birth of the Republic.* Jefferson, N.C.: McFarland, 1995.

Buel, Richard, Jr. *Securing the Revolution: Ideology in American Politics, 1789–1815.* Ithaca, N.Y.: Cornell University Press, 1972.

Burgess, John William. *The Middle Period, 1817–1858.* New York: Scribner, 1897.

Burstein, Andrew. *America's Jubilee.* New York: Alfred A. Knopf, 2001.

Bushman, Richard. *The Refinement of America: Persons, Houses, Cities.* New York: Alfred A. Knopf, 1992.

Butler, Frederick. *Memoirs of the Marquis de La Fayette . . . Together with His Tour through the United States.* Wethersfield, Conn.: Deming & Francis, 1825.

Butler, Jon. *Awash in a Sea of Faith: Christianizing the American People.* Cambridge, Mass.: Harvard University Press, 1990.

Butterfield, L. H., Marc Friedlaender, and Mary Jo Kline. *The Book of Abigail and John: Selected Letters of the Adams Family, 1702–1784.* Cambridge, Mass.: Harvard University Press, 1975.

Carnegie Endowment for International Peace. *The Controversy over Neutral Rights between the United States and France, 1797–1800.* New York: Oxford University Press, 1917.

Carruth, Gorton. *The Encyclopedia of American Facts and Dates.* New York: HarperCollins, 1997.

Cayton, Andrew R. L. *Frontier Indiana.* Bloomington: Indiana University Press, 1996.

*Chronology of the American Indian.* Newport Beach, Calif.: American Indian Publishers, 1994.

Clark, Christopher. *The Roots of Rural Capitalism: Western Massachusetts, 1780–1860.* Ithaca, N.Y.: Cornell University Press, 1990.

Clinton, Catharine. *The Other Civil War: American Women in the Nineteenth Century.* New York: Hill and Wang, 1984.

Cobbett, William. *Peter Porcupine in America: Pamphlets on Republicanism and Revolution.* Reprint ed. Ithaca, N.Y.: Cornell University Press, 1994.

Colton, Calvin. *The Life and Times of Henry Clay,* 2 vols. New York: A. S. Barnes & Co., 1846.

Combs, Jerald A. *The Jay Treaty: Political Battleground of the Founding Fathers.* Berkeley: University of California Press, 1970.

Commager, Henry Steele, ed. *Documents of American History,* 9th ed. Volume 1. Englewood Cliffs, N.J.: Prentice-Hall, 1973.

Cott, Nancy F. *The Bonds of Womanhood: "Woman's Sphere" in New England, 1780–1835.* New Haven, Conn.: Yale University Press, 1977.

Coues, Elliott, ed. *History of the Expedition under the Command of Lewis and Clark,* 3 vols. New York: Dover, 1965.

Crackel, Theodore. *Mr. Jefferson's Army: Political and Social Reform of the Military Establishment, 1801–1809.* New York: New York University Press, 1987.

Crallé, Richard K., ed. *Speeches of John C. Calhoun Delivered in the House of Representatives and in the Senate of the United States.* Volume 2. New York: D. Appleton, 1883.

Craven, Avery, Walter Johnson, and F. Roger Dunn. *A Documentary History of the American People.* New York: Ginn, 1951.

Cremin, Lawrence A. *American Education: The National Experience, 1783–1876.* New York: Harper and Row, 1980.

Cunliffe, Marcus. *The Nation Takes Shape.* Chicago: University of Chicago Press, 1959.

Cunningham, Noble E. *The Presidency of James Madison.* Lawrence: University Press of Kansas, 1996.

———, ed. *Circular Letters of Congressmen to Their Constituents, 1789–1829,* 2 vols. Chapel Hill: University of North Carolina Press, 1978.

Curtis, Benjamin R., ed. *A Memoir of Benjamin Robbins Curtis, LL.D.* Volume 1. Boston: Little, Brown, 1879. Reprint ed. New York: Da Capo, 1970.

Cushing, Harry Alonzo, ed. *The Writings of Samuel Adams.* Volume 4. New York: G. P. Putnam's Sons, 1908.

Cutler, William Parker, and Julia Perkins Cutler. *Life, Journals and Correspondence of Rev. Manasseh Cutler, LL.D.* Cincinnati: Robert Clarke & Co., 1888.

Dangerfield, George. *The Awakening of American Nationalism, 1815–1828.* New York: Harper and Row, 1965.

Daniels, George H. *American Science in the Age of Jackson.* New York: Columbia University Press, 1968.

Davidson, Cathy N. *The Revolution and the Word: The Rise of the Novel in America.* New York: Oxford University Press, 1986.

Davis, David Brion, ed. *The Fear of Conspiracy: Images of Un-American Subversion from the Revolution to the Present.* Ithaca, N.Y.: Cornell University Press, 1971.

Davis, Matthew L. *Memoirs of Aaron Burr with Miscellaneous Selections from His Correspondence,* 2 vols. Freeport, N.Y.: Books for Libraries Press, 1970.

DeConde, Alexander. *Entangling Alliance: Politics and Diplomacy under George Washington.* Durham, N.C.: Duke University Press, 1958.

———. *The Quasi-War: The Politics and Diplomacy of the Undeclared War with France, 1797–1801.* New York: Scribner, 1966.

Dowd, Gregory Evans. *A Spirited Resistance: The North American Indian Struggle for Unity, 1745–1815.* Baltimore, Md.: Johns Hopkins University Press, 1992.

Ducas, George, ed. *Great Documents in Black American History.* New York: Praeger, 1970.

Dudley, William S., ed. *The Naval War of 1812: A Documentary History.* Washington, D.C.: Naval Historical Center Department of the Navy, 1985.

Dunn, Susan. *Sister Revolutions: French Lightning, American Light.* New York: Faber and Faber, 1999.

Egerton, Douglas. *Gabriel's Rebellion: The Virginia Slave Conspiracies of 1800 & 1802.* Chapel Hill: University of North Carolina Press, 1993.

Elias, Robert H., and Eugene D. Finch. *Letters of Thomas Attwood Digges.* Columbia: University of South Carolina Press, 1982.

Elkins, Stanley, and Eric McKitrick. *The Age of Federalism: The Early American Republic, 1788–1800.* New York: Oxford University Press, 1993.

Elliott, Emory. *Revolutionary Writers: Literature and Authority in the New Republic, 1725–1810.* New York: Oxford University Press, 1982.

Ellis, Joseph J. *After the Revolution: Profiles in Early American Culture.* New York: W. W. Norton, 1979.

Elting, John R. *Amateurs, To Arms! A Military History of the War of 1812.* Reprint ed. New York: Da Capo, 1995.

Eslinger, Ellen. *Citizens of Zion: The Social Origins of Camp Meeting Revivalism.* Knoxville: University of Tennessee Press, 1999.

Faragher, John Mack. *Sugar Creek: Life on the Illinois Prairie.* New Haven, Conn.: Yale University Press, 1986.

Feller, Daniel. *The Jacksonian Promise: America, 1815–1840.* Baltimore, Md.: Johns Hopkins University Press, 1995.

Ferguson, E. James. *The Power of the Purse: A History of American Public Finance, 1776–1790.* Chapel Hill: University of North Carolina Press, 1961.

Fields, Joseph, ed. *"Worthy Partner": The Papers of Martha Washington.* Westport, Conn.: Greenwood Press, 1994.

Ford, Worthington Chauncey, ed. *The Writings of John Quincy Adams.* Volumes 6–8. New York: Macmillan, 1916.

———, ed. *The Writings of George Washington.* Volume 11. New York: G. P. Putnam's Sons, 1891.

Freeman, Joanne B. *Affairs of Honor: National Politics in the New Republic.* New Haven, Conn.: Yale University Press, 2001.

———, ed. *Alexander Hamilton, Writings.* New York: Library of America, 2001.

George, Carol V. R. *Segregated Sabbaths: Richard Allen and the Emergence of Independent Black Churches, 1760–1840.* New York: Oxford University Press, 1973.

Gilje, Paul A., and Howard B. Rock. *Keepers of the Revolution: New Yorkers at Work in the Early Republic.* Ithaca, N.Y.: Cornell University Press, 1992.

Gilje, Paul A., ed. *Wages of Independence: Capitalism in the Early American Republic.* Madison, Wisc.: Madison House, 1997.

Gilmore, James. *John Sevier as a Commonwealth-Builder.* New York: D. Appleton, 1887.

Gordon-Reed, Annette. *Thomas Jefferson and Sally Hemings, An American Controversy.* Charlottesville: University Press of Virginia, 1997.

Greene, Jack P., ed. *Colonies to Nation, 1763–1789: A Documentary History of the American Revolution.* New York: W. W. Norton, 1975.

Greenfeld, Liah. *Nationalism: Five Roads to Modernity.* Cambridge, Mass.: Harvard University Press, 1990.

Gunston Hall Plantation website. URL: http://gunstonhall.org/documents/objections.html. Downloaded on January 20, 2002.

Hammond, Bray. *Banks and Politics in America.* Princeton, N.J.: Princeton University Press, 1985.

Hannay, James. *History of the War of 1812 between Great Britain and the United States of America.* Toronto: Morang, 1905.

Harris, Niel. *The Artist in American Society: The Formative Years, 1790–1860.* New York: G. Braziller, 1966.

Harris, Sharon M., ed. *Selected Writings of Judith Sargent Murray.* New York: Oxford University Press, 1995.

Hart, Albert Bushnell, ed. *American History Told by Contemporaries.* Volume 2. New York: Macmillan, 1926.

———. *American History Told by Contemporaries.* Volume 3. New York: Macmillan, 1925.

Hazen, Charles Downer. *Contemporary American Opinion of the French Revolution.* Baltimore, Md.: Johns Hopkins University Press, 1897.

*The Herald: A Gazette for the Country.* July 8, 1797.

Hickey, Donald R. *The War of 1812: A Forgotten Conflict.* Urbana: University of Illinois Press, 1989.

Hiltner, Judith. *The Newspaper Verse of Philip Freneau: An Edition and Bibliographical Survey.* Troy, N.Y.: Whitston, 1986.

Hofstadter, Richard. *The Idea of a Party System: The Rise of Legitimate Opposition in the United States, 1780–1840.* Berkeley: University of California Press, 1970.

Horsman, Reginald. *The New Republic: The United States of America, 1789–1815*. New York: Longman, 2000.

Howe, M. A. DeWolfe. *The Life and Letters of George Bancroft*. Volume 1. New York: Charles Scribner's Sons, 1908.

Humphreys, Frank Landon. *Life and Times of David Humphreys*. Volume 2. New York: G. P. Putnam's Sons, 1917.

Hunt, Gaillard, ed. *The First Forty Years of Washington Society in the Family Letters of Margaret Bayard Smith*. Reprint ed. New York: Frederick Ungar, 1965.

Hunt, John Gabriel, ed. *The Essential Thomas Jefferson*. New York: Portland House, 1996.

Hutchins, Catherine E., ed. *Everyday Life in the Early Republic*. Winterthur, Del.: Henry Francis du Pont Winterthur Museum, 1994.

James, Janet Wilson. *Changing Ideas about Women in the United States, 1776–1825*. New York: Garland, 1981.

Jensen, Merrill. *The New Nation: A History of the United States during the Confederation, 1781–1789*. Reprint ed. Boston: Northeastern University Press, 1981.

Johnson, Charles, and Patricia Smith. *Africans in America: America's Journey through Slavery*. New York: Harcourt Brace, 1998.

Johnson, Michael P. *Reading the American Past*, 2d ed. Volume 1. New York: Bedford/St. Martin's, 2002.

Johnson, Paul E., and Sean Wilentz. *The Kingdom of Matthias: A Story of Sex and Salvation in 19th-Century America*. New York: Oxford University Press, 1994.

Jones, Dorothy. *License for Empire: Colonialism by Treaty in Early America*. Chicago: University of Chicago Press, 1982.

Kaestle, Carl F. *Pillars of the Republic: Common Schools and American Society, 1780–1860*. New York: Hill and Wang, 1983.

Kammen, Michael. *A Season of Youth: The American Revolution and the Historical Imagination*. Ithaca, N.Y.: Cornell University Press, 1978.

Kaplan, Sidney, and Emma Nogrady Kaplan. *The Black Presence in the Era of the American Revolution*. Rev. ed. Amherst: University of Massachusetts Press, 1989.

Keller, William F. *The Nation's Advocate: Henry Marie Brackenridge and Young America*. Pittsburgh, Pa.: University of Pittsburgh Press, 1956.

Kerber, Linda K. *Federalists in Dissent: Imagery and Ideology in Jeffersonian America.* Ithaca, N.Y.: Cornell University Press, 1970.

———. *Women of the Republic: Intellect and Ideology in Revolutionary America.* Chapel Hill: University of North Carolina Press, 1986.

King, Charles R., ed. *The Life and Correspondence of Rufus King.* New York: Da Capo Press, 1971.

Klamkin, Marian. *The Return of Lafayette, 1824–1825.* New York: Charles Scribner's Sons, 1975.

Koch, Adrienne, and William Peden, eds. *The Life and Selected Writings of Thomas Jefferson.* New York: Random House, 1993.

Kolchin, Peter. *American Slavery, 1619–1877.* New York: Hill and Wang, 1997.

Kornfeld, Eve. *Creating an American Culture, 1775–1800.* New York: Bedford/St. Martin's, 2001.

Kowaleski–Wallace, Elizabeth. *Consuming Subjects: Women, Shopping, and Business in the Eighteenth Century.* New York: Columbia University Press, 1997.

Kramer, Lloyd. *Lafayette in Two Worlds.* Chapel Hill: University of North Carolina Press, 1996.

LaFeber, Walter. *The American Age: United States Foreign Policy at Home and Abroad since 1750.* New York: W. W. Norton, 1989.

Lee, Richard Henry. *An Additional Number of Letters from the Federal Farmer to the Republican . . .* Reprint ed. Chicago: Quadrangle Books, 1962.

Lewis, John D., ed. *Anti-Federalists versus Federalists.* San Francisco: Chandler, 1967.

Library of Congress. American Memory Project website. URL: http://memory.loc.gov. Downloaded on September 10, 2003.

Link, Eugene Perry. *Democratic-Republican Societies, 1790–1800.* New York: Octagon Books, 1973.

Madison, Dolley Payne Todd. *Memoirs and Letters of Dolly Madison.* New York: Houghton, Mifflin, 1887.

Madison, James. *Letters and Other Writings of James Madison,* 2 vols. Philadelphia: J. B. Lippincott, 1865.

Martyn, Charles. *The Life of Artemas Ward.* New York: Artemas Ward, 1921.

Matthews, Jean V. *Toward a New Society: American Thought and Culture, 1800–1830.* Boston: Twayne, 1991.

McCoy, Drew R. *The Elusive Republic: Political Economy in Jeffersonian America.* New York: W. W. Norton, 1982.

McCrackan, W. D. *The Huntington Letters.* New York: Appleton, 1905.

McCullough, David. *John Adams.* New York: Simon and Schuster, 2001.

McCusker, John J., and Russell R. Menard. *The Economy of British America, 1607–1789.* Chapel Hill: University of North Carolina Press, 1985.

McLaughlin, Jack, ed. *To His Excellency Thomas Jefferson: Letters to a President.* New York: Avon Books, 1991.

Mellon, Matthew T. *Early American Views on Negro Slavery.* Rev. ed. New York: Bergman, 1969.

Merrill, Michael, and Sean Wilentz, eds. *The Key of Liberty: The Life and Democratic Writings of William Manning, "A Laborer," 1747–1814.* Cambridge, Mass.: Harvard University Press, 1993.

Minot, George Richards. *History of the Insurrections in Massachusetts in 1786 and of the Rebellion Consequent Thereon.* Reprint ed. New York: Da Capo Press, 1971.

Moore, Glover. *The Missouri Controversy, 1819–1821.* Gloucester, Mass.: Peter Smith, 1967.

Morrison, Alfred J., ed. *Travels in the Confederation, from the German of Johann David Schoepf.* Philadelphia: William J. Campbell, 1911.

Nagel, Paul C. *John Quincy Adams: A Public Life, a Private Life.* New York: Alfred A. Knopf, 1997.

Nash, Gary B. *Forging Freedom: The Formation of Philadelphia's Black Community, 1720–1840.* Cambridge, Mass.: Harvard University Press, 1988.

Neimeyer, Charles Patrick. *America Goes to War: A Social History of the Continental Army.* New York: New York University Press, 1996.

Nelson, William H. *The American Tory.* Rev. ed. Boston: Northeastern University Press, 1992.

Newman, Simon P. *Parades and the Politics of the Street: Festive Culture in the Early American Republic.* Philadelphia: University of Pennsylvania Press, 1997.

Newmyer, R. Kent. *The Supreme Court Under Marshall and Taney.* New York: T. Y. Crowell, 1968.

*Newport Mercury* (Rhode Island). December 31, 1799.

Norton, Mary Beth. *Liberty's Daughters: The Revolutionary Experience of American Women, 1750–1800.* Boston: Scott, Foresman, 1980.

Nye, Russell Blaine. *The Cultural Life of the New Nation, 1776–1830.* New York: Harper and Row, 1960.

Oberholtzer, Ellis Paxson. *Robert Morris: Patriot and Financier.* New York: Macmillan, 1903.

Owsley, Frank Lawrence, Jr., and Gene A. Smith. *Filibusters and Expansionists: Jeffersonian Manifest Destiny, 1800–1821.* Tuscaloosa: University of Alabama Press, 1997.

Pace, Antonio, ed. *Luigi Castiglioni's Viaggio: Travels in the United States of North America, 1785–1787.* Syracuse, N.Y.: Syracuse University Press, 1983.

Palmer, Dave R. *1794: America, Its Army, and the Birth of the Nation.* Novato, Calif.: Presidio, 1994.

Parker, Freddie L. *Stealing a Little Freedom: Advertisements for Slave Runaways in North Carolina, 1791–1804.* New York: Garland, 1994.

Parsons, Lynn Hudson. *John Quincy Adams.* Madison, Wisc.: Madison House, 1998.

Pease, William H., and Jane H. Pease, eds. *The Antislavery Argument.* New York: Bobbs-Merrill, 1965.

Persons, Stow. *American Minds: A History of Ideas.* New York: Holt, Rinehart, and Winston, 1958.

Pessen, Edward. *Jacksonian America: Society, Personality, and Politics.* Rev. ed. Urbana: University of Illinois Press, 1985.

Peterson, Merrill D. *The Jefferson Image in the American Mind.* New York: Oxford University Press, 1960.

Phillips, Ulrich B., ed. *Plantation and Frontier, 1649–1863.* Volume 2. New York: Burt Franklin, 1969.

Pole, J. R. *Foundations of American Independence, 1763–1815.* Indianapolis: Bobbs-Merrill, 1972.

Purcell, L. Edward, ed. *The Vice Presidents: A Biographical Dictionary.* New York: Facts On File, 1998.

Purcell, L. Edward, and David F. Burg. *The World Almanac of the American Revolution*. New York: World Almanac, 1992.

Purcell, Sarah J. *Sealed with Blood: War, Sacrifice, and Memory in Revolutionary America*. Philadelphia: University of Pennsylvania Press, 2002.

Purvis, Thomas L. *Revolutionary America, 1763 to 1800*. New York: Facts On File, 1995.

Quaife, Milo Milton. *Chicago and the Old Northwest, 1673–1835*. Chicago: University of Chicago Press, 1913.

Ransom, Stanley Austin, Jr., ed. *America's First Negro Poet: The Complete Works of Jupiter Hammon of Long Island*. Port Washington, N.Y.: Kennikat Press, 1983.

Remini, Robert. *Andrew Jackson and His Indian Wars*. New York: Viking, 2001.

———. *The Election of Andrew Jackson*. Philadelphia: J. B. Lippincott, 1963.

———. *Henry Clay: Statesman for the Union*. New York: W. W. Norton, 1991.

———. *The Jacksonian Era,* 2d ed. Wheeling, Ill.: Harlan Davidson, 1997.

———. *The Life of Andrew Jackson*. New York: Harper and Row, 1988.

Resch, John. *Suffering Soldiers: Revolutionary War Veterans, Moral Sentiment, and Political Culture in the Early Republic*. Amherst: University of Massachusetts Press, 1999.

Rhodehamel, John, ed. *The American Revolution: Writings from the War of Independence*. New York: Random House, 2001.

Risjord, Norman K. *Jefferson's America, 1760–1815*. Madison, Wisc.: Madison House, 1991.

Robertson, Douglas S., ed. *An Englishman in America, 1785: Being the Diary of Joseph Hadfield*. Toronto: Hunter-Rose, 1933.

Robinson, Raymond H. *The Growing of America: 1789–1848*. Boston: Allyn and Bacon, 1973.

Rollins, Richard M. *The Long Journey of Noah Webster*. Philadelphia: University of Pennsylvania Press, 1980.

Rosenfeld, Richard N. *American Aurora: A Democratic-Republican Returns*. New York: St. Martin's, 1997.

Rowland, Kate Mason. *The Life of George Mason*. Volume 2. New York: G. P. Putnam's Sons, 1892.

Rutland, Robert A. *The Ordeal of the Constitution: The Antifederalists and the Ratification Struggle of 1787–88.* Norman: University of Oklahoma Press, 1966.

Sargent, Nathan. *Public Men and Events from the Commencement of Mr. Monroe's Administration, in 1817, to the Close of Mr. Fillmore's Administration, in 1853.* Volume 1. Philadelphia: J.B. Lippincott, 1875.

Schoultz, Lars. *Beneath the United States: A History of U.S. Policy toward Latin America.* Cambridge, Mass.: Harvard University Press, 1998.

Schudson, Michael. *The Good Citizen: A History of American Civic Life.* Cambridge, Mass.: Harvard University Press, 1998.

Schwartz, Barry. *George Washington: The Making of an American Symbol.* New York: Free Press, 1987.

Seale, William. *The President's House: A History.* Volume 1. Washington, D.C.: White House Historical Association, 1986.

Sellers, Charles. *The Market Revolution: Jacksonian America, 1815–1846.* New York: Oxford University Press, 1991.

Shalhope, Robert E. *Bennington and the Green Mountain Boys: The Emergence of Liberal Democracy in Vermont, 1760–1850.* Baltimore, Md.: Johns Hopkins University Press, 1996.

Shanks, Henry Thomas, ed. *The Papers of Willie Person Magnum.* Raleigh, N.C.: State Department of Archives and History, 1950–1956.

Sharp, James Roger. *American Politics in the Early Republic: The New Nation in Crisis.* New Haven, Conn.: Yale University Press, 1993.

Shields, David S. *Civil Tongues & Polite Letters in British America.* Chapel Hill: University of North Carolina Press, 1997.

Shy, John, ed. *Winding Down: The Revolutionary War Letters of Lieutenant Benjamin Gilbert of Massachusetts, 1780–1783.* Ann Arbor: University of Michigan Press, 1989.

Silverman, Kenneth. *A Cultural History of the American Revolution.* New York: T.Y. Crowell, 1976.

Slaughter, Thomas P. *The Whiskey Rebellion: Frontier Epilogue to the American Revolution.* New York: Oxford University Press, 1986.

Smelser, Marshall. *The Democratic Republic, 1801–1815.* New York: Harper and Row, 1968.

Smith, Richard Norton. *Patriarch: George Washington and the New American Nation*. Boston: Houghton Mifflin, 1993.

Smith, William Henry. *The St. Clair Papers*. Volume 1. Cincinnati: Robert Clarke & Co., 1882.

Sparks, Jared. *The Life of Gouverneur Morris, with Selections from His Correspondence and Miscellaneous Papers*. Boston: Gray & Bowen, 1832.

———. *The Writings of George Washington*. Volume 10. Boston: Rusell, Shattuck, and Williams and Hilliard, Gray, and Co., 1836.

Sprigg, June. *Domestick Beings*. New York: Alfred A. Knopf, 1984.

Stinchcombe, William. *The XYZ Affair*. Westport, Conn.: Greenwood Press, 1981.

Story, William W., ed. *Life and Letters of Joseph Story*. Volume 1. Boston: Charles C. Little and James Brown, 1851.

Sugden, John. *Tecumseh's Last Stand*. Norman: University of Oklahoma Press, 1985.

———. *Tecumseh: A Life*. New York: Henry Holt, 1997.

Switzer, Richard, trans. *Chateaubriand's Travels in America*. Lexington: University of Kentucky Press, 1969.

Sword, Wiley. *President Washington's Indian War: The Struggle for the Old Northwest, 1790–1795*. Norman: University of Oklahoma Press, 1985.

Szatmary, David P. *Shays' Rebellion: The Making of an Agrarian Insurrection*. Amherst: University of Massachusetts Press, 1980.

Taylor, Alan. *Liberty Men and Great Proprietors: The Revolutionary Settlement on the Maine Frontier, 1760–1820*. Chapel Hill: University of North Carolina Press, 1990.

Thornbrough, Gayle, ed. *The Correspondence of John Ballodet and Albert Gallatin, 1804–1836*. Indianapolis: Indiana Historical Society, 1963.

———. *Outpost on the Wabash, 1787–1791*. Indiana Historical Society Publications, Volume 19. Indianapolis: Indiana Historical Society, 1957.

Thorp, Willard. *A Southern Reader*. New York: Alfred A. Knopf, 1955.

Tompkins, Daniel D. *Public Papers of Daniel D. Tompkins, Governor of New York*, 3 vols. New York: Wynkoop Hallenbeck Crawford Co., State Printers, 1898–1902.

Travers, Len. *Celebrating the Fourth: Independence Day and the Rites of Nationalism in the Early Republic.* Amherst: University of Massachusetts Press, 1997.

Tyler, Lyon G. *The Letters and Times of the Tylers.* Volume 1. Richmond, Va.: Whittet & Shepperson, 1884. Reprint ed. New York: Da Capo, 1970.

Ulrich, Laurel Thatcher. *A Midwife's Tale: The Life of Martha Ballard, Based on Her Diary, 1785–1812.* New York: Alfred A. Knopf, 1990.

United States Office of Naval Records and Library. *Naval Documents Related to the United States Wars with the Barbary Powers.* Washington, D.C.: Government Printing Office, 1940.

University of Oklahoma Law Center website. URL: http://www.law.ou.edu/hist/transmit/html. Downloaded on September 10, 2003.

Van Every, Dale. *Ark of Empire: The American Frontier, 1784–1803.* Reprint ed. New York: Arno Press, 1977.

Veit, Helen, Kenneth R. Bowling, and Charlene Bangs Bickford, eds. *Creating the Bill of Rights: The Documentary Record from the First Federal Congress.* Baltimore, Md.: Johns Hopkins University Press, 1991.

*Vermont Gazette* (Bennington), July 17, 1821.

Wade, Richard C. *The Urban Frontier: Pioneer Life in Early Pittsburgh, Cincinnati, Lexington, Louisville, and St. Louis.* Reprint ed. Chicago: University of Chicago Press, 1964.

Waldstreicher, David. *In the Midst of Perpetual Fetes: The Making of American Nationalism, 1776–1820.* Chapel Hill: University of North Carolina Press, 1997.

Wallace, Anthony F. C. *The Death and Rebirth of the Seneca.* New York: Alfred A. Knopf, 1970.

Warner, Sam Bass, Jr. *The Private City.* Philadelphia: University of Pennsylvania Press, 1968.

Warren, Mercy Otis. *History of the Rise, Progress and Termination of the American Revolution,* 2 vols. Lester H. Cohen, ed. Indianapolis: Liberty Classics, 1989.

Watts, Steven. *The Republic Reborn: War and the Making of Liberal America, 1790–1820.* Baltimore, Md.: Johns Hopkins University Press, 1987.

Webster, Fletcher, ed. *The Private Correspondence of Daniel Webster,* 2 vols. Boston: Little, Brown, 1857.

Weeks, William Earl. *John Quincy Adams and American Global Empire*. Lexington: University Press of Kentucky, 1992.

White, Richard. *The Middle Ground: Indians, Empires, and Republics in the Great Lakes Region, 1650–1815*. New York: Cambridge University Press, 1991.

Wilentz, Sean. *Chants Democratic: New York City and the Rise of the American Working Class, 1788–1850*. New York: Oxford University Press, 1984.

Wilkins, Roger. *Jefferson's Pillow: The Founding Fathers and the Dilemma of Black Patriotism*. Boston: Beacon Press, 2001.

Williams, Frederick D., ed. *The Northwest Ordinance: Essays on Its Formulation, Provisions, and Legacy*. East Lansing: Michigan State University Press, 1989.

Windley, Lathan A., ed. *Runaway Slave Advertisements: A Documentary History from the 1730s to 1790*. Volume 4, *Georgia*. Westport, Conn.: Greenwood Press, 1983.

Wood, Gordon S., et al. *The Great Republic: A History of the American People*. Volume 1, 4th ed. Lexington, Mass.: D.C. Heath, 1992.

Wood, Gordon S., ed. *The Confederation and the Constitution: The Critical Issues*. New York: University Press of America, 1979.

———. *The Creation of the American Republic, 1776–1787*. Chapel Hill: University of North Carolina Press, 1969.

———. *The Radicalism of the American Revolution*. New York: Alfred A. Knopf, 1992.

———, ed. *The Rising Glory of America, 1760–1820*. Boston: Northeastern University Press, 1990.

Yazawa, Mel. *From Colonies to Commonwealth: Familial Ideology and the Beginnings of the American Republic*. Baltimore, Md.: Johns Hopkins University Press, 1985.

Young, Alfred F. "The Framers of the Constitution and the 'Genius' of the People." *Radical History Review* 42 (1998): 8–18.

Zagarri, Rosemarie. *The Politics of Size: Representation in the United States, 1776–1850*. Ithaca, N.Y.: Cornell University Press, 1987.

# INDEX

Locators in *italics* indicate illustrations. Locators in **boldface** indicate main entries. Locators followed by *m* indicate maps. Locators followed by *c* indicate charts.